Sex the Measure of All Things

Sex the Measure of All Things

A Life of Alfred C. Kinsey

JONATHAN GATHORNE-HARDY

INDIANA UNIVERSITY PRESS
BLOOMINGTON AND INDIANAPOLIS

This book is a publication of

Indiana University Press
601 North Morton Street
Bloomington, IN 47404-3797 USA

http://www.indiana.edu/~iupress

Telephone orders   800-842-6796
Fax orders   812-855-7931
Orders by e-mail   iuporder@indiana.edu

This edition first published by Indiana University Press 2000.
Originally published in Great Britain by
Chatto & Windus Ltd 1998; Pimlico edition 1999.

The paper used in this publication meets the minimum requirements of
American National Standard for Information Sciences—Permanence
of Paper for Printed Library Materials, ANSI Z39.48-1984.

Manufactured in the United States of America

Library of Congress Cataloging-in-Publication Data

Gathorne-Hardy, Jonathan.
Sex the measure of all things : a life of Alfred C. Kinsey /
Jonathan Gathorne-Hardy.
p.   cm.
Originally published: London : Pimlico, 1999.
Includes bibliographical references and index.
ISBN 0-253-33734-8 (alk. paper)
1. Kinsey, Alfred C. (Alfred Charles), 1894–1956.
2. Sexologists—United States—Biography.
3. Sexology—United States—
History.   I. Title.

HQ18.32.K56 G38 2000
306.7'092—dc21   99-052918
[B]

1   2   3   4   5   05   04   03   02   01   00

Contents

Preface to the American Edition

The reactions to the first hardback edition of this book were unlike those to any other book I have ever written. The reason for this is that, even after being dead over fifty years, Kinsey still remains a symbolic figure for the liberal attitudes he preached. How critics responded to my book, therefore, depended much less than usual on its merits or defects and much more on their own attitudes to sexual behaviour.

The first biographers of Kinsey were not greeted in this way. These were Cornelia V. Christenson and Wardel B. Pomeroy. Christenson's *Kinsey, A Biography* came out in 1970; Pomeroy's (and John Tebbel's) *Dr. Kinsey and the Institute for Sex Research* in 1972. Probably one reason for the way they were received is that both Christenson and Pomeroy had been close colleagues of Kinsey and their books were very much those of admiring subordinates. The *New York Times* described Pomeroy's book as "an affectionate memoir."

It was James H. Jones's *Alfred C. Kinsey – A Public / Private Life* (1997) which revolutionised the picture of Kinsey and, more significantly, revolutionised the status and evaluation of his work. Here it is necessary to give a somewhat personal account. I became aware very early on in 1995, while in Bloomington, Indiana, researching this book, of Jones's endeavour, and viewed it with the mixed feelings common in such situations and not difficult to imagine – and was, no doubt, so viewed in my turn. However, since I also learnt that Jones had been engaged on his book since 1970, I was relieved to realize there could be no question of us being in a race as to who should come out first.

Jones and I had, on the whole, spoken to the same people. Some were less open with me than with Jones; some more so, but as a result I already knew a good many of Jones's discoveries. Again to my relief, I found I did not have to alter my *view* of Kinsey. Yet as I read Jones's long and in some ways admirable book, I became more and more dismayed. There soon began to emerge a totally different Kinsey, not so much because of new facts but because of radically different interpretations. This would perhaps hardly have mattered, on the contrary indeed, since different interpretations are the stuff of literary and critical discussion. Such skirmishes usually take place in the footnotes, as they would have here except for one thing. Jones belongs to what one might call the Kenneth Starr school of biography. That is, he decided to mount his attack, since that is what his book in the end amounted to, from Kinsey's private sexual behaviour. Jones's Kinsey was a man appallingly warped and distorted, driven by vicious personal 'demons', to such a degree and in so many ways that eventually he almost ceased to be a moral being, and largely ceased to be an objective researcher, his data 'skewed' and 'flawed' to such an extent that, in effect, essential parts of his science were fraudulent.

I returned to America in November 1997 and saw once again the people Jones and I had seen already. Those who had been cagey with me before decided that, since so many beans had been spilt, they might as well spill the lot – and I was given a great deal more material. More importantly, I confirmed that these key witnesses, upon whose information Jones had based his radical new view of Kinsey, were as dismayed as I was. While on the whole not disputing the facts, they did dispute the interpretation – and sometimes the facts as well.

Jones's line, as I explain in the text, was to a considerable extent followed by reviewers, especially in Britain. Yet it was clear to me that, despite my own considerable reservations about Kinsey, he was a much more complicated, interesting, valuable, surprising, moving and profound man than the caricature reflected by the reviewers. And, as I also point out, in ironic imitation of its subject, far more people read the comments on Jones's biography than read the book itself. The point about attacks in the press is that eventually they fade away. But a book is a more permanent record. From now on, those seeking to know anything about Kinsey would refer to Jones's biography – and find there substantially the same attacks. The only effective way of providing an equally permanent corrective, a balancing view, it seemed to me, had also to be in book form.

Though, obviously, only a very small part of my book, I decided that I would have to be more open than is customary when I disagreed with Jones's interpretation, and this I have been.

Acknowledgments

I would like to thank, first, the staff of the Kinsey Institute for Research in Sex, Gender and Reproduction, where the vast bulk of data relevant to this book still resides. It would be invidious to single out this member of staff or that and I have therefore included their names among those at the end, but I would make an exception for the Director, Dr John Bancroft. We arrived in Bloomington together, and without the office he gave me, and the full access (always, of course, respecting the strict personal confidentiality promised those who co-operated with Kinsey) to the vast correspondence, interviews, tapes, memoirs, 'Kinseyiana' and all other relevant material, my task would have been impossible.

Kinsey's family papers are in the care of his surviving children, and I am extremely grateful to his daughter Joan Kinsey Reid (Mrs Robert M. Reid) for allowing me access to significant correspondence and youthful memorabilia and to her and her sister Anne Call for numerous lengthy and illuminating conversations about their father and mother. The co-operation of Kinsey's four main colleagues – William H. Dellenback, Paul H. Gebhard, Clyde E. Martin and Wardell B. Pomeroy – was invaluable, and I am especially grateful to the (alphabetically) first two – Bill Dellenback for endless patience locating examples of his fine photography, Paul Gebhard for hours of useful (and often amusing) conversation, discussion and lengthy correspondence. Allied to these four were, in turn, their own old colleagues and surviving friends of Kinsey's: I owe a deep debt to Clarence A. Tripp, Vincent Nowlis, John Tebbel, Frank Edmondson, Sixt Kapff and Dorothy Craig Collins.

Much was new to me, and I therefore relied on experts. I would like to thank Dr Charles B. Heiser for his advice on gall wasps and Kinsey as

an entomologist; to Dr Noretta Koertge who gave me sound guidance to
the literature; once again to John Bancroft, and to Dr Kaye Wellings, one
of the joint authors of the recent British survey into sexual behaviour –
Sexual Attitudes and Lifestyles (London 1994) – who corrected my many
errors in this complicated field. Above all I am deeply grateful here to
Lynn Gorchov, who with great generosity allowed me to see much of
her unfinished thesis on Kinsey, and also painstakingly read and altered
my original manuscript. There will be mistakes still in all these areas,
but they will be where I had the temerity to override the suggestions of
these readers, which I very occasionally did. As generous as Lynn
Gorchov with unpublished material, was the biographer and editor of
Glenway Wescott, Jerry Rosco; and Clare Beaven of the BBC, who also
did much to enliven my stay at Bloomington for too short a number of
weeks. Abundant help, as well, and often hospitality, came from the
Chancellor of Indiana University, Herman B. Wells, and from Henry
Remak, Michael Shelden and James Madison. I would like to thank
Richard Sorrenson and Helen Sword, with whom my wife and I
swapped houses, and William R. Cagle who readied the already highly
efficient Lilly Library, which at that time he headed, and to him and his
wife Terry for much generous entertainment; and I am grateful to
Nancy and Robert Rayfield for equally generous hospitality extending,
in the end, to actually housing me in Bloomington on the last lap of my
research. Dolf Mootham has, as he has done before, provided invaluable
statistical expertise, evidenced in Appendix A, without which all financial statements made during Kinsey's life would be, to the ordinary
reader, foggy. Renna Nezos provided many penetrating and suggestive
insights; and I am grateful to Kenneth Anger and David Leddick for
material and introductions. I had to see people and material not only all
over America but at widely separated places in Europe. Despite the
usual generous support from my then publisher, now my agent,
Christopher Sinclair-Stevenson, I ran out of money. I am therefore
extremely grateful to the British Academy for financial assistance with
the research costs and I would thank Victoria Glendinning, Paul Preston
and Hugh Cecil for their effective sponsorship in this regard. This was
not their only help. Although, in the event, I was unable through pressure of time to take up the offer of a Donald C. Gallup Fellowship from
the Beinecke Rare Book and Manuscript Library at Yale, I remain grateful to them for that offer. I am grateful to Penelope Hoare, for her support in the often rather difficult circumstances that accompanied the

finishing of this book. I want to thank, also, Douglas Matthews for his excellent index. Marion Steel suggested innumerable useful and clarifying corrections, nearly always, but not invariably, followed. I would, as usual, like to express my admiration at Sandra den Hertog's deciphering of my notes and manuscript and the rapidity with which she consigned the latter to disk; and to thank John and Edmund Hatcher for patiently printing out those disks. Finally, although they come last, often not the least important contributions of information and help came from the following, all of whom have my sincere gratitude: Jill Adams, Judith Allen, Thomas Albright, Helen D'Amico, Philip Bantin, Dr Ian Battye, Rose Battye, William Baus, Donald Baxter, Robert Bayer, Ruth Beasley, Mary and Maurice Binkley, Dr Ray Blanchard, Jane Boling, John Bodnar, Randy Brown and his Scout Troop 136, James H. Capshew, Bobby Chance, Will Chandlee, Camilla Cazlet, Bradley D. Cook, Dr Robert M. Reid, Douglas and Elizabeth Ellson, Frank and Margeret Edmondson, Rosemary Findlater, Elizabeth Frazier, Paul F. Fuller, Dr Mary Gaither, John Gallman, Edward Grant, William Gury, Martina Hall, Sandy Ham, Margeret H. Harter, Dr Charles Hagen, Miriam Hecht, Alan Hedley, Herbert Huncke, James H. Jones, Nancy Janow, June Keisler, Denise and Thomas King, Robert L. Kroc, Consuelo Lopez-Morillas, Robert D. May, Lynda McNell, Dorothy McCrae, Earle Marsh, Abigail Mellen, William Parry, Christopher Peebles, Kath Pennavaria, Dr Michael Perring, Jerry Poorman, Lauren Robel, Miranda Rothschild, Stephanie A. Sanders, Larry Sharp, Susan Shelden, Todd Smith, B. A. Spencer, Dr Cooper P. Speaks, Thomas Swafford, Barbara Trudell, Gore Vidal, Eugene Weinberg, Robert and Dorothy Weir, Andrew Welsh-Huggins, Jennifer Pearson Yamashiro, and Carol and Frank Zeller. (It has not always been possible to check the spelling of names and the accuracy or existence of initials and I apologise for any inadvertent errors.)

Illustrations

The author and publishers are grateful to the following for permission to reproduce photographs:

Mrs Robert M. Reid for 1, 2, 3, 5, 6, 7, 8, 11, 14
The *Bowdoin Bugle*, property of Mrs Robert M. Reid, for 4
The Kinsey Institute for Research in Sex, Gender and Reproduction
    Inc. for 9, 10, 12
Indiana University for 3
William H. Dellenback for 15, 16, 17, 18, 20
Clarence Tripp for 19, 20a

Mrs Robert M. Reid for 24
William H. Dellenback for 21, 23, 25, 26, 27, 28, 29, 30, 31, 32, 35, 36, 37, 38c,
    39, 40, 42
The Kinsey Institute for Research in Sex, Gender and Reproduction
    Inc. for 22, 34, 38a, 43
R.J. for 41
Kenneth Anger for 44

'Everybody's sin is nobody's sin.'

Hans Sachs

'Few people are capable of expressing with equanimity opinions which differ from the prejudices of their social environment. Most people are incapable of even forming such opinions.'

Albert Einstein

'In the end we do not divide human nature in order to understand it. We divide it because secretly we don't want to understand it. If we did we might make the terrible discovery that we are only human after all, the only animals in the whole of evolution who like to pretend they are not animals.'

Richard Webster, *Why Freud Was Wrong*, 1995, p. 494

'In 1946 when I wrote *The City and the Pillar*, it was part of American folklore that homosexuality was a form of mental disease, confined for the most part to interior decorators and ballet dancers.'

Gore Vidal, from the *Afterword* to *The City and the Pillar*, 1965

PART I

Laying the Patterns
1903–20

I

Childhood in Hoboken: 1894–1903

1

When his children were small, Alfred Charles Kinsey used to fascinate them with descriptions of the Broadway he could remember in the New York of his childhood – a broad, unpaved muddy trackway down which cows were driven.[1]

He was born in Hoboken,* New Jersey, on 23 June 1894. He had no interests in his antecedents and virtually nothing is known of them. After *Sexual Behavior in the Human Male* came out in 1948, Kinseys from all over America wrote and asked if by chance they were related. Kinsey wrote back briefly and identically to each: it was thought they were all descended from three Quaker Kinseys who had come over with William Penn in 1682 and helped found the city of Philadelphia. One branch eventually moved, coincidentally, to the Midwest state of Indiana. Kinsey's own ancestors lived 'for generations'[2] near Morristown, New Jersey.

It seems possible Kinsey's ancestors' brothers were either Irish or Scottish in origin (the Penns had estates near Cork and William went there in 1666). The speculation is suggested by a curious circumstance of Kinsey's later life – which may also be why he himself vaguely hinted at such a descent. He was, at the height of his fame, to address very large gatherings about his sex research – several times of a thousand or more and once of over nine thousand; and on numerous occasions he had to face aggressive professional groups violently hostile to his work. It was noticed that at these times, when he was nervous, a distinct Scottish burr would enter his voice, vanishing as he gained confidence.[3] One must suppose that as their accent transformed some, or one, of the Kinseys

---

* Pronounced Hō-boken, with the accent on the first 'o'.

reverted to it under stress and that this mannerism passed on down the generations.

There are a few other scattered facts (for instance one early Kinsey was a supreme court judge in New Jersey[4]) but nothing important. One reason for this paucity is that Kinsey disliked his past and his childhood, and disliked talking about his childhood even more; none the less it is here that a number of significant and sometimes peculiar details do remain.

2

His father, Alfred Seguine Kinsey, was born in Mendham, just before the family moved to Hoboken, in 1871. In 1886, when he was fifteen, his own father, a carpenter, placed him as a lowly shop assistant in the Stevens Institute of Technology. It seems probable that he had in fact left school to find work aged thirteen, since he only ever reached 8th grade.*

Alfred senior remained here his entire working life of fifty-five years, grimly grinding his way up until eventually in 1908 he became a full professor. In his early years he worked long evenings and all his holidays in the Cooper Union School to gain extra qualifications.[5]

By 19 February 1892, when he was twenty-one, he could just afford to marry. He chose a New Jersey girl, Sarah Ann Charles, the daughter of another carpenter. Almost nothing seems to be known about the Charles family, except that Sarah's father was exceptionally able at his trade. As a young man (in the 1850s) he was employed because of his skill on the Mormon Temple in Utah, even though not himself a Mormon. When he returned to New Jersey he was escorted part of the way by armed soldiers, since they passed through Indian territory.[6]

Sarah herself was virtually uneducated (fourth grade) and, according to her son's wife Clara, was a gentle woman of great sweetness but totally dominated by her iron-hard, stubborn and dictatorial husband.[7] This young man felt that at twenty-one he could afford to rent a house

---

* To follow this and some later developments it is necessary to know a little of the American education system. Schooling begins at five or six and usually ends at eighteen, that is twelve years, and there are twelve grades, one a year. Primary (or elementary): 6 to 11, grades 1–6. Junior High School: 12–14, grades 7–9. High School: 15–17, grades 10–12.

in Bloomfield Street, number 611, within easy walking distance of the Stevens Institute. It was one of several poor, cramped, cold-water tenements the family lived in and it was here their eldest son was born.

Bloomfield Street today is in most respects exactly the same as it was when Al, as the family called him, was born. It is still respectable working and lower middle class, still long, tree-lined with pleasant, two- or three-storeyed, terraced, redbrick houses (many cramming in two or three families). Parallel to it runs Garden Street and at number 301 (number 3 in Kinsey's day, not 2 as he remembered[8]) there still stands the school that took him to his third grade. Now it incorporates a Head Start unit. And on Garden and Fourth Street is the playground he remembered, which, too, must be much the same – a big space with big, old trees, swings, an asphalt square for games, mangy grass.

Much has changed. Hoboken itself is on the east bank of the Hudson, directly across from and less than three-quarters of a mile from New York. The famous Manhattan skyline, gigantic buildings like the massive bar charts and spiked graphs of the economic dynamism that gave rise to them, extends before you. In 1894 it didn't exist. The tallest building in 1889 was the eleven-storey Tower Building. Skyscrapers proper didn't start to appear till the early 1900s with buildings like Singer Sewing Machine (612 ft in 1908) and Metropolitan Life (693 ft also 1908).

But in the 1890s nearly 60,000 people were packed into Hoboken's single square mile in conditions of Victorian squalor. From the north, smoke belched from metal, chemical and leather factories, blowing along the dirty streets. River Street, five above the Kinseys, was lined with dance halls, bars and prostitutes.[9]

The roads of Hoboken, as in most of America, were still not paved when Kinsey was born; the traffic was nearly all horse-drawn. He said he could remember the first cars and how they always broke down after a block or two. It is just possible. In 1899 there were six hundred internal combustion-driven cars in the whole of America.[10] Perhaps one or two found their unreliable way down the pot-holed streets of Hoboken.

Again, like a lot of America then, it seems likely that those same streets, indeed Hoboken generally, had poor drainage and sanitation. Kinsey's first ten years were dominated by disease. Not just measles and chicken pox and the other ills of childhood which, a delicate child, he had in abundance, but diseases now largely confined to Third World countries – rickets and rheumatic fever. Rickets is a disease of bad diet

(Vitamin D deficiency) and children with it are weak, restless and pale. It left Kinsey with double curvature of the spine. Rheumatic fever most often occurs where housing and sanitation are inadequate. It is a debilitating and painful disease; days, even weeks, have to be spent in bed, sweating with high fevers and racing pulse, unable to eat, joints aching, exhausted. It takes weeks to recover.

As a result, for much of his time in Hoboken, Kinsey was away from school, either in bed or convalescing. Sickly and weaker than his peers, kept by illness from their friendship groups, he was a typical target for bullying – and Kinsey was bullied. Years later he described to his assistant, Wardell Pomeroy, how he had once managed to escape his tormentors. Besieged in the street, he had suddenly thrown out a handful of pennies. The boys had dived – and Kinsey had fled.[11]

Such situations must have recurred. It is clear the little boy's need to escape was desperate. Just how desperate is indicated by that handful of pennies, for the Kinseys were at this time still very poor.

Poverty was the second factor which dominated young Alfred's early life. His father doled out a minute allowance by the week, and it was inadequate. His mother Sarah would get into debt and send Al to the local store with an instalment asking him to beg for more credit. She also used a store on the far side of town which issued an early version of trading stamps – and she made her son do the shopping there too. He hated these trips through muddy streets, no doubt frightened of bullying groups. But he also found begging for credit intensely humiliating.

The pressures of poverty grew worse when his sister Mildred was born in 1896 and these no doubt account for the deficiencies in diet. Pomeroy describes him as an adult still expressing a 'furious hatred' against the potato. And Kinsey never forgot the poverty of his childhood. He remained extremely frugal, not to say parsimonious, all his life – wearing darned clothes, buying cheap whenever he could, expressing 'furious hatred' at any sign that he or anyone connected to him was being exploited.[12] For the rest of his life he never went into debt. He never allowed his wife Clara to run up accounts in Bloomington or possess charge cards. When, eventually, the exigencies of his great sex research programme required him to beg again he proved virtually incapable of doing it. And both Mildred and his mother suffered from obesity – that affliction, ironically, so common among the poor.[13]

Yet perhaps the little family gained some consolation for their poverty from the teachings of Christ – blessed are the poor, for they shall inherit the Kingdom of Heaven. The third major strand in Kinsey's childhood was religion.

3

The Kinseys belonged to a group of Methodists so strict they could, doctrine apart, have been described as Calvinists. And of all that little group of Hoboken Methodists, Alfred Seguine Kinsey was the sternest, the strictest, the most unforgiving. Sundays were particularly cheerless. They went to three long services (walking – riding was forbidden), and also to Sunday school, where the father taught. Nothing else was allowed, no entertainment, no relaxation, nothing pleasurable at all – the milkman was forbidden to deliver milk, newspapers were forbidden, Sarah Kinsey had to cook all Sunday's meals on Saturday.[14] The only thing they could do was pray.

The effects of Kinsey's religious upbringing were fundamental to his character and affected his whole life. The working through of this immense force took place over time, but some aspects must have been impressed very early on. John Wesley's revival in the eighteenth century was of a passionately *personal* religion – austere, simple, personal testimony in private and public. One might note here certain strands: the vital importance of learning and education (Wesley himself started a school); fervent and frequent condemnations of smoking and drinking; speech – to be blunt and straightforward; politics – to be avoided. And, in general terms, Methodism shared that element common to all Protestantism, particularly perhaps as it expressed itself in America: unremitting work led to success and success was *proof positive* of God's favour.[15] All these particular prohibitions and spurs were to find expression in the life of the mature Kinsey.

They were impressed on the young one by stern disciplines. Aside from the strictures inherent in a Methodist upbringing (Wesley's own school, Kingswood, was absolutely appalling[16]), it is often possible to deduce from the way someone brings up their children aspects of their own upbringing, which they either replicate or react against. Kinsey brought up his own children much more strictly than his Bloomington neighbours, chastising them as he felt their behaviour required and insisting on strict rules.[17]

In passing, we should note another, odder, legacy. Alfred Seguine was strict – he was also extraordinarily egotistical. His students, who universally loathed him, used to count the number of times 'I' appeared in his one-hour lectures. A normal figure was a hundred times.[18] In later years Kinsey was virtually unable to use the word 'I', and as a result got into fearful tangles of 'we' and 'one'.

We can almost certainly assume two other things about little Al's early upbringing from the mature Kinsey's behaviour. Certainly the almost insane emphasis he was later to lay, and impose, on personal cleanliness suggested its imposition early and with a heavy hand. The same was true of his obsession with neatness. Clearly, cleanliness – and tidiness – were next to Godliness.

But father Kinsey was not just concerned with the moral rectitude of his own family. He tried, with commendable zeal, to reform the entire neighbourhood. Selling cigarettes to a minor in New Jersey was (and still is) illegal. Alfred Seguine used to send his young son out as a decoy. Once the cigarettes were sold, he would inform the authorities and the law fell on the astonished shopkeeper.

This sort of behaviour cannot have made the Kinseys very popular in Hoboken. It was a further cause of bullying. It also partly explains another significant feature of their family life.

4

The Kinseys had very few friends. They did not mix with the faculty of the Stevens Institute because Sarah Kinsey was shy and ill at ease with them. Their social life, such as it was, and apart from one or two relatives, was restricted to a few of the Hoboken Methodists[19] – gloomy gatherings, exchanging platitudinous pieties, the children enjoined to respectful silence. Dorothy Collins, one of the most perceptive and intelligent of the staff he had gathered round him by 1951, noticed at once Kinsey's social unease. 'I sensed it came from never having learnt it when small. Never having learnt to talk easily and informally. Then when they grow up – they can't learn it. It happens more frequently with scholars perhaps.'[20]

Many people were to comment on this. The effects of years of isolation through illness, with few if any close friends, the feeble role models of ordinary social life, all to be reinforced, combined to make this – the small talk of society – an area which Kinsey refused, often with considerable impatience, to enter. All his mature friendships were work-centred, and only one involved him with any deep emotion. For that, he invested entirely in his wife and children.

To say Kinsey disliked his memories of his first ten years is an understatement. He hated them. Later a skilled and fanatical gardener, he rejected the flowers of Hoboken just as he had attacked the potato. He refused to plant – or even accept as a gift – marigolds, zinnias or wisteria.[21]

Yet, deprived of such essential psychic nutrients as companions or a social life, he was to turn with compensating eagerness and intensity to those things he could get pleasure from. One of these was music.

Every so often the family would set off for Newark to visit relatives. 'We had to cross the Hackensack and Passaic meadows on the Jersey plank road (in a day when it was actually made of planks)'; but for five-year-old Alfred by far the most exciting thing about these rather rare excursions was that his cousins possessed one of the new 'talking machines'. This 'marvellous invention' was still vivid to him in an article he wrote – 'Music and Love as Arts' – just before he died:[22]

> Uncle Josh spoke from the surfaces of the cylinders that revolved in the machine. He and most other cylinder notables of that day ended their performances by announcing that we had listened to 'an Edison Rec-cord'. Even after all these years I can still hear the intonations and the exact rhythm of that phrase 'an Edison Rec-cord'.

The magic cylinders also played music and little Alfred's response to this was noticed. One of his young aunts, his father's sister, had a piano and it is possible he tried to play on this. In any event, from the age of five his parents provided piano lessons,[23] or allowed his aunt to give them. Someone had recognised a nascent and, as it turned out, precocious musical talent.

It is clear from this, and still more from events later, that his parents cared for their son and were determined to do what they could for him. The severity of his ill-health must have required from his mother years of devoted nursing – one of the most tangible expressions of love.

Nor was her husband's contribution by any means totally negative. In youth and early manhood an over-strict paternal upbringing, especially for boys, can either crush character and independence or, as it did with Kinsey, provoke angry battles between father and son. But at first, firm lines of behaviour, invariable routine, dogmatic certainty, create security and confidence. In later life, the mosaic of that sensitive and complicated man was cemented on a base of complete, almost excessive, self-confidence – a base which it is reasonable to suggest began to be laid down through a combination of his mother's care and his father's extreme firmness.

Then in 1903 he got another still more serious Third World disease, typhoid, a disease often due to poor water and sewage facilities. There was then no treatment except good nursing. The mortality rate was three out of ten; for young children, closer to six out of ten. It was, still is, an agonisingly painful disease, usually lasting about a month and necessitating lengthy convalescence.

The young boy recovered. And an unexpected result was the total cessation of his attacks of rheumatic fever which had plagued his first nine years. It is probable that the very high temperatures generated by typhoid at its crisis – 104–106°F over several days – had killed the streptococcal bacterium of the lesser disease.[24]

This recovery coincided with an improvement in the family finances. In 1903 they moved some fifteen miles further down the rail-track, already in place by that year, to the village of South Orange. Kinsey was to remain here until 1914, when he was twenty years old and stormed out of his home forever.

South Orange to Bowdoin College: 1903–14

*Let a man under the influence of strong passion go into the fields and see
how readily every thought clothes itself with a material garment.*

from *Nature* by Ralph Waldo Emerson

1

The 'village' of South Orange has now swollen and merged with other swollen villages to become part of the New York City megalopolis. But Roland Avenue is more or less exactly the same as in Kinsey's childhood. Number 102, the house the family rented, stands on a bank, with no garden to speak of, but there are a good number of huge trees along Academy Street with which it forms a corner.

Bill Gury, who lived there for seventeen years and knew Kinsey's younger brother Robert, says the house too is almost unchanged: a three-storey, yellow-painted, wood-framed house, with a kitchen and three rooms downstairs (each with a fireplace and plaster mouldings), three bedrooms on the second floor, and a small attic alongside two mansard attic rooms on the third floor of which Al had one and his brother Robert (born in 1908) eventually had the second. A 'den' was added in 1950.[1]

The house is a convenient twenty-minute walk from the station from where Alfred Seguine would have taken the train to the Stevens Institute each morning. Despite the fact that it was lit by gas and water came from the well, the Kinseys had risen in the world.

Yet at first it must have seemed to Al that everything was drearily the same. Once again he was attacked by the other boys, the seemingly instinctive picking on the weak augmented by resentment against incomers. But this time, as he returned from school or came in off the street weeping with impotent rage, his parents protested to the other parents that it was not only morally wrong to bully their son, it was also dangerous. Their doctor had told them that disease had so weakened his heart that he was unlikely to live to twenty-one. Therefore, no doubt acting on instructions, two of the local gang leaders, Girard Oberrender and Don Salisbury, took him under their wing and protected him.

The idea that he would die young, not surprisingly, made a deep impression on Kinsey. It is one reason why he flung himself with such furious intensity into anything, however trivial, that he later undertook. Subconsciously, indeed often consciously, he felt he might be snatched away before he could complete it. Earle Marsh, a friend years later, said it was as if he had to devour life.[2]

Kinsey used to describe angrily how his young aunt was once turned out of the house for playing *Cavalleria Rusticana* on the piano on a Sunday afternoon. The aggressively pious, objectionably pious Methodist fervour of the father still dominated the household. (At the same time the memory also reveals they now had a piano.)

But there was one great and overwhelming change – the cessation of ill health, something no doubt helped by the addition of fish to their diet. But Al's new health was rendered momentous by instructions from the doctor; the boy's best chance of survival was to get out into fresh air and walk. Even thirty years later Kinsey could remember the excitement, the great surge of relief he got from at last escaping out into the surrounding countryside – away from his bed, from illness, from home, from the bullying streets and cramped houses of South Orange. He was never to lose this excitement at setting out into the wild.[3]

And the countryside round South Orange *was* wild. Steeply rolling along the slopes of the Watchung Mountains, like so much of the northern continent then it was heavily wooded. Even today, thanks to the pleasant practice in America of filling their suburbs with trees, it still appears wooded as you look north-west from Roland Avenue across the valley. But then the woods grew thick and came right up to the village. On the map of 1903 the marshes, which are plentiful, are still marshes, and marked 'mosquitoes breed here' (as they are on the map of the Hoboken area – hence the plank road and hence, no doubt, additional fevers and illness).

Young Al set off alone on arduous walks, which grew longer and longer. These expeditions, his lifeline, were naturally encouraged by his parents. When he was eleven his father gave him a flower book,[4] and now the expeditions had a point – he began to collect flowers, pressed leaves, ferns. His father built a fernery, a minute glass conservatory, out the back of the house. It still had ferns (Kinsey's?) growing there in 1983.[5]

This interest in botany received a crucial boost, as did his work in general, when at the age of fifteen he went to high school.

2

At Columbia High, Kinsey discovered he was clever. If he couldn't compete with his peers fighting or at the various sports that obsessed them (and bored him stiff),[6] he could compete at work. In any case hard work was enjoined by his religion and by its earthly representative, his father.

The most important figure here was the young, bold and enthusiastic new biology teacher, Natalie Roeth. Her classes fascinated Kinsey and he joined her biology club. Now biology exploration in the surrounding countryside during school hours augmented his own expeditions. He was still writing to Natalie Roeth in 1948 and he never forgot their nature walks. Do you remember, he wrote elegiacally some years later, '. . . the meadowlark we chased over the fields, the periwinkle I brought for you to identify!'[7] He was equally fascinated by the way she drew nature into a whole – plants with animals; an approach in fact revolutionary in its day. He always credited her with his becoming a scientist.

As Kinsey found that, by hard work, he could beat his fellow pupils, his confidence grew. (And beat them he did. One remembered later, 'We called him "The Great Scientist".' Not necessarily a title indicating great popularity perhaps; more grudging admiration – an emotion Kinsey was frequently to evoke in later life.) Winning led to confidence, confidence to release. It is at last this – a more general feeling of release – one senses from Kinsey's middle adolescent years. Miss O'Hanlon (another Columbia High pupil) said her uncle remembered being nearly knocked off his feet one winter as Al hurtled past him down the steep lower half of Roland Avenue on a sledge.[8]

Release – but also intense preoccupation. As he grew older, tensions began to develop between Kinsey and his father at home. The youthful

Kinsey responded by immersing himself deeper and deeper in his work. He took it back from school and worked late into the night. It was now he began to develop his extraordinary powers of concentration. He was once seen at this time, again in the middle of an icy east coast winter – when the temperature often drops below 10°F (-8°C) – walking hatless, overcoat-less, serene and self-contained and alone, completely oblivious of the cold and his surroundings. This absorption was frequently noticed.[9]

He also immersed himself in his music. It is clear that by the age of sixteen he was becoming an accomplished pianist. Eliot C. Bergen remembers a concert at the South Orange High where he played Beethoven's *Moonlight Sonata*, a favourite piece which he quite often played. He began to give recitals at home. We can get, from another ex-pupil, a picture of him and his school world at this period.

Sophie Pauline Gibling describes the start of each day. The two hundred pupils arrived soon after eight o'clock, their lunches in 'collapsible metal boxes', and gathered for assembly in the main study hall, each at their own desk, boys and girls 'of course' separated. The nine or ten faculty sat solemnly on the platform. Like assemblies, one feels, since time began.

'Mr Freeman, the principal, would announce as the clock hands came to 8.25 exactly. Whereupon one of us – Alfred or Anne Geigor or I – would march up to the grand piano in the front, and all would rise to sing the national anthem. There followed a reading from the Bible, and another song, non-religious.'

It was a serious, unsophisticated, conscientious world. It was also a world where the Bible was taken very seriously. When Sophie Pauline and Alfred discussed Darwin and evolution and decided they believed it they felt 'daring', she told Cornelia Christenson, in taking such a 'radical stance'.

They were right to feel both. Evolution at that time was still extremely controversial. It was a mark of Natalie Roeth's boldness that she should teach it unequivocally. Darwin and his hypothesis were to be the single most important intellectual influence on Kinsey's life; that, and science itself, were gradually to replace Christianity as his spiritual centre of gravity. It was the first indication that his complete acceptance of his father's authority was beginning to crack. Another, also from about this time, is the Bunsen burner which he smuggled into the top of the house and with which he set fire to the floor. The charred hole and the piece of tin which he hammered flat, painted white and nailed over the hole to hide it, are still there, as was, till some years ago when it was found by Bill Gury, a brush handle minus the bristles.[10] This innocent object may eventually have to assume astonishing significance.

But concealed in this general picture of his school and musical life is the genesis of another, perhaps even more fundamental, certainly more noticeable, aspect of the mature Kinsey.

3

In 'Music and Love as Arts', the touchingly simple piece that he wrote in 1956 (one reads alerted, but the 'love' is only the love of music), Kinsey describes his first record collection begun about 1909, a collection of what he calls 'pancake discs'. These were extremely scratchy recordings of bits of great music by Bach, Beethoven, Verdi, Mozart, etc., usually lifted, arranged, sometimes even just imitated by the performers – Kreisler, Caruso, Paderewski and others. Kinsey persuaded relatives to give them to him; he began to give piano lessons to South Orange pupils in order to buy them himself.[11]

He was already collecting ferns, pressed flowers and leaves, and butterflies, and probably stamps[12] – now pancake discs.

Wardell B. Pomeroy, in his biography, sees being a collector as the fundamental clue to Kinsey's character (a view seemingly endorsed by Kinsey, who didn't particularly like or even approve of attempts at character analysis – at least not as far as he was concerned).[13]

Yet it is after all not an uncommon characteristic. At some stage it is almost universal. In later years it remains perhaps particularly common among scientists – indeed it is essential to them. As Kinsey's graduate school friend, Edgar Anderson, noted, without this impulse most of science would not exist – 'we should never achieve those vast stores of codified information from which the general laws and premises of science derive.'[14]

But it is true that with Kinsey it was sometimes obsessive. He dealt with things by collecting them. Simply to make a collection of whatever the problem was – adverse criticisms of *Sexual Behaviour in the Human Female*, say – seemed to solve it for him.

Nor were those collections small. When Kinsey collected he *collected*. Intrigued by a puzzling (and unknown) aspect of male masturbation, which was most easily solved on film, most researchers would have been content with fifty, perhaps, or a hundred examples. Kinsey had well over a thousand – possibly as many as two thousand – sequences of different men masturbating to orgasm.[15] Faced with this – and there are dozens of other examples – it is not enough to repeat, tautologically, Kinsey was a collector. It is necessary to look deeper.

Anderson himself observed the peculiarly cosseting physicality of the way Kinsey added to his collections (in this case gall wasps). There is a suggestion here of comforting and reassuring oneself, like eating. Dr Kroc, too, mentioned something similar – he said Kinsey had no friends in his youth and was lonely. Pressed leaves and butterflies took the place of friendship. Kroc, Kinsey's close colleague for eleven years, was one of the very few people to whom he confided details of his childhood.[16]

The element most noticeable in Kinsey's own accounts is how competitive they are. Almost the only thing he remembered about the flower book his father gave him when he was eleven was that he had found a flower that wasn't in it. Suddenly he realised – *he could beat the writer of the book*.[17] Advising young people to be collectors in his textbook on biology the chief inducement he held out was this: 'If your collection is larger, even a shade larger, than any other like it in the world, that greatly increases your happiness.'[18]

Kinsey also told Pomeroy that, weakened by illness and humiliated by years of bullying, he had felt physically inferior to other boys. We have seen how this drove him to work. But this humiliation seems to have had an additional goad.

William Parry was at school with Kinsey and was still very much alive in 1995. The passage of 103 years had blanked out a good deal but this only meant that what remained stood out in starker relief. 'Sure I remember Al Kinsey. He kept himself alone, stayed by himself. Say in sports – Al didn't join in. He wasn't one bit interested in sport. A tall guy. We thought he was a sissy guy, feminine-like, like a girl. Yeah, sissy-like, girl-like.'[19]

Collections are extensions of the self – and most, if not all, involve number. Everyone who had anything to do with Kinsey in later years became aware how intensely, even ferociously competitive he was and how this competitiveness often expressed itself in numbers. It seems reasonable to suggest that one root, at least, of this extreme competitiveness was here, in his vital need both to give vent to the bottled-up fury and aggression he must have felt against his tormentors and by beating them at the same time establish he was not a sissy, not girl-like, but a man – and a better man than them.

The strength of this need was demonstrated most nakedly now, near the end of his school days. Somehow or other Al Kinsey persuaded Oberrender and Salisbury to join him on a botanical expedition. They all carried 20lb packs. Al led them on a twenty-mile walk, up cliffs and steep hills, down into marshy ravines, pointing out items of botanical interest the while. The two youths returned completely exhausted. Kinsey had walked them into the ground.

Don Salisbury and Girard Oberrender, once they had recovered, felt humiliated in their turn – and cheated. Oberrender told his father that Al Kinsey couldn't possibly have a weak heart. Mr Oberrender, becoming angry too, went to Alfred Seguine and protested (their reaction, incidentally, suggests that the two boys had given their earlier protection under some duress). Alfred Seguine repeated that that was what their doctor had told them. Mr Oberrender was still so irate that he paid for a specialist. The specialist gave a clean bill of health (wrongly, it eventually turned out). But the message was clear – and no doubt it went round the school. Kinsey, the sissy who refused to play games, had won.

In fact, it was about now that this whole outdoor life of his took on a new and distinctive twist. Boy Scouts came to America.

4

Scouting began in England in 1908. By 1910 it had crossed the Atlantic. Al Kinsey joined immediately. In fact, he had been going to the summer camps of the Young Men's Christian Association since he was fourteen – and was to continue going to camps, on and off, till he was twenty-seven. With the YMCA, those centres of 'muscular Christianity' (their phrase), he had learnt 'woodcraft', nature studies and the rudiments of camping. Unfortunately, for some reason, possibly snobbery, South Orange never took to the YMCA. Chapters kept folding. Kinsey had to join neighbouring ones.

But South Orange, as if ashamed, threw itself into Scouting – and Kinsey threw himself too. He raced through all the possible tests on knots, first aid, woodcraft, etc., which often took people seven years, in under two – and became one of the first Eagle Scouts in America.[20] By 1912 he was assistant scoutmaster of the 52-strong South Orange troop and very soon, if not the actual scoutmaster, the *de facto* one. He now took to wearing his scout uniform – toggle, badges, shorts, hat – all the time.

Today, such enthusiasm might seem excessive. But scouting then was a serious craze, highly fashionable with young and old. (A *middle-class* craze in particular – one reason for its popularity in South Orange.) Scout troops were springing up everywhere. In this vast country still in the process of coming together, scouting was a manifestation and engenderer of patriotism, with flag-flying and saluting, the national anthem, and all those aspects of belonging to small groups which Americans still love so much – and seem to need so badly.

But scouting particularly suited Kinsey. There were fears at this time that modern civilisation was making American men effeminate. Scouting was consciously seized on as a way of bumping up masculinity, something Kinsey was no doubt still anxious to prove (the YMCA was a response to the same anxiety).[21]

Scouting was also close to another passion of the adolescent Kinsey – and here it is necessary to look at one of the remaining two sides of Methodism so far unexplored.

The major mark of all non-conforming religion – but in particular of Methodists – is a zeal (favourite adjective) for evangelising. The goal was to spread holiness over all the land. The means – zealous preachers swaying meetings, the bigger the better. In fact, every single Methodist was to be a preacher, a spreader of the Word. To this end, Alfred Seguine made his son become a teacher at the Sunday school. Here, in his learning to preach the Word of God, lie the origins of the later Kinsey's formidable oratorical powers.

Scouting in America in its early years was to a considerable extent a Christian movement. All meetings began and ended with prayers. Grace was said at meals (it still is). In a paper on scouting he prepared at college when he was still an active scout, Kinsey wrote: 'To produce Christian citizens is the only ultimate aim.'[22] Not surprisingly, the official scoutmaster of the South Orange troop was a clergyman – the Rev. D.D. Burrell, a minister of the Presbyterian Church.

As a result the whole Kinsey family became scouts. Kinsey's father was president of the South Orange troop and his mother was the second Scout Mother. In time, Robert joined. They played active roles. At the first annual banquet of the troop on 17 January 1913, Alfred Seguine took the theme – 'Pathfinding'. (Kinsey himself chose 'Be Prepared'.)[23] To begin with, his father had had grave anxieties – was it sinful to do scouting on a Sunday? The heavily religious overtones won him over and, no doubt, the middle-class ones as well.

We have an account, dating from 1910, by J.A. Woolf of the sixteen-year-old Alfred at Camp Kiamasha in the Kittatinny Mountains of west New Jersey. The young boys hero-worship him. In his tent he has twelve volumes, his library of nature books for his instruction classes and to answer questions. It is still dark when he wakes those who want to accompany him, with oil lanterns, 'On a bird, or flower, or snake hunt.'[24]

At long last, he was learning to socialise, but it was in a peculiar context. His new relationships were all that of teacher and pupil, the form of communication Kinsey teaching younger scouts or young boys at camp (and teaching them efficiently – twelve volumes is a typically thorough range of reference).

It is noticeable that in the teams and associates he was to gather round him later, Kinsey was invariably the oldest. And daughter Joan Reid said that her father always loved to get new knowledge, to extend his range – and then he loved to impart it.[25] For the rest of his life Kinsey's preferred mode of conversation was the little lecture. This can be very interesting – and Kinsey had an interesting and intensely curious and capacious mind – but over a long time it can be oppressive. There is an element of one-way traffic. Almost the only subject where this isn't boring, or at least where it is less boring, is sex.

Kinsey went to these camps not just as an instructor but as a counsellor, and this involved helping the boys (and girls, if they dared ask) with their sex questions and sex problems. He was already doing this, he told a later enemy Dr Thurman Rice, in 1913.[26] But sex was something Kinsey found just as enticing and yet guilt-inducing, just as painful and confusing, as they did; nor did his parents or teachers, scouting books or other books, help him here. On the contrary.

5

With Kinsey, sex is central. Wherever we know something of his sexuality it is at once apparent that, while it hardly ever, if ever, impaired his integrity as a scientist, it had a decisive effect on his work. And where it does once or twice seem to impair that integrity, the effect is either not very significant – or else it is obvious. There is a transparency.

So – what is known? Technically, as it were, everything. Kinsey, in a curious echo of the man he often criticised, Freud, took his own sex history. It was then taken again and again by Wardell Pomeroy and Paul Gebhard. It lies, coded and anonymous, locked and double-locked with some 18,000 other histories in the fireproof files of the Kinsey Institute, Bloomington, Indiana. One day it will be opened, decoded and read.

But in fact, apart from that, a great deal has recently become known, some as a result of indefatigable work by a recent biographer, James Jones. But Kinsey himself tells us some things.

One of his findings was that the earlier boys become adolescent the stronger their sexual drive. They begin sexual activity earlier, everything they do they do more frequently, and this pattern continues for the rest of their lives. No later research has challenged this and it has become universally accepted.*[27]

Both Wardell Pomeroy and Paul Gebhard, his two closest colleagues in later years, agree that Kinsey matured early, between eleven and twelve.[28] Photographs of him at the time – tall, gangling, shock-haired, smiling – suggest closer to eleven than twelve. His own later findings bear on this too. Early adolescent boys start their sexual activity at once, ejaculating in the first year. The majority (71.6 per cent) find their outlet, to use Kinsey's revealing but fairly blunt word, in masturbation. And these active youths reach their highest activity between fifteen and seventeen, when they can be masturbating as much as twenty-three times a week (the mean for all male adolescents combined is between three and four times a week); thereafter, for the rest of their

---

*Yet here as elsewhere it is very difficult to find other research which exactly duplicates Kinsey's and so allows one complete confirmation. (In fact, with exceptions we shall note, most of Kinsey's major findings have been accepted to such a degree that most people forget they were his.) Sometimes that particular subject is just not addressed. Sometimes the gender studied is wrong or the sample or the questions too different. Here, for example, the massive and, on the whole, excellent 1994 British survey found that early adolescence in women led to earlier sexual experience and 'early sexual experience is associated with higher levels of sexual activity in later life, which persists into the fifth and sixth decades. The relative strength of this remains undiminished over time.' The British study did not see if the same was true of men, but it would be surprising if it were not. In fact, Kinsey did not find this with women – or Females as he always termed them. But he was not testing this precise correlation. Such are the difficulties of corroboration. (See *Sexual Attitudes and Lifestyles*, Anne M. Johnson et al., London, 1994, pp. 77, 126–7.)

lives they, like all men, gently decline.[29]

There is no reason to suppose that Kinsey was out of step with the general pattern of his age and development group.[30] Where he was unusual was in the extreme conditions under which this volcanic force had to emerge.

The first of these was total, uncomprehending ignorance. It is difficult today, when all is known, all told, all shown on film or video or printed in book and play, to realise the extraordinary confusion and ignorance surrounding all sexual matters that pertained in America, Britain and over much of Europe in the nineteenth and first half of the twentieth centuries.

It was common to find girls at college in the 1930s who did not know how babies were born. Quite often they thought kissing made you pregnant. Boys were just as ignorant. When Glenn Ramsey, who later worked for Kinsey, did a study of high school boys, most aged twelve to eighteen, in 1939 and 1940, he found their ignorance astonishing at all social levels: 19 per cent knew a baby had to have a mother, but *none* realised the agency of a man was required; 91 per cent didn't know what the word virgin meant, 27 per cent didn't know the word intercourse, 96 per cent didn't know the word masturbation. Their ignorance of female physiology was catastrophic. 71 per cent knew nothing about menstruation and only 29 per cent knew the egg cell came from the mother (3 per cent thought it was provided by the hospital). And so on – the catalogue is long.[31] This all-pervading ignorance, confusion and often terror were significant features of the historical and contemporary background to Kinsey's major work. So was guilt.

In all this, as one might expect, religion played a dominant part. Essentially, as far as the Christian religion was concerned, all sex was sinful unless it was between man and wife in order to have children. This position was, in varying degrees, upheld by the American state laws. But it went deeper than that. For St Augustine, original sin was, precisely, *knowledge about sex*. Thus the confusion was created: knowledge of sex was a sin; but, paradoxically, in order to fight sin effectively everything had to be vaguely known (clearly, the vaguer the better).

Alfred Seguine was in the forefront of this battle. He tried to ensure total ignorance by seeing that his son was told nothing and saw nothing. No adult was ever seen naked in the Kinsey household.[32] He forbade all close contact with girls. He somehow sketched in forbidden areas, 'touching' oneself and so on, and banned masturbation, nocturnal emissions and, obviously, any form of intercourse. As usual, Wesley was invaluable. The preacher's longest work was actually called *Original Sin* (1757). The solution to sin was to awaken acute anxiety and guilt in order to drive the penitent to God. Here was Alfred Seguine's major weapon.

He would have had the backing of the medical profession – and no doubt he referred to it. Most of us are familiar today with the hysteria surrounding masturbation at this period (40 per cent of Ramsey's boys still, in 1939, thought it caused insanity); less well known is the effect of venereal disease.

Allan Brandt, in a brilliant study, *No Magic Bullet*, has shown what a terrifying situation had developed in America and all over Europe by the 1890s. In England in the First World War one in three soldiers was infected by VD; by the 1920s it was killing 60,000 a year. In New York, in 1901, 80 out of every 100 men were said to have it. This was an exaggeration, but it engendered a feeling that illicit sex, and so somehow all sex, was not just sinful but dangerous and frightening. Fear was certainly justified, if only by the cures.

There was essentially no cure. Treatment for syphilis was the same treatment Boswell had in the eighteenth century: the ingestion of mercury and sitting in baths as hot or hotter than could be endured. Some of the cures really seem like punishments for 'immoral congress'. Gonorrhea, for example, could cause chordee, a strictured curvature of the penis which caused pain when erect. Dr Frederick Hollick, a specialist in this area, recommended stimulating the penis to erection, placing it with the curve upward on a table and then smashing it flat with a heavy book.[33]

Nor were young Kinsey's anxieties and confusions allayed when he turned for help to scouting. The manual promulgated the received wisdom. God had given young men at around puberty a vital substance which turns boys into men. The effect of wasting this vital fluid could be very dangerous indeed. Dr Paul Gebhard much later, and for many years a close colleague, remembers discussing this with Kinsey: 'I don't know how much hell it gave young men, but a very great deal. You know, they said, well obviously we can't lose this vital fluid by doing it ourselves. But what if we do it in our sleep? My God, I'm killing myself with nocturnal emissions! You know. And it never occurred to anyone, including me, because I heard the same nonsense, it never occurred to anyone, if this is really true, marriage would be suicide.'[34]

The extent to which ignorance and conventional morality simply blanked out even simple commonsense over sexual matters at this time is continually amazing. They certainly blanked it out for Kinsey, even though it was a quality he had in abundance. It had numerous other effects, some profound.

6

Alfred Seguine had forbidden girls and his son, whatever his inner feelings, obeyed. The sometimes elaborate American practice of 'dating' was already in place at South Orange High. Kinsey never dated. The loner, the aloofness later commented on, created by early lack of social life and opportunity, was thus reinforced in a crucial area. He was not alone in this – dating was not universal – but it was noticed. 'He was,' Cornelia Christenson quotes a contemporary, 'the shyest guy around girls you could think of.' In his last year at school, the yearbook put a quotation from *Hamlet* under his photograph: 'Man delights not me, no nor women neither.'

He seemed to have no interest in girls; however, they were almost certainly interested in him. It is important to remember that all his life Kinsey was extremely good-looking. He had bright blue eyes and golden-blond hair which easily became curled, and which for that reason he cut fairly short, no doubt to avoid the epithet sissy. He was thin at this time and already full of energy and it was noticed how often he smiled. A ready smile is of inestimable value in America, as elsewhere, but Kinsey's smile, which may have evolved to disarm bullying, was more than this; it became a channel through which he expressed the warmth and sweetness of his character which, if deeply hidden, he possessed in considerable measure, a warmth and sweetness which would flash out and be gone, but which people did not forget.

Kinsey, as we've seen, rarely talked about his childhood. Paul Gebhard didn't know he had a sister until years after they'd met. But Kinsey did talk to him about his pre-adolescent sex play aged nine or so. This involved a neighbourhood group. 'There's a somewhat older girl,' said Gebhard, '... and I got the impression there were about six kids and they would go in the basement and look at one another, poke straws in various apertures, stuff like that, and that made him feel very peculiar and rather guilty.'[35] (Note that 'rather'.) One of the apertures was Kinsey's penis (the insertion apparently done by the girl).[36]

Upon this run-of-the-mill occurrence, recounted in his biography,

James Jones constructs an extraordinary, ingenious – but not necessarily implausible – edifice. The only trouble is that the foundation – the only actual *evidence* – lies some forty-six years in the future, in 1949–50. We shall, therefore, return to it then.

If the guilt over the penis insertion was relatively minor, there is no doubt that, like so many of his generation, Kinsey felt considerable guilt over almost everything else to do with sex.

Guilt, but above all frustration. What he remembered even more acutely as an adult was his terrible, torturing frustration. For years he tried, this highly sexed young man, to force the boiling lava flow of sexual feeling underground. Only occasionally are we aware of it. We know he was still wrestling with masturbation at the age of twenty. Not until he was twenty-seven was he at long last to find legitimate release – and by then, so long had he tried to stamp out his instincts, adaptation at first proved painfully difficult.

Nor would Kinsey himself have regarded a volcanic image as too extreme. At numerous times in his later writing, despite the strictly scientific pretence, the prose alerts one to his feelings. It is so now. Outlets, the means to orgasm, were not just important, he wrote to a young male correspondent, they were vital; as necessary 'as the tying off of an artery that has been cut, the provision of air for a suffocating man, or food for a starving man . . .'[37] The very word 'outlet' harks back to his youthful frustration – the sense is of something dammed up, pent, which must get free.

Kinsey told Pomeroy that he could neither forget nor forgive his father's stern and guilt-inducing morality, nor the agony it had caused him for so long. The most basic force behind his sex research was deeply personal and extremely simple and it lies here: that no one else should have to suffer as he had suffered.

7

Meanwhile, since girls were forbidden, Kinsey had only one place to turn – boys.

It is perhaps easier for a middle-class, middle-aged Englishman to understand what seems to have happened. For 150 years or so, right up until the 1960s, middle-class English boys were shut up in boarding prep and public schools, rigorously separated from girls, and kept in this proximity and seclusion for two-thirds of the year from the age of eight to eighteen. One result of this treatment was that they fell in love with each other. Usually, an older boy fell in love with a younger in what was often called a 'romantic friendship'. The root of these romantic friendships was almost invariably sexual, however unrecognised this was, but that did not mean sex took place. It did, but quite often, probably more often, it did not. Sometimes, of course, these love affairs – especially between contemporaries – were more straightforwardly homosexual; more often the younger boy was really a substitute girl. The mark of a romantic friendship was its passionate intensity.[38]

Freed from the rigours of parental control, sharing tents with bunks in close proximity for weeks on end, probably hearing each other masturbate, as James Jones vividly suggests, the American summer camp world of adolescent males was erotically charged. But emotionally charged as well. 'The mere fact of *who* went where or with whom on our various expeditions seemed to be emotionally coloured and to warrant record,' Joseph Folsom wrote nostalgically to Kinsey in 1948. 'Repeatedly it is on record [in my diary] that you had tent No. 12.'[39]

It seems likely that when he was nineteen Kinsey had a romantic friendship along the lines sketched briefly above with one of his scout troop, Kenneth Hand, aged fifteen. Kinsey kept all his letters over about two and a half years. We only have these letters, but the coin of their exchanges, as one would expect, seems to have been moral improvement. The first is Kenneth Hand's highly emotional resignation from the troop. (Kenneth is always resigning, usually because Kinsey has chided him about something, in this case probably smoking. He is always coaxed back.) The letter ends: 'PS Don't get rash on account of this but I can't help it.'

Next, on 10 February 1914, he sends Kinsey his YMCA Pledge Card to show he is contrite (their troop was a YMCA one); 'MY FORWARD STEP. *First* of these is never to touch cigarettes again. *Second*: to live more for cleaner speech and habit. *Third*: to teach a Bible class. *Four*. *To help other fellows*.' On 2 April 1914 he resigns again, '... I am sorry you cannot trust me enough to accept my approaches in sincerity. Kindly refrain from answering this letter as it is unnecessary.' On August 25 he is exhorting Kinsey to '*Read your Bible – Psalms preferably* – and then have a brotherly prayer service ... make yourself as religious as possible.' This is a frequent refrain. On 26 October he is reporting on other troop members. 'Wagner and Bodgly smoking to excess.' On 6 November 1915, he asks Kinsey, now left, to send him his photograph. There are one or two letters so obscurely worded they are probably about masturbation. 'I have had one or two old fits again though I managed to stop them in early stages both times thank goodness' (11 June 1915).[40]

The significance of these letters is that Kinsey kept them. He kept very few things. Oddly, for a compulsive collector, his daughter Anne remembers how anything not in a collection got thrown away. 'Daddy pitched things. He was always pitching them. It was mother who couldn't throw things away.'[41] Hand's letters are the only letters he kept from his childhood and youth apart from one or two of his brother's. There is quite a lot of scouting and camping memorabilia but mostly in the form of group photographs; there is only one photograph of an individual and it is of Kenneth Hand. It shows a good-looking adolescent posed rather self-consciously on the deck of what was probably a Hudson pleasure steamer. Again, between 1910 and 1914 there must have been two or three hundred weekly meetings of the South Orange troop, at each of which minutes were taken. Only one set of minutes has been preserved, that of 20 January 1913. 'We held our weekly meeting. After repeating the Lord's Prayer, the following passed their tenderfoot.' There is a list of fifteen names, among them Kenneth Hand.[42]

One can assume, then, that there was some feeling between Alfred Kinsey and Kenneth Hand – why keep these simple mementos if not? However, we should note three things, two perhaps contradictory. Though usually heterosexual in motivation, where the partners were to some degree homosexual, whether they practised or not, these affairs often alerted them to that aspect of their character. In fact, Kinsey himself was to pinpoint this moment in his life and it came many years later. At the same time, paradoxically, the exalted, emotional intensity of the relationships often completely obscured the sexuality which was their root. In Kinsey's case this would have been compounded by ignorance. Homosexuality was quite simply too horrendous for many people to be mentioned in the America of his adolescence. It had become so invisible it was the only sin ministers did not feel it necessary to attack. If one adds to them Alfred Seguine's stern moral precepts, and Kinsey's unquestioning if desperate acceptance of them, it is likely he had no real idea what was moving in him with Kenneth Hand, and unlikely that anything overtly sexual took place. Nevertheless, sexuality transposed into tenderness becomes the more intense.

And this is the third and most significant thing to note here. It seems likely that Hand created a pattern. Kinsey was to fall in love three times in his life, and twice it was with people whose relationship with him was that of pupil/follower to leader/counsellor; all but one of his known sexual affairs were with men or women younger than himself. The single exception was with a woman over sixty, when he was about fifty-five – but this, it could be argued, was more in the nature of a research episode.

Given the circumstances, and his father's prohibitions, someone like Kenneth Hand was probably inevitable. Kinsey would certainly have initiated him into the knowledge of plants and animals, since this was part of American scout training. Kenneth may well have assisted at Pine Island Camp when Kinsey set up his first recorded scientific study.

Experiment: to discover the bedtime of various species of birds.

Apparatus: none.

There follows a long list of birds and what they did between 7.15 p.m. and 8.05 p.m. 'When it was stopped on account of rain'.[43]

This abandoned experiment probably derived from his first scientific paper written when he was about sixteen. It had a faintly lugubrious, Thurber-like title, *What do Birds do when it Rains?* But it was the result of hours of careful, and presumably wet observation and was, to Natalie Roeth's excitement as well as his own, published in a nature journal.[44] At any rate, by the time he was eighteen, in 1912, he was firmly set on a scientific path. He had decided he would study biology.

At his high school commencement, the eccentric way (to the British) Americans describe what is in fact the ending ceremony, he played a piano solo – Chopin's *Polonaise* in Ab major. (There is something touching in the fact that he kept his dance programme, which was used to book girls for dances. It is completely empty.) He then returned home eager to discuss his future.

Alfred Seguine seems hardly to have listened to Kinsey's proposals about becoming a scientist. He crushed them out of hand. He had quite other plans for his eldest son.

8

Most fathers want their sons to do more or less exactly what they did themselves; and if not that then – and certainly this was so in 1912 – they want them to do what they, the fathers, tell them.

Kinsey's father had decided Alfred would be an engineer and that he would study, as he himself had done, at the Stevens Institute. This had the added advantage that the sons of faculty did not have to pay for tuition.[45]

No one in the Kinsey household had ever yet successfully stood up to its head. His mother was very subdued and bullied, Kinsey later told Paul Gebhard, which made him furious but which he did not feel strong enough to protest against. He fought, then inwardly seething he obeyed. But from this point on 'there was a great deal of tension in the house'.[46]

The Stevens Institute today, still with its 'medieval' gate put up in 1832, is a thriving, bustling college of technology set directly above the Hudson – the bar graphs of New York across from it beckoning the successful. In Kinsey's day it was much smaller and there were no girls on the campus, but it had long been a thriving, well-thought-of institution.

Christenson, a great deal of whose information came from Kinsey's wife Clara, speaks of Kinsey 'struggling' during the two years – 1912–14 – he spent there. She describes the physics professor wanting to fail him and only agreeing to a pass provided he gave the subject up forever.

However, Kinsey was already far too competitive for this to be a likely picture, and it is contradicted at nearly all points by his work record held in the archives there. At the end of his first year, it is true, he did only moderately in German, mechanics and mathematics. In physics he got 61 per cent (a pass grade in America is 70 per cent) – but he went on to advanced physics the following year and was reaching 78 per cent in his final papers.

Apart from there being no biology, botany or zoology at all, the course was quite broad, including English, foreign languages, rhetoric and every aspect of engineering.

Yet, it is clear from his results that as time passed he worked hard. As well as Scout and YMCA camps, he worked throughout the long summer holidays in 'supplementary terms'. He finally did well in almost everything. One notes, presaging the future, that he couldn't do advanced mathematics (regularly under 50 per cent). It was the only subject, with mechanics, he had to retake. He did best at 'English and logic' – getting 100 per cent three times running for his lectures, and 80–96 per cent for his essays. He was surprisingly good at mechanical drawing (75–80 per cent) and also at Shop Practice. This was his father's speciality and he may well have taught his son.[47]

The one thing Kinsey positively enjoyed at Stevens was the piano, which he played in the orchestra. For the rest, he would always refer angrily and bitterly to two totally wasted and frustrated years.[48] Yet it was not all wasted. His draughtsmanship was later used to effect, especially in his massive books on the gall wasp, where the exact if spidery drawings are not unpleasing. And his engineering skills, such as they were, would surface at odd moments. At one time he was to entrust his life to them.

During the last term of his second year at Stevens he realised he could take no more. He attended one of the evening commencement ceremonies at the end of June 1914 and, nerving himself for battle, returned to 102 Roland Avenue.

Kinsey said that up till that day he had always done what his father had wanted. He was now twenty and he was going to do what *he* wanted in future, which was biology. He intended to leave the Stevens Institute at once and go to Bowdoin College.

His brother Robert, aged six, watching and listening in fascinated horror, never forgot the row that followed. Or, more probably, rows. It seems to have gone on for several weeks. Miss Roeth remembers trying to persuade Mr Kinsey that the recalcitrant engineering student was better suited to biology.

Alfred Seguine had met someone as stubborn as himself. In the end he was forced to give way – but it was effectively the end of his relationship with his son. The one thing Kinsey would talk about with his young researchers on their long drives collecting sex histories years later was how furious and disappointed his father had been and how much, despite their differences, Kinsey had minded that sudden, total and unforgiving break.

As for his brother Robert, not only did he never forget the battle, he used it as a model. In 1924, when he was seventeen, he too had a furious row with Alfred Seguine and walked out. 'Grandfather Kinsey was a hard man,' said Jim Kinsey, Robert's son. 'No one could ever get along with him for long.'[49]

9

But there is an honesty in science which demands that the best means be used for the determination of the truth.

Sexual Behaviour in the Human Female, pp. 8–9

So what sort of young man was about to set out from South Orange?

A peculiarity of Kinsey's character until quite late on was that where many people change with time, dropping elements, refining, Kinsey just became more and more definitely what he was. His collecting grew, as did his competitiveness and related passion to work; circumstances were eventually to magnify the battling independence that had finally freed him from his father.

And here lies the final piece in that puzzlingly obsessive collecting. By collecting something, naming it, pinning it in boxes or sticking it in albums or on shelves and walls, in racks and piles, you not only impress your personality on it, extend your personality by means of it – you also control it. To collect anything is a way of imposing control. Kinsey had been completely controlled by his father for twenty years, and one reaction to this was to try and exert total control from now on over any-thing that concerned him. Subtly, he choose positions where he was as independent as possible without jeopardising his career. When the time came for him to have groups under him, his control was at once absolute. He couldn't delegate anything. In the end, when he was battling the whole world of American sexual conventionality his independence became almost exalted.

Kinsey's reaction against the control of his father extended in some respects to a reaction against all conventional authority. He was not always to be a quiescent or easy member of his faculty. And he liked to shock. He enjoyed knocking people off balance – and here another reaction sometimes came into play, a less pleasant one.

The early years of bullying, his increasing resentment at his dictatorial father, seems to have generated a great deal of buried anger. Many people commented on his liking for a fight, his aggressiveness. While he didn't often lose his temper, though he could, there was a sense of considerable impatience under the surface, and this would explode in what seems to have been bursts of almost ungovernable irritation. 'He could be very sharp indeed suddenly,' said Elizabeth Frazier, who came to work for him in 1938. 'He could stop you right short. A sharp cut off.

You just quit.'[50] Clara Kinsey, talking to James Jones, tried to excuse this by saying that at least he didn't 'keep harping on it'.[51] But there will be more extreme examples.

An over-disciplining, morally disapproving father meant that Kinsey had to keep many things secret from him – holes burnt in the bedroom floor, masturbation, his growing desire to study biology. Secretiveness became ingrained, almost automatic. It was noted as a central element by the novelist Glenway Wescott many years later.

And it was not just his father. There had been two engines of control thumping down on him from childhood. It is almost impossible to exaggerate the influence on Kinsey of his intensely religious upbringing. It made him keenly aware, as Pomeroy notes, of the tremendous and terrible power of religion in human affairs, and in particular, of course, of its repressive power over human sexuality. He became increasingly antagonistic towards this as science undermined and then destroyed his faith. In the end, when he had to confront religion again, he would rage against it. He refused to have anyone of active faith on his staff. When Clarence A. Tripp, a close friend, asked him the cause of his phenomenal drive, Kinsey located it here. It derived from the damage Christian morality and prudery had done to him. 'The whole army of religion,' he told Tripp, 'is our central enemy.'[52] Kinsey was wrong. His extraordinary drive had made itself manifest long before that and in a field which had nothing to do with religion, but there is no doubt the crusade, or anti-crusade, was one thing that fired him in the final war.

Kinsey was never able to jettison his Methodist religion completely. As its central tenets dissolved, the remaining features stood out more starkly. For instance, all non-conforming religions lay stress on social good and social reform. They also enjoin the necessity to preach. But there were more profound effects than this. Kinsey had been brought up to be a preacher. Michel Foucault, in one of his maddening but stimulating volumes,[53] sees the sermon as something that had long been essential in the West, and therefore when writer/scientists like Krafft-Ebing, Havelock Ellis and Freud came on the scene they simply took over this ancient tradition to fulfil an ancient need. The sermon has standard ingredients: chastisement of the old order, denunciation of hypocrisy, and a promise of a new city, a new day to come, a promise of felicity. This is a more or less exact description of at least one aspect of Kinsey's extraordinary volumes on sexual behaviour. The record of his life's two great works can be regarded as an enormous sexual sermon.

But his rejection/retention of Methodism was complicated. Brought up within a very strict religion, his character had been formed – as has our Western culture – with the need for a central focus, a *belief.* This is the reason he took to science so passionately – he needed a very strong absolute belief in order to carry out his task. All his lectures, not just his sex ones, had elements of the Messianic, which his audiences felt and responded to.

Since the church denigrated sex and the physical aspects of man and said that the soul and the spiritual side should mainly be studied, Kinsey made a complete reversal and studied sex *entirely*, unsullied by any spiritual or emotional side at all, including love – which he came to see as an encumbrance. It is interesting that in psychological terms sex can be almost as all-embracing as religion.

And in a final paradox beneath these half-paradoxes, Kinsey's ultimate significance as a thinker or exemplifier – and contrary to other commentators I think it is possible to consider him in this light – is that in the end his work can be seen as significantly undermining the need for an absolute belief, the very need that had given rise to it. In this respect he is a precursor of the neo-Darwinist theorists and biologists of today.

As Kinsey learnt the truth about his own sexual needs and, more particularly, about how people really behaved sexually, what particularly disgusted him about the Methodists – and about religious people in general – was their sexual hypocrisy. This disgust must have been considerably sharpened when some years later the arch Methodist, his father, went to Nevada in order to obtain a quickie divorce to go off with another woman – a Miss Antoinette Van Duren. The point here is that men simply did not do that in the 1920s and '30s. If there had to be a divorce, men provided the evidence so their wives could divorce *them*. The degree to which Kinsey felt this can be gauged by the fact that he never talked about it and his children only learnt about it after his death.[54]

If you drive down something as powerful as sex then a good many other things get sucked down too. Kinsey always had difficulty expressing intimate personal feelings, especially in public. Indeed, he didn't express them. There seems no doubt that Kinsey's marriage was a close one. Yet Dorothy Collins could 'not remember him ever making an affectionate gesture towards Mrs Kinsey. That is rather unusual for a happily married couple, but it was his way.'[55]

As often with people who have difficulty here, Kinsey loved small children and was extremely good with them. Besides which, little children are never hypocritical and don't waste time in trivial small talk.

Kinsey's sexual suffering made him able to identify with all suffering. The three young men who later helped him gather sex histories were not insensitive, and the tales of sexual frustration and cruelty they heard were often harrowing, but they could take it. Kinsey often returned from his sessions his eyes filled with tears. And the many acts of kindness, all hidden and private, which went on all his life, encompassed people in every sort of trouble – men and women, black and white, convicts or should-have-been convicts.

There is an unexpectedly sensitive and creative side to Kinsey which could only emerge obliquely – in his curvaceous handwriting, the poetry he wrote at high school, the fact that later on it was not Mrs Kinsey but her husband who always did the flowers, in what his astute University President Herman Wells noticed as his 'flamboyance'.[56] In every preacher, every lecturer, there is an actor struggling to get out – and this side of Kinsey was not to emerge fully until twenty-seven years later, when he finally stepped on to the American, indeed world, stage.

In fact, many of these developments are in the future, but their seeds lie here. It is the working out of the patterns and conflicts they engendered in this often difficult, enigmatic, sensitive, clever and complex man which will form the shape of his whole life, and finally prematurely end it.

At the moment, however, in July 1914 he had much more urgent, if more mundane concerns.

10

The hero, Freud said, first defies his father, then defeats him. Kinsey now set about the second step with, one imagines, considerable excitement and probably pleasure.

He had already, before confronting his father, written to Bowdoin for their prospectus. He now gathered references. Mrs Mayhew, an elderly widow whose husband had been President of the South Orange Town Board, knew and got in touch with a Dr Hyde at Bowdoin. The South Orange High and Stevens sent recommendations and scholastic records. On 24 July, Kinsey wrote to Dean K.C.M. Sills, referring to Dr

Hyde and enclosing the reference material. He would, he said, have to work his way entirely through college so 'a scholarship would naturally be of great help'. There is, somehow, something touching about the letter being written on the elaborately headed South Orange Troop Scout notepaper. Kinsey has inked a minute asterisk against the post of Asst. Scout Master.

The references must have been strong. On 29 July he received his reply. He was accepted; he would receive a small scholarship of $200* a year towards tuition fees.[57] Mrs Mayhew herself added another small sum towards college expenses. (This local help suggests there was some general sympathy for Kinsey's treatment by his father.)

Kinsey then left for summer camps to earn money as counsellor and leader. It was his last visit to Camp Kiamesha and that summer of 1914 they played war games. The Germans inflicted a crushing defeat on the allies led by 'Field Marshal Alfred Kinsey'.[58] This is the only recorded time Kinsey ever showed the remotest interest in war that wasn't strictly personal. But when he set out for Brunswick, Maine, in the fall of 1914, he had made just enough to carry him through the first term.

He left in September looking unusually smart. He was wearing a brand-new suit which had cost $25 and been bought for him by his father. Alfred Seguine never helped, and hardly saw, his eldest son again.

* For a very rough approximation to today's prices throughout the book see Appendix A.

College – and First Appearance of the Gall Wasp: 1914–20

My mind has changed during the last twenty or thirty years. Now for many years I cannot endure to read a line of poetry. I have also lost my taste for pictures or music. My mind seems to have become a machine for grinding general laws out of a large collection of facts. If I had to live my life again, I would make a rule to read some poetry and listen to some music at least once a week. The loss of these is a loss of happiness.

Charles Darwin, quoted in *The Life and Letters of Darwin,*
ed. Francis Darwin, 1887–8.

1

One of the interesting things about Kinsey's correspondence with Bowdoin College (pronounced Bo-dun) is that it shows clearly that his initial ambition did not in fact lie in zoology or biology at all. He was really far more interested in his camping and scouting. After college, he wrote, he wanted 'to enter YMCA boys' work'. To that end he had decided to major in psychology, with zoology and some botany secondary.[1]

But no matter what he had chosen, the amount of work required was formidable. The high school standard of biology was not high; psychology he had never studied at all. Because of his two years at Stevens, Kinsey was allowed to enter as a junior. But this meant he had to catch up on two years' work. Moreover the degree course at Bowdoin was a broad one, encompassing, as far as Kinsey went, economics, English and philosophy. To this he added the minutest possible amount of physical training, presumably compulsory.

He now revealed in earnest the extraordinary powers of work and concentration which were to characterise and dominate his entire life. He spent sixteen hours a week on zoology alone, a comparable amount on psychology, four hours on biology. He spent all day and most evenings and on into the night working in laboratories and classrooms. He worked almost the entire time. In his second year he also worked as assistant to Dr Manton Copeland. And here – a significant development – he first came into contact with insects.

He worked because he had to; he also worked because he had little else to do. He had no friends. He had arrived two years after everyone else and friendship groups had long since formed. But one suspects this made little real difference to Kinsey. His fellow undergraduates were mostly noisy, extrovert, unstudious and only really interested in girls and sport. Paul K. Niven, a classmate, said Al took no interest in any of these: '... for example, a pre-football game student rally with its cheers, bonfires, etc., was simply not his dish! Neither were college dances, fraternity house parties and other social occasions.' And so he worked more or less totally alone.

But he did not appear unhappy, nor was he unpopular. He seemed easy and relaxed, irradiated by his dazzling smile, his hair already cut in the fashionable 'Bowdoin Brush'. *The Bugle*, the college year book, said, 'If you loosen up a bit more, Al, you will make quite a man.'

Christenson, making the most of what looseness there was, says he joined in when he wanted to. For instance, she writes, he joined the 'varsity debating team and – already a formidable debater – won the top debating honour, the H.L. Fairbank Prize. He also seems to have joined the chess club.[2] One can't help noticing that debating and chess are not so much communal skills as adversarial ones.

None the less, undergraduate Kinsey did have other outlets, if one can use the term.

2

To begin with Kinsey found rooms with two old spinsters. They seemed to spend their entire time ridiculously polishing and repolishing the silver, but at first deeply impressing this young man from a silverless background.[3]

Soon after this he had rooms in college. Still collecting stamps, flowers, ferns and butterflies, he now became fascinated by snakes. He steadily collected until he had twenty slithering about his room. He did snake experiments. Like most undergraduates who spend their entire time working he was a favourite of his teachers. Dr Alfred Gross, his biology professor, used to go on weekend bird-spotting trips with him. He now let Kinsey bury a lot of snakes four feet down in his yard. Kinsey was to start his first published book with their sleeping survival.

The social nexus of American university life then was the fraternity. 'Not to be in a fraternity or sorority was widely regarded as being nothing at all.' Larry Lockridge was describing Indiana University at Bloomington in the 1920s, but the same was true at Bowdoin.[4] Kinsey joined the Zeta Psi fraternity, in the Lamda chapter* – though not to make friends. He joined primarily because the fraternities all owned or rented chapter houses near campus and the Zeta Psi house was Kinsey's home for most of his two years at Bowdoin.[5] But they also had a good collection of classical gramophone records – and they had a piano.

The Zeta Psi upright was often used by the undergraduates. They would gather round it in the evenings and play ragtime or yell out fraternity songs and hits of the day. 'In such sessions,' wrote a con-

---

* It is necessary to know a little about the American fraternity institution at this time. They probably derived, according to Dr Henry Remak, from German institutions of the same sort (though in these duelling sometimes played a part). The transition from the strictly structured high school to the much freer university meant that many felt the need for structure. Also, for freshmen, they were the route to friendships. They were self-governing student groups who lived together. A common practice was to live in your fraternity for two years and then move out. Dr Remak spoke of their 'high ideals'. Their induction ceremonies could be less than this. At IU (Indiana University) in the 1920s they were often sexual, lavatorial and endless. Students were stripped naked and erotic literature (e.g. *Night in a Harem*) was read aloud and erections cheered. Still naked they were 'ordered to follow one another around on all fours, goosing one another and then sucking fingers'. 'Fart charts' were kept during a week when freshmen were fed on unseasoned beans. IU was at this time in many respects a hick university. It is in the highest degree unlikely that Kinsey suffered such indignities at the much more sophisticated east coast Bowdoin – but there would have been some sort of induction ceremony. Membership of Phi Beta Kappa is awarded for outstanding scholarship (in some cases students can apply, in others a faculty member nominates). It is rather like, in Britain, a starred First. It is recognised across the US and is of academic use for the rest of a person's life. There are awards for graduates – but graduates, unlike undergraduates, are by definition serious. Phi Beta Kappa, therefore, signals that someone is particularly serious and dedicated at an early age. It perhaps hardly needs saying that Kinsey was Phi Beta Kappa. (Author discussion with Dr Henry Remak of IU, July 1995; induction account p.98 of *Shade of the Raintree: The Life and Death of Ross Lockridge Jnr.*, Larry Lockridge, Viking Penguin, 1994.)

temporary, 'Al just plain preferred not to join.'

But much later in the evening or at midday when the fraternity room was empty, Kinsey would come in by himself and play classical music for an hour or more. Some of the fraternity, almost despite themselves – they 'had no interest in such "stuff"' – would creep in and listen. Even *The Bugle* became interested. It was particularly impressed by his playing of the *Moonlight Sonata* which must, it is true, have been more or less perfect by this time. Another contemporary had 'rooms looking directly into the music department'. He used to see Kinsey go in (he had been given a key) and let himself go on the college grand. 'He was an excellent musician . . . [but] the main thing that impressed me was that he often played tempestuously, and I was quite sure that this was the way he took of relieving his tensions which must have built up in him by the long hours he spent in laboratory work in his courses.'

No doubt more than work tensions had built up, but there is a more interesting aspect to this. Some of the students were literally spellbound as the music cascaded from the piano. Kinsey was a romantic and fascinating figure then – with his golden hair, his striking good looks, radiant, totally absorbed. Forty-five years later, Paul K. Niven could still remember the 'aura' round him at these moments.[6]

Someone who gives impressions such as these generates them from their own inner fantasy. There are other indications that he saw himself as The Artist. He always went hatless at Bowdoin[7] – as eccentric and unconventional then as to wear a hat would be today. As at other times of his life, Kinsey kept very few things from his Bowdoin days – but four of the things he did keep are musical. There are three large photographs of paintings of Schumann, Mozart and Liszt. And there is an unsigned typewritten short story. It is a romantic, even sentimental story about the ghost of Beethoven hearing someone play his *Moonlight Sonata*. Beethoven comes in and shows how it should be played.[8] The story, on stylistic evidence as well as content, is almost certainly by Kinsey.

In 1948 a film, *Quartet*, came out based on four of Somerset Maugham's short stories. One of these was about a young pianist whose ambition is to be a great concert artist. Finally he is told by a real great pianist (female) that he isn't good enough. The young man shoots himself. It is, in fact, a curiously unmoving piece of film. But Pomeroy recounts how in 1949 C. A. Tripp went with Kinsey to see it in New York. Kinsey sobbed like a child, to the extent that people began to stare at him. Tripp today says this was a typically wild piece of Pomeroy exaggeration. None the less, the substance is true. Kinsey was considerably moved. This was his fourth visit to the film. When Tripp, surprised, asked how he could go on enjoying it after seeing it so many times, Kinsey looked at him coldly. 'I don't intend this to be the last,' he said.[9]

There was an intensely romantic streak in Kinsey, eventually deeply hidden. For some years Kinsey had serious ambitions – or serious fantasies – of being a concert pianist. Certainly his wife thought this.[10] Later, he realised he wasn't good enough; it is possible he was advised by some professional. But the buried artist remained an important part of him.

3

As well as the four musical items, Kinsey kept his (incredibly detailed) philosophy and ethics class notes from Bowdoin. The behavioural school of psychology, which became dominant in America, did not really get going till John Watson published his *Behaviorism* in 1924. None the less, it is this which informs all Kinsey's later work on human behaviour and no doubt he picked it up from later reading. B.F. Skinner, another leading exponent, was on the faculty at Indiana University with Kinsey.

The most substantial piece of work by Kinsey which survives Bowdoin is a thirty-page dissertation from his psychology major. This is a study in (boy) group dynamics – 'The boy's chief desire is to be like his fellows.'[11] What the dissertation also shows, as in the quotation used earlier about the aim of scouts being to produce Christian citizens, is how strong still was his faith. But above all it shows the paramount practical importance that the camps played in his life. They, and related activities, were his sole economic base.

He had been going to these as ordinary camper, then troop leader, counsellor, part-time teacher and, effectively, itinerant preacher for many years now and had set up a network of contacts that enabled him to find employment throughout the summer. The local YMCA, thinking of him as a future staff member, gave him work. Through them, he found teaching jobs. He gave English classes to local French-Canadians for example, and also taught local mill workers.[12]

And he continued to answer questions about sex, sometimes thereby revealing that his own desperate, pious and fruitless struggles were continuing. At one summer camp an adolescent boy confessed to Kinsey that he was masturbating too much. Kinsey knew there was only one thing to do. He took the boy into his tent and together they knelt by the bed roll while Kinsey prayed that God would help them both stop.

There is no record of his returning to South Orange during his time at Bowdoin. He probably paid brief visits. But his camping was not restricted to summer. Christenson describes a winter expedition with some fellow undergraduates to collect live animals for the college museum/zoo. But she adds a significant detail. They all agreed to take off and hide their watches in order to feel closer to nature.

Kinsey realised that his love of nature, that whole romantic streak, was essential to him. So much so, that he made it the central element in his Commencement Address when he left Bowdoin a little later.

He graduated with very high honours – *magna cum laude*. He had gained eighteen grade As and three grade Bs (one of these in physical training). His biology teacher, Professor Alfred Gross, later thought he was the most brilliant pupil of his entire career.[13]

Kinsey gave his farewell speech at the end of June 1916. Extremely oddly spelt (never a strong point), the beginning is both revealing and fairly embarrassing.

'I owned a friend in a gray squirrel yonder,' cried Kinsey, gesturing towards the campus outside. Gradually they became acquainted, Kinsey and squirrel. Until eventually – 'We talked together; we confided our troubles. Each was a mystery to the other – but we were friends!'

But now he launches, surprisingly, into an *attack* on science – on that very concentration which had just won him such honours. It was destructive – at least to the scientist. Just as important was the love of nature: 'to know . . . the flower or fern or mountain or woodland pool – to hear the tale of the winds, or hum of the bumble bee.' The love of nature – and the *individuality* which art concentrated on. Art, the artist in man, was vital. Kinsey was already aware of the potentiality in himself of being overwhelmed by science; of becoming 'a kind of machine for grinding general laws out of a large collection of facts' as Darwin said in the epigraph to this chapter, a celebrated passage, sometimes known as Darwin's Lament, which Kinsey quoted in full in his address.[14]

He set off for his camps again soon after this to get more money and prepare himself for the next assault on his precipitous and lonely upward ascent. His prodigious capacity for study, his already impressive academic achievement, had secured him a scholarship to the Bussey Institute at Harvard.

Art and science – his music, his love of nature and his growing passion for his work – were at present in harmony; however, it was a balancing act he eventually became unable to sustain.

4

The Bussey Institute for research into applied biology was recognised as one of the most outstanding graduate schools in the United States. Although its degree was a Harvard one (Harvard paid his scholarship) the Bussey was sufficiently distinguished as to be virtually autonomous.

Kinsey found a room with full board in the house of Miss Elizabeth Weld, who lived in Roslindale, then a modest suburb on the southern fringe of Boston. She took in a few students free in return for housework (free, but we should note a familiar disadvantage. Once again Kinsey was cut off from his peers). However, Kinsey, no doubt profiting from his observation of the Brunswick spinsters, polished the silver, washed windows and dishes and on Saturdays worked in her garden.[15]

And each day – and of course long into the evenings – the Bussey Institute. It was ideal for him. An old-fashioned, high-ceilinged building, the few graduate students and fewer, in some cases celebrated, teaching scholars, lived in a state of apparent chaos: Dr W.F. Castle's rapidly reproducing colonies of rats, mice and rabbits now welling up from the basement and over-running the ground floor, other floors and rooms filled with Dr Oakes Ames' 'economic' plants and their produce, and a many thousand book library without a librarian.[16]

His tutors were professors Merrill Lyndon Fernald, Morton Wheeler and Charles T. Brues. There were no set courses but initially Fernald – short, fat, 'boyishly joyous' and a botanist of brilliance and huge energy[17] – taught him taxonomy.

Fernald and he, ostensibly together, also compiled a book of edible wild plants. It did not appear till 1943. It is a substantial book of over 450 pages with an index, and required a lot of reading, a lot of work in the Gray Herborium, a lot of cooking – and a lot of often (in my view) rather unpalatable eating. When he gave a talk, probably in 1918, to the New England Botanical Society, he told them to dispense with a caterer. He, Kinsey, would provide. No record seems to remain of the meal except a vague memory of acorn bread.[18]

According to Kinsey, and there is no reason to doubt him, he really researched and wrote the book himself, with Fernald lending his name.[19] Since it was already in manuscript by September 1917,[20] a good part of his first year must have gone into this work.

But the most important figure in his academic life was William Morton Wheeler, his supervisor. Wheeler was the most famous biologist of his day, loaded with honours, continually published (and still cited more than any other American entomologist alive or dead). He was also urbane, amusing, a blatant atheist, a lover of whisky and wine who smoked like several chimneys – pipe, cigars and cigarettes. The waning of Kinsey's faith, which in two years' time would have progressed to a loathing of everything religious, almost certainly began at Harvard and probably owed a good deal to this, in Kinsey terms, outrageous sinner.[21] But since, though he later expressed admiration for him, Kinsey barely saw Wheeler at all outside lectures, the strongest influence was the study of science itself – notorious for having such effects. Wheeler was also a fervent advocate of out-in-the-field biology as opposed to the still nascent genetic school of experimental biology. Kinsey attended his lectures on general entomology during his first year. The notes for one term's lectures have been preserved and they are very full, almost verbatim – 114 close-written pages.[22] Kinsey had at first been uncertain about the subject for his dissertation but these lectures made him more and more fascinated by insects. He chose a particular beetle, studied it, dropped it. It seems to have been in April or May 1917 that he hit on the gall wasp.

Kinsey's love affair with this tiny creature was to involve him deeply for over twenty years and bring him, if on a very narrow focus, his first great success. But before he could embark seriously on this, the second term came to an end.*

5

It seems likely that Kinsey visited his family at some point in the

---

*American universities have two terms (semesters) a year. First semester: mid-September to Christmas, short break, then start of January till the end. Second semester: early February till first week of June. Summer sessions are usually mid-June to early August. So the two or three weeks of August to mid-September are holidays. At this time Kinsey spent all his holidays and some of the summer sessions at his camps.

summer of 1917. At least there is a photograph of them all together and Kinsey is in shirtsleeves.[23]

It would have been brief. As usual Kinsey had to earn money at his camps, often now teaching elementary biology. There is, incidentally, no further indication of Kinsey being attracted or emotionally attached to anyone after Kenneth Hand. The 'privacy' surrounding his sexual life at this time is all but impenetrable. One can only speculate upon the few scraps of evidence available. We know that his years of acute sexual frustration continued till he was twenty-seven. It is certainly possible, after Hand, that he was drawn to one or other of the youths he led on expeditions. But from what we know definitely about him later – in his late twenties – it seems certain that Kinsey, however shy, was at this point at Harvard much more strongly attracted by women and girls than by men or boys.[24]

A rare and vivid account[25] survives from this summer written by Howard Q. Bunker, once of the Bethany Boys' Club. This was an offshoot of the local Bethany Methodist Episcopal Church, and Kinsey led thirteen boys aged twelve and thirteen on a week-long expedition to follow the Mohawk Trail through the Berkshires, climaxing with the ascent of Mount Greylock.

They set off early and were driven to Queenfield in Massachusetts – a full day's drive. Howard Q. was the first to request first aid. The wind and sun after eight hours in an open sedan had inflamed his eyes. Mr Kinsey, his hero, treated him that night by a roadside brook, putting cold compresses on his eye. The next morning (Howard recovered) they set off down the Mohawk Trail.

For five days they tramped through woods and over fields, camping by the little streams. Mr Kinsey taught them things about the countryside as they went. They had no tents, but just slept in blankets and ponchos out in the open. When they stopped, 'We boys had our tasks assigned and we did the chores – gathering wood, carrying water . . . and scrubbing pots and pans.'

Mr Kinsey and his assistant Mr Burke, meanwhile, carefully cooked the wild plants, gathered during the day. What did they eat, no doubt helping their leader test his recipes? Possibly a puree of Bladder Campion with its 'flavor of green peas with a slight bitterness'; or Mr Kinsey may have risked some skunk cabbage from which the Indians made bread, though, if insufficiently dried, a few minutes after eating it the Bethany Boys would have noticed their mouths stinging 'with the peculiar burning and puckering sensation familiar to all who have tasted the fresh root of jack-in-the-pulpit'.[26]

During their final night there was a tremendous thunderstorm with torrential rain. They were sleeping near a golf course and 'Mr Kinsey found the greens keeper and persuaded him to let us spend the rest of the night in the club house.'

It was still foggy and damp early next morning and the boys were tired after their night, but Mr Kinsey led them up to the top of Mt Greylock. They straggled up, reached the observation tower and then came down – and so back to Boston by train.

Howard Q. Bunker never forgot this expedition – nor others like it to the Blue Hills of Milton and then on to Ponkapoag Pond in the Blue Hills reservation. He never forgot the enthusiasm of Mr Kinsey and how they sang round the campfire at nights while Mr Burke played his zither or someone else the harmonica.

And one senses in this, not just Kinsey's care for them, his pleasure in getting out and away, out into nature, his enjoyment in teaching them about it, but one has the feeling of a boy among boys, of someone who had missed out on childhood but had found it here in camps, someone who might find adult relationships difficult still but found satisfaction in the undemanding teacher/pupil relationship. Excited at getting out – but no doubt eager to get back this summer, since he had now found what he soon took on as his life's work.

It is necessary that we learn something about the gall wasp. It will be an acquaintance which, as it grows, will be more fascinating than you might think.

6

The gall wasp is a tiny and paradoxical insect about the size of a small ant. Despite its name it can neither sting nor fly. It uses its minute wings for balancing.[27] It usually lays its eggs in oaks (sometimes roses) and deposits with them a poison which irritates the oak into producing a lumpy excrescence or gall. Here the eggs lie protected, sometimes for months. Eventually they hatch into larvae which irritate the tree (or rose) into a new gall where they live and feed for anything from a month to three years. Finally, the pupae emerge, develop into winged adults, mate and lay eggs in their turn. Within a few days or weeks, sometimes even in a few hours, the little insect has fulfilled all its functions and dies.

Kinsey fairly quickly discovered a number of things about gall wasps or American Cynipidae. For one thing, they were almost completely unresearched. There had been quite a lot of work done on the European insect, but very little on the far more numerous species of North American gall. To study something no one else had studied meant the possibility of becoming a world expert, of having an abundance of material likely to get published early. (Edward O. Wilson had had fifty-five articles on ants published by the age of twenty-nine.) Then, as now, this was how scientists made their name – and so it proved with Kinsey.

An insect family with a large number of little-researched species was ideal for practising taxonomy. To somewhat simplify a complex subject, taxonomy means naming and classifying and thereby dividing plants or animals into their various groupings – as one might split the cat family into the *Felidae* – and then subdivide these again into their main *genera*, two of which are the *Panthera* (including the lion and tiger) and the *Felis* (which includes the domestic cat and puma). The *genera*, in turn, subdivide into interrelated subsidiaries or species and sub-species – *Felis* has twenty-eight, for instance: domestic cat, wild cat, lynx, etc. The distinguishing mark of the subdivision or species is usually that, though tied into the genus by a range of characteristics common to them all, in this case cat characteristics, they cannot interbreed. A lion cannot mate with a domestic cat, even artificially. However, it is now known that there are a number of exceptions to the non-interbreeding of different species – for example, a lion *can* (in captivity) breed with a tiger, producing tigons or ligers, depending on the father.[28]

Taxonomy is vital to all the biological sciences and was once their most important primary activity, as was clearly demonstrated by the first and greatest taxonomist Linnaeus. Without taxonomy, you can do no proper studies. You cannot, for instance, trace – or even detect – evolution if you don't know in what line or group to place whatever it is you are studying.

Taxonomy is the study of variety, of variation. It was already clear from the superficial examinations carried out that the range of variation in the North American gall might be very large indeed. A range not just from the jumping galls of California to the galls used to produce tattooing dyes or the galls from which medicines and tannins were extracted, but much more subtle and more fundamental variation. And variation, of course, is the raw material of evolution. Ever since his daring talks about evolution at high school, Kinsey had revered Darwin. With galls there was the possibility he himself could contribute – and so it proved here too.

And gall variation could be very odd. Some of them breed with alternating generations. That is, the immediate offspring have no resemblance *at all* to their parents – a rare biological phenomenon which one can see might have had attractions for Kinsey. One of these generations can be agamic, which means able to reproduce without sexual union, and these agamic generations are so different that 'they have actually', Kinsey wrote to Natalie Roeth in delight, 'been placed in a separate genus!'[29] That is, not recognised as galls at all.

Kinsey's pleasure was in part because the second thing that rapidly became clear to him was that, just as he had beaten the author of his first flower book, so he could easily beat the experts in this field too, and by much the same means – by collecting *more*.

When Kinsey's teacher Fernald collected plants for his taxonomy he would collect half a dozen specimens from a tree or an area and then move. Nearly all taxonomists of the time did this. Nor did they often publish any detailed measurements from which they had deduced the different sorts of plant or insect. Rather they gained a general impression of their material and then described it.* Indeed, quite often they didn't actually take any precise measurements at all.

Kinsey, instinctively, for reasons we have examined, collected hundreds and then thousands, and then hundreds of thousands of galls and wasps; where previous researches had taken the galls from one or two states and made two or three basic measurements in their handful of galls, Kinsey was finally scouring the whole of the Northern continent from Mexico up and taking twenty-eight precise measurements, several microscopic. In all this he was unique, a pioneer not just in galls but in the taxonomy of his time.[30]

It was as if the escape into nature and nature study, with which he had partly resolved the tensions in his family and solved his own inner

* In an arresting image, Professor James Jones described this as Platonic Taxonomy. It was as if there were an Ideal Species above from whose rough and vague shadow on the earth the Scientist had to work out a description. Measurement, number, did not come into it. (James Jones, lecture, Indiana University, November 1995.)

tensions and his loneliness, became more effective as it became more detailed. The immersion could go still deeper. He could *bury* himself.

This is no mere fanciful speculation. It was precisely this aspect of his work he singled out for Natalie Roeth in the letter already quoted. 'It involves the gathering of the galls by the thousands and tens of thousands, and breeding the adults out and putting them on the trees to form the next generation of galls. You can appreciate that it means a great deal of fieldwork, and detailed observation of the tiny things...' And, he goes on, it was this detail that he loved.

And it was into this detail that Kinsey plunged in the fall of 1917; but this time, and for the first time in his life, he had a friend.

7

Edgar Anderson came to Bussey in 1917 and moved at once into the household of Miss Elizabeth Weld. He was three years younger than Kinsey, but they had several things in common, besides dedication and science. Anderson had a very quick, retentive and, especially as far as Kinsey was concerned, perceptive mind. He too liked to shock. He was an amusing man. Kinsey's daughter Joan remembered his skill at inventing limericks. He became a renowned botanist, and did later come to use large numbers and statistical proof in his work. Dr Charles Heiser, the acknowledged expert on him, thinks it likely he copied this from Kinsey.[31]

Anderson was intrigued by Kinsey at once. He noticed his very yellow hair and how the secretaries and young women lab assistants talked about him incessantly. They were drawn by his radiating attractiveness – which Kinsey was still too hamstrung by guilt and inhibition to take advantage of or even notice; and especially by his 'air of ultimate inaccessibility'. Not for the last time, Kinsey's remoteness was drawing people to him. 'He walked rapidly but without hurrying... [and] he had gentle warmness and considerable charm.' But Anderson noticed, too, his intense competitiveness – how furiously he practised in order to succeed at the piano, and how strident his voice became when determined to win an argument.[32]

The two young men started at once on long natural history expeditions, setting off early together on the Boston street car system, tramping fifteen or twenty miles in pursuit of plants and galls, and returning when it was dark. Anderson noticed how fit his companion was – 'a lithe, slender, almost athletic young man . . .'*

Thus Kinsey's time at Bussey continued. Relentless gall-studying and collecting (he was known as 'Get a million Kinsey'), while also earning additional money as lab assistant to Radcliffe in 1917–18, and in the Harvard biology labs 1918–19.

Then in the summer – the camps. In 1918 he took boys from six to eight to the Pine Island Camp on the Belgrade Lakes. He still used the boys as gastronomical guinea pigs (one could still remember in 1948 a meal of leaves). Kinsey also went on a short yachting trip with Anderson. It was not a success. Kinsey couldn't see any point in just being blown about by the wind and grew very restless and bored. Only at night when they sang songs on deck 'did he enjoy it'. It was now Anderson realised his friend could never really relax.[33]

In August Kinsey served as a woodcraft instructor to the Culver Military Academy at Plymouth, Indiana. He thought Indiana far too hot and sticky and, razored by glaciers, far too flat. He hated it.

And, again though there is no record, he no doubt paid brief visits to South Orange. It is clear he was very fond of his little brother, Bob, now aged nine. He kept all his letters from the Harvard period. Bob signs off – 'Your loving brother'. One letter says, 'I've got a gall for you.' The letters from Bob are usually after his birthdays, when Kinsey would send a blank cheque and Bob would fill it in for $1. 'Daddy bought [me] four records – one was "Good Morning Mr Zip-Zip-Zip-Zip".'[34]

8

And so Kinsey's time at Bussey came to an end. While he had been collecting far more galls than anyone there before or since,† his supervisor Morton Wheeler had been carrying his 'leave alone' policy to almost

---

* Kinsey went to the draft in 1917 and was rejected owing to the double curvature of the spine, left by rickets, detectable only by a slight stoop (Christenson, 1971, pp. 16, 17).

† No one knows how many. The figure of 17,000 has been put forward, but this is the figure Kinsey gives at the start of his first big Cynips book in 1930 and represents many years' work on this group. It is highly unlikely his Harvard collections and this one would be identical. (James Jones, lecture at IU, 27 October 1995; 'The Gall Wasp Genus Cynips – a study in the Origin of Species', Alfred C. Kinsey, IU, 1930.)

ridiculous extremes. He hardly saw Kinsey at all. When his thesis arrived, Wheeler was astounded. Edgar Anderson remembers overhearing him discussing it with another professor, Dr East. Wheeler said that, to his surprise, this graduate student whom he hardly knew was of very high calibre indeed.*[35]

This calibre and Morton Wheeler's recommendation secured Kinsey, among other things, a Sheldon Travelling Scholarship to finance travelling for as long as his frugality would allow. He graduated with a PhD from Harvard in June 1919, spent his usual two and a half months in camps, and then in early September set off into the wildernesses of America.

9

In a lifetime of expeditions of one sort or another, this was the longest Kinsey ever took. For ten months, by train and on foot, he criss-crossed America. In all, he visited thirty-six states, choosing the wildest and most inaccessible places 'inasmuch,' he told Natalie Roeth, 'as oaks, in which gall wasps occur especially, are found only on the highest mountains'.[36]

Edgar Anderson was to put a crucial development down to these early journeys, namely, the unexpected (indeed contrary to what one would have expected) gift that Kinsey later showed for being able to establish a form of instant intimacy with the most extraordinary range of total strangers. Anderson said it was the necessity on gall trips to mix with all classes, to enlist help; above all Kinsey's intense curiosity about people he met on them.

Anderson would illustrate this by recalling how, on his return from this marathon trip, Kinsey described an afternoon when he was collecting galls on an oak tree beside a rubbish tip outside Butte, Montana. A bum was lolling by the dump. Suddenly the bum said in a cultured voice, 'I perceive you are an entomologist. Pray, what kind of insect might you be searching for here?' Kinsey then gave him a little lecture on galls and in return the bum told him about his life. Shelter was possible, so was

---

* Yet he must have been vaguely aware of him. Kinsey had already, as a student, published two papers in *Psyche*, a recognised journal produced by the Cambridge Entomological Club in Cambridge, Massachusetts.

food. The really appalling problem was getting an adequate supply of alcohol since Prohibition had come in.[37]

No doubt there is truth in this, though I would suggest different roots for Kinsey's extraordinary and still latent gift. It also seems that on this trip he began his practice of asking those he met to send him any galls they might find (postage repaid), together with the details of place and time. Yet, it is not so much curiosity about people but delight in their absence one notices on these expeditions. For ten months Kinsey was completely alone. He was completely alone, completely self-sufficient and blissful. 'In one range in Arizona, for instance,' he told Natalie Roeth in the letter quoted above, 'I got off where for four whole days I didn't see a solitary man; I was about fifty miles from the nearest town, living on my own camping site.'

When they were old enough Kinsey used to tell his children about his adventures at this time. One took place here. He'd bought his provisions in Tucson and set off by foot into the mountains on the east. He climbed up and up and eventually found an abandoned cabin. He gathered wood, made a meal and settled for the night in his blanket roll. He woke – 'but it was still dark', he would say, his children enthralled. He slept and woke again – 'it was *still* dark'. He got up and went to the door. It wouldn't open. At last, he forced a crack. During the night a strong wind and a tremendous fall of snow had buried the hut above the eaves. Kinsey was trapped there two days. 'But I was fine. Thanks to my scout training I had a good supply of wood; I was warm and I had four days' food.' 'I used to make him tell that story again and again,' said his daughter Joan.[38]

He tramped up all the mountain ranges except those in the far north, concentrating on Texas, Arizona and California. He travelled 18,000 miles, 2,500 on foot (naturally, Kinsey kept a careful record of the numbers). And from everywhere galls streamed back to Harvard in boxes that he packed and sent by post and rail. In all, 300,000 specimens arrived. Many of these hatched before he got back, 'filling the building'[39] to everyone's consternation.

Kinsey rejoined his tiny insects early in July 1920.

10

Kinsey hadn't only sought galls during these arduous months. He had

also looked for a job. More importantly, Morton Wheeler was trying to place him as well, and in April 1920, on learning from Carl H. Eigenmann, head of the zoology department at Indiana University (IU) in Bloomington that he was looking for someone, recommended him to take Kinsey. It was while Kinsey was unsuccessfully seeking a post at Ohio University soon after this, that he learned he had been offered the post at Bloomington.[40] To Kinsey's objections about flatness, they had replied Bloomington was not flat.

Nor is it. When Kinsey took three days off his usual camp work to visit it, he found that the glaciers had halted north of Bloomington. The countryside is rolling, sometimes steeply, thickly wooded and then even wilder than today. Kinsey was attracted to it.

He was also wooed. Midwestern colleges were desperate then to entice teaching staff from the prestigious eastern universities. Eigenmann said he would set aside $800 for gall hunting and offered a good salary.[41] He then sent him to see Dr Fernandus Payne, who suggested he stay and attend a Sigma Xi lecture that evening.* Outside Payne's door Kinsey met briefly a small, very dark-haired girl called Clara Bracken McMillen. She said later that she was instantly attracted to him.[42]

Kinsey decided to accept. Eigenmann was delighted. Not only was he *Harvard*, he wrote to the President William Lowe Bryan, but Eigenmann felt – how little he knew! – that Kinsey would be a 'safe' instructor because of his scout work and his ten years in the camps.[43]

Kinsey finished his engagements with these, went back to Harvard to stow his galls (it took a month), and with these packages – which must have been extremely bulky – set off for IU in late September to take up the post of assistant professor of zoology at $2,000 a year. He was twenty-six and ahead lay his life's work and an end at last to the long years of sexual frustration – the two not unconnected.

* Sigma Xi was, and is, a national honorary scientific fraternity. It was presumably Payne's way of showing Kinsey some of the rather short supply of high-calibre scientific figures at IU.

PART II

Bloomington, Galls, Marriage – First Steps into Sex Research

1920–39

The Married Professor

1

Indiana University has one of the most beautiful campuses in America. The buildings – Charles Addams Gothic or Scotch Baronial or like prisons or nuclear power stations – are now often enormous, some as big as an entire English university. Yet they are not unpleasing, due to the limestone from the Bloomington quarries. IU is the same colour as Bath.

And the buildings are easily tamed by the rolling campus, sufficiently spacious to form a miniature countryside, crossed by brick paths from the 1880s (in the 1920s plank paths as well),[1] and two narrow, clear, quick-running, rapidly filling and rapidly emptying little streams (or creeks as the Americans often call them). And the buildings are hidden, the rolling campus countryside filled, with thick woods and waving trees. Today the summer air is usually pulsating with the engines of air-conditioning and in winter, when the creeks freeze, steam gushes from vents in the ground and billows from the roofs.

In Kinsey's day there were far fewer buildings and they were smaller. The campus was even more a countryside. The only sound was the chiming of bells and the wind in the trees where, shortly before he arrived, along with the squirrels, gophers and rabbits of today, cows had still wandered to keep down the undergrowth and provide milk for the students.

A beautiful place then – but not, at that time, a particularly brilliant one. Indiana then (as now) was at the stolid, sluggishly-beating heart of the American Midwest. It was deeply conservative, deeply conventional, religious (it is virtually in the Bible belt) and racist. The national HQ of the Ku Klux Klan was in Indianapolis until 1925 and there was a

notorious lynching in Indiana in the early 1930s.* It was, in the southern, Bloomington half, a farming state growing corn (maize), wheat,
barley, etc., with a good deal of livestock, a sizeable proportion (17 per
cent)[2] of whose young male farmhands, Kinsey was later to discover,
were having sex with the cows, bulls, donkeys, mules, horses and poultry
they worked at raising.

The town of Bloomington, fifty miles or so south of Indianapolis,
was deep in Indiana and in spirit deeper South than North. In 1920 it
had a population of 13,000. There were few cars and a smell of
horse dung. There were hitching posts for horses and on Saturdays
there was a regular *paseo* in the treeless square – farmers chewing
tobacco and spitting, their wives feeding babies and gossiping, quacks
selling snake oil. Mrs Edmondson 'couldn't even *understand* the
natives sometimes. The trashman had a large goitre (no iodised salt)
and between his dialect and his goitre I couldn't get one word in
ten.'[3]

Pastureland and virgin forest crowded close, the forest floor
covered in mosses, may apples, wild strawberries, poison ivy. People,
like the university, kept cows and sold milk to neighbours. Joan Reid
remembers 'you bought your chickens from the poultry house, they
killed it, drew it, plucked it – you had to wait.' The 'sin strip' ran along
the rail track with prostitutes – and then, as now, the long, mournful,
double-tone sounding from the trains as they clanked through would
echo across the little town at night like two chords from a melancholy
harmonica.

Much of this brushed off on the university. Founded in 1820, only
two years after Bloomington itself, it was still small in 1920, with 2,356
undergraduates. The faculty was not particularly distinguished. Few
departments could teach to doctorate level; even in 1938 it still had only
five starred scientists (compared to Chicago with forty-six, or humble
Illinois with twenty-two).[4] In 1920 virtually the entire student intake
was from Indiana and a good many from the farms. And a good many, as

---

* Even in the '50s, a black barber had to cut the hair of blacks after hours. 'Had
he permitted blacks to patronise his own shop, he'd have been run out of town.'
Nor, until the 1960s, would the student barber cut the hair of those still known as
Negroes. In 1995, when I was researching at IU, there was a cell of the Ku Klux
Klan twelve miles from Bloomington. (See *Shade of the Raintree: The Life and Death
of Ross Lockridge Jr*, Larry Lockridge, Viking Penguin, 1994 (p. 89), and *Concepts of
Sexual Orientation*, ed. David P. McWhirter et al., OUP, 1990, Chapter 12.)

Kinsey found when he occasionally taught them, were as thick as planks. William Lowe Bryan, a devout Presbyterian and one of the old nineteenth-century preacher presidents, had been in power since 1903. He came to work by buggy and tied his horse outside Maxwell Hall.[5] The faculty culture comprised church events, fundraising, a lot of bridge, dropping and returning of cards, and snobbery.

Kinsey was always fiercely democratic and hated snobbery, nor was he remotely racist. Once, soon after he arrived in Bloomington, he attended church, then never again. Yet in most other respects he was totally conventional and slipped easily into this remote backwater. Even his politics – though probably more because he approved of financial probity than any ideological conviction – were conservative and, like most of Indiana and Bloomington, when he did vote he usually voted Republican, according to his wife.[6]

It is this sturdy figure who, very soon after he'd settled into IU, at last enters the scene.

2

Clara Bracken McMillen – soon to be given her lifelong nickname 'Mac' by Kinsey – was nearly twenty-two (in October 1920) and the only daughter of two Fort Wayne, Indiana, teachers. She was small (5′ 2″), very dark, almost black-haired, plain, boyish-looking and an exceptional athlete, a very good botanist and extremely clever. She'd just got an outstanding degree majoring in chemistry, was Phi Beta Kappa and elected to Sigma Xi even before Kinsey himself.

Although she had forgotten his name, Mac had thought all summer about the young man she had met briefly outside Dr Payne's door. There were now two other brief meetings. Kinsey, of course, paid no attention to her but at least she learnt his name. Then Dr Will Scott told her of a zoology department picnic expedition to Spring Mill State Park. Mac had been on Dr Scott's ornithology course. So – could she come? Scott couldn't see why not.

This picnic was crucial. Kinsey, again, ignored Clara MacMillen. As they were all walking down the zigzag path, Clara suddenly left it and plunged straight down the hillside – deliberately, she told her daughters later, to attract young Dr Kinsey's attention. When they ate, Dr Eigenmann inexpertly lit the fire. Kinsey, a million fires behind him, impatiently lit his own. Mac chose to join him and his fire instead of sitting with the others.

A form of dating now began – though it sometimes sounds like a series of tests. He organised a succession of strenuous expeditions, often lengthy. But camps, expeditions, had been where he'd learnt, were indeed his main form of, intimacy, and besides, he invited other people. Strenuous was the keynote of his Christmas presents to her: a knife, a compass, and a pair of Bass hiking boots.

It is even possible that Kinsey still didn't know where he was heading – or being led. Other people knew. His landlady Mrs Foley asked him if he wanted his room next term. Kinsey replied, of course he did – why did she ask? Mrs Foley said, 'I thought you might be getting married.' Kinsey was astonished.

Mac, of course, certainly knew. She had already decided not to stay on, as she'd planned, and enrol in the entomology course. 'I didn't think,' she told Cornelia Christenson, 'it would be right for me to take a course from the man I was going to marry.' And, after a Phi Beta Kappa meeting, that diffident man now suddenly became direct, and took the plunge. Could he walk her home? Mac had come with another man but as all three walked back through a typically arctic Indiana winter night, the other man had to run back for his coat. Kinsey saw her home.

A week or so later, on another walk (again in the concealing dark), he proposed. Clara MacMillen had already had a proposal – the coat man? – and wasn't sure. Kinsey would have to wait. He was, as often in the future by what he saw as other 'rejections', bitterly hurt. It is the measure of this that Kinsey, who hated sport, took her to a basketball game. ('We never,' Mac told Pomeroy, 'went to another one.'[7]) By the end, they were engaged.

Shortly afterwards, Kinsey wrote to Natalie Roeth. He was getting married in June! His expression of love runs as follows: 'The girl is a graduate student working in chemistry at Indiana University. She is a very brilliant scholar; is one of the best athletes in the place. She knows the birds better than I do, knows the flowers and the trees etc., is a capable hiker and camper, a champion swimmer. We are to spend the major part of June hiking in the wildest country in the White Mountains.'

He also told his old biology teacher about the nickname – Mac.[8]

3

The series of tests seems to have continued through the honeymoon. Tests; or were they cloaks, defences? One senses in Kinsey's progress at this point desperate eagerness – and desperate anxiety.

The short period before the wedding was spent in preparing for a honeymoon of the toughest sort – an assault on the main peaks in the White Mountains. Mac had never even *seen* a mountain before. Kinsey took charge. Light, high-energy food – dry or non-perishable – was packed and sent ahead in small parcels to a series of drop points and resort hotels which would be shut. Prunes were stoned for lightness.

They were married on 21 June 1921 at Bookville, the home of Mac's grandparents. Just relatives and close friends. Then on to Cincinnati by hired car, Pullman to Niagara Falls, a brief visit to South Orange, on again by Fall River Boat Line to Boston for a celebratory lunch with Miss Weld. Then, at last, the real business of the honeymoon – the White Mountains of New Hampshire, the Presidential and Franconia ranges, Mt. Moriah, Mt. Washington.

The weather in the White Mountains can be hell in June, and this June it was fearsome – with tremendous winds, snow storms, hail and rain. They set off in a storm with four days' food, battling up each peak as they came to it, and fighting on to reach the next bundle of sent-ahead food. They climbed Mt. Washington in a blizzard. On the first steep ascent Kinsey selected the shortest practical route. Mac called it 'straight up'. Kinsey strode briskly ahead. Mac, athlete though she was, lagged behind. Kinsey would eventually wait. No sooner had she caught up, than he was off again.

They had to build lean-to shelters against the wind, rain and snow. The evening routine was: build a lean-to, pitch tent against it, take off belts and boots (the Bass boots now showing their worth), put on clean socks, plus all their extra clothing before climbing into blankets.[9] One can't help wondering about their lovemaking.

Intense anxiety often brings about the very catastrophe that is its source. In fact, thirty years later Kinsey told a close friend that he had been unable to make love to his young wife until they got back to Bloomington.[10] This must have come as a bitter blow after the long years of acute sexual frustration.

There is some doubt as to whether the trouble between the couple was just physical, as Kinsey later said, or a mixture of physical and psychological. As far as the physical difficulty went, there was no time to attend to it immediately since the honeymoon was followed at once by two intense months at Camp Aloha by Lake Morey in Vermont, near the western New Hampshire border. Kinsey was in charge of nature study and camp craft. Mac helped. As usual, it was a non-stop vigorous programme: bird hikes before breakfast, insect trips, outdoor cooking, songs and campfires.

Here, an interesting element, as a quick bulletin to Natalie Roeth explained, there were girls – hundreds of girls. Kinsey drove them along with his kindly but no doubt rather exhausting enthusiasm, and 'by the end of the summer we had them all in fine swing, and their interest was fine. We got into the mountains over ten times, guiding over 150 girls into them. The biological interest of the White Mountains, especially above tree level, was an endless source of good times.'[11]

It took all summer. Was there some reluctance among some of the girls? There is something touching, naive, almost childlike in Kinsey's enthusiasm, his *total* certainty that everyone would enjoy what he enjoyed. It is a streak that reappears.

Kinsey and Mac marked out a camp site at Milan, New Hampshire at this time, and for several years had serious plans of starting a camp of their own there.[12]

Then, after the camps, they both went to South Orange to collect Kinsey's things.[13] They arrived back in Bloomington in the middle of September.

It is clear that the couple immediately took steps over their sexual difficulties. Kinsey told his friend C. A. Tripp that they consulted a local doctor, Dr Thomas Reed, who diagnosed an inordinately thick hymen. This required minor surgery, which was carried out in Bloomington soon afterwards[14]. They were able to consummate the marriage after this.[15]

An over-thick hymen is by no means uncommon, nor is the fact that Mac also experienced some pain[16], though this could well have been exacerbated by Kinsey apparently possessing an unusually large penis,[17] and one imagines the whole fraught situation, enacted on mountainsides in blizzards, was not helped by anxiety and inhibition on both their parts.

Certainly the damage brought about by endlessly delayed coitus, for both men and women, was to be one of the *leitmotifs* of Kinsey's later work. It is important, obviously, to be extremely careful about reading anything personal into the two big scientific studies – and indeed it cannot often be convincingly done. None the less, it is hard not to detect some personal feeling behind the edge Kinsey's language takes on (except for one chapter in the second, he wrote both books entirely by himself) when these two aspects come up – which they do frequently. The early inhibitions concomitant with sexual frustration have long-lasting effects. Suddenly at marriage, he writes, 'husband and wife are supposed to break down all inhibitions. Unfortunately there is no magic in the marriage ceremony which can accomplish this ... a very high pro-portion of females ... a considerable number of males ... find this very difficult. It can take years to get rid of these learnt inhibitions.'[18]

With marriage, the enormous, cripplingly heavy glacier of sexual prohibition and inhibition at last slowly began to lift. In a few years Kinsey was to work on their sex life with his usual thoroughness. As for Mac, Miriam Hecht met her at IU in 1944: '. . . my Indiana friends assured me that as a student, when Kinsey met her, she had been quite the hottest thing on campus.'[19] By 1944 Kinsey was already famous – or notorious – at IU for his sex work. *Any* partner of his could have been rumoured the hottest thing on campus – or the coldest. But there is a good deal of evidence later on that this was, if anything, a considerable understatement, and that Mac's responsiveness was to stand the mar-riage in good stead.

Mac turned out to suit him in many other ways. She was a motherly woman but also had the same tough, practical mind and she shared many of his interests. She learnt to tolerate and understand his often highly eccentric ways. She had what the family saw as her Scottish side, i.e. parsimony. She was an extremely strong character and though she was often to be alone, and minded this, she was not lonely. She forged an independent life. She was as clever as he was and was well able to stand up to him intellectually and in other ways. She believed absolutely in his work and shared it with him. When, years later, he was to embark on a wide range of personal sexual experiment she was completely tolerant – and joined in. When she really wanted something, she would insist on it, and get it. And then – they loved one another. Once, in the late 1940s, Kinsey told Paul Gebhard that he had only been in love three times in his life, and the first time had been with this new young wife, Clara MacMillen.[20]

But the most important thing Mac had to come to terms with very early on was that with her new young husband work came first.

4

After her Herculean honeymoon, it must have surprised the new Mrs Kinsey when Bloomington doctors refused to certify her husband for life insurance because they didn't like the sound of his heart. Insurance was not granted until he went to the Mayo Clinic in Rochester, Minnesota, a noted centre for medical specialists.[21]

Kinsey at once set about punishing this recalcitrant organ, as he was to do for the rest of his life until it finally gave in and collapsed. His first major task was a 'general biology' course. Kinsey's Darwinian background made it obvious to him that plants, animals and human beings were all locked into the same system of living things. He also felt he was easily capable of teaching botany and zoology up to graduate level.

This last was not obvious to the head of botany at IU. Professor Mottier, head of the department since the year Kinsey was born, 1894, refused even to look at Kinsey's outline lecture plan. He told Kinsey no one knew enough to teach botany *and* zoology. Who was this upstart?[22] Kinsey's reaction was typical. In December 1921 he set out to show that, if he wasn't thought capable of dealing with botany and zoology together in lectures, he was perfectly capable of producing a biology textbook along these lines.[23]

Kinsey's teaching load fluctuated term by term up to 1939, when he gradually began to drop full-time faculty work. In 1927, for instance, he is lecturing five hours a week; in 1933 it is ten hours. Most years he offered courses on entomology and insect taxonomy. Later, in 1936, he introduced a course on 'evolution'. He gave outside lectures and held seminars on his galls.

Kinsey's great strength as a teacher was when he got his classes – graduates or undergraduates – out into the open. Here, in the forests of Brown County or nearby McCormick's Creek, or the virgin woods that still pressed close round Bloomington, in the nature which fascinated him and which he could make so fascinating, he was at his best. He had a knack of getting students to notice and work out things for themselves.

But as teacher pure and simple opinions are mixed and usually unfavourable. Certainly he was dynamic and those he liked found they were very well taught. But he was also often impatient, dogmatic and autocratic. He frightened his pupils. Dr Frank Young described him as 'a tyrant. He had a very high opinion of Kinsey, and let everyone know it. This often meant he was a lousy teacher, because he never considered his students' views at all.'[24] Robert Bugbee, one of his graduate students, enjoyed working under him but 'I sometimes had a feeling that students were something he wished he could get along without, because he was so dedicated to his research work.'[25] In fact he only had six graduate students during his entire career. Presumably no more wished to work, or rather serve, under him.

If his graduate students only sometimes tentatively had Bugbee's feeling, a lot of his undergraduates were quite certain about it. English university education in the '20s and '30s was really restricted to a few middle- and upper-class men. In America anyone of either sex who had got through twelve grades and could afford it, or would work for it, could go. However, these students did not become very numerous until after the post-war GI Bill. At IU in the '20s and '30s it was quite clear to Kinsey, and he showed it with considerable impatience, that many of them should stay on their farms and do the practical work which they could do and not pretend to do intellectual work, which they couldn't.

But these big, muscular figures furnished the sportsmen and athletes so vital to an American university. The IU Physical Education Department, as a vague gesture to *academe*, required that all footballers and basketball players take a simple biology course. In 1937 Kinsey was asked to teach it. He was so outraged at the low standard hitherto allowed that he effectively flunked the lot. The PE department thereafter dropped biology as a required course.[26]

Yet, after his indictment of Kinsey's teaching, Frank Young had added, 'Of course, he had reason to think a lot of himself. He was a marvellous speaker. I went many times. He had a charismatic personality. He made you want to hear more, to learn more, to participate. He inspired you.'[27]

Kinsey had, in effect, been training as a lecturer ever since his father had made him preach at Sunday school when he was sixteen. For ten years he had been teaching himself how to hold enthralled and silent gangs of restless boys and youths – and later girls. Everyone who attended any of his lectures – and many of the IU faculty went again and again, like Frank Young, just for the pleasure of hearing him – agree on his brilliance. Nor was he someone who just shone in a small, obscure, provincial university. He was later to exert the same spell across the whole of America and in Europe.

We can gain some impression of the manner at this time, if not the content, from Louise Rosenzweig, who went to his lectures in 1927. 'On the dot of the hour he entered the classroom ... with long, measured, rather brisk steps. He was a tall man; his blond hair was closely cut in pompadour, his shoulders slightly stooped. He had large eyes with lids that drooped slightly over them, and wore hornrimmed spectacles. His suit was dark, his shirt white, and he wore a black bow tie. He walked to the front of the room, looking neither to right nor left, went immediately to the blackboard where he wrote, in print-like letters, an outline of the important topics, with sub-headings, to be covered in the day's lecture. When he turned and began speaking, he had a precise manner in enunciation, richly modulated, as though he enjoyed using the English language. For most of the hour he stood in one spot, except when he occasionally referred to the outline on the blackboard. His restrained manner seemed both aloof and shy. As he lectured, his enthusiasm for the subject matter warmed the rather awesome atmosphere of the room.'[28]

Kinsey was aware, he could hardly not be, of his powers as a lecturer, but in his own judgement he put first among his attainments his persistence, his stubborn patience to pursue a goal for years, for decades. Later on he had a clear estimation of what he had achieved – and it was modest. He realised he was not at home with abstract concepts, and felt nervous of those who were.

But wherever he had studied so far, including IU, he had been the cleverest or among the cleverest. He had a clear, logical mind of great power, comprehension and concentration. He also had a down-to-earth commonsense intelligence not always found among the academically gifted.

Especially is it not found in the endless committees and departmental discussions of university life. Kinsey was outspoken and rude at faculty meetings[29] and seemed to enjoy it. Early on he criticised a fellow professor, Will Scott, and suggested he be replaced – in front of him. 'It naturally led to hard feelings between the two faculty members.'[30] Sometime after 1924 he accused the head of the department himself, in front of all his colleagues, of generalising from ridiculously small samples. The ageing Eigenmann, understandably furious, decided not in the least reluctantly 'that he, Kinsey, be allowed to go'.[31] Payne fought for him and only just saved him.

Kinsey's manner was superior, autocratic and so brisk that people could take offence. Mrs Edmondson remembered him on the telephone. 'He'd ring – "Is Frank there?" "No, try his office." There'd be an abrupt click and I knew he would do so, at once.'[32]

Christenson says he mellowed as he grew older. There is not the remotest sign of this. If anything, he grew sharper. In 1936, he wrote irritably to Ralph Voris, his first graduate student and by then a close friend, about a colleague, the botanist Theodore Torrey – 'less active in research than any man on the staff' who talks about 'experimental zoology' – a hopelessly vague phrase in Kinsey's view, that could lead to 'trivial work'. If it does, 'then I shall raise a rumpus'.[33] By next year he evidently has raised a rumpus and not just about Torrey, but about two other colleagues, Kroc and Breneman. And none of this is Kinsey's *business*. Payne was now head of the department (Eigenmann died in 1927). But there were rumours of Payne's retirement. 'Apparently no one but Kinsey wants Kinsey to have that post,' wrote graduate student Herman Spieth to Ralph Voris.[34]

As he grew more senior (and he rose very fast – assistant professor 1920, associate 1923, full professor 1929) he began to interfere all over the place. Notes shot like bullets about the campus on the inefficiency of the traffic police, the ridiculous parking system, the auditorium acoustics ...

> Dear Mr Pearson, I would like to enquire whether it is possible for us to get a more efficient janitor service than we are having here in Wylie Hall. In my 30 years with the university this is the worst janitor service that I have ever seen. I think part of the trouble comes from the preposterous hours the janitor is allowed to work here ...[35]

By the mid-'30s quite a number of the ruffled and disgruntled faculty were saying (behind his back) that Kinsey simply thought he was God. He was incapable of admitting he was wrong.[36] Nor was it helped by his tendency to sudden flashes of furious impatience. Theodore Torrey, who came to IU in 1932, said: 'I had two impressions: one, a very sunny, genial person, yet every so often he completely bowled me over by a kind of abruptness and aggressiveness.' And he was, said Torrey, 'as tight as a banjo string most of the time'.

On a biology field trip to McCormick's Creek, Torrey and Kinsey brought the students back to the cars for lunch. Torrey turned the radio on in his car. Kinsey suddenly stood up, stalked over without a word, 'snapped the radio off' and stalked back, leaving Torrey very surprised and humiliated under the puzzled glances of the students.[37]

But Fernandus Payne – 'Poppy Payne', a farmer's son, small, slender, with a shiny bald head and courteous old-fashioned manner, yet an extremely able scientist and one of IU's very few 'starred' scientists (work on *Drosophila*) – Payne saw through all this to someone sensitive who was easily and especially wounded by criticism. He was often irritated by Kinsey, but he admired him enough to stand by him when things got rough – and they were to get very rough.

Colleagues who could stand up to Kinsey, or like Payne who saw what he was like beneath these attacks and defences, often grew to like him. Even Torrey, although 'Kinsey made me madder than hell ... [was] personally very very fond of him and admired him and respected him enormously.'[38] Professor Edmondson: 'Oh frankly I enjoyed meeting a man who had strong opinions he was willing to defend. I was very fond of him indeed ... to this day (and this may say more than anything else) when my wife and I buy a new recording of some music, one of our first reactions would be, gosh, Kinsey would have liked this one.'[39]

The picture to hold as we investigate a little further into the eighteen years to 1939, is of this prickly, intelligent, clever man, often difficult with colleagues, deeply and conscientiously immersed in his work and in all the incessant activities of a Midwestern university. He gives outside lectures. Interviews applicants. He sits on committees – on the standing committee of the university council, for instance, from 1929 to '31. Or again, he is president of Phi Beta Kappa in the late 1930s, and also of Sigma Xi.

And there is, of course, his family.

5

Kinsey clearly enjoyed the whole buzz of married life – and was equally clearly in command. He particularly enjoyed the endless opportunities for saving money.

In July 1921 they rented 620 South Fess for a year and furnished and decorated it themselves. They dyed curtains and painted walls. They bought job lots and reduced items, but that did not mean anything shoddy. Kinsey would only buy things that would last. They bought a considerable quantity of marked-down porch furniture – sitter, rocker, straight chairs with tough 'rustic' frames. 'Rustic' was the keynote of Kinsey's decor.[40]

Mac had planned to continue her graduate work in chemistry but as soon as she knew she was pregnant, in October 1922, she gave it up. Today in Bloomington (or so it seemed to me) her children would have been in daycare by one and she would have had a career. In the '20s and '30s that was virtually unthinkable. Clara Kinsey led an independent life, to a degree, but she was perfectly happy that it should be an independence built round her children and husband and subservient to them.

Like couples seem to, the Kinseys moved to a new house a month before their first child, Donald, was born in July 1922. 615 Park Avenue South, on the corner of Park Avenue and University Street, was, and is, a small, wood-framed clapboard bungalow built in 1910. It had steep, unbalustraded limestone steps in front and three small rooms, a small kitchen, a big cellar (where Kinsey worked on his biology textbook) and a big back yard. Kinsey eventually had two little bedrooms built on for his daughters (inadvertently blocking a right of way and causing endless trouble seventy years later). He did simple carpentry work on wall cupboards and a big galoshes drawer.[41] There is a small open fire in the living room. The tiny bathroom still has the original bath with its club feet and the basin where Clara Kinsey washed her babies. No shower. One gets a strong feeling of a small family with three children, not much money, the father helping. Domestic and ordinary.

And that is how it was. Kinsey was an involved father. He changed diapers, bottle-fed the babies and gave them baths.[42] When the last two children were born, Joan on 16 October 1925 and Bruce in November 1928, he watched it happen, highly unusual at that time.[43]

In August and early September 1923 Kinsey and Mac had had an orgy of camping before Anne was born the following January. They went first to Camp Lanikila at Fairlee, Vermont (Kinsey as programme director) and then on to Camp Aloha, working together on nature programmes. And they paid a final nostalgic visit to 'their' camp at Milan, New Hampshire, before allowing the dream to vanish.

Kinsey was now twenty-nine and would go camping privately many times again with his family and after galls, but this was his last official summer camp. There were two particular legacies. For Lanikila he had designed a special item – the adaptable 'Kinsey pack'. It could shrink for a child, or stretch to take the 30lb load of an adult. Von Lengerke and

Detinold Camping Supplies marketed it. Later, with an ingenious new flap, it made the 1928 Sears Roebuck catalogue.[44]

And on this trip the boys condensed Professor and Kinsey and called him Prok. Mrs Kinsey took it up, and thus they were set – Mac and Prok.

So it continued. Kinsey wrote to Natalie Roeth after Anne was born. Donald was now nearly two and running about – 'So between them it is a merry house.' He pursued galls, he worked at his book, there was a fracas over a student article in April 1924, in June he heard that his brother Robert had walked out on their father just like he had . . .

Then out of the blue, in June 1925, Donald fell ill.

It was an exophthalmic goitre case, that is protruding eyeballs, often due to an over-active thyroid. The Kinseys took him at once to the Mayo Clinic where, expecting a long stay, they rented an apartment. Kinsey took his textbook, now nearly finished. He later described to Robert Kroc how they were out buying steak when the butcher said, 'I see you've brought your son here to have his thyroid seen to.' 'Even the butchers in Rochester are diagnosticians,' said Kinsey.[45]

The butcher, and the Mayo, were both right and wrong. It was his thyroid and Mac, heavily pregnant with Joan, returned to Minnesota in September so that Donald could be operated on. Kinsey, meanwhile, stayed behind with twenty-month-old Anne. He looked after her, fed her, put her to bed and then, while a student babysat, worked late into the night in his laboratory to catch up.

The operation was a success, though Donald still seemed unwell. In October, two weeks after Joan was born, Kinsey went to the Hotel Palmer, in Paducah, Kentucky with his first and favourite graduate student Ralph Voris for a week's gall collecting. As often, they shared a room to save money.[46]

He got back to find his son continuing to cause anxiety. In fact, Donald had diabetes. This is rare in children and the disease had been masked by the thyroid condition and later by post-operative reaction. It was not diagnosed till the end of March 1926, when the little boy suddenly fell very ill indeed, sinking rapidly into a coma. Insulin was known about then but not widely used. Donald died early in April, three months short of his fifth birthday.

Kinsey was devastated, and this usually rigidly contained man wept openly. Evelyn Spieth, wife of one of his graduate students and Fernandus Payne's secretary at the time, remembered Kinsey breaking down completely in Payne's office when he arrived, dressed in black, soon after the funeral. He sobbed uncontrollably, racked by grief.[47]

6

This terrible blow continued to reverberate in them for many years. For the rest of his life when filling in forms Kinsey invariably said he had four children – 'Donald (deceased).' Still, in 1941, the only publication on his desk which had nothing to do with his work was the journal *Endocrinology*[48] – as if, by keeping abreast of the latest developments, he could by some miracle reverse the past.

But Clara Kinsey's anguish went even deeper and was to lead in the '30s to her insisting on a profound adjustment within their relationship. However, in October 1926, there came an event which, if not an alleviation of their tragedy, was at least a distraction from it. After five years' continuous work, often late at night, and a great deal of revision (he had sent it to twenty-six biologists, to lecturers including a certain Dr Thurman Rice of the medical school, and several high school teachers), *An Introduction to Biology* was finally published by J. B. Lippincott in Philadelphia.[49]

It is possible to get from the vivid, romantic, copiously <u>underlined</u> way that this is written an insight into how Kinsey must have fascinated his camp (and undergraduate) audiences – and what, indeed, fascinated him. He starts with the <u>strangeness</u> and <u>mystery</u> of life: 'For instance, a certain kind of small beetle, one of the pests of our pantries, was once kept in a bottle without trace of food or water for five years, one month and twenty-nine days before it starved to death.' And what <u>is</u> life? '. . . one ant walked around for forty-nine days after its head had been removed . . . Is the life of a headless ant stopped when the rest of its body continues to work?'

Then effortlessly, with numerous illustrations both literally (line drawings plus 300 photographs) and from his own experience (the snakes at Bowdoin) we are carried across the whole field of life on earth – plants and animals and insects, their origin, evolution, distribution and behaviour, genetics, taxonomy, ecology, history, the scientific method . . . Practically everything is touched on in some detail except, one notices, sex in human beings.

The author is quite often visible elsewhere: 'There are the poisons of tobacco, and whatever may be said for the mature man's smoking we must admit that the practice is poisonous to the health of youth.' Since most of America smoked and virtually only Kinsey and a few fanatic Methodists condemned it, Lippincott insisted on changes. They had to be satisfied with a grudging 'may ruin' for 'poisonous to the health'.

His distant toilet training surfaces: 'If . . . wastes are not eliminated once or twice each day, headaches and a general feeling of depression are going to result.'

Belief in God may have gone but the nineteenth-century preacher was still there. Instinct must be curbed and guided by reason, and since we develop habits, we must develop the 'highest'. Kinsey underlines this: 'You will immediately want to <u>acquire</u> more of the <u>worthwhile habits</u> that are within reach of humans.'

The book was revolutionary in three ways. First, the combining of zoology and botany, odd as it seems, was often still seen as scornful Professor Mottier had regarded it – impossible. How stupid it was to separate them became the theme of Kinsey's lectures to high school biology teachers in 1929.[50]

Second, the book was clearly based on and stated as scientific facts Darwin's principles of evolution and natural selection. This was bold (and, extraordinary as it may seem, in many parts of America it still would be). Kinsey hoped he was writing a popular book, but at that time a wave of anti-evolution fury was sweeping the country – especially in Tennessee, Arkansas and North Carolina. A month after the book came out Mississippi banned the teaching of evolution in all its schools. Kinsey had to do some trimming. Where the word 'evolution' appeared he put 'changes with time'.

Thirdly, biology textbooks before had been *books*, that is to say, the pupils learnt by reading. Kinsey's aim was to get them out – whether in city or country – to explore, observe, collect and test for themselves. To this end, he brought out a companion volume for teachers, *Field and Laboratory Manual in Biology*, in December of that year.

Immeasurably, the most important of these revolutionary elements was evolution, which was fundamental to all Kinsey's later thought and research. Since evolution is about the development of later from earlier species, genera, orders, it follows that to understand man we must study animals. Man *is* an animal – if a complex one. Human intelligence and reasoning, he wrote, 'does seem related to the simpler sorts of intelligence we have already considered'. Easy for us to accept now, Kinsey's awareness of man as animal was to cause him endless trouble when he came to sex.

Evolution is about inter-relations – the struggle for niches in the environment, the struggle with the environment, with other species, within the same species. But one could extend this embrace much further. 'It requires,' Kinsey noted, 'no great stretch of the imagination to think of everything in the universe as being related to everything else.'

Like a number of people who immerse themselves in nature as he had done – and perhaps especially those who have lost a central, transcendent belief – Kinsey had very profound feelings (he would have refused to countenance 'mystical' feelings) about this. Towards the end of his life, exhausted by a hard day taking sex histories in San Francisco, he sought solace alone in Muir Woods, the great redwoods north of the city. He returned deeply moved and Pomeroy said he'd never seen him so close to reverence.[51]

This awareness also allowed him to anticipate in an astonishing way certain modern insights. 'Once in northern Vermont, I killed an insect on a weed stem. I wonder what effect that had on the cost of living in New England? Who knows?'

Kinsey told one of his graduate students, Herman T. Spieth, that 'his time was precious and, if he were going to do that sort of thing [write textbooks], he wanted to make money out of it'.[52] Kinsey did make money. His two books were, over time, bestsellers. *An Introduction* . . . went into its sixth impression within three months. In total, according to Pomeroy, it sold almost half a million copies. Figures for the *Manual* don't seem to exist, but they would be comparable. He would have made about a hundred and fifty thousand dollars, a very large sum then.

It came in the nick of time. The Depression was about to engulf American universities, cutting salaries and axing departments. In 1933 Ralph Voris, now lecturing at the State Teachers' College at Springfield, Missouri, wrote telling Kinsey he faced a salary cut of 50 per cent.[53] At IU, said Kinsey, the cuts were 10–25 per cent, and department expenses 15 per cent. However, a new edition of the *Manual* would be off the presses in two months! No wonder he could end cheerily to Ralph and his wife Jerry – 'Hasta la vista, amigos mios!'[54]

At various times in his biography Pomeroy notes in tones of astonished wonderment the almost saintlike disregard for money which

Kinsey showed – not asking for salary rises, forgetting what he had in his account and so on. It is true Kinsey always slightly disapproved of personal wealth, as a good Methodist or ex-Methodist should. (Gebhard remembered a friend of theirs married a wealthy woman. Kinsey said at once, 'That'll be the ruination of him.'[55]) He could, personally, have made enormous sums from the sex research books and he didn't. But it is relatively easy to disregard money when you have large sums of it rolling regularly in from book royalties.

In 1927 his growing family started to see some of the carefully and economically planned, and prudently deployed, benefits of this.

7

Some time before, three IU professors, including the zoology department's Carl Eigenmann, had decided to supplement their income with some property speculation. To this end they bought land on the southeast edge of Bloomington. Kinsey decided to buy a plot here in 1926 (Mac had recently come into some money after the death of her parents). This was where they would build their home.

He at once embarked on a great deal of very exciting work. It was like being newly married again. Calling on his despised engineering skills, he drew up all the plans for the home himself.[56] He found, to his delight, a large number of bricks burnt by the kiln and reduced by $2 a thousand. Kinsey bought the lot.

He supervised every detail. The builders started by laying the bricks in an orderly and symmetrical fashion. Kinsey stopped them and with considerable taste and originality had them laid unevenly with the mortar bulging out like too much cream in a cake or a stack of over-filled sandwiches. The result is the most charming and eccentric house in Bloomington – a huge Hansel and Gretel home in a ballet or an architectural fantasy of Gaudi.

And, of course, the Kinseys did all the decorating and furnishing themselves. As a result it wasn't really finished till December 1936.[57] The present owner said someone had told Mrs Kinsey that if you washed walls with tea they lasted.[58] Certainly, they are dark – but Kinsey's daughter Anne said it was done by her father. 'Daddy painted everything black. He even painted his piano black.'[59]

This was not the only Pooterish touch. Kinsey now also remembered his rug-making skills acquired years before at college: a plaiting, then twisting of six-inch strips of old cotton – sheets, shirts, dresses, etc. – and yards of plain muslin dyed by the laundry. 'He was always making rugs,' said Anne. 'When we at last moved upstairs he made more rugs.' She can remember him sitting on the floor 'braiding and listening to his gramophone and sometimes chatting to mother'. But where most braided scrap rugs are half an inch thick, Kinsey's are one and a half inches thick. Some are still being used today.

It was a reasonably comfortable house but not a luxurious one. It was frugal. There was no air-conditioning in Bloomington then, and when it came the Kinseys despised it and for years did without. But there was central heating run by a big furnace in the cellar. 'It was great fun,' said Joan. 'Daddy ordered two tons of coal and they shot it into the basement. Daddy would shovel it in. At night he'd "bank" it – then first thing in the morning he'd open it up.'[60]

The long living room, with its upright (now black) piano in the corner, and its fine wooden floor of sweet gum, also had an open fire which Kinsey, out of habit from campfire days, would douse last thing – somewhat to the astonishment of house guests and also permanently weakening the chimney.

There were few other amenities. In 1928 they gained a garage, since in that year Kinsey felt able to afford their first car – a second-hand Nash which had belonged to neighbours across the street. And there was his gramophone. He now began to collect records again and soon the shelves at the far end of the living room started to fill. But the heyday of the Kinsey 'musicales' was later.

He continued to play the piano until well into the 1930s, finally free, according to Christenson, of concert ambitions. His taste in music was in fact sophisticated, but for ease of sight-reading he preferred the classics – Beethoven and Chopin in particular. Mac gave him sheet music for Christmas. During 1927 he sometimes accompanied – how Victorian it sounds – a 'Mr Turner, a graduate who liked singing'.[61]

As far as the children went (with the addition, now, of Bruce Kinsey in November 1928) the attic was an amenity. For some years this was a big empty space used for ping-pong and rushing about.

But the most notable of what is now 1320 East First Street's assets was the large garden which soon became another of Kinsey's obsessions and which, in later years, undoubtedly saved his life.

8

The whole of the Kinsey drama was, naturally enough, played out against the background of the ferocious American climate. Americans themselves often don't seem to realise how appalling this is. Not only can the temperature in summer easily reach 104°F (40°C) or more for days and weeks on end, but water sucked up from the Gulf of Mexico is regularly and continually dumped on Indiana. The humidity equals that of Malaya in the monsoon. In winter, the temperature plunges to 0°F (-18°C) or less. There is one tiny window – autumn. Hence the American worship of the fall. Sometimes in spring, too, the climate is tolerable for a brief space.*

It is because of this summer heat that many older Bloomington houses have capacious cellars, which were often used for work, as Kinsey's was at Park Street, or in hot weather for sleeping. During the '20s and '30s women used fans – piles of which were stacked at the church doors on Sundays. And the extremes of temperature, of drought and storm, mean that gardening is not easy – which is why Bloomington gardens deserve the bleak American soubriquet 'yard'.

But not Kinsey's yard – there *was* a garden. He accepted the challenge of the climate with relish – another fight to be won. When the Kinseys moved into the First Street house, Bloomington roads were only paved up to Jordan, the street alongside them. Beyond lay forest. 'We only had to walk a block or so to find blackberries,' said Joan, 'or get out into the Maxwell woods right there for white violets.' Kinsey, who later added plots till they had two and a half acres, first planned and landscaped to fit this wildness – and the wilderness he loved. Thus he planted flowering weeds, and then poke, snakeroot and golden rod. It had a creek running through it and he built a lily pond. He also doctored the soil so that it approximated to that of New England, and planted accordingly.[62]

But his main plant was the iris. Oddly, like the gall wasp (and perhaps in his self-sufficing way like Kinsey himself), the iris comes complete with its own nutritional world, in its bulb. It was therefore well

---

* In the summer of 1995, while I researched this book, six hundred people died of heat in Chicago just north of us. The winter before, a visiting Japanese professor to Bloomington had his cheeks severely frost-bitten waiting thirty minutes beside his car for a tow truck to arrive.

suited to Bloomington's climate vagaries. It also requires sun and so was ideal for land bare of trees, which Kinsey's was for some years.*

Kinsey became crazy about irises. He grew more and more of them until they became another collection. At his peak he was growing 250 varieties of iris. He began to cover Bloomington with irises – he planted them outside the courthouse, he planted in the oval (still there, still irised) which separates the passing traffic on South Jordan Avenue. He exhibited irises and attended the American Iris Society and wrote for their *Bulletin*. For six or seven years he sold irises, printing three-page catalogues: '1929. IRIS GARDEN, A.C. KINSEY.'[63]

He tried to get Ralph Voris interested in irises. On 26 March 1935 he sent him lilies and irises. He pressed him with advice. 'Meantime, you have a guide which represents our experience in our own gardens and several of the gardens we have visited over the last four or five years.'[64] (Note the 'we' in his letters due to his aversion to writing 'I', which derived from his egotistical father's excessive use of it.)

And like all passionate gardeners, his letters to Ralph are full of weather: 1930 – 'Three months drought from May. Terrible heat. The grass crumbles as hoar frost when one walks on it. Trees and shrubs are dying to the ground.' One day the temperature reached 110°F. Anne, then aged six and a half, still remembers the heat of that summer. The whole family slept in the cellar. But then comes another year: 'Spring is here – sun is nice – lots of rain . . .'[65]

Yet, though it was technical relaxation, Kinsey of course could not take his gardening in a relaxed way. Helen Wallin, who worked with him on galls in 1937, remembered the gardening. 'Relaxation – but it obsessed him as much as anything else. Got graduate students to help him. A *wild* garden, and you'd get little lectures there, about an iris, how tall it would grow etc. But it was *work*.'[66] So did his son-in-law. 'His energy! He was difficult to keep up with. He'd set himself a goal and the work he did was colossal.'[67]

The garden satisfied Kinsey's need for violent, exhausting exercise. He later added a money-saving vegetable patch. He could be seen digging ferociously every Sunday, sweat pouring off him. Sometimes he got up at six on weekdays to put in an hour before work. In 1934, copying

---

* The only tree was a persimmon which he couldn't bear to fell and which the house was therefore built in an L to accommodate. This finally blew down on to the house – causing amazingly little damage – in a July 1995 gale.

Ralph Voris, he took to wearing the briefest of skin-coloured jockstrap shorts;[68] shirtless, barefoot (but a shoe on the right foot when he dug) the neighbours thought he was naked.

James Jones, in his recent biography, explains that Kinsey gardened like this because it served to counteract the 'fragile sense of masculinity' which 'Kinsey must have felt'. By ferocious work he managed to convert gardening into 'a vigorous male activity'.[69] This is an odd statement, though a revealing one. Possibly there is a trace of truth in it. Kinsey as a boy in South Orange had used physical exercise to prove he was as tough as other boys. Perhaps a buried element of this may have remained, but Kinsey had essentially resolved this many years ago and many hard miles ago. There is not the slightest evidence he *had* 'a fragile sense of masculinity' – now or ever; rather to the contrary if anything. But that is not what Jones is on about. This is another none too subtle nudge, based on nothing at all, to make the reader see Kinsey as totally homosexual from the start. The only evidence so far for anything like this was Kinsey's relationship with Kenneth Hand. In fact, the picture that was evolving, as we will see soon with Ralph Voris, was towards a complex bisexuality, which was to continue for many years, and then to change and shift in various ways again.

What is interesting about the statement is that it only makes sense if homosexuals are seen as somehow not really masculine, as 'fragilely' masculine. Lurking here is the old prejudice that to be a homosexual is to be, somehow, a feminised man, queer, sissy. The second assumption is that gardening, too, is really for women – which is why Kinsey 'must' have felt uneasy about doing it (it would give him away).

Kinsey, like most, probably all, men had sides to his character which our culture labelled, often still labels, as 'feminine'. His piano-playing and love of music, his flower-arranging and decorating his homes were aspects of this side of him. But there is no evidence they made him uneasy – or made anyone else so. They sat on him comfortably and without strain and brought him much pleasure.

Kinsey, then, loved his garden. His letters to Ralph are never so happy as when they contain bulletins from the bulb front: 'I have the best tan ever . . . And the most glorious fine feeling my skin has ever known.' He was swimming every day, for the first time 'since you deserted me here'.

He loved his garden and he was happy with his family – yet perhaps he was never so happy as when he left them both.

9

The pattern of escape from home into the wild, set up in his boyhood, was irresistible and Kinsey continued it all his life.

He would, in fact, dash off for a week or so whenever he could grab it, but the problem with galls was that to hatch properly in the laboratory they had to be at a certain stage of maturity, usually reached in October/November. Earlier, they might not hatch; later, the ghastly American weather made it impossible to collect them. And so nearly every year from 1925 on Kinsey would get away for two weeks in the fall.

He took his cleverest graduates and two of them, Herman Spieth (later Chancellor of the University of California, Riverside) and Robert Bugbee, have left accounts; Ralph Voris' reaction can be gauged from his letters. We can, therefore, get a feeling of these expeditions.

Both Spieth and Ralph, for example, along with Avril Holloway, went with him in October 1928 when he covered Tennessee and both Carolina coasts. A day was spent carefully mapping and dividing the area. Then – Kinsey's boyish excitement palpable, the excitement of the hunt which all collectors feel, the excitement of getting away – off they set; in this case to his graduates' consternation in the Nash, which he had only just and inadequately learnt to drive.[70]

These were not holiday trips. The routine was rigid. Up at 4 a.m., Kinsey insisting on a cold shower however cold the weather, partly to get them awake. (Oddly enough he was constitutionally a late riser – though he never indulged himself.) Then, drive and walk to the search site and collect all day, rain or snow. Every gall in sight was taken. Lunch, always eaten on the move, was invariable: a 'ration' of peanuts, chocolate and raisins, which made Ralph sick. This fact, revealingly, was hidden from Kinsey since they knew it would irritate him. A huge supper, followed – and one has from Spieth's account a sense of driving on, not a second wasted – by long hours spent sorting, labelling, packing. The next day – the galls posted to Bloomington.

They slept in the cheapest hotels, the 'crude tourist cabins', Bugbee noted, always unheated. And discipline was tight. The cold shower, which Kinsey insisted be repeated in the evening, was not now to wake them up but Kinsey's neurotic obsession with cleanliness. Bugbee (apt name for an entomologist) described how he and Oswald P. Breland were made to scrub down morning and night in freezing temperatures.[71]

And these were grown men! No wonder on one two-week expedition, to Kentucky and Alabama in March/April 1931, Avril Holloway suddenly refused. There was a row and Kinsey turfed him out, telling him to find his own way back. Holloway's unexpected return caused quite a stir at IU.[72]

Everywhere he went Kinsey recruited amateurs to help collect galls for him. As his work progressed he corresponded with gall experts abroad and got them to help as well. He gradually drew together a network of over a hundred people sending him galls from all over America and from various places round the world.[73]

The statistics, as the '20s progressed into the '30s and towards his first major gall book, became truly astronomical. From 1925 to 1929, $400 of his salary came from a Waterman appointment. His annual reports for Waterman ring with these figures: 4,200 miles this year, 3,500 the next, over 7,000 in 1929; 80,000 gall wasps collected, 62,000, 105,000; Arkansas covered, Oklahoma, Louisiana, Colorado, the Rockies, northern Arizona, Utah . . .[74]

What can be measured, counted, tested, seen in actuality or in tables – this to many scientists, to science itself, is reality. The fact. And here galls were ideal. To put it crudely, had he been studying, say, alligators such marvellous figures would have been impossible.

But of course it was what he did with his thousands upon thousands of galls that mattered; Kinsey's real quality as a scientist didn't truly emerge till he returned home.

10

We have some vivid verbal cinema verité of Kinsey at work during this 1920–30 period.[75]

His office – or laboratory as he always called it – was in the east corner facing north across the campus on the second floor of what was then Biology Hall (later Swain Hall). The entrance was past the 'lift' – a railing-surrounded hole with a platform you started and stopped by ropes which Kinsey did *not* use – through a tiny, dark, windowless vestibule into a small room crammed with books and gall wasps. Kinsey's desk was in a space facing the window. Behind him two tall olive-coloured metal bookcases reached the ceiling. When Kinsey wanted anything on the top shelves he clambered rapidly up straddling the aisle. Behind the bookcases the room was filled, all but a second small space, with shoulder-high metal cabinets themselves filled with insect cases. The second small space in front of the second window held a table for his assistant.

Kinsey would stride across from First Street or use the Nash if very pressed, run up the stairs and arrive at 8 o'clock or before, unless he had a class first, in which case 9 o'clock. He was dressed informally – in summer in scout-like khaki shorts, open shirt, moccasins, no hat. June Keisler talks of an enthusiastic boyish figure rushing into the lab saying he'd been in the garden since seven. They would listen and admire and see he was 'a character'.

Elizabeth Frazier had worked with a lot of scientists. 'Kinsey was the most precise and *definite* person I ever worked for – in the way he walked, especially the way he *talked*. He'd utter a sentence. Then stopped. That was *it*. When he came into the lab he made *straight* for his desk and started work – well straight, he had to negotiate the maze of cabinets – but then start at *once*. I've never known anyone so engrossed, completely engrossed, in what he was doing.'

Engrossed for hour after hour. Louise Rosenzweig remembers him working through lunch (the usual nuts, chocolate, raisins) reading journals, then on through the afternoon. 'In winter the ceiling light was generally off. Dr Kinsey often used his green eyeshield while using his microscope. He worked intently for long periods, then suddenly might remark: "Astonishing!" or "Remarkable!" Or simply "Wow!" These interjections were not directed at me (the only other person in the room) but merely expressions of exhilaration at his discoveries.' Sometimes he would get up, stretch, smile at her, 'and quickly continue his work'. He would leave for his dinner at six and then sometimes come back to work far into the night. As the years passed, and the children grew older, night working became more and more frequent.

And what was this work? Initially, preparation. Each insect was killed, then lifted with tweezers, glued to a 'support' of stiff paper which was in turn impaled on a two-inch steel pin. To the pin was attached a minute label. 'You had to have a magnifying glass,' said Elizabeth Frazier. 'Some of the insects were more or less invisible. Then the labels! He taught us to print *perfectly* – you had to do it on this *teeny tiny* thing.' Labels saying sex, where found, when, when hatched . . . Thousands upon thousands – finally millions – of these exquisitely prepared specimens were pinned into insect-proof boxes – 800 to a box, all facing right

– and carefully stored away.

Kinsey himself was not much good at this. He had, as Dorothy Collins noticed, 'beautifully tapered fingers. He manipulated his hands in a graceful manner.'[76] He also manipulated them clumsily. (In later years he used to fiddle with Bill Dellenback's photographic equipment and break it.) In any case, no single human being could have done it. For fifteen years, from 1926, relays of young women, sometimes four at once, all working part-time, serviced his galls.

But the real work began then. Every single specimen was examined by Kinsey under a dissecting microscope; twenty-eight difference measurements were taken, recorded and correlated, and from these the species deduced, variations, order of descent, relationships ... To speed the note-taking he developed a shorthand/positional code whereby a few simple symbols took on a separate meaning from their position on a small page.[77] This was Kinsey's task; easy to relate, it took sixteen years to complete.

He had other excitements as well as his discoveries. There were his window boxes. Kinsey loved them. They were heaped with small (5″ × 8″), very fine mesh bags into which newly collected galls were sewn. Here the wasps hatched. Several times a week Kinsey and his assistants peered at them. And Louise Rosenzweig remembered how thrilling it was when galls arrived from helpers – especially if it was France. Sometimes galls lay dormant for years. In 1934 Kinsey told Ralph Voris that his lab was literally *alive*! 'One whole genus is just beginning to emerge as it goes into its 4th!!! winter.'[78]

There were his insect boxes. The older cases, the Schmitt boxes, were of pine or oak, very strong, very tight. 'Kinsey,' said Louise, '*loved* these cases too. When a visitor was impressed he'd say casually – "Oh, they're pretty enough".'

This was all part of the deep psychic pleasure Kinsey derived from collecting – which in turn made pleasurable much that was in essence infinitely boring. His college friend Edgar Anderson noticed that this pleasure grew with the years, and also how it manifested itself physically. 'When he closed one of the tight-fitting [Schmitt] insect boxes ... there was a physical reaction ... the tension of the fingers showed that the closing was of inner significance.' He noticed how long Kinsey lingered on the cabinet drawer before finally sliding it shut.[79]

And then there were his young women, nearly always working their way through college. June Keiser worked with plump, blonde Evola van

Valor and the pert, pretty brunette Elays Kurtz. He paid them thirty cents an hour, the going rate during the Depression. As this ended, he raised it to thirty-five cents. Kinsey was a considerate, kind and fair employer – and remote. Louise worked with him for three years and he called her Rosenzweig throughout. He addressed personal matters only twice in the entire time. Once he asked if she minded missing a football game. The second time he suddenly let her join her brothers on a trip to Colorado. She felt it was the teacher that was so strong in him – it would do her *good* to see and learn about the vast plains and the Rockies. Yet these young women were perceptive. June Keiser noticed his love of shocking 'like a small boy . . . then waiting rather hopefully for the explosion'.

June just kept on and on and on and on for three and a half years 'without any particular feeling of boredom or resentment against the factory-production nature of the work'. Sometimes she wondered *why* they were doing this. But she learnt Dr Kinsey wouldn't know till he had a lot of insects what it *was* he was looking for. That was science.

This was partly true. However, right from the start with his 300,000 Harvard galls[80] he was revolutionising the entire species system in the wasps, and by 1930 his work began to reach its culmination. But it was just before this, in the mid-1920s, that we have the first real indication of Kinsey's intense interest in sex, though this is something we could have assumed. But the catalyst was his first graduate student, Ralph Voris.

5

Sex Life

PS This one was really too foul to quote when the girls were present: and maybe you've heard it anyway.

There was a young man of Bombay,
Who buggered his dad night and day.
He said 'Yes it is rather
Hard up father,
But he's clean and there's nothing to pay!
Kinsey to Ralph Voris, 27 November 1939

1

Ralph Voris was Kinsey's graduate student from 1924 to 1927. An early, rather studied photograph (no. 11) shows a young man of matinée idol good looks. Kinsey's children remember him as he was in the 1930s, when he and his wife sometimes came to stay at Bloomington. He was a big, teddy bear figure, round-faced, friendly, humorous – he once gave them a bundle of his own blank cheques for a game they were playing, which worried Mrs Kinsey.[1] He was eight years younger than Kinsey and from a similar background – small town, not rich, working his way up. Oddly enough, they shared birthdays – 23 June. And, as well as his first graduate student, he was Kinsey's man in other ways. He loved to get out in the field. He was fanatical, a man, Kinsey noted approvingly, 'who could sit all day beside an uninhabited pile of dung until it came alive with bugs'.[2] He was level-headed, commonsensical – and the only one of the young men not dominated by Kinsey.

He was also, Kinsey told Gebhard, the second great love of his life.[3]

To understand their relationship we have to know something about Kinsey's sexual attitudes and sexual orientation. James Jones is definite on this: Kinsey was 'a homosexual'. He was so from the beginning and remained so till the end.[4] It was one of the 'demons' tormenting him and causing him, later, to 'skew' his sex research.

The trouble is, despite his skill elsewhere, homosexuality is something of a blunt instrument in Jones' hands. His declaration that Kinsey was always a homosexual obliterates any idea of change, of development or regression, of variation in attitude and behaviour, indeed of any complexity at all – the very stuff of human life and character and therefore, or it should be therefore, of biography.

What is more startling is that Jones' decision (for which there are in fact reasons) to make Kinsey 'a homosexual' also obliterates a great deal that is very good in his book. I was not the only reader to be startled. Many reviewers were too. 'Alfred Kinsey was "a homosexual". Oh really?' wrote Martin Duberman for instance. 'By what definition? Jones presents evidence . . . that Kinsey was lovingly married for thirty-five years to Clara McMillen, and that their relationship was in no sense perfunctory, certainly not sexually . . . and they maintained a sexual relationship until Kinsey became ill near the end of his life.'[5] Jones presents much evidence of this sort – and there is a good deal more he didn't know about.

But the point is that we know for certain the actual, if rough, outline of Kinsey's evolution here. We know it because Kinsey was neither remotely reticent nor ashamed with close colleagues. Throughout the 1940s he gave his sex history regularly to Wardell Pomeroy.[6] Pomeroy would discuss this with Paul Gebhard, who himself trained taking Kinsey's history, 'though I didn't often get beyond his twenties since he always pulled me up for mistakes'. In 1939 Kinsey was to construct his heterosexual-homosexual scale: 0 was totally heterosexual, 6 was totally homosexual and 3 was both equally, with 1 and 2 and 4 and 5 intermediate at either end. Gebhard is clear that at age twenty-seven Kinsey was a 1, perhaps edging to a 2, on the scale (predominantly heterosexual, but incidental homosexual experience or psychic response). By about 1939/40 he was a 3, but not till 1946 was it evident he had moved toward the H end of the scale, as a 4. (H was Kinsey-code for homosexual.) He was *never* completely homosexual – a 6 in his terms.[7] Kinsey was bisexual, an almost ideal position, one might think, for someone who was studying sexual behaviour in both sexes.

It was Ralph Voris, Kinsey also told Gebhard, who first alerted him to this element in his character.*[8] But this doesn't necessarily mean that they were lovers. Evidence here is scanty.

2

The only evidence we have to go on is the correspondence between Voris and Kinsey. This has been described by Thomas Waugh, in a way rather surprising to anyone who has read it, as this 'astonishingly intimate and tender correspondence'.[9] But Waugh, one of Kinsey's cleverest and most amusing commentators, was also one of the few who guessed that Kinsey was at least partly – to Waugh wholly – homosexual. As his only source, he *needs* the letters to be intimate and tender.†

Certainly, they show that the two men wanted to get out into the field together. Here is Kinsey in 1929 trying to get Voris on an expedition: 'If you can go, there is no man I'd rather have along.' Voris: '*I will go!!* There isn't a place I'd rather go ... I have a lot to say but what a gab feast we will have.' And when they get back: 'It was a glorious trip wasn't

---

* The corollary of this, of course, is that, as James Jones posits, Kinsey almost certainly wasn't even consciously aware of this strain in his character, or at least not aware of what it meant, as a youth and young man. This is a sensitive insight and I think probably accurate. I do not see, however, how it can be squared with Jones' demon stance – that Kinsey was 'a homosexual' from the start and riven with guilt about it. How can you be riven with guilt about being something you don't know you are? (Jones, *Kinsey*, p. 170.)

† In fact, Paul Robinson also guessed Kinsey was at least partly homosexual and speculated about the emotional nature of his relationship with Ralph Voris. His evidence was a phrase in Pomeroy that Kinsey's friendship with Voris made 'these years far from ordinary for him'. In fact, I noticed Pomeroy's phrases in this context and Robinson missed what seems like the most revealing: 'One is no more than assured, after reading the above, that Kinsey's feeling about Voris was that of a father ... when another paragraph casts a different light ...' The trouble with evidence for this sort of thing from Pomeroy is that Pomeroy didn't write his own book. John Tebbel did. I questioned Tebbel closely about this, both in conversation and by letter, and he was quite clear. Both he and Pomeroy meant both passages to mean what they most obviously say; in the first that any close friendship was far from ordinary for Kinsey; and in the second that Kinsey's feelings changed from teacher/father to colleague/friend. It is conceivable that Pomeroy, knowing Kinsey's sex history, saw the scarcely detectable ambiguities and therefore let Tebbel's sentences stand – but this is speculation, not evidence. (Paul Robinson, *Atlantic Monthly*, May 1972, pp. 99–102; Pomeroy, *Kinsey*, pp. 46, 50; Tebbel, interview with the author, and letter to the author, 23 February 1996.)

it?' wrote Kinsey, '. . . and I am more than ever heartbroken that we weren't able to keep in the field.' They were always being heartbroken at the shortness of visits, so much still to gossip about, such bug talk to have. They are jokey. 'O! Yes I believe a new subject deserves a new para. Well here goes.'[10] (Voris). They share double rooms at cheap hotels to save money, and to discuss bugs. As, over ten years, tutor slowly turns into friend, the most intimate thing they talk about is sex. But Kinsey discussed sex with his other graduates and the intimacy is of a peculiar 1920–30-ish masculine, unintimate sort – locker-room jokes, and practical, technical male discussion about how to improve sex with their wives. (It is all, incidentally, relentlessly heterosexual.)

In fact, it is that particular progression, not by any means an unknown one, from tutor to close friend that the correspondence really charts. Inching over six years from 'Dear Ralph Voris' to 'Dear Ralph', Kinsey starts as a father figure: 'Were you flesh and blood of my own I could not get more satisfaction out of the research you turn out.'[11] He goes to endless trouble helping Voris, advising him about money, work, houses. He even gives him the precious fruits of his own research. Then gradually the letters get more chatty, relaxed, facetious – and they are friends. But I do not think you can call the correspondence either 'astonishingly intimate' or 'tender'.

On the other hand, it is clear that, like many others, a good many Kinsey–Voris letters have been pulled. In any case, instinctively secretive, Kinsey is almost never intimate by letter. If the existing Voris correspondence doesn't reveal that this was Kinsey's first homosexual affair, it certainly doesn't prove it wasn't. It is still entirely possible (to Paul Gebhard probable[12]). There are increasing indications towards the end of the correspondence of Kinsey pressing Voris to join him in hotel rooms at conferences and so on and of Voris holding back, which are somehow suggestive.[13]

The matter remains open.* But what the letters show, as do those between Kinsey and his other graduate students, is that during the 1930s he at long last began to follow the advice of the Bowdoin *Bugle* – 'Loosen up a bit, Al.'

---

* It was, as I mentioned earlier, a letter to Ralph Voris (20 September 1929) that I showed to the graphologist Renna Nezos. I asked her if it revealed anything about his sexual orientation at this time. 'Certainly,' she said, 'confusion.' (See Appendix C.)

3

The first indication comes in a letter from Ralph Voris to Kinsey in 1931: 'Please let loose some more gossip. The last was quite spicy. We both enjoyed it.'[14] Was this gossip about the Jim Richter who Oswald Breland, another of his students, sent an undated letter about? 'I wonder if Richter has learned anything from the last few months? I'll bet he has learned that he won't have to go far from home to do his tomcatting! Something tells me that his old lady could screw the horns off a Billy goat!!'[15]

Impossible to know, but many similar letters follow. Very occasion-ally Kinsey got away to New York. Returning from one visit he wrote to Ralph: 'If you get to New York and see what I saw during the holidays, you will wriggle as you ne'er have before – and you may warn Geraldine of that before you go. Burlesque at Broadway has the most gorgeously thrilling girls I ever except [sic] to see – and they stop at nothing. The G-strings to which they finally strip are half as wide as your little finger, and not a button wider at the strategic spot. When the audience insists strenuously enough, she will remove even the string – slipping a finger in place (to live up to the law) – with more damaging effect than the complete exposure of a nudist camp. Breland says it is criminal for such shows to go on in establishments that are not provided with side rooms where gentlemen may change their trousers and have side baths . . .'[16]

A little later Kinsey sends a pornographic poem to Ralph, which has not survived, though he has found a source which 'if you are good boy, I may let you see some day'.[17] The effect on Breland, however, is elec-tric. He feared it would lead to a local headline: 'NDAC Zoology instructor castrated for biting coeds tit!' In fact, he had quite 'a few students who made me feel like doing the things described in the little poem . . . Darn it, after reading the missive, I had to wait quite a while before I could trust myself to go to class. The middle leg for some unknown reason kept hitting me in the face! Don't be blooming stingy – let's have the rest of it!'[18]

Whatever the verses were like, those that remain are innocuous enough, like the limerick at the head of this chapter, or the PS in a letter from Ralph to Kinsey: 'It seems that the reason that Walt Disney didn't make a film about Snow White and the seven Fairies is that they couldn't whistle while they worked.'[19]

In letter after letter, they all exchange sex gossip, verses, jokes. The fact is, Kinsey had a typical, fairly aggressively heterosexual, locker-room relationship with his graduate students – male, coarse, facetious, salacious, secret. Hence all the PSs so it could be kept from the wives. He several times cautions Breland to destroy all this 'incriminating evidence'.[20]

Incidentally one gains a vivid picture of how appallingly difficult it was for these young men to get good jobs during the Depression. In a note, Breland tells Kinsey he has written sixty letters. In another: 'I would certainly like to drag someone's balls through a barbed wire fence. I wrote both to the Duck at Cornell College and the Shrimp at the Women's College of North Carolina . . . a few days ago I wrote to both those bozos again . . .'[21] etc., etc. The files are full of letters from Kinsey – literally dozens – trying to get his graduates positions. He lends them money, which they take *years* to pay back at $10 a year. [22] He eventually gets Breland into the University of Texas at Austin. Breland's thrilled letter of thanks ends typically: 'How is B's [Bugbee's] joystick teaser getting along?' The joystick teaser is Mrs Bugbee, whom Breland had previously said would be fine, provided her 'pie . . . were *chewed* thoroughly'.[23]

The loosening of attitudes which all this suggests, as the great repressive weight of his adolescence and young manhood slowly lifted, also released Kinsey to concentrate on his own sex life. And here, not only were his students involved but, obviously, Mac as well.

4

In 1941 Kinsey wrote to Dr Robert Latou Dickinson and said that he had read *A Thousand Marriages* ten to twelve years before and it was this that had first given him the idea he might 'research in this field'.[24] Dickinson's book came out in 1931 so Kinsey must have read it then.

Robert Dickinson was born in 1861 and practised as a gynaecologist from 1890 to 1920. It was from information gathered bit by bit from his 5,000 woman patients, from rudimentary sex histories he took from some of them (always, or so he said, with two nurses present), that he eventually compiled his book. He was a respected figure and, according to Vern L. Bullough, an excellent historian of this subject, both a pioneer and the most important US sex researcher up until 1930.

Which is not necessarily very high praise. Dickinson became very intimate with some of his patients and recorded their intimacies: their masturbation, their frequency of intercourse, their feelings, fears, desires and so on. How intimate can be gauged by the fact that some of his patients – nearly all rich or middle class – masturbated to orgasm while Dickinson, a small, restless, excitable man, crouched between their knees peering up a glass tube shaped like a penis. In this way, he proved conclusively (something in fact already known) that women did have orgasms which involved physiological changes.

Dickinson collected other valuable if eclectic data, but it is a ramshackle, wandering book, much of it written by co-author Lura Beam, which quotes Thoreau, Keats and Tennyson, is formed of impressions and descriptions with few facts, small indeterminate tables and it is very subjective. Dickinson was a gifted artist and designed fine rubber and plaster models to teach female anatomy and foetal development, but he had some extremely eccentric theories. He believed a woman's sexual life, particularly her masturbating life, was laid down physically like a geological formation in her sex organs. He did exquisite drawings of these, and later took photographs – a practice which at one point was to lead in the 1940s, in Kinsey's presence, to scenes of pure farce.

Highly responsive women were what seems to have particularly excited Dickinson (he introduced the electric vibrator into American gynaecological practice) and he chose thirty of his most 'passionate' patients and wrote them up in *A Thousand Marriages*. These are really just erotic descriptions of highly sexed women such as one can find in *Forum*, but often moving when they describe the torture of not having as much sex as they need.

It seems likely that Kinsey's purchase of Dickinson's book in 1931 had less to do with nascent ideas of sex research than with his own marriage. *A Thousand Marriages* is subtitled *A Medical Study of Sex Adjustment*, and he also sent it out to his old graduates to help their marriages.[25] And it was about now, in 1932 (and one notes he had already been married twelve years), that he sent Ralph a marriage manual for the same purpose: 'Under separate cover we are sending you the book. While it is not well written, and contains poor biology, it seems to us to be an honest thing. You may understand the unusual frankness of some of the later parts if you will skim thru enough of the earlier chapters to get their philosophy. If the book brings you something of the substantial good that it brought us (biologists that we were!) you will forgive us for sending it to you.'[26]

It is clear that from now on, and probably long before, Kinsey and Ralph Voris discussed their sex lives together.[27] In November 1934, for example, Kinsey wrote: 'The Voris's [sic] have shared much of our thoughts in the last week. Many thanks for letting us. It is worth more than most folk can realize to have friends whose thinking is so nearly our own. The back position has suddenly proved simple – and we have the others still to try. What damned foolishness it is that actual experience is not more often passed on among friends – what blundering amateurs we can be without it!'[28]

Ralph and Geraldine, who came as often as they could, visited the Kinseys just after Christmas that year. 'It was a grand and glorious time we had,' Ralph wrote. 'Thanks. I believe our technique is improving.'[29]

The cryptic 'back position' and even more cryptic 'our technique' (open to sinister interpretation) are probably explained by the marriage manual. This was almost certainly Theodor van de Velde's *Ideal Marriage – Its Physiology and Technique*.[30] It was published in 1930 and was by far the most successful and respected of those books at this time. It detailed foreplay, erotic parts of the body, nipples, clitoris etc., but from our point of view what is interesting is that it lists ten intercourse positions – six in which male and female face each other and four with the male behind. Two of the latter are quite complicated and would, indeed, need practice.

On the other hand, 'our technique' could refer to the man positioned on his back, and be related to Mac's orgasms. In his *Male* volume Kinsey notes that man-on-top is almost invariable in Anglo-American sexual behaviour and it is regarded as biologically normal. It is not; it is a cultural imposition. All other mammals (with some rare variations among primates) use rear entrance, female prone, face down, 'her legs flexed under her'. Then 'Among the several thousand portrayals of human coitus in the art left by ancient civilisations, there is hardly a single portrayal of the English-American position.' The one shown is women on top. This was nearly universal in Ancient Greece and Rome, it is also commonest in the ancient art of Peru, India, China and Japan. In one of the oldest depictions (Mesopotamia, 3200–3000 BC) it is, again, woman on top;[31] all this, perhaps, explained by the fact that this is the position which makes it easiest for women to orgasm.

Kinsey located the change, as he usually did (and usually rightly), with the rise of Judeo-Christian dogma. At various times, any position but man on top was a matter for confession. Why? Kinsey does not know but – and this is one of many reasons he is so much more interesting and stimulating than any subsequent sex researchers, a ponderous bunch on the whole – he speculates. Women were seen as the lustful tempters of man, the wicked Eve. Perhaps this was a symbolic dominating of her. Or the position of man on top was chosen just *because* it differed from pagans and infidels. Not clear.

Gradually round the new Christian instruction everything gathered. In numerous Catholic countries women on top came to mean the male had become effeminate and was therefore homosexual. Eventually, as so often, it entered medical practice and Kinsey notes that 'one of the older psychiatrists' in 1948 insisted that 'the assumption of such a dominating position by the female in coitus may lead to neurotic disturbance and, in many cases, divorce'.[32] (I suppose if the couple, or the man, really *believed* this he might have had a point).

Without the benefit of such knowledge in the 1930s, Kinsey pressed what he could on his graduate students. The furtive fear of nudity in the Hoboken household had led to a reaction. He and Mac took their clothes off whenever they decently could. They supported nudists, a liberal group at that time, and Kinsey's earlier mention of 'the complete exposure of the nudist camp' suggests they may have attended one. In November 1934 he sent Ralph and Geraldine two books about them. 'Are the Voris's [sic] shocked? Mrs Kinsey and I agree they have been a healthy part of our children's education. Read the Mason first, it is a broader analysis of the movement.'[33] But the Vorises weren't interested in nudists 'for the simple reason we are not interested in groups either with or without their clothes'.[34]

However, enthusiasm did not wane for on-the-back or from-the-back intercourse. Breland said the position 'surely was a humdinger'.[35] He, in fact, had difficulty with early ejaculation. Kinsey suggested masturbating but trying to delay orgasm. Breland thanked him,[36] and soon after wrote again: 'Speaking of copulation, I believe we have just about solved an important problem. We have procured a diaphragm and the results so far are excellent. Seems as though [previously] various raincoats dulled the sensation, especially on the female member of the combination.'[37] Later still the second party (his wife) is enjoying it still more, while the first party (him) 'could screw a knot hole, if there were a few hairs round it . . . as you know!'[38]

No one before or since ever dared to write to Kinsey like Breland. His letters, scattered with expressions like 'screw a duck', are unrelievedly facetious and randy. Yet deductions can be made from them and from the other graduate student correspondence.

It is a truism of behavioural psychology – indeed it is common sense – that if something pleasurable and strongly desired is prohibited it becomes an obsession. It is certainly true that Kinsey became obsessed by sex. Men of achievement often become obsessed by their subject. Indeed, it almost seems a necessary condition. But Kinsey also became obsessed by gall wasps. There was an obsessive element in his character and it was probably induced during his childhood and youth. His brother Robert shared it. (It is interesting that Robert Kinsey, also a workaholic, also found release in nature. He worked as a park planner.)[39]

But one would expect, certainly one would not be surprised, that this highly sexed man, rebelling against all the teachings of his father, when finally released from eighteen or so years of frantic sexual frustration when he must have thought about it incessantly, should eventually find all sexual expression, or nearly all, fascinating, exciting and admirable. What this correspondence makes clear is that it fuelled an almost equally intense interest in the sexual lives of his graduate students, and this began in the 1920s, long before it surfaced in the letters they wrote after they'd left. In fact, Kinsey's self-concern and interest in sex had extended, early on, to all the young men and women at IU. It was from the continuing expansion of this that his whole great enterprise was eventually, and then quite suddenly, to spring.

5

The whole sexual picture at Indiana University in the 1920s and '30s – sexual knowledge and education, behaviour, attitude, fears – derived from the confused heritage of the nineteenth century, still more confused by the impact of venereal disease.

The major cultural movement of the last two hundred and fifty years in Western Europe, and to a lesser extent in America, has been the rise of science and the parallel but opposite decline of religion. As a result, but especially during the nineteenth century, sexual matters were increasingly the concern of doctors and the laboratory.

One of the extraordinary things about this century is how difficult it has proved to throw off its religio-dictated inhibitions and prohibitions. Even rightly admired figures like Freud, who seemed dedicated to this, in fact, as Richard Webster's brilliant *Why Freud was Wrong* unanswerably proves, simply carried sin forward as neurosis from an extremely flawed, indeed non-existent empirical base.[40] The medicalisation of sex did much the same. Medicine logically requires disease; so disease had to be found in sex. Anything but common-or-garden, heterosexual, missionary position sexual intercourse to have children was at various times classified as a disease. Oral sex, homosexuality, masturbation, 'back position' sex were all pathological. Van de Velde's *Ideal Marriage* for example, while allowing oral sex as foreplay, said *orgasm* from this was pathological.

This whole process was much sharpened by the appalling venereal disease epidemic which was raging across America when Kinsey was born. This continued up to the 1940s and, even if the figures were often considerably exaggerated, much hysterical and muddled thought resulted. VD, according to Dr L. Duncan Bulkey, could be caught from practically anything – whistles, pens, pencils, toilet bowls, tattoos, toothbrushes, teaspoons . . .[41] VD was so obviously an example of divine retribution that much sex, to a lot of people *all* sex, remained sinful. The disease was morally defined and had to be fought morally – from which rose the Purity Crusade at the end of the century. The American Purity Alliance, dominated by women, was formed in 1895 to make an 'unremitting effort to root out all opportunities for moral lapse'.[42] At the same time, it was obviously a socio-medical problem and here the word 'Hygiene' was summoned, which somehow contrived a sense of medical and moral cleanliness combined, and the Social Hygiene Movement was at first largely composed of doctors.

Anxiety about 'the family' has been endemic in civilised societies since the Roman Empire, but these two anxious movements joined other social commentators in feeling that, in the 1900s in America, it was actually collapsing. Divorce, immigration, but above all, since VD was often lethal, prostitutes were physically destroying the family. They were the *cause* of VD – 'all other modes of propagation are almost *nil*,' said Dr Ludwig Weiss, a leading hygienist.[43] So much for teaspoons.

But where did prostitutes come from? The Victorian idea of female purity – based on, or giving rise to, the idea that women had no sexual feelings – still pertained. It followed that only if forced, would women submit to this frightful fate. Between 1907 and 1911 white slave hysteria swept America.

Temporarily at the centre of this was John D. Rockefeller, Jr. He sat on a grand jury appointed to investigate the white slave trade in New York. After six months' intense work they had found almost no evidence, but the young Rockefeller was now passionately involved and in 1911 he funded (to the tune of nearly $6 million by 1941) the Bureau of Social Hygiene to investigate the whole subject scientifically.

Rockefeller realised that nothing could be solved without solid data. To this end he supported the studies of Katharine B. Davis, first into prostitutes, later, realising prostitution was just part of the whole field of sexuality, into a more general study among 2,200 college women. By 1920, when approached by Earl F. Zinn, Davis and the Bureau had come to realise a large-scale study of sexuality was needed.

Meanwhile, the subject was being edged towards from another quarter. During the war, in order to use manpower effectively, the army initiated a vast programme (1.7 million men) of standard psychological testing under a Robert M. Yerkes (pronounced Yerk-ees). Yerkes was in fact an animal psychologist (mice, jellyfish, etc.[44]) but he made a success of this war task. His work was related to that of the National Research Council (NRC), itself set up to bring science to the study of war. It was natural, therefore, that after the war Yerkes should join the NRC, now devoting itself vaguely to 'social welfare'.

In 1921 the Bureau of Social Hygiene suggested their large-scale sexual study idea to the NRC. At once made extremely nervous, the NRC turned it down. But 45-year-old Yerkes, who had begun to move in a tentative way nearer human beings (he was studying chimpanzees), thought the idea a good one. He was a tall, strait-laced, reticent man, but a fighter. Eventually, after endless machinations, the medical division of the NRC set up the Committee on Research in Problems of Sex, with the money to be provided by the Rockefeller Foundation. Yerkes was chairman.[45]

In fact, as far as human sexuality went, the committee did virtually nothing for over twenty years. Out of 470 grants and $1,252,786, three were used for limited studies of students, and there were a number of grants for detailed, mostly endocrine studies, but nothing on a large scale. It was mostly animals – concentrating especially on the poor rat ('Effects of various degrees of sexual indulgence in the rat' – 1926/7, $2,000). But all these elements – the Rockefeller Foundation, the NRC, Yerkes – were eventually to play a crucial role in Kinsey's life.

They were all, however, Rockefeller aside, totally unknown to the public at large. And the same is true, though to a much lesser extent, of the various Hygiene and Purity movements. This is because there were equally strong feelings that openness was dangerous; just to mention something sexual would bring it about. Maurice Bigelow, lecturing in sexual hygiene at Columbia University Teachers' College, thought that open sex instruction encouraged day-dreaming. This was even more dangerous than masturbation since it could be kept up continually. The trick was to conceal instruction in zoology courses on fishes, plants, birds. The jump to the human was somehow implicit. Nor did the public want to hear. When *The Ladies' Home Journal* published a series on VD in 1900 it lost 75,000 subscribers.

This continuance and intensification of Victorian sexual fear and reticence was continually compounded by lack of knowledge. The nineteenth-century double standard had grown up from, or given rise to, the idea that men could visit 'fallen' women (usually prostitutes) to save wives from their 'animal' passions (animal = beasts = uncontrollable sex). But this was now seen to lead to disease. Solutions were contradictory. One was to deny that men, after all, *had* animal passions. All vice commissions, notes Allan Brandt, unanimously condemned the notion that they had, 'as a myth that encouraged vice'.

Fit to Fight, a pamphlet issued to all fighting men, particularly emphasised that the idea men needed sex '*is a lie.* If it were true, the boy who exercises them [the sexual organs] regularly from childhood on should have the greatest sex power – but he is more likely to be sexually dead . . . It is [also] not true that the absence of previous sexual experience is *any* handicap to a man entering the married state.'[46]

Other commentators, such as Dr J.H. Landis, too strongly in the grip of fears about male sexual explosions to accept they had no real sex needs at all, could contradictorily accept that the needs might be weak. One fact was axiomatic – men reached their height of sexual energy at about forty. Men of forty controlled themselves quite easily; young men therefore could and must do so too. Prince Morrow, a fanatical author on this subject, wrote: 'Perfect inhibition is the sign of perfect health.'[47]

Similar exhortation was brought to bear on young women. Social hygiene pressure meant that by 1922, 64.6 per cent of all secondary school girls were receiving some form of sex hygiene instruction – essentially, no form of sex until marriage.

It was all these matters which tangled together constituted 'the sex problem', but one might note that, since they all provoked leaflets, lectures, broadcasts, films, teachers, etc., however muffled and wrong-headed the language (the *definition* of 'masturbation' in *Webster's* in the '20s and '30s was 'self-pollution'), they were all to some extent moves to openness.

These outbursts were accompanied by powerful attempts to suppress prostitution. Draconian laws were introduced, including compulsory arrests, compulsory inspection and compulsory detention. Between 1918 and 1920, 18,000 were imprisoned, and many tens of thousands more young first offenders were put on probation following 'promiscuous sexual activities'.[48]

Since most prostitutes were poor and quite often black, it came to be assumed that those who indulged in diseased sex came from those classes; it was a short step – and one quickly taken – that sex itself, especially very active sex (which by definition prostitutes pursued), was somehow both 'dirty' and a lower-class pursuit.

Finally, during the late '20s and '30s, and through the Depression, all active measures, and so moves, such as they were, to openness, were forced to cut down or stop. All that was left was more and more vehement moral preaching. There seems also to have been an increase in stifling open discussion. In 1934 the Columbia Broadcasting Company refused to allow New York State Health Commissioner Thomas Parran to give a talk on VD because he wished to use the words syphilis and gonorrhea.[49]

It is hardly surprising, then, to find Indiana University during these years reflecting the confused, silenced, frightened, ignorant, repressive, puritan-dominated attitudes of this official, establishment sexual culture and the feelings, both in expression and reaction, that it engendered.

6

In 1924 the girls' council at Vernice Lockridge's genteel, conforming and reticent Bloomington High School issued a moral code: 'We believe that school shoes should be well-fitting with moderate heels'; 'We believe that performing one's toilet in public is ill-bred'; 'We approve of the policy of "hands-off" in friendship between boys and girls'. Vernice remembered a girl at IU then, and not the only one, who didn't even know how babies got out of their mothers, much less how they got in; she guessed the navel.[50]

University presidents and chancellors either inveighed against sex fiercely, if obscurely, like Dr Harold W. Dodds of Princeton, who much later would help do Kinsey immense harm. He was reported as warning his students that if they didn't control what he called 'emotions' mankind would be swept into a new dark age.[51] Others, like IU's William Lowe Bryan who, in 1924, had already reigned for over twenty years and also believed in sex repression, found it easier to ignore the whole matter. All girls at the university were segregated. They had to be in their dormitories by 10.30 p.m., and 'you paid your life away if you went to a dance off campus'.[52] Campus dances were beadily supervised to see that girls didn't go 'too far' with boys.

Boys too were immersed in that oppressive sexual climate which 'produced', as Edmund White wrote of a later period but which is just as relevant here, 'intense sexual isolation among nearly *all* adolescents and young people . . . these included anxieties about most aspects of sexual performance . . . Even a marginally competent sexual experience was more often a relief from anxiety and doubt than it was an expression of intense desire.'[53] And so, frustrated, ignorant, anxious, they sought excitement and picked up knowledge where they could: anywhere from catalogues to manuals, from cars to corpses.

I mean corpses literally. In 1924 the cadaver room at IU's Owen Hall used to be eagerly searched for female corpses by the under-graduates.[54] The underwear ads in Sears Roebuck catalogues fuelled adolescent fantasies. Marriage manuals provided more fuel, if you could get one. In the 1920s and '30s these had vast popular sales. For instance, the Little Blue Books, published in Kansas, sold 300 million copies.[55] The premise was: marriage was on the rocks, better sex could save marriages, therefore give sexual instruction.

One might think this would have led to more open speech and thought about sex, and to an extent this is true. But, paradoxically, it also did the opposite. Condemned by moralists as rank pornography and sought by young men and adolescents for this very reason, marriage manuals were bought and read in some secrecy (hence Kinsey's diffidence sending Van de Velde). At IU they were locked away, banned from everyone but selected seniors (there were no general bookshops in Bloomington then). They thus reinforced the idea that sex was something hidden and unmentionable.

What, then, *did* young people do as regards sex at IU? Since nobody actually knew, anything could be suggested. The Christian Right has power in America today, and makes a great deal of noise;* then the views it promulgates were in the saddle. In the pulpits the preachers in Bloomington pointed to 'sin strip' by the railway and denounced the prostitutes who plied there. The other thing they denounced was petting.

Petting! 'One cannot,' writes Paul Robinson, one of the most acute and certainly the wittiest of Kinsey's commentators, 'read Kinsey's discussion of petting without being immediately transported into the distinctive sexual ambience of the 1940s and 1950s, with its uniquely frustrating synthesis of permissiveness and restraint, of which petting was the characteristic expression.'[56]

It was not just the 1940s and '50s. America was changing rapidly. The census of 1920 showed that more people lived in cities than on farms. This was not yet true of Indiana, but the process was underway. The '20s and '30s also saw the arrival of the car as a place of courtship. More and more couples could be found in these or on campus, first at dusk or dark, later, as tolerance grew, in broad daylight, locked in each other's arms. Kinsey is at his most perceptive in his discussion of this phenomenon, pointing out, for example, that while obviously a substitute for intercourse petting was also engaged in because young people, as a result of the propaganda, were frightened of intercourse.[57]

---

* America is at once the most licentious culture since Rome and the most puritan country in the world – but it is the evidence of the latter that astonishes the transient visitor. When I was at IU in 1995 I very occasionally watched television. There is an entire channel devoted to preachers and spokespersons of the Christian Right. I remember one preacher seriously citing Solomon as an authority on behaviour today with whom it was impossible to argue. 'Do you dare cross Solomon's wisdom?' And here on earth, he went on, 'Sex is our main target. And Solomon said – 'It will harm your body.' And that is the point. It is not what they are for, it is what they are against. The Christian Right, just as it was in Kinsey's day, is against sex in all its manifestations. The stands of the pro-life movement (much in evidence round Bloomington) are not filled with evidence of suffering foetuses or similar arguments; they are filled with leaflets on how to achieve chastity, how to live without sex. Where does this nonsense come from? Is it a legacy of the Puritans and Protestants who first crossed the Atlantic so long ago? I wonder what would have happened if history had been slightly different. Let us cancel the *Mayflower* sailing and suppose that Cromwell had come after, say, 1675; then it would have been the rakes and libertines of Charles II's reign who would have had to flee. Kinsey's (possible) ancestors would have crossed with Rochester, not William Penn. Would we have a Wilmotsylvania? A licentious Right? One person we certainly would not have had would have been Alfred C. Kinsey.

Kinsey was perceptive because he was sympathetic. Although he was often irritated by the stupidity of IU's students, Kinsey, like many people of his temperament, was much nicer to those beneath or younger than him than to his peers or superiors. Somewhere around 1925 a brilliant student, Phil Rice, tried to publish something (untraceable) in the *Daily Student* that offended the faculty's standards of propriety. Up for discipline, he was strongly defended by Kinsey and let off. Kinsey was not so successful in 1927, when the *Daily Student* (twice weekly in fact) referred to 'the phallic worship on campus'. Once again there was outrage. Some faculty members, like cartoon High Court judges, couldn't understand the phrase and the classics professor had to explain. One anonymous faculty member told Cornelia Christenson that he could still remember forty years later how, totally unafraid, Kinsey had faced the massed and disapproving ranks of male faculty and delivered an impassioned defence of the young editor. He failed – and an academic career was ruined.[58]

But he intervened much more directly. There is no precise evidence until much later that it was the inadequacy of the sex research literature (always the official line) that was turning Kinsey towards the subject, but it is a deduction which can more convincingly be made from what was of far more importance to him. This was his concern over the harm the prevailing attitudes were doing to his students, just as they had done harm to him. He would often bring the subject up on his gall expeditions – no doubt not a particularly difficult task with young men in their early twenties. He would explain that masturbation was harmless, and give the same sort of advice to married students as he did with Homer T. Rainwater and Osmond Breland one October in 1934, and as he continued to do after they had left. Being Kinsey, he coupled it with various of his own frugalities. That October as they sat round the fire deep in the Ozark Mountains of Arkansas, he 'talked about condoms and how to use them, and how to preserve them, how to clean them up . . . [so] we wouldn't have to buy so many'. The trick, it seemed, was to wash them and then preserve them in alcohol. Rainwater, noting it was in the thick of the Depression, was duly grateful.[59] He was, said Robert Bugbee, 'appalled at their ignorance'. He would say to them that if they 'wanted to talk to him about any problem . . . specifically sexual problems, to feel free to come to him'.[60]

The sort of questions he was asked, among many others, were: Does it matter if I've had intercourse at my age (or not had it) with someone of this or that age? If I did it this or that number of times with this or that number of people or with someone of the same sex? Does everyone masturbate? Is my penis smaller than most penises? Is it unusual for my boyfriend to want to do this or that? Was I odd to show off my genitals when small? It was these simple questions about sexual behaviour, quite aside from 'problems', that he discovered no one had really explored. No one knew precisely what people did and therefore everyone was anxious or guilty about whatever they did.[61]

It is likely that by the early 1930s he had already begun to ask his students questions about their sex behaviour, both in order to elucidate these questions and to plumb their ignorance. He certainly did this with Ralph Voris; and was soon to do so, in 1933, with young Professor Robert Kroc. But it was in the early '30s that whole fraternity houses started to ask him to come and talk about sex. He'd reply, 'I'll come if you answer my questionnaire', since that told him what they did or did not know.[62] One of the most obvious ways of finding out what people know in this sphere is to find out what they've done.

But Kinsey could not really move decisively in this direction – he certainly did not yet see it *as* a new direction – until he had triumphed as an entomologist, and in 1930 this finally began.

6

Gall Wasp Triumph

1

O ne of the curious advantages Kinsey possessed as an entomologist (apart from apparently being impervious to insect bites)[1] derived from, or is revealed by, his dealings with young people – whether scouts, campers or students. He fascinated them in his subject because he saw living things in a particularly vivid, concrete way.

Take a seminal lecture he gave to fifteen newly elected members of Phi Beta Kappa in June 1939. His theme, at first, is individual variation. This is the most fundamental and most important of all biological phenomena, since it is the root cause for the existence of everything alive. Every single living thing is different from every other living thing. We can see how this is easily enough with human beings – but it is true of everything else as well. Take his galls, smaller than an ant 'which you have probably never seen, and about which you certainly cannot care'. He had studied tens of thousands, in fact millions of these under the microscope – and *not one* was the same. Each tiny individual gall was different from every other tiny gall wasp. And the same was true of every fish, every daisy, every worm, tomato, ant . . . Each of these, like everything else, was different from every other fish, daisy, worm, tomato, ant . . .[2]

This acute awareness of the *actuality* of biological variation, a result, of course, of his passion for evolution, would eventually lead him into demonstrating a profound philosophical position, but there were other consequences. Much of the avant-garde work in biology in Kinsey's day – as once more in ours – was being done in genetics. This was where his friend Anderson was working, for instance. But Kinsey, because he enjoyed teasing out the practicalities of variations physically, liked getting out and testing it in action, preferred taxonomy – then a relatively humble branch of study. Kinsey, not a particularly humble person, was sure that taxonomy, because it could investigate how genetic factors actually operated in the field, could in fact prove, disprove and often supplant the findings of geneticists. By 1932, he could speak of 'a new day dawning in taxonomic research'[3] precisely along those lines. He was eventually able to prove it fully – at least in his own speciality.

All this was allied to a second odd advantage – the extraordinary frailty of Kinsey's chosen subject. In order to survive at all the flimsy gall wasps had been forced to join one of the toughest, longest-surviving of all living things – the oak. As a result, impregnable in their great galls (some as big as a man's head) the feeble things had survived in a unique range of species. I earlier used the cat family as an example and said how difficult it was to see how lions, tigers, lynxes, domestic tabbies etc. could all have evolved from a single early cat. That is because the intervening species have perished. But if we could see the whole evolutionary spread, if every link survived, we would have a totally different world picture. By chance, this was the world of the gall wasp.[4]

Kinsey's particular, practical skills and fascination, the peculiarities of the gall wasp, his fever to collect, all meant – and he knew they meant – that he would not only find new species but perhaps new laws. If he found gaps in the chain of evolution between one species close to another, he suspected if he looked really hard in areas geographically close he would find the links. And as Stephen Jay Gould notes, he usually did.

He began to do all this quite early on and reported it in his first papers. 'Papers' one calls them! In 1922 *Studies of Some New and Described Cynipidae* was 141 pages long; *The Gall Wasp Genus Neuroterus* (1923) was 150 pages[5] – so short books. But his twelve years' work came to its first culmination on 27 February 1930 when *The Gall Wasp Genus Cynips – A Study in the Origin of Species* was finally published.[6]

It is a massive 577 pages, mostly text, but with twenty-one pages of bibliography (listing all his five previous papers), ten pages of photographs and sixty pages of illustrations – the meticulous, spidery, delicate drawings by Kinsey himself. And it repays a brief study. First, he sets out his *method* (in essence, vast numbers, extensive measurements, huge geographical areas, caption reference to other scientific disciplines), and one notices at once several other striking Kinsey characteristics. His aggressiveness: 'Too many systematists,' he writes, attacking his fellow researchers, as he was so often to do in the future, in stinging prose, 'attain their objectives when each species is "represented" by half a dozen specimens pinned in their cabinet... [their] definition of systematic entomology... [is] the science of transferring pins from one box to another.' One notices already his distrust of anything 'psychological'. Even in the little gall he finds things hitherto apparently regarded as 'psychologic' which must have 'a biologic basis'. One notices, too, a certain leisureliness in the writing. The prose unreels. This is partly idiosyncratic, partly because he is determined to be absolutely clear.

And he leaves no doubt when, describing the *basis* of the research, he triumphantly wheels out the big guns of his statistics, that a lot of work has been done – and who did it. 'It was in the fall of 1917 that I made my first collection of the genus, and in the 12 years that have intervened I have travelled over 32,000 miles...' The 34,000 galls, the 17,000 wasps are in 'our collections – 96 Schmitt boxes'. (The 'I', 'we', 'our' switch wildly.)

And yet the romantic Kinsey is here too – he describes using his car, then outlines a typical trip: 'The farm boy helps, and we collect more smooth galls while we wonder about the varied mixture which spreads so many miles back of us. It is drizzling now, and sheets of fine snow come whirling off the mountains...'[7] Insofar as a very dry treatise can be lyrical – Kinsey is lyrical.

But it is certainly dry; naturally enough, Kinsey isn't writing a novel. After setting out the aim – to define, find and then analyse the formation of species – the method, the base, his discoveries and argument and so on, the bulk of the book is just dense data. The lay reader is only jolted awake by the bizarre realisation that Kinsey has actually *become* a gall wasp. Although he is in fact following the conventional nomenclature here, as he proudly lists the fifty new species and varieties and subgenera he has found it seems as if an army of Kinseys, an enormous biblical family of them has appeared: Advena Kinsey, Apache Kinsey, Attriidivisa Kinsey, Abbicolens Kinsey, Anda Kinsey, Alrifolii Kinsey and on down the alphabet with, here, a wave to his best friend – Vorisi Kinsey – or, there, a polite nod to his old teacher – Wheeleri Kinsey.

Here, in fact, he was moving in tricky territory, and one which continues to exercise taxonomists today. In the evolving continuum, the range of variations he had uncovered, how was he to designate it all? Taxonomists tend to group themselves into 'splitters' or 'lumpers', and Kinsey, following Wheeler, was by instinct a 'splitter'. That is, his interest in variation inclined him to make differences important and create new species. But at this point, 'I am at a loss for a solution of this difficulty,' he wrote. He compromised by quite often using the term 'variety'.

What had Kinsey achieved? First, he pioneered the use and publication of vast numbers, wide geographical range and numerous measurements – all of which gradually became common usage. Second, and as a result, he produced a thorough taxonomy of almost an entire genus, something, as he pointed out, 'only occasionally achieved', and one which involved a wholesale revision of all previous work. Finally, he made important, even revolutionary discoveries about evolution itself.[8]

He showed that, in galls at least, new species did not appear by an accretion of small variations, but more likely by abrupt and substantial changes – thus he anticipated by about forty-two years the idea of 'punctuated equilibrium' first put forward as a serious contribution to evolutionary theory by Niles Eldredge and Stephen Jay Gould in 1972.* He also showed that, again as far as galls went, isolation was probably more important as a factor in species evolution than survival of the fittest. But Kinsey was also always quite clear that his gall findings were probably relevant elsewhere.

He was to pursue both his taxonomic revisions and these discoveries further. But his future plans were even more ambitious. Again, these derived from the hopeless nature of his chosen creatures.

In the chapter on galls in his biology textbook, Kinsey describes their locomotion. He imagines a wasp hatching 'from a gall that has blown off into an open field. It runs across the mountains of ploughed ground, and through the jungle of grasses and weeds, to an oak tree that grows along the fence-row.' Let us say – thirty yards. Unless caught by gusts of wind, most of them would only move as far as the next branch. The gall wasp was, that is to say, virtually immobile, which accounts for the extraordinary role isolation could play in the development.

Nevertheless, inch by inch, the tiny insects did move. It should be possible, therefore, tracing back over the ground from the furthest

---

* Biologists, including Darwin, and paleontologists had been aware from very early on of difficulties here. But in Kinsey's day the accepted view was that there were gaps in the fossil record and, but for this, we would see that evolution was gradual. Kinsey's view was thus revolutionary. (For a short discussion of Gould and Eldredge's work see *Life Pulse – Episode from the Story of the Fossil Record by Niles Eldredge*, New York, 1987, pp. 81–3).

distribution, relating each species to the one which had preceded it, to find the place, and perhaps the gall, which had started the whole thing off – the origin of the gall wasp, the gall wasp Garden of Eden.

It was to this end among others that, in 1931 and again 1936, Kinsey mounted two massive expeditions down into Southern Arizona, Mexico and Guatemala.

2

For the eighteen months following the publication of his first gall book in February 1930, Kinsey followed his usual intense routine – galls, lectures, seminars, tutorials, new editions of the two biology textbooks, etc., but during the summer of 1931 he began to prepare for his first extended trip south.

He was away the first half of winter, from 26 September till nearly the end of January 1932. (Joan remembers her mother taking on the task of banking the furnace at night.[9]) By coincidence, the expedition was financed by a $750 grant from the National Research Council, the medical division of which was at this moment plodding on financing sex research into rats and other animals. The actual route was into the western Sierra of Mexico, Mexico City and down into the Cordillera further south. It isn't necessary, but it would be possible – via the 132 dense letters he sent back to Mac – to follow him closely across what in many places was still a wild and dangerous country.

Snapshots are enough. Kinsey, sensibly considering the record of the Nash, had bought a vehicle specially adapted for rough terrain. It was a big coupe, with, he told Voris, a 'truck body built on it in place of the rumble seat'.[10] Unfortunately the adaptations proved disastrous. It breaks down incessantly – spring leaves snap, oil pans crack, it sinks and gets hopelessly stuck. Once they have to lever it out with a pine tree; on another occasion two yoked oxen yank it out. The food is 'horrible' and Kinsey and his two graduates get violent diarrhoea. Kinsey, as always, 'at once takes an exclusively orange diet for 24 hours'. Other familiar themes emerge: he is appalled they can only get two baths a *week*! (No doubt a relief to Avril Holloway, whose presence must mean he'd knuckled down to icy showers.) Not for the last time Kinsey struggles, choking under Avril's tuition, to smoke cigarettes in the interests of local friendliness – 'I can see nothing attractive in the taste of a cigarette.'

They are continually warned about bandits and occasionally taken for them. In Mexico City Kinsey sees his first 'erotic' movie (*not* reported back to Mac[11]). And of course – galls, galls, galls. They were even collecting galls on Christmas Day (lunch cooked by Kinsey; celery soup, rice, tuna, pineapple salad, Mac's cake).

He arrived back laden with bowls and pretty plates, to find that his father had divorced his mother for cruelty,[12] something he refused to mention thereafter; and that Ralph Voris had finally got a job in the State Teachers' College at Springfield, Missouri.[13]

Kinsey had hoped Ralph could have gone with him. 'I wish you were along, Sir!' Though he realises, he adds, that Mexico isn't the place for Ralph's bugs – his staphylinidae.[14] Ralph, when he'd written regretfully before the expedition, had agreed, but 'with all the sound reasoning I can bring to bear on the subject I will still be broken hearted when I know you have crossed the border and headed into Mexico without me'.[15]

And as the trip progresses, his desire for Mac becomes increasingly intense, finally becoming (for Kinsey) open and touching. She has bought herself a new dress and he longs to see her in it. 'Maybe, you will look real sweet when I get home.' 'I miss you, Mac, very, very much.'[16]

They were together again around 20 January 1932, and these are the last years – 1932 to 1938 – that Kinsey was really able to engage at all fully with his family, before sex finally engulfed him.

3

In fact, a good many clues to Kinsey's character can be found in his life with his family. Supporting nudity, he encouraged it in the household. After his cold shower, he would be naked while 'I would be in the bath,' said Joan, 'and would watch him shave and he would sing funny songs to make me laugh.'[17] In the hot summer nights the whole family would strip naked under the sprinkler in the back yard.[18] And on their trips to the Smoky Mountains of Tennessee or elsewhere they would all leap naked into freezing pools or remote streams – an opportunity for one of Kinsey's many little lectures, on anatomy or the wholesomeness of the nude body.[19]

In fact, nudity became a mini-crusade of Kinsey's (as it did, indeed, among other liberal reformers of the time). It entered his gall expeditions, Kinsey striding about resolutely clotheless, somewhat to the surprise of his students.[20] And it entered his writing where, in his *Male* volume, he wrote that nudity was increasing. 'There is rather free expression in the home for both sexes, including the parents and the children of all ages, at times of dressing and at times of bathing.' A hopeful extrapolation from the Kinsey household presumably, since no figures back it up.[21]

Discipline was strict, stricter than for the children's friends. Both parents would spank for persistent offences. Joan remembered the last time it happened. She was twelve and having a shower. She had done something she knew would irritate her father. Suddenly, Kinsey opened the curtain and smacked her. 'I was very angry. Twelve was too old. I drew myself up and said, "Do you think you've smacked me hard enough?" He went without speaking but after that we talked things out.' Anne said at one point, 'He was a despot.' Mac would sometimes demur, especially when they got to high school and it was about going to or coming back from dances. After discussion, Kinsey's views usually prevailed.[22]

But Mac was not dominated. On the contrary, in a crucial area she won. And, just as clever as he was, she enjoyed contending with him. At table once, Joan remembered an argument about pronouncing 'tricycle'. Mac said tricȳcle – as in the cycle of the seasons; Kinsey tricy̆cle – as in sickle. 'Mother finally had to excuse herself from the table and get *Webster. Webster* gave both – but mother's first. Daddy said, "Well, I come from the east" '[23] – as if tricȳcle was some sort of Midwest argot. Kinsey had to have the last word.

But what is interesting about this little family anecdote is 'Mother finally had to excuse herself from the table'. It was a very formal life, patterned, structured. Kinsey loved fish from his east coast childhood, so regularly every fall enough tinned fish was ordered from Boston to last a year – 'Salmon, clams – and there was something called sea moss.' 'Lights out' when small was strict and on time, but Kinsey would have bathed them and read to them. 'He had,' said Joan, 'a very good voice for Jimmy Skunk or Wolf or Rabbit.' A despot perhaps, but a benevolent one. And when they went to college it was all over. They could do as they liked. 'He thought we were old enough,' said Anne. (Kinsey sent all his children away from IU so that they could be independent.)

One remnant of childhood oddly survived. No work was allowed on Sundays,[24] yet by the 1930s he was, as both daughters remember, 'aggressively against religion'. Kinsey was completely pragmatic on such issues. As far as his children went, if the *mores* of the group were strong it would do more harm than good, especially amongst their peers, to be seen flouting them. So the children went to Sunday school and church, and were also brought up *not* to believe.[25]

This pragmatism extended to sex, which in this case meant pre-marital sex. The facts of life were conscientiously fed them at each stage. Six to seven – in the garden, reproduction of plants and insects and animals, and so to human reproduction; human again as they plunged naked into remote creeks; at ten – a little lecture on breasts soon coming or (Bruce) testicles descending. At eleven to twelve – menstruation, diagrams, more little lectures.

Little lectures were the *leitmotif* of a Kinsey childhood. Joan remembers reluctantly helping, aged fourteen, read proofs of new editions of the biology textbooks, and how little lectures flowed as she did. They each had a strip of garden: 'I can remember Daddy explaining why you had seeds and bulbs and how you had to plan a garden for colours' (Joan). 'He was a teacher always – always' (Anne). This mode of converse, which however fascinating can get adults down after a bit, is of course ideal for childhood.

Family holidays were two-week high spots, usually in late August or early September. After Bruce was two (in 1930), they went somewhere every year except 1935 when Kinsey was in Mexico again. 'We got to see most of the 48 states,' said Joan (and one detects the educational value of the holidays). 'We stayed in rooming houses. You don't want hotels with three kids.' And besides this, the Kinseys would set off in the unreliable Nash on little local expeditions. Four days in 1934 to the forests of Brown County, for example – Bruce already a 'regular fish'.[26] On these trips lunch was always Kinsey-style – chocolate, raisins, peanuts.*

Daughters' memories: on holiday in New Hampshire, round the fire, Kinsey, with his arm round Mac (something he could do, evidently, in private), saying about the other chap, ' "You wouldn't have had all the lovely classical music if you'd married him; you wouldn't have had all this camping." And after a bit Mother said, "Well, he liked classical music *too* you know".'

---

* To mitigate this monotonous fare, which eventually made quite a number of people besides Voris sick, I should point out that American raisins are not the hard little bullets fired at one in British supermarkets, but soft, fruity, luscious lumps, as big as plums.

Kinsey cooking. Joan remembers he cooked the suppers when Bruce was born; Anne, his huge concoctions – beans, tomatoes, okra, anything he found. 'It was always called a goulash. He'd say to Bruce, "Come on over and we'll clean out the fridge." He threw a banana in once.'

Chess: Kinsey didn't like losing (who does?). 'If I got his queen he'd end the game,' said Anne. 'He said it'd mean I'd win anyway.' Later, the same thing happened with Bruce.

They both had dim memories of the grandparents. With his father, said Mac, Kinsey 'had a sort of truce'.[27] He came to stay two or three times in twenty years. Christmas 1929 he gave Joan a swing. Kinsey's mother, who became very fat, came more often, always in the summer, and Kinsey used to keep an eye on things. He was worrying about her, for instance, while in Mexico.[28] When Alfred Seguine left her she took in lodgers, one of whom, her daughter Mildred, also obese and who worked as a stenographer, eventually married when she was fifty. She was still living at home.

In the late '20s, Kinsey started his second record collection and by 1937 had over a thousand. He disliked opera.[29] His favourite composers were Sibelius, Beethoven of the last quartets, Bartok's first and second quartets, the songs of Hugo Wolf.[30] Interesting preferences; romantic, complex, introverted music, often melancholy. Why the dislike of opera? Was it too unreal? C. A. Tripp, a friend of later years, said he disliked novels for this reason[31] (certainly neither he nor Mac read them[32]). He increasingly disliked anything that hid or was removed from 'the fact' – a reaction almost certainly derived from his childhood and the concealment and hypocrisy, especially regarding sex, with which he came to feel it had been permeated. He even disliked beards and moustaches for this reason – something that was to cause Paul Gebhard trouble.

His 'public performances' of records seem to have begun in 1927, when on Sunday nights he would give a little lecture to students and play selected records. Then about 1932 Professor Torrey and Kinsey together started a sort of informal record club, in Kinsey's house it is true 'but joint'. Then 'Very quickly it reached the point where Kinsey decided what we were going to listen to.'[33] It took over Sundays (the students had Wednesdays), and became formal, then very formal and to some terrifying.

There are dozens of descriptions of these weekly Sunday 'musicales' – some arch, some delighted, some extremely irritated, accounts of

Kinsey's *rage* at interruptions or lack of total, rapt silence, of people not asked back (Betsy Ellson: 'You could be expelled from the group if you *squeaked*.'[34]) They were meticulously planned – a short lecture (Mrs Kinsey nodding agreement), then the records to illustrate it, a break for Mrs Kinsey's 'famous' persimmon pie, finally lighter music and a short summing up. Two hours, the hard-back chairs in a respectful half-moon facing the gramophone, Kinsey grinding the cactus needles. The women knitted or darned; in summer they fanned. The children, said Anne, rather seldom attended, 'But you couldn't help hearing it – it was loud – he bombarded the neighbourhood. But you had to have it loud to hear the details.'

Frank Edmondson: 'He had very strong opinions. His favourite conductor for a while was Stokowski – especially doing Sibelius's fourth Symphony. Then Beecham became favourite – and also did the fourth Symphony. A serious dilemma for Kinsey. He suddenly solved it one Sunday. He played three movements Beecham, the last Stokowski.'[35] Dr Charles Hagen seems to have been there too. 'He would take one of those big records and put the needle in the middle, play a bit – then take *another* big record and play the *end*. Or he'd play the *same* bit to compare them. He thought he knew better than those great conductors how it should be played. Maddening.'[36]

Frank Edmondson – later to play a small but significant role – was a regular for many years, one of the invariable six or seven core members. Dr Hagen did *not* become a core member. Lucky Sunday visitors were asked, approved graduates or even undergraduates. One should remember that there were no radio concerts to speak of then, no television, LPs, tapes or discs. And, as Herman Wells noted, they were used to live music; gramophones and those 'big records' were rare and fairly new, almost avant-garde.[37] And if you didn't mind being bossed about, you could hear lovely music.

To Kinsey they were vital. Listening to music, his musicales, sustained that sensitive piano-playing, flower-arranging inner side of him. And he told Elizabeth Frazier that he sometimes astonished himself by how mesmerised he became, how deeply and totally 'lost'[38] (something which partly explains his sharpness).

Kinsey continued to play the piano until the end of the '30s, usually sight-reading. He encouraged his children in music, but only Anne seems to have taken it up. After a while Kinsey found her practising so excruciating she couldn't do it when he was in the house. Bruce, who could have done it (he had perfect pitch), wasn't interested.

With Bruce we strike one of the most interesting and at least partly resolved tensions in the family *gestalt*. 'Really, mother brought up Bruce,' said Joan. 'Mother never really got over Don and I think she wanted to give Bruce more of the attention she had been denied by Don's death. Mother and Daddy differed about how they should handle Bruce, but she felt so strongly she wanted her own way, not to give the discipline we'd got, and Daddy loved her and understood this – so he finally pulled out.'[39]

It is an extraordinary tribute to this strong-willed man, a disciplinarian, in a sphere – sons – where men above all like to impose their image and repeat their patterns. It was one of the dynamics of their love, reciprocated in her total loyalty to him and his tasks.

It was also rather irritating to Bruce's siblings. 'He used to go everywhere barefoot,' said Joan. 'Then when he went to grade school he had to wear shoes, so a new pair was bought and when he came out of school he took his shoes off. And he *lost* one on the way home and mother just laughed! We would have been sent back *to find that shoe*. "You don't waste a shoe!"'

Yet Bruce was very like his father. Don Baxter, a school contemporary, remembers him as quite popular, good-looking – but a loner. And Bruce echoed in ways other than shoes Kinsey's own (rather mild) rebellion over clothes. Baxter remembers him with his parents at the Cascades, a swimming pool, refusing to put on the obligatory top above his trunks. 'Teacher said, "I said put on your top". The lifeguard, aged twenty, agreed. Dr Kinsey, right there in front of us, became irate and overruled the lifeguard and the teacher. He said it was a ridiculous rule. He took it up with the authorities and from then on *none* of us had to wear tops.'[40]

They grew apart. Kinsey later longed for Bruce to enter sex research,[41] but the 'regular fish' was by then developing into an Olympic-class swimmer. At his college, Oberlin, he held twelve out of twelve Blue Ribbons. Kinsey, of course, thought to take such sporting pursuits seriously was ridiculous. In the end, said Joan, 'they grew as far apart as you can'.*

---

* Bruce Kinsey refused to be interviewed in a way which suggested strong feelings were in play. As far as I can discover he has always refused. The only time he has spoken publicly was in a film made for the Kinsey Institute by WTU Television – *Sex and the Scientist*, where he gave a short speech in praise of his mother.

During the last three or four years of the '30s, some distancing between Kinsey and his family became inevitable as his workload steadily increased. The first reason for this was his final triumph as an entomologist.

4

With hindsight, one can see the rapid and impressive climax to his gall wasp work. Out of seventeen papers published in the eighteen years since 1920, he produced nine of them between 1937 and 1938.

To Kinsey, unaware of the future, it was simply his method at last being vindicated. The method was to collect vast numbers of whatever it was you were studying, indiscriminately and from everywhere. You would thus have created an enormous reservoir of 'the fact' – and, deduced from this, endless studies and books would flow. It is, he wrote to Ralph, 'a dangerous program if one gets bumped off suddenly'.[42] Clearly.

By the start of 1935, he had finished the second gall wasp book. This now ran into difficulties. It seems that peer review had made the publishing committee of the IU Science Series suggest changes and Kinsey had refused. At any rate, he crossly put the manuscript in his bank,[43] and, after six months' mammoth preparation – including buying, rebuilding and equipping what Edgar Anderson described as a cross between a laboratory and a tank – he set out on his second and longest Mexican expedition on 30 October.

He took with him lively, randy but, it turned out, absolutely reliable Osmond Breland, and James Coon. The plan was to cover the eastern and southern Sierra regions of Mexico, then rail from Cordoba to Guatemala, criss-cross Guatemala and finally return by United Fruit Company boat.

Once again, it isn't necessary, but it would be possible to follow him in detail in the ninety-eight letters and two telegrams which, despite hiccoughs of fantastic Mexican inefficiency, streamed jerkily back to Bloomington. Nor would it be boring – the trip was ferocious. Even the International Truck-tank could hardly make it. For a month and a half torrential rains thundered down – at one time twenty inches, at another forty inches, in a few hours; the Mexican roads simply flowed down into the ravines. It took five hours to traverse thirteen miles.[44] Another time, they camped in pitch darkness at 10,000 feet, 'the highest I've ever been'. They woke to find themselves beside a large, round, crystal-clear lake, 'The crater of an extinct volcano! . . . Salt water, cold as an iceberg, so our bath is brief, but we use soap, and I am clean again.'[45]

At yet another moment the only way forward is across a deep gorge by a rickety old suspension bridge meant for pedestrians and mules, a rushing river far below. Kinsey, ex-Stevens Institute engineer, finally judges it will hold. But the night before, he is frightened. 'I wish we were over that bridge.' They take everything out of the truck – including an enormous round 40lb cheese and all Kinsey's peanuts and raisins. 'We even drained the tank.' Jim Coon begs him to let one of the natives drive. But at last Kinsey gets in, pauses to wave, and takes it at a rush. The bridge, shaking violently, sinks terrifyingly 'like an old hammock . . . the boys . . . were scared stiff' – but he made it.[46]

The trip was ferocious – and Kinsey loved every moment. Coon felt that that was what he really liked – fighting, 'Out in the wilds fighting adversity.'[47] Kinsey reports all the meals, which he cooks (endless macaroni cheese).

One gets glimpses, in the diary Breland kept of the trip, of how maddening his students often found Kinsey – particularly his obsession with forcing them to keep clean. When they arrived at the crater lake above, Breland wrote, 'K the jackass wanted a bath so down we went. Was it cold! I hardly got wet when out I came again and the others did too.' If Kinsey is irritable, Breland calls it acting 'the usual damn fool'.*[48]

In Tehuantepec Kinsey saw the girls outside the brothels and was excited by them.[49] Goodness knows how poor Breland was feeling after the months of deprivation, but once more Kinsey can't help his desire for Mac breaking into his family letters. 'The return makes this last month the hardest to be away from you. I want you so much!'[50]

Finally, they arrive at Barrios near the Honduras border and the

---

* From Breland's diary, Jones makes, in my view, a number of rather wild deductions. For example, because Breland refers irritably to Kinsey's 'prick nibbling tent' and because 'Breland was a man who usually meant what he said', Jones' imagination, now well versed in such leaps, finds it 'hard not to suspect that oral sex was going down under canvas tops'. If, following Jones, we were to take as exact everything Breland wrote, with his style of lurid metaphorical epithets, we would have to deduce he screwed knot holes or, later, thought President Bryan spent all his time on a chamber pot – and many other absurdities. (Jones, *Kinsey*, p. 282; and see reference note 48 to this chapter.)

truck is winched aboard the United Fruit Company's steamer, the SS *Titivus*. The weather is tropical. The dining-room attendant says he's sorry, but they have to wear dinner jackets. Kinsey refuses. The steward now comes and says, yes they must wear dinner jackets. Kinsey (according to him) politely 'told him we had been through months of hell' and were not going to start stifling to death in dinner jackets. If the steward likes, he can bar them from the dining room – and he leads his boys to their rooms. The steward now comes and *begs* them to use the dining room. So they do – but not in dinner jackets.[51]

And as they near New Orleans, his excitement and longing for Mac once more burst into the letter. 300 miles, 200 miles, 100 miles – 'So goodbye until I can talk to you in person. GIRL!'[52]

They arrived back around 19 January, having been away nearly four months. Kinsey at once retrieved his manuscript from the bank and started to incorporate the new material. The publishing committee seems to have come to their senses and on 9 November 1936 there appeared his entomological masterwork's final volume – *The Origins of Higher Categories in Cynips*.

5

Kinsey's second gall book, even more than the first, is a sustained polemic in which he scornfully demolishes the *idées reçues* of past scientists and replaces their fumbling and usually wrong ideas and discoveries with his own correct ones. (And thereby once again, as Morton Wheeler had predicted, presaging his later work.) He operates on two related fronts: challenging the existence of 'higher categories' as entities and correcting the 'tree-of-life' view of evolution which 'higher categories' sustain and from which they spring. Second, he continues the analyses of species origin and formation he began in the first book.[53]

The 'higher categories' of the title is confusing. It refers not to more evolved gall wasps, as one might suppose, but to earlier gall wasps, the ancestors – higher is nearer the beginning, nearer the 'trunk' of the tree of life.

The image of the tree has the primeval, ancestor galls (and so technically 'higher categories' but now died out) represented by the trunk; next come the thick branches, these are the surviving early galls or higher categories. Finally come the outermost branches – the galls of today.

Kinsey sets out to demolish the entire picture. He starts as he will finish – higher categories don't really exist. They are just 'artificial conventions for cataloguing biologic data'. For one thing 'higher' (i.e. earlier) categories are not always older at all. 'This might appear axiomatic, but it is one of the concepts which we shall subsequently show to be unsound.' In fact, the idea of a 'tree' is totally unhelpful: 'practically all taxonomic studies are warped by this concept'. The oldest species did not die out, they continued to exist with the newest ones; nor were the newest ones necessarily very different from the oldest. Individuals *within* a species could show much larger differences. And the newest species weren't even better adapted or improvements on the earlier ones – all ideas inherent in 'the-tree-of-life'. The true picture of evolution was of modifications introduced by mutation and *sustained by isolation.* The image was not a tree but a prickly pear cactus (Kinsey drew one), with the pears representing different species. It was, in essence, a demonstration of how different the world of insects looked (and by inference how different other groupings in the animal and plant world could look) when variations remained alive.

What is fascinating to a student of Kinsey, as he now pursues his argument into the origin of species, is how even here, among his minute and soulless galls, he can castigate the lack of science deriving from an unthinking dependence on ancient religious dogma; and he combines this – odd when one considers his future – with an equally ferocious attack on the reproductive organs. The attack goes like this: by saying that a species is defined by not being able to *breed* elsewhere means far too much importance is given to the reproductive organs. This is compounded because changes in these organs are once again the defining element in the search for higher (earlier) categories, since the reproductive organs, because so important, are believed to change more slowly than anything else.

But, says Kinsey, having cited a string of scientists who assume this from Darwin to Muir in 1928, why do they assume this? Has anyone actually *looked?* It is assumed in flowers and trees and in biology as well as entomology. 'That the philosophy is a survival of medieval notions of the sanctity of sex and reproductive structures would be starkly denied by most systematists, but they seem to have presented no good reason for their dependence on the conservatism of these structures.' But the assumption has no foundation in fact. Change in genitalia is just as common as change everywhere else. 'We must grapple with the realities of nature, instead of tossing about hypotheses of how species should be made.'

Indeed, Kinsey challenges what to the layman seems the actual definition of a species – namely that if a group can interbreed and produce fertile offspring they are one species; if they cannot, they are different. Not so. 'This is one field in which the actual observations are enough to eliminate the question from the field of debate. The data show, of course, that while the principle may apply to the majority of cases, the number of cases of phylogenitically remote groups which may hybridise and which are capable of producing fertile offspring is high enough to make the principle of uncertain value in any particular case.' Far more important than mating or not mating in bringing about new species are seasonal and geographic isolation. 'The current opinions have been arrived at philosophically.'*

Once again, isolation – the galls' trump card – is the clue. With animals and plants you usually require plate tectonics or islands to demonstrate the power of isolation. With galls, thanks to their feebleness, you can do it within a distance of a few miles or even on single trees in a group. Galls do to space what drosophila does to time.

Kinsey now takes this feebleness and, in his romantic, dramatic, almost flamboyant way, and using the changes he has measured, follows the progress of the ancestral cynipidae from 85 million years ago in the upper Cretaceous as they tottered on their tiny legs in a slow migration over the vast continent. Glaciation, desertification, the rise of the Rockies, the forming of the great plains, the Alaskan-Siberian land severance, the beginning of the Grand Canyon – he links his gall wasps to the great movements of geological time until they have crept into the advances of the Pleistocene only about 20,000 years ago. From this, it seems that the origins of the whole genus had taken place in southern Arizona or northern Mexico.

Once again, in a slightly shorter book at 334 pages, Kinsey had achieved significant modifications in the way evolution worked and how it should be viewed, with detailed new discoveries about species formation and differentiation, and once again he had found a mass of new species and subspecies (seventy – all, quite rightly, called Kinsey).

---

* 'Philosophically' was a term of abuse in Kinsey's vocabulary. It indicated conclusions reached in an airy-fairy, irresponsible way without proper testing or reference to proper empirical evidence, in sufficient quantity, to establish scientific fact.

It was a triumphant demonstration of the effectiveness of his pioneering methodology: vast numbers over a wide geographical area, numerous meticulous measurements all published, wide reference to related sciences.

Because, of course, all of his challenging assertions were abundantly proved in 230 pages of dense data. Once again, the big canons of statistics came wheeling out. Since the last book 'We have more than doubled our fieldwork . . . travelling some additional 42,000 miles . . . collecting 70,000 additional galls from which we have bred more than 18,000 additional insects of the group.'

'It may be asked,' Kinsey reasonably asked, 'how much material is necessary for an adequate taxonomic study.' Reviewers had praised his last book for the size of the sample. Not at all, says Kinsey. He has studied about 160,000 specimens so far. (Just think for an instant what this means – 160,000 minuscule insects each put in the killing jar, then impaled, recorded, written up, often drawn or photographed, stored . . .) But he needs *far* more. He should have had a further 57,000 insects and 170,000 more galls for the eastern US alone. From areas 'of more uniform topography' he should have had still more – at least 1,530,000 insects and 3 or 4 million galls. And this barely touches Europe or Asia (he was now leaping ahead to world studies). 'We shall,' says Kinsey with relish, '. . . continue our study of those same species until we have many more insects and galls than are yet available.'

6

Kinsey's two massive books did not pass without criticisms. Chief of these was that he had created, in Stephen Jay Gould's phrase, 'a bloated taxonomy'. That is, called a 'species' what other systematists would have called a sub-species or a variety.[54] Kinsey was, of course, perfectly aware of the dangers. He had taken the decision that confusion would be less if the lowest limit recognised was the species.

Practically everyone agreed with him.* His work was almost

---

* 'Practically everyone' – that is those qualified, and those who were interested. Alas, perhaps no more than twenty all told. Probably few taxonomists were aware of his work, and only about a dozen looked at it. He got seven reviews, all in the specialist press except for a half page in *Science Progress*.

universally recognised as that of an outstanding scientist. In October 1937 he was made a 'starred scientist'. This meant that by vote of all the leading biologists in the country (after consulting his peers), his name would have a star placed beside it in *American Men of Science*. It was a desperately sought award and at that point IU only had four starred scientists. Kinsey was the fifth – and became thereby a leading figure in the faculty. More recognition followed. He was a platform speaker at the December 1937 meeting of the American Association for the Advancement of Science (AAAS), where he joined Ralph Voris, and again in December 1938. In May 1938 he was elected to the Executive Committee on Science Teaching of the AAAS.

He was particularly pleased that Edgar Anderson was coming round. It was a *leitmotif* of Kinsey's work, indeed one of its justifications, that what he was discovering had bearing on evolutionary studies in general. And Theodosius Dolzhansky seemed enthusiastic too.[55] 'You are going to see the day,' Kinsey wrote to Ralph, 'when taxonomic contributions will be accepted as a fundamental part of biologic science, Sir!'[56]

Kinsey, as one would expect, was already racing ahead, with apparently augmented enthusiasm, into new studies – six journal articles by May 1937, a paper on Mexico, another following, monographs, 300 volumes added to his gall library . . .[57] He'd chosen in particular Xystoteres – 'a new genus [of galls] larger than cynips'. And the point was he could write the book *now*, the system of an enormous reservoir was already proving its worth. 'At long last I may be able to convince somebody that I have been laying a foundation in all these eighteen years – on which the finished structure may now rise rapidly.'[58]

This was not to happen. Under the surface, something else was going on.

One of the slightly depressing things about the two large, finely bound Cynips volumes in the IU library today, if the yellowing 'Date Due' slips in the books mean anything, is that not a single person has taken either of them out since the day, signed with his strangely flamboyant signature, that he presented them sixty-odd years ago.

In 1943 he was to tell Robert Bugbee that though 'studying gall wasps might have made some important contributions, it would never have caused people to beat a path to his door'; and to Glenn Ramsey he'd said earlier he felt his studies had never got the attention they deserved.[59]

It is clear, for example, he should have been elected a member of the

National Academy of Sciences. Why wasn't he? The supposition must be that he was several times blackballed, and one suspects that his contemptuous dismissal of his peers may have played a part. It could have been the 'bloated taxonomy' – though this was more a matter of opinion. Then, the 1930s were a time of neo-Darwinists (when isn't it a time of neo-Darwinists?), and Kinsey had been unconventional (and brave) enough to downgrade natural selection. This shocked some scientists. Whatever the reason, Kinsey minded.

But a much more general restlessness is evident. He was getting sick of IU. In 1936 President Bryan, with his horse and buggy, was seventy-six and 'unwilling', Kinsey told Ralph, 'to settle any question large or small. The whole university is in a mess . . . I would leave at the first opportunity offering comparable recompense and research opportunities.'[60]

He also wanted to get out of Bloomington, now beginning to encroach on the First Street house. He took Mac to see an empty site on a distant ridge, not a commercial development. He asked her if she'd like to live there. Mac said, 'If you promise not to go on any more trips to Mexico.' Kinsey wouldn't promise.[61]

Poor woman – she'd seen nothing yet. It was the way things were ordered then; Kinsey was a man dominated by his work and Mac had long realised this would come first. 'You can't ask a man just to give up what is his driving force just because he is your husband.'[62] And he was a considerate, conscientious husband, doing far more than most men of his time in the home and with children, capable of profound sacrifice here. Nevertheless, one quite often cannot help feeling – as one often does with people of great achievement – that he sometimes behaved in the years ahead with an almost ruthless selfishness. He felt a minimum amount of guilt, though that minimum he did feel.

Then in late 1937 and 1938 three things happened to change Kinsey's life. His mother died in 1938 (Kinsey paid the funeral expenses[63]). There is no suggestion he was heartbroken, but parental death often precipitates change. In January 1938 Herman B. Wells became the new president. Born in Jamestown, Indiana, in 1902, he was at thirty-five very young to be appointed to such a position. This intelligent, short, plump, jovial, wily figure, with thick wavy hair and carefully trimmed moustache at once began to plan sweeping changes. He was to be absolutely vital to Kinsey.

And just before this, in November 1937, a film called *Forbidden* was shown on campus. It was a sex education film and caused an uproar. Undergraduates poured in to see it. *The Daily Student* had an editorial demanding that there should be a proper sex education course at IU.[64]

It seems likely that it was this that made Kinsey feel he could at last act on something he had been thinking of for several years. By June the following year, 1938, he was to be deeply involved in his marriage course – the event that, though it did not cause the change, certainly rocketed him with astonishing swiftness into sex research.

7

The Marriage Course

To me the behavior of the penis was already awe-inspiring; now it seems even more wonderful.

Comment of female student attending
IU marriage course, fall 1938

1

In the space of less than a year this middle-aged academic (in 1938 Kinsey was forty-four), a respectable and respected entomologist at a middle-rate, Midwestern university, was more or less to abandon the work of twenty years, in which he had achieved the highest scientific distinction possible, and hurl himself recklessly into sex research – not so much a profession as a dubious, almost *demi-mondaine* activity, neither respectable nor respected, indeed regarded by many people as shocking and even immoral.

For a variety of personal reasons, including concern for his students and no doubt his own evolving bisexuality, Kinsey was already moving in this direction ten or more years earlier. We can now extend our exploration into this progress.

2

In 1933 Kinsey hired a young biologist, Dr Robert L. Kroc, who had just got his PhD studying rats at the University of Wisconsin. Kroc, whose brother Ray founded McDonald's hamburgers, at once observed something about Kinsey. 'I noticed early how he had to know everything better than everyone else and the immense thoroughness this involved. He asked Ted [Torrey] what music he liked and Ted said Brahms. Now oddly enough Kinsey didn't know much about Brahms, so at once he just *went into* Brahms. A while later, he asked one of his graduate students what he liked and he said band music. Kinsey didn't want one of his boys knowing more than him – so off into band music he went. Sousa was the great figure then of course.'[1]

The young biologist got on well with Kinsey. 'I never suffered from his sharpness – we had brown-bag lunches together for eleven years and as a result we'd chat about all sorts of things.'

One was sex. 'It gets so terribly hot here and Kinsey told me how he and Mac could lie out in the grass under the full moon, nude or partly clothed, and have intercourse.' They also discussed their own past sex lives: 'When you were small did you expose yourself to other boys? And then, how about girls? And we discussed our wet dreams and masturbation and so on.'

Most people think that whatever they do sexually is what everyone does – or should do. Kinsey, with Voris and now Kroc and no doubt with some of his students, had discovered to his amazement totally different patterns. That is to say, so far uncharted *variations*. It was this which at once moved the whole subject into a scientific area with which he was totally familiar.

At what point he made this connection it is impossible to be sure, certainly by 1937–8 since by then he was drawing the comparison himself. What can be documented is how increasingly appalled he was becoming at the sexual ignorance and sexual frustration of young students (and one feels it is young, male, Kinsey-like students).

In 1935, he took this subject for a talk to the faculty discussion group. Started in 1928, this was composed of one senior member from each department and met twice a month to hear each other's papers. Kinsey had talked to them on 'The Mason Wasp' in March 1930, for example, and in 1932 and 1936 on his Mexican trips.

Already, we see, almost fully formed, the position Kinsey was to advocate for the rest of his life: human beings are animals and their sexual behaviour therefore derives from their mammalian background. Thus, the so-called 'perversions' were 'rooted in primate behavior and, in that sense, natural'. But the main thrust of his 1935 talk was a passionate attack on the widespread 'ignorance of sexual structure and physiology', of sexual technique, but above all on 'the long frustration of normal sexual activities' from which result 'most of the social problems and the sexual conflicts of youth ... Biologically, delayed marriage is all wrong.' The result of all this was 'psychic conflicts of such magnitude as to constitute probably the most serious threat against the home'.[2] Who was to blame? The Christian Church.

He brought the subject up again in a 1936 letter to Ralph Voris. 'I am, frankly, much upset over the crazy game of sending men through a five-year training in the very years when they should be married.'[3]

What we are seeing throughout the 1930s, as the inhibitions of his youth finally slip away, is that sex in all its manifestations in Kinsey's life – his homosexual side with Voris, his heterosexual side in his sex life with Mac, his own remembered and still actual frustration, his involvement with and reformist concern over his students – all start to seethe in him, as yet only sporadically in action, but in his head. And, revealed by increasingly impatient outbursts like those above, this all took place among changes, first in the university and second in the outside world, highly relevant to Kinsey's concerns.

3

The start of young Herman Wells' presidency was an exciting time in the little world of IU. The Indiana State Legislature had just passed a state retirement law, which meant that seventeen deans and department heads had to step down at once. Out went the old head of the physics department who 'had declared publicly in 1937 that there was not an electron in the state of Indiana'.[4] Out went many like him, including Bryan and Kinsey's department head Mottier.

In 1938 Wells set up a committee to review the university in its entirety – its composition, income sources, its academic strengths and weaknesses, its achievements, failures and goals – and to make recommendations. As far as we are concerned, chief of these was – *support research*.[5] Wells agreed in 1968 that this had been his lifelong policy. A faculty member could research what he liked, 'Granting, of course, that the man was a competent, sensible man.'[6]

Meanwhile, equally fundamental events were moving in the big world outside. The Depression had forced severe cutbacks in the battle against VD. Puritanical moral crusade methods had replaced more effective practical measures. As a result, towards the end of the 1930s, VD figures were once more exploding towards epidemic proportions. Once more a VD panic swept America – 500,000 new cases of syphilis were reported a year, 700,000 of gonorrhea, the loss in working days cost $100,000,000. Several major train smashes were attributed to advanced syphilis.[7] The figures may have been somewhat hysterical – but not all that hysterical. For example, 12 per cent of Robert Dickinson's upper-middle-class women had venereal disease.[8]

One of the cities most effectively fighting the epidemic was Chicago, 200 miles north of Bloomington. It introduced pre-natal and pre-marital testing, and between 1937 and 1940 31 per cent of its population had Wasserman blood tests (the standard syphilis test*) and 56,000 cases were treated. Across the rest of the country, George Gallup – significantly, for Kinsey, just beginning his mass polls – found in 1936 that 90 per cent of people said they wanted detailed information about syphilis.[9] Schools and universities invariably mirror the societies whose children they teach. In 1938, *The Daily Student* took up a campaign to let IU students have Wasserman tests.[10] They had started to campaign for sex education – and in the late 1930s sex education meant a marriage course.

4

In an uneven way, sex hygiene courses (as they started out) were endemic at American universities (something, incidentally, unthinkable in Britain then). There is record of one at Utah in 1905, the lectures given by a woman doctor from Indianapolis. The information was so veiled as to be terrifying and a staff nurse had to attend to deal with those who fainted.[11]

IU itself had one briefly in 1913–14. Lectures, heard in an atmosphere of giggling excitement, were segregated and the course seems to have collapsed when two 'girls' were discovered to be boys trying to find out what the girls were told.[12]

In the 1930s IU once again had a series of one-hour lectures called the Hygiene Course. *The Daily Student* described it as 'the most useless course in the university'.[13] By chance, a young man called Wardell Pomeroy attended it in 1932, when Dr Thurman Rice of the IU medical school in Indianapolis gave the sex lecture, 'blue jokes at which no one laughed . . . bumbling misinformation'.[14] The only vaguely bright

---

* The Wasserman Serological Reaction test is still used routinely as a test for syphilis. It depends on a precipitation reaction produced by the antibodies to syphilitic infection.

moment came, said Cecilia Hendricks, who attended later, in President Bryan's talk. This was on what today would be called stress management. There were, said Bryan (in Cecilia's words 'a gentle, erudite, earnest old scholar'), 'little tricks to relaxing'. He had one he'd like to share with them. ' "When I find myself unable to go to sleep promptly, I like to think of all the Johns I know." '[15] Stifled collapse of audience. (Johns in 1930s parlance was slang for, variously, pimps or prostitutes' clients.)

As a result of VD scares and the resulting perceived need for knowledge, and also, no doubt, because of old hygiene courses on Rice/Bryan lines, more up-to-date marriage courses became increasingly fashionable during the late 1930s. Each time they appeared, *The Daily Student* reported them: Brown University and Pembroke College reported 15 December 1937; University of Texas, 3 October 1937; University of Illinois and Duke University, 24 September 1938. In this last 24 September issue, *The Daily Student* said by that date 250 other universities had them.[16]

There was, therefore, nothing remotely revolutionary about a marriage course. What was revolutionary was the way in which Kinsey had decided to conduct it.

5

*... there are only three kinds of sexual abnormalities: abstinence, celibacy,
and delayed marriage. Think about this.*
'Reproductive Anatomy and Physiology',
Kinsey's second Marriage Course lecture

The official line on the origins of the marriage course, promulgated by Christenson, is that in the spring of 1938 the Association of Women Students led by Cecilia Hendricks came to Kinsey and asked him if he would start a 'non-credit'* marriage course.[17]

It is notable how the official line (often Kinsey's line, as here) either seeks to minimise how active, indeed often ruthless, he was, and how far he (and later his team) went in pursuit of his goals, or else it conceals what happened altogether.

None of the key figures, in fact, remembers asking Kinsey to set up a marriage course. Cecilia Hendricks, when interviewed in 1972,

---

* That is, not counting towards a degree.

couldn't remember. In fact, under questioning, she felt 'maybe we didn't approach him ... maybe he came to us'.[18] Dorothy McCrae, also on the board of the Association of Women Students, thought the same.[19] Kate Mueller, a former dean of women, whose husband lectured in the course, was quite certain the impetus came from Kinsey, of whom she was at this time a strong supporter.[20]

The course of events at the start of 1938, therefore, seems to have been as follows. At some point quite early the Association of Women Students, under instructions from Kinsey, approached Wells and said they'd like a marriage course. Wells, according to Kroc, said, 'I am a bachelor – who would you suggest runs it?' Unsurprisingly, Cecilia Hendricks and her girls said Dr Kinsey.

Things now moved decisively. By February the outline was set: open only to married or engaged students, seniors (i.e. last year), faculty and their wives, both sexes to attend together. The six biology lectures to be frank and open; plus five additional lectures from senior faculty members on economics, sociology, psychology, law and religious aspects. By March Kinsey was writing to Breland about it. Breland's reply referred lightheartedly to your 'copulating school' – but agreed a copulating school was vital.[21]

In May, Thurman Rice wrote to say he would be happy to send all his own material garnered from years of sex education experience, but was told it was not needed. By 9 June everything was complete and Wells took it to his trustees. This body behaved as if they were being presented with some form of academic explosive. One member asked to be recorded absent. Together, they asked that 'no publicity be given this course'.[22] But they agreed.

The only thing that might have disturbed Kinsey but didn't was a letter from Voris – he had 'not had my usual good health'.[23] It was a cloud no bigger than a man's hand, and shortly afterwards, in late June, Kinsey swept into the opening lecture to address an audience of nearly a hundred.

What the establishment at IU had imagined of this moment was succinctly conveyed by Dr Beck, a member of the campus religious council. 'The course ... is expected to teach students not only the negative aspects of how to escape sex and marriage, the pitfalls, but also the positive aspects, the everlasting beauty of the sacrament of marriage.'[24]

They didn't get much sacrament of marriage, not from Kinsey at any rate. His opening speech – and one can see the agonisingly frustrated

young Kinsey standing angrily behind his present 44-year-old self –
began, 'Why offer a marriage course?' And answered, 'Society has been
responsible for interfering with what would have been normal biological development ... leading to a scandalous delaying of sexual activity
which led to sexual difficulties in marriage ... ignorance of copulatory
techniques ... ignorance of satisfactory contraceptive devices ... concepts of sex all wrong.' All this he would address.[25]

There is no need to follow his lectures, dense in detail and fact, in
full (the lectures and notes still exist) but we should get the flavour. As
usual, Kinsey strode in, faced his audience and spoke for an hour without notes. He took them through the sexual bases of society, from insects
to the prodigious anthropoids who had sex 7,000 times in a lifetime.
Delays in sex he illustrated by comparing American adolescence with
that of the Trobriand Islanders, who began to have sex as soon as it was
possible (aged 9–13) and had stable happy marriages. Next (lecture 2)
the reproductive anatomy – the functions of each organ, the erotic areas,
the penis (2–5 million sperm each orgasm), the clitoris, coitus. Close-up
and dramatic slide of the penis entering the vagina: 'The vagina must be
spread open as the erect male organ penetrates ... You will see that ...
the clitoris at this point is stimulated, thus providing the erotic stimulation necessary for the completion of the act on the part of the female.'[26]
And how to contain all this – that is, details of contraception, condoms,
diaphragms, etc. So to individual variation – in human beings as much
as 400 per cent. The concept of continuous variation, techniques of
foreplay, techniques of intercourse, how couples adjust to the back position ... And finally, how to adjust to years of delayed intercourse (lecture 4): harmlessness of masturbation (both sexes), the 'safety valve' of
nocturnal emission, petting. Here Kinsey explained the heights to which
female blood pressure would rise – and how high it would remain if it
was not allowed to dissipate in the natural climax. If they were to pet,
and they would pet, they must continue arousal through to orgasm.[27]

Throughout his career Kinsey was to find that, quite apart from his
message (often startling enough), the mere fact of *saying* sexual intercourse, coitus, masturbation, clitoris, orgasm, etc., in a society where
even the word sex was barely mentionable, and in which 'venereal
disease' had just been banned on radio, was enough to shock his audiences into electrified attention. So it was here. 'You could hear a pin
drop,' said Glenn Ramsey.

Even after fifty years those who attended remember. The Weirs remember that at one lecture, hearing about the blood pressure, a southern graduate rose indignantly and said to Kinsey, 'No southern gentleman would *ever* leave a lady in that state.'[28]Alice Binkley, with widening eyes, described how in the line of variation men and women grew closer, and closer, till they crossed over and some women had clitorises longer than some men's penises.[29]

Kinsey solicited written comments from his audiences, to some extent to provide him with ammunition when he was attacked, as he knew he would be. These are, almost to a man or woman, strongly in favour. They praise the clarity and frankness. They say they need his facts. They ask pertinent questions. 'Where does loveplay end and masturbation begin?' One girl says could they have slides of the penis too? (Kinsey obliges.)[30]

The one thing the 'comments' don't comment on is the most revolutionary thing of all about the courses. At the end of each lecture Kinsey said that in order to find out about the many things scientists didn't know so that he could inform them more accurately, he needed their help. Would they please volunteer to give their sex histories?

6

Kinsey had long thought one of the best ways he could help in IU was to find out the exact physiological facts, to find what people did sexually – a virtually unknown field – and pass all this on to his students. He had realised this, he told Paul Gebhard, as early as 1926.[31] We saw it is likely he had already begun in a small way to find out some things with his questionnaires to fraternities in the early 1930s. And we know he had decided to do this in the marriage course, and prepared accordingly, since he took his first real sex history, as he told his favourite journalist Albert Deutsch, immediately after it began.[32] He also asked Wells and the trustees that any information obtained in conferences should be confidential.*

* 'Conferences', as far as the trustees were concerned, meant the sort of sex problems Kinsey expected to hear during the course. Kinsey himself also meant it to cover sex history information, and it is likely he told Wells this privately at the time. When it leaked out, as it obviously would, that Kinsey was taking sex histories – he made no secret of it – there is no evidence that Wells was in the least surprised; and from the start and for the next sixteen years Kinsey invariably told Wells about all significant developments well in advance. 'Conference' remained a euphemism for sex history, and sometimes more, for many years.

But this was something on a modest scale. It was parochial. For some considerable time he kept the questionnaire, telling Bugbee that his first fifty histories came from this source.[33] Meanwhile, at the same time, he was developing his face-to-face interview, which he still hadn't got by heart near the end of the year. Glenn Ramsey saw him glancing at his crib then. He was still using a crib – glancing at 'sheets of printed paper on a clipboard before him' – the following year when he took Donald Broadribb's history.[34] As to the number of questions, we know the questionnaire had about five pages – say, a hundred questions. Kroc added more questions, revising and refining them.[35] By March 1939 Kinsey, Kroc and Voris together, if Kinsey's later account is accurate, had brought it to about 230. After a year, in July 1939, Kinsey told Dr Raymond Pearl he now had 250.[36]

Mrs Margaret Edmondson, who was in at the start, illustrates what was happening. 'First, I did the questionnaire. It was long, four or five pages. He was feeling his way then, testing things out. He said that people didn't write down actionable things.* But then he did another one, with me, putting the questions himself. It wasn't just a series of questions – he'd suddenly go back to the beginning and say 'this doesn't fit'. He could *elicit* things from you. You had to give the questionnaire back. He didn't want it running about loose.'[37]

What we have, that is to say, is something evolving and developing, of Kinsey's experimenting and testing throughout 1938 – not something long planned and long prepared. Not till mid-1939 does it finally seem to dawn on Kinsey that here is a whole new field of *scientific* endeavour by which, almost without realising it, he is steadily being seduced.

7

By the end of the 1938 summer session, it was clear that the marriage course was to be one of the most successful series of lectures ever run at IU. And of these the most successful, far and away, were the biology

---

* One has to remember that probably at least three-quarters – or more – of what Kinsey's informants ordinarily did was against the law and carried severe penalties. For example homosexuality was illegal in all states, any form of oral sex was illegal; in Indiana it was an offence to 'incite to or encourage masturbation'.

lectures. Asked for value ratings, students voted: biology 97, sociology 2, psychology 1. The rest don't seem to have got any votes at all.[38]

One other surprising thing took place. In his last lecture Kinsey had complained that, as elsewhere, there was virtually no information about sex education in high schools – nor on what children knew. The next day a young graduate student called Glenn Ramsey, who had been teaching at a high school in Peoria, Illinois, came and dumped on Kinsey's desk a mass of data about precisely that. 'Kinsey was astounded.' He went over the data, asked Ramsey to extend his questions to cover Kinsey's own material and 'from then on we were colleagues'.[39]

On 8 August Kinsey bought his volume of *Sexual Life in Ancient Greece* by Hans Licht, paused long enough to circulate – somewhat tactlessly one might think – the student ratings to his fellow lecturers, and on 15 August set off for a two-week holiday in Florida. It was the last all-family holiday the Kinseys were to take.

He returned to find that enrolment in the marriage course had doubled, to 207. Nevertheless, it was a small segment of his workload. Galls were still central, with measurement and analysis proceeding, two new papers about to appear, and three outside lectures in December. He was also running his course on entomology, another on taxonomy and also a new course, his favourite, on evolution.

But it was the marriage course that increasingly fascinated him – and in the course, the sex histories. He was now uninhibitedly using his lectures as a quarry for histories (each one ended, 'Have you utilised the opportunity for a personal conference?'[40]). Robert and Dorothy Weir, attending now, felt 'it was somehow a condition of taking the course that you gave your history'.[41] And Kinsey was also starting to seek histories elsewhere. Herman S. Winton took the entomology and taxonomy courses that fall, and Kinsey asked all of *them* for their sex histories too. (One girl who agreed said she and Kinsey chatted after her history and she felt he was 'genuinely interested' in sex.)[42]

Unanswerable questions thrown up in the sex histories provided additions to the interview and suggestions for exploration – how common was homosexuality, how did other boys/girls masturbate, how often, when did they start, how quickly did men/women orgasm, how early, how late could they continue, when was their sexual peak?[43]

As one would expect after his years of counselling, Kinsey once more took on this role. The correspondence files are full of advice, instructions – or just sympathy. To give one example out of dozens at this time, a young woman who came to him after the marriage course had trouble reaching orgasm. Kinsey writes at length: very common, especially with no prior experience. It could be the foreskin of the clitoris adhering (see a surgeon, and he gives the address – and price. This of course had been Mac's problem.). Or try new positions – her on top; or new contraceptive, a diaphragm, say, a doctor in Bloomington fits them for $2 – 'quarter the charge of other doctors', he adds thriftily.[44]

One of the most warming things about Kinsey is this endless stream of unseen kindness (unseen obviously, for no one else saw the letters) which was to continue for sixteen years.* We shall find him still being moved by people's sexual – and other – problems, and still trying to help, up to a few weeks before his death.

8

The comments on the fall course echoed those of the summer one. On Kinsey, his great merit was 'bringing things unblushingly into the open'; on the other lecturers – 'dull'.[45] Kinsey duly circulated them.

Three other significant events ended 1938. The first concerned a gall problem. Kinsey couldn't work out how he should illustrate clearly and at once the relative numbers of wasps defined by a combination of wing length set against body length. He took this to Frank Edmondson, a young astronomer who had recently, in 1937, joined the faculty. 'I saw at once what he needed because his gall figures were just like my star figures.' He needed, said Edmondson, a scatter graph – wing length on the upright, body length along the base.

This information, as often with Kinsey when he was told something he didn't know, deeply impressed him. 'He was very intelligent,' said Edmondson, 'but he wasn't a mathematician. He understood – but left it to others.'[46] It is not even certain he always understood. For example he

---

* Pomeroy says that after a few years Kinsey got so busy he had to give up counselling and helping, but this is not so. His letters of help get much shorter, it is true, but they increase in number up to about 1953, and there are many examples after that.

often got muddled between mean (average) and median.* However, Kinsey now decided that Edmondson, who had had some rather superficial statistical training, was a genius at the subject – and thereafter relied on him totally. Edmondson's advice, based on stars, was not invariably helpful.

That fall, Kinsey had in fact asked Dr Raymond Pearl about another statistical problem connected with galls. Pearl, an eminent biologist from Johns Hopkins giving a lecture at IU on 'Man the animal', a subject close to Kinsey's heart, now came even closer to that organ. He told Kinsey that statistical theory was really just a substitute for inadequate data. If you had enough subjects, as Kinsey did with his millions of galls – had, in fact, what amounted to an equivalent of the whole population – you needed little or no 'mathematical manipulation'.[47] This, too, sank in deep. Get enough, and the statistics would look after themselves. He also told Pearl about his astonishing sex histories. Pearl said why not publish?[48]

Oddly – and it is a sign that the narrow but ferociously intense beam of his concentration was now finally altering its aim – it seems only to have been fairly late in the fall of 1938 that he started to tell his favourite graduate students what was going on. He told Breland in October. Breland didn't reply till December: 'Am glad to hear that the course on "legalized frigging" is coming along nicely. Things certainly picked up in Indiana when old Shrivel Balls got off the pot! Please give my best to everyone.' Kinsey's reply was prim: 'It was good to have a letter from you again.' He ignored references to the frigging course and old Shrivel Balls.[49]

The first extant letter to Ralph Voris on the subject is on 28 November. On 7 December he went to Springfield, Missouri, and lectured on galls, staying three days with his friend; on 10 December he lectured at St Louis, Missouri, saw Edgar Anderson and went to a symphony concert. Then on 13 December he wrote to Ralph about the AAAS meeting at Richmond, Virginia. They were to go together in Dr

---

* Median is mid-point. Take height. If the median height of 50 people is 5′ 6″ it means there are as many people taller than 5′ 6″ as there are smaller. It is often a better indicator of a rough average than the mean. To calculate the mean, you add together the heights of all 50 people and then divide by 50. But if among the taller people you have, say, 12 of 7′ 9″ then the 'average' is violently skewed towards the tall end of the frame. This could easily happen in sex statistics with relatively few exceptionally high performers.

Beber's car except 'My going is conditional that Mrs Beber is not going.' Evidently she didn't, since he took the lift. He and Ralph shared a room at the Richmond Hotel.[50]

It was at those two meetings that Kinsey laid out in detail what he had been doing. (He later sent Ralph a summary of the findings from his first sixty histories – 'Better destroy or file out of reach . . . You have helped a lot in orienting me in the handling of a goodly number of these.'[51]) Kinsey also told him he had heard about communities of homosexuals in Chicago and that he intended to investigate this secretly in the new year. But before this he had to face the first waves of opposition.

9

It is clear that during this entire period Dr Thurman Rice had been seething with resentment over, as he saw it, Kinsey's usurpation of his own role in these matters. In February 1939 he decided to attend one of Kinsey's lectures himself, and at once exploded.

To his horror, a slide of coitus in 'the sagitel [sic] position' had sexually excited him. If he, Rice, could be aroused what on earth, he asked Kinsey, would happen to some 'little rosebud of a girl . . . pure as a drop of dew?' She would see the sagitel position, get violently sexually excited, go out, sleep with everyone and get pregnant. He went to Wells and said the same thing, adding that Kinsey was seeing the coeds (girls) privately and asking them the lengths of their clitorises (which indeed Kinsey was). What did Wells propose to do about it?[52] Wells proposed to do nothing, so Thurman Rice now set out to rouse opposition wherever he could. By 1940 he was publicly attacking Kinsey in lectures in Indianapolis.

Meanwhile, as well as other murmurings on Rice lines, some of the marriage course lecturers, infuriated by the comments Kinsey kept sending them, and the fact, as Dr Edith Schuman said, that they were so obviously 'padding', began to resign. Schuman, who gave a lecture on VD, resigned now;[53] as did Dr Mueller, the sociology lecturer (he was a professional pianist and had already been irritated by Kinsey at one of the musicales).[54]

Kinsey's scornful reaction to all this was typical. He issued a stinging rebuke in the most public way possible – the student newspaper –

and thereby both thanked and appealed to the people for whom the course was designed and who were making it so successful. Beginning: 'Together we have faced problems which sometimes have been considered too personal for serious treatment,' it ended, 'Not all of the older generation can react as you do. Some of them are still stupid. Some of them still respond with blocked emotions – that is to say, they are shocked. Whatever their chronological age, you may determine the generation to which your professors belong by observing their approach to these questions of marriage.'[55]

He widened the entry qualifications, increased the number of biology lectures and now began to incorporate the results of his research – which gave his audiences a thrilling sense both of involvement and of discovery. 'We felt we were at the cutting edge,' said Alice Binkley.[56] He used this sense to make his request for histories even stronger ('Would you now be willing to contribute your history to our records?'[57]) and between February and June 1939 took a further 280 histories.[58] This exceeded the total enrolment of the course itself and shows the extent to which he was now seeking outside. But he was about to go much further and much deeper. In June, he was at long last able to drive to Chicago in pursuit of homosexuals. No one, except Mac, knew where he was going.

10

Kinsey's entrée into the underworld of Chicago male homosexuals was a young homosexual in Bloomington who was friendly with a group of young gay men who lived in a boarding house in Rush Street. This was a street of cafés and cafeterias, of bars and restaurants, not far from the area known as the Village.[59]

Despite his later expertise, the tall, rather burly, Midwestern entomology professor, tousled, intense and serious, seems to have found it uphill work. In five days, he told Ralph later, he only succeeded in taking three histories.[60] But it was enough. He was back in July and by 13 August had put in four more 'extensive' weekend visits[61] – and this at a time when it was, he told Ralph, 'the busiest six months, I think, I have ever spent'. He was doing twenty-seven hours of scheduled teaching a week, more than that in 'conferences' (which were extremely demanding and took from half an hour to three hours), running the marriage course, frantically busy with galls.[62] 'He *drove* himself,' said Elizabeth Frazier who was working for him at this time, 'he didn't get rest of any kind. He didn't want to waste a second, and he was on to the next thing. I was frightened he'd collapse or kill himself. He'd drive 200 miles and come straight back and get straight to work. He'd work late into the night. Two or three. He completely drained himself – I'd see him come in with deep circles under his eyes. He could be short with you then.'[63]

He snatched three weeks from 25 August to go gall-hunting in Colorado and Utah. He took Mac and Bruce, now eleven, and was delighted it rained 'a cold rain' all the time – 'so Mrs Kinsey and Bruce got a typical introduction to bug collecting'.[64] It was the last holiday he was to take in his life, and no sooner was he back than in October he spent another four weekends in Chicago, leaving late Friday night and getting back early Monday morning.

Kinsey had already been astonished how often homosexual *acts* had turned up in his Bloomington histories, and also how much more complicated homosexuality was than previous sex researchers had realised. For instance, as many as a third of his clearly heterosexual histories had homosexual acts, and vice versa. Also, orientations altered at various times. His solution, already touched on, was a seven-point scale – the Kinsey 0–6 scale. (Something like this is implicit in his ideas of a biological continuum, but he told Pomeroy he had thought of the seven-point scale after his first sixty histories[65] – though it wasn't finalised till September 1940.[66]) It is often described, and can be thought of, as a sliding scale, but it is really a scale of little jumps – technically a Likert scale. To try and get a (rough) grip on the fluid situation of a continuum he used every available clue – not just behaviour, but dreams, fantasies, emotional responses to photographs and events, psychological reaction, etc.* Using Het for heterosexual and, as Kinsey did, H for homosexual, the code ran: 0 = exclusive Het; 1 = predominantly Het, incidental H experience (or psychic response); 2 = still predominantly Het

---

* As follows: H (= homosexual or homosexuality) in dream content, H in masturbatory fantasy; sexual arousal thinking of same gender, by seeing same gender, by seeing self nude in mirror, by – for males – seeing erect penis, looking at penis while masturbating, by seeing buttocks of same gender; gender ratio of companions in childhood and adolescence; H in childhood play; scarcity or absence of heterosexual activity; occupations (certain ones favoured by gays); hobbies (e.g. those commonest among the opposite gender). 'Lastly, of course, we watched for any revealing mannerisms or gay terminology.' (Paul Gebhard to author, 22 February 1997.)

experience, but a good deal more than incidental H response and experience; 3 = both equally; 4 = reverse of 2, i.e. predominantly H experience but a good deal of Het; 5 = most H, but incidental Het; 6 = exclusively H. The words 'predominantly' and 'incidentally' are pretending a precision they cannot sustain; indeed the whole concept is fraught with difficulties and contradictions. Nevertheless, the scale did allow Kinsey to get an approximation to what he was finding.

But Chicago was something else again. It was these visits that finally determined Kinsey to do sex research, though for a while he seems to have felt he could do everything else as well. What we see is the scientist in him catching fire. By July he is already telling Ralph he has, from Chicago, 'eight histories the like of which is in no published study ... [I hope] Mr Man, to prove to the world some day that any subject may be a profitable field for scientific research.'[67] He told a graduate student, W. Ricker, at this time that he might be on to a 'scientific gold mine'.[68] On one of his post-holiday Chicago visits, pouring it out in a long letter to Ralph, his excitement is uncontainable. History led to history and 'Now I can pick them up 5 to 7 a day.' He is having to do 'more drinking in single weekends than I thought I would ever do in a life-time', which he hates, but it has got him to gay Halloween parties, gay clubs, taverns – 'which would be unbelievable if realized by the rest of the world ... why has no one cracked this before?' The point is these histories are, taxonomically, like a totally different species. He has masses of material, diaries, erotic art, and it ties in with campus homosexual histories, some of these also very active, but more sophisticated, so that he gets a sense of evolution: 'The most marvellous *evolutionary* series – disclosing as prime factors such economic and social problems as have never been suggested before...' Taken with his other histories he now has 'the most complete, exhaustive record ever had on single individuals, and already 2½ times' any other published study. It was the depth and detail that were throwing up his discoveries: 'While agreeing with previous studies as far as they go, our data go much further ... It becomes clear that we need many more before we have begun to tap the true study of human sexual behavior. Will get my first thousand men in another year or so ... The thousand women will be accumulated a bit more slowly.' Not just the scientist was on fire; so too was the collector. He warns Ralph that he must judge 'How much Jerry can take'.

And he *longs* to talk to him about it, '*all* of the story – the part that has too much dynamite to get into even the most objective scientific print'.

He holds out further bait to tempt Voris – 'even the goings on in the former IU President's precincts'. But it is by no means all homosexual. He was, he says, while writing from the Harrison Hotel in Chicago, waiting for a taxi driver 'whose amazing experience of 17 years here is already almost half in my history'. He had found forty men and some women who had had sexual relations with a total 12,000 individuals. 'You can figure the average. Several with 2,000 and 3,000 each' – like, one can't help noticing, variations in the most astonishing gall wasps. And Kinsey ends, 'Your reaction [to all this] would mean much to me – as your common sense advice has so often before.'[69]

One of Ralph's reactions was indeed commonsensical, and pre-figures the obvious question, and objection, that was often directed at Kinsey, and indeed has been directed at sex surveys ever since. How could he be sure, Ralph asked, that his informants weren't 'bragging'? 'You will have to check that point sometime because you will have to defend yourself after publication.'[70]

The scientific position was almost exactly as it had been twenty years before with galls, it was an unexplored field (or unexplored as Kinsey used the term). But leaving aside Kinsey's scientific excitement – which Voris saw already meant publication – there are, almost at random, other points. In that repressed culture, where homosexuality was both a crime and a disease, Kinsey was absolutely astounded at the homosexual under-world; astounded at its existence and its *quantity*.* And Kinsey himself was nervous about it – hence his warning about Jerry (in fact Ralph didn't show his wife the letter). In November, Kinsey felt he couldn't even show his 'dynamite' material to Glenn Ramsey – because he wasn't married! And this particular exchange of letters shows how ignorant they all were. Ramsey, who is now taking histories himself for Kinsey, tells him that to his amazement, 'Out of my 25 completed histories every boy has a mas-turbation history.'[71] For the first two years or so of his exploration Kinsey was constantly being astonished by what people did – and astonished from what one can see was a very conservative base. Homosexuals con-gregate in cities, for obvious reasons, and one might have supposed the Chicago community would have let Kinsey in elsewhere. Oddly enough, it didn't really do this. He had to break into New York and Indianapolis, for example, on his own.

---

* He told Ralph he thought there were 300,000 gays in Chicago. The population in the city in 1940 was just over 3 million.

But Kinsey's gradual – or rapid, depending on how you view it – turning to sex research was not just a simple matter of curiosity and ambitious scientific zeal. It is necessary to look at his Chicago visits from a slightly different angle. It was not just the scientist who was catching fire.

11

The 1939 visits to Chicago mark one of the most important watersheds in Kinsey's life, even more important personally than professionally. The Rush Street boys also, over the months, introduced him to that other subterranean side of gay life: the side of city parks at night, of public urinals, bath houses and all-night film shows, where men went for quick anonymous sex – and then vanished, able to pass their partner or partners in the street the next day and not be recognised.

At last we have concrete evidence lacking from earlier speculation about the details of Kinsey's own sex history. From 1939, almost certainly for the first time, Kinsey was at last able to satisfy fully his longing for a homosexual physical outlet. Not with the Rush Street boys, but in this world of 'tea rooms' (US gay slang for urinals; in English slang 'cottages') that they had shown him. He continued to do this till 1948.[72]

But we should note other aspects here, since it is a complex development. Kinsey's upbringing – indeed the orientation of his whole society – would probably have always meant he would feel more at ease with men. This was true of many heterosexuals at the time too. But from now on it is noticeable how relaxedly he always fits into homosexual society, how at home he feels at once.

What do these developments tell us about Kinsey and Voris? One feels there is more to the excitement in Kinsey's letters than just science. Is he saying – don't you see, since there are thousands like this, we can do it too? That he was excited at all would probably support this. I think it possible that the tragedy of Kinsey's relationship with Voris, from Kinsey's point of view, was that it only marked a stage in his finally being able to throw off his Methodist upbringing – and that this throwing off came too late for a full relationship with Voris.

However, the meaning behind the letters could be – look, there are thousands like us, don't worry. In which case we should understand at once that, whatever they had done or not done together, Kinsey did not mean that either he or Voris was 'a homosexual'. Kinsey, like Freud, thought that human beings were basically all bisexual. Only restrictive social custom inhibited people from expressing their bisexuality. 'Without such social forces,' he wrote to Braine, one of the young men he met in Chicago later, 'I think most people would carry on both heterosexual and homosexual activities coincidentally.'[73] This insight, while obviously owing a lot to his own nature, also best explained his observations, and is supported by later research.

We can, in fact, learn more about all this from Kinsey's correspondence with the Rush Street boys:

> Dear Davie
> . . . the histories we have gotten convince me that we can get folk thinking straighter on these matters, by continuing the sort of conferences I have been having. I already have a much straighter story than anyone has yet published. So you are contributing mightily by accepting [me] in your circle and introducing me to others. Will you include all of the other boys in this? This letter is really for all of them – Clep, Undie and all. Fortune to you sir! Let me know about Sandy.
> Alfred C. Kinsey, Professor of Zoology

Ed, below, had sent Kinsey his intimate diary and with it a letter asking why, if preachers and teachers said love was so beautiful, could any expression of it be wrong?

> Dear Ed
> The only answer I can give that seems at all sense is that it happens to be out of fashion in the society through which you have to move . . . God, man, how I wish the economies of the world could be affected to give youth a better chance, more of the desired social contacts, and the other things that have been at the base of your heart aches. If I can ever serve, I wish you would let me.
> Alfred C. Kinsey, Professor of Zoology

Braine, on the other hand, was at college and pressure there made him feel he should try and become heterosexual. Kinsey sent him a three-page letter of instructions about this, including: 'In your case you will have to unlearn a lot of your mannerisms; your walk, your pitch of voice, your hand flings, your other affectations.' It ends – 'I am yours, sir, for any help I can give.'[74] As usual it is signed Alfred C. Kinsey, Professor of Zoology. This was his invariable sign off. It took him seven years before he allowed a more intimate finish with Ralph; and ten before he put 'Prok' above Professor of Zoology to Glenn Ramsey. He even signed a dictated letter to his daughter Joan 'Alfred C. Kinsey, Professor of Zoology'.*

One notices at once how at ease, even intimate, Kinsey has immediately become with these lower-level young men (Kinsey hated the snobberies associated with the word 'class' and never used it). He didn't go to Chicago solely to see homosexuals. He had already noticed, from the groundskeepers and college servants on campus, very odd differences between their histories as young men and women, and those of the students.[75] He went to Chicago in pursuit of lower levels pure and simple. This was no strain. Pomeroy, who is constantly amazed at Kinsey's amazing talents, is amazed how easily he could take histories from lower-level men and women. But it is not surprising. He was himself from the lower level and though he had long learnt middle-class manners, and was later to get on with highly sophisticated and wealthy men (by the simple expedient of remaining completely himself) we shall always find him most instinctively at ease with people from backgrounds similar to his own.

Next, the letters are thank-you ones. Kinsey realised it was difficult to take the plunge into a history and he remained extremely grateful. At first he wrote to all of them – though this soon became impossible. And gratitude sometimes led to friendship – often superficial, no doubt, but not short-lived. He was still writing to Davie twelve years later – 'the boys gave me some additional news of you';[76] Davie, who had a twee side, sent Christmas cards – the one in 1949 has an elf with 'Just for you' in frost on a window. These early (like later) contacts not only kept in touch for years, they went on helping for years. He took Derek Hobhard's history in Chicago in 1939. Derek, who worked in a furniture store then, was still getting him histories in 1948.[77]

The 'Diary' of Ed, incidentally, should be noted. Kinsey received many diaries homosexual and heterosexual (or both), but mostly from men. They contain the frankest, most detailed and graphic, most

* Joan had taken to smoking in the bathroom at First Street. Kinsey's letter began, 'It has come to my attention you have started smoking . . .' and there followed pages on the evils of this habit. He changed the signature to Daddy. Joan still smokes heavily. (Joan Reid in an interview with the author, October 1995.)

unusual, most 'shocking' and longest accounts of sexual behaviour he
was to obtain from any source. Since their owners wanted them back, or
Kinsey wanted copies (there were no copiers then), they were all typed
by Mrs Kinsey. He kept nothing from Mac. They discussed it all from
the start and the children remember how he would come hurrying excitedly into the house and start telling her things in the kitchen in his
resonant voice. 'We listened,' said Joan enigmatically.[78]

The third letter, to Will Braine, contains Kinsey's instructions for
changing from being homosexual to heterosexual, which at this point he
still thought possible. Since, in his view, both orientations were learnt
behaviours acquired by early conditioning and reinforced by various
social pressures (without which, as I say, he thought everyone would be
both) the change had to come by unlearning one pattern and learning
the other. Braine should observe how heterosexual men behaved with
girls, then get to know girls, date them (but not prostitutes, who could
excite no one, in Kinsey's view), experiment with petting and, when at
last aroused, move to intercourse. But 'the physical techniques of
heterosexual intercourse are . . . more difficult to learn than the techniques of homosexual intercourse'. (An observation now made from
experience.) Nor should he despair if he sometimes succumbed to temptation. According to Pomeroy, by 1940 Kinsey had records of eighty
successful adjustments. Yet in the end he seems to have abandoned these
attempts. He told Peter Dale in 1949 that 'neither he nor any member
of his team had ever yet encountered one man or woman who had managed, with the help of *any* kind of psychotherapy, to effect a change from
homosexual to heterosexual'. Dale was in cripplingly expensive and
protracted therapy with the psychoanalyst Irving Bieber and at once
gave it up. Bieber was furious. Dale remained grateful to Kinsey for the
rest of his life.

Finally, those 'mannerisms . . . your hand flings'. In a number of
Kinsey's letters one can detect a note of barely controlled irritation,
echoed in the *Male* volume, about this aspect of homosexuality.[79]

However, what is most noticeable about these letters, and many
others to come, is his passionate concern – 'God, man, how I wish . . .'
Kinsey didn't just morally accept almost everything his informants told
him (though not quite everything), but it moved him – the more so, no
doubt, since some of their dilemmas were his own – moved him to admiration, to anger, to pity. Above all to pity. Ten years later, when he and
his team had taken some 14,000 histories, Paul Gebhard and Wardell

Pomeroy, not insensitive men, had to some degree become accustomed – indeed often bored – by what they heard. But Kinsey would still return with tears in his eyes at some account – from man or woman – of agonising sexual frustration or sexual cruelty. It was this remaining, this freshness of feeling, that gave him, among much else, such consummate skill at 'eliciting', to use Mrs Edmondson's word, the most intimate details of sexual lives. It meant history-taking caused him more psychic strain, but it also continually fuelled him to continue his crusade.

Because, of course, it was a crusade, however skilfully Kinsey disguised it. And what is interesting about these watershed years, as he finally threw off completely the inhibitions of his upbringing, is how he first established the intellectual base from which to do this – the intellectual base from which he was to carry on the crusade for the rest of his life.

It was always possible that a biologist entering this field would do so from a stance of tolerance. In a talk he gave to fifteen newly-elected members of Phi Beta Kappa in June of 1939 – that is *before* the Chicago visits – many of Kinsey's later positions had already hardened on the biological basis alone. The point of the talk was, essentially, that variation was so great and so extreme as to make moral judgement impossible – or valueless. He also, on the same grounds, rejected the concept 'abnormal', there was only 'rare'. When people said 'abnormal', they usually meant different from themselves. Psychiatrists and psychologists (and it is interesting how early they provoked his enmity) with their 'more presumptuous [sic] labeling' (i.e. disease or malfunction) were nearly always just reasserting the *mores* of society. They made no attempt to find out how common the behaviour they condemned was, or if it was 'abnormal' in the way cancer (in fact very common) was, or how serious a malfunction in society it would produce. (Kinsey's suggestion here was in effect no malfunction.)

Variation was the linchpin. In galls it was 1,200 per cent. But in human behaviour – and with Kinsey this was already beginning to mean just sexual behaviour – 'the variation is as good as 12,000 per cent. And yet social forms and moral codes are prescribed as though all individuals were identical; and we pass judgements, make awards, and heap penalties without regard to the diverse difficulties involved when such different people face uniform demands.'

And so this Socrates of Indiana University, this influencer of the young to question the codes of their day, moved to his peroration. As far as biological functions went he was sceptical of all formulae whether governing 'the feeding of infants, the hygiene of adolescents or the social relations of older men and women'. 'Hygiene of adolescents' meant sexual behaviour of adolescents, 'social relations' meant the same for adults. 'Prescriptions are merely public confessions of prescriptionists. Argumentation *ad hominem* is bad argument . . . because it is based on unique, unduplicable experience. What is right for one individual may be wrong for the next; and what is sin and abomination to one may be a worthwhile part of the next individual's life.'[80]

The demand for tolerance was as intimately entwined, as important as scientific enquiry, *from the start* – and much will emerge in relation to this argument. It never seemed to have occurred to Kinsey, for instance, in taking his apparently non-moral stance, that tolerance *itself* was a moral position. (To Kinsey, as Paul Robinson astutely points out, 'moral' always meant condemnation and prohibition.) We should perhaps note now, however, how both pragmatic and skilful he was in his practical application of the principle.

Take, for example, premarital sex – something, although technically illegal and morally condemned, one supposes not far from the minds of his young audience – probably nearer for those very reasons. Premarital sex was in fact really the *raison d'être* of the marriage course – that is, the lack of premarital sex. In the course itself he confined himself to things that could be done to alleviate this, petting to orgasm being the main one. By the time he wrote the *Male* volume in 1948 the evidence that premarital sex helped postmarital sex (and therefore marriage, according to Kinsey) was overwhelming. Nevertheless, he wrote, great care should be taken. If premarital sex was acceptable, benefits would flow. But if the social values of an individual were against it, especially if it was thought to be morally wrong, harm could be done. Moral values 'are a very real part of life . . . They should not be overlooked by the scientist who attempts to make an objective measure of the outcome of pre-marital intercourse.'[81]

As well as being pragmatic, Kinsey was extremely skilful – as he had to be to survive – at concealing in print what he advocated in private. It was the pragmatic approach he seems to have adopted with his daughters. Both agree he did not urge premarital sex on them. 'Anyway, it just wasn't acceptable in the Bloomington of the day for girls,' said Joan. (One is reminded of them both attending church to fit in with their peers.) Yet it is clear Kinsey was already sure young people ought to have early sexual experience if they possibly could. If there were moral anxieties, he would do his best to soothe them. At exactly the same time that he was warning his daughter Anne (sixteen in 1941) about the dangers of premarital sex, he was urging eighteen-year-old Marilyn – a virgin, and brought up a strict Methodist 'to value chastity, with Godliness' – that she *should* have sex with her boyfriend of two months, G.M. Morris, aged twenty-two (both were attending the marriage course). He suggested she could use her fingers 'to spread the vulva and facilitate penetration'. Socrates succeeded. Marilyn immediately 'lost all her inhibitions and shortly afterwards we began having intercourse as often as we could'.[82]

During the fall of 1939 Kinsey took the first and most decisive step into sex research proper. He began the statistical correlations on which his work was to be based.

To do this he employed Clyde Martin, a young undergraduate who was to be of some significance in the future.

12

In the fall of 1939 an economics major, 21-year-old Clyde Martin, who was paying his way through IU, was working part-time in the zoology library. Arriving to work one day in one of the torrential downpours that regularly smash into Bloomington at this time, he coincided with a weird figure in an enormous whaler's yellow sou'wester and blurted out – 'Where on earth did you get that hat?' It was Kinsey. They chatted, and learning Martin was broke Kinsey offered him work in his garden.[83]

He clearly took to Martin. The tall, naive, good-looking boy with curly brown hair and an exceptionally amiable, uncompetitive temperament, came from the same lower-level background as Kinsey – his father was a buffer and polisher in an instrument factory in Memphis, Tennessee. In fact everyone took to Clyde. 'He was a doll,' said Helen Wallin. 'Cute as a button. He was like one of their family.' Clara Kinsey confirmed this.[84] Kinsey discovered that Martin didn't even have the money to date girls. 'I was thinking of dropping out,' said Martin. Kinsey, who couldn't stand anyone's sexual frustration, lent Martin his car to facilitate dates – to Joan Kinsey's surprise.[85] (The Nash seems to have become a sort of mobile double bed. Kinsey also lent it to a young couple on the marriage course to make love in. They were married, but had to live separately. Kinsey used to leave the key on a stone ledge.[86])

Martin retained a rather touching naiveté. Talking to James Jones in 1971 about the writing of the *Male* volume he said, 'All the text was by Kinsey. This was fortunate in the sense that I think his style of writing had quite a character of its own. The disadvantage was the rest of us, by and large, didn't gain or improve our skills with respect to writing.' He was not stupid by any means, but he was methodical (twenty-five years later he was to take six years to get a doctorate.) He was also a meticulous draughtsman, artistically gifted (Payne used him as an illustrator[87]), and he also drew gall wasps. He seems to have become one of several young men Kinsey used as son substitutes. In December he took Martin's history. (At this point, and still experimenting, he was giving examples of his own sex history to help elicit embarrassing details.[88]) Martin at once enthusiastically began to help Kinsey. He got most of his rooming house to give their histories. (G. Morris, above, was in Clyde's rooming house, for instance.)

Kinsey also decided Martin was educable. 'Clyde was no scholar,' said Wallin, 'but Dr Kinsey *pounded* at him and *pounded* at him and made him a scholar.' In the late fall, he started paying the young man (out of his own pocket) to work on sex statistics correlating his findings.

One person who was appalled at this development was Robert Kroc who realised it meant Kinsey might actually publish. Like Ralph he saw that the great flaw, among others, was bragging. 'I had never thought of interviews as scientific evidence, as scientific data. It was easy for chemists, but biology was a different ball of wax. It had been drummed into me again and again – you must have controls, controls, controls, to test *against*. On rats we did sham operations. I tried to figure it out on interviews. If you just took those who came willingly to Kinsey, who volunteered, the figures would be skewed by that. The only way I could think of was by getting 100 per cent groups. Get your figures from *groups* and get *all* of them – 100 per cent – or as near as dammit. I took it to Kinsey and he saw the point at once.'

No wonder. It was a stroke of genius. And it was a stroke of genius particularly appropriate to America. Perched on their vast continent, a polyglot, polygenous mass of different descents, colours, religions, races, Americans, particularly middle-class Americans, as they continue slowly to condense into nationhood as Europeans experience it, have turned to groups – clubs, societies, associations, social groups, sporting groups, professional, political, educational, artistic, and hobby groups.* When they die, their huge memberships are listed in their obituaries. And – except for sexual groups, when it is obvious – the one thing you can be sure of in each group is that they don't share sexual behaviours and capacities. That is not why they were formed. If you get 100 per cent of *these* groups, therefore, you don't get people volunteering for sexual reasons.

In fact, later critics such as Lewis Terman suggested that since each *group* volunteered they *all* somehow must have been less inhibited. This is inherently rather unlikely. Nevertheless, Kinsey's 100 per cent group method was not perfect. For one thing, although not a significant number, some groups were rather small. Paul Gebhard remembered with embarrassment a group of nine hikers. When he remonstrated, Kinsey snapped, 'It's a group.' More significantly, groups themselves are biased compared to other people according to the nature of the group – they might all be men, or all women. They might be especially interested in firing guns or adult education and no doubt some of the characteristics giving rise to their interests will be associated in some (usually unknown) way with sexual behaviour. One particular way could sometimes have been youth, since Kinsey did not keep a record of the age compositions of his groups. But with regard to Kinsey's and Kroc's main anxiety at this point, that he would attract those less inhibited, the taking of 100 per cent groups to test against the main body was as ingenious a precaution, at that period, as one can think of. Terman was determined to criticise Kinsey no matter what. But this particular criticism – that all the varied *groups* volunteered because they were collectively uninhibited – also shows a misunderstanding of group psychology, and indeed of Kinsey himself.

What took place was this. Kinsey always made a point first of taking the sex history of the president, or secretary/chairperson/leader of the group itself, then they would tell the group that they would like them to participate. They would also say that all of them would be asked to contribute their sex history – but this was entirely up to them. *Interest* in sex is almost universal, and at this point anyone who secretly didn't want to

---

* From this, social historians have moved to the interpretation of America as primarily a *corporate* society – dominated by ever bigger groups and societies – businesses, foundations, corporations, and so on. This is not an original observation nor a new one. Alexis de Tocqueville points it out in his *De la démocratie en Amérique* (1835). But we will notice Kinsey's skill at exploiting this aspect of American society.

give a history would decide to quietly not do so.

After his lecture, Kinsey would ask for volunteers. Remember, the president or chairperson was almost invariably present – and everyone knew he or she had already given their own history. 'We would get perhaps 30% at once,' said Paul Gebhard, later in Kinsey's team. Kinsey might then invoke group rivalry, choosing appropriately: 'At the Law Society meeting in Columbus, Ohio last month we got 70% the first evening, and by the end of the month they had all helped us. I'm surprised you let them outdo you.' 'That might add another 10%,' said Gebhard; 'then a further 20–25% would ring up and drop in, who hadn't wanted to be seen signing up.'

From then on Kinsey's tenacity took over. There are literally hundreds of letters on file pursuing individual histories to complete a group. Nancy Long 'vividly remembered' one Tuesday evening a month after Kinsey had taken the histories of her sorority – Sigma Delta Tau – at the University of Pennsylvania. It was pouring with rain. Suddenly – a knock at the door and 'there was Dr Kinsey, coming to get the late hold-outs'. At a certain point, when only six or seven remained, the group itself would suddenly exert much more extreme and telling pressure. We've all done it – it's not frightening. Why are you letting us all down? Is something wrong with you? In fact, because of the operation of these powerful group forces, Kinsey found it easier to get 100 per cent of a large group than a proper random sample from the same group.[89] Of course, technically, semantically, they were 'volunteers'. Kinsey didn't hold a gun to their heads – quite. But common sense, and contemporary accounts of the extraordinary power of Kinsey's personality and the dynamics of group psychology, all make it clear that they were not really 'volunteers' in any meaningful sense at all – or only to the degree that a fish in a shoal 'volunteers' to enter the net as it sweeps through the sea.

All sex research relies on volunteers at some stage. No matter how accurate and subtle their sampling, at the crucial point the researcher has to say – will you co-operate? At that point they either volunteer, or don't. Invariably, anything from 20 per cent to 40 per cent don't, with predictable (but very much under-acknowledged) effects on the result.* With

*In practice, such surveys – which is to say all the latest surveys in Europe, Scandinavia and America – risk missing for instance those ashamed of how little sex they have or those who have sex that is socially disapproved of or of which they are ashamed or which is against the law. Oddly enough, today masturbation has returned as one of the shameful activities (see footnote on p. 286).

Kinsey aged about three
in Hoboken (*c* 1897)

Kinsey giving a piano
lesson in his home while
at South Orange (*c* 1913)

Kinsey (*top right*) with some of the boys from a YMCA camp.
Probably about 1910, so before his friendship with Kenneth Hand

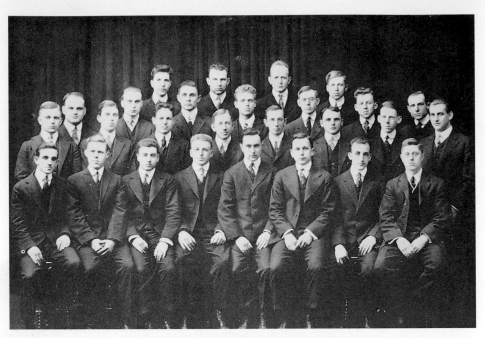

Kinsey (*middle of second row from back*) in a Bowdoin College group line-up

'The hottest thing on campus.' A rather flattering photograph of Mac
aged eighteen, about four years before she met Kinsey

Married!
Kinsey and Mac just
before setting out on
their extremely strenuous
and sexually disastrous
honeymoon (June 1921)

Left: Donald Kinsey aged about
six months being washed in the 615
Park Avenue South house in
Bloomington (*c* January 1923)
Above: Alfred Seguine Kinsey, his son
and grandson in the garden

Above: Photographs of Kinsey with his galls are rare. The collector's satisfaction is evident. *Below*: Gall wasps mounted and ranged in a Schmitt box. Each box held 600 wasps

Presentation photograph of Ralph Voris. The photograph of Voris that Kinsey kept on his desk all his life – a less formal picture – seems to have vanished

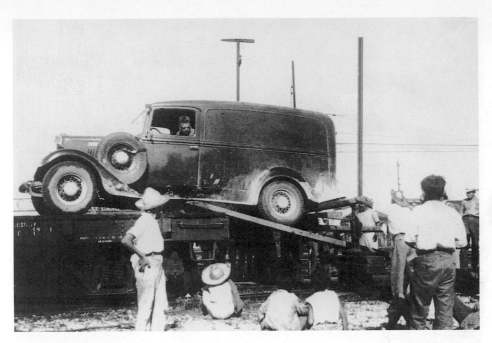

Loading 'the cross between a laboratory and a tank' on Kinsey's second Mexican trip (late 1935)

Wylie Hall. Kinsey's 'laboratory' took up most of the basement from 1950 onwards

Path and part of the garden in the First Street home. Irises in spring. Before the trees grew up, so about 1930

Glenn Ramsey at Bloomington in September 1951, carefully posed for the new photographic collection of helpers

The team about 1950. *Back*: Paul Gebhard. *Second row*: Hedwig Leser (translator), Helen Mathews, Vincent Nowlis, Clyde Martin. *Front*: Wardell Pomeroy, Elizabeth Murnan (secretary and calculator). Kinsey sits on the balustrade.

1950. Kinsey at his exercise

The code in action.
One page could hold
the equivalent of 20
pages of information

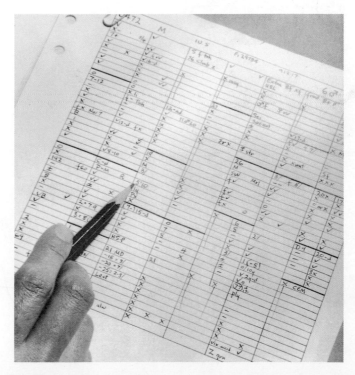

Wardell Pomeroy in 1949.
The pipe was supposed to add *gravitas*

Kinsey in 1949, at the height
of his success

Kinsey, Herman Wells, George Corner. Photographed at Bloomington in August 1951

regard to Kinsey's 100 per cent groups, this point was much more diffuse and subject to the different pressures described above. Of course, Kinsey had refusals from *other* people he asked, but in the end over a quarter of Kinsey's statistics came from 100 per cent groups. He could then compare these results with those from the rest of the sample, and draw the necessary conclusions and make the necessary adjustments. Kinsey made many significant mistakes in his sampling and in his statistics, but I think one can say he was very careful to side-step the voluntary nature of all such surveys more effectively than anyone before or since.

Kroc had a second stroke of genius. Another potential flaw in Kinsey's method was faulty memory. He would ask a forty-year-old woman, for example, about her sexual behaviour when she was fifteen and when she was married at twenty, and again at thirty-five – as well as when she was forty – and include all her replies in his figures for the various ages. If you took enough interviews at age twenty, say, then the same person again at twenty-five, again at thirty and again at forty – *but you did so without reference to the original interview* – you could, when you compared them, get an idea of where sexual memory was likely to be accurate and where not. Kinsey did 320 retakes and was able to find this out. Again, this is not perfect. If someone has repressed the truth, no amount of retakes will restore it or get them to divulge it. All surveys have checks for accuracy of recall, but this was a particularly ingenious and often successful strategy which, as far as I know, no one else has used on any scale again.

In my view, Kinsey's work, despite enormous other flaws, was superior to all subsequent sex research, right up to today, in the two fundamental areas of this tricky pursuit – his relatively low reliance on volunteers, and in particular the extraordinary, subtle and original instrument he created for interviewing. Robert Kroc was responsible for the first – and has not been properly recognised for it.

13

Kinsey put Kroc's idea into practice immediately, at the end of 1939. And it shows how deeply President Wells was *personally* involved that it was he who got Kinsey his first 100 per cent group. Wells was vice-president of Sigma Nu. Hearing at the end of 1939, probably from Kinsey himself, that he was meeting them, Wells sent an urgent message to the fraternity – they were to co-operate *totally*. 'He said "I want you to be the first". If Wells had said "Jump from the roof" we would have done so,' said Bill Armstrong. 'Kinsey came – talked – and got the whole fraternity. Even those who had nothing to tell him told him.'[90]

But Kinsey got going in earnest when the marriage lectures began again in 1940. He was, as we know, to become extremely skilful at getting 100 per cent groups, very patient, subtle, persistent. But he does now seem to have been overenthusiastic. Some of the girls were 'scandalised' and complained. Kinsey at once came up against a formidable woman now turning against him – Kate Mueller, dean of women.

The girls' counsellors said they *needn't* give interviews. 'I supported the counsellors,' Dean Mueller told James Jones. 'Mr Kinsey couldn't face the fact that he was going to be thwarted in getting all the interviews he needed.' Were there many 'scandalised' girls? asked Jones. Dean Mueller admitted the number was modest – twelve (some 350 students were now attending the course) but 'They weren't very modest in sentiment.'

It led to a confrontation. Kinsey asked her to help him persuade the recalcitrant girls. She refused. Gradually, they lost their tempers. 'Mr Kinsey became very angry with me, emotionally angry, and he shouted. Perhaps I shouted too, but he did shout at me. His face changed, he became pale. He couldn't stand being thwarted. He said I should give my history and I needed to see a psychiatrist and wasn't suited for my job. I was frightened.'[91]

Kinsey – as aggressors often do – got over it at once. Next day, he was 'very cordial'. Dean Mueller did not get over it. She was still angry in 1971. She called him 'Mr' Kinsey throughout her interview.

Criticism of the marriage course was now growing. The clergy were beginning to agitate. Egged on by Rice, the medical school was saying that they should run it. More sociologists resigned.

Kinsey trimmed – a little. He tried to add two clergymen, but the Protestant said he was too busy. He suggested Boyd of the medical school join his staff.[92] It seems, from the students' 'comments', that he had to abandon specific details of 'arousal techniques, contraception and positions'.

But in contradistinction to this he also enriched his lectures still further with his new findings – the variety of erotic outlets, their frequencies and homosexuality. As far as the sociologists went, he simply told Ralph Voris that he'd 'dropped two of the poorest lecturers'.[93] And he increased the numbers by now allowing in juniors provided they were engaged. (Attractive Joyce Cole, the campus beauty queen of 1940 and 'pretty fast' according to Mrs Edmondson, got engaged and took the course. When someone asked when she was getting married, Joyce said, 'Oh, it's not that kind of engagement.'[94]) Numbers continued to soar.

But all this was overwhelmed by something in Kinsey's life not equalled since the death of his eldest son. That cloud on the horizon suddenly left it and began to swiftly grow. On 17 February 1940 Jerry wrote and told them Ralph was in hospital with pneumonia and allergic complications. His heart was enlarged.

One can follow the whole story in the correspondence: the Kinseys only gradually realising how serious it was, Jerry's letters getting shorter and more frantic, until from 20 March to 9 May they were just a stream of pathetic and desperate postcards – Ralph 'delirious', getting better, getting worse, sinking again, sinking. On 9 May the doctor gave up hope. Jerry's postcard is followed immediately by a telegram, also dated the 9th: 'Ralph left us this morning.' She sent a last postcard on 10 May: 'I go nearly mad thinking of a future without him. I can never find a place again for myself.'[95]

Both Kinseys drove at once to Springfield, Missouri, and stayed to comfort her, while Kinsey sorted out Ralph's staphylinid collection. He was heartbroken. He turned briefly to his other old graduates as if they might perhaps replace Ralph. To Bugbee – but still more to Breland.

> I had travelled more miles with him than with anyone else … It has greatly broken me up … Man, keep yourself in physical trim, for we must carry on with the things we have started. I have never had a chance to discuss with Ralph the endless things this new study of mine has developed. He would have understood so much better than almost anyone else. Now it becomes increasingly imperative that you help my thinking on this. I am particularly anxious that you get here, therefore, sometime in the summer. Our house is your house if you will use it.

He ended, 'I will do what I can for you always.'[96] However, it was not to be. They kept in touch, but Breland never replaced Ralph Voris. No one did, though Kinsey was to fall in love once more, and have at least one significant affair, quite apart from numerous sexual encounters. He kept

Voris' photograph on his desk for the rest of his life.[97] Kinsey's emotions, apart from his family, from now on poured into his work – work which, in a small way, was about to blow up in his face.

14

In the summer of 1940 the opposition to the marriage course finally reached its climax. The Ministerial Association – all Bloomington's ministers – petitioned the university administration. The medical school, the largest outside teaching department, situated in Indianapolis, now added moral outrage to their earlier attack that a biologist couldn't know anything about human behaviour. One of the senior professors at the school was particularly outraged by the histories. In fact, he thought the whole thing appallingly immoral.

'This was ironic to us,' said Kroc, 'because we knew that Professor Y's daughter had recently been petting uninhibitedly with her boyfriend when the car, presumably parked in the dark, had been hit hard in the back and the girl's breast had been practically bitten off. The teeth wounds took a particularly long time to heal.'[98]

But matters were now moving out of Kinsey's control. Wells was about to take his decision, and it was typically ingenious. Instead of sacking Kinsey from the course, or forbidding sex histories, he gave him a choice – either sex histories or the course. Not both.

Kinsey, not recognising, as often, help when it was offered, was furious. A neighbour remembers his 'very excited' account of being forced from the course by religious bigots and comparing himself to Galileo.[99]

He waited a month – during which Wells received 164 signatures, plus many letters, begging him to let Kinsey continue both course and conferences – then on 10 September sent a letter choosing the sex histories.

And it is now, before we follow him on his turbulent, triumphant and ultimately tragic course, that we should briefly set him in his context of past sex researchers, since he is about to join them.

A Brief History of Sex Research

*If sex is repressed, that is, condemned to prohibition, non-existence and
silence, then the mere fact that one is speaking about it has the appearance
of a deliberate transgression.*

Michel Foucault, *The History of Sexuality*, Vol. I,
'An Introduction'

1

Krafft-Ebing, Moll, Hirschfeld – they might as well be distant
Austrian or German villages, or obscure generals or criminals or
species of mushroom for all these names mean to us now. Yet
these were Kinsey's predecessors. But for them, he wouldn't have
become a sex researcher.

It is not even possible to know precisely how much of them he read
for his work. This is because his reading system was unlike that of most
academics. Usually, a scholar will read all previous work and then,
partly from this base, proceed with his or her own. Kinsey's method was
the precise opposite. He would do his work first, then read what had
been done before. If it agreed with what he'd done, he would cite it as
support. If it didn't, it was wrong – and he would say so.[1]

At this point – summer 1940 – we can only be sure he had read
Robert Latou Dickinson, since he told Dickinson this later, Malinowski
and Hans Licht, because he refers these to his graduate students, and
Havelock Ellis, Katharine B. Davis and the rest of the authors on the
Marriage Course list he recommended to the other lecturers and
students on the course.[2]

Bronislaw Malinowski's *The Sexual Life of Savages* is one of the classic studies of anthropology. It depicts in careful, fascinating detail how
the totally unrestricted and uninhibited sexual life of adolescents on the

Trobriand Islands of north-west Melanesia is both extremely vigorous and 'delicate, decorous and free', and leads, after promiscuous early experiment, to successful, easy later sex lives and stable, happy marriages, based on love.[3]

Hans Licht's *Sexual Life in Ancient Greece* is interesting because Kinsey annotated his copy (bought in 1938) copiously – hardly a page is clear – obviously in part to mark material useful for his course lectures.

Licht was the pseudonym for Paul Brandt, who wrote a number of scholarly works in the late 1920s,[4] one of whose major purposes was to show how normal homosexual contact was between adolescents, young adults and older men in ancient Greece, and many of Kinsey's underlinings are to do with this. Thus, at Meleager's total opus of 130 poems, Kinsey has underlined '*at least 60 are devoted to homosexual love*'.[5] He writes *homosexuality* in the margin literally dozens of times.[6] But there are just as many underlinings concerning heterosexuality – and often just things that interest or amuse him. 'When someone said to Sophocles that Euripides was a woman-hater. "Yes, in his plays," said Sophocles, "but in bed he was very fond of them".'[7] One can trace Kinsey's rapidly evolving sexual philosophy on these pages. On masturbation: 'Widespread in Greece in men,' he notes, and on the next page: 'These passages prove that self-abuse of girls in ancient Greece also took place, either with the hand or with the use of instruments . . .'[8] (A few years later he wouldn't use the word 'self-abuse'.)

By the time Glenn Ramsey came to work for Kinsey in 1942 he said 'Kinsey had read it all' – but clearly not quite all, since he put Ramsey out reading for him for a solid six months.[9] As he did others after him. Kinsey had little time for reading, but he had an exceptionally quick and retentive mind. He would skim, get the essence, or read a *précis* – and speak so knowledgeably it would seem as if he must have read the book. When he told Voris earlier, having taken about five hundred histories, that he already had two and a half times more than any published survey he was wrong – Terman in 1938 used a sample of 2,000. Even pushing Kinsey's 'most exhaustive' still leaves out pre-1920 Hirschfeld with his 130 questions and a sample of 10,000 – male and female.

One of the earliest thinkers, if that is the word, in this field was a German aristocrat, Richard von Krafft-Ebing (1846–1902), who was so fascinated by sexual crime cases that he took to medicine, becoming an 'alienist' (the nineteenth-century term for psychiatrist) and extended his interest to deviant sex in general. In an enormous work, *Psychopathia Sexualis*[10], he explored, by 238 extended case histories, homosexuality, fetishism and – names he invented – sadism and masochism, taking in *en passant* necrophilia, incest, paedophilia, nymphomania and satyriasis.

His theory, developed from nineteenth-century ideas of the nervous system as a complex of electrical circuits distributing finite amounts of energy, was that damaging or upsetting this flow (often by masturbating) created the perversions – sadism, for example, was a pathological increase of the masculine circuit.

Krafft-Ebing established sex as a medical subject for doctors; its problems were the point (and most of sex was a problem), the case history was the method. He was also, notes Vern Bullough,[11] praised for bringing hidden things into the open. All sex researchers are praised for this; the reason it has to be done so often is that people immediately bury them again. (Krafft-Ebing certainly didn't mean to open things up; huge chunks of his book were in Latin to make sure this didn't happen.)

Albert Moll – a difficult man who had rows with other sex researchers – marks a tiny step towards Kinsey in that he also studied normal sex even if it was *in order* to understand his real interest – sex-as-perversion. Homosexuality was still a disease, but he questioned whether masturbation could be quite as fatal as Krafft-Ebing suggested. He'd noticed that little boys had erections and masturbated as early as one or two.[12]

With Magnus Hirschfeld (1868–1935) we move much nearer to Kinsey. A GP in Berlin, he was extravagant, tactless, impulsive, given to wild statements and physically repellent (Freud described him as 'flabby' and 'unappetising' – a 'not atypical Freudian put-down', Bullough dryly notes).

His life was dominated and complicated by the fact that he was both homosexual and a transvestite but it was from this, which drove him to research sex, that he gained considerable understanding. He realised, like Kinsey, that homosexuality was simply a variety of human sexuality – and campaigned all his life to have it made legal between consenting males.

Hirschfeld also used case histories but started to move these towards their final position – the statistic in a large sample. He prepared what he called a psycho-biological questionnaire with 130 questions and distributed it to 10,000 men and women. This, and similar studies, was genuine research. In 1903 he reported that 2 per cent of men he'd surveyed were homosexual – an astonishingly accurate result (whether one accepts Kinsey's findings or those of the most recent surveys), rather limply praised by Kinsey[13] and ridiculed by his critics. He couldn't quite separate himself from the nineteenth-century assumptions – for Hirschfeld, excessive masturbation could sometimes do harm – but he found 96 per cent of those under twenty had masturbated and 'in most cases the exaggerated fear of the harmful effects of masturbation is far more harmful than the act itself'.

But his most brilliant research was in transvestism[14] (a word he coined), not equalled till the 1990s. He discovered that transvestites were not necessarily homosexuals, as most people assumed. The clue was that they differed in their focus of pleasure – it was *on themselves in their clothing*. A subtle insight. He detected a masochistic element – some male cross-dressers tend to seek dominant women – but it was not a crucial one.

Hirschfeld moved sex from the realm of disease, he normalised homosexuality, and pioneered the large sample; like Kinsey he collected a mass of data and, over many years, a library of twenty thousand volumes. He also organised three successful international conferences on sexual reforms. These promoted most of the liberal attitudes which pertain, if with difficulty, today – the sexual equality of men and women, the legalisation of homosexuality, the reform of divorce law, birth control. Harry Benjamin, who would later help Kinsey, went to one in Copenhagen in 1928.

Hirschfeld's life ended in tragedy. On 6 May 1933, Nazi thugs inspired by the government broke into the Hirschfeld Institute in Berlin, smashed and threw out his data collection and burnt his library. Hirschfeld was travelling at the time and happened to be in a Paris cinema when suddenly the news film came up. His life's work was destroyed before his eyes. He never really recovered, despite trying to start up in France, and died in Nice two years later.

With Henry Havelock Ellis (1859–1939) we move much closer to Kinsey, in attitude if not character. A tall, dreamy, romantic man, Ellis was driven to study medicine and then sex by a peculiarity of his own sexuality. He was roused to passionate feelings by the act of women urinating. He called it urolognia. In late Victorian times there were still no public lavatories and for this reason women perambulating the parks wore no knickers under their long skirts. The paths were therefore made of crushed, easily drained stones. Little Ellis remembered how his nurse would stop and he'd hear a magic sound 'as of a stream of water descending to earth'. He believed, no doubt rightly, his urolognia was a consequence.[15]

Havelock Ellis married Edith Lees. Forceful where he was gentle and retiring with his high, weak voice, demonstrative where he was shy and reticent behind his beard, she was a highly sexed masochist who longed to be sexually dominated. Ellis managed to consummate the marriage but, not surprisingly, rapidly became impotent with her. Edith Lees had to turn to lesbianism to obtain any satisfaction. Finally, at the age of sixty, Ellis fell in love with a small, passionate Frenchwoman, Françoise Delisle (a surname she created from 'de Ellis'), and, like a miracle, found himself potent again.

He is significant in the history of sex research for a number of reasons. His own sexual oddness made him tolerant of anything sexual. He would not accept the concept 'abnormal'. His first major application of this was to homosexuality, to which he devoted an entire volume of his enormous *Studies in the Psychology of Sex*.[16] Arguing from animal behaviour (again the first to do so in this way), from the way it ran in families, and from its prevalence in nearly all known societies, in most of which it was accepted, he concluded it was partly congenital and partly acquired – a view many would agree with today. It was, therefore, not abnormal, just statistically rarer (he guessed about 2 per cent of men were completely homosexual). He first compared it to colour-blindness, then changed it to colour-hearing – the ability to associate sounds with colours. 'In terms of his final analogy,' notes Paul Robinson with his usual deftness, 'inversion appeared less a defect than a special talent.'

He reinforced this by his ideas of a *sexual continuum*, where homosexuality became a simple exaggeration of potentialities latent in everyone; and illustrated it by a series of thirty-three male and a number of female case histories. These were, quite simply, glowing examples of in every way successful physicians, teachers, writers and artists who were also homosexual.

Women, to Ellis, had a more elusive and mysterious sexuality because, while the clitoris dominated, behind and involved lurked the 'much more extensive mechanism of vagina and womb'. These 'intricate and in a sense distant internal organs' – I follow and quote from Robinson, on his best, slightly feline form here – meant that women's sexuality was both more massive and more diffuse; to get it all started up required the erogenous zones, of which Ellis was an architect. Another result of this diffuse sexuality was that sex played a more prominent part in the psychology of women. 'In a certain sense,' Ellis wrote, in, as Robinson notes, a rather unfortunate phrase, 'their brains are in their wombs'. Trying to redress the Victorian idea of sexless women, Ellis was in danger of lurching too far in the opposite direction and making women 'creatures so preoccupied with their sexual needs as to be incapable of functioning in any other capacity'.

There is no need to follow Ellis in detail. It is clear, and will become clearer, which of the above areas were important to Kinsey's work. In general terms, he absorbed the atmosphere of total tolerance generated. But it was a reasoned tolerance. Ellis' categorisation of sexual events, his references to animals and anthropology, in particular his image of fluids and forces building up and being released in mechanisms of sexual plumbing all gave a curiously abstract, dispassionate, *scientific* tone to his treatment of sex which contributed considerably to its effect. Kinsey absorbed this too. Except that he criticised everyone, I would agree with Robinson that Kinsey's contemptuous dismissal of Ellis[17] probably reflects an unconscious desire to hide what a lot he owed him – and shared with him. It requires no particular perspicacity to suggest that Kinsey's crusading interest in sex research probably derived in part from his own evolving sexual orientation.

Kinsey, privately (and inaccurately), despised Ellis because he thought he was too timid to conduct interviews face to face.[18] But for Ellis the interview was illustration, not the foundation of his work. Hirschfeld's pioneering of case history into sample, into statistic, was not developed further in Europe; it was left to America – that nation above all of number – to do this.* Starting with Dr M.J. Exner in 1915, a thousand students and eight questions, progressing through Katharine B. Davis with eight pages of questions and 2,200 respondents, to G. V. Hamilton with 200 people and up to 372 questions in 1929 and Dickinson with his thousand marriages and finally Lewis M. Terman in 1938 with 2,484 respondents, America in a haphazard way had begun to

---

* In fact, America had taken 'straw polls' before elections since 1824. During the 1920s and '30s very large numbers were canvassed by *The Literary Digest*, predicting election results in 1920, '24, '28 and '32. It was in the '20s that Dr George Gallup was struggling to refine sampling. (See *The Pulse of Democracy: The Public Opinion Poll and How it Works* by George Gallup and Saul Rae, New York, 1940.)

move to systematic, sizeable surveys, many based on mailed question-naires but some written-interview directed, to a degree taxonomic (i.e. collections of described data) and among ordinary people – not crazy, not odd, not primitive.

It has to be pointed out that, despite all this work, there was still very little clear, scientifically sound information. It was often haphazard, as we saw earlier with Dickinson; or solely descriptive and very imprecise as to number, as with Ellis; even Terman, who in limited areas was cer-tainly one of the scientifically most accurate, dealt largely with feelings and attitudes.

Nevertheless, albeit he reached his goals by his own personal routes – thus works the *zeitgeist* – one way of looking at Kinsey is in the context of sex research, where he can be seen as a culmination of a process that had begun seventy or so years before: his toleration, especially of homo-sexuality, his ideas of a sexual continuum, his 'scientific', taxonomic approach, his large sample, all had roots in this past. So did a number of his findings – 13 per cent of Terman's sample had multiple orgasms, for instance; so many of them had premarital sex he predicted that by 1960 no American bride would be a virgin. But Kinsey was unique in three things: the rigour of his science, his invention of a totally new form of interview, and above all, where all his predecessors had had readerships of a few thousand, Kinsey was read or known by, not just the whole of America, but at one time nearly the entire Western world.

But if we are to put Kinsey in context, we should really step back and look at a greater movement which embraces Kinsey, sex research and much else besides.

2

9 *April* 1935
Vienna

Dear Mrs . . . .
I gather from your letter that your son is a homosexual. I am most impressed by the fact that you do not mention this term yourself in your information about him. May I question you, why you avoid it? Homosexuality is assuredly no advantage but it is nothing to be ashamed of, no vice, no degra-dation, it cannot be classified as an illness; we consider it to be a variation of the sexual function produced by a certain arrest of sexual development.

*Many highly respectable individuals of ancient and modern times have
been homosexuals (Plato, Michelangelo, Leonardo da Vinci etc.). It is a
great injustice to persecute homosexuality as a crime and a cruelty too. If
you do not believe me, read the books of Havelock Ellis . . .*

> Extract from a letter of Freud's which today hangs in the
> Kinsey Institute. The name has been blanked out.

Every so often literature has to go through an upheaval in which it
throws off the stale, conventional, often stylised diction that has
developed and then ossified, and returns, in prose and poetry, to the vernacular. The Romantic movement saw itself as accomplishing this; the
next great upheaval of this sort was the one we loosely call modernism,
which began in the late nineteenth century and continued for forty
years. But this was also a return to what one might call the vernacular of
feeling. In Joyce's *Ulysses*, the novels of D.H. Lawrence and many others,
characters could defecate, swear, menstruate – and above all, make love.
This was because modernist writers, particularly in England and
America, saw themselves as reacting against, and putting right, the
moral prohibitions, hypocrisies and denials we call Victorian. The aim
was reality – the *fact* – and so we have a parallel development in art, in
which the search was for the profound, underlying reality behind the
obvious one of Victorian conventional painting. The world and feeling
behind appearance was the world of Picasso, Matisse and the Cubists.

Modernism didn't come easily. Paintings were impounded, books
banned or refused publication. Not till 1943, for example, did *Ulysses*
appear in America. Then a wily lawyer, Morris Ernst, attorney to
Random House, skilfully arranged for a copy to be imported, seized and
tried in front of Judge Woolsey, who ruled it was not obscene. It was
appealed to two circuit judges – Augustus and Learned Hand – who
again ruled in favour. The two Hands (they were cousins) went further:
no work of physiology, science or sex instruction could be judged
obscene even if people argued it produced lustful thoughts.

The way was open to Kinsey, and it seems he was aware of this
judgement. Eleven years later, given a list of the council of the American
Law Institute, he was to put against the name Hand – with who knows
what brush of memory? – a small red mark to indicate he would probably support Kinsey's attempts to change the sex laws.[19]

It is obvious that the investigation (and liberalising) of sexual attitudes and behaviour which was the task of sex research was both a part

of the modernist movement and made inevitable by it. But this movement itself was part of something far more momentous than a simple reaction against Victorian social, sexual and artistic custom. As the Church slowly lost its central position, science girded itself to take over the burden from the religion it was destroying. It is therefore a time of basic reorientation in science too – in physics, where Einstein is the seminal figure; in biology, where the implications of Darwin continue to sink in.

The figure who bridges these three worlds – the social, the literary/ artistic and the scientific – was Sigmund Freud. The figure is a towering one but I would like, at this point, to view him purely in Kinsey terms.

It might be thought that Freud, in elevating sexuality to an important, indeed overwhelming position in his thought, was a central figure both to the modernist movement and in sex research. Kinsey was early in detecting that (with one important proviso) none of these statements was true.

As far as Kinsey was concerned, Freud didn't do any sex research. What shocked him was the minuscule, really non-existent empirical base upon which Freud constructed his elaborate, city-sized, fairytale structures of conceptual thought. It was this, for instance, which allowed him to contradict himself so often and so easily.*

The second thing Kinsey felt almost instinctively about Freud and other analysts was that while apparently preaching liberation from nineteenth-century condemnations of sexuality, what they did in reality was to recategorise sins with clinical labels. He saw that phrases like 'anal erotic' or 'arrested sexual development' had strong moral content.[20]

The weakness of Freud's science had been noticed from the

---

* An ironic example of this can be found in the letter from Freud which I put at the head of this section. Kinsey was sent this letter by the mother and it is still proudly displayed in the Kinsey Institute today. If Kinsey read something he could use to his advantage he would use it, even if he disagreed with everything else the author had written. It seems likely he planned to use this letter in a projected, but never started volume on homosexuality. Kinsey had not read Freud extensively, however, and so was unaware of a later letter in which Freud more or less advocated transportation as the 'solution' to this 'problem'. Writing about another homosexual he said '... in the most unfavourable cases, one ships such people ... across the ocean with some money, let's say to South America, and there let[s] them find their destiny'. (Quoted in Webster, *Why Freud Was Wrong*, London, 1995, p. 324. See Kinsey/Dr Karl Bowman letters, November 1950, for the use of the Freud letter.)

beginning – particularly by Jung – and since then by many others. But recently both this, and Freud's wholesale but disguised carrying forward of the sins of the Judaeo-Christian tradition, especially as it affects sex, have been more comprehensively and more devastatingly exposed than ever before by Richard Webster. In these two areas Freud has been, in effect, demolished.[21]

This does not mean we can ignore Freud. It would be as ridiculous to ignore a Freud diminished by criticism in trying to understand twentieth-century intellectual development as it would be to ignore the Christian religion in studying the last 1,500 years of Western history simply because one no longer believed in the divinity of Christ. Freud was indeed a towering figure and nowhere did he rise higher, and dominate so completely, as in America from 1920 to 1950 and beyond.

The twist that Freud's thought was given there particularly suited the optimistic vein that runs so deep in American life. As the historian John Burnham wrote, the numerous 'enthusiasts of dynamic psychiatry and psychoanalysis, like the Menninger brothers, were asserting that they and their colleagues could contribute to a better world because they knew the causes of human unhappiness'.[22] In fact, by the time Kinsey came up against them – as he did; one of the Menninger brothers, Karl, was later to try and crush Kinsey; so did Lawrence Kubie, a leading Freudian analyst – the entire psychoanalytical, psychiatric and psychologic *establishment* was deeply Freud-permeated. This was to be a very significant factor in Kinsey's many battles.

Nevertheless, there remains that important proviso. Freud had succeeded in one thing. He had partially removed what Chesterton called 'Our monstrous burden of secrecy'.[23] He had lifted the taboo on mentioning sex, analysing it, describing it. Easy to say; an extremely difficult and brave thing to do. By 1939, freedom in sexual discussion was fully accepted among intellectuals. It was seen, especially in America, as a legitimate subject for study.

Kinsey was always quite clear – if Freud had not gone before, his own work would have been impossible.[24]

3

The last way to view Kinsey's move into sex is the one we have charted: first his own sex life with Mac, then his students, then the whole of IU, finally – the world. It is time, that is, to shrink the context back to the one that is the theme of this book – the working out in life of a complicated character formed and deformed in a difficult childhood.

I said earlier that it was not legitimate to ascribe Kinsey's extraordinary drive over the next sixteen years just to the fact he was studying sex. He had shown enormous drive pursuing galls. And we must see 'drive' in perspective. *All* men and women of great achievement require and demonstrate exceptional energy. Dr Earle Marsh, a friend later, acknowledged Kinsey had considerable drive and tension, 'but much less than other great men I've met'.[25]

Nevertheless, one has a sense in mid-1940, as Kinsey embarks at full power on sex research, on a routine of twelve to sixteen hours' work a day, not just of someone changing gear, but of that release of passion and energy which sometimes happens when a person falls in love with someone who incarnates some deep unconscious wish.

So here – what wish? The desire to *immerse* himself in sex, to throw off all restraints and frustrations? It is impossible to say, but it has to be suggested that the sexual element must have been very powerful. One can sense it in the *Reports* and it bursts out in his life, and we can follow it and at these points it is possible to be specific. Nor can it be irrelevant that sex research, sex science, turned out to be an ideal occupation for some of Kinsey's own sexual preferences as these developed.

Other elements we know better. 'Dear Kinsey,' Edgar Anderson wrote to him. 'It was heart warming to see you settling into what I suppose will be your real life work. One would never have believed that all sides of you could have found a project big enough to need them all . . . the Scottish Presbyterian reformer . . . the scientific fanatic with his zeal for masses of neat data in orderly boxes and drawers . . . the camp counsellor Kinsey all rolling into one at last and going full steam ahead.'[26]

The Methodist preacher determined to do good, the obsessive collector, the dedicated scientific *explorer*, the counsellor with his little lectures – Anderson knew his Kinsey. Yet there are subtleties here. We saw how the need to hide things from his parents gave Kinsey's character an instinctively secretive twist. Sex research involved, fundamentally, the keeping of secrets.

Then one often has the feeling with Kinsey of a fundamentally very warm person, no matter also impatient, whom life had blocked. Doctors, GPs, especially male ones, are also often warm, kindly people who have difficulty relating intimately; emotions disturb them. Their work is ideally suited to this since in the context of something as important as illness they can express their warmth, make often quite profound contact, but it is temporary, it remains distant, and they are always in control.[27] Something of the same sort seems to have happened with Kinsey and his sex histories.

That remoteness in him, which so many people commented on, drew people to him but as disciples rather than friends; they wanted to impress him and be liked by him. Anthony Storr in a recent book[28] has found this is a trait in messiahs and gurus and it is one clue as to how they build their followings.

And much else besides. What is fascinating about Kinsey's progress over the next sixteen years was how more and more strands of his character are drawn out and both expressed and used, until he is engulfed by it, totally involved in an enormously complex battle.

Because it was a battle. From the start it engaged that deep-seated aggressiveness and belligerence that co-existed with and contradicted his warmth. The desire to shock was clearly an aspect of this. Just to take up sex in the way Kinsey did was shocking in *itself.* But deeper still was the ever-necessary need to confront the father, the hypocritical Methodist prudes, the bullies of Hoboken and South Orange and defeat them again and again and again.

Kinsey was to get what he wanted – a fight on his hands.

PART III

Sex:
The Male *Volume*

And Besa, he was always interested! He was always aroused, always erect. He didn't let you rest! As his wife, you never rested. He'd have sex with you until you were exhausted and worn out. Your whole body was tired after he did his work. That was, he really wanted sex! I could never understand him. What do you suppose he was eating? He would make me tired! I'd think, 'Why is Besa having sex with me so often? Does he want to screw me to death?'

Nisa: The Life and Words of a !Kung Woman,
Marjorie Shostak, 1981, p. 336

How to Get at the Truth

*... underneath there was this powerful streak of crusading humanitarian-
ism which, despite his efforts to cover it, shows up between the lines in
everything he ever wrote.*
    Paul Gebhard in an interview with James Jones, October 1971

1

Kinsey may have been angered by being forced off his marriage
course; he was not in the least depressed. 'I am delighted to have
the additional time this gives for the case histories,' he told
Glenn Ramsey.[1]

It was time he now began to burn up ferociously, working fourteen
hours a day, six or sometimes seven days a week; flinging out his grappling hooks into the YMCA in Indianapolis, in Anderson, Indiana;
Peoria, Illinois; Chicago, an orphanage in Mishawaka, Indiana ... but
most exciting of all now to Kinsey – the state penal farm at Putnamville.

State farms were not strictly prisons. They were for minor infringe-
ments – petty theft, drunkenness, prostitution – and for those on
remand. The short-term inmates did reformatory farm work. But what
excited Kinsey was that at a stroke they solved two 'lower-level' problems. First, he already felt he had too few at this level – especially too
few Negroes (as they were then termed). Second – groups; Kroc's 100
per cent idea worked fine for the middle classes. Unfortunately, lower
levels did not on the whole join groups. Except, Kinsey suddenly
realised, when they did so involuntarily.

He always got on well with prisoners. Perhaps something in him
responded to anyone who came up against authority. But his solemn
promise of absolute secrecy carried particular weight in the context of
patrolling warders and strict administrators. Also, as Pomeroy put it,

those delinquent, usually young, men had been, often from birth, lectured and passed judgement on by 'parents, truant officers, juvenile court personnel, policemen, boys' club workers, chaplains . . . sweet-hearts, probation officers, wardens . . . and suddenly there was Kinsey.'[2] He didn't judge or condemn or comment at all. He just listened. The effect can be imagined.

Above all, these young people were aware of his compassion – particularly aware because, being Kinsey, it was active and practical. The files of these early years have dozens of letters recording what was essentially social service work – writing to mothers, to young wives or girlfriends, sometimes even lending (i.e. giving) money.

He noticed sexual injustice most of all. Dr Charles Hagen remembers how upset he was at finding boys in prison because they had been caught masturbating in semi-public – a park or back alley.[3] It was now he was forced, as with the Chicago homosexuals, into an appalled awareness of the cruelties of American sex law in action, especially as the laws operated on the lower levels.

Immediately after his first visit to Putnamville he startled his audience at Columbia University by saying only 5 per cent of sex crimes *were* sex crimes; or to put it another way – and Kinsey put it every way, developing this into one of his favourite addresses – 95 per cent of their fellow citizens could be in prison for what they habitually did in bed together.

British and American sex law, as Kinsey never tired of pointing out, arose from English canon law, itself based on Judaeo-Christian tribal customs going back 3,000 years. Though in America different in each state, on the whole anything outside straight marital intercourse (with the potential of producing children) was either socially condemned or illegal. For instance, homosexuality was illegal (severe penalties of imprisonment); all oral sex except kissing was called sodomy and was illegal; premarital sex was sometimes illegal; petting in public could lead to arrest for 'public indecency'. Penalties could be very harsh. 'Statutory rape' meant *consenting* intercourse with a girl under eighteen (the statutory age of consent). Kinsey quite often came upon cases where an eagerly consenting girl of seventeen had intercourse with her boyfriend, who was then shopped by a jealous father or rival or disapproving mother. The penalties were the same as for forced rape: mandatory death sentence in six states, a possible death sentence in ten more, 'life' in nineteen others, and 'ten years to life' in the rest.[4]

This was possibly going to be the fate of William Cathage who was on remand at the farm. Kinsey offered to appear as an expert witness to get the charge reduced. 'I think your boy has good material in him,' he wrote to Mrs Cathage. He could do nothing about her lawyer's 'outrageous' fees (most fees were 'outrageous' to Kinsey) but 'I will occasionally see William at the Penal Farm and help make things as good as possible for him.' He thinks there should be an organisation to help people like William when they get into trouble.[5]

Kinsey continued to go to Indiana state farms through the fall of 1940 (picking up 110 histories), on through the winter and then throughout 1941. Clyde Martin remembers driving with him to a farm when Kinsey was so ill with 'flu he could hardly stand.[6] Kinsey's eldest daughter, Anne Call, recalled: 'We'd say he was serving his sentence as he kept on going. He was so compassionate about their suffering; he was their defender. And he was fascinated how clever they were.'[7]

By the fall of 1941 Kinsey was getting into the women's penal farms, and they moved him too. 'It is a desperately lonely group of poor little girls who get into trouble with the law, isn't it?' he wrote to women's penal director, Edna Mann.[8] Some were not so meek and lonely. Christenson describes him interviewing a black prostitute, Dolores, soon to be released. Her pimp was in trouble and her friends on the farm were worried she'd be re-arrested. All at once, a solution! One of the girls said to Kinsey, 'Why don't you just take over Dolores?'[9]

And for the first time we glimpse Kinsey's ruthlessness. As far as he was concerned, the morality of the project (as he called it) far outweighed any other morality; he was quite prepared to break the law or flout convention (even scientific convention) in its furtherance. Professor Frank Edmondson remembers him coming back from a penal farm during this period. 'He had been talking to a young black girl there. He'd asked her if she was married. Yes. And your husband? He's dead. How? I killed him. She had been a prostitute and she'd found him sleeping with one of the other girls so she killed him.'

Kinsey asked Frank if he thought he (Kinsey) should go to the police. Frank didn't know. But Kinsey did. The knowledge that he would preserve confidentiality was even more vital in prisons and state farms than elsewhere. If it got out, as it would, that he'd betrayed her he'd lose the lot of them. He did nothing.[10]

2

Ever since Clyde Martin had accosted him in his large yellow sou'wester, Kinsey had been employing him in the garden. Sometime between 1939 and 1941, and probably earlier than later, this extremely good-looking, beautifully bodied, gentle young man became, as Kinsey later told Paul Gebhard, the last person he was to fall in love with.[11]

This affair was to lead Kinsey in the direction of further sexual experimentation. First, as with Voris, it clearly follows the pattern laid down by Kenneth Hand of teacher/pupil, leader/follower. It also includes the element of frustration – that wind notorious for fanning the flames of love. With Hand it was probably ignorance about what was going on; with Voris, among other things, their geographical separation. With this last love, there seems to have been an element of reluctance on Martin's part.[12]

An obsessional sexual affair appears to have continued for three or four years, but one day quite early on – and possibly as a way of side-tracking Kinsey – Martin asked him what Mac would say if he, Martin, asked her to have sex with him. Kinsey later told C. A. Tripp that he was absolutely astounded by this. It had never occurred to him that anyone might want to have sex with his wife. (What amused Tripp was that implicit in this admission was the fact that it *should* have occurred to him.) But he asked Mac, on Martin's behalf, and Mac – 'the hottest thing on campus', now married for over twenty years – was delighted.[13]

Thus began the development of something Kinsey eventually extended to the closest members of his later team. Together with those of their partners who were willing (not all were), it became a group of interacting open marriages, in which others occasionally joined. It was an experiment which seems to have been, on the whole, a success.

But – the fourth significant facet of the affair with Martin – in all this Kinsey hid nothing from Mac. He seems to have been completely open with her from the start. There is no way of knowing the degree to which she co-operated because he persuaded her, because she knew he would do what he wanted anyway or because she genuinely shared his views and wanted to join in. The serious compromises of a successful marriage are seldom easy. It cannot, for instance, have been all that easy for Kinsey to explain, and for her to come to terms with, his homosexual activities. The simplest summation is that they were able to work it out because they wanted to, and they wanted to because they loved one another.

Other things were developing or evolving in Kinsey at this time, from 1940 to '44 during his first excited exploration of the Indiana state farms.

3

We note again his daughter's 'he was fascinated how clever they were', sensing the now middle-class, Midwestern professor at last really mixing with, getting to know about, those lower levels in a way he was quite unable to do when he was much closer to them in his poverty-stricken, reclusive Hoboken childhood.

There is something else we see under way at Putnamville. Wherever he went for the next fourteen years Kinsey did what we'd call networking; he seized and then cemented by letter and invitation anyone who he thought could help the project in any way at all – lawyers, legislators, sociologists, psychiatrists, animal researchers. At Putnamville it was, first, homosexuals. One of his cons had promised to get him into the Indy (Indianapolis) homosexual groups – 'easily the equal of anything I have gotten with Chicago', he told Ramsey.[14] Another was promising him Louisville.

The second net was black, or 'the histories of all sorts of coloured folk', Kinsey told his black contact William Timber, 'the special histories you know I was interested in at the penal farm, but I'm just as interested in . . . plain, ordinary folk. Those that have very little sexuality in their histories are just as important to me as those who have a great deal.'[15] Timber, promised one dollar a history, set to immediately.

A more subtle element is revealed by Washawaka Orphanage, to which Kinsey went at the end of November 1940. Sex is such an absolutely central and astonishingly powerful force it can draw to itself almost any human activity and feeling and the further one pursues Kinsey the more one notices – though there is a paradox here – how the aims and subjects of his research constantly expand not just from the necessities but from the possibilities of his task.

Thus in the fall of 1938 he had modestly told his marriage course that he wasn't capable of dealing with children or childhood sexuality.[16] Yet here he was among orphans of twelve to eighteen, and showing his usual perceptiveness. The Principal had been surprised how quiet his charges had been when Kinsey had left. 'I wonder if the reticence of your boys and girls after my visit is not due to the fact that they are, on the whole, perfectly blank sexually. The previous regime succeeded in keeping them as undeveloped sexually as the average child four or five years younger, consequently they had as an average much less interest and had fewer problems sexually than most children that age. From that angle, such restraint has its merits. From the standpoint of subsequent development, there are serious questions to be raised.'[17]

As he realised more and more clearly how the roots of adult sexuality were to be found in childhood, so he investigated younger and younger children, discovering in himself (as people who are personally shy with adults quite often do) the ability to develop an extraordinary rapport with them.

Convicts, delinquents, university professors and their wives, black people, white people, old people, students, homosexuals, little children . . . It is time to examine the extraordinary instrument Kinsey had devised, capable, in Robinson's words, of 'an authentic *tour de force* in which every scrap of sexual information available to memory was wrenched from the subject in less than two hours'.[18]

4

When there are adequate sexual relationships, marriages become emotionally richer; when the sexual relationships do not involve sufficient emotional interchange, then marriages are threatened.

Part of Kinsey's address to the American
Psychiatric Association, 6 May 1954

'It is astonishing,' Kinsey wrote, 'that anyone should agree to expose himself by contributing his sex history to an interviewer whom he has never met before.'[19]

Setting aside the idea that perhaps that is the *only* person someone might confide in, it was obvious from the start that his entire enterprise depended on people telling him the truth, telling him everything they remembered and remembering accurately. The interview, by which all this could be found out, was therefore the single most important element in his task. Kinsey devoted a whole chapter to it in the *Male* volume –

twenty-seven pages.[20]

But before he could ask even a single question he had to establish two things. The first was the importance of what he was doing. It is difficult for us, now the work has been done, to fully appreciate this. But it was ridiculous, as Kinsey tirelessly pointed out, that less was known then about human sexual behaviour than about that of almost any other animal; less was known about sexual functioning than about the functioning of any other organ. What people did sexually was essential information for sociologists, social historians, law-makers and enforcers, educators, psychiatrists, marriage counsellors, clergymen and doctors – and nearly all the leading figures in these fields in Kinsey's day saw clearly his work was essential. It is easiest, because of AIDS, for us to see the medical importance; and VD, as I sketched earlier, was still in 1940 an epidemic with which AIDS, tragic as it is, still cannot compare, at least in the West.

We have to think ourselves back. We have all had, or have, worries about sex; but we have to multiply and magnify these many times to return, to get some feeling of the ignorance, the intense anxieties, guilts, fears and frustrations that filled Kinsey's correspondence, which he heard from his histories, and which he *knew* he could help. There radiated from him, from the buried Methodist, a simple faith, a conviction that what he did would do good – and he made everyone who gave a history feel that that was what they were doing too.

The second thing Kinsey needed was a precise unit of measurement. The one he chose was orgasm. He would study every aspect of sexual behaviour but it would only 'count', as it were, if it led to orgasm.

This was much criticised. For one thing, along with outlet, it seemed to perpetuate the hydraulic/quantitative/economic Victorian view of sexuality. This can be dismissed as semantic confusion. Kinsey himself argued fiercely and conclusively against such a concept.[21]

More to the point, his critics argued that sex was so largely a matter of 'feelings and emotions and psychological attitudes' it wasn't possible to study it and not study them too – and these were spheres beyond a biologist's training. And it is true there is sometimes a Breland–Voris–locker room coarseness of grain about Kinsey. Occasionally one senses in the two *Reports* that, spurred by his remembered frustrations, he feels people (i.e. Kinsey) should have as much sex as they want and of any sort and to hell with it – then he quickly pulls himself together again and becomes the subtle, detached *scientist* which he also was. So to critics who said a biologist couldn't study sex because of the emotions involved, he replied it was like saying a biochemist couldn't analyse cooking because it was an art. The analogy to emotions, that is, was *haute cuisine.*[22]

There is no doubt that choosing orgasm was a male-orientated choice. It was also, given his history of frustration, Kinsey-orientated. But the criticism that he ignored psychological considerations would carry more weight if it were true. In fact, Kinsey often ignored the limiting of his study of sex to its physical manifestations which he'd set himself. This is particularly true in the *Female* volume where he discovered (to his surprise) that the orgasm was often far less important than he'd supposed. He ignored this limitation, as we saw, with homosexuals; and again when looking at early adolescence in males. Really, he keeps on ignoring it throughout his studies. He was far more aware than most people that sex had a far larger emotional component than any other physical activity; he simply pointed out, as a good behaviourist, that often you couldn't believe statements about sexual emotions – they usually reflected what people thought they *should* feel, i.e. cultural assumptions. Actions were a better guide.[23] And orgasm was the only element distinct enough to measure.

Kinsey has a point here. Nor was he unaware that *behaviour* is highly susceptible to cultural influence – religion, class, education and so on. This knowledge underpins his entire research. But orgasm isn't the *only* distinct measurement, though it may be the least limiting one for a mass survey.

And it is true you get into trouble if you *don't* have a distinct measurement. Dr Stephanie Sanders of the Kinsey Institute did some research into how people responded when you asked – did you have sex? Penis in vagina – 90 per cent answered yes. (In fact one could argue this is a better distinct measurement than orgasm, especially with women.) But oral-genital – 40 per cent said no; anal intercourse – 20 per cent no. Some people simply didn't count anything as 'having sex' if the relationship didn't work out.[24] It is clear today, therefore, having an orgasm doesn't mean having sex to everyone – but without that or a similarly distinct measurement and without *numbers*, you will get very muddled figures.

This very nearly happened in the latest large-scale American survey, an excellent report in some respects, disappointing in others.[25] Here, as we'll see, they abandoned orgasm; fortunately it would seem their respondents didn't notice this and answered as if they hadn't.

Which, surely, is the point. As Robinson notes, nothing is so important to so many in sexual life as numbers. It is this that troubles couples, their incompatibility in sheer quantitative terms: one has orgasms, the other does not; one wants sex six times a week, the other six a year. It was Kinsey's 'virtue to have drawn attention to the material realities of sexual life that high-minded critics dismiss too easily as "merely mechanical"'.[26]

Robinson himself describes how before embarking on his study of Kinsey he sat staring gloomily at the *Male* report wondering how on earth he was to deal with it.[27] Suddenly a flash of inspiration – he would study Kinsey *as if he had written a book*, 'as one might . . . a major philosopher or political theorist . . . concerned to identify the assumptions, biases, the tensions and the modes of reasoning' that informed his work.[28]

It was an idea that led this clearest and most elegant of his commentators to many insights – and one or two errors. Thus he sees Kinsey's pleasure in shocking established attitudes, which I located biographically, as leading him to downgrade accepted outlets (i.e. heterosexual intercourse) and promote proscribed ones. Robinson argues that since Kinsey had made all orgasms of equal value, he was able to tuck heterosexual intercourse away 'unceremoniously into slot number four'. For good measure, he adds that Kinsey only devotes sixty-four pages to his discussion of heterosexual intercourse but allocates seventy-four to homosexual.

Heterosexual activity is only 'tucked away' (in front of homosexual activity incidentally) because Kinsey moves logically from solitary activities such as masturbation, through joint ones and finally to animal contacts. As for numbers, it depends who's counting. Robinson reaches seventy-four pages for homosexuality and sixty-four for heterosexuality by confining himself to the *Male* volume and throwing in masturbation, which seems a bit unfair to the numerous heterosexual masturbators. A more accurate guide to Kinsey's balance of interest is to take both volumes and count not crude pages but the number of times each activity is discussed. The figures then are 512 to heterosexual activity and 270 to homosexual (and this is mirrored in the questions asked in the interview about the two activities (260 about heterosexual, 136 about homosexual[29]).

The danger of a good analogy is that it takes over. Kinsey wasn't writing a novel or a philosophical treatise; he was collecting information, tabulating it and analysing it. We must now briefly find out how on earth he got the information to do this – because no one since has done it so well.

5

'Paying attention to those human actions and reactions, those spoken and unspoken utterances, those tones of voice, facial expressions and gestures ...' which psychologists and interviewers often ignore, but 'which have always been the data of all other men'.

Gilbert Ryle, quoted in Richard Webster,
Why Freud Was Wrong, 1995, p.481

Kinsey's 'victims' were first categorised by twelve 'biologic and socio-economic' factors: sex, race-culture, marital status, age, age they reached adolescence, educational level, occupational class of self and parents, rural-urban, religion and then degree of devotion, and finally geographic origin.

They were then launched into a series of about 350 basic questions with 220 extra for the unusual – such as homosexuals, pimps/prostitutes/multiple marriages, etc. These questions were, in the first instance, to elicit the weekly average and methods of achieving orgasm from the six major possible outlets: masturbation (M), nocturnal emissions (D), petting to climax (P), heterosexual coitus (C), homosexual contacts (H), intercourse with animals (Z); and all sub-categories of these (e.g. coitus marital [CM], extramarital [CX]).

Each interview was recorded on a single sheet of squared paper divided into 287 little squares, themselves contained in about twenty-five larger ruled blocks (see illustration no. 18) From his galls Kinsey had developed a (fairly) simple code. But each little square, and even part of a square, answered a different question. The symbols therefore meant different things according to which block they were in and which square in the block, and sometimes even in which part of the square itself. So M above for *M*asturbation, could be *M*other in the family block, *M*ethodist in the religion, or *M*arriage or *M*asochist. A ✓ could equal 'often', say, in the little square for cunnilingus, while it could apply to intensity in the square for reacting to a photograph of a naked man. In this way twenty-five full pages were condensed on a single squared Kinsey sheet. (The bottom of the sheet and, if essential, the back, were reserved for additional notes and details.)

The whole thing, each block, each tiny square, each symbol, its meaning in each little square, was manoeuvred, as Paul Gebhard said, in 'This compact, efficient (and to a neophyte diabolic) system'. No names appeared and, shown their sheet, people who gave their history saw something totally incomprehensible, visual proof, as it were, of the confidentiality Kinsey promised absolutely. The key and code were never written down (until many years later) and were known only to Kinsey and later his very few interviewers.[30]

It was the memorised positional code and single sheet which have made Kinsey's interviewing unique. Since then, interviewers have followed some of his rules – for example moving from innocuous to significant (it took Kinsey twenty minutes to get to his first sex question). A few have followed him in assuming everyone has done everything. Never – have you or did you ever? Always, when did you first do something – have intercourse with a woman, a man, an animal?

He was non-judgemental and even though at first frequently astonished tried never to seem surprised. Not always easy. For instance, to begin with he would tell men who had or wanted sex with children to stick to adults,[31] and Paul Gebhard remembers his amazement at his own first encounter with a coprophiliac (literally 'excrement lover'; it often involves ingestion). The man, seeing Gebhard's expression, said in a hurt, shocked voice, 'I don't mean I *chunk* it down,' indicating, with a fastidious gesture, some smaller, more dainty mode.[32]

But interviewers today are often told to give a non-judgemental appearance by keeping their distance, remaining emotionally cold, objective or impersonal (Freud gave the same advice to analysts).[33] Kinsey thought this absurd. How could you obtain sensitive material without rapport? The interviewer, he said, must convince his subject that 'he is desperately anxious' to hear the history, and minds about it. 'Sexual histories often involve a record of things that have hurt, of frustrations, of pain, of unsatisfied longings, of disappointments, of desperately tragic situations, and of complete catastrophe.' The interviewer must for a while *share* these feelings even 'though he might not be altogether neutral'.[34]

But his system made possible particular and highly effective techniques. He found that keeping constant eye contact and especially firing his questions with extreme rapidity made it very difficult to lie, especially as a person tired – it was at the end when the most difficult questions came.

And having the whole history in view meant that the various cross-checks, questions asked two or three different ways, the fourteen hidden indicators of likely homosexuality* and so on all sprang out at a glance. As experience grew so did the skill at detecting lies or exaggerations. Human sex lives have patterns and if familiar patterns were broken, the interviewer was alerted. Thus, notes Pomeroy, a young man has intercourse with 300 girls. Perfectly possible – but he also reports being aroused by thinking about women. 'People who have high numbers of sexual partners are so inundated with overt experience they usually need more than psychological stimulation (thinking or seeing) to be aroused.' So – additional checking.[35]

And, held on its single, memorised sheet, Kinsey's interviewing instrument was wonderfully flexible, making it possible to leap anywhere in the sequence and take advantage of sudden openings.

Pomeroy was taking the history of an Armenian scientist with a heavy accent. He asked when he first ejaculated.

'"Fourteen," he answered.

'"How?" I asked.'

Then, to Pomeroy's surprise, he thought the Armenian said 'with a horse'.

'My mind went into high gear. This subject was telling me voluntarily about animal intercourse, and my instinct was to jump far ahead . . . to pursue the subject.

'"How often were you having intercourse with animals at 14?" I enquired.'

Now the Armenian scientist himself looked very surprised – and also confused. '"Well yes," he said, "it is true I had intercourse with a pony at 14".'

It turned out he had said 'whores' not 'horse'. He thought Pomeroy was a genius to have somehow known.[36]

All interviewers take care over their language, but Kinsey was unique in realising how knowing the argot of homosexuals, say, or prostitutes ('On the game' in the UK; 'In the life' in the US) increases confidence; equally, how misplaced argot or the wrong language can cause difficulty. Gebhard was taking the history of a black man who was very

---

* See footnote on p. 134.

worried about the morality of homosexuality, when Gebhard was horrified to hear himself saying 'It's not a question of black and white.'[37]

The Kinsey team went further in their care, developing considerable subtlety. Yes for example, was recorded four different ways: a simple Yes, 'YES', "yes", or a hesitant 'ye-e-e-s'. And because their subject was continually in view they could catch fleeting shades of feeling as they crossed the face. It was in these nuances, indeed in the whole art of interviewing, that Kinsey did indeed show something like genius.

6

Kinsey's skills in this area should not perhaps surprise us (though at first he surprised himself). His whole working life, after all, had been spent discovering and extracting information in order to pass it on. That was the bent of his mind. He had trained himself for the rapid observation of tiny details in plants and insects, and this had extended. Pomeroy said Kinsey always noticed at once if anything – a picture, a vase – had changed in their office.[38] He now turned this to people's hesitancies, pauses, and expressions. Women (then) would rather talk about their homosexual experiences than their masturbating activity, prostitutes about 'tricks' than boyfriends – the chief skill, for Kinsey, was when to drop a difficult question, when to return to it. Then, as we've seen, he very easily identified with other people's sexual experiences, especially frustration and suffering – an empathy which must have partly sprung from the side of his nature which enjoyed piano-playing and flower-arranging. Yet it was not exactly a chameleon quality. Indeed Earle Marsh, who knew him well later, said that was the point – Kinsey was always completely himself but at once people realised his total interest in them.[39] And then there was his smile, frequently employed. It is possible to see this on film,[40] and it has more than charm; there is something almost roguish about it, a complicity, drawing you in, including you, accepting you. Robinson's 'wrenching' is the wrong verb – better persuading or inviting, eliciting, enticing.

And then there was Kinsey the actor. This was needed. Vincent Nowlis, who joined him in 1944, expressed amazement, as several people did about this impatient, often intolerant man, at the way he seemed able to like often very unpleasant specimens of humanity. 'You don't really think I like them, do you?' said Kinsey laconically.[41] At one point, as sometimes happens in the *Male* volume, his feelings burst furiously out about 'the esthetically repulsive, provokingly petty, foolish, unprofitable, senseless, unintelligent, dishonorable, contemptible, or socially destructive . . .' and he ends, taking a deep breath, 'one learns . . . to accept.'[42] But when, as happened, he realised someone was persistently lying or exaggerating or completely holding back he would terminate the history abruptly and with considerable sharpness.

I will return to the accuracy of what Kinsey was told, but anticipate enough now to say it does seem as if, seduced by skill and by the techniques I've described, the vast majority told the truth as far as they could. And the final paradoxical reason for this was that in an age when little was known and nothing mentioned most people found it an enormous relief to speak frankly about such matters.

Dorothy Collins said that it was the initial shock of it, the fact that you had 'agreed to surrender, to trust, the speed which meant you were revealing things before you realised and then, as we plunged into the intimate, all the bars were down, no further resistance – the experience, in the end it seemed to me, was an exhilarating experience'.[43] Helen Wallin: 'It was as though I was in a bubble. I told him things I'd never told anyone before or since. After the bubble burst, it was all over. I was amazed at myself.'[44]

It was often therapeutic. Respondents today are often left after perfunctory thanks – and can feel exploited. Kinsey, realising how deeply, often, people had become involved or had exposed themselves, took great care at the end, chatting, answering questions about sex, reassuring people, as they always needed to be reassured, that they were normal. It could go deeper. A psychiatrist, totally familiar with such processes, said to Christenson: 'It was a hot July afternoon . . . the questions came so rapidly and so penetratingly that I recognized some inter-relationships in my early life experiences which psychoanalysis never brought home to me . . . I have always looked back upon the giving of my case history as an outstandingly *therapeutic* experience for me.'[45]

It is not surprising, therefore, that, as Sam Steward – a sadomasochist we'll meet again – was aware, many histories experienced something analagous to 'the "transference" I'm told takes place in psychoanalysis'.[46] He remained very fond of Kinsey ever after. Robert D. May felt a bond with Paul Gebhard and used to greet him warmly on the IU campus long after Gebhard had forgotten who he was. And histories in their dozens, even hundreds, continued to write to Kinsey for years, asking advice about houses or spouses, giving details of new careers, new partners, new babies. The files are crammed with Christmas cards and increasing numbers of babies.

Kinsey, of course, rapidly became aware of this effect and would deliberately take the histories of important figures who might help or perhaps later defend him, in particular, those group leaders – chairmen or -women, presidents and secretaries. This was a major element in the forces at work which got him so many 100 per cents.

Not for nothing did Christians in the Middle Ages put the confession at the heart of their church. It was, Foucault wrote, the major engine for getting at the truth: 'one confesses one's crimes, one's sins, one's thoughts and desires, one's illnesses and troubles'[47] and, we would add here, one's loves. And, as Webster perceptively noticed, the power of the confession is that it is cumulative. Once having given and been reassured about a minor 'sin', the confessee is drawn without realising it 'into a kind of psychological intimacy with the confessor who now seems familiar with their most secret thoughts'. Thus the many things, often of terrifying power – adulterous liaisons, obscene fantasies, violent impulses, the deepest sexual obsessions – which had made people shrink from giving their history, now made them long to do so.[48]

The Church, however, was unable to reassure its supplicants that what they confessed to were not indeed sins. Psychiatrists and analysts often called them neuroses. Only Kinsey could completely fulfil the need to be accepted – to be loved in fact. No wonder he made, at first hardly aware of its force, this extraordinarily powerful dynamic, tested over centuries, the very base of his entire structure.

7

The final, in many ways the oddest, influence on the Kinsey interview, was that of his tiny, flightless gall wasp. Having had such a spectacular success with pioneering methods there, he simply transferred the entire thing to sex research. In effect, he treated human beings as if they were bigger, equally flightless, just slightly more complicated gall wasps.

Let me remind you of the gall method: vast numbers over a wide geographical area, numerous meticulous measurements all published, wide reference to related sciences.

Wherever and whenever he could, Kinsey measured; where he

couldn't, he sought precise physiological detail. He took penis measurements from the start. On a stamped postcard (three cents) was printed: Normal (soft) length and circumference; erect (hard) length and circumference. Greatest circumference is: head-middle-base.[49]* By the end Kinsey had 5,200 penis measurements and the penis, as it should be, is a minor but persistent actor in this account and will return.

The clitoris, whose measurement had so inflamed Thurman Rice, he was forced more or less to abandon, for white women at least, because it was so difficult to measure. Yet, as often with differences between the sexes in the *Reports*, the clitoris is in many ways a more interesting and more subtle organ than the penis. It is smaller, but only in certain respects; after the first inch, the sensitive erectile tissue divides and, as 'the bulbs of the vestibule', runs down for five or six inches on either side of the vaginal opening. Most of the first inch remains embedded and only the head (glans) emerges.[50] It can remain covered and undiscovered. Anaïs Nin did not discover the clitoris until 12 March 1932 when she observed it in a brothel – 'spellbound'. This was after ten years of marriage and in the middle of her torrid affair with Henry Miller.[51] White females' clitorises can stand out, but more than one inch is rare; however, they occur, said Pomeroy, in 2–3 per cent of black women. Kinsey, from 400 black women, had clitorises of 3″ or more – some capable of erection.[52]

This mechanical attitude of Kinsey's, as he wrestled to bring more than an appearance of objective science to his unruly subject, continued throughout his research, culminating in his filming. Peter Dale, a homosexual whose history he took in 1949, was intrigued how, discussing a particular penis position, Kinsey took his pen and held it at various angles so that Dale could describe it *exactly*.[53]

In fact, to follow the penis and Kinsey's mechanical interest a little further, male masturbation techniques listed manual, frictional, oral and special devices. In practice, after the obvious manual, this meant he asked if the history made coital movements against the bed? Practised self-fellatio? (This is very common in monkeys and chimpanzees, and tried by many men, it seems, but only achieved by two or three per thousand. They had one man of thirty who relied on it entirely.[54]) Put

---

* For some reason, a lot of early penis cards got sent, disconcertingly, to IU's Dr McClung – who carefully forwarded them. (Dr McClung's interview with author.)

instruments up his penis? His anus? Did anything more unusual –
melons, ropes round penis, odd mechanical devices?[55]

Kinsey then enquired further about these activities, especially the
rarest (all scientists are interested in the rare). For instance, the rarest
method of masturbation for males (2 per cent or so) is making coital
movements against the bed or similar object (pillow). Kinsey noted
that the condemnation of masturbation has for thousands of years been
fiercest among Jews – the Talmud makes touching your penis in masturbation a worse sin than non-marital intercourse. And the inhibitions
resulting continue down through three or four generations, even if
they are all non-practising, non-believing Jews. Kinsey noted in his
discussions about this, both written and with friends, that American
Jews of his day were supposed to discuss sexual matters more openly
and were therefore supposed to act more freely. He found, however,
that both believing and non-believing groups, while free in discussion,
were often the least free in behaviour. It was they above all who practised this unusual form of masturbation – presumably so that they
could masturbate without touching their penis and so avoid, or lessen,
guilt.[56]

Yet – so what? What use is this information, except perhaps
remotely to a critic discussing the work of some twentieth-century
American Jewish writers? But that is precisely the point. Science is *by its
nature* opportunistic and indiscriminate. Choose your subject – then
measure and study *everything* to do with it. In the end, something valuable will emerge – or not, and you will have blocked off one of Popper's
blind alleys. Kinsey did not find himself in many blind alleys.

8

The other gall-inspired idea which Kinsey followed was his idea of the
reservoir: collect a colossal amount of galls or histories and everything
will emerge. With galls he chose as many geographical locations as he
could get to. The equivalent to an isolated area in human sexual
behaviour was the culturally isolated group: the penal farm, college
students, middle-aged ladies in Bloomington, poor young men in
Chicago, and on top of this anyone else he could grab. (One should, incidentally, note a paradox here. Kinsey said he was following taxonomic
principles[57] – but this was only true in a limited sense. The aim of

taxonomy is to discover and describe different and discrete species; Kinsey was vehemently opposed to this in human sexuality. 'The homosexual', the 'nymphomaniac' didn't exist; the continuum was all.)

There was another problem. Kinsey wanted to discover every single thing people did sexually, to him the all-important spectrum of variation. And this he probably did – or, if he didn't, no one since has done better. He also discovered how statistically common or uncommon everything was – *in his sample.* But to what extent did this correspond to the American population? One solution, random sampling procedures, he stubbornly refused, for reasons which had weight in the 1940s. In fact, Kinsey was bored by statistics and didn't fully understand them – an attitude I find totally sympathetic. He really hoped that if he got enough histories the problems would simply vanish, as Pearl had promised with his galls. As a result, he continually upped the numbers he planned to get. But the problem didn't vanish.

However, all this was seven years in the future. What was evident now, as the fall of 1940 became winter and Christmas, was a sense of immense, contained excitement as he moved out in earnest to explore this extraordinary new world.

9

By the end of 1940 Kinsey had collected (with some of Glenn Ramsey's Peoria boys) 1,692 sex histories.[58]

They had not come cheaply either in money or time. He estimated it had cost him personally, since 1938, about $1,000 a year[59] – on a salary (1938–41) of $4,750 a year.[60] Thank God for biology textbooks.

Some money had gone to Clyde Martin. For some time he had been correlating results. Often eighty factors had to be interrelated in any one item, say the homosexual-heterosexual activity through the lifetime of 500 cases, these factors then correlated with huge amounts of other data: age at adolescence, religion, type of outlet, etc., etc. Kinsey helped, reading from the sheets, but, all done by hand, it was incredibly laborious. It took far longer to process a history than to collect it.

Kinsey realised that, apart from the drain on his finances, his entire project would be impossible without a staff – which meant more money. In December 1940 he applied for funds to the NRC. The chairman,

Ross G. Harrison, had by chance been the man who got him his Mexican grant. 'This work,' Kinsey delicately reminded him, 'resulted, you will recall, in the award of a star in the last edition of *American Men of Science*.' Harrison passed the application to Robert M. Yerkes, still chairman of the NRC's Committee for Research in Problems of Sex. This austere figure was not particularly impressed, but agreed to meet Kinsey at the annual AAAS (American Association for the Advancement of Science) meeting, held as usual just after Christmas.[61]

Christmas was now to be the only day of the year you could be sure of finding Kinsey at home in Bloomington. He remained a conscientious father but inevitably the care of his adolescent family – Bruce was twelve, Joan fifteen, Anne sixteen – now fell largely on Mac. He tried to keep Sundays for her and them, though Sundays were also essential for his two other lifelines – which he knew to be lifelines. 'It begins to look,' he'd written to Voris just after Voris had fallen ill, 'as if I need gardening to get me into shape.'[62] And, ever mindful of Darwin's lament, Sunday evening was devoted to his musicales.

There is a surprising element in his musical passion. In 1949 and 1950, Kinsey was to explore deeply into the sexual lives of artists – writers, painters, ballet dancers, actors – in an attempt to find what influence these had on their work. For some reason he never explored musicians to anything like the same depth, although it was the one art he knew intimately.* In fact, one of his rarest statistics lay here. He had one man, healthy and happy, who had only had one orgasm in his entire life – and that occurred sitting on a piano stool listening to music.[63]

One can note here another nascent development. We have seen the danger of boredom in Kinsey's little lecture style; but there was no danger of his boring anyone when he spoke about sex – and as time passed he increasingly showed impatience if people talked about anything else.[64] But to close friends he would very occasionally indiscreetly gossip. He told the Edmondsons that he had to be careful not to play too wild rhythms at some musicales because one occasional attendant became so sexually excited with such a violent erection that he had to strap his penis down to prevent it becoming visible. 'It was most surprising about this particular man,' said Mrs Edmondson, 'who was a very mild and rather elderly professor.'[65]

---

* He later took a number of histories from the Juilliard School of Music in New York.

On 26 December 1940, Kinsey left for the AAAS meeting in Philadelphia. He was about to take a momentous step. For the first time, in the full glare of a national forum, he was to reveal to, and to astonish, the world of American science with the first fruits of his sex research.

Money, Support, Attacks – The Shape of Things to Come: 1941–3

1

Kinsey, always at his smiling best at these shop-talking, hand-clasping, professional assemblies where he was now a respected figure, delivered three papers at the December 1940 AAAS meeting: one on the galls he'd collected in Utah with Bruce and Mac in 1939, one on sex education, and a third, 'Criteria for a Hormonal Explanation of the Homosexual'.[1]

This was a devastating critique of a paper by three Los Angeles researchers purporting to show significant differences in androgen-estrogen levels between seventeen 'clinically diagnosed' homosexuals and thirty-one 'normals'.[2] Kinsey destroyed the paper. First, he showed that the ludicrously tiny sample, if calculated another way, proved the exact opposite. Then he deployed his dynamite. There simply was *not* an equation (assumed in the paper) normal = heterosexual, abnormal = homosexual. There was only the continuum – and he proved it by his astonishing figures. Nor did any of the other homosexual stereotypes – effeminate mannerisms, active-vs-passive – stand up under numbers. Endocrines might be involved, but they would have to explain this variety and how homosexuals and heterosexuals switched or were both at the same time.* He ended by saying he estimated that between a

---

* In these matters Kinsey was essentially a behaviourist. If a first experience was pleasurable an individual would repeat it; if it was homosexual, he would repeat that – and each repetition reinforced the first. Early experience was more important than later. He never seems to have noticed, incidentally, that his figures of variation and switching pose problems for a straight behaviourist approach as well (an approach he abandoned when he came to women).

quarter and a third of the American male population had had at least one homosexual experience to orgasm, while there were some individuals who had had as many as twenty thousand homosexual contacts.

Kinsey's paper, despite its, to many, shocking revelations, was a triumph. Robert Yerkes was particularly impressed. Kinsey explained everything to him over several hours – his methods ('methodology' in the jargon), contents of interviews, goals, discoveries. And we see here a simple reason for his success: the *detail* of what he was finding so fascinated everyone that they wanted him to find out more. Kinsey returned delighted and immediately applied, as Yerkes had advised, for minimum and optimum sums: $1,600 and $6,500. 'Yerkes,' he told Ramsey, 'is completely sold on our programme.'[3] He was sure he'd get the $6,500.'

In January Kinsey also received an effusive letter from the now old (eighty) but still lively, even frenetic, and highly regarded Robert Latou Dickinson, to which he replied on 25 June – with the letter quoted earlier crediting Dickinson for his first moves towards sex research.[4]

The work pressure – or an element in it – was transformed in February. Seeing Kinsey and Martin plodding agonisingly through their correlations, Frank Edmondson suggested they get an IBM Hollerith Calculating Machine. All the data had to be punched on to small Hollerith data cards, and then punched again on to a 'verifier' to test it was correct. Eighty minutes a history, but then, Kinsey wrote in amazement to Ramsey, it sorted '400 cards a minute!...' It could do four additions a *second!* All sorts of calculations and correlations were possible which 'I had despaired of ever analysing'.[5]

Today this seems unbelievably primitive. Even the first (if expensive) crude computer of the early '50s, the big Atlas 5000, could do two hundred additions a second. Kinsey's IBM Hollerith was the size of a chest of drawers and went ka-*chunk*, ka-*chunk*[6] – but the two *Reports* would have been impossible without it.

Sometimes, of course, it was obvious to Kinsey what the data was pointing to – but often it was not. What was so fascinating and so exciting over the next few years, as the Hollerith ka-*chunked* away, was seeing pour from it the emerging and finally precise shapes of what they were discovering. And this made graphic Kinsey's tactic on social and sexual reform. There could, or even should, have been a conflict here. The objective scientist, as Kinsey never tired of saying, could have no moral position, no view on how people should behave or use his material. He just gave the facts. But Kinsey had plenty of moral positions. He seems to have resolved any possible conflict effortlessly. Provided he *collected* the data objectively and hid nothing, how he *presented* it was up to him. His method throughout his career was to put the facts so clearly and in such a way that it was blindingly obvious what conclusion to draw. 'I am inclined,' he told Ramsey now, 'to practically ignore the practical application of any of our results . . . until we are ready to snow them under with our scientific data.'[7] *Snow them under* – a telling phrase. Yet the element of buried conflict between scientist and reformer remained; it provides a tension in the *Reports*, generating energy. Eventually, it proved destructive.

Also in February, Thurman Rice returned to the charge in a lecture in Chicago, this time attacking Ramsey. He also repeated his 'rosebud' allegations. Kinsey told Ramsey he was considering suing.[8] In fact, at this time, desperate for 'more hands' as he always put it, he was trying to get Ramsey to join him, saying he was expecting large sums soon from the NRC.[9]

Just before these materialised, a significant meeting took place in mid-March at South Bend, Indiana, where Kinsey was lecturing to welfare workers – 'the most prudish and most restricted in their understanding of sex that you could find'.[10] One of these apparently inhibited figures came up to him after his lecture. It was Wardell Pomeroy, an extremely good-looking psychologist aged twenty-seven. He talked to Kinsey and made a date to give his history. Pomeroy arrived at Kinsey's hotel at 9 o'clock to find Kinsey wandering about in his pyjamas shaving; Martin was sharing the room to save money. Kinsey took his history and was pleasantly surprised. So far from prudish and restricted, Pomeroy was clearly extremely relaxed about sex. They agreed to keep in touch and it seems clear Kinsey was already wondering if he could be a future helper.[11]

Then in April he learnt what the NRC planned to give him in May, and it was far less than Yerkes had led him to expect – just $1,600.

2

In fact, Yerkes' committee was figuratively under sentence of death. This was due to the Director of the Medical Division of the Rockefeller Foundation which funded the NRC, Alan Gregg.

Gregg was born in 1890, the son of a minister. His interest in sex began at Harvard Medical School where (echoing Kinsey) he'd written a paper suggesting an association between sex and success. In the summer of 1909 his neurology professor, James Jackson Putnam, invited him on a holiday in the Adirondack Mountains. One weekend three other guests turned up – Sigmund Freud, Carl Jung and Sándor Ferenczi. Psychoanalysis then and thereafter had an overwhelming effect on the nineteen-year-old. He spent much of his junior and senior years recording his dreams and trying to analyse himself, in secret in case his friends thought him sexually unusual.

Gregg was happily married, a charismatic, highly cultivated and charming man, but those experiences were behind his early and passionate belief in sexual enquiry and, later, his discreet but extremely determined championing of Kinsey.

This interest and background also explain his intense disappointment that the Yerkes NRC committee, for which, as Rockefeller's Medical Director, Gregg had been responsible since 1931, had tiptoed so feebly and fearfully on the edges of human sexual research. Gregg personally felt they should support determined, even maverick individuals of worth. But all he told Yerkes now was that the Rockefeller in principle only funded the *start* of things, and that this usually lasted about 25 years – in the case of the NRC that would mean till 1943–44. The inference was clear – Yerkes was for the chop.

Yerkes received two letters outlining this towards the end of January – *after*, that is, he had seen Kinsey and *after* he had written to him. Kinsey had not been over-optimistic (an engaging trait he sometimes showed), it was simply Yerkes back-pedalling when he realised he could no longer promise long-term support. Not till he became aware of Gregg's real concerns did Yerkes realise Kinsey's work could save him.[12]

But this tiny NRC/Rockefeller Foundation grant marked a turning point. Now it was not just a lone, fairly obscure entomologist wandering about taking sex histories, but the two most prestigious and respected organisations in American scientific research. It boosted Kinsey's confidence, allowed him to approach other scientists from a powerful and recognised base, gave confidence to his group and came as a huge relief to Wells – who immediately saw to it that IU gave him a further $1,200 towards the project, which joined a minute ($200) rise in salary.

Kinsey wrote at once and thanked Yerkes.[13] He thanked all six members of his committee, two of whom, George Corner and Karl Lashley, were to become closely involved with him.[14] And as always there sounds in these and other letters, as indeed there had sounded all his working life, the steady drumbeat of the collector's numbers: in January, 1,700 sex histories; in April, 1,900; by 14 May, 2,000; his goal – 10,000.

But from our point of view most useful from now on are his annual reports to the NRC and IU each March/April (they are not always identical). We get his adroit PR with the NRC, but above all we get a clear (if upbeat) overview of each year as it passes.

In 1941 he spent 106 days travelling: 40 trips to penal farms, 20 lectures, histories from 14 colleges and universities, from St. Louis, Springfield, Missouri (where he attended a memorial service for Ralph), Chicago, Philadelphia, New York, Illinois, Pennsylvania, Ohio . . . the names rattle off and become numbers themselves.

Kinsey was still working ten to fourteen hours a day. The pattern was Bloomington Monday, Wednesday and Friday (and Sunday) and out the rest of the time. Pomeroy says he gave up teaching but this is not so. He didn't give up entirely until 1947, though his classes steadily diminished. In 1941, 17 per cent of his time was teaching, 80 per cent was sex research. He had between nine and twenty-seven students for his usual three courses.[15]

His favourite was evolution, though even here it seems his sex research reputation was beginning to impinge. During the fall sessions this year he asked one of the coeds (female students) what part of the human body could enlarge 100 times. She stood up and said pertly she didn't know but, 'You had no right to have asked me such a question in a mixed class.' Kinsey looked at her coldly. 'I was referring to the pupil of the eye, and I think I should tell you, young lady, that you are in for a terrible disappointment.'[16]

3

As everyone does, Kinsey thought he had an excellent sense of humour. A lot of people thought he had none at all. Certainly, from now on he barely countenanced 'dirty' jokes, probably sensibly. 'This is the scene,' said Bill Dellenback. 'Someone is telling a joke. Kinsey is standing foot to foot, bored stiff, loathing it. Joke ends. Kinsey raps out "Ha ha – now about that trip east . . .".' Or else, as Harry Benjamin found, he'd stare glassily ahead like Queen Victoria, apparently deaf.[17] It is true he had

many of the classic signs of the humourless. He had a very loud laugh.
There is the one famous funny story – which everyone repeats because
they can find no others. Pomeroy and Christenson both repeat it. Kinsey
was at a marriage counsellors' meeting in Boston. They were discussing
the age of peak sexual drive in the male. Someone says they'd read a
book recently by a doctor who said it was forty-eight: '"What do you
think of that, Dr Kinsey?" "I think the age of the author was forty-eight,"
quips Kinsey.'[18] Helen Wallin said, 'Yes, he did lack it. He'd never
developed one. It was tension. In a restaurant he'd sit tense, sort of disgusted.'[19] John Tebbel, who knew him well in the late '40s, said he
would tell jokes but they were terrible jokes – so terrible he couldn't
remember one of them.[20]

Yet we shall find that when he was relaxed and with friends Kinsey
did possess a sense of humour which appears not often but is authentic
and his own – dry, teasing, sardonic. And, of course, he could think on
his feet. If challenged in a lecture he'd snap back and win – 'I think I
should tell you, young lady, that you are in for a terrible disappointment.'

4

Kinsey didn't entirely give up galls until 1944 (here was the last 3 per
cent of his working time). He kept his girls working at them and in
August 1941, while their children were at summer camps, Mac and he
went on some short gall-hunting trips together. But the bulk of the
summer was sex histories. He also paid $30 a week to Ramsey to get
histories for him.[21]

The effects of his AAAS Philadelphia talk continued to reverberate
and we should not, from our (fairly) tolerant times, underestimate the
bombshell this paper represented to most people. Here is Dr Otis
Caldwell, Secretary of the AAAS, writing to Kinsey that June. 'The
feature that appalls me is . . . the raw data concerning the quantity of
occurrences. I had no idea that there is anything like so much . . . homosexuality.' Nor had he the faintest idea that homosexuals also engaged in
'normal sexual relations. What a mess it all is!' Dr Caldwell had known
only two homosexuals in his entire life.[22]

That fall Mr Wichell of the Peoria YMCA told Ramsey he was so
horrified at Kinsey's statements on homosexuality he would never let

him lecture there again.[23] (Peoria, in fact, was about to explode around both Kinsey and Ramsey.)

This sort of difficulty dogged him all the time. You will recall how earlier at the penal farm Kinsey had asked William Timber to get Negro histories for him. In October Timber wrote back proudly; he'd set it all up at Gary, Indiana. It was a fine harvest – seventy-one histories. Kinsey worked late into the night and thirty-one of them were females. The police were told. Kinsey was arrested and Dean Brisco woken at 3 a.m. by a call from the night captain. Thereafter, Kinsey travelled with an array of IU and NRC official letters.[24]

All this driving about meant that Mac, with Joan and Bruce at high school and the shops some way from First Street, had no car most of the time. In December Kinsey bought a second-hand Buick – and at once began to worry how much he'd be able to use it. Because on 7 December 1941 the Japanese bombed Pearl Harbor.

5

Kinsey did not ignore World War II to the extent Jane Austen famously did the Napoleonic Wars – but he ran her close. Yet the war was to help him. Wells, in his autobiography, says that his defence of Kinsey was much assisted by a general consciousness that the West was fighting for such freedoms – freedom to investigate and freedom to publish.[25]

And, as John Gagnon has several times pointed out, preoccupied with a war, people and therefore journalists hadn't time to bother with a professor doing sex research.[26] There is truth in this, but Kinsey *was* in fact increasingly bothered by journalists. His way of buying them off, as Martin noted, was to promise them proofs of his first *Report*.[27] The vast numbers who responded to this contributed materially to the firestorm of publicity that hit the first book.

Insofar as Kinsey thought of the war at all, said Ramsey, he thought it a total waste of time;[28] but he was, of course, aware of it, if on an extremely narrow front – how it might affect the project. He worried about petrol and tyre rationing; in particular he worried about the draft taking Martin and, soon, Ramsey.

Kinsey didn't want an independent staff but 'competent assistants he could train to be extensions of himself'.[29] He wanted 'more hands', but they had to be *his* hands. Martin was happiest, and best, at the unglamorous statistical slog. People like Martin are absolutely essential – if not particularly uncommon. But Kinsey now began to see that Martin might be moulded into something more. He therefore took him to the AAAS meeting in Dallas to meet the increasing number of scientists now joining what was beginning to seem like a bandwagon. (Dr Carl Hartman had recently visited Bloomington, given his history and recommended Kinsey's work to the National Committee on Maternal Health.) Kinsey gave a gall talk, and a talk he called 'The Frequency of Sexual Outlets' (a suitably mechanical title), in which he revealed he now had 2,500 histories.[30]

But his chief anxiety at this point was Glenn Ramsey.

6

Kinsey felt and was, in fact, closely associated with Ramsey's work at Woodruff Senior High in Peoria (about 120 miles south-west of Chicago). 'One of the common answers on the Bradley campus to the question "Where are you going?",' Ramsey had told him earlier, 'is the response "I'm going home to jerk off a quickie – Kinsey says it's OK".'[31]

During 1941 it 'leaked out' that Ramsey was taking sex histories (in fact he had told his superiors exactly what he was doing). Catholics complained. Dr Bryant Trewyn, a Protestant himself and President of the Board of Education, at once arraigned Ramsey before his Committee. Trewyn's character is illustrated by his conduct of the case: 'You know what they are saying about you? They say you ask these questions so you get sexually excited so you can go home and masturbate or screw your wife.' Dr Trewyn claimed he could 'cure' masturbation. Kinsey had rushed to Peoria and delivered an impassioned defence, but Ramsey was summarily dismissed at the end of December.

Kinsey, of course, refused to accept the decision and for three months he and Ramsey fought it. Kinsey involved all the relevant IU faculty and also Yerkes. Trewyn, assisted by the Superintendent of Schools, B.T. Wyllie, engineered frame-ups, compelling one boy to say, 'Mr Ramsey took my penis and measured it.' Ramsey was easily exonerated of any sexual wrong-doing, but the dismissal was upheld under the antiquated Illinois tenure laws (then just about to change). The lawyer charged $150. 'I suppose that is a law fee,' Kinsey wrote crossly to Yerkes later, asking if he could take it out of the NRC grant, 'although an outrageous fee for a corresponding number of hours spent by anyone else'.[32]

Ironically but typically they learnt in November that Superintendent Wyllie, who had filed the spurious charges, was soon after himself dismissed on a real sex charge.[33] But as far as Kinsey went one good thing resulted – in May Ramsey joined him as another pair of hands.

It seemed, too, as if Wardell Pomeroy might also join. In February he wrote asking if he could do so. Kinsey drove to see the Pomeroys at South Bend and offered him $3,600, which Pomeroy felt wasn't enough. But Kinsey wrote, 'Keeping the door open ...' adding 'rather cryptically I thought', said Pomeroy, that he had been 'much pleased to see the neatness of your home'.[34]

In March Yerkes encouraged him to put in a new application. Kinsey decided to chance his arm and ask for $7,500, characteristically and opportunistically now making sex studies part of the war effort: the 'present National emergency calls for ... publication for immediate use'.[35]

His pattern now was Bloomington Monday, Wednesday and Saturday teaching till 10 a.m., and the rest of the time sex research. But he could juggle this since he spent two weeks at Hays, Kansas, in March/April this year, and again in May. Bugbee was unhappily at Fort Hays State University there and got him in. Kinsey took 130 histories but what he was really after was the Negro community at nearby Nicodemus. And this is a pattern. Gebhard later compared him to an astronaut bounding about on the moon picking up rocks indiscriminately;[36] but in fact he would also concentrate on pursuing or bumping up particular groups – and after what he'd got earlier at Gary, Indiana, he felt he needed more lower-level Negroes.

Yerkes wrote to Kinsey on 27 April telling him the NRC would give him the whole $7,500. He seems to have taken and opened the letter on his way out to Hays again, because he stopped on the road and dashed off a letter: 'Dear Mac, Martin, Ramsey, Bruce, Joan – and what do you think of the research council grant? Wow! ... The doubting Thomases may sit up and think again ... largest single grant ever made ... We'll prove this is the most important piece of research ever undertaken at IU. I felt so four years ago when there were damn few of them who were not ready to knife it ...' He ends by thanking them all for their loyalty to 'the queerest and most human, the most taboo and the most important job we could have tackled'.[37] One notices the excitement; one notices also the exultation at triumphing over enemies.

His ebullience carried over into the April/May NRC Report. He has 2,800 histories; 550 from 100 per cent groups – some quite odd; drug addicts and alcoholics, 40 pimps, 60 carnival showmen, 30 taxi drivers, 140 lorry drivers and, the list ended, 'a wide variety of college professors'. Professional conferences with biologists, psychologists, sociologists, penologists, lawyers, etc. Future publications: possible Mexican study (thanks to 'my command of Spanish'), marriage, homo-sexuality. Sexual activity and athletic performance (a project not all that close to his heart, but in fact he added 433 athletes this year). In all, eleven studies and books were projected. But it was in the last one – 'Patterns of Sexual Behavior at different Social Levels' – that Kinsey hinted at one of his most astonishing discoveries.

7

One of the shapes now finally condensing from the Hollerith cards that most surprised and fascinated Kinsey was the extraordinary differences between the classes. I mean shapes literally. He represented what they did by a series of black bars and 'Even a child would comprehend that the creature represented in each of these silhouettes,' he wrote poeti-cally, 'is distinct and unlike the creatures represented in the other sil-houettes.'[38]

Radically distinct: lower levels (grade and high school) had seven times more premarital sex and far more partners, used prostitutes three times more often, had four or five times more homosexual contacts, were promiscuous in early marriage, faithful later. Upper (college) levels were the reverse: masturbation, nocturnal emissions and petting playing the part of premarital and promiscuous intercourse. Homosexuality was less, though Kinsey guessed a cover-up here. Intercourse patterns were reversed: lower levels spurned elaborate erotic technique, upper levels, trained on petting, embraced them. Most upper-level men never used prostitutes.[39] (A startling finding given the VD panic. Then, as now, upper levels slept with each other.)

At a stroke, all past sex research was rendered invalid as to the uni-versal. No one before had been able to get such information from lower levels but, assuming the classes to be homogeneous, they had all relied on college-level samples to represent everyone. Now the classes were revealed as more distinct than separate anthropological cultures.

Why was this? Kinsey speculates it could be the greater imaginative powers of the upper levels which led to greater scholastic attainment and the ability to get by on less forthright outlets.[40] The explanation is less tautologous than Paul Robinson supposes, but Kinsey neither supports it nor continues with it (in fact we see Kinsey here *en route* to his final, ingenious, but I think erroneous, explanation for some of the differences between men and women).

What is interesting is that the same pattern was found in Britain in 1971 by Geoffrey Gorer.[41] And the recent huge British survey, *Sexual Attitudes and Lifestyles* – by far the best of the modern sexual surveys – indicates a similar pattern but much fainter.[42] The classes have drawn together, as they have even more completely in America.

But again one wonders how the divisions arose. Kinsey felt they went back many centuries. It may be so. Certainly, Mayhew found similar heterosexual patterns among the London poor in the 1840s and '50s, as did the anonymous author of *My Secret Life*. Anecdotal evidence from many autobiographies would suggest similar lower-level tolerance of homosexuality then. Perhaps religion couldn't penetrate the tangled thickets of the poor; or perhaps, denied education, there were preserved there ancient and freer customs from our distant past. No one knows because no one has studied it.[43]

8

On 28 May 1942 Joan Kinsey graduated from Bloomington High. She wrote and told Grandfather Kinsey, who sent her reward by return of post – a framed one foot by one foot photograph of himself. 'Daddy's comments are unprintable,' said Joan.[44] The month before, she and Mac had toured colleges, finally choosing Oberlin. Anne had already gone to a fine art course at Washington University in St. Louis.

Clyde Martin, meanwhile, gave Kinsey further proof of his maturity by saying he planned to marry in August. Kinsey, who always tried to mastermind the minutiae of his employees' lives, said they could hold the reception in his garden but it must be May when the irises were out – and so it was. Kinsey was a good host in a genial, taking-charge way. But he also now began to train Martin as an interviewer.

Ramsey, too, joined in May. At weekends, as Kinsey gathered

histories, Ramsey and Martin worked in the garden. For the rest of the time, Kinsey had Ramsey reading everything he could find in the IU and other libraries that touched on human sexuality – taking notes and advising from this what Kinsey should buy for his research library, now numbering about three hundred volumes.

More hands didn't mean less work for Kinsey since work always increased exponentially however many 'hands' joined. 'He spent *hours* in his lab,' said Ramsey, 'often till two or three in the morning. He was a very hard task master, but hardest on himself.' He didn't order – 'You just knew'. The 45-minute, peanut-raisin-chocolate lunches were usually spent in work discussions. He now planned, he told Ramsey, to get 50,000 histories. This reflected his idea that the way to represent the whole of the American population was to get the 200–300 most important groups and then from each enough (50–300) to catch the extremes of variation.

Ramsey didn't find Kinsey over-intense. 'Intense – yes, but in a relaxed manner. Intensity was in persistence towards the goal. He would walk rapidly, he would stand alert, but this tension seemed appropriate to the task. His heart meant his time was limited. He had an insatiable desire to accomplish as much as he could in his lifetime.'[45]

Lectures mounted, miles to travel mounted and, as histories mounted, more and more letters poured in – and Kinsey answered them all, usually on dictaphone, sometimes dictating straight when (Elizabeth Frazier) 'You're going too fast – you'll have to slow down Dr Kinsey.'[46] In June a married woman writes and says how difficult and tortured she finds it trying to satisfy, and obtain satisfaction from, a girl in her office with whom she is passionately in love. Kinsey writes a long, careful, sympathetic reply – how long it takes to adjust to new patterns of thought and behaviour, ending: 'I shall think of you many times and hope to hear of a successful outcome.'[47] He even this month answers at some length a girl worried about her parents' plans to sterilise their dog.[48]

In the future, many major items – including the interviewers' and secretaries' salaries, and all equipment and offices (which Kinsey insisted on calling laboratories) – were provided by IU. But at this point not only was income from his biology textbook declining, because he was too busy to update it, but the NRC grant had to cover Martin and Ramsey's salaries. He therefore continued to charge for lectures – $15 at Purdue University in July, for example, and $25 from them again in

November.[49]

The files are full of letters in which Kinsey manoeuvres to keep his two men out of the war but in September, after Bugbee had stayed one night to discuss working for him, Ramsey enlisted in order to avoid being drafted. He was to send back sex bulletins till 1945, rather as old gall recruits had once sent galls.

Once again, Kinsey was hunting alone.

9

And loving it. 'I have almost decided,' he told Bugbee in early October, 'I am going on a spree of travelling until rationing is forced on us on 22 November.'[50] 'Spree' was the word; always, till the very end, what Kinsey enjoyed most of all was getting out and away – as he had after ferns at South Orange or later galls and now human beings. He began to take Martin with him to practise on young histories.

They spent three weeks at South Bend working around sex offenders. And here we should note a vital element in Kinsey's drive for socio-sexual reform. The people he had to convince were the administrators and practitioners: prison governors, warders, welfare officers (as at South Bend), lawmakers, marriage counsellors, educationalists, doctors, parents, psychiatrists/psychoanalysts and so on. He was to spend huge amounts of time lecturing to such people explaining how what he was discovering affected (and so should change) their work.

At the South Bend Department of Welfare, he thought that 80 per cent to 90 per cent of 'sex offenses' were not offences at all (and today nearly everyone in the UK, at least, would agree with him). He would, for instance, demonstrate how common were oral sex, premarital sex and most of the other offences. He also thought most attempts at cures, especially psychoanalytic ones, were a waste of time. 'The notion that every departure from social customs,' he wrote to the Director of Prisons in the Department of Justice, Washington, 'represents a disturbed personality cannot be substantiated in any scientific fashion.'[51] Often all that was needed was common sense. If someone wanted to tie themselves up and masturbate, teach them to do it in private.

Once more, numbers mounted, he had over 3,000 histories by 19 October. Letters still poured in. A Bob Glover at the penal farm was worrying Kinsey. His wife felt the marriage was breaking up. Kinsey (his second letter) urges her to wait till she sees him. 'Your husband, like most men on the farm, is nervously unstrung by difficulties of this sort ... when they are unable to discuss matters ... with their wives.'[52]

But by far the most significant development of the whole year was the decision by the NRC to come and inspect his work at the beginning of December.

10

So important was this visit – upon which he at once realised depended his entire future funding – that the moment he got Yerkes' letter Kinsey turned it over and, under press of urgency, scribbled on the back a possible programme: forum and questions – histories – prison – Hollerith – lab tour – het/H balance – outlets – Payne and Wells ...[53]

Yerkes had braced himself; he would have to give his history. Dr George Corner and Lowell Reed, the latter a brilliant bio-statistician from Johns Hopkins, agreed they would have to too. They must all have arrived feeling slightly apprehensive.

Perhaps Kinsey felt apprehensive too, but I doubt it. 'You felt,' said John Tebbel who saw a lot of Kinsey later on, 'you could actually *feel*, here was someone outstanding. He emanated power. The only other person I met, who seemed at first mild, but radiated power and strength in the same way was Einstein.'

Now, politely but effortlessly and completely, Kinsey, as he was to do so often with even more sophisticated and powerful men in the future, took charge. Reed had to leave early, so Kinsey dealt with the statistics at once. Then he took all their sex histories, and immediately after drove dramatically into Indianapolis, where Corner and Yerkes crouched concealed in a corner – Yerkes shrinking visibly – watching while Kinsey took the history of a black murderer. Next they saw him with prostitutes in a Negro brothel. Deeply impressed (and now to a certain extent psychologically in his power) they returned and were given a detailed demonstration and account of everything in the 'laboratory'. Finally, meetings with Payne and Wells.

It took four days and was a triumphant success. When they'd gone Kinsey wrote to Bugbee: '... the trip was worth $100,000 to us.'[54] In fact it was to be worth nearly three times that. The NRC was equally thrilled. Reed suggested Kinsey might hire a statistician and had a few statistical criticisms regarding unanswered questions. He didn't even mention the sampling that was later to cause such trouble. Corner told Yerkes they should support him 'as generously as possible'.[55]

A tall, reserved and, in Paul Gebhard's words, 'Godlike' figure,[56] Robert M. Yerkes was born on a farm in 1876 and was in all but one respect an old-fashioned American puritan. The exception was, in a strictly limited way but one vital to Kinsey, sex. Yerkes was deeply shocked, as a biologist, that so little was known factually, as regards man, about this important subject.[57] It was clear to him that a fellow biologist would best do the work. It would also seem, from a paper he wrote later this year, that despite the 1940/41 AAAS meeting, he at first considerably misunderstood Kinsey. As a result of psychoanalytic and Freudian concentration on deviant abnormality, he wrote, justifications of 'self indulgence or eroticism by authority have become conspicuous'. Moral guidance was now in order based on the 'rock of strictly verifiable fact'.[58] For several years Yerkes tried to steer Kinsey away from looking at 'abnormality', efforts Kinsey always politely but effortlessly ignored.

As far as Yerkes' personal sex life went, Kinsey characterised him as 'sex shy', which he was, to the extent that he couldn't even bring himself easily to watch animals copulate.[59] Vincent Nowlis, later to work for Kinsey, remembered how the primates in Yerkes' laboratory in Florida (now Atlanta), who seemed to copulate most of the time in one way or another, always caused him intense embarrassment.[60] But because he believed, *as a matter of principle*, that the facts of human sexual behaviour must be known, he became, with some gritting of teeth, one of Kinsey's staunchest and most important supporters.

From now on Yerkes regarded Kinsey as nothing less than 'a genius in this extremely difficult field of inquiry'.[61] He also realised he could trust Kinsey to finish. He had earlier given money to Adolf Meyer to do the same sort of thing with medical students at Johns Hopkins. Meyer got so much material it had sunk him. Kinsey would not sink. Finally, Yerkes now realised he needed Kinsey as much as Kinsey needed him. He could use Kinsey to stop Gregg destroying his committee.[62]

Certain of money now, Kinsey knew he *had* to get staff and in fact Pomeroy had written again saying that after all he did want to join him. But now Kinsey was worried he looked too young – though twenty-nine, to Kinsey, aged forty-eight, Pomeroy looked about eighteen. He delayed his reply.[63]

As the year ended, Mrs Glover wrote to say she'd decided she'd go

and see Bob at the penal farm. Kinsey says he'll give her a lift.[64] He goes
again to South Bend for a week. Christmas at First Street – and then
immediately afterwards to New York, his first major foray to the city. He
had added 816 histories this year[65] but he needed many more. From
New York – anything he could lay his hands on, in particular women
(especially Jewish women) and homosexuals.

Kinsey at his Exercise: 1943–4

Life can little else supply
But a few good fucks and then we die

John Wilkes, *Essay on Woman*, 1763

1

Kinsey's chief entrée into what one might call ordinary New York life seems to have been Miriam Hecht, about to graduate from Hunter College.* She had friends at IU who gave Kinsey her number. Miriam was twenty, an idealistic and passionate would-be revolutionary and when she met the then totally unknown Kinsey – 'nobody knows anybody from Indiana'[1] – she was at once inspired. Here was her Cause.

Leaving her to trawl on his behalf, Kinsey dashed to Chatham, New Jersey, to see in 1943 with his father. Alfred Seguine had retired in 1941 but, despite frailty, was as nasty as ever. 'Antoinette is an unusual angel to stand all . . . his cutting criticism.'[2]

He returned to find Miriam with a bulging catch. 'I asked my parents, my friends' parents, the owner of the local coffee shop, practically anyone I could and of course everyone at Hunter.' Kinsey hadn't told her at the outset that he'd pay her but eventually he gave her $1 a head. She got $71.

Some girls complained, not at giving their (often minuscule)

---

* This account of Kinsey's first contacts in New York doesn't tally with Pomeroy's (1972, p. 133). I have found that Pomeroy, while often accurate as to 'the fact', where he goes into it, which he frequently doesn't, is often far out about the dates events took place, and where there are discrepancies I have followed times and dates about which I am certain. Unfortunately, James Jones did not turn his research skills to this period in New York.

histories but because 'they wanted to talk about their feelings', and Kinsey was not interested in these. They were not the only ones who complained. These histories kept Kinsey in New York half of January and a week in February, by which time Miriam's activities had become extremely noticeable to the college authorities. The president of Hunter, Dr George N. Shuster, wrote angrily to Wells on 4 February, ending in outrage that the ' "procuress" got a dollar a head for every girl she got!' Wells wrote a soothing letter about science.[3]

Kinsey also asked Miriam if she could find homosexuals. She had, by chance, met a young man called Herbert Huncke that October in Chase's Café on 42nd Street – but Huncke seemed to have vanished (an interesting figure, he was not to meet Kinsey till 1945). However, she eventually found at Chase's 'a very thin, pale, peaked boy of 17 or even younger. I was expecting Kinsey and tried to keep the boy interested until, sure enough, he joined us. Kinsey bought the boy dinner and sig- nalled me to go. Later, he told me this was among the half-dozen most important interviews he ever conducted.' She thought the pale youth got him into the homosexual underworld.

Kinsey also spent this time in New York networking. On 7 January Yerkes came to his hotel, the Pennsylvania, and among other things they discussed the promising but dangerously youthful-looking Pomeroy. As a result Kinsey wrote to Pomeroy offering him $600 less a year than before. Pomeroy accepted immediately.[4]

But the net was now being flung higher and higher: Frank Beach, later Professor of Psychology at Yale and the University of California (Berkeley) and now curator of the Department of Animal Behavior at the American Museum of Natural History, Joseph Folsom the socio- logist, Austin MacCormick the penologist, Harry Benjamin (who, as I noted, attended Hirschfeld's conferences in the 1920s), Professor Hunt of Brown University . . . all these and rapidly others this year came his way because of and almost *immediately* upon his meeting, at last, with Robert Latou Dickinson.[5]

In some ways an odd conjunction. When they met, tears poured down Dickinson's cheeks and into his neat white beard – 'At last! At last! This is what I have been hoping and praying for all these years.'[6] Erratic, eccentric, voluble and openly emotional where Kinsey was secretive and withdrawn, Dickinson, over eighty but in no sense as far as he was concerned retired, was a livewire, appearing everywhere, speaking like a machine gun. 'Kinsey was a livewire too,' said Earle Marsh, who knew them both, 'but a *quiet* livewire. He was deliberate, he drew out the end of his sentences – aaa – "The conclusion must be – um – aaa ... that ... aaa ..." ' (There exists a very funny tape of Marsh imitating Kinsey aaa'ing and Dickinson firing back.)[7]

Yet, despite occasional impatience with Dickinson's more bizarre theories, Kinsey grew fond of him and later said no one had introduced him to more influential people or got him, indirectly, so many histories. He now, at once, offered Kinsey access to his entire life's work. (He also, incidentally, introduced Kinsey to his colleague, the bibliographer George Legman [or Gershon Legman as he preferred to be known] – whom Kinsey was later to employ and then sack.)

February saw another Glover letter, from Bob. Out of prison and out of work – so needs a further $5 to tide him over, but 'I am going to show the people of this town I can make a man of myself'. Kinsey sends $5 and says the first was a gift. Why not also get some histories – $1 each?[8]

Then at the end of the month, the Pomeroys arrived in Bloomington.

2

The medium-sized (5′ 9″) good-looking if over-youthful man with dark brown, wavy hair who now joined Kinsey was to become one of the linchpins of the enterprise. He was sociable, extroverted, full of 'zip and zap, snap-crackle-pop', as Martin put it, or brash as others did; at the same time there was considerable inner tension. This found expression in intense competitiveness and a compulsive sexuality – both were to be useful to Kinsey. Even the amiable Martin was irritated by the relish with which Pomeroy beat him at chess on their long trips (as for Kinsey, after a few games he gave up chess for ever). But, competing with each other, Kinsey and Pomeroy together were soon to more than double the rate of history-taking.[9]

It is here that Pomeroy became a linchpin. Intelligent, quick and perceptive, he turned out to be an interviewer of genius. Dr Paul Fuller, a psychologist with vast experience in this field, said he was the best interviewer he had ever observed.[10] It was upon his training that Kinsey began the moment Pomeroy arrived.

I was at pains to emphasise the cunning, care and subtlety that went into the design of the interview, and would do so again over the thoroughness of the training for it. It usually took a year or more. The code alone took several months to learn – it was never written out, but taught, like the rites and rituals of some secret mystery, by rote to the acolytes by High Priest Kinsey. Pomeroy, in fact, 'fired up', as he said, by the electric atmosphere of dedication the High Priest had engendered, taught intensely for two hours every day by him, and then working day and night himself, mastered it in a phenomenal two and a half months. There followed endless simulated interviews with Kinsey acting this history or that, and criticising ruthlessly. Then they (Martin was training too) deferentially sat in on Kinsey's histories. Finally, the trainee was allowed a simple male student, with Kinsey sitting in, and again criticising ruthlessly. (It was three years before Gebhard, who joined later, was allowed one of the complicated homosexual histories.)[11]

Kinsey was delighted with Pomeroy. For once, this contained man showed it: 'Gee, I'm glad you're going to be on the staff.'[12] The work was clearly fascinating. Martin was always astonished how there was no relationship between how sexy a girl looked and her sex life. There was a perpetual sense of discovery – and of power. Pomeroy thought this latter was one of Kinsey's main motives. On the campus alone he knew of more than twenty professors with homosexual experiences, not to speak of extra-marital affairs, and as time passed he learnt the secrets of many rich and powerful people.[13] Tripp, who still hero-worships Kinsey, said rubbish. Surrounded, he now saw, in the past and present by hypocrisy in these matters, what satisfied Kinsey was at last *getting the facts*.[14] Both could be true.

But it was not all plain sailing. For one thing, the moment he'd learnt the code, Pomeroy then broke the second code, which related the names to their histories, and then secretly ferreted out nine histories – Kinsey's, Mac's, their two daughters and five others – and read them. Then he confessed. Kinsey was understandably irritated, and disconcerted. However, he improved the second code and thereafter, since Pomeroy knew his history already, they took each other's every two years to test for accuracy.[15]

Pomeroy had to contend with Kinsey's neurotic eccentricities. Although he now once again made desperate and fruitless efforts, with Pomeroy's help, to learn to smoke cigarettes, he couldn't stand Pomeroy's pipe. He insisted on rolling down all the windows in the Buick, however cold, and also in the hotel rooms they shared. Later on, when they took to flying, they found that only cigarettes were allowed. This proved, Kinsey said triumphantly, that pipe-smoking had been found unacceptable to the general public.[16] As with his gall girls, he insisted his entire team wrote as he did, that is, legibly.* In the end he gave up on Pomeroy. Gebhard, Kinsey found, made the tail of his Q in the wrong direction. 'I remember that gave us a great deal of difficulty,' said Gebhard laconically.[17]

There was also 'the laboratory'. Kinsey was in a state of touching excitement about this, writing both to Ramsey and Yerkes about the five rooms instead of two, a 'new' (i.e. secondhand, so half-price) Monroe calculator, a new, *full-time* secretary! Pomeroy was frankly appalled. The 'three' new offices were in fact just another of the tall, gloomy Biology Hall rooms divided into three tiny, sound-proofed cubicles. Galls and gall stuff were everywhere and up to the ceiling in what Martin called 'large metal tanks'.[18] It might be thought difficult to impress visiting scientists and dignitaries – and Kinsey *did* impress them and continued to do so after the move in 1950 – amidst all this clutter. But the point is it was *scientific* clutter.

However, valuable as Pomeroy was technically, there were other aspects to his arrival which were, probably for Kinsey and certainly for our understanding of him, almost as important.

3

Pomeroy seems to have been almost as fascinated by sex as Kinsey was, but in a much less scientific, more personal and direct way. Amongst the close group round Kinsey there was no particular interest in, or importance attached to how much sex any member was having, except for Pomeroy – who boasted about it and noted his numerous conquests in a little black book.[19] His compulsive sexuality encompassed both sexes. He said to his close friend and colleague John Tebbel that 'he managed to work himself up to a weak 2 [on the H scale]', and to Paul Gebhard that he was a 1½ – much the same.[20]

Pomeroy's desire for sex, his willingness to have it with men, later

---

* Kinsey's natural handwriting was wild. He therefore developed a second style, which was really tiny capitals. He became almost as rapid in this as in the other (see Appendix D).

allowed Kinsey to use him as a sort of experimental sexual missile, firing him at subjects or into demonstrations on film which he wished to explore. Pomeroy also had sex with Kinsey – though it seems more as a favour than out of attraction (Kinsey was now nearly fifty).[21]

But this was all part of a wider development. As the endless sex histories poured over Kinsey and then his team, as they heard described the huge variety of behaviours and fantasies in male sexual behaviour (and, at this point to a lesser extent, in female behaviour), things they hadn't even imagined, much less done – complex alternatives of H and heterosexual pattern, ropes around penises and scrotums and neck, sado-masochistic practices, vast quantities of sex or none at all and all the varied and ordinary/extraordinary expressions of this seemingly irresistible and anarchic force – so a sort of indifference or, more accurately, blanket acceptance and immunity to surprise developed among them. Anything and everything could be experimented with – since it all took place. And not only could – but *should.* Kinsey realised that to understand what they were hearing, above all to enable them to extract every significant detail, he and his team must experiment to the limit. The difference this made in extracting homosexual histories was already obvious, and Kinsey continually urged the need to experiment on Pomeroy and later Vincent Nowlis – and indeed anyone who now joined him. From the point of view of his task, of course, he was quite right.[22]

It is therefore here – 1942–3 onwards – that I think we should place Kinsey's various experiments with, for example, ropes and gross penis insertion, which were to surface nine or ten years later, and which I'll deal with then. The degree to which they'd progressed by that time requires such a genesis.

Kinsey was always acutely aware that true science lay in the observation and recording of data – not in listening to people talk. Soon after Pomeroy joined, prostitutes let the two of them secretly watch them at work.[23]

In fact, Kinsey had begun to observe sex before this. Public baths in the big cities, especially in New York, were often gay meeting points (in which, as in their practical set-up, they resembled our Turkish baths of the same period). This was particularly true of the Everard. In this haunt, with its music-hall name, there was an open 'dormitory' where sex went on openly during the 1940s, and Kinsey first went in 1942. Later, he used to go to the Penn Baths, near Penn Station, where similar scenes took place. The busiest time was 5 o'clock, he noticed, when it was mostly married businessmen hurrying home. This appealed to Kinsey's sardonic sense of humour. 'He liked the naughty quality of it,' said Dr C. A. Tripp. He said that Kinsey – who no doubt sometimes joined in – also noted that the married men 'mostly wanted to be fucked; they were tired with all the fucking they had to do at home'.[24]

One would be interested in statistical proof of this, a field so far left unexplored by modern surveys. The great pioneers of the scientific observation of sexual activity were, of course, Virginia E. Johnson and William H. Masters. Yet Kinsey anticipated them by nearly thirty years, and the eventual fruits of his very thorough and meticulous work here and later formed the substance of two of the most valuable and original chapters in his published work.

But that lay in the future. Now, with his new staff, which he planned to increase, and confidently expecting more money (why else should Yerkes have authorised the new Monroe?), Kinsey forged ahead through 1943.

4

In fact, a brief hiccup, Kinsey's father died in Chatham on 7 April. The event seems not to have left a ripple on Kinsey's progress.

He was now again after new hands. A 29-year-old psychologist at the University of Connecticut (Storrs), married with three children, had been suggested – Vincent Nowlis. He had worked for three years with Yerkes, who was enthusiastic: 'He is a big fellow, of splendid physique, fine appearance and forcefulness . . . a first rate mind . . .'[25] As Yerkes' man, he had to be seriously considered, but Kinsey, as always with new hands, was tentative – too classy? Too judgemental? He would have to take his history.[26]

On the pretext of achieving another long-planned trip, he just had time to get out the annual report, his files covered in plaster and surrounded by painters and carpenters. Once again we can get an overview of the year: teaching cut by a third and beginning to vanish; more new groups, more from old groups – 28 builders, 44 miners, 60 psychiatrists and doctors, eight more pimps, etc., in all now 3,500, from Chicago, New York (63 Jewish females), Indiana state farms and prisons, Philadelphia[27] . . . Having rushed this off, Kinsey set out for Hays, Kansas.

He had at last succeeded, with Bugbee's help, in getting into

Nicodemus. This community of very poor blacks – deeply rural, in tumbledown shacks, two small stores – had been much the same since the Civil War and was therefore, Kinsey told Yerkes, taxonomically fascinating.[28] For the first time he unleashed his whole team and in three weeks they got 126 histories. A burly, 35-year-old farmhand made determined passes at Pomeroy, who fended him off with his left while taking his history with his right hand. (It was midnight and they were in a car. Pomeroy quite often had passes made at him. The best defence, apparently, was total passivity – though this was not always possible.[29])

Kinsey grew attached to this humble community, especially its mentor there, the Rev. James H. Jones. 'I like your wisdom and your quiet acceptance of so many things.' The Nicodemus pastor went on writing for years.[30]

They returned to Bloomington on 9 May, to learn that the NRC would give $23,000 – more than three times the year before. Kinsey had led up to this in a way both subtly flattering to Yerkes and completely genuine. His work had always been guided by evolutionary theory, and a 'phylogenetic' approach now – the approach to humans via their evolution from animals – obviously made primates central. In April, he'd twice suggested a meeting to discuss primates. Since Yerkes' work *was* primates, he was naturally delighted.[31]

Kinsey was now financially more secure and gave up charging for lectures, asking only that he could solicit for histories. His salary had been raised to $5,100 and this year finally saw the belated publication of *Edible Wild Plants of Eastern North America.*[32] No royalty accounts remain, and they would have been shared with Lyndon Fernald, but this must have contributed to his income – especially as it was taken up by the Army. (Yet it is an odd book to take on manoeuvres – 452 scholarly pages plus index and, as we saw earlier, often requiring quite elaborate cuisine.) On 26 July, Kinsey wrote to Nowlis – he wished he was ten years older and 'that your hand writing was better'.[33] (Nowlis had been unwise enough to write to Kinsey by hand in ink.) But, about to set off for the Primate Conference, Kinsey suggested he and the team could come and see Nowlis on the way.

They all arrived at Nowlis' house in Storrs, Connecticut – having grabbed seventy-three histories of 'so-called juvenile delinquents'[34] in Columbus, Ohio, *en route* – on 14 August. Kinsey commented on a large spruce on the Nowlis lawn, giving one of his little lectures on fertilising pines. The two had things in common; both came from poor back-

grounds. Nowlis' father had been a miner, then a salesman, both had
been to Bowdoin. But one thing worried Kinsey – Nowlis' weekly
orgasm tally was too low. Nowlis was rather aggrieved. 'I was making
love to my wife three times a week, which I thought all right.' Yet this
was a significant comment, as we'll see.[35]

In fact, they all liked this intelligent, charming and, in Pomeroy's
words, 'attractive' young man[36] and soon after the Primate Conference
Kinsey was to offer him a job. But it was to this conference, held in New
York, that the team now drove.

5

From an RNA perspective, a man and a dog are the same organism. In fact,
I'd have trouble distinguishing between a man and a wombat.

Norman Pace of IU, quoted in *New Scientist*,
Vol. 149, No. 2016, 10 February 1996, p. 27

Yerkes had gathered sixteen scientists to examine 'Patterns and
Problems of Primate Sex Behavior' (at a cost, Kinsey boasted to Bugbee,
of $1,500). Not just his entire committee but distinguished figures like
Karl S. Lashley, the Harvard psychologist, and Frank Beach (Nowlis
also attended).[37]

Kinsey had two blissful, stimulating days with them. It is easy for
most of us today to see human beings as just a particularly evolved
animal. Kinsey, as we know, never had the slightest difficulty here. Nor,
in theory, should any of the scientists gathered at the Hotel Pennsylvania.

Yet Kinsey astonished them. He took, said Beach, 'a very unorthodox view' of animal research.[38] Essentially, in New York, he outlined his
entire programme, and then asked them to search for primate roots of
everything he was investigating; not just masturbation and coitus, but
nocturnal sex dreams, homosexual behaviour, mouth-genital, 'premarital' sex (i.e. pre-adolescent), etc., etc.[39]

Beach also observed that Kinsey was able to make him feel that his
(Beach's) animal research was vital to the project.[40] But this was because
to Kinsey it *was*, if not vital, very important. He showed now he could use
almost anything they found. For instance, in Yerkes' Florida laboratory
there was a male monkey who could *only* have sex by persuading female
monkeys to sit on its erect penis. It had trained one female to be particu-

larly adept. Yet, when the male died, his female was immediately happy to mate in the usual rear-entrance primate way. Kinsey at once seized on this as a demonstration of his nascent ideas about men and women: men were heavily conditioned by society, women much less so.[41]

Although unorthodox, Frank Beach noted that Kinsey's use of animal sexual behaviour, on which he now became an adviser, was effective, especially when it came to homosexuality. He described Kinsey at the conference. After his initial address, he suddenly asked, who would like to help? 'Well, there we were, surrounded by the people actually paying for our work – who could refuse?' Beach reluctantly put his hand up, envisaging an interview in the distant future. Not at all, practically next morning Kinsey was firing questions at him with machine-gun rapidity in his hotel bedroom. Beach described, as so many people did, the method. 'It wasn't "have you ever?", it was "when did you last make love to a pig?" You said "Never!" OK – but he had you hooked if you were a pig lover.'[42]

Actually, Kinsey was at his most perceptive in the *Male* report discussing pig-lovers – and dog-, bull-, calf-, sheep-, chicken-lovers as well. He found that 17 per cent of rural farm hands, especially adolescents, had had every form of sex to orgasm with practically every animal farmed. He suspected the true figure was 34 per cent. Oddly enough, in common with other solitary pursuits, it was highest in upper, college levels. He describes sympathetically the excitement, even passion, and the strong emotions boys and young men could feel towards animals they had regular contact with – just as people have strong feelings about their pets. 'The elements,' he wrote, 'that are involved in sexual contacts ... [of this sort] are at no point basically different from those that are involved in erotic responses to human situations.' 'In effect,' as Paul Robinson observed, 'Kinsey refused to grant the human realm a unique place in the larger order of things.'[43]

Kinsey was to leave New York on 10 September well pleased with his efforts to link the various realms. He had even asked Beach to see how often primates had sex with other species.[44]

6

The team had been getting fifty histories a week in New York, but Kinsey stayed on for a more important reason – a meeting with Alan

Gregg engineered by Yerkes for 3 September.

Gregg had told Yerkes that the Rockefeller Foundation would probably cease funding his committee in 1944. Ignoring this, Yerkes, with some cunning, now suggested they give him $135,000 so that he could continue funding Kinsey without making endless new applications. The meeting was for Gregg to judge Yerkes' man for himself.

It was a total success. Kinsey was his charismatic and convincing self. Gregg, convinced before he got there, found himself saying they would support him, as Kinsey instantly wrote and told Wells, on 'an unlimited scale for an indefinite time'.[45] At the Rockefeller Foundation's January 1944 meeting Gregg got Yerkes the $135,000. He was soon deeply involved in Kinsey's progress and never mentioned withdrawing funds again.

Buoyed up by the prospect of money, Kinsey immediately offered Bugbee a job, which he accepted,[46] and followed this when he got back by offering Nowlis one as well. Nowlis: 'Nothing I would rather do than join your great work.'[47]

There followed history trips to Chicago (the first in two years) in September/October, to St. Louis, Missouri (partly to see Anne) in November, and three weeks in New York in December.

There were also two events of future significance. He had a letter from Morris Ernst agreeing to be his attorney. This small, aggressive, energetic, quick-talking crusading lawyer was excited. The whole *firm* was excited. To champion Kinsey should be 'quite rare fun'.[48] (No doubt, therefore, Kinsey would have taken in the *Ulysses* case, which broke under Ernst's direction that December.)

And Kinsey had a letter from Gershon Legman about Kenneth S. Green, one of the most extraordinary sexual figures Kinsey would ever come across. When he and Pomeroy finally got his history in 1944 they were astounded – blasé as they then were.[49] Green had recently got in touch with Dickinson about the detailed, voluminous and meticulous record he kept of his life's work – which was, essentially, sex. From these records the three of them were compiling a definitive monograph on the penis – Legman's letter talks of Green's 'zealous care'.[50]

Mrs Glover wrote. Bob was in prison again for not paying a $15 fine. But she'd got him a job at the rolling mill, 'only about three squares from my home where he could have a hot dinner. I do hope everything works out for the best ... I hope you won't think I am terrible for writing you as you seemed such a nice person to talk to.'[51] In pencil, small lined pages.

Just before Kinsey left for New York, a large Thanksgiving turkey arrived from the Rev. James Jones. 'The turkey you sent was remarkably tender and rich in taste,' wrote Kinsey. 'It added that much more to my appreciation for the windswept hills of West Kansas.'[52]

In New York Kinsey and Pomeroy got a further 325 histories, continuing to quarry homosexuals and Jewish families. This brought the year's additions to a staggering 1,501 and the grand total to 4,861.[53] (Kinsey's number obsession is catching.)

Emily Mudd had written to him on 17 November and now, on 18 December, he addressed the American Association of Marriage Counselors, having dinner afterwards with Dickinson. He asked the lively old man to stay after Christmas and returned to Bloomington on 22 December.

7

Dickinson stayed at First Street for four days. Kinsey's daughter Joan remembers him well, as small, warm and vital. He would sit calmly, rapidly sketching. He and Kinsey talked sex almost the entire time (it was becoming more noticeable now that Kinsey wasn't really interested in talking about anything else[54]). Among other things, Dickinson probably discussed the lecture he was giving on vulvas at Philadelphia at the end of the year and certainly they must have talked about Green and the study of penises Dickinson, Green and Legman were engaged on.[55]

He left on 4 January, his thank-you letter ending 'Yours all ways' – one of many eccentric Dickinson signings off including 'Yours heartily', 'Yours ever more so', once 'More power to you! More ball bearings and personnel!'[56]

Hitherto, it has been possible to follow Kinsey fairly closely. From 1944 it ceases to be feasible. The press of engagements, lectures, letters, of numbers, all become, literally, overwhelming. Take two and a half weeks towards the end of the year, a busy period but not unusual and soon to be typical. Kinsey, Pomeroy and Martin arrive in Philadelphia on 28 November: 29th – Kinsey lectures to the University of Pennsylvania Medical School; 30th – to the Baldwin Schools (several schools in one room) and the Department of Psychology at Temple University; 1 December – University of Pennsylvania Faculty Research Club; 4th – probation officers and the university marriage course; 6th – Emily Mudd's marriage counsellors; 6th – to the Philadelphia Psychiatric Institute; 13th – Mudd's counsellors again; 14th – Wilmington Friends School; 15th–16th – to New York and Laidlaw's American Association of Marriage Counselors. (Lecture topics at the time – prostitution, masturbation, sexual factors in marital adjustment, patterns of sexual behaviour at diverse social levels, homosexuality, techniques of interviewing and analysis of data) ... and, packed in between, busy breakfasts, lunches, dinners, and of course, endless histories which he would go on taking up to twelve at night and the planned numbers of which he continually increased: 20,000 in January, 50,000 in June.[57] This volume of work increased steadily until late 1946–early '47, when he started to write the *Male* volume.

The pattern that had evolved by 1944 was three weeks away, usually with Pomeroy, sometimes Martin, soon Bugbee and Nowlis, three weeks at Bloomington, when the histories were processed, letters answered, state penal farms and prisons trawled, visitors shown round. And as Beach, Laidlaw, Emily Mudd, Dickinson, Lashley, Yerkes, and all the others in a steadily growing band of helpers accreting round him urged other scientists and influential figures to visit him, more and more did so – compelling Kinsey to work later and later into the night. By the time Nowlis arrived in June he was regularly working sixteen hours a day.

Unable to follow in detail, we can continue to indicate the chronological thread and we can pick out patterns. Mrs Glover writes almost for the last time. Bob has quit his job and been drinking ever since. He's been 'raving' and abusing her. Police. Her ulcerous leg. 'So Mr Kinsey if he happens back in the penal farm I am through with him.' They have four children. She is desperately poor.

Kinsey replies four days later, very concerned. 'If it were a question of sexual difficulty I might be able to give you a more expert answer. But when it is ... alcohol, someone else will have to take charge, although I'm not sure anyone knows the answer yet.'

I have followed this sad human story not because it was unusual but because it was typical. He received many letters like this, and far more about sexual pain and sexual catastrophe, and he always answered and tried to help. The last letter arrived from Rose Glover eight years later. Bob was dying of TB and in a terrible state. Could Kinsey send money for a bathrobe and cigs before he goes into hospital? 'You know we've been divorced ten years but that doesn't make any difference ... I still feel sorry for him.' But she forgot to give an address and Kinsey couldn't reply.[58]

Frank Beach came for four days in February 1944. He remembered Pomeroy's car – a jazzy convertible – and how his entire visit was scheduled hour by hour. Kinsey took him to Indianapolis, calmly entering dives which would have terrified Beach alone – 'Hi doc – gotta new history for you.' They talked solid sex research, or rather Kinsey talked while Beach listened, till 2.30 a.m., until exhausted, if fascinated, he begged to go to bed. 'Kinsey – "All right – I'll call you 6.30" – and he did.'

Kinsey had hardly begun to analyse the female data yet, but already, to his astonishment, another totally unexpected shape was emerging as the Hollerith cards whirred through the Monroe calculator. It had long been axiomatic that women (one had only to look at them) matured sexually before men, who in turn, the other *idée reçue*, reached their sexual peak at about forty. Kinsey now told Beach the opposite was true. Women were not fully sexually responsive till near thirty, while men reached their height at between fifteen and seventeen and then steadily declined.[59] These findings were to be modified slightly later (women staying on a plateau till their fifties for instance)[60] but remained essentially the same, prompting Paul Robinson to observe sadly that 'from a sexual standpoint, men and women were like ships passing in the night'.[61]

But the most interesting development in 1944 was Kinsey's increasing concentration on children.

8

I said earlier that like numbers of people who are uneasy in intimate relations with adults, Kinsey loved children and was very good with them. Henry Remak, a young colleague at IU, took a home movie in 1952 of a Kinsey staff picnic in Martin's garden. Kinsey is careering about grinning with Clyde's little girl *standing* on his shoulders.

By 1944 he had realised how extraordinarily early – three, four or five years old – sexual attitudes and responses (and therefore future happy or unhappy sex lives) start to develop. He decided they must investigate little children *directly* and not rely on adult memory of childhood. He found, however, that Pomeroy, Martin and, later, Paul

Gebhard were unable to develop the requisite empathy.[62] All this work, therefore, fell to him.

I am talking here of attitudes and feelings, not child sexuality and activity, a topic we'll come to. Kinsey had a favourite illustration. He was taking the sex history of a little girl. She had drawn a child for him. 'She poised her pencil over the genital area and said "I guess I'll make it a girl", and she didn't do anything.'[63] That is, she had *already* begun to absorb the idea that women had no sexual feelings or entity.

This was how he worked, with dolls, toys, drawings, games, puzzles, telling stories and eliciting them. He learnt how subtle and insidious the pressures were: the 'nervous amusement' of adults expressing approval which was really disapproval, the 'disdainful ridicule of other children', peers always the most important influence on attitudes – both things 'that even a three-year-old does not wish to experience again'. He partly blames the 'analysts' where, for instance, they class as masturbation what in small children is often just exploratory touching, gaining tactile experience. It is not masturbation till it is clear the child is purposefully 'reaping an erotic reward for his activity'. The discussion of all this in the *Male* volume is long, sensitive and acute.[64]

Kinsey, in Socratic mode once again, had an effect. 'Shortly after you left,' wrote Mrs Trend, 'Jane appeared flitting about the room naked . . . [announcing] jubilantly, "Now I can run around the house like this, because Dr Kinsey said I could."' Kinsey's reply, ignoring Jane, said, 'The nursery school has done a very significant thing introducing children to common toilets . . . [our research] shows that this has done a lot in the acceptance of sexual differences at a very early age.'[65]

Kinsey followed to the letter later 'standards' in these things,[66] but with small children, though parents were usually present, they were not invariably so, as Pomeroy asserts.[67] Ruth Weinberg arrived at the Bureau of Juvenile Research in Columbus, Ohio, as a newly trained psychologist in 1943. She had no task so they sent her along to see Dr Kinsey. To her amazement he sat her down and began to fire questions at her: 'I assumed that when you start work as a psychologist all your most intimate personal experiences are subject to question.' But she said during the two years she worked there Kinsey saw the children alone.[68]

The Ohio children ranged from five to eighteen, and it was with adolescents that one of Kinsey's most mystifying findings began now to emerge. Lifetime sexual patterns in males were set by sixteen/seventeen and never really altered.* But lower-level boys who were going to move up assumed the sexual pattern of the class above them *long before they moved.* A lower-level boy who was going to move up, already, by thirteen/fourteen/fifteen, was demonstrating the high masturbation/ low intercourse pattern of the level he would eventually reach. And the same was true, though less clearly, in reverse – upper-level adolescents destined to slip down the social scale were already manifesting lower-level patterns beforehand.[69] C. A. Tripp said Kinsey could predict future grades from early sexual patterns.[70]

How could this happen? It cannot have been parental pressure to adopt a 'smarter' sexual pattern, since no one knew the patterns existed till Kinsey found them. Paul Gebhard thought that lower-level men with high levels of intercourse were by definition extrovert. It was the reclusive, introverted ones who preferred to stay at home and work who were likely to go to college. They masturbated from this root *faute de mieux.*[71]

Some oblique confirmation of this comes from tests done in the 1960s/70s. Walter Mischel, a psychologist at Stanford University, gave a marshmallow each to four-year-olds, promising that anyone who didn't eat it would be given a second in twenty minutes. Some years later, he found that those who had resisted temptation had been academically far more successful than those who hadn't.

But this was more than a simple demonstration of powers of delayed gratification (the classic Victorian recipe for academic excellence). The marshmallow delayers did so by telling themselves stories, singing, tapping their feet, imagining the marshmallow was something else. That is, they demonstrated extra imaginative and behavioural complexity.[72] This in turn reflects back on another Kinsey finding, that nocturnal emissions, which one might suppose beyond conscious control, also correlate with educational attainment – 51 per cent of grade level boys having them compared to 91 per cent of college level. Kinsey speculated that more intelligent boys were more imaginative and so had more powerful dreams[73] – not the only indication that Kinsey was an elitist. The observation might elicit disapproval on these grounds alone, and

---

* Though there seems to be some inconsistency here with Kinsey's other finding that sexual (in particular) homosexual patterns did change over the years, with periods of homosexual outlet alternating or co-existing with heterosexual ones. It was this that made the idea of permanent sexual 'orientations' inaccurate; it was also the basis of the o–6 scale. (*Male,* pp. 610–66, especially p. 639.)

one should note, as well, that it assumes dream content precedes and causes the emission, whereas the contrary could be the case.

This begs to be pursued, but biographers cannot follow every detail in their subjects' lives – especially where sex is involved. But that shouldn't inhibit those whose business it is. Do these class patterns persist? As far as I know no one has bothered, or been able, to find out.

9

On 7 March 1944 Kinsey lectured to the Wistar Institute in Philadelphia. Lawrence (Larry) S. Saunders, president of the medical publisher, W. B. Saunders, was there and was deeply impressed. However, he was one of only three who didn't give his history. Kinsey wrote to him and Saunders agreed to give it later in the year.[74]

In April Kinsey learnt that the NRC would give him $25,000 – a small increase. And in May Yerkes asked him to evaluate a proposal that the NRC fund a research project to test if homosexuality was inherited. The clarity, power and sarcasm with which Kinsey demolished the entire project was devastating.[75] However, one can't help noticing his refusal to countenance any suggestion – however objectively put – that homosexuality might be anything other than a perfectly normal variant of sexual behaviour.

In June he was in Princeton, New Jersey, interviewing headmasters. Five of them, it turned out, were paedophiles.[76] Their histories had such a significant effect on Kinsey I will defer an examination until we look at this area a little later.

Then in June, Vincent Nowlis joined Bugbee, who'd already been there several months, as a second pair of 'hands'. It is time we had a look at what it was like working in what he later described as Kinsey's submarine. It will come as no surprise to learn that Kinsey ran a very tight ship indeed.[77]

Determined since early manhood to dominate any sphere in which he found himself, his domination now became total. Nowlis says he found a guru surrounded by disciples. There were staff discussion meetings, it is true (usually on Fridays), but these almost invariably took the form of a Kinsey lecture. The staff could express their views but everyone knew he had made up his mind and everyone knew his view would prevail.

He could delegate nothing. He answered all letters, however trivial, even (or especially) those addressed to other members of the team. He cornered all important interviews. He checked the smallest detail: 'We got sent porn books,' said Helen Wallin, who had previously held a number of responsible jobs. 'Dr Kinsey said send those ones back. I'd pack them. Then he'd come out and unpack them. To see if I'd packed them right! I'd get *mad* at him.' He'd check their arrival and departure – 'Gebhard, you came in at 8.12 yesterday.' (Paul Gebhard joined in 1946. The despotism hadn't altered an iota.)

Kinsey invaded their private life. He tried to get them to live near him (he found the Nowlises a house a few doors from his own). In his appointment diaries you find entries like this – 'Thursday 2.30. Martin dental appointment.' They all had to fill in sex calendars, detailing their orgasms and their source. (Gebhard is still keeping his today – at eighty.) He invaded their dreams. 'I would be about to have intercourse, might have begun,' said Gebhard. 'Suddenly the door would fly open and there would be Kinsey staring at me with this air of stern reproach. In every dream he would point at me and say "Gebhard!" He ruined more erotic dreams for me over the years than I like to remember.'

They could never win an argument. Pomeroy and Gebhard would plan their attack. Kinsey twisted, manoeuvred – and always defeated them. 'I never saw anyone get the better of him – and I doubt anyone could,' said Pomeroy. (Kinsey attributed his skill in argument, probably correctly, to the days at South Orange when his only weapons were verbal.) In the whole thirteen years he had a team, they mounted only one successful rebellion.

How did they take it? Some couldn't or wouldn't. In fact, Bugbee was already fed up by the time Nowlis arrived (he had been using Bloomington as a stepping stone east). Kinsey was to pursue numerous capable people, including Frank Beach, Glenn Ramsey and Nowlis after he'd left. They always refused. Scientists don't like despotisms. By 1950 Kinsey had gathered round him over a hundred people – Friends of the Research – in a series of concentric circles, who moved more or less close as he required their services. It is significant, as one of the band, Earle Marsh, noticed, that they were practically all younger than Kinsey.

There were tensions, especially when Kinsey relieved the strains of outside attacks by exercising his whip-like sarcasm; and even more so when Paul Gebhard arrived, an intellectually more substantial figure than the others.

At the same time, they remembered his sudden warmth, his smile when he returned from a trip – 'How *are* you?' 'You felt it was meant,' said Pomeroy. The despot's kindnesses are always craved, always loved – none the less it is true, it was a benevolent despotism. Kinsey was unfailingly polite. He was a kind man and if they had a genuine grievance he would listen and comply. He arranged staff picnics and luncheons, though it has to be said even the benevolence was sometimes tinged with dominance. His calculated generosity with Christmas presents was so excessive it embarrassed them – especially Martin. 'He would take us all out to lunch at the Tudor Room,' said Dorothy Collins, 'then without even asking would dump extra helpings of salad cream and dressing. What he liked was good for everyone.'

But the real point is, they were a completely dedicated band locked by a charismatic and administratively gifted leader into an enormous and dramatic task. Nowlis found a superbly efficient, smooth-running machine: 200–250 histories were processed each month, letters, visitors poured in, interviewers streamed out, long-distance telephone calls, telegrams . . . 'Pomeroy and Martin worked 10 or 12 hours or more, Kinsey often 18, five or six days a week.' And they were locked together as well by a common language and ritual, sometimes even conversing in code. The talk was entirely about the project or sex. 'We would talk very freely,' said Gebhard, 'since we knew each other's histories. Wardell could say "Dickinson says the clitoris disappears into what's around it, but I don't find that." I'd say, "Yes, when I stimulate my wife I'd say it swells if anything."' Or one of them would say his wife was having trouble with her masturbation. Kinsey occasionally joined in, but usually with one of his little lectures. Dorothy Collins said that one of the reasons she left several years later was the relentlessly sexual nature of the conversation.

So, ferocious hard work, a single focus, a benevolent autocrat – yet to what extent was Kinsey really in control? Beach said, 'His motivation? Basically, as a psychologist, my intuitive judgement is that Kinsey underneath it all was a fairly rigid person. He was extremely compulsive. I don't think it was clear whether he ran his research or his research ran him.'

Someone in whom it was crystal clear that they were run by their 'research' was Kenneth S. Green. It is time to look closer at this curious figure.

10

A secret life must not leave out anything; there is nothing to be ashamed of
... one can never know too much concerning human nature
                                        My Secret Life, anon., New York, 1966

There have, historically, been a small number of men of quite exceptionally, astonishingly strong libido whose resulting obsession with (and
overriding need for) sexual release has driven them to write detailed
books or diaries about their activities. One thinks of de Sade, Casanova,
the anonymous Victorian author of *My Secret Life*.

It is not surprising that some men* of this sort got in touch with
Kinsey after *Male* was published. But the most extraordinary of them
was before this – Kenneth S. Green. He, in fact, got in touch with Robert
Dickinson in 1943, who told Kinsey about him. In 1944, Green was
sixty-three.

He was, essentially, an obsessive recorder. Not just of sex. In his
rooming house he will look through a knot-hole. A woman is gargling
with Listerine. Braun notes it.[78] But since his life consisted almost
entirely in a highly excited and urgent pursuit of sex with boys and girls,
men and women, animals, even mechanical devices, the diaries are full
of this – in literally thousands of case histories and autobiographical
accounts. (The whole colossal work was typed by Mac. She didn't finish
till 1956.)

The record takes two forms. It is clear that, as with the historical
figures mentioned above, recording what happened – erotic description
– was a way of experiencing it a second time. But – like a distorted mir-
ror-image of Kinsey himself – Green was equally obsessed with recording the exact physical proportion of everything he experienced: length
and circumference of penises, time to reach orgasm, duration of it and
intensity, volume of semen, distance of ejaculation. I take only male
characteristics since Kinsey used some of these, but Green did the same

---

* There are women with equally strong, or stronger, sex drive, but they do not
seem to keep diaries. Paul Gebhard thinks it is because, while men have been
proud to be so driven, women have been ashamed. Perhaps this will now change.
Yet, who knows they have not kept them? Diaries have been coming into the
Kinsey Institute for the last fifty years. They are coming still. They fill a small
room. One stretches an entire shelf. Many have not been opened since the day
they arrived. There is a thesis here.

for women. Operating as he did in the sexual equivalent of the front line he had evolved various rules of thumb – literally, sometimes: thus his thumb measured 2.5″, a standard cigarette was 2.75″, an ordinary teaspoon held 5cc and could be used 'to scrape semen off a body'.

By such means he compiled elaborate and detailed statistical tables. (He was a university graduate in government employ, possibly a forester at one time, and seems to have had some form of scientific training. Details from the Kinsey Institute are kept deliberately vague.) For instance, out of 1,200 penis measurements, taken from men aged sixteen to seventy-seven, the longest was a 37-year-old white man's at 10.2″, diameter 2.4″; the shortest was 2″ erect, but diameter 3″ – that of a 27-year-old American Indian. The mean was 6.14″.* Green from his years of experience, said that a large penis brought happiness from increased self-confidence; but men with small penises were more active sexually since they were determined to prove they were as good sexually as (they imagined, often wrongly) men with large ones.

But Green didn't only observe, sexually excite and measure men and women; he did the same with 317 pre-adolescent boys (I will look at girls later). 'Pre-adolescent' is perhaps misleading. Green seems to have done a lot of babysitting; he also persuaded a good number of mothers with whom he had sex to co-operate, lending them his stopwatch.

---

* As with so much in this inexact field, penis length seems to depend on your authority. Kinsey, too, with 4,000 self-taken measurements, gave the average as 6.3″. But oddly enough only in letters (here to a J. Healey, 24 March 1948). The figure appears in neither of the *Reports*. But if you follow the encyclopaedic Edgar Gregerson the average seems 'generally' to measure 4″ with 14″ the 'maximum reliably recorded'. Recently, researchers at the University of San Francisco injected sixty men with an erection-producing drug and measured the results. The average erect penis was 12.8 centimetres, or just over 5 inches. But there are some unusual and interesting data, based on Kinsey's findings but not published, that homosexuals have penises between a quarter and a third of an inch longer than heterosexuals. This has been corroborated since by the Czech researcher Jan Raboch, where in a study of 20,000 Czechs he found homosexuals' penises exceeded those of heterosexuals by 10 per cent in length and 8 per cent in circumference. I learnt about this late and didn't have time to read the two studies. I cite them only after discussion with Dr C. A. Tripp. One would like to know a) if homosexuals have, as I suppose, a more intense interest in the penis and b) whether or not this affects self-measurement. (p. 52, *Sexual Practices: The Story of Human Sexuality*, Edgar Gregerson, Mitchell Beazley, London, 1982; a report in *New Scientist*, 6 May 1995, p. 9; for unpublished figures in connection with Bell and Weinberg, see Bell, Weinberg and Raboch, 1981, in the Bibliography.)

He masturbated, and got the mothers to masturbate, twenty-eight children from two months to a year, and similar numbers for each year up to the age of fifteen. He gathered a great deal of material: orgasm, physiologically identical with adult orgasm except for ejaculation, began as early as five months; between two and five years half of Green's subjects could reach orgasm. He recorded multiple orgasms from five months to fifteen years; the more, the younger the child. He described in detail the varied physiological reactions to orgasm, which were sometimes extreme: 'legs often become rigid with muscles knotted and toes pointed, muscles of abdomen contracted and hard . . . breath held or gasping; eyes staring . . .'

This particular account, only much longer, was used by Kinsey verbatim.[79] In fact he lifted large chunks of Green's pre-adolescent material and it furnished a considerable proportion of Chapter 5, 'Early Sexual Growth and Activity', in the *Male* volume.[80]

The question arises – should he have done this? It is an interesting reflection on the changing fashion of concern that this chapter is almost the only one that was totally ignored on publication.[81] Vincent Nowlis, at the time, was quite clear – Kinsey should not use the material. Not so much because he, Nowlis, disapproved of Green, which he did, but because he thought it was scientifically disreputable.

Kinsey totally and flatly disagreed with him. Dickinson and Legman, working with Green on the penis monograph, vouched for his scientific accuracy. The material was unique and was impossible to replicate. This, to a large extent, is still true. Floyd M. Martinson did a study in 1972 and found that most children have the capacity for self-stimulation to orgasm by the age of five. No one would publish his work and he had to do so himself.[82] Professor Timothy Taylor of Bradford University cites recent authorities on ultrasound images of a baby boy masturbating in the womb, and for finding that the *average* age for children to be observed starting masturbation in the West is 18 months.[83]

Kinsey/Green have, therefore, been at last partially substantiated as to the fact. My own view, for what it is worth, is that Kinsey cannot be blamed for using the material. What one can say is that he should have stated clearly where it came from and the possibly uneven nature of the sources his authority used. Instead – and one can understand why – he buried Green among the nine paedophiles, the work Ramsey had done at Peoria, the pre-adolescent memories of large numbers of male case histories, and some mothers of little children, all of whom also contributed to the chapter. It is one of the very few times it is to some extent possible to impugn Kinsey's scientific integrity.*

This also raises the further question of Kinsey's attitude to child-adult sex in general. At its most basic Kinsey saw sex as simply a matter of physiological reactions and sensations which were fundamentally pleasant. It followed that anything else, or anything adverse (guilt, fear, dislike, inhibition), had to be learnt and were human and social additions which had nothing inherently to do with any sexual act itself. Theoretically, therefore, as far as Kinsey was concerned, there was nothing automatically wrong with child-adult sex.[84]

None the less, this was one area, he told Glenway Wescott, that when he started out shocked him. He thought he would have 'to fake tolerance to get the history'.[85] Actually, as we saw, he didn't even do that. He told them to stick to adults. However, he went on to Wescott, and it is interesting to observe how he *learnt* to be tolerant, as time passed he began to notice that in histories with child 'abuse' the subjects of it disapproved – but actually in their cases it had done no harm. He noticed how it was often the poor, unloved boys whose only affection came from such contacts. Then he was deeply impressed by the four paedophile headmasters' relationships.[86] The upshot was that, to put it no higher, Kinsey always, to use Robinson's words, put in a good word for the molesters – pointing out, that the 'molesters' were frequently impotent old men not interested in anything but an affectionate cuddle, or that the subjects sometimes enjoyed these encounters.[87]

It should go without saying, but should nevertheless perhaps be said, that Kinsey was fiercely against any use of force or compulsion in sex. And there are cross-cultural examples which support his stance on child-adult sex. Until very recently, the military organisation of the

* His use of Green's findings formed the basis of recent attacks on Kinsey so scurrilous and shoddy in manner (equating him with Mengele for instance) and so ludicrous in argument – ignoring the fact that all the material was collected many years before Kinsey had even heard of Green – that it neither deserves nor requires refutation. It seems that the religious Right in America attributes all the liberal development of the last fifty-odd years, which it so hates, to Kinsey and thinks that if it can destroy Kinsey everything it hates will vanish. As idiotic, John Gagnon said recently, as supposing that if you could prove Jesus was a child molester somehow Christianity would vanish. More disturbing, since it did not have the excuse of the same ideological platform, was the equally shoddy TV film put out by Channel 4 in their series *Secret Lives* in 1998 which took essentially the same line. (*Kinsey, Sex and Fraud*, Judith A. Reisman et al., Lochinvar-Huntingdon, 1990; John Gagnon, interview, BBC TV series *Reputations*, 1995; Channel 4 *Secret Lives*, 1998.)

Zande in central Africa, where homosexuality is widespread and accepted, allowed their soldiers to take boy-wives, sometimes as young as twelve, often for years, as a matter of course. It was not regarded as remotely wrong or disgusting.[88] The same sort of thing was true of the armies in ancient Greece, in Sparta and Crete.[89] And throughout the Middle East, particularly in Morocco and Egypt, young boy prostitution has been common for centuries and still is.[90]

But the primacy Kinsey gives to attitude and custom also means you cannot simply transpose these examples from central Africa or ancient Sparta into North America or Western Europe. The trouble with adult-child sex, as everyone knows, is that it is almost impossible to know when pressure has compelled children into acts they didn't want. You certainly can't take the word of paedophile headmasters. In this area, the proviso in Kinsey that no one should be forced or harmed is there, but it is weak. He is very ready to believe they will *not* be harmed and have *not* been forced.*

It is possible to discern at work here, as well as Kinsey's on the whole admirable tolerance going somewhat over the top, the Puritan idealisation of the individual conscience, so powerful an element in American culture in general and particularly so in Americans of Puritan

---

* Events today in this field are perhaps not wholly relevant, but one wonders what Kinsey would have made of them. Increased concern with the subject has resulted in a good number of horrifying paedophile cases being unearthed and Kinsey would have been as appalled as anyone. On 'recovered memory syndrome' I guess he would veer to 'implanted memory syndrome'. He would certainly notice some of the classic signs of a witchhunt – the isolation of paedophiles, reviled by gays, heterosexuals, lesbians alike, the forgetting that they are also human beings. The air of general hysteria, the mere fact that everyone was against it, would have irritated him and brought out again, as it did in his own day, that pugnacity that was probably as much at the root of his attitude as tolerance. In 1950 the FBI was talking about a 'terrifying increase in sex crimes' and similarly stirring up public hysteria. Kinsey wrote impatiently, 'The FBI's figures are based on records of arrests and, consequently, merely reflect police activity. What the country is calling heinous crimes against children are things that appear in a fair number of our histories.' Kinsey, who often looked to Europe for a lead, would also have taken note of the much more relaxed attitude in one European country. In the Netherlands sexual intercourse, homosexual and heterosexual, is legal for and with anyone over 12, provided there is mutual consent. 'Child abuse,' said the Amsterdam police spokesman Klaas Witting in 1990, 'is not a problem in Dutch society – three, four, five cases a year.' (*The Independent on Sunday*, 18 November 1990, Home, p. 5; Kinsey to M. Feinstock, 24 February 1950; *FBI Law Enforcement Bulletin*, February 1950 issue.)

upbringing. What Richard Webster calls 'the Puritan tendency to transfer the doctrine of scriptural inerrancy from the "Bible without" to the "Bible within" of the individual human being'.[91]

At any rate Kinsey's encounter with Green's work, where this discussion started, left him with an urgent desire to see him and get his history – a desire which by mid-1944 had become even stronger because he kept fearing Green might die. It took a good deal of arranging but finally the omniphile agreed to see him at a secret point fifty miles from his home. Kinsey and Pomeroy set off in the middle of June.

11

They drove the old Buick south to Memphis, Tennessee, and then deeper and deeper towards Albuquerque, New Mexico. It was still very hot.

I can do no better than copy the Pomeroy/Tebbel account of what they heard when they got there.

> When we got the record after a long drive to take his history, it astounded even us, who had heard everything. This man [Green] had had homosexual relations with 600 pre-adolescent males, heterosexual relations with 200 pre-adolescent females, intercourse with countless adults of both sexes, with animals of many species, and besides had employed elaborate techniques of masturbation. He had set down a family tree going back to his grandparents, and of thirty-three family members he had had sexual contacts with seventeen. His grandmother introduced him to heterosexual intercourse, and his first homosexual intercourse was with his father . . . At the time we saw him, this man was 63 years old, quiet, soft-spoken, self-effacing – a rather unobtrusive fellow . . . At one point in his history-taking he said he was able to masturbate to ejaculation in ten seconds from a flaccid start. Kinsey and I knowing how much longer it took everyone else, expressed our disbelief, whereupon our subject calmly demonstrated it to us.[92]

It took them both seventeen hours to record the history, while Green refreshed his memory from his enormous diary. Then four days later they left, arriving back in Bloomington on 7 October. They had driven 3,141 miles and 'felt', said Pomeroy, 'that it had been worth every mile'.

12

Nowlis began trainee interviewing, just as Bugbee gave up. Numbers continued to rise – 6,100 by July.

It was not all plain sailing. Thurman Rice still fulminated in public whenever he got a chance. In fact, he and Kinsey had recently bumped into each other by chance in Indianapolis and at once got into an argument. Suddenly Rice said, 'I guess the only way I'll learn what's in a history is to give my own.' He did so, but unlike most people did not succumb and remained bitterly opposed.[93] (Rice, incidentally, was a popular, burly, happy-go-lucky rough diamond – 'a hick as to the English language', according to Edith Schuman.[94])

Dean Kate Mueller, still smarting over her passage with Kinsey over the marriage course, returned to the attack this year, telling Wells that Kinsey was now interviewing girls in the IU dormitories and there would be an explosion if it were not stopped. Wells soothed her with his usual adroit charm.[95]

But a more significant row broke in July/August. As soon as the Rockefeller Foundation began to support him, Kinsey dropped its name wherever he could – that is, everywhere. In July, Alan Gregg told Yerkes that 'someone' had recently addressed a gathering of headmasters in Princeton (the paedophiles among them) on 'A New Research Program Supported by the Rockefeller Foundation and Indiana University'. Gregg was appalled. He gave various reasons, but in fact he did not want the Rockefeller, a tax-exempt foundation, taking sex research flak. The NRC must do this. At the same time he didn't want Kinsey to feel his support was waning – hence the 'someone'.

Yerkes agreed. He himself was also worried by something else – Kinsey's reckless use of his results to enliven his lectures, instead of waiting in the somewhat more accepted scientific mode for accredited publication. He wrote a sharp letter to Kinsey on both matters – particularly stressing that the NRC must be the acknowledged official body who would deal with enquiries.

Kinsey's response was interesting, and reveals the same furiously wounded reaction he had when, over the marriage course, he'd failed to see Wells was trying to help him. He simply assumed Yerkes was jealous. After admitting he'd given the talk (but not the title) he wrote a passionate, highly emotional personal letter to Alan Gregg begging for support. Did the Rockefeller Foundation wish to repudiate him? Did Gregg not realise the terrifying amount of work they were doing – the harassment, the colossal effort of seeing tens of thousands of people, the sixteen hours a day, six days a week, required to get where they now were, with 6,300 histories? If they wished to support him they must be prepared to defend him.

Kinsey won (he may later have wished he hadn't). Gregg, clearly moved, made significant concessions: Kinsey must say the money came from the NRC, but he could say the Rockefeller Foundation supplied the NRC and also approved of what Kinsey was doing. Kinsey, therefore, continued exactly as before and also completely ignored Yerkes' strictures about unpublished material.

But the row showed how difficult it might be, if it came to the crunch, to have both the NRC and the Rockefeller Foundation identified with his work. Eventually, it did come to the crunch – and proved impossible.[96]

13

In October, during one of their visits to the Bureau of Juvenile Research in Columbus, Ohio, Vincent Nowlis suddenly stopped interviewing. Kinsey wrote at once to Yerkes, who was 'amazed and puzzled'.[97]

Nowlis' letter to Yerkes, sent just before Kinsey's on 21 October, is a good deal more pointed, if enigmatic. 'My training and background have proved to be in sharp conflict with the requirements for history-taking in this project . . . [At Columbus] it became very clear that the complete role of interviewer . . . was basically incompatible with any role I am prepared to assume and maintain.'[98]

What went wrong? Pomeroy said that, first, Nowlis didn't approve of Kinsey using, in publication, material obtained from Green. Second, Nowlis was ill at ease taking homosexual histories. Martin agreed: 'We could see beads of sweat on his upper lip.'[99]

Nowlis' own account is rather different. He confirmed that Kinsey felt that he was uneasy with homosexuals and about his lack of sexual experience generally. He arranged for Nowlis to see a homosexual sex show in Indianapolis with him and the team. Then late one night when they were all in Columbus, Ohio, he asked Nowlis to come to his hotel bedroom. Nowlis found Pomeroy and Martin there too. Kinsey, kind but concerned, repeated what he had already said, and added that it was his view that good interviewing could only come from someone with actual experience of some of the various forms of sexual activity with which they were being presented. Nowlis badly needed homosexual experience and he, Kinsey and the team, would help him here.

J.G-H.: 'You mean – you were to have sex with them?'
Nowlis: 'Yes.'

Nowlis said that later he realised this was meant as a 'nurturing experience', and indeed he now felt Kinsey was correct – this *was* the best way, if it could be arranged, to train interviewers to get at the truth in the difficult area of homosexuality.

At the time, however, he was shocked. His feeling about sex then (and now) was that it 'requires previous love – first love, then sex'. He told Kinsey, ' "I feel like going back home to see my family." And I took the train back rather than wait for the Buick.'[100]

On 26 October Kinsey wrote again to Yerkes about Nowlis: '. . . it is lack of experience with groups outside an academic circle that is the problem.'[101] A somewhat economical description of what had happened.

Racing for the Male Report: 1944–7

1

It is perfectly possible, even likely, that as well as wishing to help Nowlis become more at ease with homosexual activity, Kinsey was attracted to him. I noticed how emphatic Pomeroy's account in his biography was about Nowlis' physical appearance – describing him as 'personable' at one point and 'this attractive young man' at another.[1]

But whatever had passed between him and Kinsey left no ill-feeling. Nowlis, who later went on to have a long and distinguished career at the University of Rochester, continued to work on the project for over six months analysing and processing data. He was soon to help correct the *Male* volume. He remained fond of Kinsey, admired and supported him and, as I said earlier, only refused to rejoin him because he felt Kinsey was too dominant a boss. 'I wanted my own ship.'

2

Meanwhile, back at the ranch, so to speak, in Bloomington, work proceeded in what Kinsey once described to Nowlis as 'a continuous whirr'.[2]

In November, to his surprise, another large turkey arrived in time for Thanksgiving from the Nicodemus pastor, the Rev. Jim Jones.

Then on 27 November the team, now minus Bugbee and Nowlis, launched into the packed Philadelphia/New York three weeks I have already outlined.

It was here that Kinsey finally took Lawrence Saunders' history. He also saw a certain amount of Dickinson. The vigorous old man (at eighty-three 'kinda proud,' Nowlis remembered, 'that he could still get an orgasm or two per year with the help of his long-time assistant'[3]) was at this time pursuing another of his pet enthusiasms, mentioned earlier, the sex history of an exceptionally highly sexed woman. Dickinson had probably heard of Alice Dent from Robert Laidlaw, whom she had just joined at the American Association of Marriage Counselors. She was an amusing and lively young woman but seems to have deliberately mis-understood Dickinson. 'I was tremendously surprised,' she had written to him in September, 'at your offer of $100 for a completely worked up sexual history of myself.' She thought she could write it up but – in what form?[4] *Write* it up! This was not at all what Dickinson had in mind and he was to pursue Alice Dent for two years.

It is necessary, in view of the slight aura of farce that can hover round Dickinson, to remember his genuine concern for women and his labours on their behalf – against the stereotypes of the period, in relation to their sexual pleasures, menstrual troubles and so on. He was also a pioneering crusader for birth control and frank sex education.

Nevertheless, farce was uppermost at State College Philadelphia. The three-day conference at Pennsylvania State University was the largest professional gathering Kinsey had so far addressed. But almost as much interest had been aroused by Dickinson's lecture, which Kinsey attended, where he was at last to unveil the results of his massive study into the physical effects of masturbation on the sex organs of women.

The lecture hall was absolutely packed (I paraphrase Pomeroy's – or rather John Tebbel's – very funny account here[5]). Dickinson began at once, tapping the floor sharply when he wanted a slide changed. Unfortunately, the young male projectionist, a university employee, had not been told the nature of the talk, and as one after another of Dickinson's hugely magnified vulvar studies sprang on to the screen, he became unnerved. He muddled the slides and dropped them; they began to appear upside down, back to front and sideways. Dickinson became more and more agitated and impatient, banging his pointer and shout-ing 'No! NO! *Not* that way!'

Confusion grew, there were louder and louder sounds of desperately stifled and hysterical laughter from the distinguished figures present, when all at once, now seriously panicking, the projectionist somehow picked up a slide from a previous lecture and, to the astonishment of everyone, there suddenly appeared a panoramic and peaceful view of wheat waving in the wind in Kansas.

It says much for the respect in which Dickinson was held and his grip on his audience that he was able, eventually, to continue.

Kinsey, incidentally, despite their friendship, refused to countenance any of this nonsense. Some years later when Dickinson sent him an article on the subject he briskly and totally demolished it – there was no causal relation, all the changes had taken place first, besides which, how on earth did he expect to tell anything from five cases?[6]

It was after Kinsey's second lecture at this conference that a young editor at Doubleday, John Tebbel, took his friend Vance Packhard, Kinsey, Pomeroy and some others back to his hotel room. Tebbel got on very well at once with Kinsey and Pomeroy and they stayed up talking till 3 a.m. 'I realised,' said Tebbel, 'that something very exciting and very important was underway.'[7] Tebbel was to become very close to the research and he eventually ghostwrote Pomeroy's biography for him.

Kinsey's letters to Mac when away on these trips are short and follow an invariable pattern: he loves her, an account of what histories they are taking and his lectures, promises he is getting enough rest and sleep (Mac was understandably already worrying about this), he loves her – and that's that. On the Philadelphia/New York trip this year he was so busy he delegated Pomeroy to write to her: 'He still loves you very much and would be writing himself if it weren't for the other work.'[8]

Kinsey was back in Bloomington for Christmas, in time to start dictating letters again on 26 December.

3

In 1945 Kinsey officially announced to the NRC the final goal he had in fact fixed on some time before – 100,000 histories. It would take twenty years.

His idea was that he would take the 200–300 or so major social subgroups and get from 400 to 1,000 in each – something he called 'stratified sampling'. But in fact, Kinsey made no effort to find out which groups were 'major'; he simply assigned his histories, after he had taken them, to various groups which he had often invented. Thus this year janitors, porters and maids were lumped together as a significant social group. It was really a rationalisation of his gall method of grabbing as many histories from as many places and levels as he could, hoping (a) that like galls he would form a huge reservoir from which many future studies could be written; and (b) that huge numbers would solve everything now as they had then.

Once again he criss-crossed America: Topeka, Kansas; Santa Fe, New Mexico; Princeton, New Jersey; Cleveland and Columbus, Ohio (children); six solid weeks in New York in November/December; a month in Philadelphia; Indiana penal farms and women's prisons ... the team added more histories this year than ever before – 2,668.[9]

He started off February/March 1945 with six weeks in Chicago and New York, lecturing, among many others, to five psychiatric groups (he already had the histories of 150 psychiatrists[10]). He took Mac with him to New York – and there is something touching, so rare was this, how she still remembered the trip twenty-five years later.[11]

While Kinsey was in Chicago, Dean Kate Mueller pounced again. She rapped out a memo to Wells on 17 February: the mother of one of her girls now at the University of Chicago, a Mrs Fred Hugill, had complained, not at the taking of a history, but at Kinsey volunteering information like 'a very large percentage of college girls were not ignorant of sexual experience'. Wells scribbled on the memo – 'see Kinsey on return'.[12]

Back home, Kinsey had a distasteful task to perform. For some time he had been employing Gershon Legman, the bibliographer who had worked with Dickinson and Green on the penis, to go through the New York Academy of Medicine and New York Public Library and send him lists of books connected with sex. According to Bill Dellenback, he had discovered that Legman, an irascible, difficult and extremely egotistical man, chronically short of money, had 'allegedly', in Dellenback's words, been inventing titles and authors of books for Kinsey to purchase and then charging considerable fees. In fact, it seems that Dellenback was probably maligning Legman. What Kinsey accused Legman of was not doing work he had asked him to do. Legman also wanted more money and to be paid under the table to avoid taxes. They were also arguing about Kinsey's invented system of bibliographic cards (all Kinsey's librarians argued about this). But the upshot was that Kinsey sacked him. Unfortunately, as often happened when he was angry, his vocabulary wobbled. Instead of saying, as he meant, that Legman had been 'mulcting' the funds, he wrote 'mulching' – a mistake Legman gleefully and sarcastically pounced on.[13]

However, on his return, he also found that Nowlis, working in Bloomington, was now proving 'very definitely valuable . . . in the process of analysing our data', Kinsey told Yerkes, just after telling him they'd reached 7,500 histories on 4 February.[14] Nowlis' keen eye rapidly spotted the sort of errors and anomalies which, had he stayed, might have been eliminated, particularly in the figures for old-age sex, which bored Kinsey because there was so little of it. For instance, Nowlis pointed out how: 'The interesting reversals in the female curves at [age] 80 and 85' was entirely due to 'the two active little old Negro ladies in the High Plains . . . What price statistical glory!'[15]

But mostly it was continuous, dawn-to-dusk, very hard work. Pomeroy describes Kinsey's workload this year as 'unbelievable'.[16] It is worth pausing a moment to see how he sustained these pressures.

4

Paradoxically, one of the things that kept Kinsey going was also the most exhausting – his lecturing. He had always enjoyed this; he enjoyed the buzz of adrenaline, the praise, the power. This last could backfire, as Pomeroy noted. If he had a hostile audience, he would dominate them, they would comply with histories – and three days later resent it.

It happened this year. Suddenly, Kinsey realised he had far too great a preponderance of lower-level blacks. He therefore went to the all-black Howard University, only to find after his lecture a resentful resistance to histories. He realised why – a *white* man was getting black histories for a *white* book. They also resented the division white/black. Kinsey said he made dozens of divisions, an explanation angrily dismissed. 'Now we're going to do this project no matter what happens,' Kinsey said finally, 'and you should know that we already have a large body of histories from lower-level Negroes. When we publish our findings, we will be careful to state that these *are* lower-level histories, but people won't remember that. The only way to correct this impression is for you to co-operate so we can get the whole spectrum.' Reluctantly, the upper-level black audience did so.[17]

But resistance was rare. For one thing, as I've said, just to hear penis, clitoris, orgasm spoken straight out in public, electrified and exhilarated people. 'You'd be sitting up there on the platform with him,' said Nowlis, 'and there would be intentness and tension. There would be surprise – and then dismay that someone with prestige was talking about such things.'[18] And it was a subject that aroused emotion. Kinsey was by now very good at it; so familiar was he with his material that he seemed to improvise. And to an extent he did, feeding in new discoveries, *pace* Yerkes, as they emerged, so they were almost as fresh to him as to his listeners.

Then, with his resonant voice (often pushing aside a microphone other speakers had needed[19]), he was dramatic, colourful. Frank Beach described how, if he had a wall-length blackboard behind him, which he often did, he would start at the end with one orgasm a month and then slowly walk along, the line very gently rising – an orgasm every three weeks, two weeks, a week – slowly rising until, at the end, he'd suddenly throw his arm as high as he could reach, to the peak – the individuals, usually lawyers or distinguished scientists, who had had twenty-five or thirty orgasms a week for twenty-five years. 'This was the sort of thing he did,' said Beach, 'and did very, very well. I think he was a superb lecturer.'[20] What amused him, Kinsey told Mrs Edmondson, was how he could tell the orgasm rates of his audience from their expressions: 'They would get this disbelieving look as he passed their particular rate.'[21]

But the feelings he stirred were more profound than astonishment or fascination. Just as he was lifting guilt, inhibition and ignorance from individual homosexuals, masturbating girls and youths, non-orgasmic women or inept male lovers, so he did this collectively in his lectures – and this pleased him too. 'There was a glow about him,' said Henry Remak.[22]

But Kinsey also benefited from and employed a range of more or less conscious strategies to keep going. If the fundamental pedagogic element in his character responded to his lectures, the equally strong scientific one was charged and sustained by a direct current of genuine insights. In addition, he carefully alternated concentrated work with work that was easier. He told Glenway Wescott how important the gap at supper was, when he talked family trivialities before returning to the laboratory to work through the night.[23]

Every now and again he was able to get out to concerts or plays. He continued, if rarely, to go to burlesque shows; to the Rialto in Chicago (twice in 1945), the Old Howard in Boston, the Fox Theatre in Indianapolis. But this was now also in the line of business and, with his customary thoroughness, Kinsey listed the references to, for instance, balls (3), goosing (1), foreskin, condoms, marital troubles, pelvic thrusts, kiss-my-ass, fuck-a-duck and, in the end, Kinsey himself.[24]

He both relieved tensions and fired himself up by talking to colleagues. Whenever Frank Beach (among many, many others) saw him, Kinsey launched into what he was doing. Even during a musicale, while

Sibelius was playing, he 'drew me apart to talk sex research'. In New York he'd ask Beach to the Hotel Astor (only once did he go to Beach's hotel) and 'the upshot was not that I told him what I was doing, but he told me what he was doing; I liked it because I learned a lot.' He didn't feel he was a sounding board. 'Kinsey just wanted to talk about what he was doing.'[25]

Then, Kinsey was enjoying himself. A very common feature of depression is the person who floods themselves with work to drown all other feelings. There is no evidence this was true of Kinsey. 'He was doing,' said Pomeroy, 'what he most wanted to do.' He became depressed at the end of his life, but there were good reasons for this.

He steadily widened the scope of the research, rekindling enthusiasm as the prospect of each new field opened. This happened particularly from 1948 on, as the project became wealthy; but even now he was buying more and more books to do with sex. From 1943 he spent 'hours' in secondhand bookshops, according to Pomeroy.[26]

The 1945 *Progress Report* plans nine complete volumes: the two preliminary ones, at this point called *Sexual Outlet in the Human Male* and *Female*, and then *Sexual Outlet in the Negro*, and volumes on sex offenders, the heterosexual-homosexual balance, marriage, sexual adjustment in institutions and prostitutes.

Just as with galls Kinsey had had people sending specimens from all over the world, so now his network began to reach out from America. He asked Dickinson to get him 'a list of the signs in Italian brothels'; Dickinson responded with a man, Van Hecht, who would get him data from China.[27] And Glenn Ramsey now regularly sent back information from the front, writing about the ease of sex in war-ravaged Europe (a woman for a packet of cigarettes). The GIs, he told Kinsey this April, 'say the French are a funny people – they fuck with their mouth and fight with their feet'. Later, he says the word for oral sex from a woman is 'blow job'.[28] Kinsey's later perception that Europe was a paradise of sexual freedom seems to date from this period.

And, of course, Kinsey kept up his main defences against overwork, his garden and his music. But with the new three-week programmes, this had at a stroke been halved.

The reason they chose three weeks is that this was the most they could stand. The effect of the intense concentration required in a history, closely following individual after individual for anything from one to four or exceptionally five hours, eight or nine hours a day, can be imagined. Martin used to feel he had been 'pulled through the eye of a needle'.[29] Lectures, as well as exhilarating, exhausted.

Despite all his prophylactics, as 1945 got under way, for the first time Kinsey began to falter.

5

Kinsey was to be fifty-one in June, and in a very heavy year, the first few months were not the lightest, as I've already indicated.

The climax came at the end of April. Although Kinsey's only real concern with the war had been to keep his men out of the draft (even the atom bomb, to which he was himself to be compared, failed to ruffle his correspondence), he had none the less been irritated for some time that his expertise had not been called on. Many of his findings – especially on homosexuals and prostitutes (and so VD) – were highly relevant. Now, he got his chance.

In June the previous year Kinsey had spent a week at Menninger's well-known psychiatric clinic at Topeka, Kansas. Brigadier General William C. Menninger was chief psychiatrist to the Army. He put Kinsey in touch with Colonel Thomas B. Turner of the Surgeon General's office. As a result of this meeting and considerable correspondence, Turner got the NRC to arrange a conference for top figures in the Army and Navy, but including representatives from the US Public Health Service and the American Social Hygiene Association and, of course, the NRC.

Over two long, very demanding days Kinsey addressed them: the Army on 26 April, the Navy on the 27th. He displayed his whole programme, partly, he told Yerkes, in order to educate the NRC Committee. He responded to anxious questioning on 'sexual abnormality': sexual patterns were set for most men by age sixteen, so the services would have no significant effect here, besides which, most sexual deviations were common, perfectly normal and no threat to military discipline. As a result, using Kinsey's work as a guide, the military put in train their own investigations into sex.[30]

Kinsey returned to Bloomington on 28 April completely exhausted. On 29 April he collapsed, just as Nowlis had finally left. Pomeroy (partially backed by Kinsey) says he now spent several weeks in bed.[31] He certainly should have done this, but in fact he was up by 5 May, since his appointment diary shows him at Indiana State Farm all that week. And he was in New York again from 14 May to 6 June, and yet again from the end of June to 13 July.

No wonder he told Yerkes he was still very tired at the end of that month. He was trying to do more in the garden and getting Mac to help him elsewhere. He also hoped writing the *Male* volume, soon to begin, would be less exhausting.[32] He missed Nowlis a lot[33] (Nowlis was now at Iowa State University in the Child Welfare Research Station), and in August, when Bugbee left, Kinsey was back to himself, Martin and Pomeroy. He wrote anxiously to Dickinson in pursuit of 'hands'.

None of this was yet very serious. Money improved – the grant increased to $28,000, his salary to $5,750. Numbers increased – 8,800 by July, 9,500 by the end of October.[34] On 3 August, a Dr Carpenter sent him some gall studies to check, which Kinsey returned on 20 September.[35] For a moment, it must have felt rather strange.

By mid-September he was back on full throttle and, amidst the 'whirr' of histories and lectures, was grappling with Kenneth S. Green's study of the penis.

6

In October, Kinsey was sent the first Army-sponsored sex investigation; the subject – VD. The text is heavily marked in red in his hand where he agrees or disagrees. For instance, he questions the non-use of the car as a locale for sex, and below that he has underlined 'half the Negroes matured sexually before their 15th birthday'.[36]

From 20 September to 27 October the team had an extraordinarily fruitful stay in Chicago, only pausing briefly to go to burlesque shows at the Rialto on 22 and 24 October. They got 450 histories – men and women and children, black and white, ranging in age from three to eighty-three. By the end, Mrs Mary Lou Ketten of the Council of Social Agencies of Chicago became so enthusiastic she wanted to give up everything and come and work for Kinsey.[37]

In fact, the lack of interviewers was now becoming serious. One hindrance was that the genuine and very difficult demands of the job were compounded by various Kinsey idiosyncrasies. So difficult was it that, though he interviewed literally dozens of applicants over the next five or six years, he found only one man who suited him.

It had to be a man. He was often urged to have a woman interviewer for women and a black one for blacks. On that basis, Kinsey said, he should have prostitutes for prostitutes, criminals for criminals, drug addicts for drug addicts, and so on. Mary Lou Ketten was therefore, like all women who applied (and many did), rejected out of hand. But Kinsey had good reasons. He felt all interviewers should be happily married (a lot of people suspected someone not married) yet still be able to leave home for half the year, something Mac regarded as really 'a contradiction in terms'. Also, people would feel that a woman with the intense interest in sex that interviewing implied would be better (safer) contained in the home. In fact, a later Kinsey staff member, Cornelia Christenson, was trained and did some interviewing, and another, Alice Field, might have done had she not had to leave through ill-health. He also asked Dorothy Collins but she didn't want to. But in the context of the 1940s Kinsey was probably right.*

There were further hurdles. New interviewers had to have an MD or PhD in a related science; but they also had to get on with lower levels. They had to be American. Kinsey also wanted them to be middle-aged (that is, his age), though the extravagant strenuousness of the job clearly indicated younger people. They all had to give their histories and at the merest flicker of moral judgement or area of unease – out. The same was true of their wives (Nowlis' wife was the only one who refused, on principle, to give her history). No one religious need apply. 'He couldn't,' said Gebhard, 'even stand a slightly religious secretary.'

He would ideally have liked them all to have had previous homosexual experience and, one can't help suspecting, want, or be willing, to have sex with Kinsey himself, though in the end only Pomeroy and Martin were satisfactory here. And they also had to be prepared to have sex outside marriage.

Then names were problems. Kinsey felt odd names could block intimacy. There was an ideal man called Tatin-Pottberg who was told he would be hired, provided he dropped either Pottberg or Tatin. Tatin-Pottberg wouldn't. Nowlis remembered another ideal candidate called Birdwhistle. 'We just can't,' Kinsey said, 'go into town with someone called Birdwhistle in tow.' He really felt, said Pomeroy, that only WASP men could interview. What it amounted to was that Kinsey wanted all

---

* It is interesting that out of six authors of the massive recent British survey, five were women.

interviewers to be replicas of himself.[38]

In fact Kinsey was to get the fourth and, as it turned out, final member of his team quite soon, in 1946.

The last six weeks of 1945, meanwhile, were spent in New York, putting up at the respectable Lincoln Hotel. It was on this visit that another of the ardent, book-carrying college girls who scoured the streets for Kinsey picked up a thin, ashen-faced, good-looking, thirty-year-old hustler/drug addict/petty thief called Herbert Huncke in the Angle Bar on 42nd Street and Eighth Avenue. Huncke (rhymes with junkie) was an interesting character (he died in 1996) who liked Kinsey and said that he was grateful to him for lifting his sense of guilt, something that sounded odd somehow from someone of such an unrestrainedly dissolute life. Huncke later 'pimped', as he put it, William Burroughs, Jack Kerouac, Allen Ginsberg and similar figures for Kinsey.

In November/December 1945 it was meatier fare. 'I certainly knew a goodly crew, ha-ha, to put it mildly – thieves, pickpockets, a few stick-up men, prostitutes male and female ...' It was this gang, in return for $2.25 each ('I made it clear from the jump I wanted my cut'), that Huncke steered into the Lincoln. As more and more of those louche figures sidled into the staid hotel the manager became more and more agitated. Finally, he could stand no more and late one night he turned Kinsey and Pomeroy out. He would not, he told Kinsey, who recounted the incident in the *Male* volume, have him undressing people's minds in his hotel. It was wartime conditions still, and rooms were hard to get. The Salvation Army put them up.[39]

Thereafter, they usually stayed at the Astor in Times Square, partly, no doubt, because the bar on the ground floor was a famous pick-up point for homosexual partners. 'At any time of day or night,' wrote Gore Vidal, a frequent attender, 'hundreds of men would be packed six-deep around the long oval black bar within whose center bartenders presided.'[40]

Kinsey and the team saw their time out at the new hotel, finally returning to Bloomington, as usual, just before Christmas.

7

On 25 January 1946 Kinsey wrote exultantly to Dickinson – 10,000 histories!

It was for him a major landmark, a tenth of the projected twenty-year goal. But in fact as the year went on he began to cut back on taking histories himself in order to write the *Male* volume. 1946 saw an addition of 'only' 1,467, 1,201 less than 1945. And for the same reason he taught only one academic course this year – a ten-hour total for his 'Evolution' course.[41] But his correspondence rose inexorably, as it did every year till 1948 – when it rocketed.

In fact, a clear pattern of preference is emerging in Kinsey's letters by this time. He writes more relaxed, chatty, longer letters to intelligent lower-level young men who are trying to better themselves (and with whom, one feels, he can therefore identify), and to young, preferably lower-level, male homosexuals. It is not that he doesn't do this with women. He does. There is, for instance, a charming short exchange with June Viner who is on parole from Westfield penitentiary and addresses him as 'Mr Shamrocks'. She sends long chatty letters asking advice about this and that and especially getting married. '[I hope] you will be as nice in your letters as you are in person.' Kinsey kept up a correspondence for a while – 'Dear Miss Shamrocks' – just as chatty, but also giving the advice asked.[42]

But the weight is clearly towards men in the above categories.*

Kinsey and the team left for New York on 8 February and were to spend, at various times, over three months in the city (plus four weeks in Chicago, several weeks in Philadelphia and the rest of the histories from here, there and everywhere). A visit in early April to Washington was partly for Kinsey to address the Medical Division of the NRC, headed by Lewis H. Weed, which had been funded by the Public Health Service to study VD – causing much anxiety again as GIs returned from the war. A letter after this visit, where Kinsey had addressed the Superintendent of Women's Prisons, gives us a clue to one of his specific legal reforms, in this case that many so-called sex offenders could be treated non-institutionally.[43]

---

* Unfortunately, I cannot substantiate this with hard statistics since it didn't occur to me until too late, but the impression gradually became overwhelming. I did, however, test a related reaction to the correspondence. Judith Allen, head of Women's Studies at IU, who had also read some of the Kinsey correspondence, said her impression was that Kinsey found it easier to relate to male problems than female problems and was therefore more sympathetic to them (like most men, one might think). Her impression was borne out by my analysis, but so minutely and with an interesting contradiction, that I concluded it was not significant. I have put the details in Appendix B.

On 11 April, he returned to Bloomington, via Philadelphia, to learn that the NRC had nearly doubled their appropriation to $40,000.

This marked the climax to over a year's complex manoeuvering, in endless, often secret meetings, letters and conferences by and between Alan Gregg and Yerkes and Lewis Weed. For Kinsey, the result could hardly have been better. The Rockefeller Foundation now undertook to give a special $120,000 grant to the NRC specifically earmarked for Kinsey over three years, i.e. $40,000 a year. It meant the NRC was no longer independent – they *had* to give the money to Kinsey. It meant that the Rockefeller Foundation was now bound even closer to him.

What is astonishing is that all this really rested on and resulted from two intangible factors – the power of Kinsey's personality and the gripping nature of his subject. Kinsey hadn't published anything of consequence on it yet. There had been nothing in the nature of 'peer review'. Gregg, despite his Board's frequent and intense anxiety that the whole thing was 'decent', or that Kinsey was pursuing ridiculously large numbers (which he was), had, he told Kinsey, simply presented most of his extraordinary findings to the Rockefeller Board and they, like everyone else, had been completely fascinated. It was almost as if they paid to find out – what will he discover next? And this had been backed up by Corner and Yerkes testifying almost hysterically to Kinsey's fantastic powers and skills. 'Alfred Kinsey,' cried the usually staid Yerkes to Weed, 'is in the midst of an epoch-making socio-biological inquiry.'[44]

Kinsey was, of course, absolutely delighted and wrote personally to them all. It boded well for the next tricky problem already looming: the separation and protection of all Kinsey's work by embodying it in some sort of independent corporate identity.

In fact, Kinsey's own financial position improved this year along with that of his project. His salary went up again to $6,500. And, with some astuteness, he managed to sell all his gall wasp books to IU for $5,000. It may have been his success here which led him for the first time to value his growing sex library (all bought with his own money) and put the figure in his report to IU. And on top of all this, IU, as if to reward this further imprimatur from the Rockefeller Foundation, bought another Monroe Calculator, new electrical punches and fireproof filing cabinets for the Hollerith cards.[45]

It was a definite peak on the route to the first towering summit which was now distantly in sight – the publication of the *Male* volume.

8

Kinsey had, as always, seen Dickinson in New York and his friend now metaphorically pursued him down to Bloomington with a possible huge penis. A Dr Bocking had written to him, and Dickinson now forwarded the letter to Kinsey, that he had seen a photograph of a South American Indian with a penis (pendant) measuring seventeen inches. Kinsey has scribbled tersely in the margin – 'Write.'[46]

And Dickinson had revived his intense interest in the female orgasm and also wrote to Kinsey now seeking 'two extremely intelligent young women' to help him find out *exactly* what contact the clitoris made in female-female intercourse.[47] In fact, Dickinson's interest in female orgasm was never precisely dormant – it seems that in March, whether he paid her or not, he had finally got the highly responsive Alice Dent to let him take her history, because she wrote to Kinsey about it then: 'to say RLD was *elated* is rank understatement'.[48]

But this exchange of letters has a more interesting significance. Kinsey was of course just as interested in the female orgasm as Dickinson, as he was in all aspects of sex, and was indeed to make some of his most profound discoveries here, although he didn't go deeply into it until researching the *Female* volume in earnest. Or so the bulk of the evidence suggests. But in his reply to Dickinson, Kinsey refers to two women they seem to have in mind, adding 'We will have to go slowly with the two subjects from the former conference.'[49] ('Conference' was an elastic euphemism in their jargon.) It is possible Alice Dent was one of these subjects.

Kinsey always felt that listening to accounts of sex was not real science in the way observing it would be; he had already observed some and later he was to observe more, including Alice Dent, among many others. In these exercises he sometimes used an enthusiastic Wardell Pomeroy. Dent, in her letter about Dickinson's elation, also says she is quite happy to give a 'retake' history but thinks 'in this particular case more would be gained by your taking' it than Pomeroy. She goes on, 'Pomeroy mentioned yesterday your interest in another type of "demonstration". I told him I was perfectly willing but could not of course promise what the value might be as the presence of a third person might mitigate the spontaneity of the situation but if it's worthwhile to you to take a gamble on that I'm glad to cooperate.'[50]

These exchanges, in view of later developments, suggest that

Kinsey, through Pomeroy (who had also taken Dent's history), had already embarked on his investigation into the orgasm facility and other responses of highly responsive women and now wanted to observe Pomeroy and Alice Dent in intercourse himself.

But these matters, if to a minor degree, were now impinging on his own family.

9

> *To have or not to have pre-marital intercourse is a more important issue*
> *for more males than any other aspect of sex.*
>
> Male, p. 559

To this *aperçu*, no doubt true but offered, as often in Kinsey, without any written evidence, he could well today have added females. Kinsey always regarded marriage as the bedrock in relation to which everything else must be judged – and he was always clear sex was not the most important element in it. The main force that keeps a marriage going is the determination to keep it going.[51] Slightly begging the question, what then leads to this determination? – Kinsey would add, uncontroversially, that sex was none the less a very important element.

We saw earlier that, while discussing premarital sex with apparent balance, Kinsey would advocate it in private. It is also a battle which has been largely won (or lost, depending on your stance). But so significant had the lack of it been in his own life, and so central was it to his belief in the primacy of successful (i.e. orgasmic) and guilt-free sex which did not harm anyone, that it is worth briefly following how he made it clear it should be allowed while appearing judicially impartial. Particularly because it is the method he followed in many such presentations.

First, he shows that if successful sex helps marriage then early sex helps later sex. 'The coital adjustments of this group [college males] in marriage are frequently poor.' This is because of their 'tardy acceptance' – revealing phrase – 'of heterosexual coitus'. It follows without saying, and it is therefore not said, that a less tardy acceptance from that point of view is to be encouraged.

Next, as he always does, he points out premarital sex is very common cross-culturally, universal in all mammals (if an odd concept), and indeed more or less universal among lower-level Americans. A tone almost of wonder comes over Kinsey when he comments on this, which he does more than once. In some communities the only people not to have premarital sex are the mentally deficient or homosexuals. Some boys have sex 'with several hundred or even a thousand or more different girls . . . sometimes coitus does not involve any interest in the girls themselves at all'. It is pure pursuit and pleasure. That 'tardy acceptance' begins to seem more and more unnatural and ridiculous.[52]

With women he took the same balanced approach. Gradually, the argument swings. Pregnancy? True, 18 per cent of his sample had become pregnant. But his sample would have had coitus approximately 460,000 times (a typical Kinsey calculation) – so the chance was of one pregnancy every 1,000 copulations.[53]

The swing becomes decisive over orgasm. Future orgasm success (not to have orgasms is almost invariably a 'failure' to Kinsey) depends on early orgasm success, which is a learnt behaviour. And, insofar as success in orgasm leads to successful sex in marriage, and insofar as unsuccessful sex in marriage helps to explain its breakdown, the (unspoken) conclusion has to be to help prevent marriage breakdown everyone should have premarital sex.[54]*

Sometimes in his discussion we glimpse again the romantic Kinsey, the Kinsey who was moved by the snow whirling off the mountains as he gathered galls. In an eloquent passage he notes that in the past the great love affairs of literature revolved around *teenagers*. Helen was twelve when Paris carried her from Sparta; in the great pastoral romance of Daphnis and Chloë, Daphnis was fifteen, Chloë thirteen: 'Heloise was 18 when she fell in love with Abelard: Tristan 19 when he met Isolde and Juliet less than 14 when Romeo made love to her.'[55] It is the only time the phrase 'made love to' appears in his books.

The earlier the orgasm the better leads logically to infant orgasm. Kinsey had similar accounts for little girls as for little boys (but not from Green as far as I can gather). One mother described her three-year-old

---

* Which most people in the West now do and there have never been more divorces. There are too many elements for this to be a sequitur, but in fact, the accepted wisdom in Kinsey's day on this is no longer seen as accurate and most studies seem to show that sex becomes more important as a symptom of marriage breakdown than cause. It is a huge subject and one not touched on in Kinsey's one-dimensional extant works – though perhaps he would have done so in the projected volume on marriage. For a dated but reliable survey see my *Love, Sex, Marriage and Divorce*, London and New York, 1981.

daughter: 'Lying face down . . . pelvic thrusts . . . smooth and perfect rhythm which was unbroken except for momentary pauses during which the genitalia were readjusted against the doll on which they were pressed . . . marked concentration and intense breathing with abrupt jerks as orgasm approached . . . Her eyes were glassy and fixed . . . relaxation after orgasm . . .' (This was in fact a Bloomington mother, the doll a teddy bear.)[56]

Kinsey had four cases under a year, twenty-three cases of little girls under three, and various longitudinal follow-up studies, but in fact he did discover by another route that very early orgasmic experience carries over. He heard in 1949 from Dickinson, who had been told about it by Green, of a little township in deep Kansas where all the women were reputed to have orgasms easily, routinely and always in ordinary intercourse. This was not usual. Kinsey drove down and found that they had developed a way of soothing their little girls, a rubbing and petting technique of the genital area which did soothe them but also brought them to orgasm, a learnt reaction they thereafter retained. He did not, perhaps wisely, put this forward as advice in his *Female* volume.[57]

But Kinsey's most ingenious and unscrupulous argument for premarital sex was to set one abhorred behaviour against another. No matter he also argued for the more or less complete normality of homosexuality, he now threatened that prohibiting premarital sex 'forced' men and women, adults and adolescents in large numbers, into homosexuality. Of the two, in America, homosexuality was the more dreaded.[58]

Given the stigma that attached to women having premarital sex, it is not surprising that, when his daughter Joan, soon to be twenty-one, decided in 1946 she wanted to marry her childhood sweetheart Bob Reid, Kinsey urged her to do so at once. Joan planned to wait, for various financial reasons, but Kinsey was extremely insistent. 'Don't wait a year and a half.' He would pay everything. He also brushed aside Bob Reid's feelings that they should wait while he finished medical school. 'It all showed how in favour of Bob he was,' said Joan.

No doubt that was another reason. In fact, Bob Reid said that at first Kinsey was rather distant, only dealing with him in little lecture mode. One question he used to ask, followed by a little lecture, was 'Do you know what birds do in the rain?' There was no waste with Kinsey. But 'everything changed when I gave my history. I volunteered – and from that moment he was my best friend.' 'And he liked the fact Bob was a doctor,' said Joan.[59]

They were married on 29 June 1946 in the garden of First Street, in time for the last of the irises. But even this brief family interlude was tangled with work. The day before the marriage and the day after it Kinsey spent interviewing Paul Gebhard and his wife.

10

In fact two months before, Gebhard's professor at Harvard, under whom he was just about to finish his doctorate in anthropology, told him it would be a good idea if he learnt something of Alfred Kinsey's work. It was a reasonable idea to suggest to a young anthropologist, since cross-cultural studies are difficult at a sexual level, but – something Gebhard did not know – Professor Clyde Kluckhohn also sat on the Committee for Research on Problems of Sex of the NRC, all of whom seem to have been trying to get Kinsey 'hands'.

Gebhard had met Kinsey late in the evening in New York at the beginning of April. After taking his history, which Kinsey did immediately, wincing from Gebhard's belching pipe, he asked him his usual probing questions, among them how common he thought homosexuality. 'Very rare,' said Gebhard, emitting clouds of smoke.

'Really?' said Kinsey. 'Come with me.'

Although it was already after 11.30 p.m., he then took Gebhard on a tour of Times Square, starting at the urinal. Let Gebhard take up the story:

> We stood halfway down the stairs where we could watch. He said, 'Gebhard, how long does it take a man to urinate?' I said, 'Oh, not long, a couple of minutes I guess.' He said, 'All right, stand here and watch.' So I did. And I saw to my amazement there were 8 or 9 guys just spending their time migrating from urinal to urinal, washing their hands and circulating around. He said, 'Gebhard, those are homosexuals. They are looking for partners. So, now what do you think of the incidence of homosexuality?' He then told me the true figures. I was mighty impressed.

It was 2.30 a.m. before they got back to the Astor.[60] In fact, this was a favourite tour of Kinsey's; he'd taken his daughter Anne on it the year before.[61]

Kinsey wrote to Kluckhohn on 2 May asking about Gebhard. Since the fiasco with Nowlis, Kinsey had sensibly added to his list of qualifications the phrase: 'We can not use anyone who is afraid of sex.' Kluckhohn replied laconically, 'Mr Gebhard is not afraid of sex.'[62] Gebhard (always Gebhard to Kinsey – all the team were surnames to him) had, in fact, already done work involving interviewing – for the Air Force and at the Massachusetts General Hospital – in all about 700 interviews. He and his wife fulfilled all Kinsey's criteria – happily married, non-judgemental, tolerant of any behaviour, of erotica, pro sex education, etc. Kinsey took the leap and offered him the job. Gebhard had, in fact, a job pending. 'What are they paying?' '$4,200,' said Gebhard. 'I'll give $4,400,' said Kinsey, clearly feeling generous.

The Gebhards had planned an August holiday but had to cut it short after a barrage of telegrams. Gebhard's wife and son could not come till later, but Paul himself arrived in Bloomington on 15 August. He seems to have rapidly taken to the liberal 'open marriage' situation Kinsey encouraged and soon began an affair with Clyde Martin's pretty wife, Alice.

We should note, incidentally, that this state of affairs was not one of unbridled, unprincipled licence. Kinsey believed that, freed from (usually religiously) imposed, conventional, artificial restrictions, most people would lead much freer sexual lives. He wished to create this utopian possibility in his own circle. But no one was to be coerced, no one was to be hurt.

Separating sex from its various entanglements in his work, Kinsey believed the same was possible in life. It was not always so easy. The utopian encounters were meant to be for sexual pleasure, but after a month Alice Martin began to fall in love with Gebhard. Seeing Martin's distress and that the marriage might be threatened (and the whole venture thereby disturbed) Kinsey told Gebhard apologetically he would have to stop. The affair came to an end, but Alice Martin was furious. She was to take her revenge much later.[63]

11

Gebhard's family arrived in Bloomington in November, and Kinsey at once helped them look for a house. He found one near him. 'That suited him fine,' said Gebhard. 'He liked to have all his troops in one place. So he liked it, he was extolling everything. Then he said, "What are you asking?" "$12,000," said the man. Kinsey drew himself up and glared at him and said, "I hope you starve! Come on Gebhard, let's go." Actually, it wasn't a bad price. I eventually found one, not near Kinsey, for $12,500.'[64]

'Not near Kinsey' – this new, and as it turned out final member of the team, was already learning what it was like to be employed by him. There were to be many such lessons.

In fact, two days after Gebhard had arrived in August, Kinsey had shot off with Pomeroy for his first brief visit to the West Coast. And it was there – or just possibly on the second four-day visit a year later – that we learn of another significant event in Kinsey's sexual odyssey.

Some time before, Dickinson had introduced him to a young, extremely bright, good-looking, lively and likeable West Coast gynaecologist, Dr Earle Marsh. Marsh came from a stern, sexually repressive religious background similar to Kinsey's, and like Kinsey – like converts famously everywhere – had reacted violently in the opposite direction. His history, when Kinsey took it, as of course he soon did, was diverse and active and included sadomasochism and a good deal of homosexuality.

On the visit, Kinsey invited Marsh to see him in his hotel room. While they chatted, Marsh suddenly told him he'd had a fantasy of having sex with him '[I told him] with no idea in mind except to report it'. Kinsey looked at him, and then 'He sort of said "Take off your clothes." So I did,' said Marsh, 'and we started right there. So every time we met from then on, we had sexual contact.'[65]

But what is significant about this is not the event so much as the manner in which it occurred. One of the things Pomeroy noticed about Kinsey was his extreme diffidence in proposing a sexual encounter. He was excessively terrified of being rejected, and this relates to that oversensitivity to criticism Payne had noticed years earlier, to his misery when Mac delayed her answer to his proposal – and, one can suggest, to his earlier rejection by his father and perhaps earlier even still, to the rejection implicit in his mother's failure to shield him from that father, and possibly nurture him as he needed.

But whatever the genesis and its ramifications, Pomeroy said that – outside, of course, anonymous and casual 'tea-room' sex – this strongly sexed and idealistically promiscuous man only had about nine other partners during his life.[66] The intuitive skill of Marsh was to present the event as though it had already happened.

But 1946, as well as these events, saw the whirr continue unabated. Kinsey, as well as interviewing four other applicants, writing the *Male* volume in earnest, lecturing, taking histories, was also now in the thick of the next NRC/Rockefeller/IU development – his incorporation.

12

It seems to have been Wells who first suggested that Kinsey's project be set up legally as an independent, separate, corporate body. He had no intention of repudiating Kinsey, and never did so, but he saw – as publication came closer – advantages in putting distance between IU and Kinsey. In fact, they were all getting slightly windy about the attacks they knew were inevitable. From Kinsey's point of view he would be independent and so free from the danger of public inspection which a state university was liable to. It also solved the problem of whether IU, the Rockefeller Foundation or the NRC owned the histories, the library, or was due any royalties (though few were expected). And Kinsey saw independence as giving him a chance to deal yet more directly, as he was always trying to do, with the Rockefeller Foundation, the real source of prestige, money and, perhaps, effective defence. Alan Gregg and the Rockefeller Foundation, on the other hand, saw incorporation, as Wells did, as a distancing move. It also promised some form of permanence to their already considerable investment. Finally, Yerkes – who suggested the name of the nascent body, the Institute of Sex Research (ISR) – also saw advantages, in that it would take the fire from attacks. Besides, about to retire in 1947, it set a seal on the project he'd spent so much time supporting and defending.[67]

Thus each partner had slightly different aims, the resolution of which required endless meetings and letters and whose negotiations continued for the rest of the year and into 1947.

There were other preoccupations. Kinsey had been asked to arrange the zoologists' contribution to the AAAS meetings in Boston in December 1946, and in August he'd roped in Frank Beach. Now, in September, he asked Nowlis to join them: 'You could put some life into the thing, and that cannot be said of very many people who have worked with primates.' Nowlis got the point. 'I see I am to be the *scherzo* preceding the combined third and fourth movements.'[68]

But Kinsey was also worrying about Green. He wanted him to check the data he had taken from the diaries and also, it would seem, from his August letter to Beach, investigate Green further using Beach's immense zoological expertise. There was considerable urgency, he told Beach – 'Our man is ageing.'[69]

In the event, Beach was too busy, and on 3 October Kinsey made a special trip just to drop off his manuscript, which Green duly went over.[70]

13

Almost immediately, on 15 October, they all drove to Chicago, partly in pursuit of upper-level Negroes, male and female, in the Parkway Community Home.[71]

'All' included Paul Gebhard who was actively learning to interview. Although, as we saw, it was a year before Kinsey let him tackle a complicated homosexual history, he was now allowed the most straightforward female histories. Even these were not necessarily simple. He was interviewing a young woman this Chicago visit and had reached – he had most of the interview by heart – frequency of intercourse. The young woman said, 'Four or five.'

'A month?' enquired Gebhard.

'No, per day,' she replied, blushing deeply.

So Gebhard learnt not to put words into people's mouths.[72]

He was learning a great deal more. Quite soon after he joined Kinsey, he began to suspect that 'this man was somewhere on the H Scale. I asked Wardell, who said, "Yes – a 4." '[73] Nevertheless, some of Kinsey's most vigorous and pleasurable heterosexual activity was still to come.

Then there was the work. Gebhard supposed he had been hired as a trained anthropologist to investigate cross-cultural patterns and social structures. He rapidly found he was just an assistant interviewer and 'a card puncher. We couldn't let secretaries learn the code so we had to punch the bloody cards ourselves. Of course, Kinsey didn't do it.'[74]

In the dynamics of the group, Martin was professionally the least important, Pomeroy was Kinsey's extremely junior colleague, who never questioned him; Gebhard did question him and at the beginning strongly and angrily. Eventually, he put up with him, just because he, like them all, was convinced of the absolutely vital importance of what they were doing and because he too was fired by the drama of it. And suddenly, with his dazzling, beguiling smile, Kinsey would soften – and Gebhard would succumb to his charm.

And then – where else except possibly Hollywood was it possible as a young man (or woman) to enjoy such a liberally sexual *professional* regime? We must remember that Kinsey didn't have to coerce his staff into this – they entered in enthusiastically.[75]

Also, very slowly, things got better professionally in other ways. The world of academia – with its graduates and researchers, its junior or senior lecturers, its assistant professors, full professors, deans and department heads and holders of chairs, who are dependent on those above for promotion and on 'peers' (read, often, superiors) for publication – the world of academia is irredeemably hierarchical. Kinsey, however paradoxical his reactions sometimes, was no exception. Dr Henry Remak, a professor at IU who often helped Kinsey by summarising the secondary literature in German, Dutch, French and Spanish, remembers his reverence for German scholarship. 'He would *announce* – "And Dr Remak was educated in Berlin!"'[76] Kinsey respected Gebhard's Harvard doctorate, that he had published, and always regarded him, rightly, as the academic of his team. He gradually treated him more and more as an equal and, by the time they came to the *Female* volume, was allowing him to write some of it.

It took a long time. Meanwhile, the team remained totally dominated by Kinsey. In 1947, when the Institute for Sex Research was finally incorporated, they were all made equal directors, and could, wrote Pomeroy, technically have combined, 'insisted and outvoted Kinsey' – and one senses the dreams of the crushed – 'but as Gebhard remarked later "it never came to a vote".'[77]

But it was far more than work. Kinsey didn't only invade Gebhard's dreams. Easy-going, amusing, both intelligent and commonsensical, fond of the outdoors, Gebhard was twenty-nine, a fit six foot, with reddish hair – and a moustache. Kinsey hated moustaches. He felt they were disguises, physical analogues to hypocrisy, cover-ups of 'the fact'. (He wouldn't employ anyone with a beard.) He said to Gebhard, 'Look at any movie – the villain is always the one with a moustache.' 'Nonsense,' said Gebhard. 'Only if it is a *thin* moustache.' He wanted us all, said Gebhard, to be clean-limbed, clean-cut, ideal Americans – '*astronauts*'. He refused to shave his moustache.[78]

Then Kinsey still had his cold shower every morning, for himself as much to wake up as anything (oddly, for a man who got up at six or seven all his life, he was naturally a late riser[79]). But for the team, as it had been for his graduate students, it was still obligatory and for cleanliness. It infuriated Gebhard that Kinsey would come and check if shower and towel were wet. 'Gebhard – I'm afraid you smell.' They argued about it. In the end, Gebhard ran the shower while he shaved, then dried his face. Kinsey said, 'Do you know, Gebhard – you are not offending me any more.'[80]

There was also the domination of the work. The wives suffered here as much as the men. 'My wife used to get pretty angry,' said Gebhard. Mac used to tell them they had to build satisfying, independent lives for themselves. She herself started the Bloomington Girl Scouts Day Camp in the early '30s and ran it for thirty-eight years.[81]

And it was into work they ploughed again while 1946 came to an end and, as was almost becoming a habit, they were in New York. But this year was significant. For the first time since the project began Kinsey at last brought himself to address a gathering of psychoanalysts.

14

One of the most noticeable things in both the *Male* and *Female* volumes is Kinsey's unconcealed hostility to, and contempt for, psychoanalysis and in particular Freudian psychoanalysis.

This can partly be explained. For one thing, Kinsey was aware, long before most people, of the degree to which Freud had simply transposed sins into neuroses and psychoses and continued their punishment in the guise of treatment. Thus to Kinsey homosexuality, since neither rare nor abnormal, could not be 'evidence of neuroses or even psychoses'. Nor, as Freudians then maintained, was it anything to do with mother-fixation when a survey of non-homosexuals 'shows that most children, for perfectly obvious reasons, are more closely associated with their mothers'. Even age at adolescence was more significant than 'the much discussed Oedipal relations of Freudian philosophy'.[82]

He attacked the Freudians head-on again over masturbation; in view of its harmlessness and its universality at all ages it was clearly ridiculous to say it was a sign of immaturity. Freud's views were, as usual, simply a continuation of the old 'Talmudic tradition'.[83]

In fact, his real quarrel with the analysts and Freud was that they had erected an, on the face of it, completely absurd 'philosophy' – to use Kinsey's favourite term of abuse – on virtually no empirical data at all. Indeed, wherever Kinsey had data, it demolished the philosophy.

Then the idea of sublimation underlay, as Freud noted, his entire structure of 'abreaction', hysteria and other psychosomatic manifestations.[84] Kinsey showed that as far as objective examples went, sublimation just wasn't demonstrable.[85]

Freud, it is true, did introduce the idea of infant sexuality but in such a bizarre form – the baby boy wishing intercourse with the mother and terror of the avenging father – that it seemed neither believable nor sexual. Kinsey found nothing to substantiate this, nor penis envy, nor castration fear, nor sexual development proceeding from narcissism via homosexuality to heterosexuality. Kinsey had demonstrated that the 'latency period' (roughly five to thirteen) didn't exist – quite the contrary.* And in his discussion of all this he frequently castigated 'Freud and the analysts' for shoddy scholarship and non-existent evidence.[86] In short, by the end of Kinsey's work much of the empirical base of Freud had gone.

But Kinsey's hostility to 'Freud and the analysts' – and to a much lesser extent the psychiatrists – was more intense than mere criticism of their science would warrant. It also had a profoundly emotional and irrational base. He told Pomeroy once that he had a feeling that they could somehow divine his innermost and most secret thoughts. He was therefore frightened of them.[87]

Fortunately, at this time, from November to December 1946, he was able to make friends with one of the most prominent and most perceptive of the American Freudians, Lawrence S. Kubie, head of the New York Psychoanalytic Society and Institute. He was a man of limited charm but Kinsey brought him his research problems and they discussed the interaction of the physical and the mental. On 26 November, Kubie arranged for Kinsey to lecture to, and solicit histories from, his institute. Less fortunately, no one told Kinsey that Kubie had a reputation for unreliability in friendships.[88]

---

* Adults are often fearful of child sexuality, equating it with their own – no doubt one reason Freud's rigmaroles arose. Kinsey's much more balanced view was that the sexual life of the pre-adolescent 'is more or less part of his other play . . . the sexual life of the older male is, on the other hand, an end in itself'. The same distinction applies to females (*Male*, p. 182).

There remained in 1946 only another possible large penis to pursue. Dickinson told Kinsey that a Lt. Commander Jack Simpson of the US Navy had measured a nineteen-year-old black rating at 12.5 inches. 'You would,' Kinsey wrote to Simpson, 'be contributing materially to science if we can follow through on these cases.' Simpson replied that the huge penis was white and it was only a *report*, but he'd check up. He didn't write to Kinsey again for two years.[89]

Christmas – and then the AAAS in Boston, meetings fraught with significance for the future.

15

Kinsey left for the Statler Hotel on 27 December. No doubt Nowlis, Beach and he discussed the first chapters of the *Male* volume, since Nowlis had already read them.[90] But it was now that Kinsey was threatened for the first time seriously with the blasts of national publicity. Journalists from all over the country finally heard some of his findings – and were electrified. They immediately wanted to publish but, with the exception of *Newsweek* which did a piece on the age differences of men and women at sexual maturity being sixteen and twenty-eight respectively,[91] which astonished everyone, Kinsey persuaded them to keep silent. In return, he promised full facilities before publication. Amazingly, they acquiesced for a year.[92]

He returned to Bloomington on 6 January 1947 to fling himself into writing his book. He thought he had won himself peace from the press, which he had. He had also set off by so doing an almighty time bomb.

Writing the Male Volume – Science and Self-expression: 1947

1

I 947 saw a dramatic fall in histories collected – only 720 (bringing the total to 12,214). One reason was that selected groups were now nearly completed. In his NRC/IU Annual Reports Kinsey said, for example, that he now had enough male and female alcoholics (514), enough heterosexual prostitutes and enough male and female taxi drivers. (This statement of Kinsey's indicates the extremely rough and ready way by which his so-called 'quota' or 'stratified' sampling proceeded.)

But 720 is none the less not a negligible figure, and the reason there are as many as this is that there continually appeared groups Kinsey couldn't resist: there was a colony of 100 castrates available, obviously very interesting, or religious groups which were always hard to get into (he'd managed Yale Divinity School at the end of 1946[1]). And one notices again, and as usual, the meticulous attention to detail. On 17 February he addressed the American Orthopsychiatric Association in the Hall of Mirrors at the Netherlands Plaza Hotel in Cincinnati, Ohio. The effect of the mirrors and the stage lighting was dazzling. Saul Rosenzweig, who was there, noticed how Kinsey was wearing make-up to counteract this.[2]

But the main reason there were fewer histories was, of course, that Kinsey was frantically trying to finish the *Male* volume. We must now look briefly at the manner in which this was presented, since this was just as significant as the contents themselves.

2

> *[The orgasm record of single males] is evidence of the ineffectiveness of*
> *social restrictions and of the imperativeness of the biologic demands. For*
> *those who like the term, it is clear that there is a sexual drive which cannot*
> *be set aside for any large portion of the population, by any sort of social con-*
> *vention.*

Kinsey, Male, p. 269

The *Male* volume was organised into three parts. (1) 'History' – of past research – 'and Method' – of compiling the present one. (2) 'Factors Affecting Sexual Outlet' – age, social level, religion, etc. And (3) 'Sources of Sexual Outlet'. Here Kinsey moved from solitary activities – masturbation, nocturnal emissions; to common heterosexual joint ones – petting, intercourse; and lastly rarer activities – the homosexual and animal contacts. It took 735 pages and twenty-two chapters, ending in a final chapter of clinical summaries for doctors and clinicians. Apparently, no one used or read these and Kinsey, according to Pomeroy, was so hurt at this 'rejection' that he refused to have similar tables in the *Female* volume.[3]*

Despite some of his usual entanglements in I/we/one/he, Kinsey's style is clear and forceful, if not particularly concise. People complained of its laboriousness, but compared to some recent surveys it positively dances along. What makes it difficult to use are the vast number of tables, graphs, bar charts and the whole marshalling of the statistics, which are sometimes confusing to professionals and to the layman, frankly, often incomprehensible.

But these are not the elements I want to discuss. Kinsey wrote the whole book entirely himself, and he took enormous pains over it. The Kinsey Institute has preserved some of his page proof corrections and they are as dense as those of Proust: 'perhaps' is changed to 'probably' to 'certainly' to 'inevitably'; commas became semicolons and go back to commas; whole sentences or paragraphs are crossed out and rewritten or additional ones are added. Helen Dietz, who later edited, or rather tried to edit, his endlessly reworked text, remembered hearing him reading it aloud to himself to test for euphony and effect.[4]

---

* Yet oddly enough my father, who was a doctor, used them and found them helpful.

One of the peculiar things about writing, particularly when the writer is deeply involved, is how profound aspects of the character emerge without the writer being aware of it. We soon realise when reading the *Male* that here is someone who loves teaching (by page sixteen we are already getting a detailed four-and-a-half-page lecture on taxonomy), who enjoys clarity and who enjoys even more putting (and winning) an argument. Especially winning it.

We saw in the gall books how Kinsey seemed to derive the energy for his writing by using it as an outlet for his deeply, if controllably, aggressive personality. The same is true here. He uses the same swingeing sarcasm to dismiss his sex research predecessors as he had his gall wasp ones. Lewis Terman would have been far 'more reliable' if he had interviewed instead of using a questionnaire, and got 'totally different' results if he'd pinpointed educational levels, i.e. shoddy technique and hopelessly confused sampling.[5] 'Millions of dollars have been spent by certain organizations' to curb prostitution. The only result has been an increase in masturbation and nocturnal emissions and a 'transference of . . . pre-marital intercourse from prostitutes to girls who are not prostitutes.'[6] So much for all the vast social hygiene expenditure. In fact, later, Kinsey can't resist wondering if it isn't more transformation than transfer: 'The girl who has to be taken to dinner . . . before she will agree to intercourse with her boy friend . . . is engaged in a more commercialized relationship than she would like to admit.'[7]

But as well, in every section throughout the book, Kinsey launches passages of sustained, sarcastic and often successful polemic, so much so that, even though a humane reader today would probably agree with 90 per cent of what he says, it is almost impossible to resist arguing back. Despite a probably greater number of calm and rational expositions, this aggressive stance certainly accounted for a good deal of the opposition to him.

At the same time, you become aware of the much more attractive sides to Kinsey. Here, also, is a man of great *general* curiosity about human beings – expressed always, of course, via their sexuality. Odd information surprises one in every section: female virginity is so much prized in the Jewish religion that, in 1947, 'First generation immigrants . . . may still send the blood-stained napkin back to relatives in Europe . . .' Or drug addicts undergoing withdrawal experience spontaneous orgasm and nocturnal emissions several times in twenty-four hours (in fact, in a letter, Kinsey elaborated on this: cocaine has an erotic effect; marijuana, like alcohol, lowers inhibitions, but usually prevents orgasm and sometimes erection; opium derivatives reduce erotic responsiveness and in addicts eventually remove it; and finally alcohol will do so for those 514 alcoholics – yet he has a few examples of very heavy drinkers remaining highly active to the end).[8]

Kinsey looks at that end as well, although with considerable boredom. He 'never', as Paul Robinson put it, 'developed the enthusiasm for geriatric sexuality that has characterized the work of William Masters and Virginia Johnson'[9] – simply because there wasn't enough of it. He only had eighty-seven white males over sixty and thirty-nine black, so cannot, as he often says, generalise and at once, also as often, proceeds to do so. By sixty, 18.4 per cent are impotent and find nothing erotic at all (yet this seems contradicted – typical of how the statistics muddle one – by the fact that only 5 per cent were totally inactive at that age[10]); by sixty-five, 25 per cent were impotent; by seventy-five, 55 per cent. Yet there were records even here, so gradual is the male decline – one black man of eighty-eight was still having intercourse with his ninety-year-old wife (one of Nowlis' active little old ladies no doubt) from once a week to once a month.[11]

At the other end of the scale, the earliest ejaculation Kinsey had was by a Negro boy of six; but there seems to be doubt as to how 'normal' this was. Earliest 'normal' was eight.[12]

There is acuity of observation, as when he notices from his retakes how as people got older so the age at which they did anything – kiss, masturbate – became older too, as if they wanted to drag their past up with them.[13] Or his vivid picture of extramarital affairs (his figures about to horrify America) as furtive, sporadic, guilty – 'on an occasion or two with this female, a few times with the next partner, not happening again for some months or a year or two . . . then occurring several times or every night for a week . . . on a single trip or in a few weeks of the summer vacation'.[14]

Leitmotifs appear – the boredom older people feel for sex with the same partner[15] (and one cannot help reflecting that in June Kinsey would be fifty-three, married twenty-six years). There is a distinct, not quite anti-female feeling, but certainly impatience with women for not being as enthusiastic or responsive as men would like them to be.[16]

There is one extraordinary outburst here. Why should men always have to wait until females are ready, especially with upper-level women who are so inhibited with their tardy acceptance that they require endless stimulation and even then can't climax? 'It would be difficult to find another situation in which an individual who was quick and intense in his responses was labeled anything but superior, and that in most instances is exactly what the rapidly ejaculating male probably is, however inconvenient and unfortunate his qualities may be from the standpoint of the wife . . .'[17] It is an interesting demonstration of how *automatically* provocative Kinsey was (as well as the fact that, for his time, he displayed unusual flexibility in his attitudes) that we shall find him making precisely the same sort of utterances in the *Female* volume, only this time from the point of view of women and directed against men.

It is, I think, now generally accepted by all commentators, and has been for some time, that Kinsey had a range of social and legal reforms – his 'social agenda' in today's jargon.[18] Of these, the only one we need to look at further is homosexuality.

It is here, above all, sharpened obviously by autobiography, that there is passion in the *Report*. Kinsey had seen how these men had been harmed by society for their sexuality – he had seen them in prison, blackmailed, made to feel guilt and anxiety, even made outcasts, and it had made him very angry. This never led him to falsify his figures; it did dictate his presentation.

Kinsey is famous for three statistics: 37 per cent, 10 per cent and 4 per cent. 37 per cent is the percentage of men who have **'at least some overt homosexual experience'** to orgasm (Kinsey's emphasis) between adolescence (thirteen) and old age. 10 per cent is the number of males who **'were more or less exclusively homosexual** for *at least three years'* (Kinsey's emphasis, plus my italics) between sixteen and fifty-five. 4 per cent is the number of men **'exclusively homosexual throughout their lives'**.[19]

It is obvious that this method of presentation was specifically designed to make there seem to be as much homosexual activity as possible (and it is equally obvious Kinsey's own bisexuality played a role here). Hence the inclusion of adolescence, when libido and experimentation are at their highest; hence that arbitrary three-year period. Paul Gebhard agreed, adding: 'I wish to God he had *not* chosen that 3-year calculation for that purpose for it has given me years of trouble trying to explain it.' Yet this obviousness, surely, is the point. There is an openness, a transparency. It is not difficult to straighten up (and lower) the figures. You can remove the adolescents. If you take out, in those arbitrary three years, those who had some heterosexual experience the 10 per cent drops to 8 per cent for example.[20]

The second point is that another reason Kinsey chose to record and measure through individual homosexual acts was that it was single homosexual acts which brought down the rigour of the law. The more single homosexual acts he could demonstrate, therefore, the more ridiculous he could make the law look. Thirdly, he showed practically every animal has given evidence of homosexual behaviour.* At one point, by including early maturing adolescents, he pushes his 37 per cent to nearly 50 per cent. But the upshot is that while on Kinsey's figures prostitution provided about 4 per cent of the total male outlet and homosexuality scarcely more, at 6.3 per cent, the way he presented it made prostitution appear negligible and homosexuality overwhelming.[21]

The other area where there is general agreement is that Kinsey was, as Paul Robinson put it, an 'enthusiast' for sex. And Robinson pointed to one device, deriving from Kinsey's liking to shock, which leads him to 'inflate' cover-up and minimise exaggeration in his histories, thus allowing him to suggest that many behaviours were more common than his figures. His *Report*, he asserted, was really conservative.[22]

No doubt Kinsey was often quite conscious of his moves. He must have been so when he characterised the highly sexed, highly active early adolescent maturers (himself) as 'often the more alert, energetic, vivacious, spontaneous, physically active, socially extrovert, and/or aggressive individuals in the population'; compared, in their parade of social virtues, to the late-maturing, low-rating figures – 'slow, quiet, mild in

---

* Kinsey's homosexual animal behaviour seems to be mostly either male animals aroused by the presence of females but kept from them, or in highly artificial and temporary circumstances, and chasing other males *faute de mieux*, or in dominance exchanges. In the *Male* volume Kinsey partly acknowledges this and is circumspect in his deployment. He shows no such restraint in the *Female* volume. Only very recently has exclusive long-term homosexuality been observed in animals under natural conditions. Anne Perkins, in her *Sexual Orientations: Towards a Better Understanding*, describes how as many as 10 per cent of rams refuse to breed with ewes and devote themselves exclusively to homosexual intercourse; and *Nature*, in 1995, carried a report of two male octopuses caught engaging in sexual intercourse several miles down on the bed of the Pacific, where they must have at least supposed themselves safe from observation, though this might have been a single illicit engagement. New research at the University of Montreal, however, has discovered long-term lesbianism amongst Japanese macaque monkeys. The rams in particular would have pleased Kinsey because of their symbolic value, except that the main factor seems to be genetic, something he refused to countenance (*The Sunday Telegraph*, Review, p. 4, 9 March 1997, Ron Clark, *Male*, pp. 613–16, *Female*, pp. 448–51).

manner, without force, reserved, timid, taciturn, introvert, and/or socially inept'.[23] It is true that this finding, based really on no more than the necessarily fairly vague impression the interviewer got from each history, was put forward quite tentatively. Nonetheless, it is a telling indictment of the late-maturing, sexually inactive.[24]

But Kinsey's bias is often unconscious – and perhaps the more effective for that. We've seen that bias in his language – the 'tardy acceptance' of coitus, the 'reaping an erotic reward' for masturbation. Failure to orgasm (always female) is precisely that – 'failure'; low raters are almost invariably 'apathetic'.

Then, in any taxonomy extremes are important since they define the range and the variety. (And Kinsey was therefore perfectly sensible to seek out large penises.) But, though Kinsey always includes the lower ends of every range, he doesn't single them out. It is the high raters who get this treatment. (Equally, we don't find such enthusiastic effort to pursue tiny penises.) And here another factor comes in. Since one of the ways the social hygienists had of denigrating sex had been to suggest in veiled terms that it was really either a lower-class or Negro pursuit, Kinsey always took pains to impress the opposite. One of the most active males – over thirty orgasms a week for thirty years – was, by the way, 'a scholarly and skilled lawyer'. While in the league tables of the SIX MOST ACTIVE MALES (Kinsey's capitals) 'one is a lawyer, one is an educator, three of them are scientifically trained persons'.[25]

One might note here that Kinsey doesn't really have any firm suggestion as to why some people are so much more active, and some so much less – but then nor has anyone since, so far as I'm aware. He says at one point that he thinks it is connected with differing rates of metabolism but if so, and he produces no evidence, this just moves the question back a stage. Perhaps it is a function of character, of psychic motivation – and again one regrets (if understanding) this lacuna in Kinsey's approach.

The league table was all white. As for blacks, Kinsey left them out. He said the sample was inadequate. Gebhard said it was a 'grotesque' sample and too heavily weighted to the rough lower levels, a statement somewhat contradicted by Pomeroy who says they did get enough upper-level histories to compensate. Perhaps C. A. Tripp's statement holds the clue – that many lower-level blacks conformed too closely to the vulgar stereotype. Upper-level blacks were effectively the same as upper-level whites, so this may have been a cultural imposition, but it meant, specifically, that lower-level blacks had more sex and were better at it. Kinsey told Beach, 'The average lower-level Negro may take 15 to 20 minutes to reach orgasm' – which some women no doubt found more enjoyable than Kinsey's quick-firing whites. To Peter Dale, in 1948, he was even more open. He said he did not dare publish his figures because blacks had larger penises and higher frequencies and American neo-Nazis would say, 'We told you so.'[26]

Kinsey refers to humans as animals so often it is impossible to reference – four times on page 327 alone, for example. (The Kinsey Institute today must be one of the few places in the world where the toilets are labelled 'Male' and 'Female'.) And it was fundamental to many of his arguments. The law and convention, the prudes and the moralists, described a lot of activities as 'unnatural'. Kinsey countered by demonstrating they occurred in 'nature', among animals, human beings were animals – ergo, they were natural to us.[27] But beyond this was a sense of sex as an imperious, irresistible, biological force sweeping aside the pathetic efforts of society to crush it – as he said outright in the epigraph which began this section.

And the cumulative effect of all this on the reader is rather curious. You gradually, and then increasingly, begin to sense something enormously powerful pulsing in the *Reports* and driving them forward, an impetuousness of the blood, a force to which many people were to respond and from which many people were to shy horrified away, and which derived ultimately from, and expressed, Kinsey's own intense sexuality.

3

The writing went ahead with rapidity, but they still had no publisher. Wells had suggested in 1946 that they choose a well-established *medical* publisher to deal with their 'special problems in keeping the book identified as a very sober, scientific contribution ... much needed in the medical field', as Kinsey put it turning down a not yet well-established firm.[28] Another medical publisher suggested by Alan Gregg was turned down in February.[29] Then on 25 April 1946 Kinsey lectured in Philadelphia. Lawrence S. Saunders, the president of W.B. Saunders, one of the oldest and most respected of medical publishing firms, was again in the audience. For the second time, he was deeply impressed. He went up to Kinsey afterwards – had he by any chance got a publisher? Meetings followed at once.

Wells also suggested they publish when the state legislature was not sitting. He'd noticed they were prone to over-excitement, even hysteria at these times.[30] Both suggestions show the plump, wily university politician taking various defensive steps as apprehension grew before publication.

But they were all doing this, Kinsey not least. In October, Alan Gregg told Kinsey the Rockefeller Foundation would give $14,000 to pay Kinsey back for the library ($10,000) and finance further purchases. Kinsey had now bypassed the NRC and dealt directly with the Rockefeller Foundation just as he had earlier seized a chance to persuade Gregg to write a preface to the *Male* volume, identifying them with him even more closely. This was compounded by the incorporation* which at last took place in April, since it gave Kinsey still more independence to wheel and deal.

Kinsey, incidentally, saw his ever-closer association with the Rockefeller Foundation as a triumph of wheeling; in fact it was to prove a crucial tactical error. In the long term, it meant that if things went wrong, the Rockefeller Foundation would be associated with that too, and be tempted to withdraw. In the short term, it led to considerable tension between the Rockefeller Foundation, the NRC and Kinsey as he played the first two against each other. Yerkes, who was handing over to George Corner, was hurt that he, who had fought so hard for Kinsey, had not been asked to write the preface – particularly as Kinsey had specifically asked Corner in June 1946 if the NRC would do this. It took Corner till June 1947 to get Gregg, in effect, to apologise and agree to leave things to the NRC,[31] and for Kinsey to respond more politely to Corner's clearing up what he politely called 'misunderstandings'. Corner did, however, manage to get a grip on things again. He used to refer to Kinsey later as 'our problem child'.[32]

All this manoeuvering took time, and a lot of Kinsey's sharpness during this period was because he was now frantic to get the *Male* volume finished.

* i.e. to establish the Institute for Sex Research as a separate, autonomous, legal entity or corporation.

4

On 16 May, the contract with Saunders was signed. Publication was tentatively fixed for early 1948. On 22 May, Kinsey told Beach that the first draft of the manuscript was 'almost' finished,[33] like all authors anticipating that event by several months. Early in June he expressed the first nine chapters to Saunders; at the end of June Nowlis had accepted $200 to read critically what Kinsey was writing.[34]

In fact, the chapters were sent more or less straight to Saunders. Kinsey almost totally ignored what his team said, as he ignored most criticism. After he had read the first two and a half chapters in January, Nowlis had written to say that it was already so obvious that Kinsey was writing a book to change society, which therefore 'is going to raise strong emotional responses, sympathetic or otherwise, in practically all of your serious readers', that he should put these chapters at the end and start with the science. Kinsey promised to consider it, and did nothing.[35]

The title had now been fixed – *Sexual Behavior in the Human Male.* This, too, was criticised, both now and later, as suggesting he was writing about the entire population of human males, as indeed, naturally, it was taken to mean (and as it often reads). Kinsey's defence was grammatical; 'in' meant 'within'. If he'd meant the whole human male population he would have said 'of'.

This defence, as well as being disingenuous and irritatingly pedagogic, was symptomatic of a much more fundamental contradiction of which Kinsey at all times seemed blithely unaware. He wanted his book to be read by millions, he also wanted it to be read only by scientists and professionals. His use of 'in' was standard in science ('Mating Behaviour in the Yellow Baboon'); it was not anywhere else. By trying to produce a book which was both good science and would also carry his several messages to a large totally unscientific public Kinsey wrote something that was so dense rather few ordinary people could get through it. They thus relied on the press and to this extent Kinsey forced out the sensational – since clearly this was what the press would concentrate on.

The obvious solution* in fact occurred to Kinsey now, when he wrote to Yerkes in May suggesting it might be a good idea if they pre-

---

* Or obvious to us, with our experience of Masters and Johnson, who learnt from Kinsey's mistakes. In 1947 the whole situation was, as far as I know, unprecedented.

pared a simplified, much shortened trade (i.e. popular) version of the book. This would have provided the public with something authoritative they could have read, counteracted the selectiveness of the press, and diverted to the new ISR (Institute for Sex Research for which Dickinson had designed the book plate) the considerable sums which in fact went to the various books extracting from or based on the *Male* findings which soon began to appear. At this point (the idea kept recurring) it was Wells who argued against it – thus helping to bring about exactly the vulgar sensationalism he thought he was preventing.[36]

5

During July and early August galley proofs flowed from Saunders, were corrected and sent back. By 27 August they were sending page proofs – seventy pages every three days. The whole staff worked furiously – Sundays, holidays, nonstop. Envelopes were addressed, lists made – Pomeroy made lists of psychological journals, Gebhard of sociological and anthropological ones. Mac was reading proofs. Kinsey was working sixteen to eighteen hours a day. Publication was now fixed for 5 January. Saunders had to have completed copy by 15 September at the latest, and on 27 August there were five chapters still to write. Kinsey had to dictate the last chapters straight to a special stenographer hired from Chicago.[37]

And during August the press poured into Bloomington – magazines first, newspapers second. The idea was that each should be given a set of galleys and talk to Kinsey. But because, as Martin observed earlier, Kinsey had for years kept journalists at bay by promising this, galley proofs ran out. They were reduced to being allowed to read but not keep a set and listening to Kinsey. But the time bomb had been set ticking.

Although there were national magazines then, America had and has no national press as in Britain – there are therefore a far larger number of newspapers. At the same time, the press has always been more powerful in America than Britain – and at that time, before TV was established, it was as powerful as it would ever be. None the less, Kinsey imposed his will. He made them all sign a (completely spurious) 'contract': articles had to be vetted for factual accuracy and copyright had to be respected (i.e. no actual quotations were allowed before publication).

Kinsey often afterwards, especially to scientists, deplored the

amount of popular publicity his work received. In fact, he actively engineered it – to sell copies, to make money, to carry his crusade to millions. After the magazines had gone – including *Life, Time, Reader's Digest,
Look* and *Ladies' Home Journal* (from about half of whose staff Kinsey, with
strategic cunning, got the sex histories the year before) – he wrote to
Saunders pointing out this was 10 million readers: 'This should be worth
a great deal to us in advance publicity.' He was also aware that concentrating publicity into one blast and as near publication as possible was
best, and engineered this too. Corner, who saw clearly what Kinsey was
after, worried that such publicity would excite the prurient and arouse
the suspicions of the prudes and moralists. He thought that Kinsey
thought he was capable, single-handedly, of persuading the nation of the
scientific necessity of his work just as he had already persuaded so many
important individuals.[38]

The final sentence was written, to time, in the middle of September.
Choosing, like Proust, to end on the word that for him contained his
whole endeavour, it has a certain bleak, almost elegiac dignity. 'As
scientists, we have explored, and we have performed our function when
we have published the record of what we have found the human male
doing sexually, as far as we have been able to ascertain that fact.'[39]

Most authors feel tired, psychically drained, after a long book. No
doubt Kinsey did too; he wrote furiously just after this to the treasurer
of IU, railing against the racket – '. . . loud speakers, airplanes and sound
trucks. They are a perfect nuisance to the continuity of our thought and
our work when they blare over the campus from early morning until as
late as 11.30 at night.'[40]

But there was no let-up. In mid-September, Helen Dietz, Saunders'
most efficient editor, arrived with a mass of little alterations to go over
the final proofs. Pomeroy describes how they all listened to the 'endless
arguments', nearly all finished, as theirs had done, with Kinsey saying
flatly, 'This is how it has to be.'[41] Dietz remembered his disregard for
normal working hours and his extraordinary attention to detail. How he
chose a special pencil to make his corrections (now very few – he didn't
believe in messing up proofs) and how, though Martin drew the graphs,
tables and bar charts, it was Kinsey who dictated the width and weight
of the lines, the spacing of the figures.[42]

George Corner stayed at Bloomington 26–28 September to read the
finished book. He was, Kinsey told Alan Gregg, 'quite convinced that
there can be no reasonable complaint unless people are going to deny

science the right to present objective data'.[43]

On 16 October the *Male* volume finally went to press. Saunders had done careful market research among their usual customers and decided on a print run of 10,000 copies.[44]

Just before this, on 14 October, after a request from Kinsey,[45] his chief analytic friend and ally, Lawrence Kubie, arranged to review it for *The Psychoanalytic Quarterly*. Kinsey, of course, was delighted. 'Frankly and very honestly, I should say that we are very much honored in having you undertake this review.'[46] Kinsey himself wrote to numerous scientific publications, and among others got Dr Kluckhohn (who'd sent him Gebhard) to review it for *The American Anthropologist*. In some of these letters, too, Kinsey subtly boasts of having got Kubie.[47]

And as 'the great event', as Kinsey now described it,[48] approached, so they all grew in turn more and more nervous, excited and tense – and showed it in their various ways.

On 31 October Wells delivered a stirring eve-of-battle speech to his trustees. Kinsey was about to be published and they must prepare to stand firm.[49]

Saunders suddenly thought they should only allow the book to be sold to those over twenty-one. Since this struck at the fundamental source of his entire work – his sexual sufferings as a youth and young man – Kinsey absolutely refused: 'The book is very specifically needed by young people who are under 21.'[50] Then, as more and more magazines and papers started to ask Saunders for review copies, the publishers increased the print run to 25,000.[51]

Corner and Gregg thought some of the advertising was too 'racy', too close to 'erotica' (it was in fact extraordinarily staid, essentially a scientific announcement with a giant blow-up of the *Male* volume). Then Gregg wrote angrily because some advertisements mentioned the Rockefeller Foundation.[52]

Thurman Rice started to write furious letters to as many people as he could, including Kinsey. Dean Brisco wrote to Rice and begged him to calm down and in particular *not* to let his views reach the public.[53]

Lewis Terman, on the other hand, sent Kinsey a warm, pre-publication letter: 'I can hardly wait to see your first volume...'[54]

And Kinsey? The indications are that, while on edge, he confidently expected his work to be welcomed.[55] A little earlier he had written irritably to Robert Dickinson about an article on the penis which Dickinson planned to publish with some of Green's drawings. 'I think the drawings are quite inadequate,' Kinsey wrote testily, '. . . the chief error is the fact that the most usual type of penis is not shown at all.'[56]

But Dickinson sailed easily through all Kinsey's strictures of this sort – in any case, he probably wasn't all that interested in the normal penis. He came to stay for three days now, just before Christmas. And just after it, Kinsey left for the annual AAAS meeting in Chicago where, in fact, a few copies of the *Male* volume would be on advance sale.[57]

When he returned to Bloomington he would know at last how the world was taking this work which, while it had been in active preparation for the past ten years, had really sprung from and been shaped by his entire life.

Publication: Criticism, Praise, Success!

1

Not since Byron's celebrated comment on what happened to him in March 1812 had another writer awoken, as Kinsey did on 6 January 1948, to such universal clamour. IU's President Wells, in his autobiography, described it as a 'steady national uproar that continued over a number of years'.[1] The time bomb had gone off.

Despite the throngs of journalists at Bloomington in 1947, whose reports were now splashing across the pages of their magazines, broadsheets and tabloids, the fragmentation of the American press meant that nearly as many waited to see how successful this extraordinary book would be.

They hadn't long to wait. By 19 January, sales were 40,000 and Saunders was reprinting on the 22nd and at once increasing the run on the 23rd. On 27 January the British contract was signed – where it eventually sold 10,000 copies. In February there were the fifth and sixth reprintings, the Swedish contract was signed, 83,000 copies had gone (at one point Saunders was running two presses round the clock and receiving orders for 6,000 a day) and it was at the top of all the bestseller lists except that of the *New York Times*, where it was second. By the middle of March 100,000 copies of this large and expensive ($6.50 compared to the typical $3) hardback had sold and by June 150,000 copies, as well as the French and Italian editions. It was into its eighth printing and was now topping all the bestseller charts, including that of the *New York Times*.[2]

And so it went on. In the end the *Male* volume sold about 270,000 copies, with eleven translated editions and the English-language edition selling in eighty countries.[3]

The cuttings resulting from the publication fill six shelves of carefully bound volumes and the same number of shelves with some thirty large unbound files tightly stuffed with loose clippings, including twenty radio transcripts. It is almost as daunting a task to immerse oneself again in this deluge as it must have been to submit to it during those first months of 1948 as it poured on to Kinsey's desk. Perhaps only one man ever since has dared to do so – Paul Delbert Brinkman, who wrote his PhD on the subject in 1971 and whose account I will use freely.[4]

Kinsey was compared to Darwin and (as he had once compared himself) to Copernicus – in that they too provoked both moral and scientific outrage. The popular press compared the effect of his book to the atom bomb, which had exploded, uncommented on by Kinsey, in August 1945.

And the popular press, of course, seized on all the bombshell elements: his sexual advocacy, the homosexual figures, men maturing sexually ten years before women, premarital sex, human beings as animals (or 'beasts' as the many religious commentators usually put it), that, as *The Indianapolis Star* (always and still anti-Kinsey) headlined: '50% OF MARRIED MEN UNFAITHFUL!'[5] John B. Chapple, editor of the *Ashland Daily Press*, Wisconsin, accused him of being part of a Communist plot – he attacked the family, therefore undermined the State, therefore he was part of a red plot. He was a mad dog and should be shut up forthwith. This attack was taken up.[6]

But few things are less interesting than rehearsing long-ago headlines. Brinkman's conclusion was that the press and magazines were very largely favourable. The responsible press behaved on the whole responsibly. The *New York Times*' view was that, ultimately, the effect of the book would be healthy, even if shocking to some and to some an invitation to licence. *The Washington Post* swallowed Kinsey's line that he made no recommendations, only provided facts upon which changes could (or could not) be made, but suggested that in the long term changes *would* be made – in social attitudes and sex laws.

A poll conducted by Gallup some months after publication showed that out of those who had read or heard about the *Report*, 78 per cent thought it 'a good thing' and 10 per cent disapproved.[7] Similar surveys of smaller groups like students also found it was overwhelmingly supported.[8] Princeton ordered 400 copies for class use, and Southern Methodist University, Dallas, ordered 135 copies. It became, said Frank Beach, 'the fashionable book to have around'. No doubt there was a huge amount of skimming but, 'Everybody was buying the book,' said Miriam Hecht, 'everybody was furtively turning the pages.'[9]

However, what concerned Kinsey far more was the scientific reaction, since he knew that on this depended his future.

2

It is possible to make a great many legitimate criticisms of the *Male* volume as a scientific document – and many criticisms were made, and are made still.

For example, there is a striking lack of historical perspective. Kinsey had a poor grasp of history and seemed unaware of the alternating patterns of repression and liberalism in recent (400 years) Western civilisation – though this was not a focus of historicism in the 1930s and '40s. The data had been gathered over eight years and changes in attitude and behaviour during this period probably slightly skewed results, undetected by Kinsey.

He noticed, in fact, virtually no change between the behaviour of different generations.[10] Paul Robinson sees this as a way of allowing him both to batter the one historical element he did know about and hated – the Judaeo-Christian sexual tradition – and also to champion youth against age, 'Whose criticisms of the young were inspired by waning sexual powers and simple envy.'[11]

There is truth here, no doubt, but I think it is really Robinson's Kinsey-as-novelist again. This is an ingenious and fruitful analogy and I borrow it myself, but, though Kinsey was certainly wrong, he failed to detect generational change adequately because he didn't tabulate his informants by decade of birth. This was a major omission and one he corrected in his next volume.

As we have seen, there were no blacks and far too few old people. Even Paul Gebhard allows that, while their statistics gave a reliable picture of middle- and upper-level America (except for black people and the old) they were far less accurate as regards the more extensive lower levels. 'Our lower level sample stank,' Gebhard says now. 'We should never have used it.'[12]* The conclusion has to be that Kinsey was not justified in generalising his conclusions to the whole American population which, despite his disclaimers, he frequently did.

Yet, in fact, at this distance, nearly all the scientific criticism Kinsey received, though some of it was eventually to damage him, dwindles into insignificance. I would agree with Paul Robinson that Kinsey's dismissal of a lot of it as disguised prudery, while no doubt maddening to the critics, was probably true.[13] It is certainly true of the criticism by Lawrence Kubie, Lionel Trilling, Geoffrey Gorer, Margaret Mead and others, though with Trilling and Kubie anger at Kinsey's attacks on Freud were also involved.

One should note here an aspect to these attacks which reveals an attitude probably not uncommon today – and one which demonstrates the chameleon cunning of the old prohibitions. When Trilling attacked the *Report* for narrow 'materialistic' thinking, i.e. for trying to study sex only through physical facts, and Margaret Mead did the same (adding wittily, 'The book suggests no way of choosing between a woman and a sheep' or, she could have added, a man), what lies behind such statements to a considerable degree is the feeling that sex *alone* is wrong – you can't do it just for pleasure. It has to be sanctioned, has to be 'enriched' by love, or 'deepened' by emotion. The same feeling, a watered-down version of sex pure and simple being disgusting and wicked, is really,

---

* It stank, perhaps literally, because such a large proportion came from prisons and state farms. Kinsey was aware of dangers here, since he did not use any prison frequencies in his tables. ('Incidences' are how many people do something, 'frequencies' are how often they do it.) He did not use prison frequencies, presumably, because he realised that in those artificial circumstances men would do some things, like masturbate, more often, and others, like heterosexual coitus, less often (*Male*, p. 210). But then, more of them, one supposes, might have had more homosexual contacts and he should therefore have left them out of homosexual incidence figures as well. That they were not left out is a further indication, if it were needed, of how determined he was to boost the homosexual statistics (though in actual fact we shall find they made little difference here). In fact, the logic that led him to leave prison figures out of some, should really have led him to leave them out of all calculations. The prison sample should have been kept for the sex offenders book.)

perhaps unconsciously, behind James Jones' quite frequent castigation of Kinsey for his 'mechanistic approach', his 'mechanical' fixes, his 'reducing' of coitus to mechanics.[14]

Most informed commentators today are clear that, provided one leaves out cultural change and accepts the fact that not all his findings can be generalised, Kinsey's major conclusions, and including those encompassing the lower levels, remain unchallenged and, despite tinkering, unaltered.[15] Dr Anke Ehrhardt, in a talk she delivered in 1982, said the most important thing, and also the most difficult, was to get truthful information; percentages of population were not so important (and today with sophisticated sampling techniques not difficult). 'In re-reading the endless criticisms about imperfect sampling strategies of the Kinsey studies,' she writes, 'I was struck by how pedantic these attacks were considering the fact that for the first time 18,000 people [or 5,300 for the *Male*] from many different groups of the population had revealed their sexual histories.'[16]

And this, as Brinkman's analysis found as well, was what the majority of the scientific comment also concluded. The NRC, at this point, was content. Lowell Reed, for instance, wrote to George Corner about the sampling criticism, that they all knew Kinsey's sample wasn't perfect – for his material an ideal sample was impossible. (An interesting aspect of this letter, incidentally, makes clear that the whole NRC Committee supported Kinsey's desire to reform sexual attitudes. 'If the book does that,' he wrote, 'it has served its purpose.' They were *all* reformers.[17])

But this calm was not echoed by the primary subject. On the contrary, Kinsey's reactions were often fierce. Yet he had reason. Let us for a moment consider the curious behaviour of Lawrence Kubie.

3

Kubie's review, which eventually appeared in *Psychosomatic Medicine*, was a twelve-page critique, sandwiched, as such attacks often are, between two thin slices of fulsome praise.

In 1970 Paul Gebhard thought of organising a *Festschrift* for Kinsey, and wrote to Kubie about it. Kubie replied he couldn't contribute because of the circumstances surrounding his review of the *Male* volume. In 1948 he'd sent the review, which Kinsey had asked him to write, 'begging' for Kinsey's comments. Kinsey merely asked him to delay publication till they'd discussed it. Finally, it got so late Kubie was about to send it in, when Kinsey rushed to New York to see him, keeping him waiting from two till five. 'He arrived,' wrote Kubie, terrified and 'sweating with anxiety'. In later years, Gebhard said, Kubie would describe Kinsey weeping; in his letter he has him pleading with Kubie not to publish the review. It 'would cut off all his Foundation support'. 'I really had to deal with him,' Kubie goes on, kindly but perplexed, 'as though he was a patient.'[18]

Now, there are minor inaccuracies here, of no great moment. Kubie had freely agreed to write his review;[19] the date they made was for the 'evening', not 2 o'clock;[20] Kubie didn't 'beg' for comments, he merely apologised for his attack, though a later note would 'value' Kinsey's reactions.[21]

But the real point is – did anything of this sort ever happen? It is so out of character as to be unique in Kinsey's history. There are a great many instances of this aggressive man attacking people, wounding them, reducing them to silence or to tears; not one of him being reduced to tears himself. Certainly, Kubie behaved towards Kinsey later, not with the Olympian detachment he assumes here, but with the animus of someone who had been humiliated. He talked of Kinsey's 'paralyzing influence' on those around him. He referred to Gebhard and Pomeroy as 'Kinsey's handmaidens' and urged a journalist to publish the remark.[22] He circularised his review and did his best to persuade Gregg and Corner to stop funding Kinsey unless Kinsey agreed to accept his criticisms.[23]

I think Kinsey and Kubie met in 1948, had an argument, Kinsey finally lost his temper and attacked Kubie with the savagery and sarcasm of which he was a master – and this letter to Gebhard, after Kinsey was safely dead, was Kubie's revenge.

Kinsey was to be stabbed in the back like this more than once but, in fact, everyone associated with him agrees that his reactions to criticism – rage, despair, pain, anxiety – were excessive. (C. A. Tripp remembers him at this time talking obsessively about Kubie.[24]) *Any* criticism was both a personal attack on him, a rejection of him, and the result of deep emotional and psychological flaws and prejudices in the critic.

Yet, he had good reasons. Kinsey was deeply bound up with and into his book – and this was so obvious that it was already being called *The Kinsey Report*, against which he protested in vain.[25] (In Sweden it was actually published as *The Kinsey Report*.[26]) All writers feel an attack on their book as an attack on them – and in varying degrees, so it is.

Then, despite their assurances, he was terrified of the effect on his funding – again, with good reason since in the end this sank him. (And we should note that *already* Karl Lashley of the NRC Committee was talking about funding ending in five years or so, after the *Female* volume, while Corner, a year later, only envisaged three more years.[27])

Kinsey worked frantically, with endless letters, to counteract the effect of bad reviews on his funders. When Kubie's critique came out, for instance, arguing that Kinsey should have psychoanalysed some of his 5,300 sample,* Kinsey sent some calculations to Corner: 'It would take 223 analysts to do this sort of thing that they demand on the population which we are handling. That is one-half of the entire supply of analysts in the United States.'[28] When Lewis Terman's statistical broadside was eventually fired, Kinsey rushed copies of all the good scientific and statistical reviews to the whole NRC Committee, and, after a later attack, a six-page letter to Corner.[29]

We see beginning that acute paranoia which still, fifty years later, haunts the Kinsey Institute in Bloomington like the afterglow of the Big Bang. For goodness' sake, he writes to Dickinson, don't let on about our erotic material – it's too difficult to explain its significance.[30]

But Kinsey's main reaction was anger. Corner, Gregg, Saunders, indeed everyone, urged him to calm down, not to reply, that it wasn't important.[31] He could do none of these things. One outlet was letters – on Geoffrey's Gorer's 'vicious slant' to Dickinson, to Saunders on Kubie – 'we have not attacked their precious doctrines'. He frequently wonders if he can sue his critics.[32] He let drop dark hints that he knew many of his critics' sex histories, where lurked hidden moralities, hidden flaws

---

* Part of Kubie's criticism was that while Kinsey's data might be correct, his analysis was wrong. The motivation was usually not biologic (or 'animal') but unconscious, accessible only to analysts. Kinsey should therefore have had psychoanalysed a spectrum of representative individuals. Kubie here, as one would expect, was reacting to Kinsey's demolition of Freud's empirical base. This was behind several attacks, including almost certainly that of the influential Professor of English at Columbia, Lionel Trilling. Trilling was not the architect of the great Freud temple in America – it was well in place – but he was a prominent worshipper, to the extent that he eventually took on, with Steven Marcus, the huge task of abridging Ernest Jones's three-volume hagiography of Freud – and then wrote an equally hagiographic introduction. (See *The Life and Work of Sigmund Freud* by Ernest Jones, edited and abridged by Lionel Trilling and Steven Marcus, Penguin, 1964.)

and prejudices about sex. Terman in particular, he knew, was motivated by 'moralistic ideas'.[33]

(In fact, Terman was, understandably, probably more motivated by ideas of getting back at Kinsey for the curt dismissal of his own work.)

And his friends in turn sent letters of support and came to his defence. Nowlis, in November 1948 – 'Dear Prok' – wrote that no one was swayed by Terman and enclosed a quotation which is one of the epigraphs to this book – 'Everyone's sin is nobody's sin.'[34] Karl Menninger was part of that ring of defence Kinsey had been consciously gathering over the years. Menninger wrote letters of support to Kinsey, wrote to the editor of *The American Journal of Psychiatry*, who had published a damning review, that the *Male* volume was 'probably the most important book published in our lifetime', and in a later review/defence called it 'one of the great scientific documents of the century'.[35]

But the chief method of counter-attack came, oddly enough, through a medium about which Kinsey also bitterly, and quite unjustifiably, complained. This was the very rapid compilation and publishing of a number of books specifically designed to answer his critics and put Kinsey's 'case'. The books were *Sex Habits of American Men*, edited by Albert Deutsch, a journalist on *PM* and a fanatic supporter; *American Sexual Behavior and the Kinsey Report*, by David Loth and Kinsey's lawyer Morris Ernst; and *About the Kinsey Report*, edited by Donald P. Geddes and Enid Curie.

Kinsey actively helped with all of these, suggesting contributors, correcting errors and so on.[36] The books made enormous sums of money. Geddes' first printing, for example, was 500,000 and Ernst's *reprint* was a million.[37] It was about this that Kinsey complained. The money should have been his. But had he published his own condensed version it *would* have been his. They were probably more efficient (if not always quite accurate) at spreading his gospel widely, and were an extremely effective way of answering popular attacks. 'They should be of inestimable value in swinging the pendulum the other way,' was the view of Saunders.[38]

But Kinsey was not the only one engulfed in what Dickinson, loving it, called 'the whirlwind'.[39] Hundreds of others were facing these tremendous gusts with him – or helping cause them.

4

One of the latter was Thurman Rice again, goaded beyond endurance by the attention the monstrous *Report* was receiving. What absolutely infuriated Rice was that, similar in build, he was now quite often mistaken for Kinsey on campus. There is a bulging file of his angry letters to Wells in the IU archives.[40]

Rice wasn't the only faculty member bombarding Wells. Dr Haddon (also in the Medical School) expressed his feelings frequently – 'repugnant to the point of nauseation' – with Wells invariably polite in reply.[41] And letters poured in from everywhere; from anxious mothers and angry fathers ('I think he [Kinsey] should be imprisoned for life'), and from cranks – 'Sodomy Education!' On these, Wells scrawls an angry – 'No Reply.'[42]

Wells and Kinsey kept in constant touch throughout the campaign (Kinsey was now calling it 'a battle'). When President Dodds of Princeton compared the *Report* to 'small boys writing dirty words on fences', Wells offered to deal with him. (This was that same Dodds who twenty years before had issued dire if vague warnings of a new dark age if his students didn't control their 'emotions'.) Kinsey was concerned about this because Dodds was a trustee of the Rockefeller Foundation, but Corner reassured him and Kinsey told Wells he needn't bother.[43] And Kinsey made sure Wells received copies of all the good reviews.

Which Wells in turn passed on to his own trustees. But, in fact, there was never any danger of Wells wavering. Apart from anything, many of the letters to him were in favour of the *Report*, and he knew that Kinsey's own correspondents were overwhelmingly in favour. He was a man of great good humour and unusual commonsense balance. And he was used to controversy – in the university, the state, the legislature: 'We always have issues that come up there. You know, money issues, issues of irrelevance, and you have issues of immorality, and somebody always gets raped in the middle of the legislature – and that's without Kinsey ...' This astute, calm man kept his trustees calm too: 'They never moved – they would squirm occasionally, in pain, but never moved.'[44]

In IU itself, feelings were decidedly mixed. According to Dorothy Collins, wife of the Vice President of IU, Ralph L. Collins, Kinsey wasn't taken nearly so seriously on the campus then as now. But few people really enjoy their colleagues becoming nationally, and finally internationally, famous – especially if that colleague has, like Kinsey, put a lot of backs up. Wives, in particular, often disapproved and Kinsey's friends – the Edmondsons, Henry Remak and others – frequently had to defend him. At the same time, everyone shared in his fame. Professor Torrey remembered how wherever he went people saw his IU number plate and asked if he knew Kinsey. And as Fernandus Payne said – 'it brings in students'. They all knew that their university, thanks to Kinsey, was famous too.[45]

In Bloomington, indeed in the rest of rural, racist, conservative, religious Indiana, the reaction was not mixed. Don Baxter, now over seventy, who had lived there all his life, and gone through high school with Bruce Kinsey, put what was felt mildly: 'A sense of shock. People felt these were very private matters and they had made them public. People wished that, if it had to be done, it didn't have to be done in Bloomington. And the Kinseys, good ordinary folk, the last people in the world you'd think would . . . well, thinking of the whole family . . .'[46]

How did the whole family itself, meanwhile, react? The clamour round them was not confined to press and letters. Strangers telephoned in the middle of the night. Kinsey was joke-of-the-year for cartoonists and comedians and in burlesques; in communities up and down the country and on the radio* it became the fashion to hold 'seminars' – often chaired by a clergyman – where people 'discussed' the *Male* volume. Kinsey had reports of two hundred of these, but there were hundreds more. A record *Ohhh Dr. Kinsey!* was put out by Martha Raye and, banned by the big broadcasting companies, sold half a million copies.

It was a strain on his children. At college, knowing his professor hated his father's book, Bruce replied, 'Never heard of him,' when asked if he was a relation. Later, the professor found out. Anne used to answer – no relation, her father made whiskey, prompted no doubt by an ad campaign the Kinsey Whiskey company was running to cash in. (Later, they sent her a crate of whiskey.) And it was not only his children. All over America Kinseys took ads to explain they were not related to him.[47]

What, then, had it all achieved? I want to leave a full discussion of this until after the *Female* book, since the effects of Kinsey's work were

---

* Kinsey refused to appear on radio. Paul Gebhard said microphones made him uneasy and radio journalists always brought up his 'social agenda'. He refused television as well, except once near the end of his life. Cameras once got into his hotel room in Los Angeles, but he threw them out. (Gebhard, in conversation with the author.)

slow, complex and cumulative, but there is one aspect we should look at here and that is what light has been thrown on the *Male* volume by more recent surveys.

5

It is an axiom of the scientific method that any experiment, any discovery, can be proved valid only if it can be duplicated by other scientists repeating the same experiments or same procedures.

This is often difficult. Darwin's theory of natural selection, for instance, cannot be 'tested' by the usual 'scientific' methods. And, despite what I said about Kinsey's major findings, it is extraordinarily difficult, and often impossible, in sex research – at least in any precise way. For one thing, since Kinsey there have been remarkably few mass surveys of comparable scope. Geoffrey Gorer did one in the UK in 1971, though he was more concerned with attitudes. Only fairly recently has AIDS prompted new large-scale surveys; in the UK – *Sexual Attitudes and Lifestyles*, 1994; in the US – *The Social Organization of Sexuality*, 1994; in France – *Les Comportements sexuels en France*, 1993. There has also been one in Norway.[48]

What can one learn about Kinsey from those who have tried to duplicate his 'experiments'? One is that people tend to give answers they feel the interviewer is seeking. Gorer wanted to diminish sexual behaviour, and he succeeded. 'England still appears to be a very chaste society' – 26 per cent of men and 63 per cent of women were virgins at marriage, according to Gorer. By pushing marriage back to 'betrothal' he got his virginity figures up to 46 per cent men and 88 per cent women. His bias is revealed by his questions and the let-out he always allows: 'How old were you when you first (if ever) had intercourse?' In fact, he managed to find almost no homosexual behaviour at all; at least, he found one man, a 38-year-old welder, who replied tersely: 'Yes, that's my business.' So, homosexuality in England in 1971 – 0 per cent.[49]

One understands the fierceness of Gorer's attacks on Kinsey much better after reading his own survey. But correspondingly, one must assume that Kinsey and his team induced a bias the other way. His prison sample enhanced this, since they were by definition against the *mores* of society, especially in areas like premarital sex, and Kinsey later admitted this.[50] One could, I suppose, argue that in the 1930s and '40s, when attitudes were so much more inhibiting than today, Kinsey's bias was a corrective towards getting truthful information.

One interesting thing you can see operating after Kinsey is that, so violent and continuous was the criticism of his sample, all subsequent surveys have been determined to avoid it. They are, today, near-perfect random probability samples – perfect profiles of the populations they are investigating. Kinsey was aware of random sampling – he rather charmingly called it 'pinpoint' sampling – but he said it wouldn't work for sex surveys. For one thing, it would probably mean you would miss the extremes, which as a taxonomist he required. Moreover, if you just appeared out of the blue and asked X or Y, picked at random from the telephone book or electoral register, intimate questions about sex, a lot of people would refuse. 20 per cent refused in the US survey (even offered $100); Gorer failed to get 35 per cent of his sample; 25 per cent refused in the UK survey, plus an average of 3.8 per cent on 'sensitive' questions, which takes it up to 28 per cent. That is an average rate from all the surveys of 27.7 per cent.

It seems that in one area Kinsey was undoubtedly right about probability sampling, especially for his time – the areas covered by that adjective 'sensitive'. If you are looking for behaviours affecting smallish percentages of the population – 2 per cent, 4 per cent, 8 per cent – and those behaviours are also stigmatised or illegal – cross-dressing, homosexuality, incest, child-adult sex – and you *then* get 20–30 per cent refusal rates your survey is, as far as those behaviours go, dead in the ground. (No social statistician I have discussed this with has convincingly refuted it.)

But what were Kinsey's refusal rates? He kept no record of them, though they were not high, certainly not approaching 27.7 per cent. He kept no record because his 100 per cent groups made up a quarter of his sample. While one has to allow some biases in these, in unknown directions, as we discussed earlier, they none the less supplied a corrective. If refusals had markedly skewed the results he was getting for the rest of the sample then it would have shown up when he compared these results to those of his 100 per cent groups, which he invariably did. There were differences, but they were small – well within the 2–5 per cent error he allowed himself – and he was able to discount them.

Kinsey's refusal rate was low because he was so persuasive. This brings us to volunteers again. It is extraordinarily maddening to anyone who knows anything about Kinsey to read the strictures on his sampling in the 1994 US survey (repeated in much milder and politer form in the 1994 UK one). This was, the American authors write, 'Essentially volunteer and purposive in character...' and therefore, they imply, useless.[51] *All* surveys are essentially volunteer and purposive, but we saw in our long and detailed discussion of this (p. 134) that of all subsequent surveys, Kinsey was less dependent on straight volunteers than any of them. I would refer the reader to this discussion again.

The second thing the volume of criticism directed at Kinsey did, was to make later sex researchers wary of choosing orgasm, seeing it as an unsubtle measure for sexual activity. Gorer barely probed 'behaviour' at all; instead of orgasm, the 1994 US survey chose a vague genital contact that involved excitement. (So that, theoretically, it would be possible for their highest raters, in Kinsey terms, to have had no actual sexual intercourse, heterosexual or homosexual, at all.) But the authors of this survey also erected an excitingly elaborate theoretical structure of social 'scripts' (essentially induced social patterns), of 'choice theory', 'networks' (patterns of interlocking scripts), finally planning a whole reordering of their material into 'clusters' of behaviour – or they would have done all this, had they attempted any of it. In fact, the whole thing proved completely impossible and all their complex refinements collapsed, even though they could only bring themselves to admit it in a footnote.[52] In the end, they did *exactly* what Kinsey had done: they tried to gather statistics on sexual behaviour dividing their quest under the same simple but vital headings of sex, race, age, education, religion, geographical area and so on.

The 1994 UK survey did the same, and I would conclude here, with them and with Kinsey, that for mass surveys it is not possible to do anything more complicated or subtle than he did – and that all criticisms on these grounds were, and are (they are still made), mistaken. In fact, one can but notice how much richer and more ambitious the Kinsey surveys were. His two volumes only used about 10 per cent of his data,[53] and his 'reservoir' concept meant that from it books and studies continued, and still continue, to flow.

As regards comparing the actual findings of these surveys with Kinsey's, other difficulties appear. For one thing, society changes, and with it sexual patterns. This applies to premarital sex. One would expect the huge rise in divorces to affect figures of extramarital sex, and this seems to be so – though the jungle of charts and tables in the US survey becomes all but impenetrable here. (And so inadequate was their questioning, that 65 per cent of their conclusions here had to be left blank because of 'Fewer than 30 cases.'[54]) But one might deduce that in this area Kinsey caught America just as the institution of marriage was about to start cracking up.

But the figures I'd like to look at closer are those for homosexuality, though a difficulty here is of non-comparability of question and sample between the *Report* and later surveys. None of the surveys, for instance, uses the same number of years for which homosexual activity has to last to 'count', as it were, and so we cannot really compare Kinsey's 10 per cent (though 6.1 per cent of UK men reported some kind of homosexual experience[55]). None the less, generally speaking, it does seem significant that instead of Kinsey's 4 per cent figure for exclusively homosexual, *all* the recent surveys have figures ranging from 1.4 per cent (UK) to 2.8 per cent (US), with similar figures in France and Norway.[56]

Leaving aside my earlier strictures on probability sampling in this area, all the recent surveys agree their figures are too low. The US sample was so small (3,432 compared to 20,000 in the UK and France) that the authors admit it is inadequate for the purpose but promptly use all the figures.* Social patterns may have changed.[57] But in fact a general distrust of Kinsey's figures (so far, as we've seen, misplaced) has become focused on and symbolised by his 4 per cent.

And to discuss it further allows us to step back and take a broader view of sex surveys in general. The US survey came under some fairly devastating criticism. Some of the most effective in a review in the *New York Review of Books*, by Richard C. Lewontin.[58]

Richard Lewontin is a distinguished evolutionary geneticist from Harvard, author of several celebrated studies.[59] His criticism fell into two halves. The first was the uselessness of the survey as regards AIDS (its aim), a uselessness 'made all the more objectionable by the air of methodological snootiness assumed by the authors when comparing their techniques with all the studies that have gone before'. This does not concern us.

The second of his criticisms can be directed at all sex surveys. How

---

* In fact, in order to get accurate information about homosexuality, more or less the same team as did the US survey once again had to use what was essentially Kinsey's method – now sometimes called 'snowball sampling'. That is, they went into the cities and deliberately sought out homosexuals and homosexual groups. (See Edward O. Laumann et al., 'Monitoring the AIDS Epidemic in the US: A Network Approach', *Science*, 266: 1186–9, June 9, 1989.)

can you be sure people are telling the truth? There is only one certain test – if the figures add up. For instance, the figures of heterosexual intercourse in a lifetime have to be the same for both sexes. But they were not. In the 1994 US survey men reported 75 per cent more partners than women. And, said Lewontin, this is true of all sex surveys. In the French survey, Frenchmen reported four times as many partners; in the 1994 UK one (which he did not mention) twice as many.[60] Lewontin's conclusion was that *no* sex survey gets at the complete truth.*

There are answers to this. Logically, it only applies to a closed population – for example, all the people in a college. Where one can find such a population in Kinsey the results might have surprised Lewontin. With married couples he found that wives said they had *more* intercourse with their husbands than the husbands did. Kinsey thought it was because the husbands *wanted* more intercourse and the wives were complaining about it. (In fact, in the *Female* volume when he had a larger sample – 706 couples – the figures were almost equal.[61])

Then, though Lewontin dismisses this, I don't see why discrepancies wouldn't result from men boasting and women covering up, or from the exclusion of prostitutes. Also, if respondents think (or know in the case of Kinsey) that it is *orgasms* which count, then men and women could have intercourse the same number of times, but men would report more orgasms.

But, of course, in general terms Lewontin is quite right. You cannot be sure everyone will tell the truth; in fact, you can be sure only that some unknown number won't – or won't tell everything. And Kinsey was perfectly aware of this: 'For the remainder of this volume it should, therefore, be recognised that the data are probably fair approximations, but only approximations of the fact.'[62]

All one can do, then, is to try and judge which surveys come *closest* in their approximation. And here we have to return to the interview, since this is the tool which extracts the information. So important is the interview that I was at some pains to explain Kinsey's methods in detail. You will recall the single sheet and memorised code and questions which allowed such flexibility, such rapid questioning, the intense and continuous eye contact. You will remember the arduous year-long training,

---

* Actually, Gorer's survey had equal figures here, but Gorer's figures are so low and his questioning so innocuous that it doesn't really signify as to rates and incidences.

Kinsey's urging of rapport and sympathy, and the enormous difficulty he had finding people capable of doing it.

One turns, therefore, with some eagerness to this aspect of the recent 1994 surveys. No difficulty in getting interviewers, at any rate. The US survey chose women – 220 of them. They were in fact middle-aged women who did interviewing part-time all over the country. (They were known internally, apparently, as 'The Blue Rinse Brigade'.) As they fanned blithely out across America, especially attractive matrons were given 'assistants' (i.e. chaperones) but their Blue Rinse status took care of that. No passes were made. Quite a task, though, one might think, to train these amiable figures and indeed 'This project required extensive training before entering the field.' In fact, the training took *three days*! The importance attached to this whole area can be gauged by the fact that where Kinsey devoted an entire chapter to the interview alone, the US survey's account occupied a single page.[63]

The same extraordinary picture emerges with other surveys. The UK survey employed 488 interviewers, of whom 421 were women. There was some improvement here. The interviewers were at least chosen from groups trained in dealing with sensitive topics – drugs, pay, etc.; additional training was specifically on interviewing for sex. It, too, took three days. The 1993 French training also took three days, and the adequacy of the interviewing, compared to Kinsey's, can be guessed at when one learns the whole thing was done on the telephone.

This state of affairs was compounded by other things. With an eye, one might almost think, to giving respondents an excuse to avoid questions, in the US survey 21 per cent of the interviews took place with other people present – 15 per cent with children, 6 per cent with spouses or partners.[64] The same was true of the UK survey, though no percentages were given. They had no idea how reliable memory was when subjected to their methods since they did no retakes. Rapport and sympathy were actually *discouraged* in favour of a cool, objective detachment. Instead of a quick, flexible, learnt interview, both surveys employed cumbersome forty-page questionnaires through which the interviewers lumbered – 'If the answer to 16b is "Never", move to 19c.' Both surveys found it so difficult to get people to respond to 'sensitive' questions, they had them write answers down (both the US and UK surveys used a special sealed envelope), though Kinsey and others[65] have found that people shrink from committing things to paper. (The fact that the UK survey found their respondents reported more homosexuality in this way than when they were asked directly is simply an indictment of their interviewers, not a proof that the written system is better. If it were really better why did they not employ it for the whole exercise?)

What seems to have happened is that since Kinsey's interviewing methods did not come under the same serious attack as other aspects of his books, present-day practitioners have relaxed about it. By ignoring it they have rendered all their other refinements pointless, since if you can't get the information properly in the first place it doesn't matter who you get it from or if they do or do not correspond to your national population.

Three last points should be made. Long before anyone knew of Kinsey's bisexuality, his homosexual sample was criticised a) for including figures from his state farm histories and b) for the way in which he sought out homosexuals. It was perfectly obvious to Kinsey and the team that, left entire, his data would bias the results. They therefore sharply weighted down these figures by comparison with their 100 per cent groups, a quarter of the total sample and in which no homosexual bias could exist. Nevertheless, this criticism still exercised Paul Gebhard and during the 1970s he removed *all* suspect data – that from prisons, specially selected groups etc., re-examined the weightings in relation to the 100 per cent groups, and then recalculated all the findings. To his surprise, this 'cleaned' data produced homosexual percentages only marginally less than before. Thus, where Kinsey had 37 per cent, Gebhard had 36.4 per cent; the 10 per cent sank to 9.9 per cent for white college males; though it was somewhat lower for lower levels, where of course much of the 'cleaning' had gone on. None the less, Gebhard was able to conclude that the cleaning 'has not yet caused us to recant any important assertion'.[66]

Second, whether the figure for exclusively or partly homosexual behaviour is 2 per cent or 12.7 per cent or anything in between makes not the slightest difference to Kinsey's argument. Two per cent of US or UK males is such a vast number it is quite absurd to suggest they should be prosecuted. Everyone's sin is indeed no one's sin.

Finally, it is clear that because of Kinsey's interviewing technique, the mass surveys since him are less effective than he and his team were at extracting details of sensitive matters like homosexuality, extramarital affairs, masturbation, child-adult sex and so on. I would go further. *All* sex is sensitive. I would conclude that, with the provisos I have made – and I should perhaps emphasise Kinsey's sample

deficiencies in the lower levels – Kinsey's two volumes, as far as 'approximating to the truth' goes, were superior to anything that has come since.
And the fact, averaged out, that the three main surveys that have come
since have, as regards exclusively homosexual men, hovered at about 2.1
per cent,* is a measure of how they were all equally wrong, not that
Kinsey was.

Nor, in general terms, was Kinsey thought wrong in 1948 and 1949.
As the press, public and scientific clamour gradually died down, he
emerged triumphant, ready to set out in earnest after a far more elusive,
fascinating and baffling figure – the human female.

---

* A figure prominent among New York gays in 1994 said on reading reports of
this conclusion – 'But I've slept with 1% myself.' Paul Gebhard had a gay friend
whose criticism of the US survey was equally concise, if coarser. 'Do they think
I'm going to tell some old woman who reminds me of my mother that I'm a cock
sucker?' The inclusion of masturbation above as 'sensitive', incidentally, is
interesting. Both the UK and US surveys found that once again this had become
something people were ashamed of admitting. Is this because, as it has become
easier to get sexual partners, solitary sex is an admission of failure? Or is it just
another reflection on the Blue Rinse Brigade and the other female interviewers?

PART IV

Sex:
The Female *Volume*

*Women are strong; women are important. Zhun/twa men say that women
are the chiefs, the rich ones, the wise ones. Because women possess something
very important, something that enables men to live: their genitals.*

*A woman can bring a man life, even if he is almost dead. She can give
him sex and make him alive again. If she were to refuse, he would die! If
there were no women around, their semen would kill men. Did you know
that? If there were only men, they would all die. Women make it possible for
them to live. Women have something so good that if a man takes it and
moves about inside it, he climaxes and is sustained.*

Nisa: The Life and Words of a !Kung Woman,
Marjorie Shostak, 1990, p. 288

15

Money – Branching Out – Kinsey's Sexual Experiments: 1948–9

Thank heaven for having given me the love of women. To many she gives not the noble passion of lust.

John Wilkes, *Essay on Woman*, 1763

1

A great deal of 1948, and much of 1949, was of course taken up with the tumult of the *Male* publication and its aftermath. 'We have spent an entire week,' Kinsey was already writing irritably (but excitedly) to Larry Saunders in January, 'at the cost to us of endless man hours, entertaining an extraordinary top journalist, Mr St. Clair McKelway.'[1] The 'top journalist' was doing a big piece for *Life*, with a photographer who was to get into trouble with Kinsey later.

But under the beneficent sunshine of fame, a certain relaxation became evident. Shortly after the *Male* volume came out, around 15 January, Earle Marsh, the young gynaecologist who had effectively seduced Kinsey in California some time before, arrived to stay with the Kinseys.[2] Although he was to help Kinsey professionally, his chief role at this point was sexual.

Marsh fulfilled this task with pleasure, and described it graphically. But on this visit – and on subsequent ones – he also had sex with Mac. Still very close emotionally, the Kinseys now 'slept in different bedrooms', said Marsh. 'I don't think he had sex with Mac to have sex, but if I was there we'd all have sex. Kinsey and I'd be having sex upstairs and I'd go down and have sex with Mac in the same house. She accepted what went on, you know ... They totally accepted what the other one did, totally.'

She accepted what he did, Kinsey told Marsh, because 'She knows that when I make up my mind to do something I do it.' Yet it seems it would not necessarily be accurate to see Mac having to compromise too much here, since compromise implies an element of reluctance, a giving way in the interests of harmony. Mac seems to have entered in eagerly. Marsh was astonished and delighted at how she enjoyed herself. '[She] was tremendous.'³

Let us pause an instant here. This information was one of a number of similar items James Jones uncovered with skill and persistence. Some reviewers were disgusted. It depends how you view such things. One of the reasons Kinsey celebrated sex was the way it automatically brought with it a charge of affection – and its power, like a spring, of endless revival.⁴ Here, it re-awoke for a while a 27-year-old marriage, and Marsh was also struck by the atmosphere of generosity, of warmth, in the home, between the two.

During his Bloomington visits, Marsh joined in the various staff encounters. 'I also had sex with everyone else round there too . . . we all sucked one another.' But he became aware that while Kinsey joined in, with husbands* and wives equally – one wife always refused him.⁵ It seems likely that this was Alice Martin, still harbouring her resentment.

One further thing we should notice. Kinsey by this time had evolved, when strictly on his own, a much closer association between pain and sexual pleasure than is usual – and in the secondary and limited dictionary meaning he was certainly a masochist. But Jones goes much further than this. It is his contention that Kinsey was a masochist in the much more graphic, clinical sense used by S/M practitioners and those who study them. Since this contention underpins his whole case against Kinsey, we must examine it. It is time to return briefly to Hoboken and South Orange, since the origins of Jones' argument lie there.

2

Let me just remind you of those distant events. At age nine or so, a group of Hoboken kids, including Kinsey, used to play about, among other things inserting straws up various orifices including their penises. Then,

---

* Except Paul Gebhard. Conscientiously, as we'll see, Gebhard tried a number of times but could never enjoy H sex. (Gebhard in conversation with the author.)

at about age sixteen, Kinsey set fire to the floor of his bedroom with a smuggled-in Bunsen burner. In the hole under the burnt floorboards there was found, many years later, a brush handle minus the bristles (see pp. 14–15 and 23–24).

These are the bones of Jones' case. Here is its outline.

Kinsey always made a point in his later work of emphasising how early sexual experiences set the pattern for later ones. Jones assumes the penis insertion was painful and now takes a quantum leap of some magnitude. He imagines that the brush handle discovered in the South Orange attic became part of a masochistic ritual developed by Kinsey during adolescence and which had started with the straw insertion at Hoboken. Riven by guilt over masturbation, he was only able to do it if he punished himself at the same time – and he punished himself by using the brush end and causing himself 'exquisite pain', augmented by vivid fantasies of group 'humiliation directed at him by others.'[6]

This development is one of the central pillars (the other is homosexuality) in Jones' interpretation of Kinsey's character. Masochism became, according to Jones, one of Kinsey's 'demons' – driving him and distorting him, and eventually becoming one cause of his later deliberate concentration on 'perversions' which 'flawed' – a favourite word of Jones' – Kinsey's research.

Now it is perfectly true that during the late 1940s it emerged that Kinsey practised a form of masturbation which did indeed involve urethral insertions, and that by this time he had evolved certain patterns in which pain and pleasure were closely associated (see pp. 336–7).

But the operative word here is *evolved*. You must be very sure, when you transpose behaviour in a man of forty-five or fifty-five back, unchanged and entire, on to the boy of nine and the youth of sixteen, first, that you are accurate about the adult behaviour and, second, that you have some solid, *contemporary* evidence to support the link (in this case from 1899 to 1910). Jones is wrong on the first count, and distinctly shaky on the second.

Take those lurid 'fantasies of humiliation'. Turning to the references it is startling to find they have nothing to do with Kinsey at all – what is cited are studies of *other people's* fantasies, and these done seventy or nearly a hundred years ago by Havelock Ellis and Krafft-Ebing.[7] On this basis you could cite studies of arsonists and point, in Kinsey's case, to the hole scorched by his Bunsen burner. In fact, such evidence as we have of Kinsey and masochistic fantasies, again dating from more than forty years ahead, is that he didn't have them, couldn't have them and, when asked, refused to have them.[8]

Then, urethral insertion is not, for some males, particularly painful, at least when done with a straw or, say, narrow rubber or plastic or glass tubing. On the contrary, the urethra for these men is an erogenous zone and the activity takes place in pursuit of pleasure.* Cases in the medical literature usually have this origin. What sometimes happens is a slow desensitising of the urethral passage, and the necessity, therefore, of inserting larger and larger objects. It is then that pain may gradually enter in. This is probably what happened with Kinsey – but over many years and, in my view, much later than early adolescence.

And masochism – left unexamined by Jones – is complex. Certainly the idea that religious prohibition produces guilt which can be circumvented by self-punishment sounds plausible. But it seems to have nothing to do with true masochism. In fact, we shall find, when we look again at this subject at the appropriate time, that *none* of the central elements in masochism apply to Kinsey.[9] And so, already alerted to Jones' use of sources, one looks to these again. Here the citation is not just startling; it is irrelevant. He refers us to passages in a fascinating book by Philip Greven, *Spare the Child.* These do indeed relate masochism to strict religious (or other) upbringing – *but only where this involves persistent and violent corporal punishment, usually inflicted when young, and usually by some loved figure.* Whipping, beating, physical abuse and humiliation are the *essential* ingredient for the effects to result in masochism. Nowhere does Jones attempt to suggest this was Kinsey's lot; rightly, since it was not. The citation is not just irrelevant; it contradicts the whole masochistic case.[10]

And Kinsey himself, who eventually came to know a great deal about the subject, as he did about all matters sexual, and who was always totally open and not in the least ashamed about this aspect of himself with his colleagues, never called himself a masochist.[11]

Indeed, perhaps this suggests a different way of looking at it. Between 1940 and 1946, Kinsey managed to throw off his childhood and adolescent guilts so completely that Paul Gebhard had never known

---

* By a coincidence my father, who was a doctor in the Navy, had a rating from whom he had to extract a length of thin plastic tube which had vanished into his urethra. The rating's aim was pleasure. Dr John Bancroft, with whom I discussed this, said that in some females the urethra was also an erogenous zone. He thought this could be the explanation of the elusive 'G spot'.

anyone with fewer sexual inhibitions.[12] Germane to this may be cases studied by Dr. C. A. Tripp. People who lose their religion, as Kinsey did, also as a corollary lose the pattern of inhibitory barriers religion has set up. But often the pattern has become ingrained and has to be put back and sometimes the barrier chosen is pain. Tripp calls it 'the reincarnation of prudery'.[13] If this is relevant to Kinsey, the process cannot have started till he lost his faith, many years after South Orange.

The South Orange brush handle was a good half-an-inch across.[14] It would have taken time to learn how to accommodate it (in fact Kinsey never inserted objects of this size). Also if it were the tool of such essential, secret and demonic activity, why leave it behind?

This is very speculative, if interesting territory, but rather than Jones' ingenious but essentially invented presentation, one has to see Kinsey possibly discovering an original form of pleasurable masturbation when young. Nothing else. Not till well into manhood, and then over many years, did he slowly evolve his later practices. I would assign the humble brush handle to the more mundane role of stirring whatever Kinsey concocted on top of the Bunsen burner which at some point set fire to the floor underneath it.

As for demons, there are no demons here (come to that, there are no 'demons' anywhere in Kinsey's life). He was never a masochist in this particular sense – a physically abused childhood, association of love and pain, a *partnership* of humiliation with someone else doing the humiliating, the need to be whipped and hurt – which Jones uses, and his case requires.* And confirmation comes with Earle Marsh. He, who enjoyed a sadistic role here, found Kinsey 'was kind of punk when it comes to S/M'. He shrank from being beaten. He refused to be humiliated. He refused to dress up. He refused to enact staged fantasies. Paul Gebhard remembers that Kinsey, in fact, actively disliked watching S/M scenes and would walk out on them.[15]

Marsh had been invited to Bloomington. But now the whole world did indeed begin to beat a path to Kinsey's door. One of the first was C. A. Tripp, who rang Kinsey up the moment he had finished reading the *Male* volume.

---

* All this is detailed in the excellent 1994 review of all S/M studies since 1987 by Thomas S. Weinberg. Indeed, Weinberg found pain was not the core of S/M sex at all, but only a symbol and a means to express the submission in the relationship. (See Weinberg, 1994, in bibliography.)

'Tripp,' said his close friend Jack Tebbel, 'would ring the President if he wanted to.' Something about this directness, a challenging quality in the 28-year-old New York photographer, that he said he was planning a book on homosexuality, the very fact he *was* a photographer, all this appealed to Kinsey, and he asked him down to Bloomington at once.[16]

Tripp stayed with Kinsey from 2 to 4 February – and the visit changed his life. Tripp found a hero and a mentor: 'Anyway, I am with you for life and everything I can do is not enough,' he wrote on his return.[17] Under Kinsey's guidance he was to leave photography, take his PhD, and become a psychotherapist. He did indeed finally write one of the most perceptive books about homosexuality ever written.[18] On Kinsey's side, he found he enjoyed Tripp's repeated 'challenges' about the facts and deductions in the *Male* volume, and Tripp became one of only two people (the other was to be the writer Glenway Wescott) he always visited in New York. And as time passed he came to confide things to both men he told no one else.

But work was the real significance here. Kinsey, as we've seen, was perfectly aware of the scientific shortcomings in his field of study. Science meant observation, and observation here required film. 'Within hours of my arrival,' said Tripp, Kinsey was asking him if he could film sexual activity. Tripp said he could.[19] The research was about to enter a new dimension.

In fact, Kinsey's mind was running strongly towards film at this point. He already had film from Frank Beach of rats, pigeons and mink mating, now in January he was about to get cats. But he also suddenly started to write to Dr Albert R. Shadle at the State University of New York at Buffalo (shortened to SUNY Buffalo). He hears Shadle has a film of porcupines mating – is this so? Shadle – plump, timid, sixty-four – writes back at length, not answering the question: '. . . the porcupine has a number of very interesting points which are probably peculiar to the porcupine.'[20]

There is something touching about the relationship that developed between Shadle and Kinsey. Shadle is passionate about porcupines, but infinitely restricted, infinitely humble. Kinsey, apart from fruitless efforts to get the porcupine film, is always encouraging him to expand, boosting him, praising him – he persuaded him at one point to try for an NRC grant (mostly for green stuff for his porcupines). Shadle only asked for $300. The NRC itself had to tell him to ask for more. But now, about to come to SUNY Buffalo anyway, Kinsey made a date.

One senses the relief when, on 16 February 1948, Kinsey was at last able to leave Bloomington for New York State, followed swiftly by New York City, and plunge once again into the hectic whirl of lectures and history-taking. But there was more than just this behind these visits, and indeed behind the acceleration in his film plans. Kinsey was beginning to realise the project was now rich.

4

In February, Saunders had offered Kinsey an advance on royalties. Kinsey answered not to bother – he'd borrow from Indiana University. But by 2 March when Saunders asked him if he'd like a cheque for $25,000, Kinsey snapped it up by return of post.[21]

As the sales soared, so did the team's expectations. In his annual *Report* of April 1st to the NRC, Kinsey wrote, 'it is quite probable that in time the entire project could be supported from this source . . .'[22] Now very much getting favoured-author treatment, when Larry Saunders offered a gold cigarette lighter to whoever came closest to the year's sales, they were all wildly out – Kinsey (presumably not after the prize) guessed 300,000, Pomeroy 425,000, even Saunders guessed 350,000.[23]

None the less, a good deal of money was flowing in. It is instructive to see where it went. None, not now or ever, went to Kinsey or the team. It was all ploughed back into the project. But out of a first year's total of $93,672 from royalties, under $3,000 actually went on the project proper. This continued to run on the NRC's regular $40,000 and on the salaries and facilities being paid by Indiana University. $55,480 went on deposit as a reserve, and a whacking $35,237* was spent on the library and other collections of erotica and pornographic materials. You will recall that the total in 1947 for *ten years'* expenditure on this had been $10,000. This vastly increased concentration was to continue for three years until new anxieties made themselves felt – but collector Kinsey had finally got the bit between his teeth.

---

* Figures are taken from the Income Tax returns held in the Indiana University archives. They are, no doubt, as accurate as such things are. On the return of 1949–50 someone has panicked – 'reduce expenses etc.', and a second set of figures has been prepared reducing both these and royalty income. But they can be taken, like the *Male* volume itself, as approximations to the fact.

It was in connection with the collections that he had arranged to meet Andrey Avinoff in New York. Avinoff was an intriguing figure. He had, like his fellow lepidopterist and aristocrat, Vladimir Nabokov, fled Russia after the Revolution with his sister, and, a man of great charm and energy, became a success – vice-president of the Entomological Society, director of the Carnegie Museum in Pittsburgh, one of those men who 'knew everybody'. Like Nabokov, too, he was an artist – but a painter, a homosexual who had, as he said with considerable understatement, 'tried my hand at the favorite subject of our brotherhood'.[24] (His sister became a well-known portrait painter and was painting FDR when he had his stroke.) Avinoff left all his erotic paintings to Kinsey.

Having heard he was after groups, Avinoff had in fact written to Kinsey late in 1947, wondering if he'd considered the world of artists, singers, musicians, ballet dancers – 'an interesting group to study'; also 'interior decorators should not be omitted'.[25] At their first meeting* in Avinoff's Century Club on 11 March 1948, Kinsey agreed. Lifting off, as Avinoff's acute social antennae instantly detected, with the irresistible buoyancy of fame, Kinsey could now be introduced to anyone – and Avinoff at once got to work on his ballet dancers, artists and interior decorators. He also raised the idea of a history of erotic art. He was to see a lot of Kinsey this year.

Insofar as anyone could see a lot of Kinsey. He was frantically busy – but he did manage to see Tripp. One of the things Tripp realised, or stumbled on, was that the bully in Kinsey would respond to Tripp's argumentative approach. His 'list of challenges' was ready.

But Kinsey had an aim – photography. He was struck, according to Thomas Waugh, the best historian of this subject and period, by Tripp's 'sharp and compelling' homoerotic work. Especially by 'a stunning set [depicting] anal intercourse between a famous male model and a Broadway singer [which] ... impressed Kinsey with its contrast of sexual outlawry and social respectability'.[26] However, at this point Kinsey, who had decided to test an odd observation of Kenneth Green's about male ejaculation, wanted more down-to-earth data. 'I need 2,000 orgasms,' he told Tripp briskly. 'All I want is the genitalia – close up. Some form of masturbation. I have to see the semen coming out.' Tripp and his 31-

---

* Actually their second. They had met briefly before over a small gall wasp collection Avinoff had, as Kinsey reminded him. Avinoff had forgotten. (Kinsey to Avinoff, 20 (?) December 1947.)

year-old business partner, their hearts slightly sinking, agreed to try and set it up.[27]

Thereafter it was two and a half months' hard graft for Kinsey – apart from the Philadelphia *Bulletin*'s 'famous author' lunch on 19 April. He gave some fifteen lectures: at Buffalo, then to New York, dashing back to Bloomington for a psychology symposium, to Baltimore to talk to the Johns Hopkins Medical School, back to New York to give the Herman Biggs memorial lecture and to talk to Dr Guttmacher's committee on sex law reform ... and he still managed to take 350 histories.

The meeting Kinsey was most terrified of, and to which he was pointedly not asked, was that of the American Social Hygiene Association on 30 and 31 March. Since he had shown their decades of lavish spending to have been totally useless, he was quite sure they were out to destroy him – Margaret Mead was a speaker and other 'enemies'. Letters flew about[28] as Kinsey rallied his forces, especially from Dickinson, who began to sign off 'Yours rather incessantly'. Dickinson himself attended, so did George Corner and various allies. In fact, the meeting passed off relatively harmlessly.

But Kinsey's intense anxiety and activity around it were symptomatic. He was under attack; he had to fight back. Two additional outlets now appeared which he used with some ferocity.

5

From now on Kinsey used his lectures and speeches to get back at his critics. Thomas Clark, historian of Indiana University, notes how belligerent and provocative they often were after the *Male* volume came out.[29] He would also use these lectures from now on to answer his critics directly – counter-attacks which must sometimes have mystified his audience.

Then there were the weekly staff meetings on Friday mornings when they were in Bloomington. Here he would pour out his frustration at the recent attacks and ask for suggestions as to what they should do; sometimes, it seemed, he would simply vent his anger on the team. Especially on Martin. Martin's relationship with Kinsey could be fraught. Kinsey was still attracted to him, so his position was privileged. But by now Kinsey had had to accept Martin's rejection – which could suddenly irritate him.[30] Martin, from his privileged position, would sometimes defend one of the critics who, he thought, had a point. Or he would continue, stubbornly, to bring up a solution Kinsey had already rejected. He might even make a joke.

We have a record of Martin in one of those situations, though in a slightly different context. Gebhard remembered a conference of distinguished penologists at Bloomington. All at once Martin, usually silent, burst out – *locking up* was wrong. Why bars? Why locked doors? Why walls? If everything was open a lot of pressure would be taken off the prisoners, there would be an easing of atmosphere where rehabilitation would be easier.

After a startled pause, one of the penologists said gently: 'But some of these men are very dangerous, Mr Martin. How would you suggest we stop them escaping?' 'Why that's easy,' said Martin. 'How about a minefield round the prison?'[31]

But in staff meetings, as Martin rambled on, Kinsey would suddenly start shouting, '*You* are holding up the project, *you* Martin.' 'I've seen Martin come out of those meetings,' said Bill Dellenback, who was soon to join the team, 'figuratively covered in blood.' Kinsey would shout at Pomeroy too. Only Paul Gebhard, *Dr* Paul Gebhard, was spared.[32]

By June, when Kinsey was fifty-four, he was exhausted. 'You look more tired than I have ever seen you,' Dickinson (now eighty-seven) had written earlier.[33] A trip to California which would include rest was arranged for the Kinseys together at the end of the month.

Till then, of course, he drove himself as usual. Two weeks in New York, where he saw his old biology teacher Natalie Roeth (he sent her irises in August).[34] He also met Avinoff again, and from now on, as their art idea expanded, the Russian sent a steady stream of erotic gifts, new plans and suggestions for purchases. There is an urgency about Avinoff which makes one wonder whether he was not aware in some way that he had only eighteen months to live (he had a bad heart). He stayed at Bloomington this month, sending Mac roses.[35]

There were lightning dashes to Chicago – once to 'a gaie stag reception for their honored guest Dr Alfred C. Kinsey' from Derek Hobhard and his new boyfriend Harry Kohnoke. 'Appointments for case histories are obligatory ...'[36] These were some of the early Rush Street, Chicago, boys, to whom Kinsey remained as loyal as he did to his old teacher.

Then he spent a day in Chicago seeing Jim Edden, fifty-eight, who liked sucking off married men and then masturbating; nothing unusual in that – and it is strange how run-of-the-mill it seems – but his letter in

April had outlined such a huge history since he was seventeen that Kinsey felt he had to take it himself. Then he and Mac left for California.

They went on 30 June and stayed till 3 August. And, once again – lectures, speeches, histories. One of the speeches was significant – this was held at the University of California at Berkeley on 12 July. Three large halls, wired up, filled to capacity an hour and a half before he began, 2,000 people, Mac among them. But after it, August Vollmer, who headed the Department of Criminology, set up contacts for Kinsey in the famous, or infamous, San Quentin prison. This was destined to play an important role in his life.[37]

It was not quite as usual. Mac, Kinsey told Emily Mudd, did what she loved doing: exploring, botanising, 'mostly on the mountains, and on the seashore, with lots of hiking and camping. I got some of it with her.'[38]

Yet it is not these rare breaks, but the usual trips we must get some idea of, since they occupied half his time.

6

Kinsey and his team travelled hundreds of thousands of miles together, the Buick (never replaced) getting steadily more battered.[39] Miami, Boston, Philadelphia, St. Louis, Chicago – all over America. It was exhilarating – the chase – and exhausting. Here, above all, applied Vincent Nowlis' image of the submarine. 'We were in a very isolated, self-contained world,' he said, 'sliding through dangerous waters on a difficult mission, desperate for time, with the commander directing every move and the crew utterly dependent on him and on each other. No one could afford to make a mistake.'

And one can only speculate about the curiously powerful and unusual nature of the bond that bound them – indeed bound the whole of the top staff and their wives – with the threads of intimately shared sexual experience that ran between them. But it is perhaps significant that when the nature of the bond finally began to surface it was, as far as the team went, via the two who had not had sex with Kinsey.

Paul Gebhard said the bond was 'close', without elaboration – but then Gebhard was one of those two. Not that he didn't make heroic efforts in the H direction. 'I said to myself, "I am an anthropologist, I must participate in the local customs."' Kinsey took him to some baths. Gebhard looked about him; eventually – 'I had to wrestle with myself' –

he chose the oldest figure there, 'he'll die before the end'. Gebhard was
still young enough to be responsive to any physical stimuli and managed
a semi-erection, but he could never – he tried four or five times – get a
full one and never had an orgasm during an H encounter.[40]

There were a few other sexual encounters on trips. Mac very occasionally came with them. On one of these, both Pomeroy and Kinsey
himself had had sex with her, and Kinsey asked Gebhard if he'd like to.
'You don't tell someone you don't want their wife.' Mac was perfectly
willing, and perfectly passive. Gebhard felt she had been manoeuvred
into it; but it is also likely she realised that Gebhard, unlike Earle Marsh,
had been himself manoeuvred. Where once Kinsey had rejoiced in her
responsiveness, telling Kroc and others about it, he now sometimes
complained to Gebhard she wasn't as interested as he, Kinsey, was – an
odd complaint since it was a natural declension, after near thirty years
of marriage, which he often charted in his writings.[41]

But in fact there was little time, or energy, for sex on these trips; the
project was all.

As they drove, they would discuss it, or else talk about sex. The real
differences between male and female sexuality. What would be the ideal
sexual world? That was easy – a world without guilt. In the early days,
Kinsey had very occasionally talked about his childhood and youth.

It was monotonous, sometimes boring. Wherever they arrived, the
commander of the submarine would deliver a little lecture on the
ecology, the flora and fauna. It was exhausting because Kinsey worked
them so hard – starting at 9 a.m., finishing at 11.30 p.m. He could neither
stand nor understand time passed doing anything else. Pomeroy remembered once in Miami, trying to unwind, he and Gebhard played a round
of miniature golf before the course closed at midnight. Kinsey stood
watching gloomily in the neon glare, not joining in, wondering how they
could waste time like that.

They took trains more often and then planes. Even here, Kinsey's
parsimony made it exhausting. Pomeroy remembered walking with
heavy suitcases in the hot sun from Broad Street Station in Philadelphia
to the Ritz-Carlton Hotel because Kinsey wouldn't take cabs. This only
changed when the team pointed out they were wasting time walking.

The commander's eccentricities occasionally enlivened things. In
Philadelphia again, in the Thirtieth Street Station, a vast railway cavern
several storeys high, Kinsey suddenly stopped and began sniffing.
'Someone's been smoking here.'

For Kinsey himself, apart from the almost endless fascination of the histories, the trips were enlivened by food. At home a frugal eater, he now became a gourmet. He made a collection of restaurants, his friends helping – try 'Formos on 52nd near 7th', wrote Beach; Kinsey told Beach about the Balalaika in San Francisco.[42] He loved Italian food, and seafood – especially oysters and lobster.

Yet perhaps gourmet isn't quite the word. He had to impose himself on food, stamp it with his personality, control it, as he did with every-thing else. He did so by covering it with salt or mayonnaise. In O'Donnell's Seafood Restaurant in Washington the speciality was turtle soup. Kinsey invariably swamped it with sherry.[43]

He seemed immune to the snatched late meals or hurried snacks, but the team often got fearful diarrhoea. Kinsey's prescription hadn't changed since he'd almost destroyed the stomachs of his graduates – starvation plus large quantities of fresh or canned orange juice.

And how well he knew America! The remote mountains and wilder-nesses from his gall wasp days, now the cities and townships, and the secret lives of their inhabitants. The opportunistic nature of his search, while it caused considerable chaos in his sampling,* led to an extra-ordinary richness. And gradually, as time passed, he held in his head a sort of sexual map of America. When Derek Hobhard left Chicago for Houston in 1950, Kinsey was sad but commented, 'I have heard enough about the city to understand.'[44]

He was already beginning to move among some of the most brilliant and sophisticated figures of his time in New York. But writing to Dickinson about abortion in 1944, he said it wasn't induced abortion that ended pregnancies, nor VD. There was a 'terrific amount' of spon-taneous abortion. It was too early pregnancy, appalling poverty. 'We got histories from women who have delivered half their children alone ... lack of care after birth, generally poor nutrition, experience of disease of all sorts ... These conditions are probably true for as much as half our population.'[45] He had been to the depths.

And when, after three weeks, they all set off back for Bloomington very tired, great care was now taken since for the only time in the pro-

---

* And I have perhaps been lenient on Kinsey here, though it seems to me that his carelessness, there is no other word, is only rarely of significance. There is a good (and amusing) account of it and the degree to which it matters in *The Kinsey Data – Marginal Tabulation of the 1938–1963 Interviews* by Paul Gebhard et al., W.B. Saunders, 1979.

ject the sex histories and the names of who had given them were held together. Gebhard once nearly had a fight with a black bellhop trying to wrest his briefcase from him. Also, if all four had been killed in an accident the unwritten code would have been lost. On the rare occasions this happened, Kinsey would sometimes travel separately – but usually Martin was left behind as repository of the code.[46]

7

When Kinsey and Mac got back to Indiana University in August he was still suffering from exhaustion, and therefore put himself, he told Emily Mudd, on what he called an 'easier schedule'.[47]

How much easier? One result of his success was an explosion in Kinsey's correspondence. His letters got shorter after 1948 – the shortest I've found was to Mr B.B.D. who'd asked what fellatio meant: 'Dear Mr. D, Fellatio is mouth contact with the male genitalia.' But only lunatics were not answered – and even lunatics, or at least the highly neurotic, were answered if anxious. Does sex while pregnant lead to polio? No. Tampons were new and there was general (and revealing) anxiety – they might prove 'an excitant'. No – all they do is stretch the hymen. Does suppressing sex lead to stuttering? Kinsey didn't know, but from several hundred stuttering sex histories he'd noted that once sexually aroused, people cease to stutter.

Many people wrote about being persecuted or prosecuted; Kinsey always replied, giving advice, encouraging. They wrote about their sex lives: a young black woman of twenty-three who'd had forty men and loved sex and men; an airline pilot, full of guilt, who'd first ejaculated at twelve (self-fellatio).

And we suddenly glimpse in these letters the post-history *general* curiosity of Kinsey. A female history writes to say she had been interested when, after the interview, he'd suddenly asked 'Why I married a certain kind of man. There was not time to answer. Anyhow, I didn't know the answer . . . [but it] gave me something to think about.' She had thought, and now realised why. She was married to an Egyptian and was far happier.

Odd letters arrived. Mrs Mary Downside wrote and asked for Kinsey's *Life of the Frog*. Henry Zchloch from Switzerland, on a typewriter with a mauve ribbon, wrote about the problems of men who couldn't get sufficient intercourse. His solution was a very large number of masturbatory machines of 'absolutely incontestable hygienic quality' set up all over Europe like urinals. There was a good deal of animal correspondence, much from a Dr M.C. Klang – rams ejaculating six times, a dog continually for ten days ('very important,' said Kinsey).

But of course the vast majority were ordinary letters, from married homosexuals, people with simple and less simple questions and problems, letters from old Bowdoin alumni (calling him Al), criticism, praise, from histories in gratitude or offering other histories, and autograph seekers (always granted). Some of them could be answered by formula. Many begin 'Thank you for your interest in our research . . .' and end '. . . I hope our paths may cross (or cross again) in the future,' when his correspondents have expressed no interest in the first, and the last thing Kinsey wants is the second. Many of the letters are completely unnecessary. He thanks people for a visit, they thank him for having them, he thanks them for their thank-you letter, they write again to say *how* useful it had been . . .[48]

Analysis of the figures in Appendix B shows that in the five years 1948 to 1953 his correspondence leapt twentyfold over the previous ten years. Every letter was answered personally by Kinsey although 80 per cent of them could have been answered by the team.*

Only two further points should be made. As I read file after file of correspondence in the Kinsey Institute there was gradually borne in on me the huge preponderance of despair, the mess of lives, the frustration and pain of those who wrote, until sometimes the great *weight* of it and the endlessness became overwhelming in its sadness. Kinsey must have felt this cumulative burden, as doctors do, and counsellors.

And this was compounded because, the second point, he now often took to doing letters (and other work) even later into the night and early morning, which was itself a consequence of another exponential increase – the stream of visitors who came to Bloomington to see the ISR (Institute for Sex Research).

* I was struck by how often Kinsey wrote a letter where we, until recently and even still, would have telephoned. Are there figures for the rise in telephone use in America (or England for that matter) from 1940 on? In 1955 he was still writing irritatedly, 'This sort of thing has happened before. Can we count on your more prompt service in the Bloomington Post Office, or do we have to turn to the telephone as a means of communication?' (Kinsey to Bloomington Post Office, 4 May 1955.)

8

The 'tour' had a threefold function. First, and most obviously, PR.
Guests would often take the *Spirit of St. Louis*, leaving New York at 6.05
p.m. and arriving Indianapolis 8.45 a.m. the next day, to be met and
whisked at once to Bloomington.

The extent of the tour slightly depended on the status of the visitors. When Marshall Balfour of the Rockefeller Foundation came in
May 1948 with his colleagues from the Medical Division, they got the
works: all the files and statistics and tabulations and charts, the library,
the collection (selected items); the full- and part-time staff produced
and introduced with hyperbolic panache – 'this is Dr Remak ... degree
in *Berlin*', 'Professor Edmondson, our *statistician*'. A two- to three-hour
continuous lecture as Kinsey took them round. Then Wells, the vice-
president, and Payne. Meals in the Tudor Rooms, Kinsey discoursing
on the project, helping them lavishly to bottled mayonnaise. Future
plans. Had it been a weekend, they would have been asked to a
musicale.

Lesser visitors got less. Tripp, for instance, who also came in May,
much less. But the idea was to impress, particularly to impress, as we
noted, how scientific it all was, how clinical. And it was impressive.
Wells made a point of bringing round the legislature's budget committee so that ISR glory should reflect on to Indiana University.

Though the tours expended a good deal of Kinsey's energy, paradoxically their effect was the reverse of tiring. Gebhard noticed how
scientists invited down for their advice were often disconcerted not to
be asked it. Instead, they had Kinsey lecture them, and he got the
same charge out of this, the same lift, as Beach had observed
whenever Kinsey talked about his work. Bill Dellenback, who,
although he didn't officially arrive to join the team till April 1950,
was already working for Kinsey in late 1948 and through 1949,
noticed this aspect. The tours were 'a way of recreation under the
guise of work'.[49]

And the tours themselves, finally, became another collection. Once
Dellenback was installed, everyone who came was photographed and
sent a copy; then Kinsey obtained photographs of anyone who had ever
done sex research; then of anyone who had co-operated with him; then
of anyone connected at any *point* with sex research – all the important
figures in biology, animal studies, marriage guidance, in law and law

reform, psychiatry, psychology . . . Kinsey collections always expanded, not to fill anything, but to infinity.

And it was to concentrate on his more significant collections that Kinsey saw so much of Avinoff during the four months up to Christmas.

9

Over the next three to four years that drumbeat of rising numbers, with increasingly numerous trips out west, is continuous and relentless: with over 12,500 on *Male* publication, by April 1948 they had added 1,500 histories; by March/April 1950 Kinsey had a total of 16,500, 8,000 of them women; and by March/April 1954 17,000 (a striking indication of how much of 1951–3 was spent calculating and writing the *Female* volume).[50]

But it was the collections that, if at a tangent to the main task, now began to interest him more and more. Of course, all scientific disciplines need libraries relevant to their subject, but Kinsey went way beyond that. In part it was the voracious appetite of an obsessive collector; he was soon buying every and any work of erotica, sex research, sex history from any period and any country. And spending large sums – $2,250, for instance, in one go for 'several large cartons' of French erotica, according to Gershon Legman.[51]

Kinsey wrote or went to the dealers. They sometimes victimised him. 'He'd be in L.A. or somewhere,' said Gebhard, 'with half an hour to spare. The dealer would say – "Dr Kinsey, I have this four-volume set of Brentôme, and this and that – these merit a place in your library." Poor Kinsey didn't have time to appraise it all, he'd simply say "Well great, pack them up and post them." We bought some stuff that was pretty damn peripheral actually.'[52]

But this was exactly the same reservoir principle that had animated everything else – get enough, and eventually something would come of it. And Kinsey, by 1954, had a reservoir of erotic literature (not to mention objects and illustrative material) to rival the British Museum or legendary Vatican collection (legendary because, according to Legman, there are relatively few erotic works in the Vatican[53]).

There were other motives. Over the next three years, Kinsey sometimes grew bored with history-taking.* It is often noticeable in the correspondence how long and lively the collection letters are compared to others, especially when, as quite often, Kinsey is catching out those victimising dealers. 'We already own Genet's *Querelle de Brest* which you offered at $75.00. We paid $50 for our copy last spring.'[54]

In all the collections, Kinsey was rapidly building a worldwide network, stretching in the end to China, as he had with galls and to a lesser extent with sex research. But another, and fascinating, evolution was taking place which is most easily demonstrated by Avinoff and the art collection.

Throughout the summer, fall and winter, Avinoff sent a stream of (undated) letters – about an illustrated Omar Khayyam, about Genet, Cocteau, Dali, Beardsley. Gifts poured from his own collection, photographs of Nijinski as he was in 1915, prints, etchings, objects, paintings – till by January 1949 he estimated he had given the ISR $1,000 worth of material.[55] He came to stay in June, and saw Kinsey in New York in September, October and December. The Kinseys chose an Avinoff sketch for their Christmas 1948 card.

Preserved on three sheets of Indiana University Union paper, we can see how their ideas developed by discussion and letter. Avinoff has outlined, not just the simple history of erotic art he'd first suggested, but a map extending across Egyptian, Cretan, Assyrian, Persian and Sino-Japanese art, and then down from each of these heads; thus from Cretan to Greek-Etruscan, to Roman, the Hellenistic and Byzantine to the Romanesque, Gothic, Renaissance, Baroque and so to the nineteenth century and the Modern. Superimposed on this interconnected overview is the whole range of erotic/sexual behaviours and fantasies – heterosexual, homosexual, sado-masochistic, animal and so on – as manifested, via myth and legend, in art (which includes jewellery, sculpture, ceramics and so on) and as it can be traced back into pre-history.

It seems to be the beginning, as yet in sketch form, of an extraordinary enterprise to present the whole of world art, across space and through time, interpreted both erotically and sexually, and to see how it illuminates, expresses, and suggests, as far as is known, actual practices.

---

* The interview had long since ossified and he refused to allow changes – though odd things, like tattooing, would get tacked on for a while. Though he would pursue an interesting case with his customary brilliance, the team would be disconcerted to find there were large gaps in the other histories with nothing to put on to punch cards. (Paul Gebhard, in an interview with the author.)

We shall see related endeavours, including the forays Kinsey was now starting to make into observing and filming the physiology of sex.

10

Kinsey had observed sexual activity long before he began to film it. Pomeroy described to Dr Paul Fuller how prostitutes used to let him and Kinsey hide and watch them in action with their 'tricks', including the stealing of wallets. (In 1949 they asked Fuller to join the team.[56])

But one trouble about prostitutes, as far as Kinsey went, was that all their orgasms were faked. Nor did they help his immediate concern, which was, as I noted earlier, to test one of Green's more extraordinary observations: men didn't 'ejaculate' – i.e. 'throw out' – their semen, but that usually it just fell out.

Clarence Tripp and Bill Dellenback found their task, to their great relief, surprisingly easy. 'I gave a German boy, a male prostitute, $3 to masturbate,' said Tripp, 'and asked him to get more and he went out and grabbed everyone he knew.' By 3 November 1948 there were, literally, queues going round Tripp's apartment block in Greenwich Village's fashionable Sheridan Square, all eager to masturbate for $3 a go.[57]

They got some 300 of them on film, but rapidly branched out. They filmed someone Wescott described as 'a husky, Jewish, very attractive young man' who could lie on his back, hands pressed to his side, get an erection and ejaculate spontaneously. They made films of two Puerto Rican lovers and of other homosexual couples. Tripp himself starred in two films, and Kinsey would sometimes observe him perform with new lovers.[58]

In 1949 the filming was to move to an attic room in Kinsey's house on First Street, though some more filming was done in New York apartments. Wherever it was done, Dellenback became adept at setting up a powerful cone of light such that the performer(s) felt cut off, invisible to observation. It wasn't always easy – especially in winter, when the attic was cold. Earle Marsh couldn't do it till they left him alone with a timer to set off the camera. Wescott had similar difficulties.[59]

The filming of masturbation went on for four years. Just as 'Friends of the Research' – as these participants/helpers were now known – had before been asked for their sex histories (and still were), so now they were asked if they would masturbate, and many did. In the end, Kinsey had films of about a thousand men masturbating.[60]

And the result? To get some details of male reactions in orgasm,[61] and to find that Green had been right (and that many commentators today are still incorrect[62]). The sperm do the work. In 73 per cent of men, the semen just falls out; 25 per cent can go a little further and, very rarely, six to eight feet further.[63]

And in this huge effort for apparently rather small return, Kinsey is not just like all scientists, but like biographers too, whose days or weeks of research can result in a single sentence – or often nothing at all.

11

On 17 December 1948 a telegram arrived for Kinsey at his New York hotel (the Commodore): 'Anxious to meet you please telephone me Warwick Hotel – Mae West.'[64]

He ignored it – but he was now well and truly famous. Kinsey enjoyed his fame. He felt justified; it showed, he told Dickinson, 'the world has wanted this thing done'.[65] He enjoyed things like the banquet given for him on 7 May by the Sigma Delta Chi chapter at Indiana University as the faculty member who'd brought most distinction that year to the University. He liked, said Dellenback, being the figure all heads turned to when he came into a gathering, the one who'd been eagerly awaited.[66] One senses a greater ease, and pleasure in the friendliness fame calls forth.

Not that Kinsey stopped being difficult. He was furious, for instance, with the Condé Nast photographer who'd taken the photograph for *Life* in January. 'I think it is very bad and essentially slanderous,' he wrote. 'I very much wish you would destroy the negative and all prints of it.' Pomeroy attributes this to vanity.[67]

It is true there is something about how people describe Kinsey – the bow ties always slightly askew, the stubby hair 'tousled', through which, as Dorothy Collins observed, he was always 'rippling' his 'beautiful hands'[68] – that makes one feel he was conscious of how he looked. There is a certain confidence in the way he always dressed the same no matter how smart the company – always the same scrupulously clean but neatly mended clothes, the same polished but old shoes. But vanity is perhaps too strong a word – just as 'slanderous' is a strong word. I think the reason Kinsey was so angry was that he had a sensual face (an aspect

Glenway Wescott noticed at once) and certain photographs could catch an expression that seemed little short of lascivious.

Because, a final aspect of fame, he had to take care now. When C. A. Tripp put out his hand and rested it on his shoulder as they were coming out of the Astor, Kinsey gently removed it. 'It's gotten so that people recognise me to such an extent it isn't even safe to put an arm on me.'[69] He had to give up casual sex in bathhouses and tea-rooms. 'A lot of valuable research opportunities have had to be forgone,' he said to Gebhard, perhaps only half-joking.[70] He could no longer even hint that he approved of certain things he did approve of. 'We are of more value to everyone if we maintain our position as fact-finding and reporting scientists,' he wrote to one of dozens of such requests. 'We would immediately stir up trouble if we attempted to interpret or apply our material.'[71] It was the stance Corner had taken in his defence at the hygienists' meeting the year before, for example, and which Wells invariably took. It baffled opponents if it did not convince them.

The team too. 'Suppose someone had come up at a party and said did I think Marilyn Monroe looked sexy,' said Paul Gebhard, 'and I'd said "Yes". It'd've been all over the papers. "Kinsey team says Marilyn's got it!" or something. We had to be damn careful.'[72]

But as they continued on into 1949 and 1950 with their still immense task, they were all, at least, boosted now by the adrenalin of success.

16

Expansion – and Discovering the Female: 1949–50

Even if you do not like it, I still cannot guarantee anything less than 90 –
for we have active histories at that age.

Kinsey's reply, on 29 April 1949,
to Mrs Blanche Simone Strauss (aged 50) asking
when she could expect release from her intense sexual desire

Dear Dr Kinsey, What a long sentence! 30 years after a 42-year 'term'
... nocturnal orgasms, dreams of lovely girls and youths and of my husband
... my 'record' of 23 love episodes over a weekend and 20 orgasms during
one entrance, probably will be a (too) slow subsidence! Yours B.S.S.

Mrs Strauss to Kinsey, 3 May 1949
(The dots are Mrs Strauss')

1

In fact, success came to Kinsey again early in 1949 – and the occasion of it in some ways marks a peak.

In July 1948, the University of California at Berkeley had written asking if he would address them once more. Kinsey was now, of course, actively pursuing histories again and had other burgeoning interests on the West Coast, but what probably counted most was, as the special assistant delicately pointed out, that the President Robert G. Sproul was a trustee of the Rockefeller Foundation.[1]

Kinsey, Mac and the whole team arrived on 15 February 1949, staying at the Hotel Durant. Enormous excitement had been generated by the announcement of his speech, scheduled for 17 February, to such an extent that the university had to move to the field house – a vast indoor stadium where the basketball games were held. Even this was not enough; it, too, rapidly filled and when they closed the doors there was such an outcry, reported the *San Francisco Chronicle*, that they opened them again, cleared out all the gymnastic equipment and allowed people to sit in the aisles and on the wide window ledges. When Kinsey, Mac and the team arrived, 9,000 people had crammed in – 2,000 more than the record attendance at a basketball game.

It must have been a daunting moment for Kinsey, as he waited to begin. Even the photograph in the *San Francisco Chronicle*, (see no. 34), is terrifying enough. He was introduced by the vice-president, Dr Claude B. Hutchinson, who observed with interest the large number of faculty wives sitting in the aisles, most of them knitting, 'who had suddenly decided to attend a university meeting'. 'Of course,' Dr Hutchinson ended, 'most of us [the faculty] must view the subject to be discussed largely in retrospect.'

Kinsey stepped forward and, as always without notes, plunged straight in – the only sign that he was nervous the slightly more emphatic Scottish burr in his accent. He started with variety – of outlet, of frequency. Those who required one orgasm a year, or a week, to those who had several a week, or a day. At which point one of the male students let out a long, low whistle.

Pomeroy, appalled, thought he had lost them, but not for nothing had Kinsey been dominating his student audiences for twenty years. He did not pause. 'And then there are some,' he said smoothly, 'whose outlet is as low as that of the man who just whistled.' There was a huge cheer and then, the burr now vanished, he continued in total and electrified silence. The only other sign from the 9,000-strong audience, the *San Francisco Chronicle* noted, was when all the knitting needles suddenly stopped as Kinsey described how, while male sexual powers gradually declined from the teens on, female sexual powers did not, continuing unabated, ignoring the menopause, till the late fifties or early sixties – the whole subject perhaps for some suddenly not so much in retrospect after all.[2]

He spoke for over an hour, and the applause was tumultuous, and as it rises around him one is suddenly reminded of other great preachers in American history, austere and passionate Methodists like Robert Strawbridge in eighteenth-century Maryland and Virginia, or the hosts addressed so fervently by Francis Asbury in the North. Kinsey had at last become the preacher his father had started him out to be forty years before in South Orange, albeit in the subject of his sermons standing the self-denying doctrines of Alfred Seguine and the Methodists completely on their head.

2

Kinsey, and no doubt Mac too, was justly proud of his performance, and he sent a copy of the *San Francisco Chronicle* to his publisher Larry Saunders.[3] He had also written to warn the sales department at Saunders to expect increased orders of the *Male* volume, something he frequently did before and after a big speech.[4]

Two other things exercised him with Saunders. The first was that foreign publishers were always asking if they could cut the *Male* volume (particularly graphs and tables); Kinsey always refused. By January 1949 he'd decided he was wrong. The fact was, he in effect told Saunders, this was a crusade. His findings had to be known. 'The German-speaking world needs this book.' From 1949, cuts were allowed, provided reference was made to the US edition for full details.[5]

The second matter was Saunders' discount. Instead of the usual 40 per cent they had fixed on 20 per cent. Standard for medical books, Kinsey, with reason, saw it as unfair on what was turning out to be, in effect, a trade book. He continually inveighed against this. People couldn't buy it because they couldn't get it in little shops and they couldn't because Saunders had made booksellers so angry they wouldn't stock it.[6]

Saunders, making huge profits, wouldn't budge, but Kinsey, with his usual adroitness, while continuing to complain, turned this to his advantage in his annual reports to the NRC and IU on 1 April, pointing out, by inference, how scholarly and restrained he was by confining the book to 'the larger and more respectable book stores'. In his IU report he also seems to realise that he should perhaps justify his huge expenditure on his collections, putting a valuation on them of $100,000. (A figure, one suspects, more or less off the top of his head, since scribbled above it in the IU report is a pencilled $150,000, which he didn't actually use till 1950.)[7]

This was, in fact, somewhat in contradiction to his main anxiety which was, once again, that the Rockefeller Foundation would cease to support him. In the annual reports Kinsey states flatly that withdrawal of support now would be taken by the public as a sign of no confidence; also that it is clear royalties, in the long term, won't amount to more than $30,000 a year. Once again, agitated letters flew – and one can sense how Gregg and Corner feel they are dealing with a highly volatile, even explosive figure. Finally, at the end of May, Corner told him Gregg had managed to swing it – a further $120,000 to cover three years. But, his letter ended, Kinsey 'should take strongly into consideration' that this support could end.[8]

None the less, at this point money was still pouring in, and Kinsey spent it. He extended his travel budget ($8,500 compared to $2,000 in 1948). In April, he, Gebhard and Pomeroy spent a week in Cuba, going again late in November. One object was to observe sex in another culture, benefiting from Kinsey's expertise in Spanish. But the trip had one curious result. At last Kinsey found a drink whose taste he could tolerate – rum.

He dealt with it in his usual way, by forming a collection of rum cocktails which he shook up himself. He even built a bar in the First Street house, and now, instead of harmless fruit drinks and, according to Professor Torrey, extremely nasty coffee, Zombie, Dancer's Bottom and Planter's Punch circulated. Torrey now suddenly saw 'a relaxed Kinsey! With a couple of drinks under his belt he could be a very genial, small-talking host.' 'He never drank much,' said Bill Dellenback, 'he played with it.'

Not everyone approved. Mrs Hedwig Leser, his translator, told Bill she could 'remember ven liqueurs ver not allowed in the house'. Paul Gebhard's heart used to sink. Longing for a straight Scotch and soda, he would even have settled for a Scotch and Benedictine – 'but those great glasses of green and mauve ... purple ...'

But this too is symptomatic of the more general relaxation which fame and success brought. One is struck by how fond the young men and, if fewer, women became of Kinsey as they gathered round him now. The dedication of C. A. Tripp, or Kenneth Anger, the avant-garde film-maker some of whose work Kinsey bought, who would have made Kinsey his choice for President; soon Glenway Wescott, Monroe Wheeler and Alice Field, all became devoted to him. Earle Marsh, at this point when he first knew Kinsey a heavy drinker, was allowed as much as he wanted. 'He never got at me, but when I told him in 1952 I was giving up he gave a heartfelt "Thank God".' A tolerance in this matter, incidentally, that he always extended to Frank Beach, who enjoyed a drink.[9] Alice Field, an extremely attractive young woman, also drank a good deal and eventually died of a liver complaint as a result. Surprising Kinsey had so many drinkers in his circle.[10]

The Cuba visit had also been intended as a holiday for Kinsey, but he spent exactly one day 'vacationing', said Pomeroy, on Veradero Beach, when he talked entirely about 'the project'. They spent a lot of time watching simulated sex exhibitions, but Kinsey didn't even take notes.[11] He knew he could, and would on his return, organise far more genuine and valuable demonstrations.

3

Most males and some females become erotically aroused when they observe other individuals engaging in sexual activity.

Female, p. 648

In the course of his interview for BBC TV in 1995, John H. Gagnon made several shrewd observations about Kinsey and the *Female* volume. One was to note that Kinsey 'was sort of mystified by women'. In the *Male*, orgasm was everything. Now he finds, in the female of the species, some who don't have, or want, orgasms at all. Many others can stop sex for two or three years, and not miss it, and then have lots, and lots of orgasms. He therefore has to develop 'a more social vision of sexuality – and it is part of his intellectual honesty that he doesn't try and force them into a male format'.[12]

Kinsey found other things that surprised him. The *Male* volume, as we saw, quite frequently expresses what amounts to irritation at women: for their ignorance of the needs and power of adolescent male sexuality, for instance; for not wanting orgasms enough; or for not having them quickly enough for vigorous men. But as the *Female* patterns began to emerge from the IBM sorting machine's whirring Hollerith cards, he found a good number of women far *more* responsive, and far more intensely responsive, than any man. Multiple orgasm had been known about before Kinsey – but not till him was it widely known, nor realised that it was common. 14 per cent of his sample responded in this way, of which 3–5 per cent were extreme.[13]

Kinsey, as always, was very curious about these extremes. We have already met Alice Dent, but even more unusual was, coincidentally, another Alice – Dr Alice Spears. She was a gynaecologist in New York and later at Monterey, California, and as one of the close 'Friends of the Research' helped Kinsey in several ways. Wardell Pomeroy has described her:

> I remember one woman who was capable of from fifteen to twenty orgasms in twenty minutes. Even the most casual contact could arouse a sexual response in her. Observing her both in masturbation and intercourse, we found that in intercourse her first orgasm occurred within 2 to five seconds after entry . . . Another remarkable thing . . . was her ability to achieve full relaxation as soon as her partner did. Immediately after his ejaculation, she relaxed in complete satisfaction.[14]

Not the least surprising (and comforting) thing about Alice Spears was that she didn't have her first orgasm till she was forty and was in her sixties when they observed her. In the Kinsey Institute today there are still numerous photographs of her as she was then – an elderly, smiling lady, rather thin, with big uneven teeth. You could not possibly tell from looking at her what a rare creature she was.

By 'observation' Pomeroy means film. Clarence Tripp remembers how 'Kinsey was staggered. They made a number of films with her – you could make a 7-hour movie out of them – with every sort of partner.'[15]

One of the partners was Pomeroy himself, who was therefore writing about her from personal experience. John Tebbel remembers watching some film of Pomeroy and Alice Spears. 'Wardell going like crazy but far far behind his partner and her effortless flow of orgasms.'[16]

In fact, when Tripp says 'every sort of partner' he actually means the entire team. Kinsey was both fascinated and attracted by these highly responsive women and had sex with a number of them. He had what amounted, not to an affair quite, but a sexual liaison with Alice Spears, often lunching or dining her in New York and later when she moved to California.[17] Paul Gebhard also had sex with her once. He found her machine-gun orgasms distracting.

But this brings us to a contentious issue. Thomas Waugh, in the paper already referred to, is furious that Pomeroy tries to pretend that neither he nor any of the team were in the least aroused by anything they saw. Why should they alone, he argues, not be excited when one of Kinsey's major formulations was that men, especially well-educated men, were far more sexually stimulated by psychological and visual stimuli than women?[18] In this particular instance Waugh was, of course, quite right.

After Kinsey died, Paul Gebhard solicited memories of him from close Friends of the Research. Robert W. Laidlaw, the psychiatrist and marriage counsellor, wrote to Gebhard on 2 May 1968.

'You will probably not be able to use the following anecdote,' runs the last part of the letter:

> but I've remembered it warmly for many years as it so illustrates the human side of Kinsey. AD [Alice Dent] told me this herself. She told me that Kinsey had many times questions [sic] her minutely in regard to her strong sexual responsiveness (this was at the time of the debate between clitoral and vaginal types of orgasm) and that once in her own apartment she had intercourse with you-know-who, with Kinsey as observer. Both AD and her partner threw themselves into the situation with the fullest vigour and intensity, and immediately following a tumultuous simultaneous orgasm, AD looked up and caught Kinsey's eye. The light of sexual arousal was in it.* Instantaneously, as he saw that AD was aware of the situation, he flushed scarlet, pulled his mask down again and became once more the detached, objective, scientific observer. This was never subsequently mentioned between them in any way.[19]

Alice Dent was being discreet. In fact, Kinsey's 'light of sexual arousal' was probably sparked by experience. As with Spears, he used to lunch and dine Alice Dent in New York and had sex with her on a number of occasions.[20] Both liaisons were suspected at the time, as was one with another Alice – odd the number of Alices – Alice Field. Kinsey had plans for this attractive young woman to run a branch of the ISR in New York, but unfortunately she died before this was possible. Paul Gebhard is not certain here, but thinks it likely she and Kinsey had sex together too.[21]

But, to return to the subject of their excitement when observing,

---

* It seems that Frank Beach was also present, either on this or on another occasion, when Pomeroy was demonstrating with Alice Dent. Becoming sexually excited himself, Beach also thought he detected desire in Kinsey's eyes. (Jones, *Kinsey*, pp. 502, 503.)

Waugh goes much further than his simple, indeed, as he says, common-sense, deduction. He says this means Kinsey was incapable of being objective.

How can the pleasure of men [or women] fucking for the camera . . . how can the pleasure of scientists watching them . . . be mistaken for evidence of unmediated physiological fact rather than input into a collaborative dynamic in which knowledge and desire inextricably interplay, to use Foucault's formulation? How can the pleasure of scientific looking be separated from the pleasure of erotic looking . . . the drive for visual pleasure, in which knowledge and desire are inter-locking terms of power? How can sexual science in Western society be separated, to invoke Foucault once more, from erotic art?[22]

When Waugh, or anyone else, writes like this – like Foucault in a word, or rather a great many words – you know they are trying to swamp you, to put one over. 'Power' – power over whom? To what end? In what way? This is pure Foucault and, as we'll see in a minute when we return to the collections/films where Waugh's main 'power' thrust comes, totally irrelevant to Kinsey.

But as regards the more general attack of lack of objectivity – why should the two not co-exist? The fact that Kinsey and his team were occasionally turned on does not mean they invariably were, or even often were,* or could not also observe objectively. So ubiquitous is sex that sexual arousal enters into all sorts of situations and professions: doctors, psychiatrists and psychoanalysts, gynaecologists, casting direc-tors, pupil-teacher relationships, the armed forces, boy and girl scout troops, offices . . . indeed it is difficult to think of somewhere it *doesn't* enter. And when it causes men or women to act unobjectively, which of

---

* In sex research this is at times an almost inevitable trap or perk – depending on your stance here. But as with everything, familiarity breeds, not contempt, but boredom. Kinsey himself warned C. A. Tripp, when asking him to film sex, 'that any scenes which, at the outset, I might find "sexually stimulating and enjoyable" would soon lose their appeal (as indeed they did) after constantly seeing and handling such material'. Dr John Bancroft, the present director of the Kinsey Institute, said that when at various times he has had, for professional reasons, to watch films of couples in sexual activity he has more often been worried by how he was not being aroused than the reverse. (See Tripp, 1998. Bancroft, in conversation with the author.)

course it can, then it is usually obvious and detectable. If it is not, it isn't significant.

The only thing Waugh doesn't do, again resembling his mentor, is to produce any evidence. Unsurprisingly, because it would be difficult to find a more objective collection of fact than that demonstrated in Kinsey's books,* and especially in the *Female* volume when it comes to detailing the physiological reactions which were the fruit of his filming, and observation, and nearly all of which have been corroborated subsequently by Masters and Johnson.[23]

Indeed, Kinsey demonstrated it as clearly as anywhere right here, as it were at the heart of the subject under discussion, with his exploration into the female orgasm.

4

Physiological studies into female orgasm went back many years. An early example, oddly enough, also came from Indiana. One hot afternoon on 8 August 1872 a Dr Joseph Beck was examining a woman he was treating for a collapsed uterus, which he was sustaining with a mechanical device. As a result of the collapse and the device, her cervix was clearly visible through her labia and he was about to probe here when she told him to be careful. She had such a passionate nature that she would almost certainly have an orgasm when he touched her.

Beck suddenly realised he might have a chance to see the female orgasm in action. He ignored her and

> separating the labia with my left hand, so that the os uteri [vaginal opening of the cervix] was brought clearly into view in the sunlight, I now swept my right forefinger quickly three or four times across the space between the cervix and the pubic arch, when almost immediately orgasm occurred . . . Instantly the height of the excitement was at hand, the os opened itself to the extent of fully an inch, as nearly as my eye could judge, made five or six successive gasps, as it were, drawing the external os into the cervix each time powerfully . . . At the

---

* But it is important to make a distinction between *collection* and *listing* of data and sometimes Kinsey's mode of *presentation*, as we saw with the *Male* volume. I shall deal with this aspect of the *Female* volume later.

near approach of the orgiastic excitement the os and cervix became intensely congested, assuming almost a lurid purple colour . . .[24]

Beck thought sperm got sucked into the uterus like this, and Kinsey had wondered the same thing,[25] but such details were not elucidated until Masters and Johnson twenty years later (sperm are not sucked in).

Simpler, though in the context of his time far more revolutionary, was Kinsey's suspicion about the contemporary version of the female orgasm, especially since it derived from Freud. For many years, doctors, clinicians and 'the psychoanalysts' had distinguished between a clitoral orgasm and a vaginal one. A clitoral orgasm was immature and wrong; the point was to stimulate the vagina and relocate the orgasm there – failure to do so was neurotic. Thousands upon thousands of women had struggled with anxiety and conflict to do this. 'Under frigidity we understand the incapacity of women to have a vaginal orgasm,' wrote Dr Edmund Bergler in 1936.[26] (Bergler, an irascible New York analyst not unlike Thurman Rice in character, also dismissed multiple orgasm as a chronic form of frigidity.[27]) Freud, too, struggling to relocate, spoke of the clitoris 'stubbornly maintaining' its sensitivity.[28]

To Kinsey, this all sounded highly dubious, as he had already indicated in the *Male* volume, thus incurring further the ire of Freud's biographical abridger, Lionel Trilling.[29]

For one thing, it ran directly counter to what Kinsey discovered about female masturbation. Very few did this by deep vaginal penetration. Kinsey went as thoroughly, and as mechanically, into female masturbation as he had male. 84 per cent of his masturbation sample gently stroked or stimulated in some way the inner lips (labia minora) and/or clitoris. 10 per cent crossed legs and exerted a steady rhythmic pressure affecting the whole area. Others employed vibrators or rubbed against pillows, beds, tables 'and other objects'. A very few (2 per cent) could orgasm from fantasy.

Muscular tension was interesting (if rare). Orgasm itself is a series of powerful, rhythmic muscular tensions and relaxations, and spasms; it turned out it worked in reverse. That is, inducing a rhythm of muscular tension – relaxing and tensing buttock and thigh muscles – could produce an orgasm. It was the reason some women went to the gym; and also why some didn't – a refusal which could puzzle ignorant instructors, Kinsey added helpfully.

A few (20 per cent) had tried vaginal penetration, but not gone far and only in conjunction with some other method. Many had done so because they felt they should, or had been told they should by 'the psychoanalysts'. 'Vaginal orgasm', that is, was really an expression of male dominance; women were supposed to *need* a huge cock inside them – and if they didn't they must learn to. Hence men 'upon their conceit as to the importance of the male genitalia', wrote Kinsey, fantasised about women habitually using deep penetrative objects when in fact they didn't.[30]

He decided to go into the whole subject. He organised five gynaecologists (one of them Earle Marsh) to test nearly 900 women. The results were conclusive. The vagina had practically no nerve endings and 86 per cent of his sample felt nothing at all when probed, the remainder almost nothing. As for the huge cock, Freudians had identified the thumb-sized cervix in the depths of the vagina as crucial, but again, the cervix proved to be nerveless; 95 per cent felt nothing. Vaginal orgasm was a 'biologic impossibility'.

Which did not mean the vagina was irrelevant. It took part in the general spasms and convulsions which often engulfed the whole body at orgasm. Nerves close to it could be stimulated (and so deceive): rectal nerves, nerves between anus and genitalia, 'the perineal muscle mass', sensitive in both sexes; there were also psychological elements, knowledge of satisfying the partner, the weight and contact. Orgasm is complex. But as a discrete event in a single localised place, which itself required stimulation – as angrily insisted on by Bergler, and other psychoanalysts – the vaginal orgasm was a myth.[31]

Once having got his teeth, so to speak, into the penis, Kinsey continued in his usual way. 'It has even been suggested . . .' he wrote, 'that a female who had a phallus as large as the average penis might respond as quickly, as frequently and as intensely as the average male.' But the penis, though bigger, was no more sensitive than the clitoris. On the contrary, it was 'equalled or surpassed by the greater extension of the tactilely sensitive areas in the female genitalia'.[32]

As for speed, any slowness was due to the hopeless way men wielded the big penises they were so proud of – 'the ineffectiveness of the usual coital techniques'. Women masturbating or making love to each other, aware of what *was* effective, came as quickly or quicker than men: 45 per cent in three minutes or less, 25 per cent in four to five minutes. What women wanted (and got from each other) was a generalised emotional and physical stimulation of the whole body, stimulation of the genital area, carried through, without extended foreplay, as a continuous rhythmic course that 'leads directly towards orgasm'.[33]

There were things Kinsey got wrong and things he didn't understand – which we still don't understand. It is fascinating to see how throughout the *Female* volume he retreats from the orgasm, hitherto so central. 'It cannot be emphasised too often,' he writes, and does so often, 'that orgasm cannot be taken as the sole criterion for determining the degree of satisfaction which a female may derive from sexual activity.'[34] When Frank Beach wrote to him and asked if the clitoris wasn't, as Dickinson said, all-important to female orgasm,* Kinsey replied it was important, but 'I attach a great deal more importance to psychological background ... than Dickinson does.'[35] Today, there are American therapists who see pleasurable non-orgasmic coitus for women as simply a normal variant of female sexuality.[36]

Kinsey said that women could not, strictly speaking, ejaculate, but this is not so. A good many women, according to Vern Bullough, ejaculate fluid unrelated to urine, sometimes quite a lot. Many women have prostate-like tissue surrounding their urethras and this may be the source.[37] We still don't know why some women are so extremely and so instantly responsive and some so much less so, any more than we know why some men require thirty orgasms a week for thirty years and some almost none. But Kinsey's approach on these matters predated, and is often identical to, that of feminist writers twenty or thirty years later.

The research around the female orgasm continued up to and beyond the publication of the *Female* volume. But during May and June 1949 there was a totally unrelated development in his social/work life (and all social life was connected to work with Kinsey) which was destined to be of sufficient significance for us to learn something about the two protagonists.

---

* The exchange was in pursuit of an interesting idea Beach had had. Female animals were often able to satisfy (or exhaust) a huge number of males. Beach thought it could be because they rarely had orgasms and this could be because rear entrance didn't stimulate the clitoris (Beach to Kinsey, 16 January 1950). At the same time quite a lot of female animals can have orgasms – rabbits and rhesus monkeys for example. The *purpose* of mammalian female orgasm is a rich field, though it would take us too far off course. But see, for instance, Timothy Taylor, 1996, pp. 50, 58, 79, 279; or Stephen J. Gould, 1985, pp. 41–58.

5

*Kinsey is a strange man, with a handsome good sagacious face but with a
haunted look – fatigue, concentration and (surprising to me, if I interpret
rightly) passionateness and indeed sensuality.*

Glenway Wescott in his journal,
after his first meeting with Kinsey
(*Continual Lessons*, 1990, pp. 245, 246)

Glenway Wescott was also a Midwesterner, born in Wisconsin in 1901.
He was a precocious, sensitive, highly intelligent boy who soon had rows
with his father – a small-time pig farmer – and all his early writing is
dominated by the need to escape the Midwest (as is much Midwestern
writing). He had had his first passionate love affair aged thirteen for two
years with a fifteen-year-old boy at his West Bent High School.

In 1917 he went to the University of Chicago and there met Monroe
Wheeler. They began a love affair which after twelve years became sexless, allowing both of them innumerable sexual affairs, a familiar homosexual pattern, but which endured until they died within eighteen
months of each other in 1987–88.

In 1920, they left Chicago together and spent thirteen years wan-
dering, partly in New York, but mostly in Europe. They met Robert
Frost, the Sitwells, Ford Madox Ford, Jean Renoir, Somerset Maugham,
Rebecca West. Glenway wrote poems and reviews for *The Dial* and the
Transatlantic Review and then, in 1927, his second novel and his best
book, *The Grandmothers*. The hero (Wescott) is 'consumed . . . by a kind
of fatalistic and helpless susceptibility to love' and trapped in the
Midwest. It was a huge success, winning several prizes including the
Harper Price Award. Wescott became one of the top four or five expa-
triate American writers.

The couple settled in Paris; Wheeler beginning another life-long
affair, with the brilliant fashion and erotic photographer George Platt
Lynes, Wescott a shorter-lasting fling with a young French aristocrat,
Jacques Guerin. More success, more people: Colette, Cocteau, Picasso,
Stravinsky, Chagall. Gertrude Stein wrote, 'He [Wescott] has a certain
syrup but it does not pour'[38] – whatever that means. But whatever it
means, Glenway agreed it was true.

In 1933, the couple – or rather now a threesome – settled in New
York, and in 1937 the heiress Barbara Harrison married Glenway's

brother and gave Glenway, Wheeler and Platt Lynes a country house, Stone-blossom, in New Jersey. She also gave Glenway a private income, and this may be one reason his creative flow began to dry up. There were two more novels; *The Pilgrim Hawk* in 1940 and *Apartment in Athens* in 1945. Then silence, apart from a few reviews and essays. Wescott became establishment: President of the National Institution of Arts and Letters, receiver of honorary degrees (Rutgers University, for instance).

What were they like? Wheeler was charming, clever, worldly and very ambitious. He became Director of Exhibitions at the Museum of Modern Art and, with a genuine insight into and feeling for painting, wrote several highly praised studies.* He was, like Kinsey, a work addict who, though tough, periodically collapsed through overwork. Wescott was a talk addict. There is sometimes something slightly precious about him. He turns up at a friend's with two hundred daffodils picked 'impulsively' as he left the house. When *The Grandmothers* was reprinted in 1986 he'd tell young friends whimsically, 'I had nothing to do with it. It came through the trees, looking for me.' He sometimes affected an English accent.

But neither of them was in the least effeminate and both had been very good-looking; Wescott, especially, was sultry, masculine, sensual. He had a hot temper, an obsessive interest in sex, a subtle, penetrating and calculating mind. He was deeply read, and clearly entertaining – he could hardly have kept the friends he did otherwise. Thomas Mann wrote in his autobiography, 'Being fond of civilised people, I always relished his company.' He was almost too loquacious and, like all successful gossips, indiscreet – you don't get something for nothing – but, like all successful gossips, could also keep a secret – or in the end, people won't divulge.

When Kinsey met them in 1949, they were at the height of their social power in their apartment at 410 Park Avenue. More parties, more people: Isak Dinesen, Thornton Wilder, Cecil Beaton, Tennessee Williams. In February of that year Somerset Maugham's arrival had been upstaged by that of Marlene Dietrich. The novelist Frederic Prokosch remembered a party where Edmund Wilson knocked a shrimp off his plate into the high-piled hair of Edith Sitwell. Everyone politely pretended not to notice. They went to Joe Louis fights, the opera, the ballet.[39]

* *Modern Painters and Illustrators*, 1946; *The Last Works of Henri Matisse*, 1961; *Soutine*, 1966.

There is no record of how Kinsey met Monroe Wheeler, though it was certainly in pursuit of histories from modern artists, this itself part of his expanding interest in the influence of sex on art, and it is likely through Andrey Avinoff. But it probably took place in 1948.* It was followed up in June 1949 by a formal dinner, when Glenway Wescott met him for the first time. Wescott gave some of his impressions to Rosco: 'This huge old body with this heavy chest and heavy belly, muscular old legs. He looked much older than I, and wasn't.'[40] (Kinsey was almost fifty-five, Wescott was forty-eight.) But his most interesting comments were in his notebooks, part of which head this section: 'a handsome good sagacious face . . . passionateness and indeed sensuality'. It is worth finishing the paragraph, since it is one of the few accounts we have of Kinsey's effect on a (at this time) disinterested and also practised observer. 'With all his scientific conscientiousness and pride and faith in science, he has the temperament of a reformer rather than a scientist; fierily against hypocrisy and repressive law of every sort, censorship etc., and against Judaism and Catholicism and Irishry.'[41]

The dinner party was a success. Monroe and Glenway had asked E.M. Forster and his life-long friend the policeman Bob Buckingham. Kinsey held forth on, among other things, the differences he thought he was discovering between the sexes, which were essentially the stronger role imagination and fantasy play in male desire. This struck Morgan Forster and next day, when Bob Buckingham was describing a gay friend so womanish he couldn't imagine him *not* being like that, Forster said, '"Oh no, Bob, no. That is what we learned from Dr Kinsey. Extreme as some men are in their effeminacy, still they are men. Because – they all

---

* Wescott, in the long interview he gave his biographer Jerry Rosco in December 1976, places their meeting in 1947, but this is extremely unlikely. For one thing, Kinsey paid very few visits to New York in 1947, and these were short. He was far too busy writing and then overseeing the publication of the *Male* volume. For another, Kinsey invariably wrote at once to anyone important (or unimportant come to that) immediately after meeting them – and his first letter to Wheeler is dated 16 June 1949 (about work). Nor would Wheeler have kept so interesting a new acquisition for two years from his friends, necessary in a 1947 dating. Wescott is not reliable regarding dates, and this extends to his journal, *Continual Lessons.* The book is amusing, honest, nicely written, if sometimes overwritten, and particularly vivid in its sexual accounts, but it is in no sense a journal. It is a collection from his voluminous notebook entries, and sometimes these were dated. I suspect the editors, who did a fine job, have often guessed when events took place. For this reason the book lacks the narrative drive chronology can give a genuine journal.

love smut!" He added softly . . . [giving] his characteristic small laugh – "Indeed I was rather comforted to hear it."[42]

Kinsey also saw Gore Vidal, possibly through Glenway, this May, on the 16th. Vidal's courageous, ground-breaking and fascinating novel, *The City and the Pillar*,[43] had been published in 1948 and Kinsey admired it. After taking Vidal's history at the Astor, Kinsey gave him a copy of his *Male* volume inscribed in his flamboyant hand, 'With congratulations on the quality of your work.'[44] Vidal, in his equally ground-breaking and equally fascinating memoir *Palimpsest*, gives an interesting example of Kinsey at analysis post-interview. 'When Kinsey had finished with my history . . . I asked, "If you didn't know who I was – what – *who* would you say I was, according to my sexual history?"

'"I'd rate you as a lower-middle-class Jew, with more heterosexual than homosexual interests." Curiously, I have lived most of my life with such a person.'[45]*

Monroe Wheeler and Glenway Wescott, with perhaps a half to a dozen gay figures in that New York of the late '40s and early '50s, were to give Kinsey an enormous amount of help. One notices how swiftly (for Kinsey and the period) he moves to intimacy. Excluding young, lower-level men, it usually took Kinsey anything from four to six years to use Christian names. In a few months now it was 'Dear Glenway' and 'Dear Monroe' – followed at once by 'Dear Alfred'.[46] These two took him up and helped him at first, of course, because he was the celebrity of the moment. But they stayed with him because they grew very fond of him.

There was another consideration. To American society, to *Western* society, Kinsey's homosexual statistics came as a bombshell; but to homosexuals themselves they came, if this isn't too mixed a metaphor,

* Gore Vidal and Kinsey, though they only met once, clearly got on. In an interview he gave to the BBC, Vidal said that another thing they chatted about was a man he (Vidal) had met in the Army who'd boasted he could pick up anyone, which Vidal thought nonsense. But Kinsey said he had a guy in Chicago who could do this. Kinsey would walk down Division Street and point men out at random, and nearly always his guy would succeed. 'He was quite awed by this.' But not in fact totally unused to it. Vincent Nowlis described how 'in New York, Kinsey would say to Pomeroy, "OK, now show Nowlis" – and we'd be on the north side of 42nd Street, west of Broadway, and he'd do a certain eye and swagger thing, and my God, there'd be four or five homosexual guys descending on him.' (Vidal, BBC interview transcript, 1995; Nowlis, interview with the author, October 1995.)

as a thrilling bombshell. Kenneth Anger remembers a group of gays, among them Wescott and Wheeler, meeting in Paris soon after the *Male* volume came out. The point of the meeting was to decide what they should 'do' about Kinsey's findings. The conclusion – somehow to use them to improve their lot, the recognition of homosexuals in America. The first organised pressure group devoted to this end, the Mattachine Society, called its first public meeting to discuss Kinsey's findings.[47]

Kinsey was perfectly clear that Monroe and Glenway were joining his crusade to get 'this thing done right'; and they in turn, in numerous letters, were equally clear they were in the battle, as Monroe Wheeler said, for 'understanding and tolerance which will some day bring peace to this planet'.[48]

In fact, through an independent arrangement, Glenway was giving six talks at a writers' conference at IU in July. Unfortunately, Kinsey was away the whole time – but his absence marked another stage in his odyssey, to be almost as important as the meeting at 410 Park Avenue. He had flown to California with Pomeroy and Gebhard for his first visit to San Quentin Prison.

6

Rumbling criticism of Kinsey's use of prisoners in his main sample continued for years after the *Male* volume came out. Gebhard and Pomeroy had felt, and still felt, they skewed the results. Kinsey had always refused, and still refused, to give way. He really felt *all* lower levels had been involved in crime of some sort. It went with poverty. Besides, this man or woman of fifty has one lapse – are you to chuck away his/her entire past history? If so, how do you know this man of twenty-five *isn't* going to have a lapse? Could Gebhard or Pomeroy *prove* prison inmates were different from others? They couldn't. 'If you can't prove it,' Kinsey would say, 'shut up.'[49]

When William C. Cochran tackled him on the subject in 1951, Kinsey said he had recalculated 'strategic' bits of the *Male* volume, taking out the prison population, and it made little difference.[50] Gebhard says that at that time they hadn't done this.[51] Kinsey often dealt with his internal critics by saying he'd made changes when he hadn't, or else by promising changes he'd no intention of implementing.

But this first visit to the notorious San Quentin Prison in

July/August 1949 had a different aim – and was to develop others. It was primarily for his sex offender book.

Pomeroy's description (slightly misdated), which I follow, is fascinating.[52] The administration had got together a gang of prison leaders – the chief Negro, toughest fighter, top Mexican, etc. Kinsey lectured these, then, having won them over (and his reputation had preceded him on the con grapevine), took their histories.

The prison leaders secured their entrée. Next – rooms for interviewing. This was difficult. Even the chaplain's room was just partitioned. Finally, old cells dating from 1852 were found soundproof. The walls were two feet thick, the doors quarter-inch solid steel with tiny, barred peepholes. Here, in a cell each, the team settled to work. They were allowed Coke in bottles. In prison, only cardboard cups were allowed, and the bottles, the fact that they had chosen *cells*, deeply impressed the cons. Nevertheless, the warden was nervous and wanted the team to wear whistles. Kinsey refused.

There were incidents. One con cut his throat in front of an appalled Pomeroy – but turned out to be a professional throat-cutter, able to produce maximum blood and minimum harm. Another pulled out a ten-inch file sharpened into a knife and said he was going to kill X, who hadn't paid gambling debts. The team debated what they should do – as always when conventional morality clashed with project morality, project morality won. Besides, if X was to be murdered, he'd get murdered whatever they did, so they did nothing. But it was in fact a test. The prison waited to see if the file con would be 'shaken down' that night, or X hurriedly moved. Nothing happened – and confidence in Kinsey was secure.[53]

In this two-month California visit he took 450 histories.[54] 100 per cent samples from women counsellors at the University of California, and of children (two- to four-year-olds) in a nursery school; he also got sidetracked into a 'group of amputees'[55] – but the most important to Kinsey were the convicts. He could, wrote Pomeroy, have taken the entire prison, warders included.

Kinsey, as he had at the Indiana State Penal Farm, and for the same reasons, got on instantly with these tough, often violent men. That element in him which wanted to shock authority responded to those, like homosexuals and criminals, whose way of life inevitably involved that – and therefore intimately involved, as did the dictates of his own character (and for some time now behaviour), a strong element of secrecy. But above all, they were in trouble – and his aims expanded accordingly. He both wanted to study, and then help, prisoners adapting to sex deprivation inside and how they adjusted when they came out.[56]

'Some of them,' wrote the assistant warden, Douglas Rigg, 'were in the awful predicament of being able to trust no one'[57] – and suddenly they could trust Kinsey. Once again, as in 1940 and 1941, the files fill with letters from prisoners, of gratitude, with problems; and, though he was now three times busier, Kinsey rose to them as he had then: '. . . Robert G. Ingleton (No. 8054),' he wrote, apologising for 'meddling' to Doug (it was already Doug), 'wants a job which involves heavy physical work, and my protracted interview with him makes me think that such heavy work is what the boy needs.'[58]

When he was back in Bloomington in September, he wrote and thanked the convicts for helping him and promised to return, which he did, many times. And it is impossible not to rise oneself to the sheer humanitarian kindness of Kinsey in these circumstances. Yet the conditions, once he'd won their trust, were ideal and no doubt his view of them was sometimes over-rosy. He continued to say that 90 per cent of sex offenders could quite safely be let out, but Dorothy Collins remembers him returning from San Quentin once in a state of indignation saying 90 per cent should be kept *in.*

'He'd asked some rapists what was the first thing they'd do if they got out and they told him the first thing they'd do would be to rape another woman. Kinsey was never so surprised in his life.'[59]

7

In October, he was back in New York and Washington, lecturing and taking histories (some from lobotomy patients), addressing the National Press Club, and seeing a great deal of Monroe Wheeler, and also Glenway Wescott, whose history he took (a 6 on the H scale – exclusively homosexual, one of only 4 per cent. Wescott was delighted at his rarity[60]).

But Kinsey also had work for the loquacious writer. Up to now, he had been interested in how a culture's sexual attitudes and practices manifested themselves in and influenced its art. What also seems to have interested Kinsey at this point was *how,* or *if,* the particular sexual history of a particular artist – painter, writer, actor, dancer (but hardly ever, for some reason, musician) – manifested itself in his or her own art. This was a question that might be tested empirically and seems to have been one of the tasks he set Glenway.

I think it is possible to glimpse more here. Kinsey had a theory, Wescott told his own biographer, Jerry Rosco, that the closer an artist came to autobiography (and with Kinsey autobiography could now only mean sexual autobiography) 'the warmer, more vivid and penetrating or profound the result would be'. For this reason he often tried to persuade Wescott to write about homosexuality. Wescott agreed there was truth in this idea, but there were so many exceptions it didn't stand up.[61] No doubt Kinsey accepted the judgement, yet there is something revealing about the almost naive assumption we can sense lurking behind the theory. Kinsey's feeling was always Rousseauesque – man was born sexually free and everywhere was in chains. Only release those chains, and *everything* would be all right, including art. It was a feeling that derived, once more, from his own acute frustration and suffering bound for so long in sexual chains.

8

1950 was to see rapid expansion in two areas: the first was that of staff, the second filming sexual activity. Kinsey and his team had been getting ever more squashed in the tiny 'laboratories' of Biology Hall for ten years. During 1949, IU rebuilt the entire basement floor of Wylie Hall (at a cost, Kinsey boasted to Beach, of $70,000[62]) to rehouse them, a process which of course Kinsey oversaw minutely. Memos flowed, on soundproofing, on security, on heat: how did they expect him to exist hermetically sealed when the temperature control proposed was 'nothing but a simple fan delivering outside warm air?'[63] He got his air-conditioning.

The new quarters, in one of the oldest ivy-covered buildings of the University (1884), were ready in the New Year and they were all in by March. Everyone had their own office and there were offices to spare; there was a file room, a darkroom, a large room for the 8,000-book library. It was so spacious all the galls moved too, and one new staff member was surprised to find that the test for a sex research job was to write out one of the tiny gall labels.[64]

And hermetically sealed it was. All the rooms were fireproofed and

also soundproofed for interviewing. No one could break in since, apart
from heavy locks everywhere, the windows were wire-meshed; no one
could see out or see in, since they were opaque or, in the library, provided with blinds. It was like a bunker or, to President Wells, a busy
hospital.[65] Wells, in fact, was now their nearest neighbour in another of
the old, nineteenth-century red-brick buildings, handy for Kinsey who,
much to the irritation of the IU administration, always took his problems
straight to the top (he once used Wells to sack a janitor[66]).

But, from several points of view, they had moved in the nick of time.
One problem was the continuing criticisms of Kinsey's sampling and
statistical techniques. For the first three months of 1950, letters passed
between Corner, Kinsey and Gregg. Gregg said to Corner that if Kinsey
just ignored the criticisms (which he did and was to continue to do) and
repeated the mistakes – the grant would end. Why didn't he take on new
(statistical) staff? Where were the royalties going? Finally, Kinsey faced
up to the whole tiresome thing in April. He proposed that a group of
prominent, recognised statisticians should go over his entire system and,
'when practical', he would accept their recommendations. He would
also discuss it all with Gregg 'on the ground'.

Corner and Gregg accepted the idea of a statistical committee with
relief. The point was not so much, for Corner at least, that Kinsey should
do anything drastic, but he and Gregg had to satisfy the Rockefeller
Foundation that at least something was being done. The NRC set aside
$4,000 to cover the cost, and it took five months of letters and meetings
(Gregg to Bloomington in July) to set it all up.[67]

In fact, Kinsey was already rapidly expanding his staff. By April
1950 he had added three full-time and one part-time (all women). One,
Dr Jeannette Foster, was the first full-time, professionally trained librar-
ian (who eventually resigned because, despite her battling with him,
Kinsey refused to change his own invented cataloguing methods to stan-
dard library procedure[68]). None was a statistician, though as a sop to
Corner, Kinsey gave $500 to his old friend the astronomer Frank
Edmondson and pretended he was active on the staff in this capacity.[69]

However, in 1951, with the institute's annual budget now running at
over $100,000, Dorothy Collins joined the staff, which had by then
expanded to fifteen (from seven in 1949 and eleven in June 1950), and
one of her tasks was indeed meant to be helping handle statistics. She
rapidly gave up. They were not doing statistics. They were doing
mathematics. When she suggested an improvement, 'Kinsey would

ridicule it. You soon stopped making suggestions of that sort.'[70]

But she gives a picture of what it was like being one of the increasingly numerous 'fringe' workers. Kinsey expected, and got, very hard work. 'When I came, I had to choose between Christmas and Thanksgiving.' But he was a considerate employer, kind, understanding of those doing part-time (as all his gall girls had done). He left her alone. He was, except at the very end, always optimistic, cheerful, 'bouncing in, saying good morning though it was often afternoon'. He would try and visit everyone more than once a week, sitting by their desk, his fingers 'rippling' through his hair, now beginning to grey, unconsciously straightening their pencils and aligning their paper. He was generous (or generous with Rockefeller Foundation funds) – standing lunches, paying for picnics. Yet, although she liked him – 'he had a warmth you felt rather than experienced' – she also had a curious feeling that his kindness and attention weren't particularised; it wasn't *her* (or even Gebhard or Pomeroy) he was generous to, or talked to, but her (or them) as part of the project.[71] Perhaps, one wonders, to some extent, or ultimately, as a part of, an extension of, himself.

Eleanor Roehr joined in 1950. She was tall, solidly built, powerful, 'in early days a bit blowsy', said Paul Gebhard, who clearly remembered her with extreme vividness. 'She walked like a man. She had been married to someone called Gorman but she was too dominant to be married. After Kinsey's death, she left to take up a post as an administrator in a Thai university. She dumbfounded the Thais. They were used to delicate little Thai women, subservient and quiet. Eleanor came at them like a tank. She once walked right in, past secretaries and guards, into some high ranking Thai's office and thumped his desk and said, 'Why haven't you answered my memo?' They called her Sergeant Roar.[72]

Eleanor Roehr took a grip on things from the start, and then went on tightening it. She was appalled to find that the hundreds and thousands of Rockefeller Foundation dollars had frequently been, and were frequently still being, simply paid into Kinsey's personal account, from where he dished them out. (He kept them apart in his head.) She also stopped him wasting time checking up on her. 'I said when he asked me to do something he must realise that is what he had done – delegated.' No one before had even attempted that. When the years of murderous overwork at last began to tell on him, Roehr took over more and more until Kinsey eventually began to let her answer some of the hundreds of routine letters.[73]

She clearly worshipped him. She had come with personal, presumably sexual, problems which 'he helped sort out'. She too had wanted to be a professional pianist until she broke her hand and she attended the musicales with particular zeal. 'We were a family.'[74] She was an excellent, brisk cook and now visitors were given delicious meals which she cooked outside and had brought in. She guarded Kinsey jealously, as top secretaries are supposed to do. She even kept the team from him, much to their annoyance. Gebhard she could get on with, but Pomeroy maddened her. She used to say, 'He can't put one sentence in front of the other.' In the end, her accumulated irritation found fairly devastating expression. Bill Dellenback, on the other hand, she fancied. It took all that astute photographer's skill to escape her.[75]

Kinsey's iron, headmasterly hand, inside the rather threadbare velvet in which he still contained it, continued to rule over his team as before; but now the school also had a headmistress.

9

Alan Gregg's slightly irritated query about royalties would have been answered had he been shown the year's tax returns: $10,780.36 were spent on sex research from that source, and another $34,993.27 went on the 'collection'. But by far the largest sum, like the year before, was put cannily on deposit and carried forward – $85,348.16.[76]

Buoyed by this money, with his staff now rapidly growing, Kinsey was at last able to start implementing in earnest his most wide-ranging plans. In June 1950 he produced a six-page paper setting out concisely his extraordinarily ambitious programme for the next two decades.

I want now to single out Project 7 – 'Physiological Studies of Sexual Arousal and Sexual Orgasm'. This was, essentially, the same programme Masters and Johnson were to undertake twenty or so years later. He notes unspecifically that 'a considerable body of observed data' was already available.[77]

In May and June he set out, resolutely and in secret, to make this body of data very much more considerable. Homosexual and heterosexual filming began in Bloomington.

17

Filming – 'Philosophy' – Women – Writing – Wescott: 1950–1

1

N ot till the publication of Pomeroy's biography in 1972 was it generally known that Kinsey had taken films of sexual activity – and Pomeroy only revealed the tip of an iceberg. Since it was clear there would be an uproar if it leaked out great care was taken. Appropriations for Bill Dellenback's film (he had been resident since April 1950) were always earmarked 'for mammalian studies', and most of the filming took place secretly in Kinsey's house on First Street.[1]

You can still see the little attic-sloped gable bedroom on the second floor which was the studio. It had a plain pine-board floor, and a mattress. Nothing more. Outside there was a narrow primitive bathroom – a shower, a lavatory and a sink. It must have been needed, since the room with its single small window would have been very hot from June onwards.

Samuel Steward has left a vivid account of one session, covering two days.[2] He had met Kinsey in 1949 in Chicago, where he was a lecturer at the little Catholic college of De Paul. He was then about thirty-nine, thin, good-looking, cultured; he translated Genet's *Querelle de Brest*, wrote two erotic novels and a large number of pornographic short stories (which in those days circulated secretly in samizdat typescript). He was a close friend of Gertrude Stein and Alice B. Toklas.

Even though there was a considerable element of the acolyte in these relationships, once again one notices the devotion. 'I suppose,' Steward writes, 'that to a degree I fell in love with him.' They seem to have got on well from the start. His history took five hours – one great advantage was that he kept detailed records – and at the end 'he looked at me thoughtfully and said, "Why don't you give up trying to continue your heterosexual relationships?" I abandoned my phony "bisexuality" that very evening. Poor Emmy.'

Gay society held several advantages for Kinsey. Having overcome the stigma of homosexuality, which required courage then (it still does), gays were often freer and less inhibited in their behaviour. They had also learnt to keep it as hidden as possible from the outside world. To these, Steward added friendship.*

None the less, he never discovered Kinsey's bisexuality, which led to moments that must have caused a certain frisson to run through members of the team. For example, Steward describes a lunch with them all in the Tudor Room. A small container of monosodium glutamate was on the table and, sprinkling some on his finger and licking it, he asked if any of them had noticed how it tasted like semen. In the electrified silence that followed 'the enormity of my *gaffe* turned me rosy as I slowly realised that I had spoken to three presumably straight heterosexuals. Kinsey grinned. "I do believe," he said, "that not a single one of us here has ever noticed the similarity . . ." Everyone laughed. '"I thought," I said, "that certainly this time I might trap someone into admitting he was a club member." He grinned. 'I mustn't say. We must preserve the confidentiality of the research." '

Steward was also a masochist. Kinsey had become increasingly interested in this and in June 1950 he asked Steward if he would co-operate in a film. His partner was to be Mike Mikshe, a gifted freelance fashion illustrator with extremely strong sadistic tendencies found for Kinsey by Glenway Wescott.

'It was quite an experience,' starts Steward's account. Kinsey, it seems, got Mikshe, described by Wescott as a magnificently bodied giant, 'half drunk on gin', while they were both lounging under an apple tree in the First Street garden (Steward had given up drink). For some, no doubt masochistic, reason, Steward flicked undone Mikshe's bootlace and said provocatively, 'You don't look so tough to me.'

There followed two afternoons of blood-stained, bruising violence

---

* Steward meticulously logged 700 hours in Kinsey's company, meeting him whenever he came to Chicago. Kinsey taught him enough of the code for them to continue their sexual discussions (they didn't have any other discussions) in restaurants and so on. One item of this was S/M for sadomasochism. Steward credits Kinsey for introducing this acronym into the language. He may be right. At least I can find no more convincing origin.

and unrestrained sex from which not the least extraordinary thing is that Kinsey did manage to extract some minute fragments of scientific observation. Mikshe was a ham who overacted outrageously whenever he heard Dellenback's camera whirr; to accompany every conceivable form of homosexual intercourse they had, apart from mirrors, only rather crude aids – a tawse, two whips and a leather belt.[3] The team took notes, 'While Mrs Kinsey – herself a true scientist as well – appeared in the attic and once in a while calmly changed the sheets on the workbench.'

Mikshe, with whom Wescott later fell in love, eventually committed suicide; thus proving, according to Steward, that sadists were more unbalanced than masochists.* He himself left university teaching and started a lucrative tattooing parlour on South State Street, whence derived Kinsey's rather short-lived exploration into the sexual motivation of getting tattooed.

But their film was only the first of the homosexual films among the many homosexual and heterosexual films he took, since, as with everything, Kinsey had to have as much as possible. Wescott continued to suggest participants for three years and Kinsey used eighteen of them, providing partners from other sources himself.[4] Sometimes interviewees would volunteer and were accepted. Earle Marsh and Alice Spears both did this.[5]

But Kinsey again used his close staff and their wives here. Mac was filmed with Pomeroy. Only one wife, anonymous in James Jones' account, refused to be filmed with her husband. She told Jones she was under 'sickening pressure' and 'felt her husband's career... depended on it'.[6] Both Paul Gebhard and Bill Dellenback agree that, aside from Kinsey's usual expectation or hope of total liberation, nothing justifying the epithet 'sickening pressure' was ever exerted, and no one's career depended on co-operation of this sort. If you didn't want to do something – as with Gebhard and H behaviour – you didn't do it.[7] Internal

---

* Kinsey used to warn masochists to take care with sadists because they could get seriously hurt. But Paul Gebhard discovered that in fact it is the masochist who is in charge during these encounters. The sadist serves the masochist, who is interested in being hurt – and the masochist's rarity gives him or her an added power. 'All our masochists have been big ruthless creatures, tough, successful business men and that sort of thing,' said Gebhard. But Kinsey might have been right as regards Mikshe. Wescott describes in a letter to Kinsey how his friend had just broken several ribs of his current lover. The spelling of Mikshe, incidentally, seems to vary. I follow Wescott. (Gebhard, interview with the author; Wescott to Kinsey, 1 March 1953.)

evidence suggests the 'sickening pressure' wife was once again Alice Martin.

'Herself a true scientist' – it scarcely reads like science sometimes. Yet it is important not to forget, because of the peculiarities of his subject, that if you are to study some field scientifically, you must know as much of it as possible. Nothing can be evaded – and Kinsey didn't evade. He not only filmed every variant of sexual behaviour that he could, he observed where he couldn't film.

One of Wescott's chief pleasures at this time was to give dinner parties for men, usually in their twenties, and try and provoke orgies, in which he would participate or more often watch (there was a strong element of the voyeur in him). Kinsey sometimes attended these and Wescott described to his biographer how he seemed on these occasions to completely disappear. 'Everyone said that.' He sat silent, motionless, his face stern, almost lugubrious. 'And suddenly he'd get up and move and you'd think, "My God, he's been there a long time."' [8]

And masturbation filming also continued, for many years in fact. We must now look more closely at certain aspects of this.

2

The association between pain and pleasure can be close; particularly perhaps with sexual pleasure. Certain cultures expect passionate kisses to draw blood (this used to be true in Wales for instance), and in our own a 'love bite' carries an element of this. Kinsey himself observed that orgasm can itself in many respects resemble an intense reaction to pain; it also, almost in contradiction, involves a loss of sensory perception requiring, or enjoying, ever more powerful stimulation and bringing an increased imperviousness to pain. [9] (All stimulation becomes painful beyond a certain point.)

Kinsey experimented with this pain/pleasure/sex connection in various ways. One, no doubt learnt from his histories, was the tying of a rope round his genitals and tugging, sometimes combining this with a rope round his neck – both while masturbating. [10] This has initially two effects. The stimulation leads to an engorgement of the penis, prolonged since the blood cannot drain, and results in a more intense ejaculation. It is also possible, in the view of Dr Bancroft of the Kinsey Institute, that the semi-strangulation – 'auto-erotic asphyxia', a lack of oxygen to the cerebral cortex – reduces inhibition and so increases pleasure.

The practice is not all that unknown because every now and again prominent figures are discovered strangled having got carried away. But the tendency is to push the practice to the point of pain, a bridge is thus built between pain and intense sensation, reinforced each time and gradually increased. Kinsey seems to have followed this path, at some point experimenting with the rope round his testicles alone. By 1954, it is clear years of pulling had strengthened these fragile tissues to an extraordinary degree.

We must also have in mind, when we come to events in 1954, that a time can eventually come, according to Dr Michael Perring, when the sexual element can't function without the painful supplement.

Some of the same considerations can apply to someone, like Kinsey, who finds that his urethra is erotically sensitive. Beginning we don't know when but possibly, as we discussed earlier, quite late, Kinsey began to develop this. Getting pleasure from inserting thin objects, as the years passed and the passage grew insensibly larger, and also less sensitive, the size of the objects increased, until by 1949–50 he was able to insert pencils and even a toothbrush, bristle end first.

How should we view Kinsey's experiments? As usual, we can admire his courage. Michael Perring said the potential association of sexual pleasure with pain is universal; rather few dare explore it. Also, 'Popular acceptance of such experiment is still very limited.' No doubt.

There are other ways of looking at it. You may recall Clarence Tripp's 'reincarnation of prudery'. A seriously inhibiting sexual upbringing creates a pattern of barriers; when, or if, the barriers are removed the pattern remains and barriers have to be reimposed – sometimes pain is chosen.[11] I am not convinced this applies to Kinsey, though it might.[12] For one thing, there are whole areas of his sexuality where it doesn't apply. But Kinsey certainly fits one observation made by Tripp. The greater the past inhibition, the higher the pain barrier can rise. In the end, Kinsey's rose high. Both Gebhard and Dellenback recall that by 1949 there were holes visible in his foreskin which, one supposes at the exquisite peak of his orgasm, Kinsey had pierced.[13] But if one follows Tripp, then Kinsey had developed an ingenious if unusual form of self-therapy, something enabling, which helped him surmount his childhood trauma.

Or we can, something Dr Bancroft suggested, simply view both practices as idiosyncratic methods of self-stimulation which we have no

real reason to label masochistic – indeed, as we saw, they were not
remotely masochistic in the sense that S/M practitioners and those who
study them use the term.

One last observation has to be made. Kinsey was always scrupulously careful that no private interest of his should distort either the
research or his published work. He would record on film, and write
about, rare practices because they existed – but, because they were rare,
he did so sparingly. Thus, there was only one record each of his own
forms of masturbation, and – out of the total of twenty-four couple films
they made – only four were S/M.[14] In the *Male* report there are only two
significant but glancing references to masochism; in the *Female* report
there are three references, which are to S/M and which acknowledge a
connection between pain and sexual pleasure but are uncertain as to its
precise nature and etiology.[15]

Finally, it is important to remind ourselves now that in the summer
of 1950 and thereafter, the filming and observing of sex took up a very
small amount of Kinsey's time.

3

Eleanor Roehr listed some of the demands, over and above his vast regular correspondence, made on Kinsey in a typical week in June this year:
9 requests for information, 2 for lectures, 15 letters about future visits, 7
questions about *Male* statistics, 7 questions about the *Female* volume –
and all these often requiring several letters and telephone calls.[16]

Kinsey himself wrote to Deutsch about his schedule this year, and
said he had to deal with visitors from two-thirds to three-quarters of his
time.[17] Since he was now actively writing the *Female* volume it meant
that night working was now invariable. The staff would leave at 5.00.
Kinsey would remain till Mac called to say supper was ready. He would
go back to First Street for an hour or so, and then return to his desk until
Mac rang again at 11.30, telling him to come home to bed. Kinsey might
or might not comply.[18]

At the end of June he flew to Los Angeles and San Francisco (there
was now a daily flight from Bloomington to Chicago which speeded
things up). Partly, he wanted to continue the work at San Quentin he so
enjoyed. Also, Doug Rigg, the humane and intelligent assistant warden,
had become a friend, and on this visit he asked Rigg to join his staff as an

The Statistician's Conference at Bloomington, 23 and 24 February 1952. Corner, Kinsey, Pomeroy, Martin and Gebhard, all under considerable strain, face Cochran, Mosteller and Tukey. Dellenback is on top of a cabinet, photographing

Typical of the packed, totally absorbed meetings Kinsey addressed for sixteen years all over America. Here a gathering of GPs in San Diego (Hotel Coronado) in October 1953

Alice Field (*left*), Mac, Kinsey and Clyde Martin's children. Kinsey's basic physical frailty, conquered by his indominatable will, is visible

Mac at home in First Street (*c* 1952)

Robert Laidlaw, his wheelchair (from polio) not visible, and Emily Mudd, discussing the *Female* volume

Robert Yerkes

Harriet Pilpel, Morris Ernst's partner. Her attractiveness both concealed her toughness and won her cases

Karl Lashley, with his musician's hands

C. A. Tripp late 1951

Eleanor Roehr – the smile on the
face of the tiger

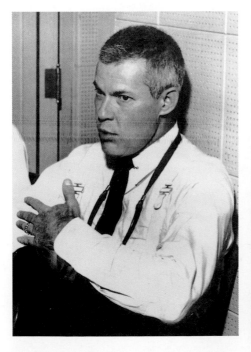

Glenway Westcott on the crucial visit
to Bloomington in July 1951

Monroe Wheeler. As always,
immaculately dressed

Kinsey addressing his massed
audience at the University of
California, Berkeley

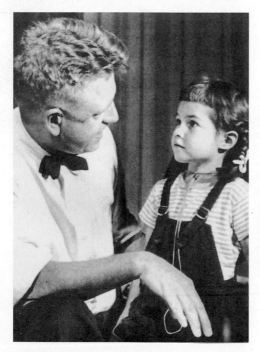

Kinsey and Clyde Martin's daughter.
His *rapport* with small children, their
trust in him, was immediate

Facing page: Kinsey, Professor Fred McKenzie of Oregon State College and Albert Shadle – watching the film of porcupines. *Above*: Also watching. Back row: Kinsey, Dorothy Collins, Jean Brown's husband, Clyde Martin (?). Middle: Cornelia Christenson (Kinsey's biographer), Martha Pomeroy(?), Mac, Jean Brown (assistant librarian). The expressions on the faces of Kinsey and some of the children bear examination

Kinsey collected obsessively for the Kinsey Institute Collection. This little scene (three inches in diameter) is painted on ivory on a gilt frame covered in glass. Probably Paris, date uncertain – 19th century, but could be much later (1950s?)

Decorative condoms existed in ancient Egypt. These examples are from 20th century Germany and America. The originals are highly coloured

Kinsey had film of this, shot by Dellenback in Oregon in 1951; one of many examples which showed, in his opinion, that homosexual acts were not 'unnatural' since they occurred in nature

Kinsey, completely exhausted, escaping to San Quentin prison on publication of the *Female* report in 1953

August 1954. Dellenback photographing during the visit to Peru

Kinsey chatting to RJ in Naples on his European tour

Kinsey with Eric Dingwall during the latter's visit to Bloomington in June 1954

October 1955. Kinsey lectures to the University at Århus in Denmark on his European tour

Kinsey with Kenneth Anger in Aleister Crowley's house, Cefelu, Sicily. Photographed nine months before his death, Kinsey seems to have become one of the demons that have been imagined pursuing him

interviewer. Rigg didn't feel he'd be good enough.[19]

But Kinsey was also very bound up with sex law reform in California, using as his principal mouthpiece Dr Karl Bowman of the Langley Porter Clinic. There was a committee examining the whole subject at this time and they now asked Kinsey to advise on an ongoing study of sex crime, particularly as it involved children.[20]

He flew back on 6 July, just in time for Alan Gregg's visit on 8 July to discuss the statistical committee. Dellenback made this flight with him quite often and remembers the pilot announcing the weather: ' "The temperature as we leave LA is standing at 98°; at Chicago it is presently 93°; and at *Bloomington, Indiana* it is 90°." Kinsey would laugh and say "That's his way of saying 'Hi Doc! I know you're aboard'." '[21]

In fact, fame had struck, or tried to strike, just before he left. The magazine *New York Close-Up* wrote to Mac about a book they proposed. Would she be one of the wives of 'thirty famous men – from Mrs Eisenhower to Mrs Sarnoff to Mrs Pinza . . . As a chapter in our book, you should be wonderful!' Kinsey wrote back declining: 'Our job . . . would be simplified if we did not have more publicity.'[22]

This summer, among the stream of visitors, little Dr Albert Shadle of the University of Buffalo came, forgetting to bring the films of his porcupines mating which Kinsey had begged him to remember: 'We do need these for our study and meditations.' Shadle didn't even mention the films in his thank-you letter of 8 August, just rattling on, perfectly at ease with Kinsey now, about whether his porcupines will give birth: 'Am pinning my hopes on Dannie the yearling and Peterkin the two-year-old which wed last 17 December.'[23]

Kinsey was also carrying on a lively correspondence with Dr William Field (lively on Field's part at least). Field was studying artificial insemination and had been much struck by the *Male* volume. The effect of artificial insemination on bulls, he wrote, is that every bull 'masturbates frequently' and continually tries to mount other bulls. Kinsey asks for film of this, which Field doesn't have, but, in his jaunty style, writes vividly of how some cows are highly sexed, while others 'just stand'. Then suddenly, apropos of nothing they were corresponding about (at this point it was homosexual cockerels from whom Field was collecting semen), he writes asking if there is any aphrodisiac effect if he and his partner (a woman) both swallow his semen? Kinsey says no.[24]

Slightly more weighty was his continuing row with Dr Edmund Bergler. Bergler had now written, in an article on premature ejaculation in the August 1950 issue of the *International Journal of Sexology*, a violent attack on Kinsey's view of the female orgasm. Kinsey demolished him in a scathing letter: 'I have emphasized abundantly that orgasm involves the whole nervous system and not merely the vagina, which happens to be the organ that is least supplied with nerves.' He answered each point and ended, 'Your treatment of the material smacks much more of a dogmatic effort to win a point than a Scientist's effort to discover the fact.'

Other reviewers might have replied in kind, but the irascible New York psychoanalyst was so furious that he set to and started to write an entire *book* in an attempt to destroy Kinsey's case.[25]

On 10 August, Robert Dickinson, now eighty-nine, had gone into hospital to be operated on for a neoplasm of the prostate. He recovered, but collapsed again with pneumonia on 30 August. Kinsey sent a telegram: 'Worried about you. Will come fast if I can be of use.' Dickinson had cancer, but the prognosis was good, though treatment, somehow ironically, had meant castration. Indeed, the tough old man again seemed to be recovering. 'So quick is my regaining strength that I can now make plans,' he writes, and letters began to flow from the hospital bed, some fairly eccentric. But then his letters had always been that, with tiny scraps of paper suddenly pinned to them: 'Women who are pianists – do they have especial skill in playing with male genitals – RLD has case histories of men who discovered this.'[26]

Kinsey was very fond of Dickinson, despite or even because of his eccentricity, and wrote several concerned letters, but he too was now bracing himself for a crisis. In October, the statistical committee, vital for his future funding, finally arrived in Bloomington to examine his sampling and statistical methods in detail.

4

The members of the statistical committee, picked (subject to Kinsey's veto) by Dr Lubin of the Committee on Statistical Standards of the American Statistical Society, were high-powered: William Cochran, professor of biostatistics at Johns Hopkins University School of Hygiene; Frederick Mosteller, associate professor of statistics at Harvard; and John W. Tukey, professor of mathematical statistics, Princeton University.

In fact, it wasn't nearly as difficult, at this point, as Kinsey had feared, the reason being that the committee was there to learn, not comment.

They arrived on 9 October and were given the works: tour, lectures, Hollerith cards, Payne and Wells wheeled out, musicale, Roehr's meals – and every single detail of Kinsey's project.

Frank Edmondson, Kinsey's 'statistician', said that everyone realised the funding was at stake. But what really struck him was how the committee clearly hadn't the faintest idea before they arrived of what Kinsey was up to. It was fascinating to watch them learn. They knew nothing about 100 per cent groups, nothing about interviewing. And as they learnt, said Edmondson, they became more and more friendly.[27]

It was not, in fact, quite as simple as it seemed to Edmondson, though it became much easier after all the committee had given their sex histories (one of Kinsey's conditions). Sensibly, he shared this with Pomeroy and Martin and so demonstrated that all the Institute's interviewers were equally good at it. 'The KPM interview,' the committee was eventually to write in their final report, 'impressed us as an extremely skilful performance.'[28]

They left on 14 October, and from then on Kinsey was consumed with impatience to read their conclusions. He had still heard nothing by 9 November. On 2 January 1951 Cochran said it would be a report in depth.[29] In fact it wasn't published for three years.

And soon, once more, events were sweeping him along – writing the *Female* volume, endless visitors (Karl Bowman on 18 October), endless letters, still more histories. Then, on 10 November, a week in New York.

5

Kinsey was now energetically following up his plan to explore the effect of their sexual lives on the work of as many artists as he could lay hands on.

He saw Herbert Huncke on this visit, and possibly some of his friends. In any case, it was over this period that Huncke introduced him to Jack Kerouac, William Burroughs and Allen Ginsberg. They all gave their histories and Ginsberg helped in more concrete ways on film. He remembered, wrote his biographer, 'not knowing what Kinsey meant when he asked the 24-year-old poet if he'd ever "browned" anyone'.*[30]

---

* My gay informants were not sure either. Probably active anal sex. Possibly anal-oral sex.

Kinsey had lunch with Thornton Wilder and tried to see Paul Cadmus – both introductions from Monroe Wheeler (who had to duck dinner on 14 November, Glenway went instead). Cadmus, who became a friend and from whom Kinsey bought, and by whom he was left, many pictures, was staying at the Villa Pinkipo in France. He sent a postcard weeks later.[31]

During 1949 and 1950, Kinsey had been taking all the histories he could gather from casts of *A Streetcar Named Desire*, and since January 1950 had been trying and failing to meet its author. They finally succeeded on this visit.[32]

It didn't really work out, though Kinsey wrote thanking Tennessee Williams 'for your excellent help' ('excellent' was a favourite adjective of his). Williams didn't give his history and, according to the files, there was no further communication until 1954, when Williams asked for the name of an analyst Kinsey had mentioned. Kinsey couldn't remember but said to the playwright's secretary that 'if he wants to see a psychiatrist, towards which I am inclined rather than an analyst' – Robert Laidlaw.[33]

Yet, what was Kinsey up to? What significance did all this have? Obviously, in the net sweeping to capture the whole of American humanity, artists had a place. But a number of those close to him talked of far more than this, of Kinsey's 'vision'. However, when you try and see precisely of what this vision consisted, it seems to fall apart. Pomeroy says that after getting three entire casts of *Streetcar* more or less 100 per cent, they demonstrated 'at least to our own satisfaction' that any particular part – Blanche, Stanley – emerged differently when played by different actors 'because of differences in the actors' sexual backgrounds'.[34] Yes – or every actor is different and therefore acts differently and these differences are also expressed in their sex lives. 'Because of' is the crucial phrase here, and this is never explained.

Similarly, nothing coherent ever emerged from all Avinoff's labours. Glenway Wescott was to spend many hours trying to correlate writers' works with their sexuality, but Jerry Rosco, who saw some of the results, wrote 'an interesting listing, with no particular conclusions'.[35]

In 1954 and 1955, Kinsey took the histories of a great many ballet dancers. Yet the only result, as far as I can see, was something he once said to Dorothy Collins. 'Kinsey said he'd never interviewed a male ballet dancer who wasn't a homosexual.'[36]

It is true, Avinoff died in December 1949 (leaving his entire erotic collection to Kinsey). Avinoff didn't finish. Indeed, he'd hardly begun. Kinsey, too, died before he could really get to grips with this aspect of his huge, self-imposed task. Perhaps, given his enormous creative energy . . .

And it is also true you can sometimes seem to glimpse something, something grand, something extraordinary, over-arching. Glenway Wescott was one of those who used the word vision. Christopher Isherwood was proving resistant to Kinsey's charms (this in autumn 1951). Wescott longs to get him down to Bloomington. 'The history is not much for candid men like ourselves,' he wrote in his journal. 'Whereas out there, one gets a certain vision; a new objectivity, with implications in morals and philosophy.'[37]

Wescott was partly referring to the tolerant, practical, humane sanity – not common then – with which Kinsey regarded sexual matters, the removal of moral judgement from almost the entire area. But this extends to the extraordinary scope of what he proposed. In his proposal for the next twenty years I referred to earlier, he set out nine complete books: the *Female* volume, which he was now completing; sex law and sex offenders, including historical exegesis and comparisons with Europe; child upbringing and development of sexual attitudes and behaviour; marriage; physiological studies; prostitution, male and female; institutional sexual patterns (prison, schools, hospitals, Army, Navy, etc.); the whole field of the arts and culture from an erotic standpoint; and homosexuality. But even this didn't cover Kinsey's reach. It ignored his collections, now moving well beyond the erotic in art. He seems, also, to have envisaged the whole world coming under his scrutiny. 'Yours is the first first-hand report we have had from Russia since the new sex laws went into effect,' he wrote in 1952 to RJ, one of several 'agents' sending him lengthy bulletins from abroad. RJ eventually sent him long letters from North Africa, India, South America and Scandinavia. Then there was Van Hecht, whom Dickinson had found for Kinsey in China. And quite soon, in 1954, Kinsey was to thrust his research deep into the past, into 'the sexual life of an ancient people' – the pre-Columbian, pre-Christian, Peruvians.[38]

What it amounted to was that Kinsey proposed that *everything* should be studied from a sexual standpoint, if possible by him – a pan-sexual vision, the world seen entirely sexually where the continuum, the patterns, were imposed by the *mores*. And here it is interesting to look at another disciple, Dr C. A. Tripp. Tripp's view is that the point, for

Kinsey, was that sex is a *factory of affection.* It is one of very few biological forces that work in this way. And this is most clearly seen when it is cleared of accretions like romantic love or religion or morality. Once this is done, society's behaviour hangs together as a continuous, coherent unit of biology and conditioning. In our nearest primate relative, the Bonobo chimpanzees, sex is not just the general coin of social commerce, like a smile or a handshake only more pleasurable; it is the glue of social cohesion and peace. For Tripp *that* is the philosophy that permeates both the *Male* and *Female* volumes.[39]

We can approach this from yet another angle. To the Greeks and Romans sex and love were separate (an attitude still partly preserved in the Middle East). Then two things happened: the Church, recognising the power of sex, took it over and declared it evil. Second, the rise of Romantic Love exalted sex and finally joined it to love. Kinsey, in essence, was returning us to an earlier, now rarer view of sex – 'demystifying it' in Paul Robinson's phrase.

Only the mystic, religious impulse in man seems to have the same power as sex to invade, pervade, every aspect of behaviour. This is why sex quite often in the past, in the form of Dionysiac/Aphrodite/Pagan fertility rites, took on the forms of religion. What seems to have happened (and to be still happening) is an echo, or a resurgence in sharpened form, since shorn of fertility, of those ancient patterns. And of course they are naturally clothed in the language of our other religion – science. Michel Foucault fits here, a man who 'tried to experience through his own life, particularly through his own search for sexual pleasure, the kind of salvation that a traditional Christian might well have sought by immersing himself or herself in religious devotion'.[40]

So, too, does Kinsey. The phenomenon of the intensely religious figure who loses his religion but retains the need for some equally all-explaining central idea is familiar. It seems plausible to suggest that Kinsey was psychologically impelled to replace the love and dictates of God with the sexual love of man and woman – and this is another reason sex rather than galls became the driving force of his life.*

I want, for the moment, to leave the discussion there. It is enough

---

* Kinsey is archetypically American in a number of ways: in working his way from poverty to a position of world renown entirely unaided – twice; in his optimism; in his individuality and his elevation of the individual; in his disregard for rank or status. And perhaps in this tremendous elevation of science and sex as well.

now to indicate that there are more profound, or at least quite different, ways of looking at Kinsey's work. I am not sure, as Tripp is, that you can precisely call it a philosophy; it is too incoherent for that. But I also think we'll find that very incoherence may be the point.

Meanwhile, to return to Kinsey at the end of 1950, three events now took place, two involving his oldest and his newest close friends, and the other which was to dog him till his death.

6

Kinsey received a telegram that Dickinson had died on 29 November 1950. 'Thanks for wire,' he responded immediately. 'Will come East whenever needed. Meanwhile please guard our property.' He then telephoned Tripp and told him to do the same at once.

There was, apparently, a real danger of theft here. Dickinson had long ago left everything to Kinsey – manuscripts, models, case histories, drawings, notebooks, etc. Tripp rushed across New York and, together with Dickinson's daughter, packed it up and guarded it for three days.[41]

The element of eccentricity continued to hover over Dickinson even now. Some years before, Green, who was not surprisingly having rows with his wife over his activities, packed his most explosive accounts into cylindrical metal containers and buried them in the Arizona desert. He had willed this to Dickinson and he left the details of the various locations with a Dr Werner, Green's companion in many sexual jaunts, telling him to give the containers to Kinsey if he, Dickinson, should die. Dr Werner did now send one to Kinsey, but then unfortunately died himself. There are still canisters of explosive sexual material lying buried about the Arizona desert.[42]

The second event had taken place a little earlier. On 19 November a news story broke in Indiana that Customs officials had seized a quantity of pornographic goods which Kinsey was illegally attempting to import from abroad. Paul Gebhard says, as do other accounts, that the ISR had an unofficial arrangement with a Customs officer in Indianapolis always to let stuff through to them. In November, he was on holiday and a new officer, Alden Baker, opened some of Kinsey's crates, was outraged, and acted accordingly. But IU's historian, Thomas Clark, says that Baker had been put up to it by the Archbishop of Fort Wayne. The Archbishop himself then personally sent material to the

Indiana Governor, Henry F. Schricker.[43]

Kinsey's chief fear, he told Corner, was the effect this might have on the Rockefeller Foundation. By 13 December he had managed to get back 80 per cent of the material, or so he told Corner and Wells.* But much was retained – including books like *The Memoirs of Dolly Morton* and, ironically, Gershon Legman's *The Horn Book*.[44]

Kinsey decided to fight. Customs might seize other material (as indeed they did); if he didn't fight, the Rockefeller Foundation might assume he felt guilty of something; and it was a clear case of principle – whether the government had the right to seize materials, of whatever sort, imported for genuine scientific and academic purposes. It didn't only affect Kinsey. 'The Boston Museum, the New York Public, the Metropolitan . . . had all complained,' said Wells. Harvard had been unable to import modern literature. The case was to generate an appalling amount of correspondence, at some points it was costing IU (who joined Kinsey and helped pay his fees) $1,000 a day, and it wasn't settled until after Kinsey had died.[45]

7

The final event of 1950 was a four-day visit to Bloomington by Glenway Wescott, during which he began reading and evaluating some of the library's collection of erotica. He also talked.

At one point in his journal, Wescott, without undue modesty, mentions that his friends sometimes compare him to Dr Johnson. But it is clear from the journal itself, from the calibre of his friends and acquaintances, not the sort of people to tolerate bores, that he was an accomplished and amusing conversationalist. Several people – including Kinsey's daughter Joan, Dellenback and Gebhard – all agree that Kinsey very much enjoyed talking to him.[46]

* I think it is possible that Kinsey was simply trying to minimise the event, make it lighter, by saying this, and that he didn't get anything back then. It seems highly unlikely that the Customs would just admit they were wrong about 80 per cent of the items after a month, especially since it was no longer their responsibility but now higher up in the Treasury Department in Washington. In the letters which that department sent Kinsey's lawyers, Greenbaum, Wolf & Ernst on 13 February 1956, which is a resumé of the whole case since proceedings began in 1951, there is no mention of returned material until the date of the letter, when five items were restored to the ISR.

At the same time, Glenway told his biographer Jerry Rosco, Kinsey was nervous that he was indiscreet, that he would 'babble'. 'You well might be,' Glenway agreed – but he proposed a test. Kinsey was to tell him a secret and see if he told Monroe – the man 'most determined to get things out of me'. Kinsey did so, an item innocuous enough – the name of some 'very, very important' (but herself not named), very highly responsive business woman's partner.

Wescott seems to have passed the test (he says he had guessed the business woman's name but he told neither to Rosco).[47] And, as far as I can discover, although he couldn't resist rather obvious hints, he never revealed to anyone, except eventually and inevitably Monroe, certain confidences and events about to transpire in the summer of 1951 – although the effort required was sometimes clearly heroic.

8

1951 began with Kinsey putting pressure on Albert Shadle for the films of porcupine mating, which he'd now been after since 1948. He had also been gently suggesting Shadle could branch out and the little zoologist had made a tentative move into guinea pigs. But it was the film Kinsey needed. This is 'its last chance to influence our thinking as we write about the nature of sexual response and orgasm in the human female'. He offers to come to Buffalo and pick it up. Or could he send Bill Dellenback to film mating himself? Kinsey is clearly desperate.

Shadle replies with one of his chatty letters about Dannie and Peterkin – *and doesn't mention the porcupine film at all!* However, it must have eventually arrived since there is a record later of Kinsey paying $50 for eight films, and of Bill copying them.[*48]

* One should never forget the scientist in Kinsey, the zoologist, endlessly fascinated by the complexity, variety and ingenuity in the behaviour of *all* mammals in his chosen sphere. He loved these films of Shadle's and often watched and showed them. And the porcupines were ingenious enough: the foreplay – standing on hind legs, embracing, seeming to kiss – was followed by the male pressing the female down, at which she dramatically and completely opened up all her quills and the male descended over her, entered with a number of rapid strokes, jack-knifed over to suck his penis clean, and relaxed. Wescott described their approach as 'more human than monkeys – slower, moodier, soberer – in their great overcoats, only their shining eyes and occasionally bared teeth showing through their all-over beards; like nineteenth-century men of genius, Tennyson, Ibsen, Whitman' (*Continual Lessons*, p. 293).

But in fact a great deal of 1951 was taken up with what Kinsey described to his publisher as the huge difficulty of getting all his female data 'crystallized in the text'.[49]

Kinsey had been puzzled to discover that many women, unlike almost all men, seemed able to have no sex for long periods – and then suddenly a great deal. As the patterns increasingly emerged, there appeared what were, to him, stranger and stranger anomalies. Women seemed unaffected by class differences (except as regards extramarital affairs[50]). They were unmoved by pornography, fantasised less while masturbating, were far less involved in S/M, fetishisms, and trans-vestism.[51] Kinsey's solution had in fact crystallised while writing the *Male* volume (we saw one result in his dinner with E.M. Forster): male sexuality was predominantly mental and imaginative, while women were much *less* affected by conditioning and psychological pressures. They became aware of physical need only when actually locked in their lover's arms. This explained female passivity, female abstinence, female resistance to variety.

It was an astonishing and astonishingly bold conclusion. For one thing, it completely reversed the popular stereotypes of women tangled up in their emotions and men coarsely and only physical.

But even internally, Kinsey's theory – genuinely trying to solve what seemed, then, to be fundamental differences, and argued with some subtlety and greater length – was hopelessly contradictory. For instance, in those females impervious to psychological and imaginative forces, religion and generational change had far greater effect.[52] 2.3 per cent of women were far *more* stimulated psychologically than men and 33.3 per cent were the same as men – which left an odd picture of some 36 per cent of women being like men and the rest not.[53] Then, while women responded *less* to photographs they responded *more* to film.

In fact, as it became clearer and clearer that all the differences between the sexes that worried him were examples of learnt behaviour and therefore likely to be cultural impositions, Kinsey was forced to consider this. He did so, briefly, but dismissed it on the bizarre basis of female *animal* response.[54]

Kinsey was a man of his time, as were Robert Kroc and Ralph Voris who had helped him design his interview. The tests of what stimulated the female human animal psychologically, to use his terms, were what sexually stimulated Kinsey, Kroc and Voris psychologically in 1938. Also, though it is true males are more quickly and readily aroused,

Kinsey did not realise how important the mode of presentation was. Gebhard later found that women would respond just as positively if stimuli were presented gradually and especially in a romantic context. 'We got the female sexual responsiveness hopelessly wrong.'[55]

As the culture has changed, so have women. In England, in 1987, women and girls committed 10 per cent of violent crime; by 1995 it was 16 per cent. Oliver James, a clinical psychologist, was reported as saying, 'If the rate of increase goes on women will be as violent as men within twenty years.'[56] Women, including Nancy Friday, who has written with great insight of her own early conditioning, publish *books* of female sexual fantasies.[57] That young women and girls are behaving more and more like young men and boys, sexually and in other ways, is one of the clichés of our time and there is no need to belabour it.[58]

There are still basic biological differences, or seem to be differences, between the sexes. Female homosexuality seems to run, as Kinsey found, at about half the rate it does in men.[59] Yet, is this true either? Women seem to be invading, or about to invade, where once Kinsey seemed most certain there was difference. 'There seems to be no question but that the human male would be promiscuous in his choice of sexual partners throughout the whole of his life if there were no social restrictions.' (And one can't help feeling autobiography lent energy to this passage.) 'This is the history of his anthropoid ancestors and this is the history of unrestrained human males everywhere. The human male almost invariably becomes promiscuous as soon as he becomes involved in sexual relations that are outside of the law. This is true to a degree in pre-marital and in extra-marital intercourse, and it is true of those who are most involved in homosexual activities.' Females were far less so, and thus often found extramarital affairs 'incomprehensible'.[60]

But one might ask (something that struck Kinsey) if men want or seek sexual variety to this extent, which is what this is about, where are they going to find partners if fair numbers of women didn't want the same thing? Evidence is patchy, but the 1994 American survey (though not the 1994 British one) seems to suggest that they *do* want the same thing.[61] Some extremely complex but fascinating (and controversial) work has been done concerning the ability of women to 'up-suck' sperm and of some sperm to block other sperm, all of which points to far greater active manoeuvrability of married women (or women wanting to conceive) as regards partners.[62] (They will *marry* those who will support and protect them, but *conceive* by those whose looks/health/intelligence etc.

attract and appeal to them.)

In 1997 the *British Medical Journal* came out, albeit at an exalted genetic level, in favour of this: 'We have evolved for conditions of mild female promiscuity or multiple mating. Sex with a regular male partner, it seems, is not a sound genetic investment for the female of the species: infidelity ensures a wider gene pool and better sperm quality. And this is widely reflected across the animal kingdom . . .'*[63]

Kinsey did his work on the cusp of momentous change. The second great theme of his *Female* volume, that as far as physiological, orgasmic sexual response went, women were in fact almost the same as men, seemed to detect and foreshadow the seismic events beneath the cultural surface which Betty Friedan's *The Feminine Mystique* crystallised in 1963 to start the feminist revolution. At the same time his first equally revolutionary if erroneous theme – that women were not influenced sexually by imaginative and psychological forces – came in the last years of continuing, and even increasing, male-dominated *mores* at the start of the 1950s.

Nothing that exalted men, even giving them women's traditional attributes, was therefore surprising then; at the same time nothing that exalted women, like equating their sexuality with that of men, could yet be accepted. As a result, both themes were completely ignored.

---

* There are contradictions in our Western culture in this sphere. On the one hand, by genital indulgence and easy toilet training when children are small, tolerance of adolescent experiment and so on we encourage a free sexuality. In many ways we encourage divorce. At the same time we value deep and intense relationships with our lovers and our children, a major reason for the first being our domination by the tenets of romantic love. We bring this about by forming powerful and exclusive bonds with our children which they repeat as adults. Thus we create conditions which encourage freedom for romantic sexual love but where the expression of it, especially in divorce, causes maximum pain for everyone involved.

Not all of this need happen. All cultures share problems caused by the search for sexual variety, but in many they are minor problems. In Samoa, according to Margaret Mead, the *emotions* involved are minor. To some extent the same is true of the !Kung; at least, they are manageable. The clue lies in child upbringing. If babies are brought up by a number of (but the same) people they are secure, but don't form over-deep bonds with either parent and so don't need or form them later on. There is a trade-off between intense (romantic) love feelings and a freer sex life and stable marriage. I sometimes wonder if the explosion of early all-day nursery care across the West isn't the (unconscious) start of a move in this direction. (See my *Love, Sex, Marriage and Divorce*, London and New York, 1981, pp. 122–50, 328; also Mead, 1928; Shostock, 1996, in bibliography.)

9

Despite his writing, which he worked at hard all this year and next, Kinsey still found space for a good many other things. He always tried to give some time to IU and twice, in January and again in February, talked to the Faculty Club; he also gave two lectures on evolution in March.

Pomeroy, little help in the writing, was away for one term working towards a doctorate at Columbia University. Kinsey and Gebhard took four days off in March to collect histories in Chicago, where they squeezed in a burlesque at the Rialto.

On 1 April, as usual, Kinsey presented his annual reports to IU and the NRC. One notices two items: spending on collections is still high – $25,593 – and they are valued at $175,000; and how deeply woven into the project are Friends of the Research. They now begin to be mentioned by name. Wescott is named as a 'visiting specialist' for example. The following year there were to be forty-five names in this category, including C. A. Tripp – 'psychology student'.[64] John Tebbel, later Pomeroy's colleague, and another very close Friend of the Research, was told by Kinsey that he, Tebbel, knew more about sexual behaviour than anyone not on the staff.

After a quick four-day visit from 22 June to the Oregon State College Agricultural Experimental Station to study and film animals, particularly some bulls in homosexual activity,* Kinsey hurried back to fly to San Francisco on 27 June. Partly this was San Quentin, but partly a more serious development.

America, like other countries, has quite often had recourse to, or considered, castration as the solution to sex crimes. Or not even crimes – in 1901, at Palmer, Massachusetts, it was 'persistent masturbation . . . unpleasant for a refined woman to see . . . it seemed an absolute necessity

---

* There is a minute but telling example here of how, though he never remotely falsified evidence, Kinsey would always interpret any doubtful fact to support his own crusades. Pomeroy describes how Dellenback filmed 4,000 feet of animal behaviour, including a bull mounting another bull 'achieving complete anal penetration and ejaculating as he withdrew'. This is how Kinsey would present the film. But Dellenback, in conversation, said, apart from the fact the bull was excited by the presence of cows, it was not at all clear what exactly went on. He thought it was not penetration but friction on the outside which caused ejaculation (Pomeroy, 1972, p. 183; Dellenback, in an interview with the author).

to try something which we [Dr Flood] had not yet tried'.[65] The most recent attempt was in California in 1996.[66*]

It was about to be raised in California again now, in June/July 1951, for a sex offence with girls under fourteen. Kinsey had, of course, studied the effects of castration. Female castration (ovaries removed) made no difference sexually at all. For males it was less precise. From their sex histories he knew many could still respond erotically, and a fair number were able to continue intercourse. And as a legal course he was absolutely clear that this barbarous remedy was far too deeply flawed in other ways. All sex offenders had a low rate of recidivism, but in fact castrates had a *higher* rate than those not castrated; that is, it had the opposite effect to that intended. The fullest study (done on war wounded) found that desire often exceeded potency, hence 'the fallacy', wrote Kinsey, 'of castration as a cure for sex criminals, since such criminal violence is often the result of the conflict of weakened potency and strong sexual impulses'.[67]

The proposed Californian law was also badly drawn up. 'Sex offense' could mean standing too long by a children's playground or exhibitionism (in fact one of Kinsey's correspondents had been castrated for this some years before and had more or less 'completely recovered'). Karl Bowman, armed with a long letter from Kinsey, eventually with the help of others persuaded the governor to veto the bill.[68]

Kinsey was back in Bloomington to greet his 'visiting specialist' Glenway Wescott who arrived to lecture to the university on 13 July and then returned again on 17 July to stay with the Kinseys for two weeks.

10

Almost as soon as he had arrived, it seems, Kinsey asked him if he would be filmed masturbating.[69] Wescott, as he several times notes in his journal, felt he had an inadequately small penis – though this also makes him something of a stud.[70] In interview he was more open still. He told Kinsey, he said to Jerry Rosco, 'I couldn't stand my horrid little penis,

* Castration has quite often been proposed as a solution in Britain too, and regularly appears after particularly appalling paedophile murders. It was used in Denmark throughout the 1950s.

and that I lost one of my testicles at the time of writing my first book.'
He felt Kinsey wouldn't want him.

Kinsey was clearly very gentle with him. He said it was just as interesting, just as valuable *scientifically* (Wescott was deeply impressed by 'science') if he failed. He could take things from the collections to stimulate him. Glenway, typically, didn't choose pornography but 'marvellous old German books of the erotic Greek vases'. Determined not just to be cultured in this stressful (Wescott was fifty that year) and rather bizarre task but original as well, he asked Kinsey if he had 'ever had anyone bugger himself with a dildo'. Kinsey said 'No'. He also told Kinsey that he *never* wanted to see the film of himself.

In the event, it only went fairly well. Kinsey said, of *course* he could pull out, but after breakfast with Mac (Kinsey himself long since up), and armed with plates of archaic erotic Greek vases and *two* big, but not 'monstrous', dildos with their 'seats of very naturalistic testicles', Glenway found himself sitting within Dellenback's 'curtain of lights ... It took forever' – but he managed it.

Unfortunately, he had to do the whole thing again the next day.[71] It seemed he had 'jack-knifed' at orgasm as he had told Kinsey he did, but 'the boys think you faked that' (no doubt with Mike Mikshe's histrionics in mind). Glenway indignantly said he hadn't but agreed to do it again. This time Kinsey was satisfied: 'Well you know it isn't as crucial as we thought, because the boys have found rabbits do it and guinea pigs.' Glenway was pleased to find human beings doing it was 'very rare'.

For the rest of the time Wescott worked. He had a small outer office in Wylie Hall, from where Kinsey, still preoccupied with the Californian castration law, occasionally called him in for 'a few minutes conversation'. He worked through the erotic books and also started on his compilation of contemporary authors and their sex lives.[72]

Wescott observed Kinsey's method of conserving himself: ten hours' work, then home and trivial conversation about records or talk about gardening, then back to work ... (In fact so little actual physical gardening did he have time for that trees were now growing thickly round the First Street house, as if to hide it.)

One thing that always upset Kinsey and which he invariably tried to put right was anyone ashamed or guilty or anxious about any part of their sexuality. It seems clear that he was determined to alter this aspect of Wescott, with his small penis and single testicle; which in any case combined oddly with his continuing good looks and complete lack of inhibitions.

Late one night shortly before Wescott left, Kinsey took him to Wylie Hall and together they watched a number of the ISR's erotic and 'observational' films. 'One of a German boy and a Cuban boy who was almost black, and that was as beautiful as anything I've ever seen.' There was another of a man fellating himself, another of a 'beautiful man' doing it over a stool and several more. 'And suddenly, there! What's that? My God, looks like me!' It was, and Kinsey said he'd included it on purpose, because Glenway had to learn to see himself objectively, and also, now 'very solemn', must 'learn to love the way you look . . . And then,' said Wescott enigmatically, 'and then came some very interesting experiences.'[73]

It was as close as he ever came to telling his future biographer that he had at that point begun his affair with Kinsey, an affair which, soon after this, became what Glenway really always preferred, a three-part affair, with Monroe Wheeler also becoming Kinsey's lover.

subject of Kinsey came up. John Tebbel mentioned Kinsey's affair, and was shortly after rung up by an extremely agitated Pomeroy telling him he should on no account mention the subject again.[4]

Today, all but four of Glenway's letters have been removed from the Kinsey Institute files. Kinsey's letters are still there, frequently thanking 'for your letter, and a long one' – which letter is not there. (An apt comment, incidentally; when I eventually got hold of some of the letters they ranged from two pages up through 10, 13, 14, 51 and 55 pages.)*

Sometimes the excessive precautions taken to inter Glenway were slightly ludicrous. Working in the Institute on the art collections, I came across an excellent article on the photographs by James Crump. Here he used the same observation about Kinsey by Wescott I quoted earlier, including 'fatigue, concentration and (surprising to me, if I interpret rightly) passionateness and indeed sensuality'. Crump's use goes like this: '. . . fatigue, concentration and (surprising to me, if I interpret right) [he is] passionless and indeed [without] sensuality'.[5] Crump was for a period curator of photographs at the Kinsey Institute.

The fact is, the whole team was appalled by Kinsey's affair. Not on moral grounds – quite the contrary. But because they were terrified Glenway Wescott would, as he had put it, 'babble'.

As far as I can discover, Wescott did not babble, but we learn at least two things from his letters, published journals and the Rosco interview. First, they show it is likely the affair began where I place it, in July 1951. The Rosco interview strongly suggests it was after he had seen the film of himself masturbating (which it also made clear was done at Bloomington). We can pinpoint this to July 1951 because the accusation of faked jack-knifing continued to irk Glenway and he wrote a thirteen-page letter explaining he *hadn't* faked, in January 1952.[6] Since there was no visit to Bloomington between July 1951 and January 1952, the filming and its sequel must have been then.

But, even though he plainly took a colossal grip on himself, Glenway couldn't resist a few delicate winks in Kinsey's direction. His thank-you

---

* Thanks to the generosity of Wescott's biographer, Jerry Rosco, I was able to see most of the letters, since Wescott himself eventually recovered copies from Paul Gebhard or, in some cases, took copies before sending them. In all it looks as if fifteen full letters have been removed, and there are a further twenty pages of 'letter fragments' which Rosco can't match up. But even the 'full' letters are not complete and I think it probable that Wescott himself destroyed the missing portions.

18

Bisexuality* – and the Case Against Kinsey

[Homophobia and hatred of sadomasochism] are as central to the ideology and psychology of the Christian Right as anti-Semitism was to the Nazis in the 1930s and 1940s.

Philip Greven, *Spare the Child*, New York, 1992, p. 184

1

It is one of the contentions of James Jones that Kinsey loved, indeed needed, an element of danger in his work to such an extent that he recklessly and it seems deliberately risked discovery, exposure and ruin to feed his appetite for it.[1]

The man Jones identified as Anonymous A told me that he had put Jones on to this and that Jones had misunderstood him. Anonymous A had not meant Kinsey courted danger, only that he liked excitement in his life – as many people do.[2] Possibly – nevertheless, though Jones exaggerates here, one can see his point.

It is fascinating to observe the whole play of this in the repercussions that accompanied and followed Kinsey's affair with Glenway Wescott. What the team felt, then and for years, can be deduced from what happened later. Soon after Kinsey died John Tebbel, who was my initial informant in this matter,[3] happened to be chatting to a New York psychotherapist who knew both Kinsey and Wardell Pomeroy, and the

---

* Kinsey, of course, would not have countenanced this, any more than he did the designation 'a homosexual'. There are homosexual acts and heterosexual acts; not discrete, identifiable types. As we'll see in a moment, modern research continues to substantiate this. I use the term as shorthand.

letter after the July visit includes 'Monroe listened delightedly to my account of the fortnight in Bloomington – no indication of jealousy or anxiety. I did not confess all . . .' (Glenway's dots).[7] In his next letter he says in the same arch way that anyone of his 'loquacious' habit must feel on returning from Bloomington: 'On trial as to discretion . . . Therefore I have made a little exercise, and demonstration for you of not talking even to Monroe about some of the things that we found of interest.'[8] And in later years there were quite a number of references to 'that happy day in 1951'.[9] In his published journal he allowed himself only one overt entry: 'I love Kinsey, and I aspire to his particular virtues: laboriousness, secretiveness, and neatness.'[10] Had he seen this, Kinsey would undoubtedly have underscored 'secretiveness'.

Because the second thing we can deduce is that Kinsey took steps to instill discretion. It is clear that as far as he was concerned Glenway's nudges were a great deal too obvious, and he took a hold on the writer himself. One can see this, too, operating in the letters. Wescott's first letters begin 'Dear Dr Kinsey'; then, after the Morgan Forster dinner, move to 'Dear Alfred', after the July 1951 visit they start 'Dear Friend' and end 'yours devotedly', but from then on move sharply back to 'Dear Dr Kinsey . . . Yours Glenway.'[11]

Kinsey, in fact, took great care in general that events inside his circle, or about himself, should not get out. He didn't, Dellenback and Gebhard are clear, swear anyone to secrecy. Apart from other considerations he had no need to since, as Gebhard noted, complete confidentiality about anyone's sexual behaviour was axiomatic and automatic.[12] But Kinsey also exercised a form of selective secrecy within the circle itself. He would tell Pomeroy or Gebhard something and no one else. For instance, the rope round Kinsey's testicles was complete news to Gebhard. John Tebbel knew about them making heterosexual films, but had no idea there were homosexual ones as well.*[13]

Nor, as far as we can judge, did Kinsey or Mac tell their children anything about their experiments in sexual behaviour.[14] They may have thought them still too young to be trusted. Or Kinsey may have remem-

---

* And Tebbel was an intimate of the research – perhaps nearly very intimate. He wrote that late one night he and others were talking as often in the Astor Hotel with Kinsey and the team. John Tebbel had to catch a train. Kinsey urged him to stay. '"Plenty of room," he said. "You can bunk in with me." The beds in the Astor were not all that large. I decided to catch the train.' (Tebbel to the author, 8 April 1996.)

bered his own anger against his father and worried what Bruce's reaction would have been. Or it is possible that, just as he had sent them to Sunday school to fit in with their peers, he may have felt his example, if followed, would have rendered them unfit for Bloomington society – and he would have been right. Whatever the reason, his decision was to cause considerable havoc among his children later on.*

Paul Gebhard felt there was never any great likelihood of the team or anyone else letting things out, and indeed no one did so – at the time.[15] Nevertheless, it seems to me there was, as it were by definition, a considerable risk just entering the group round Glenway Wescott. Wescott's three obsessions in life were snobbery/gossip/society, writing (usually his) and sex, and it would be hard to choose the most important. And the whole homosexual group which revolved round him was charged with sex and fascinated by it. They were all equally charged with gossip about sex and Kinsey didn't just observe them, at Stone-blossom,[16] in New York and Bloomington; he also, if rarely, joined in. He had sex with Bill Miller for example[17] – a young man 'of absolutely stunning physique when young'.[18]

There was a definite strain of bravado in Kinsey, born of flamboyance, defiance and supreme self-confidence. The way he'd shoot off in front of experts knowing virtually nothing about their subject used to curdle Paul Gebhard's blood. 'I remember he got totally out of his depth over the erotic element in Egyptian art.' Kinsey, talking about the lack of nudity in Egyptian art, suddenly became angry and said it showed how prudish they were. An expert present piped up and said that was nonsense. There was a lot of nudity in Egyptian art. Kinsey went completely blank. ' "Oh yes," said the expert, he'd seen "lots of tomb murals with nude slaves and workmen." Immediately, Kinsey recovered – exactly, *artisans* and *slaves* were nude, that was *precisely* his point. He almost never got caught,' said Gebhard.[19]

This strain of defiance also operated to some extent in his homosexual activity. At the same time one might ask – what else was he to do? The reason it was risky was because of unjust laws he was trying to remove and prejudices, ignorance, fear and hatreds he was trying to change. Was he once again to go through the agony of trying to repress this side of his nature as he had once struggled to repress his whole

* The decision is also, incidentally, an indication of how slowly Kinsey expected the *mores* of America to change.

sexuality? One could argue that *not* to have tried to live something of the life he believed in would have involved cowardice, a loss of integrity.

But it is how this side – the bisexual side – affected his research and writing, his science, that is obviously one of the most significant things about it and this is what I'd like to look at more closely now.

2

The first thing to say, or admit, is that, once alerted, one quite often notices how the H element informs the actual writing of his two books.

It explains, for example, the drive in the prose, that ringing eloquence with which the passages about homosexuality are frequently touched:

> If all persons with any trace of homosexual history, or those who were predominantly homosexual, were eliminated from the population today, there is no reason for believing that the incidence of the homosexual in the next generation would be materially reduced.* The homosexual has been a significant part of human sexual activity ever since the dawn of history, primarily because it is an expression of capacities that are basic in the human animal.[20]

Kinsey's feelings surface suddenly, and often in curious ways, in images, sentences, even single words. Some exclusively homosexual men are very discreet, but others 'are active wolves who are in continual trouble because of their open affronts to social conventions'. 'Wolves' – so brave, so fierce and dangerous, even romantic. Or: 'The lower level male . . . may find it difficult to understand that a sex study should be concerned with anything except heterosexual coitus, unless perchance he is interested in homosexual relations.'[21] That wistfully hopeful 'perchance' is the giveaway here.

Angry memories of 'sissy' stir, appearing as it were in reverse; and to help him here Kinsey evokes, if from an unusual angle, a fantasy about

---

* Something that has been tested. The German Nazis murdered between 220,000 and 500,000 homosexuals, with no detectable later effect. (Edgar Gregerson, *Sexual Practices: The Story of Human Sexuality*, London, 1982, p. 175. Other authorities, however, dispute these figures, though not the facts.)

one of America's most potent and most enduring myths. There is, he writes, 'a type of homosexuality which was probably common among pioneers and outdoor men in general ... among groups that are virile, physically active ... Such a group of hard-riding, hard-hitting, assertive males would not tolerate the affectations of some city groups that are involved in the homosexual.' He returns to this theme again: '... there is considerable homosexual activity among lumbermen, cattlemen, prospectors, miners, hunters and others engaged in out-of-door occupations.' No urban mincing here, no anxiety or guilt – just good honest-to-God, straightforward sex. 'It is the type of homosexual experience which the explorer and pioneer may have had in their histories.'[22] This must have come as something of a surprise in the land of John Wayne.*

But all this, though interesting in a lit-crit way, is not at all how Kinsey's detractors approach the subject. He and his work have been the subject of seemingly much more lethal attacks.

3

Earlier I questioned a recent study of Kinsey by Thomas Waugh,[23] not for his conclusions (which were at least partly correct) but about his characterisation and use of the Kinsey–Voris correspondence.

Waugh, however, lays much more serious charges. He alleges a) that Kinsey was not an objective scientist but a subjective and biased homosexual. The evidence is the extraordinary bias in his collections where male 'homoerotic' elements are disproportionate 'in terms even of the stunning statistics that Kinsey himself had claimed in the *Report*'.[24] And b) that this had a significantly damaging effect in Foucaultian terms where sex research = power = sex repression.

Leaving aside that 'claimed', which suggests a falsification Waugh nowhere even tries to substantiate, and also that the collections were not

* I, too, am surprised, but only that in these more liberal times this particular avenue has not been more deeply explored by a *genre* always seeking new avenues. In fact, the big man, or his company, did write to Kinsey about a new film – *Big Jim McLain* – in which John Wayne was to star in the title role. But it was only for permission for Big Jim to say 'You investigating for Dr Kinsey?' Kinsey wrote back grudgingly that he couldn't see any legal objections (having in his first version of the letter said he couldn't see they had any legal right). (Wayne–Fellows Productions to Kinsey, 14 May 1952; Kinsey to Wayne–Fellows, 26 May 1952.)

part of Kinsey's published work, Waugh's allegation about the collections is, quantitatively, quite simply wrong. To a limited extent it was true of the few films Dellenback shot, but it was not true of the far more numerous commercial and amateur films;[25] nor was it true of the photographic collection, according to the last curator.[26] Taking the collection as a whole, the balance is overwhelmingly heterosexual.[27] The fundamental reason for this is plain: the collections, all but the films, reflect the market-place, over many decades and centuries and many countries, going back to ancient Peru and Africa; and the market-place, then as now, is to a vast extent heterosexual.

As to power = oppression, once again Waugh falls under the disastrous spell of Foucault, disastrous not least for his prose style:

> How did 'Power' move through these pictures, power conceived of not only in the traditional sense of political imposition and control, but also power in the sense of hegemonic socio-sexual discourses, and, most important of all for a historian of the gay imaginary, power in the sense of the cultural and corporal resistance of lived experience.[28]

It is indicative that the question mark was omitted at the end of all this by Waugh. When you search to find *precisely* how this 'power' expressed itself, you read it had 'concrete ramifications in the classificatory systems of the military and the FBI, anti-obscenity vigilantism by state agencies, the sex hysteria of the media, and the further entrenchment of the psychiatrization of perversion and other means of repression'. And his evidence? That the collection contains one police film of men having sex in a public toilet which is, moreover, 'similar' to some other films in the collection.[29] *That is all.* Examined, the whole case collapses.

As it was bound to do. One of the most striking things about the film collection is that virtually no one – certainly not the military, the FBI, vigilantes, etc. – ever saw it or sees it. And from all the other items in that vast array only one or two sometimes trickle out into expensive scholarly publications or tiny exhibitions, usually at IU. During the 1980s nothing whatever was seen anywhere.

If in these instances Waugh can be discounted, the rest of his excellent and illuminating (and amusing) essay stands. But his attack was nothing like as damaging, even in intent, as those we must discuss now.

4

At numerous points during his recent biography James Jones accuses Kinsey of deliberately seeking out male homosexuals and as a result – and also deliberately – his work is seriously 'flawed' or 'skewed'. Jones is often a little vague as to the precise nature of this sinister 'skewing' and 'flawing' but taking some of the more specific references the reader is clearly being led to believe that Kinsey collected far too many male homosexual histories.[30]

Jones is, of course, correct here. Kinsey also deliberately collected (a fact unmentioned by Jones) far too many sex offender histories and far too many juvenile sex histories. He collected all three groups in excess because he planned, as we saw, full-scale books on homosexuals, sex offenders and the influence of child upbringing and sex education on future sexual development. Indeed, so important were the last two that the projected homosexual study kept on being pushed further and further back.[31]

But Jones goes much further than this. By 'his methodology and sampling technique [Kinsey] virtually guaranteed that he would find what he was looking for'.[32] That is, too many homosexuals. What the reader is meant to infer (and so what most reviewers *did* infer) is that Kinsey collected too many male H histories so that he could make out there were more homosexuals than there were. By his search for extremes he deliberately 'skewed' his results.[33]

Now this is an extremely serious allegation; yet oddly enough Jones nowhere attempts to support it with figures or analysis or comparisons. Yet, as we saw in some detail, it isn't true; indeed, it is the reverse of the truth. Kinsey weighted down his H figures by comparing them to his 100 per cent groups; he didn't use his sex offender and juvenile histories except in specific instances. And when, as far as is possible, the H figures are compared to those of subsequent surveys not only are they close (2.8 per cent exclusively H in the recent US survey, to Kinsey's 4 per cent for example) but we concluded that Kinsey's findings, on all counts, were likely to be the closest approximation to the truth. We also noted that the 'cleaning' of Kinsey's sample of specifically H and prison histories made surprisingly little difference. Certainly, as we again saw, Kinsey's sampling was not representative, but that had nothing to do with any of this.

Since this 'skewing' and 'flawing' were two of the major conclusions drawn by readers of Jones' book, I should perhaps emphasise the true state of affairs.

Kinsey told Wescott he was terrified fellow scientists would accuse him of bias,[34] not because they knew of his orientation, which, unlike Wescott, they didn't, but because of his discovery that homosexual *acts* were very common. This, as his letters to Ralph Voris in 1938 showed, had astonished Kinsey as much as it did everyone else. He therefore, *on this ground alone*, took enormous pains to guard against bias. There is no doubt that he succeeded.

Kinsey's bisexuality is the final, and probably most potent, element in his success at extracting the truth from homosexuals. It gave him an edge quite out of reach of the Blue Rinse Brigades. It is never the sole explanation, but it is also this that explains the rapidity with which he worked out his 0–6 scale (though in fact such scales are not uncommon either in biology or the social sciences). It is behind his repeated insistence that there is no such thing as 'a homosexual' – there are only homosexual acts. It is behind his insistence that nothing can be considered stable here: men and women can, in his terms, be a 2 at one point, spend three years as a 4 or 5, ten years later be 1 and end as 0.

It is *behind* all this – but Kinsey didn't invent or falsify to reach these conclusions. Precisely the same ones were reached by the recent (1994) British survey. They found no 'profile' of homosexuals, they found the same impermanence of patterns, and they decided that Kinsey's continuum (or some version of it) was still the most accurate way of looking at it.[35]

James Jones must have known all this. Why then did he leave his allegations (purposely vague to embrace as much as possible) intact? Something odd is going on here.

5

It is difficult to characterise the atmosphere of a book without lengthy quotations, but early on, the language of Jones' biography indicates that something more than mere distaste for its subject is operating. You may remember that, in connection with Voris, I said it seemed likely, given Kinsey's idealistic attitude to nudity, that the Kinseys had been to nudist camps – an innocent enough activity. Faced with the same evidence, Jones came to the same conclusion, but he puts it like this: 'Suspicion lingers that he was speaking from experience', and Jones goes on to imagine, on no evidence at all, that Kinsey is suggesting group sex.[36] On the marriage course Kinsey's poor, duped students 'thought he truly cared about their problems'.[37] (Kinsey's real concerns, according to Jones, again on no evidence at all, were prurience and to see if other people shared his sexual 'demons'.[38]) Kinsey is not allowed to lecture to them without 'sneering';[39] if he pays a bill he's a 'check grabber';[40] he is not allowed to express pleasure at good reviews but is 'unable to resist tooting his own horn'[41] or 'boasting' about them;[42] good reviews which in any case he 'rigs', thereby 'corrupting peer review';[43] if Kinsey is pleasant at some point he has a 'congenial façade' concealing the domineering, driven man 'lurking' within;[44] he 'postures' as objective, but actually the *Female* volume only has 'the trappings of heavy-duty science', while in fact Kinsey's 'private demons came dangerously close to howling in public'.[45]

These 'demons', which weave in and out continually, howling and pursuing the reader as they are supposed to have pursued poor Kinsey from about the age of fifteen, are 'masochism' and 'homosexuality'. We saw, from Jones' own evidence, that Kinsey was neither a masochist nor a homosexual in the sense Jones' book uses the terms. The distinction I made as regards masochism may not have seemed particularly important, but we now see how vital it is to Jones' purpose that precisely these terms are insinuated into the reader's mind – the rampant 100 per cent homosexual, the '6' from youth, the masochist of popular image, begging to be beaten, cringing in a fantasy of humiliation – in order that the reader will be the more ready to believe, *of course* Kinsey would seek out *all* bizarre sexual extremes and so 'skew' his science.

These are not the only instances where Jones stretches to breaking point the meaning of words in a way not compatible with scrupulous scholarship.

Take another 'demon' – exhibitionism. Kinsey, as a matter of policy, encouraged people not to be ashamed of nudity and, in his family, out camping, in his hotel rooms and so on, would lead by example. Jones therefore feels justified in dubbing him an 'exhibitionist', thus conjuring up in his reader's mind someone who, for perverted sexual thrills, exposes his genitals at inappropriate times and in inappropriate places including, especially, public places.

The same is true of 'voyeur'. Kinsey was certainly sometimes aroused on the infrequent occasions when he, quite openly, observed couples in sexual activity* – and this is likely to be true of all sex researchers in this field. On this basis Jones calls Kinsey a voyeur, that is (according to *Chambers Dictionary*), 'a sexual pervert who derives gratification from surreptitiously watching sexual acts or objects: a peeping tom: one who takes a morbid interest in sordid sights'.[46]

It is instructive to see Jones at work here. At one point he quotes Vincent Nowlis in order to accuse Kinsey of using his musicales as opportunities for voyeurism. The paragraph starts with Nowlis saying that, discussing music, Kinsey asked, ' "Which music have you heard that aroused you erotically? . . ." ' Jones now continues, 'As his thoughts returned to those Sunday evenings, Nowlis painted a vivid portrait of thinly veiled voyeurism: "in those musicales, with this piercing glance of his, he would scan the intimate audience for potential signs of responsiveness . . ." '[47]

I rang Vincent Nowlis to check on this rather surprising view of the musicales not noticed by any other observers, most of whom commented only on Kinsey's rapt absorption and his intense irritability if this was disturbed. Nowlis said it was quite true he was asked the question about music; sexual response to music was rare and Kinsey was interested to see how rare (exceedingly, was the answer). He also talked to Jones about Kinsey as a teacher and how he would sometimes check on how people had responded to his lessons and take pleasure if they had taken them in, in this case his preliminary music lessons. Jones had simply joined two totally separate and distinct parts of their interview with his own 'Nowlis painted a vivid portrait . . .' sentence. 'The idea Jones puts forward here,' said Nowlis, 'is, of course, ludicrous.'[48]

Jones' references to Kinsey as a voyeur and exhibitionist are not glancing or incidental: they occupy thirty-one pages.[49]

Now, though it is Jones' invention, perhaps Kinsey did 'sneer' while lecturing, nor would half-a-dozen or a dozen such derogatory verbs or denigrating adjectives much matter in a long, combative biography. However, when they pour in an unrelenting stream, pejorative page after pejorative page, when they are accompanied by accusations of corrupt research and 'flawed' science, of voyeurism and exhibitionism, misogyny, 'masochism', and homosexuality, steadily accumulating throughout 937 pages, the final effect is overwhelming and there

---

* It is interesting, incidentally, that our only hard evidence of this – from 'Alice Dent' and Frank Beach – is when he was watching heterosexual activity.

emerges a portrait of someone so unpleasant as to be actually grotesque – and I use the word deliberately. Jones' final jab at Kinsey is to describe what he looked like when 'having sex', and that is the word he chooses to emphasise – 'grotesque'.[50] Few of us would like our portrait, verbal or otherwise, painted in such circumstances.

It is hardly surprising, then, that a great many reviewers both here and in America, recoiled with disgust and condemnation when confronted with this creature. 'During his career at Indiana University, he forced his etymology [sic] assistants to masturbate with him ... Later, this monstrous scientist would volunteer his wife for gynaecological experiments ... The reason Kinsey's private life matters ... is that it corrupts his research over 20 years ... he had partialities which seriously skewed the sample ...' wrote Laura Cumming in *The Guardian*. In the *TLS*, Christopher Hitchens declared that Kinsey 'began prostituting his wife to some of his male colleagues ... His own voyeurism meshed awkwardly with that of a wider society ... in this bleak and joyless piece of methodological unsoundness ...' Kinsey chose people 'either on the margins or beyond the pale: homosexuals, sado-masochists, voyeurs, exhibitionists, paedophiles, transsexuals, transvestites, fetishists ... the statistics which cram the doctor's books must now be regarded as decidedly "skewed" ... perverted bunkum ... the doctor was driven by his own tortured compulsions ...' wrote Sharon Churcher in *The Mail on Sunday*.[51]

The Times actually devoted an editorial Third Leader to the attack: 'Nobody, perhaps, has so shamelessly exploited the opportunities [of sex research] as did Professor Alfred Kinsey ... [He] was a voyeur, a masochist, a homosexual ... his science ... vitiated by his disregard for proper sampling methods. He was simply too interested in bizarre or extreme sexual behaviour to resist the temptation to seek out its practitioners ... driven by demons ...'[52] And even reviewers sympathetic to Kinsey felt obliged to acknowledge Jones' 'evidence'.[53]

The same was true in America. Alan Wolfe in *The New Republic* wrote: 'An inveterate exhibitionist ... a voyeur ... Kinsey's approach to sex was as scientific as *Peyton Place*.' Dozens of papers took verbatim news service columns like this one from the *Gannett News Service*. 'Kinsey was ... a closeted homosexual and masochist obsessed with sex and driven by his own sexual demons ...'[54]

In ironic imitation of its subject's books, the massive review coverage of the biography has been more widely read than the book itself. The public reputation of Kinsey and his work has been badly damaged, though I hope not irretrievably.

Yet Jones' attack is odd too. Not only does much of it fly in the face of evidence found in his own book, the standard is often not what one would expect of such a man. He is a professor at a distinguished university; he has one fine book to his credit and no doubt many equally distinguished papers. I would like finally, and very briefly, to try and see if we can find some explanation for what happened.[55]

6

I think the first clue lies in that first fine book of Jones'. This was *Bad Blood*,[56] which publicised the racist scandal of the US Government's Tuskegee syphilis experiment from the 1930s to the 1950s. This was a polemical journalistic work about something self-evidently wrong. It was a success.

Morton Wheeler told Kinsey that his first book would set the pattern for all the others – and so it proved. This is very common, especially where that first book is well received. It would be surprising if Jones had not come to his second book with some form of exposing polemic not already in mind as a strong possibility.

But what could be exposed? Here we have another clue – those demons. It is perfectly clear now that there was nothing in the least 'demonic' about Kinsey's masochism nor his homosexual element. The first is probably best seen as a progression where, in the search for intense sexual sensations, pleasure finally became associated with pain; and it can be looked on as an enabling development in the ways I described. His homosexuality was part of his changing and evolving sexuality. There is no evidence that he was the slightest bit guilty about either and a great deal of evidence that he enjoyed both. 'Angels' would be a more accurate personification.

But 'demons' don't just torment and drive people against their will – they also come from hell. To attach the word 'demon' to those sides of Kinsey, that is to say, *is to categorise them as sins*.

When he talked to James Jones in 1988 Vincent Nowlis became more and more appalled by his interviewer's obvious homophobia. 'I realised when he had gone that he might well use, probably would use, what I had told him to damage the cause of sex research and also Kinsey.

I wrote to him about this, saying that I hoped he would not.' Jones did not reply.[57]*

That Jones has a strong distaste for homosexuals and homosexuality was noticed by several reviewers. Kenneth Lewes, for instance, noted how he 'articulates some rather parochial, almost homophobic, views. He assumes, for example, that Kinsey harbored deep doubts about his masculinity and felt enormous guilt about his homosexuality, simply assuming that these feelings are intrinsic parts of the homosexual condition, without reliable evidence.'[58]

Martin Duberman comments on the difference in Jones' treatment of Gebhard – 'characterised as "a free spirit", "a very likable man" with "a terrific sense of humor" ' – and Pomeroy. Pomeroy is 'a kind of equal opportunity Don Juan . . . a character of little substance.' 'Get it?' writes Duberman. 'The exclusively heterosexual Gebhard wins the kudos. Pomeroy, a man by other accounts of great charm . . . is discussed as a vain creature . . . "He just fucks everybody and it's really disgusting," says one of Jones' informants, who clearly speaks for Jones.'[59]

It is possible the animus is unconscious. Certainly, the extraordinary, almost automatic, bias in the language would suggest this. (And see again p. 76, where I pointed out how Jones unwittingly gave away his prejudices about homosexuality.) But once engaged on a second work of uncovering and investigative polemic Jones was in a sense trapped. Hardly any opportunity to drive home his points could be missed. Of course, it is not *all* against Kinsey. Jones is careful to include a good deal of appreciation. But the purpose of this in an investigative work is quite different from what it is in a biography. In the first, it is to show that the writer is objective – but the end remains paramount. In the second, appreciation and condemnation have to be carefully

---

* During my conversation with Nowlis about this he said that it was very evident, also, how Jones encouraged him in anything in the least critical or pejorative he said about Kinsey, by smiling and nodding. I had noticed myself how Jones' style as an interviewer, clear even just reading the transcripts, was to lead his subjects in the direction he wished them to take. It would require rather lengthy quotations to demonstrate this, but one can see him in action in his book where he tries to persuade Rainwater, a graduate student of Kinsey's, first that Kinsey was an exhibitionist (p. 273) and second to get him to say that Kinsey got them all to masturbate together (p. 275). Rainwater, apparently a 'gentle soul', 'self-effacing', and in his eighties, managed to stand firm; Jones was forced to rely on the 'prick nibbling tent' as his evidence for this sort of thing (p. 282).

shaded and mixed with much else to create an accurate *balance*, the result of which, one hopes, will be a portrait approximating to the truth. By the time Jones gets to balancing, the scales have been irretrievably and far too steeply weighed down.

7

Freed of its demonic primacy, Kinsey's bisexuality now sinks back, very important, it is true, but once again just one of all the other biographical elements – his remembered sexual frustration, his desire to shock authority and convention, his preaching and so on. It does, finally, with them explain the extraordinarily personal feeling that flashes continually through these two books as Kinsey, like an artist, expresses in the form of his science some of the deepest parts of his nature. It is to the last stages of the final work, approaching its climax, we must now return.

19

Writing and Publication of the Female *Volume* – Science as Sex and Literature

A random number generator is like sex. When it's good, it's wonderful – and when it's bad it's still pretty good.

George Marsaglia, *New Scientist*, 22 July 1995

1

Immediately after Glenway's return to New York, Kinsey's engagement diary for August 1951 shows six dates with his dentist in seven days, which may or may not be significant.

Visitors passed through as usual, driving writing deep into the night. Manfred Guttmacher, who came now, was shown a film of coitus;* he also remembered Kinsey 'holding forth at length against Terman and ... Kubie' (Dorothy Collins said of Kinsey and his critics, 'He would carry a slow burn for a long time'; just as he never forgave his father, and retained his rage against the potato well into adult life.)[1]

Psychologists Albert Ellis and Ruth Doorbar came on 24 August. They arrived at 8.30 a.m., Kinsey long at work. He now spent the entire day with them 'alert and enthusiastic' – talking, listening, displaying; lunch, LP records (his new collection), supper, then he took them back to Wylie Hall till 11.30 p.m. when he finally said he had work to do,

---

* But not his psychiatrist wife. Great care was taken as to who saw what – and most people saw nothing. Children, obviously, were not shown Wescott masturbating, but invariably, for educational and 'wonder-of-nature' reasons, the porcupines. Dorothy Collins has a photograph of her son, aged four, watching with his eyes wide and jaw dropped. (Collins, in an interview with the author.)

resuming where 'we had presumably interrupted him at 8.30 that morning'.

Ellis, in his short memoir of the visit, noticed the 'iron hand' with which Kinsey ruled and also felt Kinsey could have had very little time for sex – at least with Mac.* Ruth Doorbar, meanwhile, was rapidly yanked in to collect female graffiti from toilet walls.[2]

In fact the iron hand was about to be challenged. Glenn Ramsey came in September, so did Tripp and his friend Oliver Kostuck. There was always trouble with men pretending to be Kinsey interviewers and the NRC issued a press statement. Then in October little Albert Shadle visited, about to launch out with considerable boldness into homosexuality in buck rabbits.[3]

But it was about now that the team broke into their first (and last) act of open rebellion.[4]

2

It had been some time in preparation. Gebhard, like all of them, was often extremely exasperated by Kinsey and he had been particularly stung by the brutal way his questioning the use of male prisoners had been rejected out of hand. He, Pomeroy and Martin had therefore secretly embarked on a thorough analysis comparing female offenders with the rest of the female population. Martin, in particular, enjoyed the work.

The results were conclusive. They differed significantly and in all the ways you'd imagine. By definition set against the *mores* of society, female prisoners had sex earlier, with more partners, more unstable relationships and marriages and so on (and clearly this reflected back, too late, on the *Male* sample). The team came and presented their evidence. Kinsey listened, argued, and finally, to his credit, accepted with good grace. He also realised its retrospective significance for the *Male* volume, and later checking, on his instructions, showed that the male prison population should have had separate treatment, though this was something he never admitted publicly.[5] (Nevertheless, as we saw, as far as

---

* Deducible, perhaps, from thirty years of marriage. But a recent survey by the University of Chicago found that 'workaholics' have more sex than other people. (*The Daily Telegraph*, 15 January 1998, p. 4.)

homosexual incidences are concerned, removing the prison sample made surprisingly little difference.)

Kinsey's acceptance meant thousands of hours of work, all the women state farm offenders, among his earliest histories, had to be jettisoned. It was impossible now for him to give a picture of females below high school level in the *Female* volume – and his regret sometimes surfaces there.[6]

But far more serious threats to Kinsey's research were gathering. It was becoming increasingly clear to George Corner how very worried the Rockefeller Foundation was getting about supporting Kinsey – Alan Gregg had only won the last grant by a single vote. In August, Corner suggested Kinsey invite Dr Henry A. Moe, Secretary General of the Guggenheim Foundation, to Bloomington. In September he began wondering about the Ford Foundation taking over and by February 1952 was actively exploring this with Ford.[7]

Then, on 22 December, Corner received the draft statisticians' report.* Kinsey was fairly appalled by it, particularly its obsession with random probability sampling, and he began to draft his reply and counter-criticisms at once.[8]

It must have been a considerable relief to escape from all this into the civilised and stimulating world of Wescott and Wheeler.

3

Kinsey spent the 9th or 10th to the 18th of November in New York, staying at the Statler Hotel. Glenway had worked himself into a perfect fever of plans before the visit: strings of possible meals, dates, tickets, Isherwood, Trilling (!), Inge, e.e. cummings . . . And, in fact, Kinsey saw a good deal of him and Monroe – dinner with them on the 11th, then lunch alone with Glenway, as his journal records, dinner the same day with Glenway and his 'young man' (Mike Mikshe). Two days later Glenway took him to the première of the Stravinsky/Balanchine ballet *Apollo.*[9]

Kinsey seems to have got out of Trilling, but he met Isherwood and

---

* The point of these drafts is that they were sent to all interested parties, including the Rockefeller Foundation. This meant that though the report was not *published* till 1954, its *effect* was felt long before, increased by repetition and the fact it was modified *en retard.*

Auden, both in town for rehearsals of Van Druten's play *I Am a Camera* (from the 'Sally Bowles' sections of Isherwood's *Goodbye to Berlin*). The two had some experience of sex research, having visited Hirschfeld's Institute in Berlin in 1929 (where they noticed a prominent photograph of Wilde), but the meetings now don't seem to have been much of a success. 'No one is more notably opposed to the research than Auden,' recorded Glenway, and Isherwood was heard to remark at a party in his gentle, feline, ambiguous way, 'Glenway and Dr Kinsey, those two saints of sex . . .'[10]

Glenway's journals were now beginning to resound with his growing passion for the wonderfully passionate Mikshe – 'certainly a splendid enough creature . . . powerful in the flesh . . .'

The journals also, incidentally, start to show clear signs of Kinsey's influence. Autumn 1951: 'An intelligent reasonable and self-respecting man can indeed learn *not* to be ashamed of masturbating, yes indeed, I have learned; in fact at this age I am inclined to feel that I ought to masturbate more than I do.'[11] (That 'yes indeed' is typical of the un-diary-like style of Glenway's diaries.)

But the real focus at this point is on Monroe Wheeler. Kinsey had been trying for months to get him to Bloomington. Glenway's visit, he'd written earlier, 'was most profitable and a great delight to us . . . When can you come?' The date was finally fixed now and by 7 December, Kinsey was looking forward to it 'with considerable anticipation'. Monroe arrived in Bloomington on 26 December and stayed four days.[12]

Monroe Wheeler did not keep diaries, or at least publish them, and this urbane man was a much more discreet character than Glenway, to the extent that the Kinsey Institute did not feel they had to remove his letters from file.*

---

* Which is more than can be said of Mike Mikshe's letters, all of which have been pulled (twenty-three over four years, as can be counted from Kinsey's replies, which remain). Why? Kinsey did not have a sexual relationship with Mikshe – at least there is no evidence he did. Perhaps because in a 1953 letter Kinsey refers to letters, presumably erotic, which Mikshe was to send him. Or else his letters may have been too open about the filming. Mikshe and his boyfriend Dick (once again Glenway was getting into a three-way situation) came to Bloomington 17–19 December, a little before Monroe. It may have been now that Kinsey filmed him, as Glenway describes, 'drawing pornography in the air with a flashlight' – an interesting technique pioneered by Gjon Mili and copied from him by Picasso. (Kinsey to Mikshe, end of October [?] 1953; 8 January 1952; Wescott, interview with Rosco, 1976.)

None the less, it is these that indicate this visit was significant. Before the visit, the letters are typed, start 'Dear Alfred' and end 'Yours Monroe'. The letter after it is handwritten and starts 'Dear Friend', and quotes Marianne Moore: 'And these are the words in her same poem that describes *you* – "Whose spirits and whose bodies all too literally are our shield".' The emphasis is Monroe's; he signs off 'devotedly yours'.[13]

If not now, then very soon, the affair between them became, as Glenway always preferred, a three-part one.[14]

4

I never fed a group of men that I would have so much liked to poison.
Clara Kinsey in interview with James Jones, December 1971

Kinsey saw Glenway, Mike Mikshe and Monroe several times again on his visit to New York at the end of January 1952. But the first two months of the year were taken up by the statisticians' draft report. Kinsey had said they couldn't publish until they had discussed it with him – and doubted they'd do that.

William Cochran replied to Corner – the secretary's typo revealing the effect Kinsey was having on them all – on the contrary, they would be delighted to attend 'a no-holes-barred' meeting.[15]

It took place at Bloomington on 23 and 24 February. Six people came from outside: the three authors Cochran, Mosteller and Tukey; Allen, Corner and Moore from the NRC. Kinsey, as always, had prepared meticulously, working together with Corner: a detailed four-page critique of the draft report, a carefully reasoned (and convincing) argument against random probability sampling in his sphere, and he had also rewritten the draft digest. As far as he was concerned, he was fighting for his project's financial life.

Everyone still alive who was there remembers it vividly. 'Kinsey,' said Gebhard, 'was under one hell of a lot of stress, and it showed.' In fact, everyone was tense. And it shows, too, in the photographs Dellenback took while it was in progress (see no. 21). To do this – a bizarre touch – Dellenback, not a small man, clambered along the tops of the filing cabinets. He remembers the antagonism in the air.

Kinsey was violently defensive, which with Kinsey means aggressive. At one point, when he left the room, Cochran said to Gebhard it would be much easier if he'd just relax and admit *some* defects. In fact, it seemed to resolve itself into a battle between Kinsey and Tukey. Mosteller and Cochran were quite sympathetic. But Tukey was one of those totally cerebral, totally unrealistic academics. He had maddeningly pontifical mannerisms. 'He put his fingers together like a bishop,' said Gebhard. At one point he remembers Tukey saying he'd happily sacrifice all 17,500 histories for just 400 from a random sample. Gebhard thought Kinsey would explode. Corner, who agreed Tukey was 'reckless in his criticism', had to engineer the compromises.[16]

When the statisticians left, Kinsey confessed to Wells, as he seldom did to anyone, that his work was 'sometimes nerve-wracking'. That night, instead of working late, he went to Cocteau's *Orphée*.[17]

Mac said Kinsey felt the meeting hadn't gone well. Yet, on the whole the committee accepted most of his alterations to their draft. Their later suggestions that he try a small pilot study on probability sampling was effectively what he'd suggested (his draft said 'a very small pilot study'). And the NRC, in this sort of context Kinsey's men, were quite satisfied. Even before the meeting Karl Lashley had told Corner, 'In any less emotionally charged field, Kinsey's study would be accepted as meeting good scientific standards.'[18]

But in the end, Kinsey's instincts about it were probably right. It is significant, at any rate, that immediately afterwards on 28 February we find Corner writing to the Ford Foundation more or less asking them to take over the funding.[19]

5

Kinsey plunged immediately back into what had really dominated his time during and since 1950 – the writing of his *Female* volume. He made very few concessions to the statisticians. What concessions did he make to his public?

Few. Essentially, he was doing for women what he had done for men, and quite often from their point of view – we saw for instance their failure to orgasm now placed on the incompetent penis. But naturally enough many of the same aspects of Kinsey appear. The female human animal is often set in context with other female animals. Kinsey worries how uncommon masturbation is here. He can only find it in 'the female rat, chinchilla, rabbit, porcupine, squirrel, ferret, horse, cow, elephant, dog, baboon, monkey and chimpanzee'. Not that uncommon, one feels. The fact that he was comparing American Womanhood to the female horse, elephant, cow, baboon, etc., doesn't seem to have struck him – or bothered him if it did.[20]

His sexual tolerance and encouragement are just as evident and in the same ways. All frequencies and incidences are, of course, always given, but in the text, which is what people read and where commentators dug, he again prefers to quote the highest rates – the 'individuals who were having coitus in their marriages on an average of four times a day, every day of the week';[21] or with masturbation he gives two lines to low frequencies and nine lines to 14 orgasms a week, 30 orgasms a week and 'females who had regularly masturbated to the point of orgasm 10, 20 or even 100 times an hour'.[22]

His heartfelt comments on the sexual boredom of a long monogamous marriage appear several times again, as do his frequent and irritable (and justifiable) swipes at religion.[23] He cannot resist a provocative stance. On adult-child sex, he found there was very little between adult females and children, but, to repeat Paul Robinson's phrase, he once again put in a good word for the male child molester. 76 per cent of females had no experience of what we'd now call 'abuse'; of the remainder, 80 per cent only had one experience, usually exhibitionism or fondling, only 3 per cent involved actual coitus. The most common ages were eleven and twelve – Lolita's age.* Kinsey's conclusion was that the hysteria surrounding these events usually did more harm than the events themselves, which sometimes gave pleasure.[24]

On rape he appears even more outrageous – comparing the situation to that pertaining among baboons – where the females eagerly seek out other males but if caught by the dominant male at once attack the new partner, as if to say 'I *did not* want it.' 'A high proportion of the human "rape" cases which we had the opportunity to examine,' wrote Kinsey, 'involve something of the same motifs.'[25]

These are fraught areas. It is, as earlier, an interesting indication of changing *mores* that neither of these viewpoints were even commented on in 1953. However obvious, I should perhaps stress again that Kinsey was implacably opposed to any sort of violence, coercion or pressure of

---

* Nabokov's novel, in which the heroine Lolita did the seducing, was written the same year as the *Female* volume was published, but was not itself published in the Olympia Press edition till 1955, and not published in New York until 1958.

any sort in sexual matters.[26] None the less, here as elsewhere, his sympathy for those in prison made him gullible. Violent rapists invariably allege their victims 'wanted it' and it is invariably a lie. At the same time, one has to recognise complex interactions of pain and pleasure in sexual desire – in both sexes. In Kinsey's day, when women were still often not supposed to want sex outside marriage, there were conventions of saying 'no' while meaning 'yes', leading to misunderstandings in what we now call 'date rape'. When women can say yes, then no can mean *no*. (And yes, *yes*. In Britain only 1.7 per cent of female adolescents gave 'coercion' as the reason for their first coitus.[27])

Child-adult sex is also complicated. Perhaps violence is more common today (there are no figures in the recent surveys). There are problems of definition. Large age differences are clear (and more dangerous), but what if the abuser is thirteen and the victim ten? Or even, as Kinsey sometimes found, the other way round? It can be the culture – the age of consent in many countries (as in a few states in America fifty years ago and in Spain, for instance, today) is twelve. It is also complicated because it has become, among sections in America especially, a feminist issue – of dubious rationale. It is argued that little girls are allowed, indeed encouraged, to be sexually abused because it breaks them in for the later dominance, sexual and otherwise, of men. This, and gradations of it, have led to a climate very different from Kinsey's.[28]

Kinsey found that the majority of cases (52 per cent) were exhibitionism and (22 per cent) 'fondling', sometimes of genitalia. Since in Kinsey's view there was nothing *inherently* unpleasant about male genitals, and the only thing inherent in genitals being touched was pleasure, adverse reactions had to be learnt. It was these (inappropriate) learned reactions that caused distress. Similarly, he was irritated by the way the hysteria surrounding the tiny minority of violent cases (he found only one out of 4,441 females*), which he abhorred as much as anyone, spread out to that vast majority of cases where it was not just inappropriate but was what did the damage.[29] There is a considerable body of fairly recent research to suggest he may be right.[30]

Kinsey told the statisticians he had already accepted a hundred suggestions for improving the *Female* volume. As regards statistics, it is difficult to see he accepted anything; none the less, though it was a less passionate and less idiosyncratic book than the *Male*, in some ways it was

* One would like to see this astonishing figure re-checked.

a better one. Kinsey was sure of this: '... it is going to be magnificent,' he told Glenn Ramsey in April.[31]

It was more scholarly. Where the *Male* had almost no footnotes, for instance, in the *Female* they are on almost every page; supporting him in depth, often giving the entire history of the topic under discussion, attacking his critics (and sometimes accommodating them). It is easier to read, since there are many fewer tables and graphs and they don't interfere with the narrative. As to style, the continual references to myth and history, to law and literature and anthropology give it a feeling of richness. Though dense, as with the *Male*, the book is so thorough, explores so much and explains so carefully, the feeling is almost leisurely. Kinsey's prose, because careful, requires time; it is not long-winded but it is certainly full-winded.

And as he unreels over five pages the occupations of the women who have helped him you suddenly see a panorama of American society in the 1930s and 1940s – its variety, its perspectives, its oddity, the way it had, this supposedly male world, already been invaded by women: 'art critic, berry picker, burlesque performer, bus girl, cigarette girl, dice girl, dramatic critic, Girl Scout executive [Mac?], glass blower, inventor, judge, male impersonator, mannequin maker, odd jobs, poet, puppeteer, riveter, taxi dancer, truck driver, U.N. delegate, welder...'[32] (A taxi dancer was a woman in a public dance hall whom you paid to dance with. When Paul Gebhard was young in 1935 it cost ten cents a dance.[33]) Women invading the male world as riveters etc., because of the war, as they had in England (e.g. the famous cover of *Picture Post* in 1943 of a woman riveter); and, the war over, now being cynically dispatched back to stove and sink.

In response to critics (and to what he found) Kinsey tacitly diminished the importance of the orgasm by widening his enquiry into social and psychological areas, but it remained the chief unit of measurement.[34] Similarly, he restated what he saw as the causes of homosexuality, which were (1) the ability of the human mammal to respond to any sufficient stimulus, (2) the importance of the first experience, modified or increased by conditioning.[35*36]

---

* This begged many questions even then. There is no doubt that Kinsey's figures, since they showed that homosexual experience was just too numerous to condemn, played a large part in the slow move to tolerance won by homosexuals. But in order to wage the battle, homosexuals had to unite, and by uniting and in order to, they found an identity. This had in fact to a considerable extent already happened. People don't feel themselves to be a collection of acts, as Kinsey

In slight deference to much critical irritation at dogmatic and unsupported generalisations, he remained just as dogmatic but said they were *supported* but not possible to tabulate.[37]

Finally, he sprinkled his book, as he did his talk, with odd or surprising items he had turned up on his way. That breasts, for instance, were as sensitive in men as women and that, though rare in both, both could orgasm by breast stimulation. Or that, analysing 1,378 toilet wall inscriptions, though far fewer women indulge in graffiti, there were still almost as many (3.52 per toilet) as with men (4.05 per toilet), and that if you remove those from men that are clearly (to me, though not Kinsey) homosexually inspired, the messages are nearly identical from both sexes: 17 per cent heterosexual female, 21 per cent male; coital contacts – 7 per cent female, 8 per cent male; and there were actually *more* depictions of male genitalia by females (5 per cent) than vice versa (3 per cent), though this could be because male genitalia are easier to get a grip on, as it were, pictorially.[38]

---

argued. They construct entities for themselves and one component is their same- or opposite-sex experiences. They actually live and feel the social types, as Gagnon has ably put it, that Kinsey 'fought so hard to dissolve'. That the conception 'a homosexual' is relatively new (the word wasn't coined till 1868) makes no difference; as new dimensions, new possibilities of feeling and being are conceived, so people take them up. This will be compounded by recent (and controversial) discoveries of a genetic component – at least for men – in the complex interactions between biology and environment which influence sexual orientation. This was always possible – Havelock Ellis observed how homosexuality ran in families. It is gradually being narrowed down, but no one knows how it works or the proportion of influence to be assigned to it – anything from 5 per cent to 20 per cent has been suggested. I suspect it will increase, if for no other reason than this is still a fashionable biological bandwagon. A recent Swedish study has shown that 62 per cent of intelligence is genetic, leaving only 38 per cent for Kinsey's conditioning in an equally complex area. Gays often fight the genetic component because they fear there might be attempts to force them out of existence. I think this is unlikely. The gene may well be linked to other faculties and qualities. And a number of women (and men) want gay children. Nor are human beings so easily controlled or predictable. Downs Syndrome has for some time been genetically pinpointed and is detectable in the womb, but the number of Downs Syndrome children is rising, in Britain at least. If any society did take such a mad decision it would be the loser. There are more gay people than you would expect from random mutation so one has to conclude that if homosexuality has a genetic base this has survived because it is favourable. It is not difficult to think in what ways. (The various authorities supplying a discussion of this fascinating subject, which cannot be done properly in a footnote, are so numerous I would refer the reader to reference note 36 for this chapter.)

Yet, as he wrote day after day and night after night, there is always the feeling from his letters that he longs to get out and away again – after histories, lecturing, lobbying – and sometimes he does.

6

At the end of March Kinsey took Mac out West when he gave the four Jacob Gimbel lectures at the University of California at Berkeley and Stanford University. One gets a sense, from the endless correspondence setting this up, of the *excitement* a Kinsey lecture now generated – several hundreds were turned away. (Significantly, for the first time in many years he accepted the $1,000 fee, either evidence of his anxiety about further funding or to please the Rockefeller Foundation, since he gave it to them.)

He gave other lectures, saw endless people (including, briefly, Lewis Terman), he and Mac had supper with Karl Bowman to discuss sex law reforms, and were back in Bloomington by 14 April, in time to greet a training group from the Menninger Foundation.[39]

But there were beginning to be ominous signs. Albert Deutsch said he'd never seen Kinsey look so tired as in California – the schedule was 'murder . . . too much, too much'. One notices how rambling his year's reports to the NRC and IU are. He was up, Frank Beach said, at six each morning. And that April, crossing the campus late at night – 'dark, and here and there couples were piling up statistics for Prok on park benches' – Eggert Meyer, a Chicago high school biology teacher and a friend, found Kinsey's light still burning at 11 p.m. It was often still burning at 2 a.m. Where once he'd sought interviewers over forty, now it was too gruelling unless they were under thirty (Kinsey was about to be fifty-eight).[40]

He managed to get four days in New York on 10 May, when he saw Monroe for a two-hour lunch in a private room at the Museum of Modern Art. Later, in Chicago on 24 May, he managed something even rarer – a joke. He was staying with Eggert Meyer and was late. 'We have to address the Chicago Patrol Officers tonight. You know where this address is – 69th and Normal? "Say," said Kinsey, "say, this is a good one – 69th and Normal!" '[41]

His relentless schedule was compounded by multiple editing, and multiple rewriting, and then re-editing and rewriting again, and all in the blazing, stifling Indiana summer.

7

The editing: at first, Kinsey gave relevant staff copies of a chapter.* They would read it, then all gather to criticise it. 'It takes a brave man,' said Dorothy Collins, 'to have his precious English criticised by eight people.' But it was impatience not cowardice that made Kinsey change this system. Gebhard had to gather the criticisms and they went over them together. 'If Kinsey didn't agree he'd say "Pass on".'[42]

Kinsey was *determined* to make the *Female* volume as near as possible perfect. He engaged the best consultants he could get (paid by Saunders). In June 1952, he arranged to employ Emily Mudd, in July, Karl Lashley and in September, Robert Laidlaw. Laidlaw was becoming, Emily Mudd was already, very prominent in marriage counselling. This lean, highly intelligent woman also had the advantage of being one of the few people not overawed by Kinsey.

As for Lashley, there is something oddly naive about Kinsey's 'He is rated as having one of the highest IQs in the United States', writing to Saunders about him.[43] But everyone spoke glowingly about this brilliant ex-member of the psychology department at Minnesota, who since 1942 had been director of Yerkes' primate laboratory in Florida. He was a good-looking, cultured man who spoke several languages and played in a string quartet. He smoked Egyptian cigarettes and Vincent Nowlis remembered how he once blew a tuba at a tank of alligators and one of them tried to mate with him.[44]

Glenway Wescott told his biographer he visited Bloomington this summer, but there appears to be no record of it. July and August were packed with editing – Dr Earle Marsh for two weeks in July, Helen Dietz from Saunders in August – and with conferences, lectures and writing. And at the end of August, for the first time in years, Mac had a holiday.

She joined Joan and Bob Reid, who'd just finished his internship. For two weeks the three went touring across the West. Mac was blissful. Bob

---

* This did not include Pomeroy, with whom this sort of work was not a strong point. He therefore again spent a lot of the year working on his PhD. But earlier he had helped Dorothy Collins check all the figures. 'He was strange,' she said. 'He'd work intensely for twenty minutes – then have to shoot off. But it was very boring – boring, boring, boring.' Pomeroy, a brilliant interviewer, impatient, volatile, used to say of himself, 'Well, I may not get it done right but I get it done fast.' (Collins and Gebhard, in interviews with the author.)

Reid remembered 'her go – rushing naked into a glacier runoff'. When they got back, Joan said, Kinsey thanked them for taking her. 'He felt guilty he'd cheated her out of so many expeditions like that, which they'd once done together and which she loved.'[45]

Glenway may not have come out to Bloomington but Kinsey did write in July and rather tentatively asked him if he'd check his prose. Glenway turned the suggestion down, partly because he was writing his tenth new novel (never finished, like the other nine), but really because he didn't think Kinsey's prose needed checking.[46]

If he didn't come to Bloomington, Glenway sent a great many letters there, as the huge gaps in his file testify. But it is worth looking briefly at some of those that survive.

8

He copied a number into his journals. Some of these are 'science': for example, 'Michael [Mikshe] and I especially regret your not knowing Ronald, because he also clenches his fists and strikes his partner during his orgasm . . . A very strong orgasm, with marvels of the muscles, though not as wild as Chuckles', none of those leaps like a black bass on the hook.'[47] He also wrote about the complexities of his sex/love life and the blissful agonies of romantic love, though he knew Kinsey didn't altogether approve of the last.[48]

In fact romantic love struck at Kinsey on a number of levels, some profound. One of the aims, or at least tools, of science is to simplify: the gall wasp is reduced to twenty single elements whose measurement defines them; muscle responses are analysed by severing a frog's leg and wiring it to electrodes. Sex was far more complex, and Kinsey felt he could only study it by stripping away all but its physiological functions, first removing moral judgements, second, even harder, emotions and feelings. For both he was ideally equipped psychologically and for both he was savagely criticised. Even the psychoanalyst Kubie said of the *Male* volume, 'On every page I can find the word penis; nowhere the word love.' (In fact, though Kinsey only uses the words 'to make love' once [see page 244] the word 'love' appears 109 times.)

Then Kinsey knew only too well, from his histories and his correspondence, as he told Tripp, the terrible damage romantic love could cause in carefully built lives; house, secure children, contented wives or happy husbands – all in an instant destroyed. Indeed, Tripp remembers two exclamations from Kinsey, at about this time, on this very subject. One was jubilant – it *was* possible to have a purely sexual affair without the encumbrance of romance (a beneficent aspect he drew attention to in his *Male* volume). The second was an irritable outburst about the reverse – the trouble love could cause. Tripp didn't know (or wouldn't say) what had led to those exclamations.[49] Perhaps the first was a comment on Kinsey's affair with Wescott and Wheeler. The second could have been Kinsey remembering the havoc Paul Gebhard's affair with Alice Martin nearly caused.

The major sphere, wrote Octavio Paz, is sexuality, and the force behind it is reproduction. But within this, or from this, come eroticism, which engages the imagination and has little or no overt connection with reproduction; and second, romantic love, which singles out one person – 'I chose you.' So love and eroticism form 'a double flame fed by the original fire: sexuality'.[50]

Romantic love is, therefore, a branch of sexuality – but a curious one, since it acts to curtail sex (one of the reasons the Romans objected to it). Sex now requires legitimising by love, and is restricted by it to one person. Perhaps one could argue that it is, at root, the Trojan horse that carried the medieval Church's disapproval of sex into the modern age. No wonder it irritated Kinsey. He disliked the French language, said Clarence Tripp, for this very reason. It had no word for sexual intercourse. '*Faire l'amour*' or '*faire la cour à*' were precisely what he did *not* mean.*

He would have been pleased to learn from the recent British survey that romantic love is rapidly declining here as a motive (or excuse) in both sexes for having first coitus. 51.6 per cent of older women gave it as the reason, while only 37.5 per cent of those younger (16–24) did; older men – 22.4 per cent; younger men – 16.7 per cent.[51]

---

* There are two additional French words Kinsey does not seem to have been familiar with: *baiser* (to kiss) has a slang usage – our 'to fuck'. There is also *rapports sexuels. Rapports* is 'relations', so 'sexual relations'. Kinsey would no doubt have thought that they too really skirt the situation. One sees his point but it is not a valid one. The root meaning of 'intercourse' is 'communication with' or 'commerce with', so sexual intercourse gains its force from the way we use it, not from its real meaning, just as *rapports sexuels* does. What Kinsey wanted, no doubt, was some literal portmanteau word like 'Penis-moving-in-vagina', which may exist in some African tribe or South Sea island, but nowhere else, if there, as far as I know.

Kinsey had strong feelings about romantic love and argued about it with Wescott, though he did once grudgingly agree that if you had discipline and luck perhaps it *could* lead to maximum sexual pleasure – but only if.[52] But their differences in no way disturbed the relationship. Indeed, it is noticeable that even at the height of his work Kinsey wrote to Glenway regularly once a month or so and the letters were, for Kinsey, long.

And as autumn arrived to slightly soothe the savage heat of Bloomington, so the work steadily increased in intensity.

9

By September Kinsey was working seven days a week; the twin lifelines which, though diminishing, had together kept him going for so long – music and the garden – now temporarily severed.[53]

Karl Lashley stayed for two weeks editing this month. Dr Harold F. Dorn and Jerome Cornfield, both recognised and distinguished statisticians, also stayed two weeks (among other things cutting out 150 pages of printed tables). Being edited is not a passive process, as anyone who has undergone it knows, and very tiring. Those visits, Kinsey wrote, 'completely exhausted us physically and mentally'.[54]

And as the *Female* volume came nearer, so the first rumblings of publicity, which had begun distantly in 1950, now like approaching gunfire began to shake the ground in Bloomington. Reporters rang in the middle of the night. Harriet Pilpel, the slim, dark and attractive young attorney in Morris Ernst's firm now handling Kinsey's affairs, put a stop to Dr Pinsey, a character – essentially a slavering sex maniac – in a strip put out by [Andy] Capp Enterprises.*

In October, Helen Dietz came for three weeks' editing. She just coincided with Auden who arrived to read his poetry at IU on 28 October. Kinsey had already written to ask him to drinks, but Auden had drinks scheduled by the English Department.[55] They met, however, and Kinsey showed him round the Institute. Whether this changed his views or not is not known.

---

* Mrs Pilpel used her looks to advantage. There was, she said, one judge before whom she could always win her cases, especially if she wore a particular red dress. (Paul Gebhard.)

Timing the writing of the *Female* volume is complicated; partly because Paul Gebhard wrote some of it – many of the notes, all the anthropology and Chapter 17 for instance. But mainly because Kinsey's pattern of writing, editing, rewriting, re-editing, were all mixed up at the same time. No one seems to know precisely when it was finished, but it was probably November/December this year. And it was these final chapters, especially Chapters 14 and 15 – 'Anatomy and Physiology of Sexual Response and Orgasm' – that he regarded as the most important and the best in the whole book, as he told several people, including, for instance, Vincent Nowlis.[56]

10

> . . . *a description of the respective positions of the partners, the postures*
> *assumed, gestures, places touched, caresses, the precise moment of pleasure*
> . . . *an entire painstaking review of the sexual act in its very unfolding.*
> Michel Foucault, *The History of Sexuality*, Vol. I, 'An Introduction'

Foucault's description of the confession manuals in the Middle Ages is in fact an equally accurate one of Kinsey's Chapters 14 and 15. These chapters still make extraordinary reading, and we see from time to time scenes from his biography and also at last the fruits of those long sessions in the attic, the hours motionless on the edge of Wescott's orgies.

Some we have covered. The power of the clitoris, the insensitivity of the inner vagina, the potential rapidity of the female to orgasm . . . but now he emphasises the perineal nervous system, between anus and genitals, sensitive to touch; the anus itself, its surfaces rich in nerve endings, in some of both sexes an area of erotic arousal. And sometimes, too, of pain 'which may intensify the sexual responses of some persons . . . As a matter of fact, contractions of the anal sphincter appear to produce contractions of muscles in various remote parts of the body, including areas as far away as the throat and the nose'. The nose flares, the subject inhales deeply.[57] Even music can arouse, 'e.g. march and waltz time . . . variations in volume' and there follows a whole musical list[58] (was he thinking of the professor at his musicales who had to strap down his penis?).[59]

Steadily, from arousal, he moves towards orgasm. In the female, the amount of mucus from the Bartholin glands – 'a clear, quite liquid, and somewhat slippery secretion' – evidence of arousal, its lack evidence of non-arousal, varies sharply in quantity. It is most considerable just before and after menstruation, the time of maximum responsiveness.[60] While with men, practically all the secretions (3cc) come at the last moments, from the prostate and Cowper glands at the base of the penis. The popular idea of grossly swollen testicles desperate to discharge is 'quite unfounded'. The sperm contribution is infinitesimal.[61]

As orgasm approaches – loss of sensory perception; one feels that for Kinsey it expressed the all-embracing and uncontrollable nature of sex, contemptuously tossing aside all Judeo-Christian restraints. He records loss of feeling, hearing, sight – finally sometimes complete if momentary unconsciousness.[62] Blood flow is less from wounds (hence the violence possible in sado-masochism). Stutterers stop stuttering, spastics move freely – 'they may be surprisingly capable in coitus'. People can have terrifying strength, not acquired but released as inhibitions vanish. Men can suddenly double in half so that self-fellatio becomes possible. All this shows how the whole central nervous system is brought into play.[63]

The expression, as orgasm now irresistibly approaches, becomes nearer to agony than pleasure. Unresponsive wives who try to smile and look pleased are in error. 'On the contrary, an individual who is really responding is as incapable of looking happy as the individual who is being tortured.'[64] 'The eyes of sexually aroused persons acquire a distinctive glare, particularly at the moment of orgasm.'[65]

And thus it arrives – for some relatively quietly, but 'In some individuals the whole body may be thrown, or tossed, or rolled over a distance of several feet or yards. On occasion the sexual partner may be crushed, pounded, violently punched or kicked during the uncontrolled responses of an intensely reactive individual.'[66]

It is, really, the climax also of both his books, in a way of his life, and the prose takes on an epic quality: 'Sometimes the recession from the high peak of orgasm is accomplished in a single great sweep. Sometimes there are momentary pauses ... some brief resurgence ... Sexual orgasm constitutes one of the most amazing aspects of human behavior.'[67]

And *post coitum omnium triste est*? Kinsey will have none of it. 'There is neither regret nor conflict nor any tinge of sadness ... on the contrary, a quiescence, a calm, a peace, a satisfaction with the world ...'*[68]

---

* Kinsey says the Latin tag is a corruption of Galen (c. 130–200 AD): '*Triste est omne animal post coitum, praeter mulierem gallumque*' (every animal is sad after coitus, except the human female and the rooster). (*Female*, p. 638 fn.)

They are unusual passages – and there are many more of them – to read in a scientific treatise. Not that they are unscientific; unique at the time, practically all the painstaking science has been confirmed since Kinsey, most notably, of course, by William Masters and Virginia Johnson. But there is not only science here. Wescott described it as 'an extraordinary piece of writing and in a spiritual way a kind of pornography'.[69]

I'm not sure that is correct either, though quite a number of Kinsey's correspondents found it erotic.[70] And perhaps, if we do now re-interpret Paul Robinson's idea, that is how to look at it, behind what it obviously is, scrupulous pioneering sex research, behind the science, the measurements, even the polemic, we can discern the form – or the feeling – of something else: a massive, two-volume, Boccaccio-style work of erotic literature. It can be seen as episodic, almost picaresque: first a series of male heroes are taken on a long odyssey of sexual adventures – masturbating, petting, dreaming, fornicating, coupling – coupling with children, with women, with men, with animals of every size and description; followed by a troop of bacchantes, heroines replicating and joining in the adventures of their partners and counterparts – with the sudden appearance of creatures of extraordinary voracity – until the climax, to which all these adventures ultimately tend and finally reach, the orgasm itself, is described in graphic detail (graphic literally, with graphs and drawings). And the work ends on the long, almost too long, dying fall of the chapters on psychologic factors, neural mechanisms and hormonal factors. Few people read them, it seems, exhausted by what they had been through and satiated by it.

11

Kinsey was certainly exhausted, and wrote and told Saunders at the end of November that he was on short-time to try and rest. But he was also increasingly excited by his book. '[We] are more and more convinced,' he said in the same letter, 'that this is an infinitely better book than the male volume.'[71]

Kinsey's short-time was everyone else's full-time. At the beginning of December he was in New York and then Boston for a series of lectures (one of the New York lectures, at Columbia University, had taken one and three-quarter years to set up). He managed to see Mike Mikshe and he also had dinner with Monroe. Kinsey had become interested in a German photographer, Baron Von Glodon, and they had been corresponding about him. (Von Glodon took thousands of erotic homosexual photographs between 1870 and 1928 – mostly in Taormina, Sicily.)[72]

Thus Kinsey refreshed himself. His letters to Wescott and Monroe are always longer and livelier than business letters, as are the letters about his collections. Robert E. Skutch, a Baltimore art dealer, had just sent him Adhemar's *Portraits Français* in a 1950 Paris edition by Fernand Hazan. Note plate 23, says Skutch, Flaubert commented on it. Kinsey does – it is a scene of homosexual lovemaking between two women – and then comments himself:

> Even the simple contact shown between two females in the painting suggests that the male who was the artist was aroused at the notion of anybody making such a contact with a female. You may be interested to know that heterosexual artists less often paint scenes of heterosexual contact, because that would require a painting of a male in which they are not interested.[73]

But he was very tired. Paul Gebhard said that it was from now on that his health began to deteriorate in earnest, and did so steadily until the end.[74] One of the most upsetting side effects from this for Kinsey was that he increasingly suffered from erectile impotence, something which appears to have started earlier.[75] One has the feeling now of an exhausted racehorse being mercilessly flogged towards the winning post, and as he moves into 1953, the winning post – or at least a winning post – was at last in sight.

12

The president of the printing firm chosen by Saunders for the *Female* volume, E. W. Palmer, had been the officer commanding all Army printing, much of it top secret, in World War II. Clearly in his element again, and much enjoying it, full military measures were now adopted: the presses were fenced off, every sheet accounted for and then locked up with the others until they were actually bound. Bound sheets were then themselves locked up. Transport of proofs or bound copies was in unmarked vehicles.[76]

At Bloomington, too, all proofs and manuscript were kept locked up. Waste-paper baskets were searched before being emptied, or their contents simply burnt. When a janitor left a door in the Institute unlocked by mistake, Kinsey rang Wells and had him transferred 'as of that day'.[77]

Into this charged atmosphere flowed a constant stream of editors. The statisticians Dorn and Cornfield again for the first half of January, Earle Marsh at the end of it. Then Emily Mudd and Laidlaw in February, Helen Dietz and little Dr Shadle in March (Kinsey too busy even to see him); Karl Lashley and Frank Beach also this month. Even when his editors had left, Kinsey sent chapters winging after them as they came off the presses.[78]

Whereas with the *Male* volume, he'd taken little or no notice of suggestions, now he did – sometimes. He let Emily Mudd, for example, tone him down. At 'the females [sic] *failure* to be aroused' she said, 'Isn't failure an emotionally charged word? Could this be said more objectively by 'the female's lack of arousal through any sort of ...' This holds for other places in the book where 'failure' is used in this way. Kinsey took out a few failures. But she also often tried to make him less dogmatic, advice he ignored. As he did when, equally often, she asked if he needed to use 'human animal' so often. 'Could you use human or human being? Although technically you are of course correct, many negative emotional responses will be stirred up I think unnecessarily.'[79] Kinsey did not take out a single animal, and a lot of negative emotional responses were stirred up.

But, once again, he was certain this enormous labour was improving the book. 'It will be a very great book,' he told Saunders in February. And to George Corner, about to go to Oxford for six months, 'It will be a much better book than the first one.' The letter to Corner was in reply to one telling him that the Ford Foundation would not be taking over his funding. His increasing anxiety over money is reflected in the tax returns for this year, where money spent on the collection is slashed from $25,000 to $6,000.[80]

Kinsey was now working ninety hours or more a week and this additional financial worry, as well as all his usual work, were imposing enormous strains on him. On 25 April he collapsed and had to go into hospital for two-and-a-half days. But he forced himself up and on the evening of the 28th delivered his 'Sexual Problems in Youth' talk to a conference of social workers.

He was still very tired, and money was still weighing on him, in May.

'It has become apparent,' he told Saunders, 'that neither I nor the rest of the staff can continue to work at the rate we have for the several last years.' Can Saunders, recipient of 'the major profit from the [*Male*] book', think of some way to help him financially? There is a rather long pause, then Saunders pulls himself together and says he will increase the royalty to 15 per cent on the first 100,000, thereafter 18.5 per cent provided he has 'first refusal' on all books for ten years. Kinsey said no. If that was the condition, he wouldn't accept the increased 18.5 per cent royalty. There had been set in train one of those 'slow burns' which, in time, was to find him pursuing other publishers.[81]

Saunders had also suggested, rather tactlessly considering the hectic point they'd reached, that Kinsey take a two-week holiday. In fact, he was about to embark on the course to which Mac, later, attributed the major role in his collapsing health.

13

Kinsey's solution to the hyperbolic, inaccurate and slanted reporting endured with the *Male* volume was entirely in character – total control. It was essentially the same method evolved for the other book only more so.

In 'the late spring' he sent letters to all the journalists over the last six years who had asked for, or been promised, access to the new book.[82] Sixty replied and arrangements were made for them to come in groups of ten for four days each during May, June and July. As before, they had to sign a contract: no article over 5,000 words, all copy submitted for factual checking, no release till 20 August. The actual date of publication was kept secret.

It was the procedure with each group that proved so exhausting for Kinsey. Soon after they arrived, at 9 a.m., they gathered in Wylie Hall, had a lecture by Kinsey, then the tour, met the team, lunch, a further lecture from Kinsey, the contract, and were then given the galley proofs and had that evening and three days to take notes, plan their articles – and talk to Kinsey.

Kinsey realised it was *vital* they understood exactly what he was doing and flung himself into intense interaction with them, often till very late at night.

Meanwhile, early in June, Associated Press had given the 20 August release date and a brief account of activity at Bloomington. At once journalists (and their editors) who hadn't booked in became frenzied. Immediately after the AP release there was an avalanche of telephone calls – 100 new requests for access on the first morning alone. Three new operators were hurried on to the university switchboard. It was Eleanor Roehr who met the attacking hordes – 'No, we cannot accommodate more writers. It is physically impossible. Sorry, sorry.' Grace Naismith, who watched her and wrote it all up for *This Week Magazine*, described the press attack as overwhelming.[83] It didn't overwhelm Miss Roehr.

Some excluded papers became absolutely furious. One was the *New York Times*, despite the fact that the paper had been offered a chance to attend the briefings and had ignored it. It would take too long to describe the protracted battle between Kinsey and the editor-in-chief, the assistant editor, Harvey Breit, the review editor Francis Brown and finally the publisher Arthur Hays Sulzberger, but the root of the fracas was that no journalist, particularly perhaps no American journalist, likes being controlled and Kinsey was not going to relinquish either control or his form of it. The result was, when 20 August broke, the *New York Times*, almost alone of the nation's press, had no new news story, and had to run the AP news announcement. Their review (a favourable one) by Paul Gebhard's mentor Dr Clyde Kluckhohn was published later.

Kinsey was also overseeing lists of review copies, the advertising schedules and all promotional material. His I/we syntax more or less broke down. Protesting to Saunders that their use of 'Kinsey Report' in advertisements would mean he had written it and not his team, he wrote 'it will make it appear . . . that we have written the book instead of someone else'.[84]

In fact, just before he had written this at the end of June, it had suddenly become too much. He had only been out of hospital three weeks when three clumps of journalists arrived in May one after the other, followed by a fourth on 7 June. Then on 23 June (Kinsey's fifty-ninth birthday) Christine Jorgensen, a transsexual ex-GI who had had one of the earliest sex-change operations, came to see him. The press, desperate to release *anything*, besieged them both. Dr Cooper P. Speaks remembers the uproar of the Jorgensen visit. 'When she appeared at the local cinema there was nearly a riot.'[85]

Kinsey somehow dealt with all this and then took the whole of 24 June interviewing her and showing her round. Earle Marsh remembers the particular delicacy and charm with which he treated her. Kinsey got his son-in-law Bob Reid, Joan's husband, over to examine her.* But he was spent. The following day he collapsed and had to be taken into the Robert W. Long Memorial Hospital.[86]

Kinsey's extraordinary need to work, which had probably partly arisen to relieve, or use, or evade the tensions in him caused, as we have explored, by his upbringing and the homosexual elements in his character, had now continued for a great many years. It had become such an integral part of him that he was incapable of changing – and didn't want to. Kinsey was begged by those close to him – by Mac, by his team, by Earle Marsh, C. A. Tripp, Glenway, Monroe – to work less hard. He sometimes protested that he was doing so, or would. But both begging and protestation ring slightly hollow, since each side knew it was impossible. Indeed, to refuse probably satisfied that deep anti-authority streak in him; and even, more speculatively, that need for attention (love) detected by the graphologist Renna Nezos (see Appendix C). Certainly, Bob Reid remembered how from 1954 on Kinsey would encourage doctors to listen to his heart. He liked to see them blench. 'It sounded,' said Dr Reid, 'like a concrete mixer.'[87]

When Edgar Anderson went to see him in hospital on 29 June, he found his friend considerably 'slowed up' by tranquillisers, and over the next two years Kinsey began to rely increasingly on drugs – tranquillisers to relieve tension and then amphetamines to reverse their effect. He started using Coca-Cola as a stimulant in the afternoons, and at night he took Nembutal (long use induces depression). He now always carried digitalis. And he seems effectively to have ceased gardening.[88]

---

* It is an interesting case because one of the first. After military service, George Jorgensen worked as a laboratory assistant in New York. His desire to be a woman was so desperate that he shaved his pubic hair and gave himself oestrogen from the lab. Finally he went to Copenhagen and, in 1952, was castrated and had his penis removed. At first there was no attempt to construct a vagina or reshape his urethra (Bob Reid would have had little to see). Today extremely skilful surgery uses penile tissue to mould a sensitive and responsive vagina (and vaginal tissue to make a functioning and feeling penis in the opposite operation). Kinsey's friend Harry Benjamin specialised in transsexuals and he recognised extreme cases such as Christine Jorgensen's, which he speculated were due to pre-natal brain changes, probably hormone induced. He may well have been right. Quite recently, autopsies have revealed brain differences between men who have had sex change operations and other men. (Vern L. Bullough, *Science in the Bedroom*, New York, 1994; *New Scientist*, 4 November 1995, p. 6.)

Kinsey emerged from hospital at the start of July into the stifling heat of an Indiana summer, just in time for the first batch of proofs pouring in to be checked. One marvels at his power of work, even though exhausted. He checked nearly all the copy himself. There were two more groups of journalists to engage with on 20 July and 27 July. There was a course for prosecuting attorneys to be addressed in Chicago on 9 August. And yet, on 14 August, he still found time to write a long letter in support of a pauper Negro on a 'sodomy' charge (mouth-genital with a black woman).[89]

Everything was now converging on 20 August. Movietone News asked if they could interview him. Kinsey refused. On 19 August, Saunders, caught up in the excitement, decided to bind 200,000 copies instead of 150,000. On the same day, Bloomington's *Herald Telephone* lead column said, 'If you hear a roar like thunder at 6.30 a.m. tomorrow, it will probably be the various magazines hitting the local news stands with their articles on the new Kinsey book.'[90]

20 August came, and whether or not there was thunder on the newsstands, there was certainly a frantic ringing of telephones as the reporters sought comments from Kinsey. The telephones rang unanswered. Kinsey's staff had all fled on holiday. The whole of Wylie Hall basement was empty.

Only Herman Wells was left to respond. This staunch, plump figure issued a dignified statement: 'Indiana University stands today, as it has for fifteen years, firmly in support of the scientific research project that has been undertaken and is being carried on by one of its eminent biological scientists, Dr Alfred C. Kinsey.'

And where then was the eminent biologist? Kinsey, once again on the point of collapse, had left four days before to rest in the one place he could be certain no reporters would think of looking – the San Quentin Prison in northern California.

There was a gap of three weeks between 20 August and planned publication on 14 September, but so many bookshops were selling copies by 9 September that publication was effectively advanced to this.

Kinsey, after his rest, and after a series of lectures in California and Washington, had returned to Bloomington briefly on 6 September, and then flown to his retreat in San Quentin for two days, to rest again and to ride out the second firestorm of publicity. But he was already becoming aware of the extraordinary nature of the conflagration his new book had set off.

20

The Paper Explosion

Murder is a crime. Describing murder is not. Sex is not a crime. Describing it is.

Gershon Legman
(Quoted in Richard Webster, *Why Freud Was Wrong,* 1995, p. 1)

1

We can deal as briefly with public and critical reactions to the *Female* report as we did with the *Male* – and for the same reasons.

None the less, they are important. People bought the book; few read it thoroughly. For some years Kinsey's reputation (even with scientists) rested on what had been written about him by reporters and journalists, many of whom had only themselves skimmed the book.

The press reaction came in two mighty waves – the first, and largest, after 20 August. The coverage was surpassed only by the death of a president in power or war; it was unprecedented for a book then and has never been repeated since. Every leading national magazine came out with long illustrated accounts. *Time* devoted the cover and six pages; *Life*, nine pages; *Newsweek, Collier's, McCall's, Redbook* . . . Something like 80 per cent of the entire country's newspapers carried it, most with banner headlines and lead stories, and the silence of fifteen or so large newspapers was as startling in this context as the banner headlines. And then, as now, news fed on itself – for many months, the papers and magazines reverberated with the reactions of readers, celebrities, and with their own re-reactions.

The second wave, smaller, came after 9–14 September publication, with reviews which themselves sparked off further reports. Kinsey and Saunders could not have hit on a more effective method of generating publicity had they tried – and there is no evidence that they did try. After the *Male*, why should they?

Kinsey evolved his two-tier method to ensure journalistic accuracy, and he was by and large successful. Paul Brinkman's painstaking study, which I again follow here, found that the press did a better job of explaining the *Female* report than the *Male* one. *Time*, though it gave a rather lugubrious picture of Kinsey himself, was actively complimented by him on its coverage.[1] Analysis of the leading magazines found all but one (*Cosmopolitan*) favourable, and of 124 leading newspapers 64 per cent favourable to 31 per cent not.[2] At first the public seemed to be following suit. Gallup found that people thought it was 'a good thing, rather than a bad thing, to have this information available' by a ratio of three to one (compared with five to one for the *Male* report). Even a majority of women approved 'of making available the information on female sex habits'.[3]

But all serious reporting and favourable public response were gradually overwhelmed by violent eruptions of public and then press disapproval and disgust. At one level, the reason for this is clear. Victor Cohen, who in 1953 worked on the *Washington Post*, had just before joining them covered a 'notorious guy in Chicago named William Herons who broke into women's apartments, strangled them, put on their underwear and masturbated and we – my editors agonised over that. How could one say masturbated? Finally we said: "He engaged himself in satisfaction." '[4]

The American public had just been able to take Kinsey's terrible language about the appalling activities of men; about American womanhood they could take neither the language nor the activities. American womanhood masturbating, having orgasms, *pre*-marital sex, *extra*-marital sex, sex with each other . . . This simply could not *be* American womanhood. Kinsey had clearly confined his enquiries to prostitutes.

All over the country the churches rose in fury. Catholics, Kinsey had expected; but now Protestants were equally furious. Billy Graham (without reading the book but responding to reports he'd read) wrote: 'It is impossible to estimate the damage this book will do to the already deteriorating morals of America.' Dr John W. Wimbish, of the Calvary Baptist Church in New York, reacting as negatively as Emily Mudd had predicted, compared Kinsey to a 'deranged Nebuchadnezzar' leading women 'out into the fields to mingle with the cattle and become one with the beasts of the jungle'.[5]

As these angry attacks increased and spread, papers which had been favourable could join in in their reporting of them. The *Washington Post* ran a headline: ' "New Kinsey Study Degrades Science," Archbishop Charges.' More ominously for Kinsey, the attack spread to Congress. Representative Heller, a New York Democrat, who said he hadn't read the book but had a full knowledge from reporters, promised to demand a Congressional investigation. And he, like a number of the accounts (e.g. *Harper's*), commented on the close association with the Rockefeller Foundation and Indiana University.

Indiana and Bloomington reacted like everywhere else. The Bloomington *Herald Telephone* told its readers to turn to the Bible. Like angry cartoon colonels, distinguished IU alumni gave press conferences. Judge John L. Niblock of the Indianapolis Superior Court declared: '[Kinsey is] guilty of wasting the funds of my dear old Alma Mater. What IU needs so badly are some stalwart halfbacks to furnish good, clean mayhem on fall Saturdays.'

IU was threatened directly when the Indiana Provincial Council of Catholic Women – representing 150,000 Catholic women, mostly mothers – wrote a horrified letter to Wells. Their point, gleaned from the press, was premarital sex – the *besmirching*. '. . . that the chance for happiness in marriage may be in direct proportion to the amount of sexual experience they have as teenagers . . . appalled . . . forbidden fruit . . . sordid pleasure . . .'

Wells replied, with considerable bravery considering his large Catholic enrolment, with his usual academic freedom/IU neither approving nor disapproving letter, but at the end, with wily Jesuitical skill, managed to yoke Kinsey to God: 'To deny this right and this objective [the search for knowledge] would seem to deny the belief in a divine order as it pertains to man and the universe.'

Four fat files bulge with such letters sent to Wells, all of which, except crackpots, he answered. You can read them in the IU archives. Mrs Carol Reavley: 'I demand that those women interviewed by Dr Kinsey be given a lie detector test.' The Knights of Columbus: 'Mr Kinsey's . . . peddling [of] lewd and obscene literature . . . smut . . . his dastardly deed.' And there, dated 24 August 1953, is the letter from the Council of Catholic Women – 'We have, of course, not read the latest book . . .'[6]

But what is significant about this sustained and often incoherent opposition is the degree to which it infected scientific and scholarly criticism as well.

2

Compared to the *Male* volume, the criticism of the scientific community was harsher for the *Female* report, but often harsher on the same outraged grounds as the popular press. There was also, probably for the same reason, much less coverage. There was confusion and, like the serious newspapers, some journals solved this by printing two reviews. The *Journal of the American Medical Association*, for instance, did this in its 19 March 1954 issue. One was against: the *Female* book was 'not scientific, psychologically inept' and like a layman 'who tries to give an authoritative voice to his prejudices'. The other was for: 'This report is a detailed, careful, scientific analysis of a fairly large sample of our feminine population . . . a study still in progress, which is being diligently pursued by a group of experts well qualified to carry out the project.'

Margaret Mead, author of a book famous for making adolescent and youthful sex healthily attractive, wanted Kinsey's book banned as corrupting: 'the sudden removal of a previously guaranteed reticence has left many young people singularly defenseless in just those areas where their desire to conform was protected by a lack of knowledge of the extent of nonconformity'. An extent, one might add, which reached deep into the private life of the distinguished anthropologist.[7]

But Karl Menninger's betrayal was the most wounding. Menninger, who had shown he knew how to jump on to a bandwagon, now showed he thought he could tell when to jump off. At a widely reported panel discussion on 6 May 1954 of the American Psychiatric Association, repeating an earlier attack, he said the book had nothing to do with American women. 'It should be labelled "What Five or Six Thousand Rather Attractive Ladies Told Me, In The United States of America, Under Certain Conditions".' Kinsey's brief reply was controlled and dignified, ending, 'It is a sorry day for psychiatry when it publicly disclaims any connection with science.'[8]

Earle Marsh remembers being present later 'when Kinsey said, "Let me ask you, Karl, have you ever read my book?" "No," said Karl. "I didn't need to. I read a great deal about it." He had the grace to blush.'[9]

One is often struck by Kinsey's restraint under these attacks and innuendoes, which continued till he died. On 2 September, just after the 20 August explosion, he addressed the Women's National Press Club in Washington, DC. Only one reporter, Ruth Montgomery of the *New York Daily News*, dared ask what all the papers were full of. 'Can your statistics be accurate when they are based on questions some women are not in the habit of answering for men? Particularly, nicer women, as compared with our sisters of the street.' Kinsey simply said, 'I'm sorry, but these are not terms a scientist uses.'

But Kinsey was, as with the *Male* book, bitterly and personally hurt by the ferocity of the attacks on him. He could not stop thinking about them and at night, answering them in his head, couldn't sleep. He became much sharper with Gebhard, Pomeroy and Martin.

It was not just anger and hurt feelings, it was also, said Bill Dellenback, who used to talk late at night with him in Wylie Hall, sometimes something close to despair. He could not understand how furiously he was opposed even by rational, non-religious people when all he was trying to do was get at the scientific truth.[10]

The Midwest is not exactly the world centre of introspection, none the less Kinsey must have realised that that wasn't *all* he was trying to do. Yet it might have helped him understand his opposition had he seen – which people so rarely can in the moment – how he and his work stood, to repeat a phrase used earlier, on a very peculiar cusp of time.

3

It is almost as easy for us, immersed in his life and work, as it was for Kinsey, to forget his context. The hydrogen bomb (to which the *Female* volume was predictably compared) went off on 1 November 1952 and once again not a page of Kinsey's voluminous correspondence fluttered.

After the Second World War, there was a strong feeling in America (especially among Republicans) of getting back to the *true* America. And peace was quite soon under the same general who had won it – in November 1952 Ike was elected President. For men like these, the same generation as Kinsey (Eisenhower was the last President born in the nineteenth century), America meant the America of their childhood.[11]

This conservative tide was enormously enhanced, of course, by the Cold War. The Berlin airlift to surmount the Soviet blockade began in the summer of 1948. This whole conflict was an extraordinary phenomenon – despite fierce and prolonged conflicts (Korea, Vietnam), these were localised. It was in effect another world war without global destruction. It brought many of the benefits of war, particularly in scientific and technological progress, but also the same feelings (sometimes paranoid) a war engenders – the country must unite, non-conformity is dangerous, fears of conspiracies and enemies within.

These feelings were exploited and fanned by Republicans for political reasons. By men like B. Carroll Reece, a Tennessee congressman and later chairman of the Republican National Committee, and Joseph McCarthy – who made his first significant speech on 9 February 1950.

At the same time, under this surface, ultimately more powerful forces were at work in quite different directions. Over a long perspective, America had undergone profound change between 1910 and 1950. At the start, it had been a patchwork of regions, natives and immigrants, with different customs and religions, and more rural than urban. By the end, partly as a national process, partly as a result of slowing immigration, as a consequence of mobilising for two world wars, and economic growth, it had become a predominantly urban population, whose divisions – class, education, colour, money – and whose sense of itself were national, not local.

Against this background of deep change, shorter-term, but equally strong pressures were operating. The hydrogen bomb was a symbol of America's huge economic power. In 1948–50 the country had half the world's wealth, more than half its productivity and two-thirds of the machinery. 'No other power,' said Robert Payne, 'at any time in the world's history has possessed so varied or so great an influence on other nations . . .'[12] US oil production rose from 5.8 million barrels a day in 1949 to 16.4 million in 1972. Low oil prices fuelled a surging economy at all levels. There was, wrote David Halberstam, whose informative and interesting book *The Fifties* I follow, a hunger for goods and for pleasure after the long years of the Depression followed so quickly by the war.

And of all goods, the most important was the car. Roughly 49.3 million cars were registered in 1950, by 1960 it was 73.1 million. The car meant freedom, independence. The car was where people (and to an extent Kinsey[13]) said teenagers necked, petted – and made love.

Ten years of middle-class, solidly based prosperity from 1945 to 1955 meant wealth came right down to teenagers – in fact, *principally* to teenagers. This had never happened before in history. A great many, of course, earned their money but as parents grew richer they *gave* money to their teenage children. By early 1956, 13 million teenagers in America had a total income of $7 billion a year, a disposable income of $10.55 a week each – the same as the average US *family* in 1940.

Youth means sex, and it is no accident, therefore, that the popular culture that grew on this economic base was highly charged with sexuality. Elvis, with his sultry, sulky good looks, his thrusting pelvis, carried on, or himself carrying, with his perfect pitch (like Bruce Kinsey) the change from white to black music, music whose beat meant dancing, but *wild* dancing. His 'That's All Right Mama' came out on 5 July 1954. Or James Dean, equally sulky, equally sexual, but bisexual. Even the language of rebellion was sexual. Once, in the mid-'50s, Kerouac and a friend got drunk and 'drafted a message to the President. "Dear Eisenhower, We love you – you're the great white father. We'd like to fuck you."'

Yet it was not just sex. James Dean was a product of method acting. At a more profound level, what was emerging – with Lee Strasberg, Tennessee Williams, Marlon Brando, and many others, even in the end Marilyn Monroe, and then out into society, where it flowered in the 1960s – was an evolution of modernism, an attempt, a determination, to be more honest, more open, to face *the fact.* That was what Kinsey had recognised in *A Streetcar Named Desire.*

The battleground was age-old – unconventional, outspoken, rebellious youth against conformist age. The sultry heroes were always 'misunderstood'. In Dean's films the parents are the enemy. But for the first time youth, or the sexuality of youth, was going to win, was indeed already winning. Analagous movements were going on in Britain, though not driven by so early or so large an economic engine. One of the most interesting findings of the recent 1994 British survey was that there was no evidence 'of a sexual revolution coterminous with the decade of the 1960s'. Median age of first intercourse, for example, fell in the '50s as much as it was to do over the next thirty years. It seems that people became *aware* of sexual changes in the '60s which had taken place in the '50s.[14]

And America, in fact, saw in the late 1950s the first movements of openness and toleration in all sorts of other areas: towards black people, with Martin Luther King and civil rights, towards (or from) women, soon to be articulated by Betty Friedan.

It was at this cusp, on this tension point, one perhaps not fully appreciated, that Kinsey stood. It now becomes much easier to understand why he provoked such anger. It came from those older generations, the majority, who were frightened by the continued threats generated by the Cold War, and almost equally tense about the profound cultural revolution they could sense, or see, taking place all around them.

But it is therefore also clear that compared to the vast and fundamental forces helping to create this revolution – unprecedented wealth, wealth centred on the young, a general feeling of pleasure having been held too long at bay, a vast self-fuelling culture of books and films and plays and music, many of them developments of modernism, deep currents of toleration – compared to these, it is ridiculous to see Kinsey as in some way bringing it all about. It is more accurate to see him as effect, as part, rather than cause. Indeed, by the very nature of his work, he couldn't bring anything about. He could only detect changes which had already taken place in his field. And Kinsey himself was always quite clear that the decisive factors in social-sexual change in the twentieth century were the two world wars.

Nevertheless, Kinsey's contribution was not negligible. By revealing, he crystallised and focused attention on what was happening, and books that do this to a social process in progress have a considerable, if unmeasurable, effect in speeding it along (and insofar as she meant this then Margaret Mead was quite correct). The most influential books, as Orwell pointed out in *1984*, are those that tell you what you vaguely knew already. History has a number of examples from Rousseau in the middle of the eighteenth century to Betty Friedan in the middle of the twentieth. And to Kinsey's effect must be added the effect of all those he directly influenced: the many writers urging greater sexual tolerance and understanding, like Albert Ellis; the sex researchers, like Masters and Johnson, whose work he made possible; or, at a different level, publishers like Hugh Heffner and his numerous imitators.

* 4

One thing the volume of attack did not affect was sales. The *Female* report, indeed, sold far faster than the *Male* one – Saunders was already into its sixth printing, of 185,000, two weeks after it came out, and it reached in two years the figure reached by the *Male* book in six.[15]

Foreign editions began to appear very quickly – in Britain soon after America. It was news in Britain but not hysterically so. It received respectful reviews in the serious papers (nothing in *The Times*); the *Lancet* was particularly favourable: 'The new book . . . is a serious, well-conceived and courageous attempt to provide factual information about a branch of social psychology in which legend and emotion still predominate over knowledge and sense.' It especially praised the stance on homosexuality.[16] The book caused a certain sensation in the tabloids. Only the *Daily Mirror*, *Sunday Dispatch* and *Sunday Pictorial* had sent journalists to Bloomington. The *Daily Mirror* had a three-inch headline WOMEN. The *Daily Express* retaliated with an editorial on 'Our sex-sodden newspapers'.[17] The book sold about 10,000 copies in Britain and in total roughly the same, a quarter of a million copies, as the *Male*.[18]

The next three years were eventually to be dominated for Kinsey by two tremendous battles. To one, the fight for the financial (and so actual) life of his project, the flow of royalties was vital. The other battle – for his life – he seems to have decided to ignore.

PART V

Decline and Fall

Those who have some means think that the most important thing in the world is love. The poor know that it is money.

Gerald Brenan, *Thoughts in a Dry Season*

21

Money – and Deterioration: 1953–5

1

The 'whirr' of Kinsey's life seemed to continue as usual after the *Female* report came out, but there were significant pointers to the future.

At the end of October he was to address a large meeting in Philadelphia of the American Association of Marriage Counselors. 'If . . . I find at the last moment I should conserve energy for the 8.30 meeting,' he warned Emily Mudd, 'I will let you know . . . I find it very bad policy to let myself be worn out for two or three hours in dinner meetings, cocktails and meeting people before going on to the platform before a big audience.'[1] Only a few years before it had scarcely seemed possible to wear him out.

Just before this he spent four days in New York, seeing Mike Mikshe and Glenway (Wheeler was away*). Then, after Philadelphia, he went to California to be guest of honour at San Quentin's Inmate's dinner, a humble distinction he prized so highly he missed his second award as 'Hoosier of the Year' from Indiana's journalists.

A sentimental Christmas letter arrived from Glenway, longing to be at First Street 'listening to the recorded music, watching, perhaps, as in

---

* Yet it is noticeable how often Kinsey saw them separately. It may be that a letter Glenway wrote this year about a possible joint meeting in Bloomington throws light on this. 'Have you a purpose or particular interest in having us there together? There is an odd reticence between us about everything erotic.' They *tell* each other secrets and scandals – but don't describe anything that happens sexually. 'My feeling towards him in this connection is . . . complex – something like an incest taboo.' And complex, now, also to three-sided affairs. 'It was not always so, indeed I must have narrated something of my triangular desire in the days of George Lynes, and the incident of the unintentional glimpse of them in intercourse . . .' (Glenway Wescott to Kinsey, 1 August 1953).

1951, dear hands strongly and skillfully composing a rug . . .'[2] (Glenway's dots).

Of far greater significance was a letter George Corner sent him now. In November he had put out feelers for a further $80,000 from the Rockefeller Foundation, $40,000 of it for Kinsey. On 2 December he wrote to say the Foundation was being extremely cautious. 'They held out no certain prospect as to the continuation of . . . support.'[3]

The question of money was about to overwhelm everything.

2

In fact, 1954 began ordinarily enough. Kinsey was giving talks about three times a week and taking histories again. Plans were going ahead for an expedition to Peru in August. Emily Mudd received a really charming letter from India – a Mr Rai Chopra, 'in absence of dollars', asking for free Kinsey copies. Completely enchanted, she wrote to Kinsey and Saunders, saying how 'very happy' it would make her if they would send copies of Alfred's books to Mr Chopra. Alfred was less enchanted. 'Dear Emily . . . we average several letters a week from India, all asking for free copies . . . Frankly, I have a very bad impression of the ability of Indians to comprehend the realities of the world.'[4]

Dr D.E.J. Dingwall, an authority on erotica and erotic literature and curator of rare books at the British Museum, wrote offering a very rare eighteenth-century condom in its original wrappers. Kinsey invited him to Bloomington.[5]

Then, in February, the first of three bombshells struck. Dean Rusk, who had earlier been appointed president of the Rockefeller Foundation, summoned George Corner and told him he was extremely worried by rumours of a Congressional committee about to investigate his Foundation, especially pertaining to its support of Kinsey. Thus began the culmination, over a few short weeks, of a series of complex and interlocking events, some going back to July 1952, the date of Rusk's appointment.[6]

Let me, at the risk of some simplification, try and condense these. Chief among Kinsey's attackers post-*Female* was Harry Emerson Fosdick of the Union Theological Seminary. He, with many others, had bombarded both Congress and the trustees of the Rockefeller Foundation with angry letters. B. Carroll Reece had received similar letters – and seen mileage in them.

In fact, it seems likely that Reece wasn't really interested in Kinsey *per se* at all. Robert Taft had promised him the position of Secretary of State provided he won the Republican nomination in 1952. In the event, Eisenhower got it and Reece, furious, decided that the Foundations in the east, using their huge revenues, were largely responsible, especially the Rockefeller Foundation (Foster Dulles, the chairman at that time, was a fervent Ike supporter and later his Secretary of State). The club Reece would use to batter the Foundations would be the Rockefeller Foundation, and he would batter the Rockefeller Foundation with Kinsey.*[7]

But Reece's manoeuvres, already underway in 1953, coincided with changes in the Rockefeller Foundation itself. There had always been considerable opposition to Kinsey among the trustees, and his case had only survived because of the eloquent and powerful advocacy of Alan Gregg. Gregg only won the decision to continue Kinsey's support for two years from 4 April 1951 by one vote. In May, he was 'promoted' to vice-president. His place was taken by Dr Andrew J. Warren, in favour of Kinsey – but not passionate. Then in 1952 the Board voted in principle not to go on supporting Kinsey 'at the same rate as before', as Robert S. Morison put it.

As the storm of public disapproval roared on, as the angry letters from Emerson Fosdick and others poured in, the position hardened. On 17 January 1954, a clearly guilty and ashamed Robert Morison came to George Corner, 'like', said Corner, 'a spy into enemy territory', and said they would not give any more funds to the NRC Committee if any of these were earmarked for Kinsey. This was confirmed in late February. Corner reluctantly withdrew his request for any specific Kinsey money, and the Rockefeller Foundation then granted him $50,000. But it was, at a stroke, the end of Kinsey's funding.[8]

Corner, long since deeply bound up with Kinsey's work, was so upset by all this 'that I proposed that we should dissolve our committee'.

---

* There was an interesting parallel to this while I was in Bloomington in 1995. Representative Steve Stockman, a Republican of Texas, tried to get a Congressional hearing into possible child abuse in Kinsey's collection of data in the 1940s. His target was not really Kinsey but funding for sex education in schools. By saying this was based on Kinsey's research, which he would discredit, he would discredit school sex education. He failed, but it is a demonstration of how emotive Kinsey's name in America still is to the Right.

He was only dissuaded when it was pointed out what a lot of other bodies would suffer.[9] Kinsey himself wrote an impassioned letter to Rusk: this was the worst possible moment to abandon him, since it would just confirm public opinion; his royalties would only last three years – not time to complete any of his proposed studies; the whole fifteen years of pioneering work would have to be jettisoned just as they were about to bear fruit.'[10] The point here is that Kinsey had reached the position he had with gall wasps in 1936–7: the data had been gathered, the reservoir filled – now he could pour out studies.

But Rusk was adamant, and all those involved who have been questioned agree why: the fundamental reason the Rockefeller Foundation abandoned Kinsey was because it didn't like to be associated with what he was researching – sex. It was the *subject* they detested. Even John Foster Dulles, the chairman, had said that sex should not be *touched* by the Foundation.[11]

There were exacerbations. As a non-profit foundation holding public trust (i.e. exempt from taxes) Dean Rusk said they had to take account of public opinion. Though Reece didn't begin till May, he had contacted Rusk in February 1954 and it is clear the Foundation, and especially Rusk, had not surprisingly got the wind up. (In fact, Reece was so incompetent, the hearings so biased, journalists – especially on the *New York Times* – demolished them so effectively, that the sittings were ridiculed and Reece's conclusions ignored.) Also, the statisticians' report was now finally published. It is often oddly chatty and informal and obviously in favour of Kinsey. His survey is outstanding compared to all other surveys. But it did include various sampling and statistical criticisms and at one point says that where he is dogmatic without evidence, even where 'most interesting', he falls below the level of 'good scientific writing'. It gave just enough scientific respectability to Kinsey's opponents.[12]

But the root cause of the Rockefeller Foundation's defection was deep distaste for Kinsey's subject, barely concealed and not requiring these justifications. And, of course, both Corner and Kinsey had suspected and dreaded this outcome ever since the *Male* volume, and especially since 1950–1. They had been actively seeking new backers for a long time.[13]

Because you know something terrible is going to happen doesn't make it any less terrible when it does happen. In the tragedy of the next two and a half years – and there is tragedy here as the vast parabola of Kinsey's heroic endeavour now plunges inexorably down towards death

– inevitability plays its part. Indeed, it is the essence of classical tragedy that all is known beforehand; audience and central actors watch in mingled terror and pity as what is known or been foretold unfolds. And the catalyst, the spring, is always some fatal flaw in the hero himself.

To what degree did Kinsey bring this catastrophe on himself? It was now clear that his getting Alan Gregg to write the preface to the *Male* volume, the earmarking of Rockefeller Foundation funds especially for him, the continued public association of the Rockefeller Foundation with his work were all major tactical errors. But these sprang from various roots: first, the Rockefeller Foundation was the most effective brand name to validate his research. Second, was Kinsey's need for total control in anything he undertook, brooking no dissent and accepting no advice. He *wanted* the close association of the Rockefeller Foundation with his project and he obtained it.

Then the extraordinary public exposure he sought and got was also central. It was the *news* splash coming first, said Robert Morison, that so startled the Rockefeller trustees and seemed so unscientific.[14] Yet this was really an expression of the deep contradiction in his work, mentioned much earlier, between science and social-sexual reform. The second needed publicity, the first did not.

And the social-sexual reforms derived not just from the humane side of his character but from his highly sexed (highly *bisexually* sexed) nature and its grievous frustration till he was twenty-seven. This, too, explains what one might call the *sexuality* of his sex science. Much later, in 1955 while Kinsey was in Europe, Robert Morison visited Bloomington. He told Gebhard it might have helped if Kinsey hadn't always been so 'evangelistic', so obviously approving of all forms of sexual activity in his public lectures.[15]

Yet it was from here that Kinsey drew the psychic energy that drove his project, and it is doubtful if he could have succeeded in it without that total, autocratic control by which he functioned. That is to say, it was, ironically, the very forces in his character bringing about his success which also helped to bring about his downfall.

It is plain, the Rockefeller Foundation had, as Rusk endlessly pointed out, a perfect right to end its support of Kinsey; it had supported him generously for thirteen years, it had long decided to disengage.[16] It is equally plain that the abrupt timing and brutal manner of its going were a cowardly and panicky reaction, not least on the part of Rusk. But Kinsey had played a not inconsiderable part himself.

Kinsey and Mac had a week's 'holiday' in Peru from 7 March 1954. No detailed record remains, but it was partly for him to reconnoitre the much longer visit planned later; and partly no doubt for him to get some rest from the battering.

It is unlikely he got much. Pomeroy describes Kinsey as a chronic worrier. Having lost the Rockefeller Foundation, he knew it was vital to keep, if he could, some sort of prestigious official backing and as soon as he was back he and Paul Gebhard applied to the NRC for $3,500 to pursue the studies in Andean (Peruvian) art – a complete and unique record 'from 1,000 BC to 1,000 AD . . . of the sexual life of an ancient people . . .'[17]

The tax return for 1954–5 shows $20,000 from the NRC – the last of his old grant. One notices the massive $309,079 royalty returns and equally massive amount immediately put into reserve – $243,440. Collection spending was $7,620 – compared to $35,000 at its height.[18]

In the past, Kinsey's natural buoyancy and optimism, his extraordinary energy, had carried him through everything. Now, he wrote to Dr Carl Hartman, inaccurately but showing how abandoned he felt, 'there is practically no scientist outside of yourself and the NRC committee that has commended any aspect of any single item in our volume on the female'.[19] And this about the book he had been quite certain was the best he'd ever written.

The solution was, as always, incessant work. Once again he lectured two or three times a week[20] – and now, as in the early years, whenever he could for money.[21] He and the team forged ahead towards 100,000 histories, taking 1,000 this year.[22] From 26 March to 3 June, with brief returns to Bloomington and other short trips, he was away in California and New York.

Saul Rosenzweig remembered seeing him in St. Louis, Missouri, at the 6 May 7 p.m. meeting of the American Psychiatric Association – the meeting of Karl Menninger's betrayal. Kinsey was no longer 'the enthusiastic investigator', but seemed bitter and disenchanted. Yet Rosenzweig thought he effortlessly mastered Menninger in debate. (Not quite effortless. When he'd arrived at 10 a.m. he told Robert Laidlaw he hadn't slept all night. Laidlaw gave him a strong pill, put him to bed and let him sleep eight hours.[23])

And another of the later leitmotifs of this period, as Kinsey's money anxieties increase, now appears – letters from friends (in this case Monroe Wheeler) trying to think of rich new patrons.[24] Soon Kinsey would start to go out fund-raising himself – a task at which he was absolutely hopeless.

On 4 June Dr Dingwall arrived in Bloomington, bringing his eighteenth-century condom,* and stayed a week. Eric Dingwall, at this time aged sixty-three, was a highly intelligent, sprightly, sceptical figure, who knew something of sex research. He had known Magnus Hirschfeld in Germany and been irritated, as he had been by Krafft-Ebing, by the unscientific, sloppy 'anecdotal tittle-tattle' of it. He arrived just as sceptical about Kinsey, with 'the gravest doubts'. He went away convinced – wherever he doubted, Kinsey produced hard, clear, scientific evidence. He sensed at once the 'sterling character and integrity'. When he wrote his account years later, he said: 'In my long life (and I am now over 90) I still think Alfred Kinsey was one of the greatest men I have ever met.'[25]

He was to meet him again. Ding (as he rapidly asked Kinsey to call him) was determined to get Kinsey to England. No doubt he began his campaign now; certainly, he continued by letter as soon as he'd left.[26]

Soon after this, and just before his sixtieth birthday, Kinsey left for California – to pursue law reform work and San Quentin. He also went to the New York City ballet in San Francisco with Cornelia Christenson on 29 June. Christenson said going to the ballet with Kinsey was more interesting than with most people because he knew the sex lives of all the dancers.[27]

Finally, as the long-planned, much-looked-forward-to expedition to Peru in August drew near, Glenway Wescott arrived for ten days in Bloomington on 5 July. He worked with Paul Gebhard on the artist-writer project. Essentially, this seems to have been Glenway spouting intimate gossip. 'Fascinating,' he called it in his journal; 'a great bore' to his biographer. Gebhard only remembered he had to keep asking if the subjects had had any heterosexual life, an aspect Glenway tended to forget.[28]

---

* It is still there. Made of sheep's gut, eighteenth-century condoms were worn against VD rather than for contraception, which explains Madame de Sevigné's often misunderstood remark that they were gossamer against infection, steel against love. Boswell, who had a very large penis, wore his tied on round the scrotum with red ribbons, but left it off as often as he dared precisely because of its steely qualities. (See my *Love, Sex, Marriage and Divorce*, London, 1981, pp. 36, 43.)

In August, the Rockefeller Foundation, in response to repeated questions from journalists, issued two official statements regarding Kinsey. Funding had been ended because he now had 'other sources', and because 'he did not request a renewal of support'. Apart from the second statement being a flat lie, their motives were more eloquently revealed by the fact that at the same time they ended Kinsey's grant they gave Harry Fosdick's Union Theological Seminary $525,000 – one of the largest grants they had ever given, and more than their total thirteen-year support for Kinsey.[29]

But by the time these announcements were made Kinsey, Paul Gebhard and Bill Dellenback had left for Peru.

4

Not since gall wasp days had Kinsey set off on such an adventure. It was to last nearly a month and promised to be fascinating. Paul Gebhard had some years before learnt about the Mochica, a Peruvian tribe who could be traced back to prehistoric times and who had left a great deal of extremely explicit erotic pottery.

As long ago as 1947, when they had their first glimpses of the material, Kinsey had written, it 'portrays every conceivable thing. It completely discounts any theory that the so-called perversions are a development of our modern civilization ...'[30] It rather depends what you mean by so-called perversions. The one thing that was not depicted was homosexuality.*[31]

But in fact from Kinsey's point of view the expedition was little less than disastrous. He had, he told Eric Dingwall, been feeling unwell before he left.[32] The loss of the Rockefeller Foundation, the continuing attacks and betrayals, his insisting on working as hard as ever – were all now coming home to roost. He managed a little work. Bill Dellenback remembers him watching some Peruvian labourers peeing into the

---

* Kinsey was therefore probably, as so often, arguing the homosexual case. But recent research has shown that, paradoxically, the absence of evidence almost certainly proved him right. It seems that the sixteenth-century Spanish invaders of South America were so outraged by the widespread homosexuality and transvestism they found in the indigenous people that they destroyed all artifacts depicting these practices. (Timothy Taylor, *The Prehistory of Sex*, London, 1996, p. 17.)

gutter by a building site. 'If they did that in America,' said Kinsey, 'they'd be clapped into jail. Always, it's a matter of the *mores*.'[33] Then, after ten days, his throat infection transferred and his illness developed into a full-blown pelvic infection – either of the urethra or prostate, according to Gebhard.[34] He went to a hospital in Peru and spent the last two-thirds of the time in bed.

This was a serious collapse, and it continued. Just how serious is indicated by an entry in Wescott's journal this September. Soon after their return on 31 August, Kinsey was expected at Stone-blossom for the weekend but had to cancel. Wescott rang Gebhard. 'They expect ACK to pull through all right, but he was in bad condition.' (And just how flippant this crowd often was is revealed by the next entry. 'Someone,' on hearing about Kinsey's infection, said '*Pelvic* infection? Oh yes, of course, llamas . . .')[35]

Kinsey had been expected to die before he was twenty-one. It seemed to him his entire life proved doctors were wrong and he was right, and this was, to some extent, behind his attitude to his heart. He treated his heart – the usual culprit – like a recalcitrant employee. He would *force* it to behave. He would collapse, recover – then work as hard as ever till he collapsed again. As now. He got up, worked – and soon, as he told Ramsey on 24 September, was back spending more time, help-lessly weak, in bed again.[36] He remained in Bloomington most of October.

In Peru, Gebhard and Dellenback had shared a room. Late one night Kinsey, lying ill in the next room, had gone to the bathroom. Dellenback was writing a letter under one small lamp. As Kinsey returned, Dellenback looked up and smiled at him through the open door. Kinsey stuck his head in and hissed, 'Bill, for heaven's sake, you're keeping the entire household awake with the scratching of that pen.'[37]

From now on his irritability and sharpness, especially with his team, became increasingly pronounced. But there was wider deterioration: '. . . he had always,' wrote Sam Steward about this last period, 'used "we" and "us" when referring to the work . . . now it suddenly became "I" and "me" . . . Formerly, Kinsey would listen to you, nodding, agreeing, or raising objections. Now his statements became authoritative, almost ex-cathedra pronouncements; he no longer listened quietly. Instead, he interrupted, issued dicta dogmatically, often turning impatient and snappish, sometimes arrogant . . .'[38]

It is here necessary for one last diversion into the byways of Kinsey's sexuality. James Jones, in a way to which we have become accustomed, has a more melodramatic version of events in Peru.

Just before leaving, he writes, Kinsey went into the basement of Wylie Hall, slung a rope over an overhead pipe, tied one end round his testicles, gripped the other end in his hands, and jumped off a chair. 'For what length of time he stayed aloft, caught between heaven and earth, remains unclear.' Jones has medical expertise which proves it took place at this time since 'a physician friend' said the illness was 'orchitis' and came from the testicles. Jones also ascribes the incident (and pinpoints it further) as a response to attacks in the Reece Committee – it was, he implies, analogous to an agonising, agonised suicide attempt.[39]

Let us look at this. 'Orchitis' simply means inflammation and usually, in this area, comes from bacterial or viral infection. Since it did not manifest itself for *ten days* in Peru[40] it can have had nothing to do with prior wrenching of testicles or leaping off of chairs, to which the response, if there was to be a response, would have been very rapid. The pelvic infection was therefore, as Kinsey said, almost certainly the result of his throat infection.[41] This is further born out by the infection lasting into October – far longer than any inflammation would have done.

Nor was there any chair, an effective dramatic touch but an invented one. The authority for the account of this incident was Anon A. I discussed it with Anon A. He said *his* sources were Earle Marsh and Pomeroy, neither of whom actually saw it but, he assumed, heard about it from Kinsey. The point here is that, not only was there no chair, but it had happened innumerable times before. To toughen those 'fragile tissues' to the extent of being able to bear his weight had taken years. It was not, that is, a particular, focused event.[42]

Removed from pre-Peru and despairing, near-suicidal response to the Reece Committee, this event, or succession of events has, I think, a different significance. Sometime during this final period, Kinsey told Dellenback he had 'circumcised' himself in the bath with a penknife.[43] Since we know he had pierced his foreskin numerous times before in pursuit of intense sexual pain/pleasure sensation, this was probably the last of such incidents (last because there was now nothing left to pierce).[44] What this series of activities shows is, first, that in these last years Kinsey reached very considerable heights of extreme sexual pain/pleasure sensation; second, that he was rather intrigued by and proud of just how high. (Why talk about them otherwise? It would have been most unlike Kinsey to point them out as indications of despair.)

And third, we should bear in mind Dr Michael Perring's observation earlier that self-inflicted masochistic practices combined with sexual ones can, after a time, mean the second cannot function without the first.[45] Kinsey's increasing erectile impotence from 1953 may well have been the penalty he now paid.

5

Kinsey recovered. But, once up again, having for some time given up gardening, he now abandoned his last defence against the fear he'd expressed so long ago when he read out Darwin's lament at Bowdoin. He stopped giving his musicales.[46]

In October he wrote and told Dingwall he would definitely be coming to Europe within the next twelve months.[47] And in November and December he was again frantically busy flying between New York, Bloomington, and California.

Kinsey saw a good deal of the Wescott–Wheeler circle on this New York trip. He had lunch with Monroe on 20 November; he may have managed a short visit to Stone-blossom just before this – certainly he met Glenway and also Glenway's benefactors, his brother and sister-in-law.[48] He was still collecting,* and partly to this end (though it is clear he was also fond of him) he had dinner with the painter Paul Cadmus. In his letter to Cadmus afterwards he apologises for his 'physical condition' interfering with the evening.[49]

* As regards the collection, there is a rather curious letter which is undated but which I think can be placed here; it is from the 'Countess Dorothy de Labouchier'. In February 1954 he had taken the countess's history. She had been so stimulated she did a series of erotic drawings. These were clearly powerful. 'I was showing the drawings to three men (for they are aesthetically good and I am not in the least reticent about them) a prominent analyst [difficult to read. Could be artist or even dentist], my assistant, and a well-known art dealer. Suddenly the art dealer (of Sicilian descent) unzipped his pants, his eyes became glazed and in a kind of trance he proceeded to masturbate, completely unconscious of the rest of us. I shook him and slapped him and gave a sharp "Stop it" – and he immediately zipped himself up, came out of his trance, and went on talking, seemingly unconscious that the incident had occurred. I believe he was in a hypnotic state.' One wonders at this point if it wasn't the countess who had fallen into a hypnotic state, but she adds, to show how alert and scientific she was at the time, 'No orgasm occurred.' Kinsey's reply is polite but non-committal. The drawings are somewhere in the Kinsey Institute collection but when I asked for reproductions of them for this book, could not be located.

Glenway also comments with some asperity in his journal on Kinsey's physical condition on this visit leading to sudden changes of plan without warning: 'Of course he isn't old, nevertheless is nearing his end, with a terrible cardiac deterioration. Perhaps the circulation of his blood in his brain is irregular, causing lapses of memory . . .'[50]

Another result of this deterioration is common at more advanced old age. As the tides of energy subside, the sharp rocks of the personality, laid down in childhood, once again emerge. Kinsey had every reason to be anxious about money – he could only keep staff if his future was secure, he had an enormous programme to fulfil, and indeed royalties did begin to run low in three years. At the same time, a great deal of money was still pouring in during 1954, three years was a long time to find a solution, and in fact there was an obvious solution to hand which he totally refused to consider – government funding for specific projects. He refused because government funding carried the right to inspect and he would not – on the grounds that so much was confidential – even allow that as a possibility.

The intensity of Kinsey's anxiety makes it likely that he was returning to the anxiety about money which had dominated his first eleven years of poverty in Hoboken. And a possible confirmation of this comes now. Monroe and Kinsey's one-time sexual partner Bill Miller, had fixed on the extremely rich Dr Cary Walker as patron. Kinsey saw him on this New York visit. 'I saw Cary Walker once and talked to him on the phone several times,' he told Robert Laidlaw, 'but no question of finances came up.'[51]

This was to happen time and again. Friends, particularly Glenway and Monroe, would arrange a meeting with a possible benefactor – and Kinsey simply could not bring himself to mention the subject of money *at all.* He was a proud man and no one much likes asking for money – but what one is reminded of is his acute humiliation as a little boy when his mother sent him out again and again into Hoboken to ask for credit from the local shops.

Whatever the underlying forces, by the end of 1954 he was getting desperate again. He still couldn't quite believe the Rockefeller Foundation had really abandoned him. He kept asking those on the board he believed to be his allies down to Bloomington – at this point Dr Robert S. Morison for instance.[52] In 1955 he was to start making indirect overtures again, through the NRC.

History-taking, lectures, conferences – flying with the team between Bloomington, New York, California, Chicago, Philadelphia – went on for three-quarters of 1955. Thereafter, now fixed for October, Europe loomed.

Mac, who was to go, saw Europe as the last chance for the holiday Kinsey so badly needed. However, Dingwall had alerted the Maudsley psychiatric hospital, Kinsey suggested prisons, letters flowed to and fro – and in fact all spring his correspondence was devoted to making quite sure a holiday was what it would *not* be.[53]

But money dominated everything. He was in New York in February (and saw Mike Mikshe) to talk about it with Monroe and Glenway.[54] Monroe, in the letters following these meetings, said the embarrassment of the institute for *sex* research was one problem, particularly as regards wills. 'It might make it easier [speaking to lawyers] if it were ... "The Research Institute for Animal Behavior" or Something . . .' But for Kinsey, this was an issue of principle: 'There is therapy involved in forcing our society to use the term sex objectively' – besides, no one would be fooled (not quite Wheeler's point). He was still discussing this with them when in New York for an abortion conference in April.[55]

Kinsey was searching for money everywhere, but his main hope was still the Rockefeller Foundation. He had drawn up a list of schemes and in February presented them to George Corner for the NRC. Both men had long realised *specific* projects of social concern, as opposed to just generalised and embarrassing sex, were the only possible route back to Rockefeller Foundation funding – one reason for Kinsey's emphasis on sex offenders. Corner thought that abortion, on which Kinsey was already working for the Planned Parenthood Federation, was the most likely subject and promised to try for $5,000. There is something touching about the gratitude which fills Kinsey's letters to Corner now. 'Best of everything to you. Thank you for the many ways you have helped in our research.'[56]

Even his sleeping pills could not overcome his many anxieties. Kinsey also had a New York doctor, William Waterman, who gave him phenobarbitone and told him to exercise more (which Kinsey pretended he was doing).[57] But when he attended the Planned Parenthood New York abortion conference at Arden House in April, he wrote asking for a single room since, sleepless, he was often up for two hours in the middle of the night 'doing other things'.[58]

Then, in May, Corner wrote and told him delightedly that he'd got $3,000 for abortion research. He'd told Robert Morison at the Foundation that he proposed to treat Kinsey like any other applicant and, said Corner, 'I can tell you privately' he didn't think they would mind.[59]

He was wrong. The Rockefeller Foundation soon began to panic again. On 10 June, Corner had to tell Kinsey that Morison was laying down conditions. His work must be 'directly useful to physicians'. Would he please publish in a scientific journal – say the *American Journal of Obstetrics and Gynecology*? The same day, another letter arrived. Kinsey could only acknowledge the NRC, there must be no *mention* of the Rockefeller Foundation. With these repeated and humiliating instructions, Kinsey had to comply.[60]

Letter after letter is about money. He ropes in Larry Saunders, who sends a list of professional fund-raisers – none of whom seems any good. In fact, in search of money, Kinsey was about to change publishers, from Saunders to McGraw-Hill – and wrote and told Saunders so in July. They still exchanged one or two friendly letters after this.[61]

July was spent in Bloomington. Mr Cummins Catherwood, a possible benefactor, came down. Lionel Trilling came to lecture at IU and was shown round the ISR. Dr Cooper Speaks, who remembers the visit, says how impressed Trilling was by the library.[62] Whether it was Kinsey who showed him round is not recorded.

Half of June, all of August and half of September were spent taking histories in Californian prisons – Soledad and Folsom. But once again, Kinsey – sixty-one in June – was becoming exhausted.

7

One of the people he saw a good deal of whenever he went to San Francisco was Harry Benjamin, the doctor who specialised in transvestites and had known Hirschfeld. He was one of the many people Robert Dickinson had introduced to Kinsey.*

---

* Harry Benjamin was also one of the few people who failed to appreciate one of Kinsey's rare expressions of humour – perhaps because it was directed at Kinsey himself. They met one year in the Sir Francis Drake Hotel, where Kinsey often stayed when in San Francisco. A new decorator had just done up the dining

Harry Benjamin, during one of these 1955 trips, visited Kinsey in hospital after he had had a heart attack. He was appalled at how ill he looked. Paul Gebhard said they were not yet strictly speaking heart attacks so much as episodes of 'congestive heart failure' – but they could be frightening enough.[63]

Having given up exercise, Kinsey began to put on weight, and his blood pressure was rising. He started to get violent cramps in his legs and Wardell Pomeroy had to massage them. In the steep streets of San Francisco, where Kinsey had once strode ahead, he now panted in their wake until, refusing to acknowledge what was happening, he'd call out, 'Gebhard, Pomeroy, just a minute – I need to look at this window display of lingerie.'[64]

In May, Dingwall had written that when he got to England Kinsey could have a really good rest in his house. In August he repeated this – '*You need* a holiday.' Kinsey wrote on 19 September to say he would like a hotel with a lift.[65]

At the end of September he flew to New York for six days, to lecture, having dinner, separately, with Glenway and then Monroe. Harriet Pilpel and Kinsey also had a meeting with McGraw-Hill.

On 17 October he and Mac set off from Bloomington *en route* to Europe.

rooms and Benjamin showed Kinsey round. In 'The Tavern', which was tough-style – oak, leather etc., Kinsey said decisively, 'Obviously, this has been done by a homosexual who loves masculinity.' Benjamin took him to the next dining room, which was a mass of frills and daintiness and femininity. Kinsey laughed and laughed and 'laughed so heartily that it actually surprised me because I failed to see anything funny in this pleasant room'. (From the file 'Kinseyiana' in the Kinsey Institute.)

22

Europe: October–December 1955

The histories of persons born and raised in Continental Europe usually
involve a great deal of extra-marital intercourse.

Male, p. 593

1

E urope was Kinsey's swan song. It is astonishing to see this sick, exhausted man suddenly revive. Once more the taxonomist found himself in a new world of different specimens and new patterns. One can detect the energy in the vividness and detail of his descriptions – especially in Italy – and, as the only long verbatim record of him speaking, it is as close as we can ever get to a rough idea of how Kinsey must have been when speaking off the cuff and at ease with his staff.[1]

If not famous worldwide, he was certainly so Europewide. His path was eased by the care and facilities granted celebrity. And, away from American censure and prying journalists, Kinsey relaxed and dropped his guard.

The precise dates of their itinerary are not always completely certain, but the route was Scandinavia (Norway, Denmark), England, France, Italy, Sicily, Spain, Portugal.

He talked to 'scores of people' wherever he went and to some extent found the sexual paradise Europe had always seemed from afar. In Norway, landing at Oslo, he discovered, to his delight, that premarital sex took place in 90–95 per cent of all marriages. The Norwegians regard sex, not like Americans 'as something dirty . . . [But] one of the best things that can come out of one's developing a nice relationship with a girl . . . They begin intercourse at a rather early age – 16,' and often earlier.

He felt still more at home in Denmark, where he lectured at the two leading universities – Copenhagen and Århus. In Århus he even found a man 'making a tremendous toilet wall inscription study', and another (a dentist) who was in the course of proving Hans Andersen was homosexual – which Kinsey saw at once was obviously so.*

On homosexuality, though there was still some disapproval, it was legal and the approach was sane. As to his statistics, the Danes agreed with Kinsey – 2 per cent or 4 per cent, 25 per cent or 37 per cent was irrelevant, 'it is the trend that counts'.

But he noted with surprise how Scandinavians 'have just as insane a horror of' sex between adults and children. The real danger, he pointed out, was other adults making an issue of it. He told his Århus audience he 'was amazed to find they were still having inhibitions regarding contact of homosexuality and older persons with children in spite of their great acceptance of most things sexual'. Kinsey clearly felt able to be much less circumspect abroad.

He crammed Norway and Denmark into five days, including two nights in Copenhagen up till 2 a.m. with the vice squad, mainly watching them *not* arrest homosexuals. About 22 October he and Mac flew to London.

Eric Dingwall had become considerably over-excited about the Kinseys' arrival and at one time had arranged a visit to a nudist club run by a friend of his. 'I doubt if anyone there would recognise you although the application of a heavy black moustache might be advisable!'[2] But the programme for the week in England was in the event sober enough, if heavy: a day round the British Museum erotica, a day at Wormwood Scrubs, two lectures to the psychiatrists at the Maudsley, whose Dr Trevor Gibbons arranged for him to testify to the Wolfenden Committee; on top of this various sexual explorations.

The British Museum did not overly impress him. The curators

---

* 'The original manuscripts are straight-out homosexual stories,' said Kinsey. For instance, as the dentist pointed out, reading rather wildly between the lines, the story of the mute nymph – the beautiful statue by the sea who cannot speak – clearly symbolises Andersen not being able to tell the world of his homosexuality. The dentist also said there were three bodies in Andersen's grave – Andersen, his wife, and Andersen's male lover. Modern biographers agree that he was low-sexed and hypersensitive – the princess and the pea is a better symbol for him – but convincingly reject any real homosexuality. The grave contains no male lover. (See Bredsdorff, 1975; Helweg, 1927/1954, and Reumert, 1971.)

couldn't buy 'anything that smacks of sex' and had to rely on gifts. There was a lot of junk and he had to peer about to find that. 'One way of finding anything erotic in the British Museum is to look for anything upside-down or turned backwards.'

He was critical, too, of Wormwood Scrubs – still beating men, up to '20 lashes on his bare back'. He was horrified that 30 per cent of men were in for sex offences, of which 60 per cent were homosexual charges. 'Some men have done as much as 6 years for homosexuality.' He attended a group therapy session in one of the dormitories, was impressed by how open the young psychiatrist had got the prisoners to be, and astounded, it seems almost impressed, at the masturbation figures achieved by the eighteen-year-olds. 'I have never seen such high rates.' Yet the animus of the group was against a man, forty-two, who had fallen in love with a twenty-year-old. They wanted to beat him up, but were frightened because he was so strong. Also, the twenty-year-old wouldn't object. Kinsey lectured them on tolerance.

As he clearly did to the Maudsley psychiatrists. After one of his talks, Mrs Haldane, wife of Professor J.B.S. Haldane, said to Mrs Kinsey, 'You can see that he is just seething underneath with anger at the way these people are treated by the law.' Mac agreed that he was.[3] And he carried his message to the Wolfenden Committee, where it was clearly also sympathetically received. 'As a commission there is no doubt of their liberality.'

But all this was, as it were, just the official side of Kinsey's visit. Someone had the bright, if slightly bizarre idea of bringing him together with Vyvian Holland. 'Had luncheon with the son of Oscar Wilde, rather a sober and dullish business man . . .' Kinsey talked about homosexuality in rabbits.

And after the day's work, he hit the beat. He and Mac spent most of one night – from 8 p.m. to 3 a.m. – patrolling Piccadilly with Dingwall. Kinsey had never seen such aggressive soliciting or so many prostitutes of both sexes. He observed every detail: the lack of arrests, the beating up of 'queers' often by the very people who had had sex with them. These last sometimes the guardsmen – 'dare devils, wear skin-tight uniforms' – going all out for sex. By 3 a.m. when Mac, that selfless, loyal woman, must have been dropping, Kinsey was still alertly watching; by now 'all the prostitutes – male and female – were letting their hands dribble across the crotches of passers-by'.

Two more nights were given to pubs. Kinsey was in fact exploring the London sexual underworld as he had that of Chicago, New York and other cities. The first pub Ding took them into Kinsey at once spotted an American homosexual model he knew. 'We carefully avoided each other.' He found no exclusively homosexual pubs, but a number were centres of picking up. He seems to have had trouble over drinks – 'mostly beer and occasionally Scotch whiskey sold'. He several times noted how attractive English prostitutes were, how 'trim and neat' – high praise.

Before they left for Paris he commented in general: 'I am quite convinced at this point that we inherited a lot of our attitudes from our English forebears.'

Their three days in Paris were, on the whole, a failure. He refused his publisher's request to publicise his book, and his single lecture to a medical group was badly attended since it was the French equivalent of a bank holiday and all the professors had pushed off.

They noticed the animosity towards homosexuals. Both Mac and he felt the French adoration of women was patronisingly male-orientated. And when they went together to the *Folies Bergère* – a touching picture, somehow – Kinsey was impressed by the size and flamboyance but not by the sex. The humour, which he rather surprisingly relayed, was well up – or rather down – to Kinsey's view of such things. 'Girl meets three men: "What do you think of Amour?" Englishman says it's a waste of time. Frenchman faints. Italian went into ecstasies.'

Not, in fact, it turned out, an inaccurate condensation as far as Kinsey's Italy went. It was to there they both flew on 2 November, and at last he was to find his sexual Eden.

2

Kinsey's guide in Rome was Kenneth Anger, the young, good-looking, avant-garde filmmaker he'd met several years before. Anger was the *auteur* of the celebrated *Fireworks*, which he had made in 1947 aged seventeen, as well as, later, numerous other films. Kinsey rapidly realised, under Anger's tuition, that, unlike Scandinavia, sex meant prostitutes and/or money. 'The families keep the decent girls pretty well locked up at night . . . In the lower levels it is not uncommon for a lower level girl to refuse intercourse before marriage, but she may prostitute to raise money for her trousseau and no one would think anything of it.'

Since regulated prostitution was, outside of marriage, the main outlet, Kinsey spent a lot of time in brothels. His account is vivid. The
typical house had a waiting room with a wall bench, chairs and men
waiting. The girls, when not occupied 'in the deeper recesses of the
house', would come and exhibit themselves – elaborately dressed, in the
best houses, 'in the poorest they were down to a little triangle'. Madam
would be on a raised platform at the end, suddenly chanting: ' "There are
three girls available" or "Come on boys – let's go".' But the girls, except
from Turin, 'were rather sloppy, fattish Southern Italians, nowhere near
the attractive girls in London'.

There was a large turnover, men and youths coming in to window-
shop, as it were, and leaving. A scene of indifference. 'There is no attention paid to the male, who may come to erection and wildly masturbate.'
Kinsey could sit and observe unnoticed, as he had at Wescott's parties,
scribbling on his little pad. He noticed the 'lordly' disdain of the men
compared to the frenetic French. 'Interestingly enough some of the
homosexual males have found the brothels are good cruising places for
males.'

And of course, expertly led by Kenneth Anger, Kinsey, the observer,
cruised too. Italy exactly exemplified his ideas that homosexuality was a
potentiality in *all* men and also the harmlessness, indeed mutual benefits, of adult/child sex. Everyone he talked to told him males at all levels
had homosexual activity – pre-adolescent and adolescent, married and
unmarried – but 'you seldom find an exclusively homosexual male'. A
man looking for sex would take it from either – paid if he had it with a
man, paying if he had a girl. This often happened in succession 'and
since the girl would cost less than he had been paid by the male, he
would still make a profit'.

At night, Anger took him to the Spanish Steps, but above all, fascinated, Kinsey stalked the Colosseum. The Colosseum! In ancient Rome
prostitutes plied their trade all over the place, but often in the spaces
between the arches which held up the theatres and circuses, and most
notoriously of all in those of the Colosseum itself. The word *fornicate*
comes from the Latin word for those arches – *fornices*.

Kinsey found inscriptions deeply incised into the stone of those
magnificent, sexually haunted ruins, some going back to the Middle
Ages. The commonest was 'W, ancient symbol for Viva – "anything".'

In 1955, it mostly seemed homosexual anything. He watched a
priest 'cruising for sexual contact for two hours'. Going with Anger

down a blind alley they found two soldiers masturbating each other –
but not necessarily homosexuals, just needing relief. 'Does not fall into
the same category as anal intercourse.' Another time, they came to a
dungeon with an iron fence – 'a male on one side exhibiting his erect
penis to a male on the other side. We disturbed this and one man went
away but the other immediately followed him.'

And it extended out and out. 'Fields around Rome are filled with
copulating couples both homosexual and heterosexual on a balmy night.
Police make no attempt to hold down sexual activity. Probably 95 per
cent of the time money is involved.'

Kinsey's European tour was a defining moment in two processes
which had been becoming more and more evident, the second for twelve
or more years.

The first can be demonstrated by a significant exchange he had had
with Dingwall in London. Noticing how exhausted he was, Dingwall
begged him 'not to push himself so hard'. They argued about this, and
suddenly Kinsey fell silent. Then he said, 'Ding, I'm sorry but I must go
on. I just can't help it.'[4]

The second is best approached through Shelley. When he first came
to Rome in November 1818 (by coincidence the same month as Kinsey)
Shelley was overwhelmed by the great ruins of the Colosseum, and
especially by the way nature had reasserted herself – 'an amphitheatre
of rocky hills overgrown by the wild olive, the myrtle and the fig tree . .
. and the wild weeds of this climate of flowers bloom under your feet'.[5]

Seventeen years before, even sixteen, the first thing Kinsey would
have noticed would have been the botany of wherever he went, his little
lectures then would, too, have been on the myrtle and wild olive. Now,
sex had become the measure of all things, his yardstick, his lodestone.

He is not the first person by any means to have been so taken over
by their vocation, nor, of course, was he incapable of other reactions to
other things – he was soon to spend what he described as 'two solid days'
in the Prado in Madrid. But when he went into a gallery, what absorbed
him most was how the paintings reflected or indicated sexual behaviour,
when he went to the theatre the possible (or actual) sex lives of the actors
were more interesting than the play. Sex was the only thing he really
wanted to talk about, sex was his way of judging people and his way of
getting to know them – and so it was with everything: books, art, laws,
politics, countries, cultures – as we can see soon in Naples, to where on
8 November Kinsey and Mac took the train south.

3

Kenneth Anger stayed a day or two in Naples and then went south to Sicily. Mac had taken him aside and told him how worried she was that Kinsey was pushing himself too hard, and Anger was aware of Kinsey's deep underlying weariness. He did take a sort of vague care. In hotels he continued to ask for rooms 'nearest the elevator', and when there was a suggestion of Pompeii – in the heat, lots of walking – he said, 'I prefer to spend my energy on the living.'[6]

Kinsey had not been in Naples long, when the mayor sent 'his top man' and offered him every facility (just as in Rome, Alberto Moravia had sought Kinsey out to talk 'for several hours' about Moravia's plans to do his own sex survey). Kinsey at once asked the mayor if he could gather sex material. 'Of course.'

His plan to carry on sex research, which is what it amounted to, was much facilitated by his second guide in Naples. This was R.J., the highly active homosexual businessman who had been sending copious accounts to Bloomington from all over the world – Europe, North Africa, Russia, India, South America – since 1948. (Many of Kinsey's observations about Italy he took from his guides R.J. and Kenneth Anger.)[7]

R.J. stayed, as Anger had, in the same hotel as Kinsey. It was the first time they had met, though they had exchanged over a hundred letters. 'He was able at once to eliminate all barriers – a charming man. After five minutes we were into sexual topics – Mrs Kinsey was there. It was obvious she was completely familiar with it all. She was rather a motherly figure to him, not possessive.'[8]

And now, as in a mini-*Report*, Kinsey explored the cultural background and conditioning. Italy was a totally male-dominated society. He looked hard for resentment, but found Italian women were proud of the dominance of their men (the only resentment he found was among 'American females' living in Italy). The pride extended to their men's large genitals, for which trousers were specially cut to accommodate the largeness – or simulate it. He thought possibly the genitalia *were* large. 'We have no average yet.'

The root of Italian sexual freedom lay, he saw at once, in the adoring parents' permissiveness towards their children. As he picked his way through the narrow, smelly, noisy slum streets he noticed the kissing and cuddling. They were propositioned the whole time. 'When a woman makes a pick-up she takes him home to their one-room home and if the husband is asleep she would root him out and the children may stay around but also anybody passing could also watch.' And here, somewhat belatedly, he comments on the poverty which one feels was a considerable element in all these Hogarthian scenes.

R.J. showed him a few brothels but 'girls were not on his program so much – that is to say, I was not the right guide'.[9] Mac did not accompany them as they pursued homosexuals, setting out at 9 o'clock and returning between 12.30 and 1.30 a.m.[10]

They went two or three times to the Galleria, a big arcade, four storeys high, wide as a street, with cross passages, shops. This was the Naples Colosseum, where people hunted for sex. Kinsey watched it all – 'a girl completely nude to the waist, had a very thin gauzy shawl which kept slipping off.' As darkness fell he saw at fifty yards 'a rather straight and rather well-groomed boy of about 14 with a gang . . . doing a bit of tussling. Through their thin shorts, no pants, you could see this 14-year-old masturbating.' Dusk, fifty yards – one is suddenly reminded of his letter to his old biology schoolmistress in 1921 recalling his extraordinary sharpness of observation and memory for anything that interested him outside – a flower, an insect.[11]

They explored the toilets. In one, an older man with an erection became quite desperate at Kinsey's lack of assistance. 'I have to come to orgasm! If you are too tired I can see you at 2 a.m.' Kinsey speculated that often it was not poverty, but that they would lower their station if they offered themselves without asking for payment. He thought it was probably an historical carry-over from Greek and Phoenician backgrounds.

In the gloom of another toilet, he watched R.J. at work. ' "R.J. – now you have had five." "No," I said, "four". He was pleased to see I was not the sort to exaggerate.' R.J. didn't seem in the least surprised that Kinsey should stand and watch him fellate or masturbate or whatever he did to these Italian men. (Both Anger and R.J. said, incidentally, that as far as they could see Kinsey was not in the least aroused or involved by anything he saw, nor did he show any preference between homosexual or heterosexual observation.[12])

But one thing that did surprise Kinsey was R.J.'s astonishing ability to pick up almost anyone. 'I of course can always find someone who is willing.' This also fascinated C.A. Tripp, who also came to know R.J. well, and he thought it was because R.J. always brushed their thigh or shoulder at his approach, but R.J. said he hadn't noticed he did this and carefully avoided it – and was still successful.*[13]

On about 14 November, Mac and Kinsey continued south to Palermo, where they met up with Kenneth Anger again. They went to Cefalu to see Aleister Crowley's house and Anger managed to find someone who, as a boy, had spied on the Beast at his exercise.[14] Kinsey's long account, lecture almost, has a journalistic vigour. 'Aleister Crowley,' he begins, 'was physically big, dirty and offensive on that score . . .' It ends, 'Crowley was a drug addict: the doses he took of heroin and cocaine etc., are almost unbelievable and the same is true of the amount of sex he had.' Once again, Kinsey found a picture of open acceptance of sex – especially, traditionally, homosexuality. But they were getting pressed for time. Anger whizzed them across Sicily: 'We passed through the town of Catania on the way to Taormina. All you have to do is to give one look at it and see that it is teeming with sex.'

At Taormina he looked for the Von Glodon photographs of male nudes he had discussed with Monroe Wheeler in 1952.[15] The fascist government had destroyed 7,000 plates, but Kinsey located and bought hundreds that had survived. They saw no erotica – 'When sex is so free you do not have this sort of thing.' Kenneth Anger also managed to find one of the models, now aged seventy, who had posed for Von Gloden, and told them the photographer particularly liked boys and youths with giant genitalia.[16]

The last week-and-a-half of their tour was something of an anti-climax, partly because they lacked an Anger or R.J. or Dingwall to guide

---

* By chance I was witness to this power, undimmed at eighty-three. Driving from the airport, an Arab youth came up to try and wash our windscreen at some lights. R.J. addressed him in Arabic and on the *instant* indifference vanished. The youth chattered volubly. 'I may meet him later,' said R.J. 'I now know where.' 'But can you . . .?' I asked. R.J. said it was true his erections were a bit shaky now – 'But I can still give pleasure.' He was an interesting, amusing, cultivated man, a Dane of distinguished family who had been brought up in Germany. He had joined the German Resistance, been discovered, imprisoned and only escaped execution by the Russian invasion. He lives with his gay, 72-year-old Italian working-class friend and we spent a morning, a lunch (his friend is an amazing cook) and an afternoon talking about Kinsey. R.J. was grateful to him for validating his extraordinarily vigorous sex life and kept meticulous records from 1948 to 1994. I noticed with some amazement, and perhaps envy, on the long graph of his orgasms, that one peak was in 1966 when he was fifty-three, only a few years younger than I was when I saw him – a peak of 515 orgasms that year. Yet the great love of his life had been when he was twelve, his lover a boy of sixteen. He had been looking for such a love ever since and had never found it.

them. In Barcelona, which they reached on 22 November, Kinsey did at least meet Dr Ramon Serrano, with whom he had had a long correspondence, mostly about female masturbation - Dr Serrano's speciality (he had 1,237 case histories).[17]

But the Spaniards under Franco seemed tight-lipped, the men's buttocks were a different shape (an odd thing to notice, one feels – an observation from his gay side), they 'Are a silent, dull, beaten people ... there isn't any doubt they are a church-ridden people.'

After Madrid and the Prado they went on to Portugal, which was even more disappointing. He asked a Lisbon taxi-driver about homosexuality. 'He said there was none in Portugal. Men are men in Portugal.' This dispiriting, if ridiculous information was compounded by the buttocks changing shape again – 'long-waisted, rounded buttocks but low'.

They flew back to New York on 5 December, staying at the Statler Hotel. They had dinner with Glenway and Monroe that night and it seems that Kinsey later telephoned Glenway suggesting he join them for breakfast, which he did before they finally flew back to Bloomington.[18]

23

Death

All deaths are sad except one's own.
Gerald Brenan in a letter to V.S. Pritchett, 14 August 1966

1

When Kinsey returned to work at the end of 1955 it was to a completely different locale. While he and Mac had been in Europe, the ISR offices (including all the gall wasps) had been moved to new quarters on the third floor of Jordan Hall – whose preparation had taken most of 1955.

Much has changed but you can still see how spacious they were, one or two of the many sinks, put in anticipating extensive physiological research, remain, and the glass window is still there in the office guarding the entrance through which Eleanor Roehr could see who came in and grab them before they got to Kinsey next door to her.

It is the only stretch of offices on the third floor whose walls are not steel. They *were* steel, but Bill Dellenback noticed how they resonated and told Kinsey, who insisted that, for interviewing, all offices had to be soundproofed to 90 decibels.[1] At vast expense, the walls were all replaced. But, during Kinsey's first history, every intimate detail was carried loudly into all the other rooms of the complex. All the air-conditioning had to be replaced too.[2]

And 'return to work' should perhaps be qualified. On 9, 10, 12, 16 and 17 December, Kinsey gathered his entire staff and for two or three hours each day gave the account of his travels from which the previous chapter was drawn. But Dorothy Collins said that around April/May 1956 this became a regular pattern and she felt it was because he had by then become too weak to do proper work.[3] At these rambling addresses, where he reminisced about the past, Kinsey often became emotional. It was as if he could no longer contain the pain and pity at all the suffering that had been laid on him. Collins remembered 'the tears pouring out of his eyes' as he talked about the injustice done to a young man incarcerated for eighteen of his twenty-nine years in Chino for some minor sexual 'offence'.[4] This emotion also now entered his letters and his public lectures – Cornelia Christenson describes him addressing an audience at Johns Hopkins with tears running down his cheeks as he told them about a similar case.[5]

As this went on, and as he became more and more paranoid about the attacks on him, the staff, said Paul Gebhard, became demoralised. Some wanted to leave, but realised they must stay. Paul Gebhard was offered a position in Southern Illinois which he felt he had to turn down.[6]

Up till the end of April, Kinsey somehow managed to work nearly as hard as usual. It is true that not much of this was on any of the projected books. He could manage only nineteen draft pages for Chapter 3, nineteen for Chapter 4 and a few pages on religious affiliations for the abortion book.* He did no work at all on the sex offender book.

Meanwhile, Kinsey continued to take histories and gave at least seventeen lectures during the first four months of 1956. He wrote to everyone he had seen in Europe, and carried on his vast general correspondence, often with something of his old vigour.

But his most desperate battle was, still and until the end, to get money.

2

In January and March 1956 Harriet Pilpel and Kinsey were negotiating with Edmond C. Aswell of McGraw-Hill about a plan to publish *all* Kinsey's future work – 'apparently' twenty-four books, including cheap editions, condensations, etc.

---

* These forty-odd pages are written on the back of old sex histories. The Institute's habit then of writing everything, even draft letters, on the back of something else was not just Kinsey's parsimony, which it was, but a hangover from the war, when paper was scarce and expensive. I also found something endearing in the way that, despite their paranoia about confidentiality, the draft abortion pages were partly written on a long list of histories identified by name against their history numbers. On another sheet backing something else I found Kinsey's own history number. It is safe with me.

Regularly now he would sally forth to woo some rich possible benefactor, and return defeated. He revealed further deficiencies in this role,
apart from his inability to ask for money. He was so used to, and so good
at, asking for sex histories that quite often his meetings with the very
rich just resulted in very rich histories. He returned from Havana with a
lot of very rich histories. When he met the famous (and appropriately
named) Philadelphian philanthropist Mrs Bevan A. Pennypacker, his
thank-you letter simply said he hopes soon 'to get your own history'.[7]

Then, rich men like to talk, like to take centre stage and hold it, a
position Kinsey was not good at relinquishing. When the A & P heir,
millionaire Huntington Hartford – a particularly promising catch engineered by C. A. Tripp – was asked down to Bloomington, he arrived
with a bevy of giggling girls, obviously expecting to see eighteenth-
century condoms and the like. Kinsey, appalled, ignored the condoms,
and just gave them the tour, holding forth for two hours. After each of
these failed attempts, said Dorothy Collins, his decline was more
marked, he walked more slowly – 'a sort of sleepy appearance'.[8]

We can witness this ourselves. Driven by anxiety, on 20 March
Kinsey did what he had always sworn never to do – he appeared on
television. He gave an interview to Arlene Francis for her *Home* programme. He moves as if in treacle, very weary, very patient. 'Kinsey:
"We – aaaa – went into this research because we discovered a gap in our
knowledge. And – aaaa – I repeat, it is the history of science that whenever we fill in a – aaaa – gap in the knowledge, mankind, ultimately,
may profit." Interviewer: "Thank you Dr Kinsey." '[9] And one notices,
however automatic it must by now have become, the immense charm
of his smile.

He still, pathetically, clung to the hope that perhaps the Rockefeller
Foundation might relent and in April he wrote to Alan Gregg begging
for help. Gregg, who had retired in 1953 and was in fact to die of cancer
in 1957, wrote a long and sympathetic letter. He had hated the trustees'
reaction. He still believed totally in 'your abilities ... [and] the importance of the investigations you were a pioneer in starting'. As for help,
he couldn't, the Foundation wouldn't, try other trusts. Kinsey's reply
was short and bleak: 'It does encourage us to know that you still have
faith in the sort of thing we have been doing.'[10]

George Corner and the NRC remained loyal, and wrote in April to
say they would give another $3,000 for the abortion study.[11]

Kinsey was on the point of leaving for New York, for more, in this case final, humiliation at the hands of the very rich. He saw Glenway, who repeated what Monroe had said – that wealthy gays would find it easier to bequeath if they didn't have to say 'sex' research.[12] He had another indeterminate dinner with Cummins Catherwood. Then, at the beginning of May, he had an absolutely disastrous dinner party at the Huntington Hartfords.

This, too, had been engineered by Tripp to clinch matters. He made, he said, a great mistake in not going himself. It was precisely the sort of setting Kinsey loathed – candles, being waited on, New York socialite company, social chat. Also, he was very tired. It rapidly became clear the whole subject no longer interested Huntington Hartford at all. Nevertheless, Kinsey ploughed on with his careful, detailed account of what he was doing, why it should be done, what money was needed. Marjorie Hartford, the current wife, seeing how badly it was going, kept saying, 'But honey, what he means is . . .' Finally, bored out of his mind, Huntington Hartford simply turned away and talked to someone else about some other scheme. Kinsey, his face drawn, ended the evening in a state of total exhaustion.[13]

He managed to make it to Glenway. 'He came to me afterwards and almost died in Monroe's apartment!' said Glenway. 'He had the worst heart attack I've ever seen anyone have, turned green and panted, lying in the bed, and I thought he was going to die right then and there. We were pushing the nitroglycerin pills down his throat and eventually he was coming to life again. I was so angry and he was so angry. But that time it was like that and we knew he was going to die and he was very unhappy.'[14]

He was back in Bloomington, via Chicago, by 10 May, but Mac said he never recovered from the Huntington Hartford dinner and its aftermath.[15]

3

From now on, like the stations of the cross, we are aware of Kinsey doing things for the last time. On 24 May he was back in Chicago again and here he took his last two sex histories – numbers 7,984 and 7,985.[16]

Yerkes had died in February; and that same month Mac had finally finished typing Green's Masterwork and her typescript was bound in board and cloth. On 1 May George Corner wrote his last letter to Kinsey suggesting someone who might join his staff.[17]

Preparations were already underway for a reunion with all his first graduate students, and he was clearly thinking about Ralph Voris again. On 11 May, after a gap of fifteen years, he wrote his last letter to Jerry, Voris' wife, telling her that Ralph's staphylinid collection had been taken by the State Natural History Survey Division at Illinois.[18]

Letters still streamed in and out on all his old topics; Kinsey's still sharp, unaware that this was his final word. 'In regard to your remark about vaginal orgasm,' he told a Mr George Norton, 'your comment is, frankly, reminiscent of the philosophers who were still insisting that the world was flat in a bygone day.'[19]

One of the saddest documents of these last months is *The Right to Do Sex Research*, found among his papers after he had died. It is a long, rather rambling *cri de coeur* in which, in despair, he rails against 'the multiplicity of forces which have operated to dissuade the scientist, to intimidate the scientist, and to force him to cease research in these [sexual] areas'. And *still* he harps on the agony of frustration suffered by teenage boys and young men 'and fifteen per cent of teenage girls' by denying them a legitimate sexual outlet – his old agony, the major root of his work.[20]

4

The summer that year in Indiana was particularly ferocious, and on 1 June Kinsey had another small heart attack and went into hospital.

He spent most of June in bed, and the steady worsening of his condition put paid to another scheme of making money – journalism. In its way, it was as desperate an attempt as his television appearance. He wrote to *Woman's Home Companion* (where Albert Deutsch placed his articles): 'Let me try my hand at writing for your sort of audience.' His idea was a piece on the significance of early attitudes to sex. The *Companion* was delighted and offered $5,000.[21] But this, and a proposal from *Time* that he write their music column,[22] fell through because he was not well enough.

He did manage to get up for the dedication of Jordan Hall on 7 June. It was a sentimental occasion because his favourite old pupils were there – Herman Spieth, Breland and Bugbee. Kinsey and Mac gave a 6 o'clock supper for them in the overgrown garden of First Street. When they'd left, Spieth wrote hoping, 'you have gotten some rest'. They must all have been worried.[23]

Kinsey was still spending a lot of time in bed when Albert Shadle came at the end of the month. The extent to which he had liberated the little zoologist can be measured by the fact he had now burst free from his porcupines and was filming coitus in dogs, guinea pigs and rats; also by the way he had suggested a two-*month* visit. He stayed a week, seeing little of Kinsey and working in the library.

However, Shadle did meet Wescott, who came from 22 to 24 June, mostly to continue his work with Paul Gebhard. Glenway talked intimately with Kinsey, mostly it seems about the moral aims and implications of Kinsey's work. He found Kinsey 'severe and sad', but, he told his biographer Jerry Rosco, 'we were very, very close'.[24]

By July, as though taking wing again at last to leave their master, some of his gall wasps left to go to the Carnegie Museum in Pittsburgh.[25]

In July, also, he finally consented to some primitive air-conditioning in his bedroom to combat the fierce summer heat.[26]

And still Kinsey fought on. He was once again, he told Harriet Pilpel, managing four or five hours a day, by dint of two or three hours' work, then two hours sleeping on the office bed, then a further two hours' work.

On 7 July he gave his last lecture. Henry Remak still remembers it. It was to biology teachers on how to teach sex in high schools. He spoke noteless and 'it was well nigh somnambulist perfection'. His replies and retorts were brief and pungent.[27]

At the end of July, Edward Aswell stayed two days. He had left the publishers McGraw-Hill and was now pursuing Kinsey on behalf of Doubleday. He was a friend of Glenway's and later described the visit to him. Kinsey showed him round Jordan Hall with pride. As they went down a corridor of photographs, Kinsey said, 'These are the people who have given me the greatest help.'*

'An hour or so later, after the tour of inspection was over, Kinsey took me back to his office. He had obviously overtired himself. Slowly he folded his hands behind his head as if to support the weight of it, and leaned back and half closed his eyes. 'So you know Glenway do you?' he said in a musing sort of way. 'How well do you know him?'

---

* Today, in the Kinsey Institute, you pass exactly the same photographs: Herman Wells, Karl Lashley, Robert Laidlaw, Emily Mudd, Monroe Wheeler, Glenway Wescott, various staff line-ups . . .

A difficult question. Aswell knew him well enough to answer it and they discussed Glenway – Kinsey 'with admiration and affection'.

Aswell said he could see that Kinsey realised he was dying. 'He repeated several times, "I have managed things so this work will go on no matter what happens to me".'[28]

Yet did he realise it? There is doubt in that statement. To most people he spoke with total confidence of his recovery. He told Harriet Pilpel he'd got his heart under control again. To a friend in Tulsa, 'I shall prove to them, as I have in the past 30 years, that you can do more with a physical handicap than they sometimes think.' To Frances Shields he said he'd lost 16 pounds and talked of 'permanent improvement'.[29]

Yet his June visit to the hospital had shown that – like Ralph Voris years before – his heart was dangerously enlarged, his pulse wildly erratic, and, with the primitive diuretics of the day, he had serious water retention problems. His doctors continually told him he would die if he didn't let up.

A part of Kinsey seemed bent on suicide. Certainly, Mac sometimes felt that.

5

Herman Wells remembered how, at this time – late July, early August – Kinsey had forced himself out of bed and made Mac take him in the summer heat to see some man at IU about money. Wells was passing as Kinsey started to drag himself up the stairs. 'Mrs Kinsey said to me, "You've got to help me stop him." 'I said, "I can't stop him, but he's got to stop himself, otherwise he'll kill himself." Mrs Kinsey said, "That's what he's doing." '[30]

Kinsey told several people that if he couldn't work he'd rather die, among them Harriet Pilpel and Theodore Torrey.[31] Yet at the same time almost to the end (he dictated his last letter on 17 August) he was arranging letters and visits far into 1956 and 1957.

To die, to refuse to die and prove those authority-figure doctors wrong, to recover and work again, to pretend none of it is happening – contradictory and conflicting reactions are common close to death.[32] A sort of franticness took hold of Kinsey near the end.

On 14 August – the temperature now regularly soaring to 105°F – he insisted on being taken to a meeting at Purdue of the National Deans

Association. He also became as desperate about what they were spending as about how they were to be funded. In May he had written to John Wise, a New York art dealer, saying he thought the Customs case would cost them $30,000 before it was over.[33]

This had been rumbling on for years, and by 4 June Treasury Department dilatoriness decided Harriet Pilpel that private libel action was the only solution.[34] IU was fighting alongside Kinsey, and about the 18th of August Wells called a meeting at IU with the leading Indiana law firm of Barnes, Hickam, Pantzer and Boyd. He thought they should look round the collections at Jordan Hall to see the sort of thing they were dealing with. Kinsey was meant to be there but was too ill. Suddenly the telephone rang. It was Kinsey. He said they must come to his house at once. The senior partner, a younger partner and Wells went to First Street.

'We went over,' said Wells, 'and went into – he was in bed, propped up. Having trouble breathing. His heart was failing, of course. And he started discoursing on this case with all the intensity that he had. This was an intensity which was unbelievable. He would grow so emotionally and intellectually tense that he was unbelievable really.' Kinsey set out the importance of the case, how they must co-operate with Harriet Pilpel and so on.

'I called Mrs Kinsey outside,' said Wells, 'and said, "He is just consuming himself, can't we get this stopped? Can't we break this off?" She said, "No, it is impossible to do it. He went to Purdue last week when he shouldn't have and there is nothing you or I can do. He is just – this is his obsession." '[35]

The final act was precipitated, ironically, by Kinsey's trying to renew the lifelines that had kept him going before. Lying in bed, he had just begun a new catalogue of his records. Then, in his brief moments up, he struggled to do some work in the garden. 'He knocked his ankle,' said his daughter Anne Call, 'a bad bruise and a clot broke free. His specialist was away and the substitute doctor failed to spot it.'[36]

On Wednesday 22 August he suddenly worsened and was taken into hospital. On Thursday, Anne arrived. It was on this night that for the first and only time Mac, that stoical woman whose loyalty to him had been like steel, broke down and wept publicly, so terrible did her husband look near death.

Clear now, to them all, to Kinsey himself, that he was dying, Mac sent for Bruce. Anne was in a precarious stage of pregnancy and on

Friday it was felt that to see him would be too upsetting. Bruce had still not arrived. But Joan had a long, calm talk with him that Friday afternoon about how she could best help the family. That night, Kinsey was put into an oxygen tent. He died at 8 a.m. the next morning, Saturday, 25 August.

The funeral was on Monday. Pallbearers were Bruce and his second son, Dick, and 'the boys' – Bill Dellenback, Clyde Martin, Wardell Pomeroy and Paul Gebhard. (Kinsey's last words to Gebhard as he was being carried away to hospital had been, 'Don't do anything till I get back.')[37]

Theodore Torrey gave the funeral oration – 'It wasn't the easiest task I've ever performed I might add' – and they read Kinsey's address to the prisoners of San Quentin. It is about sex offences and about his gratitude to the prisoners. Robert Laidlaw came, on crutches and wheelchair (he had had polio). And Glenway was there. 'My heart,' he told Gebhard later, 'so full and heavy.' It was the summer holiday and most of IU was away so there were fewer people than there might have been.

Mac asked people not to send flowers but instead money to the Institute for Sex Research.[38]

24

Conclusions

Because our intellectual habits – our habits of belief, and our habits of thought – are, no less than our muscular habits, physically encoded in complex patterns of interconnecting neuronal groups within the brain, patterns which become stronger each time they are used, it is extremely difficult for us to unthink our orthodox assumptions and to rethink old problems in terms of radically new categories and assumptions. Unlearning cultural responses, orthodoxies and theories to which we have been habituated since the cradle is something which comes no more naturally than dancing the fox-trot backwards or systematically inverting the word-order of every sentence that we speak.

Richard Webster, *Why Freud Was Wrong,* p. 498

1

Kinsey died a bitter man who, while disguising it, was almost, in the words of Dr. C. A. Tripp, 'crushed by disappointment'. He was fearful his Institute would founder, certain that his last and best book had not been properly recognised, or even, often, read by his fellow scientists. The forces of repression and prudery had triumphed.

So – what came after? Had he in the end achieved anything at all?

Kinsey's Institute survived, eventually, after twenty-five-odd years, *as* the Kinsey Institute. The NRC remained loyal – $4,000 in 1957 for a pregnancy study, $5,000 in 1958 and 1959.[1] Hugh Heffner, who regarded the *Female* report as the foundation of his 'philosophy',[2] gave money. But the main reason was that Paul Gebhard decided very soon that they had to accept government funding. The National Institute for Mental Health gave a series of grants – and saved them.[3]

Gebhard decided. The succession was fraught. Kinsey had agonised over it for several months. He'd discussed it with C. A. Tripp and Tripp said his preference was plainly for Wardell Pomeroy, except... Except, said Dorothy Collins, with whom he also discussed it, although Pomeroy was a brilliant interviewer, was he steady enough? Joan felt her father had fixed on Gebhard. In the end, Kinsey couldn't face it and did nothing.[4]

The decisive figure now became Eleanor Roehr, long irritated by the ebullient Pomeroy. On Kinsey's death, Gebhard and Pomeroy announced a joint leadership. Immediately, Roehr hurried to Herman Wells and told him Kinsey had made it quite clear to her that Pomeroy was not at all suitable, not a scholar, not scrupulous about getting sufficient back-up data. Gebhard – the scholar – was Kinsey's clear and definite choice. Thus it transpired. IU reversed the joint leadership and Gebhard took the crown. Soon after that Eleanor Roehr left. 'I did not feel that Wardell, particularly,' she said, 'would have agreed to my becoming a full member of the Institute.'[5] But by then she'd done for Wardell.*

The team had always had mixed, wildly veering feelings about Kinsey: loyalty, exasperation, hate, admiration – 'and, yes, fond feelings', said Gebhard.[6] There was certainly some apprehension once the iron fist in its iron glove had gone – but also elation, relaxation, and peace. Above all relaxation. Vincent Nowlis knew 'a very fine anthropologist from the University of Washington – Jennifer Innes – and she said, 'Vincent, you worked with this Kinsey. After his death I attended one of their regular workshops and it was the most openly free set of sexual behaviours encouraged among the participants I've ever encountered.'[7]

Relaxed or not, valuable work was done. Freed from his shackles, Gebhard was able to explore the psychological and sociological elements in sexuality he had often felt Kinsey too much ignored. And gradually some of the books Kinsey had promised appeared: *Pregnancy,*

---

* Wells, incidentally, had no recollection of his meeting with Eleanor Roehr when he was interviewed just before he was seventy by James Jones. But there seems no reason to doubt her account, except to note that it is odd Kinsey was not emphatically anti-Pomeroy to anyone else at all. Perhaps that is why Roehr put an embargo on this part of her interview for twenty-five years – an embargo which ended in 1996.

Birth and Abortion in 1958, *Sex Offenders* in 1965, *Studies in Erotic Art* in 1970. In all, by 1972, six complete books using Kinsey data had appeared and over fifty articles and studies in professional journals.[8]

The books don't perhaps have the *éclat* of Kinsey's work; deliberately, according to Gebhard. Thus *Erotic Art* is not the great overarching vision glimpsed by Kinsey and Avinoff. It is a series of monographs on Picasso, ancient Greece, Rome, Japan, the Renaissance, Peru (by Gebhard) etc.; but it is a lavish, well-illustrated book.

Then the defects of Kinsey's work can sometimes be detected. In the *Sex Offenders* book, for instance, what one chiefly notices is that the sexual behaviour, aside from their offences, of the offenders is much the same as everyone else. Despite this, and largely because of additional work by Gebhard and his associates, it made valuable discoveries, especially as regards sex offences with minors. The *Abortion* book was the first serious scientific blow in the long battle to get sane abortion laws in America – a battle that continues. All the books were well-received and are still cited.

The books and studies are also a complete vindication of Kinsey's 'reservoir' method. Collect a large and deep enough reservoir of material and use will be found for it. The *Male* and *Female* volumes had only used about 10 per cent of the data he had collected. The other 90 per cent is still being used today. It is used either because it can provide a baseline, and/or information in sufficient quantity, which can be found nowhere else.

Take Dr Charles Peek, at the Department of Sociology, Texas Technical University. As a result of AIDS he needed to see if multiple partnership sex had altered between 1939–43 and 1989–93. 'We *had* to use Kinsey data to establish a baseline.' (Result – it had altered; for example, women are now having as many extra partners as men.)[9]

Dr Ray Blanchard, at the Clarke Institute of Psychiatry in Toronto, tested a hypothesis quite often advanced, based on small samples, that homosexuality and left-handedness are associated. Using Kinsey's much larger unused data Blanchard found there was no difference. He also did a more extensive and significant study testing for other variables associated with homosexuality.[10]

Dozens of other examples could be adduced. Since e-mail, the use of the Kinsey data has soared. While I was in Bloomington in 1995, Tom Albright, in charge of computerisation and all data storage, retrieval and analysis, was receiving about four requests a month.

Gebhard put the data on cards in the 1960s and then on tape.*
Currently it is being transferred to disk. The Kinsey Institute also has
a worldwide web site (http://www.indiana.edu/~kinsey/).

Kinsey's institute survived, and survives. What of the more peripheral matters and people we have followed?

2

The Customs case was decided in 1957. On 8 November 1956, Harriet
Pilpel issued a libel writ against the Treasury Department in the names
of Mrs Alfred Kinsey and IU. The case came before Judge Edmond L.
Palmieri on 15 July 1957 and resulted in complete victory for the plain-
tiffs – the ban on pornography did not apply to material collected for
bona fide scientific and scholarly research.[11]

Harriet Pilpel, who had been as emotionally involved as Kinsey, saw
to it that her firm's fees were halved. She later went on to become prominent in civil liberties and First Amendment cases.

Chests of musty gall wasps were still cumbering the cellars of First
Street in 1971, when Frank Beach gave Mac the name of a man at the
American Museum of Natural History in New York. The millions of
specimens were eventually deposited there.[12]

The other of Kinsey's collections – books, artefacts, pictures, etc. –
which, though supposed to be peripheral, quite often became central, is
now easily the largest conglomeration of erotica in the world. Leaving
aside the library (also the largest and certainly the best of its sort in the
world), it was, in 1995, housed (crammed is a better word) in three
moderate-sized rooms. The display room: with glass cabinets holding
statuettes from West Africa, objects from Pompeii and ancient Peru, a
medieval chastity belt, etc., and paintings, etchings and drawings well-

* Not without difficulties. Mary G. Winther, who joined a month before
Kinsey died, was in charge of the transfer of histories from sheets to cards, an
enormous task. 'We employed a Mrs M. She'd read *Male* and *Female* and thought
they were just *great*.' Mrs M had to learn the code to effect transfer. Now she
discovered homosexuals. 'Somehow she'd missed these in her perusals.' She was
appalled. Next she discovered homosexuals in the Navy, figures not used in the
Male. She was even more appalled because her son was in the Navy. She began to
crack up. 'I had to let her go,' said Mary Winther. 'She was upsetting everybody
with her psychological problems over it.' (Winther, in interview with Jones, 11
March 1971.)

lit and carefully hung – Renoir, Picasso, Matisse, Paul Cadmus, Chagall, Tassaert... A second room is full of locked cabinets with 45,000 photographs neatly boxed and catalogued (in code) as to physical positions, sexual act, aspect, etc.; a further 30,000 still unprocessed.

In the third room, it is almost impossible to squeeze between the shelves and tall, steel, green Berger cabinets themselves all jam-packed with every conceivable erotic artifact: charming, tiny, often exquisitely made couples copulating (one, a 1½″ cunnilingus); dildos of every size, shape and colour (somewhere among them Glenway's two); condoms in condom-shaped vacuum flasks, one (Dingwall's) in its original eighteenth-century wrapper; phalluses; statues; statuettes from every country and period; erotic toys (a delightful one from which, when opened, a cockerel springs out and mounts a hen); books with lascivious scenes on the inside or in secret panels; masturbating machines; Japanese and Chinese erotic scrolls and paintings, with great, wrinkled genitalia and twinings of indescribable intricacy. There are stacks upon stacks of elegant late eighteenth-century and nineteenth-century erotic paintings and etchings (coloured), often nineteenth-century French. There are fifty-five boxes of prison 'art', crude cartoons and comic strip narratives of desperate wish-fulfilment.

On the one hand, you have the feeling that Kinsey's collecting mania finally got completely out of control, an indiscriminate grabbing of everything to create another of his huge reservoirs. The photographic collection, mostly gathered in the '50s and '60s, especially seems to have no direction whatever (which does not mean there are not many beautiful photographs, and also very odd ones. 'Who,' asked James Crump, at one time curator of photographs, of a scene snapped in the 1880s, 'are the dapper gentlemen in tweed, one masturbating the other as they stand together upright in a field?'[13]) But Tod Smith, curator for several years, felt that as regards paintings and drawings, of necessity limited to representation, Kinsey showed a real feeling for art and chose with skill and taste.[14]

And in a material sense, the collection is in one way the most successful of Kinsey's enterprises. As I write, it is about to be valued for insurance, estimates varying between $20 and $40 million.[15] If we include the library, probably the upper end of those figures.

It is valuable, and possibly that is what lies behind the paranoia that continues to hang about the Kinsey Institute like a miasma. Every room is locked, every outside door barred, as if erotica and pornography were hard drugs. The cleaning 'female', who in her innocence is allowed everywhere, comes with a vast bunch of keys swinging at her belt like a medieval gaoler. *All* the senior figures clank about with these enormous bunches of keys jingling and clinking. The most junior, on the other hand, biographical researchers for example, wait for tens of minutes, or longer, to be let in or to pass, briefly, into some inner sanctum. But, of course, erotica and pornography are not hard drugs. It is William Masters' dictum about the effects of sex research on its practitioners, still as true today as when he made it.*

Two of those past practitioners, sex researchers emeriti, you occasionally meet in the corridors – Paul Gebhard and Bill Dellenback. It is, of course, absurd to call such figures peripheral. But, just as Napoleon's marshals have been eclipsed by the dominance of their master, so, unfairly, is it here.

Paul Gebhard remained in charge of the Kinsey Institute till the early 1980s, doing the work sketched above. Pomeroy, understandably disappointed, left in 1963 to become a psychotherapist in New York. He also published two successful books, again ghost-written by his friend John Tebbel. Clyde Martin, who had clearly found it difficult with erstwhile colleagues above him, resigned in 1960, took a PhD at Johns Hopkins, and continued a career in research.[16] (Interestingly, all three made the extraordinary interviewing technique learnt from Kinsey the centre of their work.) Dellenback became, and still is, a successful photographer.

Herman Wells was still alive and sharp, if rather immobile, at ninety-three in 1995, an *éminence énorme* of the university whose reputation and future were so much enhanced by his courageous and cleverly manoeuvred stand on Kinsey.

Glenway Wescott and Monroe Wheeler continued to live together, squabbling, gossiping, travelling, partying into their eighties. In 1986 a new edition of Wescott's best book, *The Grandmothers*, came out. He died at home on 22 February 1987, two months before his eighty-sixth birthday. Eighteen months later Wheeler died in New York. The Museum of Modern Art has dedicated a reading room to him.[17]

---

* Masters once said that it was impossible to work in sex research for twenty-five years and not become paranoid. Taking Kinsey's eighteen years and their own forty-two years, the Kinsey Institute has now had sixty years to become paranoid. (*Ethical Issues in Sex Therapy and Research*, Vol. 1, Boston, 1977)

Kinsey's daughters are still alive and as well as can be expected of people in their seventies. But when I returned to Bloomington it was clear they were considerably shattered by the still recent revelations about their parents' private lives. It was a different age then and Kinsey must have expected these would remain private. We today know better. I wished he and Mac had found some way, even posthumously, to let their children know.

As for Mac, it is, naturally, also absurd to call her peripheral. Yet one cannot help feeling that she had had increasingly little real marriage during the last sixteen or seventeen years. It had been consumed by Kinsey's crusade just as, eventually, it had consumed him. Some years after he died she said the hardest thing to get used to had been 'being alone a lot'.[18]

Mac had bent her life to Kinsey's wherever and whenever needed, but she had not sacrificed herself to it. She had a strong will, could have a sharp tongue, had had to build an independent life and continued to live it – her family, birds, scout troops, hiking groups, summer camps and swimming expeditions. 'But she definitely expanded after he died,' said her daughter Anne, 'collecting antiques, for instance, and so on.' Whether she had enjoyed her forays on to the wilder shores of behaviour, as Earle Marsh says, or had been manoeuvred into them as Gebhard felt, she had shown considerable spirit. The forays now came to an end (as far as we know) and she joined, for the remainder of her life, the conventional ranks of Bloomington widows. As she grew older, she became mildly eccentric. In old age, she would stand in the garden in her dressing gown watching the traffic pass, and hurl pans of water at cats to save the birds. She dropped dead in her living room after taking a shower on 30 April 1982. She was eighty-three.

3

Kinsey is, of course, assured of immortality – the great family of Kinsey galls has seen to that: Apache Kinsey, Avida Kinsey, Anceps Kinsey, Alrifolii Kinsey and the rest of them. (At least in a small way and for as long as man remains interested in North American gall wasps.)

But two things make it, in the first instance, difficult, in the second nearly impossible, to assess precisely Kinsey's long-term achievements.

The first reason was put neatly by Miriam Hecht: 'It's like seeing a movie you've been told is seminal, changed all movies, but you've seen so many of these other movies by then that the first one seems old hat.'[19] Many of the things Kinsey tried to bring about have become part of the climate, conventions of good sense and, his battles won, his part in them is forgotten, by social histories, by ordinary people. Few people under forty have ever heard of Kinsey, even at IU and in Bloomington.[20]

Which leads to the second difficulty. Kinsey needn't have worried – he was on the winning side. The liberal revolution of the last half of the twentieth century has been a result of deep forces acting upon and moving in our culture, affecting everything, but perhaps especially sexual behaviour. All one can say is that it is hard to think of any *individual* who had more influence than Kinsey here.

We have covered most of the areas during the course of the book but, as it ends, a very brief, not so much résumé as short discussion is warranted.

Some idea of what Kinsey did can be gained if you imagine what a difference to how many millions of lives it would have made if, by a miracle, his books had come out in 1848 and 1853. Even in 1948, you only have to read some of the 40,000–50,000[21] letters of his correspondence to see what enormous relief to many thousands of people he provided with his simple information – that masturbating was harmless, that homosexuality and homosexual acts were common, that vaginal orgasm was rubbish, that wanting a lot or having very little sex was normal – this deeply humane man, easily moved to pity, personally affected. And it spread out in waves of alleviation, as his correspondents spoke to other people, as his books came out, as their contents were reported. Unlike his predecessors, Kinsey reached the masses.

No doubt Kinsey was influential in bringing about plainer speaking. So were, for example, Henry Miller and D.H. Lawrence. This was an aspect, as we saw, of the modernist movement. But the *New York Times* did not dare use the word penis till the mid-1960s, shortly before Kenneth Tynan created uproar saying fuck on the BBC. Speaking about 1967, when his *The Naked Ape* appeared, Desmond Morris boasted recently, 'If you read about sex before *The Naked Ape* all you find are these euphemisms, like "member" for "penis" ... I thought: "To hell with it: I'm going to tell it like it is." '[22] In 1996, Steve Jameson, a lecturer at the Maudsley, said, 'Until quite recently, talking about sex was taboo.'[23] The tides of embarrassment, prudery and concealment continually reform and surge back. Kinseys, it seems, have as often to reappear.

Once something has happened, it is easy to look back and say – of course, it had to happen. Indeed, it often seems impossible to do anything else. The social forces of which Kinsey was a part also made someone like him seem inevitable.* As Frank Beach pointed out in 1971, William Masters had already started to plan his work in the 1940s, before he knew anything about Kinsey.

I think this is a dubious argument, at any level, from the NRC upwards. Masters' work, fine as it was, was very different from Kinsey's; it was small-scale and on a narrow physiological front, and to a considerable extent therapeutic in *response* to sexual goals, particularly among the ageing, which derived from the social climate Kinsey had helped to create.

Then, would a different Kinsey have had the desire to raise up and then the courage to brave the firestorms of publicity? Would he or she have invented as effective an interviewing technique? Would he or she have had Kinsey's maniacal collector's passion or the obsessive energy

---

* It is a diversion, but I'd like to look briefly at one force sometimes put forward, since it too makes a Kinsey inevitable. The argument is essentially Marxist and in two stages. First, industrial capitalism's explosive rise in the nineteenth century required from its driving class delayed gratification and financial frugality, so that (a) it had time for capitalist enterprise and (b) the money saved could be invested as capital. Thrift in semen is analogous to thrift with money – by denying sex till late, society released forces, which sex would have consumed, to create wealth. Stage two is the result of overproduction. Now the emphasis is on consumption, leading to pursuit of gratification by purchase of goods and pleasures and, again by analogy, sexual freedom. The dialectic of materialism therefore requires a Kinsey. Perhaps there is truth here, but I am always suspicious when analogy and theory take over from evidence. Sexual abstinence is not the same as thrift; sex does not take much energy or necessarily money (marriage – a religious institution – takes money, but that is different). Steven Marcus has shown that Victorian England was far less chaste than supposed – and England is important in this context since capitalism started here in the sixteenth and seventeenth centuries and was roaring by the eighteenth century. If the rise of capitalism had such profound effects on sexual behaviour, why did it not show up in England? Lawrence Stone has demonstrated that in England in the 'driving class' there were waves of sexual liberalisation in the sixteenth and eighteenth centuries and repression in the seventeenth and nineteenth centuries and that these coincided with the fall and rise of evangelical religious influences. Kinsey also found that religion was by far the most powerful cultural force operating on sexual attitudes and behaviour. If one has to choose a social force, I would prefer the fluctuations in the aims and power of organised religion. (The Marxist case is well put by Regina M. Morantz (1977, 1983) and see Steven Marcus (1970) and Lawrence Stone (1977).)

to drive it through? Would he or she have been bisexual? I think the answer to all these questions is no, except the last where the answer is, who knows? Far more likely would have been a series of *small-scale*, increasingly efficient, surveys, resulting in minimum publicity, probably surveys of college students, using the questionnaire and thus getting totally inadequate and/or untruthful answers – especially in the homosexual, as Kinsey would have put it.[24] Indeed, we *know* this last to be true from the 1994 surveys.

Which brings us to one place where it is possible to be more precise about Kinsey's influence. My own view is that Kinsey and his team, to their eternal credit, were one of the decisive factors enabling homosexuals to win a measure of tolerance. From the muddling and frankly propagandist presentation of his homosexual figures the one that was fixed on was not 4 per cent but 10 per cent. Despite the moderately significant flaws we looked at, Kinsey's reports became the source of the numbers that society, particularly American society, agreed on when talking about sexuality. One per cent would have been sufficient; 10 per cent was overwhelming. This and his other figures enabled gays in America, sometimes using them rather loosely, to produce some very powerful arguments in the form of slogans. If you took *predominantly* homosexual in both sexes (4s, 5s, 6s on the H scale) you got 20 million potential voters: 'The voting lobby is the world's safest closet.' Every family had gays: 'We *are* your children.' How could 10 per cent be unfit for military service? 'We are everywhere.'[25]

A *measure* of tolerance. Society changes with difficulty and slowly on this, as in most fundamental areas – for reasons partly explained by the epigraph to this chapter. 'I differ from you,' Kinsey had written to a friend in academia, Fowler Harper, in 1946, 'primarily in believing that social changes come very slowly and as a result of greater complicity [sic] of processes than we academic people usually realize'.[26] As regards the short term, the 1950s – the flood tide of conservative defensiveness in the US – Lynn Gorchov has done some very penetrating, detailed and original research, with special reference to the psychiatric community and to political reactions to homosexuality in the military and the civil service. Her conclusion is unequivocal: 'it is clear that Kinsey lost the debate over homosexuality in this country'.[27]

Lost the debate perhaps; but temporarily, and not the war. And certainly not to the same extent as regards sex laws in general, where we re-enter the area where it is not possible to be exact about Kinsey's effect.

It is even harder to be at all precise about Kinsey's effect in Britain, though it was not inconsiderable, especially as Britain seems to follow America in many of its social trends. The latest 1994 survey showed that the British tolerate homosexuality, but still stigmatise it. Gradually, the main institutions are giving way – it looks as if the Church will eventually allow practising gay priests. Even the Army (unlike the US military) is beginning to face up to it. Only ballroom dancing is still holding out.[28]

In America, the situation in general is far more complicated because sex law is largely state law. It is possible to argue that Kinsey was decisive here too. The American Law Institute's *Model Penal Code* of 1955 is virtually a Kinsey document. 'We deem it inappropriate for the government to attempt to control behavior that has no substantial significance except as to the morality of the actor ... It must be recognized, as a practical matter, that in a heterogeneous community such as ours, different individuals and groups have widely divergent views of the seriousness of various moral derelictions.' The *Male* volume, pages 390 and 487, is cited here. At one point, Kinsey is cited six times in twelve pages.[29]

But states did not have to follow this and have been slow in ceasing to regulate private sexual behaviour between adults. One of the first was Illinois in 1961. Many others have done so since, but in 1994 'sodomy' (a catch-all word) was still illegal, with widely differing penalties, in twenty-two states.[30] (Yet this, too, is complicated. These laws are sometimes kept on the statute book for criminals the police can't catch but know to be guilty of other crimes.[31])

It is extraordinary how squeamish establishment America still is about Kinsey. He is totally ignored by the *Dictionary of Scientific Biography* which, in sixteen volumes, sets the seal. There is a single two-word reference, in Volume IV, the entry under his old tutor Lyndon Fernald, about the *Edible Wild Plant* book, written 'with A. C. Kinsey'. Nothing else. No mention in the most recent supplement.[32]

The recent digging up of Kinsey's private life, incidentally, is not going to help him here; yet if moral judgement on personal behaviour is going to be a major yardstick of scientific achievement what do we do about Newton's pathological vindictiveness and possible homosexuality, or the way Jung used, at one time, to keep eight women on the go – to mention just two of dozens?[33]

Bloomington seems equally reluctant to honour its once most famous son. The aim here is the Monroe County Hall of Fame – a brass plaque in a Bloomington shopping mall. Kinsey finally made it in 1994.

Hoagy Carmichael ('In the Cool Cool Cool of the Evening'), at IU in
1929, sailed on to the wall in 1981. He even has a hall named after him,
ironically actually in the Kinsey Institute building.

Even the science which, if he did not start, he certainly established
as a science, is still to some extent stigmatised, at least in America. Vern
Bullough, a veteran figure, has been investigated by the FBI and labelled
a security risk.[34] But only in this sphere is Kinsey given anything like the
honour which is his due.

4

> *I am a [biological] female with a predominantly male gender and social sex*
> *role identity, and I am attracted to males with male gender social sex role*
> *identities. Therefore I consider myself, basically, a gay man.*
>   Eli Coleman, in *Homosexuality/Heterosexuality: Concepts of Sexual*
>   *Orientation*, ed. David P. McWhirter, OUP, 1990

Kinsey's pioneering, often founding, contributions to sex research have
been the subject of earlier chapters. Here I would just like to make some
last glancing comments.

As a result of the long dominance of the psychoanalytic school there
grew up what one might call the Standard Social Science model of
behaviour which has as its base the belief that most of our behaviour and
thought is culturally determined. Biology is almost irrelevant. These
ideas were behind the 1994 US sex survey.

Kinsey was aware of social and cultural determinants of course; most
of the influences on sexual behaviour whose effects he measured were
precisely that – class, religion, education and so on. In the *Female*
volume, he attempted to show that these influences had little or no effect
on women compared to men. He was wrong. *But the proof that he was wrong
lay in his own data.* You can take Kinsey's facts and reinterpret them if you
want to.

The biological base is something measurable and, however mal-
leable, at some quite high point – and for most people – immutable. It is
the essential knowledge without which you cannot properly examine
what the culture is doing. Today, with the genome, a model where
biology is central is once again becoming dominant in its turn. Dr Lewes

Wolpert wrote recently: 'We are born with a much more sophisticated brain function, all programmed by genes, than anyone previously thought. At birth we already have a concept of numbers and relate to human faces in a very definite way.'[35] It would be surprising if this did not at some point start to impinge on human behaviour – indeed with the postulated 'gay gene' (or genes) it already has.

Second, sexual science has been driven over the last twenty-five years or so by feminism, AIDS and, partly as a result of these two, the gay movement. It has also become a branch of journalism and junk publishing.

Freed from the constraints of having to seek the biological behavioural base, already provided with it by Kinsey, sex researchers have been able to go out and explore the complex interactions of biological, psychological and social factors which Kinsey was sometimes accused of avoiding. One great focus has been gender studies – analyses of cultural and psychological masculinity and femininity aside from biological maleness and femaleness (the seminal figure here, if now superseded, has been John Money).

Take Kinsey's 0–6 scale. This is now regarded as something of a blunt instrument, partly because 'masculine' and 'feminine' elements can co-exist in individuals of either biological sex, and partly because there is now a far greater range and subtlety in the description of those 'masculine' and feminine' gender components. The modifications to the scale seem, essentially, to be to make a series of little scales. Thus 1. Behaviour of X; 2. Fantasies; 3. Who X falls in love with; 4. Which sex most attractive, etc. etc. Then take each of these and have another scale for them. Under *1. Behaviour,* have (a) numbers of partners, (b) nature of activity, (c) frequency, (d) number of orgasms, etc.[36] Then these too can be refined.

Say orgasm is refined: 'In a funny way, when two gay people of opposite sexes make it, it's still gay sex.'[37] Indeed, for many lesbian and homosexual male researchers 'the sex act itself is not a fruitful area for study'.[38] So now you get grids, charts, pie charts, diagrams, scales to try and test and measure the infinite variety of men and women.

Or consider Ms Artemis Moonglow, a real person but not a real name in what is in many ways the most perceptive of the essays (this by Noretta Koertge) in the collection I am here following (though I think I would question the strictness of her 'social scripting' approach). Ms Moonglow 'chose to become a lesbian after working for three years in a

battered women's shelter. She experiences varying depths of erotic intimacy with different women at different times, sometimes leading to
orgasm. She denies she ever "has sex", because that is a phallic concept.
For men, the principal organ of pleasure also happens to be the organ of
reproduction and the organ of penetration. But women's genitals (i.e. the
parts principally involved in biological reproduction) have nothing to
do with the bodily sources of their sensuality. And for Artemis, erotic
fulfilment is inhibited by penetration, or feelings of being "had" or
"possessed".[39]

Artemis is now a political, committed, left-of-centre lesbian. There
are more complex characters, also often women – those, for example,
who have long-term, alternating relationships with first a man, then a
woman, while their fantasies alternate too, but in the opposite direction.
Why, Noretta Koertge wonders, as Kinsey wondered before her, is there
not *more* variety, given the infinite possibility? Why so few Moonglows?
Probably because society expects stability, so people don't try. And
people are *inherently* conservative. Yes, but if this is reality, would it not
be simpler to accept it? Noretta would say, but we are after the *real*
reality.

And so on. It would be fascinating to follow and discuss the avenues
of modern sex research, and the commentators thereon, but it would
take us far from Kinsey. What one notes, however, is that it makes nonsense of accusations that Kinsey, given his purpose, was unsubtle in his
approach. For one thing, Moonglows are indeed thin on the ground and
even less extreme figures are not thick (it seems that in 90 per cent of
people gender/sex/identity cohere and conform.[40]) But the main point
here is that analyses of this complexity and subtlety are simply not
applicable to a mass survey. As we've seen, the only time it was tried the
attempt fell flat on its face.

It is clear what has happened. As in all fields – as with Darwin, as
with Freud – after the wide-ranging general thinker and pioneer, the
field expands exponentially into innumerable specialists. But can one
equate Kinsey with such profound figures? Paul Robinson was clear you
could not. I wonder. It is here I would make one last comment.

5

I tried, in Chapter 17, to show that there were other ways of looking at

Kinsey's work: in the context of Greek and Roman views of sexuality, as replacement for religion, as, in Dr. C. A. Tripp's phrase, analyser of 'the factory of affection'. There is still one more dimension to explore.

Since Plato, Western thought has been dominated by his cave and its shadows. Plato's theory was that there was an 'ideal' version of everything in the cave, that is of things in the world, outside it. What we saw were merely shadows of this outside world. Reality consisted in the 'pure', 'the ideal', the 'essence' existing outside. But since the 'essence' was what was real, what was good, it allowed, indeed necessitated, judgement. The *intellectual bias* of essentialist thought tends therefore to intolerance. What is judged near the essence is tolerated, what is not, is not.

But Plato's thought also heavily influenced Christianity, and here a second control element was introduced into Western thought – monotheism. A habit of mind which came to need overarching total theories, a desire to repeat monotheism in every sphere. Intolerance/intellectual monotheism: the potential route to totalitarianism is clear.

Kinsey came into this from a complex and contradictory personal background. On the one hand, he was brought up as a strict Methodist, his whole mind fashioned to overarching, monotheistic systematising; on the other, he was marked by a deep and lasting fury, sharpened by his sexual orientation, against the intolerance and dominance of his father and of his father's religion. He solved the dilemma neatly; by embracing an overarching system, but one that was the intellectual opposite of his father's – the system of Darwin. Darwinian natural selection has as its most fundamental element the variation of species and in species. The *intellectual bias* of infinite variety is towards toleration.

Variety does not imply intellectual chaos; on the contrary, it means particular forms of order and unity. As early as his biological textbook, you'll remember, Kinsey wrote: 'Once in northern Vermont, I killed an insect on a weed stem. I wonder what effect that had on the cost of living in New England? Who knows?'[41] Or, when discussing the splitting of mind from body, he wrote, 'The distinctions can never be sharp, and they probably do not represent reality.'[42]

A number of thinkers, particularly perhaps Isaiah Berlin,[43] have decided that, partly because of the route it opens to totalitarianism, partly because it does not reflect reality, essentialist thought has to give way to pluralist thought – whose overriding idea is that there is no simple answer.

It is this, according to Richard Webster, that characterises post-modernism. He quotes Gilbert Adair: 'Post-modernism is less a genuine doctrine than a ruefully ironic recognition that the doctrinal era has passed.' And the search, Webster goes on, for some intellectually totalitarian theory involves, inevitably, a second strand. 'From Aquinas to Marx, from Plato to Lévi-Strauss' – and certainly including Freud and psychoanalysis – 'our intellectual culture has again and again demonstrated a seeming predilection for global, theory-centred doctrines of human nature in which empirical evidence has been either ignored or eclipsed.'[44]

What Kinsey devoted his life and work to fighting could hardly be better put. The application beyond his sphere is, of course, not explicit in Kinsey; nor is it explicit in Darwin. Both are thus less global thinkers than exemplars, demonstrators; though of the two, Kinsey, with his social reforms, is the more explicit. But I would agree with those who see this opposition – fundamentally between Plato and Darwin – as the most significant intellectual struggle today.

There let us leave Kinsey: social reformer, liberator, pioneer scientist in two totally different and unrelated fields. A much maligned, courageous, difficult and great man; his first three adjectives are self-evident – I do not see why he should be denied the fourth.

Comparative Values of the Dollar and the Pound

T hese figures have been prepared for me by Dolf Mootham from statistics provided, for Britain by the Central Statistical Office; and for America by Professor James Madison of Indiana University, including *Statistical Abstract of the United States*, Washington, DC; 46th edition, 1923, pp. 582, 584; 62nd edition, 1940, pp. 328–9; 116, edition, pp. 479–81, 483. They must be regarded as impressionistic; nevertheless, they give some idea of changing money values during Kinsey's life. The values are calculated from 1998. Thus one dollar in 1900 is worth 19 of today's (1998's) dollars and 12 of today's pounds.

Year	Dollars	Pounds
1900	19	12
1905	18	11
1910	17	11
1915	16	10
1920	8	5
1925	8	6
1930	10	6
1935	12	7
1940	11	7
1945	9	6
1950	7	4
1955	6	3.75
1960	5	3.50

A Short Analysis of Kinsey's Correspondence

This analysis is based on 2,755 letters, comprising the D, S, M, W and about one-quarter of the C letter files at the Kinsey Institute. I did it to test Judith Allen's impression from reading the A file that Kinsey found it easier to respond to male problems than female ones and was therefore more sympathetic to male problems, particularly the problems of younger males. Judith Allen was Head of Women's Studies at IU when I researched there.

I categorised the letters as Kind or Brisk, and I found that a good measure of these was often the number of lines devoted to each correspondent. Using these three measures, Judith Allen's impression is born out, but so marginally and with a small but interesting contradiction that I do not think it is significant. Thus, while the average answer to males is 18.07 lines and that to females is 15.16 lines, there are in contradiction more 'brisk' replies to males than to females (though this could be the Roehr affect – see below).

Categorisation	Male problems	Female problems
Numbers	50	55
Nos. where lines counted	43	50
Kind	43	48
Brisk	7	7

(The point here is that from the start I divided into Kind and Brisk; it was only after 12 letters that I counted lines.)

Average lines	18.07	15.16

Three additional points might be made:

1.   If one excludes Q, U and Z, the 4¼ letters of the alphabet analysed represents 18.47 per cent of the total letters; in fact, probably slightly more since a disproportionate number of names begin with S and W. Although a very large number of letters are missing (I estimate about 5 per cent) this still suggests that Pomeroy's estimate that the correspondence totals 40,000 letters is an exaggeration.

2.   I discovered rather late that from about 1952 Kinsey left an increasing number of routine letters to Eleanor Roehr. Sometimes this included problem letters. Roehr's letters to problems were invariably extremely short, brisk and formulaic. But since she was equally brisk with male or female correspondents this should not overly affect the findings. If anyone else wishes to pursue these matters in the files it is possible to recognise Roehr's letters since they have her initials alone on them ('erg' or 'ERG' or 'e/r') and not her and Kinsey's ACK combined.

3.   Many of the letters are fantastically boring, but many are also fascinating, from a social point of view as well as a sex research one. I think an interesting social-sexual 'Selected Letters' could be compiled from the Kinsey correspondence.

Kinsey's Handwriting

Kinsey had two handwritings. His normal hand (or what would have been normal had he not tried to tidy it up) and the one he used when he wanted to be clear; this was the one he used when demonstrating how he wanted his gall wasp labels written and the style he endeavoured to press on his team. Specimen 1 is an example of the first; specimens 2 and 3 examples of the second.

Opinions vary as to what you can learn from handwriting, but it is interesting to read what two experienced graphologists made of these Kinsey specimens, analyses which I did not have done until after I had completed the first draft of my book.

Renna Nezos: She saw two fundamental things at work in Kinsey; his lack of a close, physical nurturing as a baby and child and his sexuality. The first, which was the strongest, left him emotionally stunted, longing to attract people to him and seeking fame as a substitute for love. In compensation, too, he was excessively self-centred, over-estimated himself and would counter-attack very aggressively if he thought this self-estimate was threatened. There was also a physical narcissism, itself allied to the actor in him, the need to perform.

All this helped compensate and comfort him, but the primary comfort and compensation was sex. He was driven by his sexuality. He had suffered from guilt, but this disappeared and he loosened up too much. All limits went. He tried to rationalise his sexuality but really just lived it. At the point of the handwriting (1929) he was confused sexually.

Other characteristics: dry, ruthless, stubborn, sentimental, more clever than intelligent, in argument he liked to split hairs, a degree of emotional sadism, manipulative, intuitive. Imagination – not artistic but wide-ranging. Able to bluff people – and this gave him pleasure. A complicated man.

(But graphologists never completely agree. The distinguished

DEPARTMENT OF ZOOLOGY
INDIANA UNIVERSITY
BLOOMINGTON, IND.

ALFRED C. KINSEY, Ph.D.
Associate Professor

Sept. 20, 1929.

Dear Ralph Voris — It was a glorious — wasn't it? Now that I have had a chance to rest and try out civilized clothes again I am more than ever sorry broken it we weren't able to keep in the field. I am headed out again into the south and the Ozarks as soon as the God. can be moved. — Many thanks for the good help on the trip. I would mighty much like to use it again on some of the future trips. Your help in training the other boys was fine. It was a hard trip in some ways — but I have no regrets that we didn't plan it otherwise. — We reached Bloomington just at 12 P.M, Sunday. 503 miles makes it from Springfield. The trip ran smoothly, one small puncture at Terra Haute. Between renewing acquaintance with family and entertaining my father who visited for several days — I am still short of sleep — but certain the our work out in the Northwest has put in

I trim than that of 80

Specimen 1

A B C D E F G H I J K L M N O P Q R S T U V W X Y Z

a b c d e f g h i j k l m n o p q r s t u v w x y z

1 2 3 4 4 5 6 7 8 9

6 ⸸ 7

this is an example of the way

Specimen 2

culous prihting he
~~against~~

law + custom
(Non-particip of obsen/
Psycholog inhib suly
Maintain confid
Eg rape us human film
complx. interal Biol. Ψ. soc. dathr
Naccesity use large no.S

Diverse discipl involved
Biol
Medic - var
anthrop
Soc -
Etc.

Public intrst.   Eg. Statistics of
Press relat.   Dollard Meringer
Public + scient obj.
E.g. Psychnyl
e.g. Relig.

eg. Customs case
Fate corporal Case hist std
Diffic do+ rpt obs studies.

Specimen 3

Hungarian practitioner, Klara G. Roman, saw Kinsey's extreme concentration on sex starting much earlier, in youth. C. A. Tripp was for nine years Director of Huntington Hartford's Handwriting Institute. When he showed Roman a specimen of Kinsey's handwriting [blind] in 1948 'she let out a kind of shriek, saying "Never in my life have I seen such a fierce obsession with sex! It is not now, either, it has been there for decades." ')

Rosemary Findlater of Graphology Associates, London: The subject was a powerful personality, taking over and dominating and needing to be the centre of attention. Gifted and resourceful, shining particularly when faced with unforeseen events, when he would create inspired solutions, capable of manipulating others to his own advantage. Intelligent, with high aspirations, and with considerable bonhomie. Attractive in many ways but difficult to live with, because behind this sociability there is a dry heart, without real responsiveness or warmth or much ability to give himself. Craves praise and attention to bolster basic insecurity and uncertainty. Argumentative and aggressive. Seeks excitement and activity and possesses a vital, almost manic energy. Meticulous, with very high standards, great concentration and attention to detail, with a strong need to investigate in depth.

Sexually he would need to dominate and there are signs that he possessed an aggressive sexuality. At the same time there is a contradiction between his strong sensuality and an inner defence – even coldness. His sexual imagination was very fertile and inventive – even to excess. There are signs of possible sadism.

A very complex man. People would be excited and impressed by his charismatic personality, with such a liking for a multiplicity of social contacts, but would be disappointed to find they could not get close to him and that he would have little real sympathy for the predicament of those around him.

Brief Note on Sources

rimary sources: The two main deposits of Kinsey material are located in Indiana University, Bloomington, Indiana. The largest is in the Kinsey Institute and consists of most of his correspondence as a sex researcher, memoranda of telephone calls and meetings, lecture notes, reminiscences of friends and colleagues, taped notes, bookcases of clippings, files, etc., etc. Slightly smaller are the IU Archives, which include Herman Wells' correspondence on behalf of Kinsey, popular Indiana reactions, staff details, and, very useful, financial records – salaries, work records, income tax returns, royalty statements, reports to the NRC and the IU administration, expense sheets, and so on. Glenway Wescott's papers are held in 100 unsorted boxes by the Beinecke Rare Book and Manuscript Library at Yale. Here I relied on the researches of Jerry Rosco.

Institutional sources: These are extensive and, based mostly in Britain, despite seven months' research in America, I was only able to examine personally the Stevens Institute of Technology Archives, Hoboken, New Jersey. I received extensive information by letter and photocopy from the Bowdoin College Archive, Brunswick, Maine. I relied on Lynn Gorchov's searches in the Archives of the National Research Council in Washington, DC, and the Rockefeller Foundation records at North Tarrytown, New York. These institutional sources were used in exemplary fashion, as I indicated, by James Jones in his biography.

Interviews: Oral history, despite its dangers and limitations, is vital to the understanding of Kinsey. Those I found most useful are detailed in the References, but the sources were as follows: 26 interviews conducted under the IU Oral History Project in 1971–2 by James Jones for his PhD and housed (in 1995) in the Lilly Library, Bloomington, Indiana; 18 interviews made available to me by the BBC after their *Kinsey* in the BBC 2 series *Reputations*, which are with the BBC; 34 interviews conducted by me personally, which remain in my possession.

Family archive: After Kinsey and, later, Mac had died the family papers were split equally between Joan Reid, Anne Call and Bruce Kinsey. Of these, Joan Reid allowed me to see a large proportion, though not all, of her share.

The remainder of the primary sources I used, consisting mostly of my very large correspondence, are detailed in the References and the Bibliographies.

Secondary sources: Many of these can be found in the Reference Notes and the Bibliographies. The major ones, the previous biographies of Kinsey, I have dealt with in the Preface.

References

Key

Bib = Bibliography.
K = Kinsey.
A = Author.

Pom = Wardell B. Pomeroy's biography of Kinsey (see bibliography).
Geb = Dr Paul Gebhard.
Martin = Dr Clyde Martin.
Ch = Cornelia V. Christenson's biography of Kinsey (see bibliography).
JB = James Jones' biography of Kinsey (see bibliography).

The date at which interviews took place will be included only the first time.
Int J = Interview with James Jones. I would like to acknowledge the kind permission of the Lilly Library, Indiana University, Bloomington, Indiana to use these interviews.
Int A = Interviews with author.
Tel Int = telephone interview.
Int BBC = Interviews done by the BBC for their film 'Kinsey' in the series *Reputations* in October 1995.
BBC letters = correspondence with the BBC in connection with the above programme.

Mac = Clara Kinsey, Kinsey's wife.
Joan = Mrs Robert M. Reid, Kinsey's second daughter.
Anne = Anne Call, Kinsey's eldest daughter.

IU = Indiana University.
KI = Kinsey Institute.

Letters cited use the initial letter of the correspondents if they are cited immediately; otherwise names are spelt out. All names obtained from Kinsey Institute sources are pseudonyms, and these, and other pseudonymous names, are placed between single quotes in the reference notes.

Books are cited by author's name only and date of edition, see bibliography for full title. Kinsey's works are listed separately.

I have used ibid. and op. cit. rather more freely than is usual, but I think it is always clear. Thus Int cit = Interview already cited.

Male = *Sexual Behavior in the Human Male* (see bibliography).
Female = *Sexual Behavior in the Human Female* (see bibliography).

1 Childhood in Hoboken: 1894–1903

1 Joan, ints A, August–November 1995.
2 Ch, p14.
3 Geb, ints A, July–November 1995. See also Pom, Chap 1. A David Kinsey came from Bristol in 1682, and a Ralph Kinsey said he had property in Pennsylvania in 1682. They could be brothers. A Hugh Kinsey went to America in 1659; another Kinsey was transported there in 1751; a Ben Kinsey went to Maryland in the mid-nineteenth century. At least five separate Kinseys are known to have gone, therefore, and all no doubt started families. There are a number of Kinseys in Scotland and in Ireland but the origin of the name is English, from Kinsey in Bucks and Kilmsea in East Yorkshire. The root of the name is 'King's man' (source: Records at Debretts Peerage in London).
4 Note scribbled by K on the back of an envelope to James T. White & Co. who were compiling a biographical volume. Postmark – 3 January 1951.
5 *The Stute* (Journal of the Stevens Institute), 10 April 1943, vol XXXIX, No. 13.
6 Joan, int A, and JB, p10. Kinsey, who kept very little from his past, kept an ashtray, made in Japan, of the temple in Salt Lake City.
7 Ch, pp15, 16.
8 Details in Chap 1, Ch and Pom and, especially, JB, p777, note 38, plus visits by A.

9 JB, p12.
10 *Encyclopaedia Britannica,* 13th edition, New York & London 1910, 1926, vol 17, p920. JB, p811, note 39 (quoting Lynd, 1954, p251) has a figure of 8,000 for 1900, which compares with the *Encyclopaedia's* 10,576 for 1903. It is possible the Lynds included steam cars, which were popular at first in the US.
11 Pom, p40.
12 Details Pom, Chap 1, and Ch. Credit cards, Geb, int BBC.
13 Mac, taped int; Pom, 1970.
14 Joan, int BBC. See also Ch, Chap 1.
15 See David M. Thompson, ed., 1972. Also

Encyclopaedia Britannica, op. cit., article *Methodism,* sub-head *Methodism in the United States.*
16 A, 1979, p55 (New York, 1978).
17 Anne and Joan, ints A, August–October 1995; BBC October 1995.
18 JB, pp20, 21.
19 Mac, taped int, op. cit.
20 Dorothy Craig Collins, int J, 9 December 1971.
21 Dr Clarence A. Tripp, int A, 28 October 1995.
22 Quotations here from K, 1956, pp27, 28.
23 *Time,* 24 August 1953. Also Ch.
24 Consultation Dr Ian Battye.

2 *South Orange to Bowdoin College: 1903–14*

Any quotations or information not sourced come from Ch, Chaps 1 & 2.
1 A's observation; Bill Gury, tel int A, December 1995.
2 Dr Earle Marsh tape sent to Geb, 25 November 1961. Dr Frank Young, int A, October 1995, Dr Robert Merrill Reid, int A, 15 November 1995.
3 IU's *Daily Student,* 4 December 1937, int K; also Mrs Frank Edmondson, int J, November 1971; Dr Robert Kroc, int A, November 1995.
4 *Time,* 24 August 1953.
5 Bill Gury, int cit.
6 William Parry, tel int A, December 1995.
7 K to Natalie Roeth, February 1921, quoted Ch.
8 Bill Gury, int cit.
9 Ch, p19.
10 Bill Gury, int cit.
11 Ch, p18.
12 Joan, int A cit.
13 Pom. pp155, 156.
14 Edgar Anderson, quoted Ch, p178.
15 Tripp and Martin, ints A. See also Thomas Waugh in Jacqueline Murray, ed., 1993.
16 Kroc, int A cit.
17 *Time,* op. cit.
18 Kinsey, 1926.
19 William Parry, int cit.
20 Family papers in possession of Joan. See also JB, pp52–7. In the interests of biographical knowledge, I spent some fairly nightmarish time under canvas in the scout camp near Bloomington, Indiana in August 1995. The temperature reached 110°F, the humidity was 90%. Rather garbled versions of my presence got around and I became aware that one group of Scouts was clearly

regarding me as an object almost of worship. I learnt later the boys had been told that I had been one of the first Eagle Scouts in America.
21 Michael Kimmel, 1996, p196; JB, p52.
22 Joan, family papers.
23 Ibid.
24 J.A. Woolf, from Pom.
25 Joan, int cit.
26 K to Rice, February 1939, quoted Jones 1972. (See note 4, p. 472.)
27 *Male,* pp303–13; Anne M. Johnson et al., 1994, pp77, 126, 127; Martin, 1975, 1981.
28 Geb, int A, July–October 1995; Pom, int A, September 1995.
29 *Male,* pp220–3, 302–13.
30 I should note here that in January 1998 I showed the world-renowned Greek graphologist, Renna Nezos, a specimen of Kinsey's extraordinary handwriting as it was in 1929. She said that the most fundamental element in his character was not his sexuality – though this was clearly a fundamental engine of his action – but the fact that he had no close *physical* love as baby and child, and that the need for lost love of this sort augmented his need for sexual outlet. There is no way to prove or disprove this analysis, but if true it does help illuminate certain aspects of his behaviour. See Appendix C for examples of Kinsey's handwriting.
31 Glenn Ramsey, April 1943.
32 Geb, int cit. Dr Henry Remak, int A, August 1995. One can also deduce a good deal from K's behaviour with his own children in the way he reacted against all this.
33 Allan M. Brandt, 1985.
34 Geb, int BBC, October 1995.

35 JB, p23.
36 Geb, int A, November 1997.
37 Quoted in Pom, p77.
38 A, 1979/New York 1978, pp156–72.
39 Folsom to K, 15 February 1948, quoted JB, p73; and see JB, pp72–5.
40 Joan, family archive.
41 Anne Call, int A, August 1995.
42 Joan, family archive.
43 Ibid.
44 Pom, p25; JB, pp46, 784, note 18. I see no reason to doubt the Pom account, though the two are not incompatible.
45 Mac, int J, 11 December 1971.
46 Geb, int A; Mac, int J; Pom.
47 Stevens Institute of Technology, Castle Point Station, Hoboken, NJ. I differ slightly from Jones in my assessment here, but that is because Jones only gives Kinsey's first-year marks, not his second. JB, pp90–2, 792, note 23.
48 Joan and Anne, ints A cit.
49 Jim Kinsey, tel int A, November 1995. See also Ch and Pom.
50 Elizabeth Frazier, int A, July 1995.
51 Mac, int J.
52 Tripp, tel int A, 28 October 1995.
53 Foucault, 1979.
54 Joan, int A. Decree No. 36693, Dept. No. 2, filed at the Second Judicial District Court of Nevada, 18 August 1931 and 21 September 1931.
55 Collins, int A.
56 Anne, int A cit.
57 Stevens Alumni Archive; Bowdoin College Library, alumni biographical files.
58 Pom, pp27, 28.

3 College – and First Appearance of the Gall Wasp: 1914–20

For facts or quotations not sourced in this chapter see Ch, Chap 2, pp25–39.

1   Bowdoin College Library, alumni files. See also, for example, K to R.L. Dickinson, 25 June 1941.
2   Joan, int A.
3   Anne, int A, August 1995.
4   Larry Lockridge, 1994, p98.
5   JB, p121.
6   Niven to Geb, 22 December 1961.
7   W. Norton to Geb, 13 December 1961.
8   Family archive, Joan.
9   Pom, p188; Tripp, tel int A, 28 October 1995.
10 Mac, int J, December 1971.
11 Family archive, Joan.
12 Pom, p28; JB, pp118, 119.
13 Bowdoin College Library, alumni files cit, esp. Dean Paul Nixon to K, 21 February 1945.
14 Commencement Address at Bowdoin College by ACK, June 1916. Alumni files cit.
15 Notes Edgar Anderson, 'Kinseyiana' file, KI.
16 Ibid.
17 Ewan, 1970, pp583, 584.
18 Ch, p34.
19 K to Roeth, 20 January 1918.
20 Anderson, op. cit.
21 JB, pp136, 137.
22 'Kinseyiana' file 11.
23 Ch, pp50, 51.
24 James Jones goes much further than this in his biography, and in the opposite direction. He is already moving towards his position that Kinsey was totally homosexual very early on. He writes, for instance, of his 'punishing secret', his 'private turmoil'. Yet there is no evidence for any of this. Indeed, Jones actually invents Kinsey reading about sexuality while at Bowdoin to resolve his torments. In my view, this whole picture is totally contradicted later by the very evidence Jones himself has so skilfully uncovered. I shall deal with this when we come to Ralph Voris, Kinsey's first graduate student, when it finally becomes relevant. All one might note additionally here, not as evidence so much as an observation, is that there are as many group photographs of girls in the Kinsey family archive, which Jones was unable to see, as there are of boys. Girl Scouts (our Guides) came to America in 1912. Kinsey was asked to help plan their programme, and later ran camps (JB, pp123, 125, 171; family archive, Joan Reid; Ch, pp34–5).
25 'Kinseyiana' file quoted Ch, pp36–7.
26 Kinsey, 1943, pp31, 32.
27 Ch, pp33, 34. Also Kinsey, 1926. For full details of gall books and papers, see K's bibliography.
28 Macdonald, 1984, pp26–55; Sanderson, 1962, pp160–7.
29 K to Roeth, quoted Ch, pp33–4.
30 Dr Charles Heiser, ints A, October– November 1995; see also Young, 1983. But it is likely that Kinsey received rather remote encouragement from Morton Wheeler in his pursuit of numbers, since this was an aspect of Wheeler's own pursuit of ants. Remote, since Wheeler left Kinsey more or less to himself until he had finished

his dissertation. See below and JB, pp135, 203, 147.
31 Heiser, Joan, ints A, August–November 1995. And see Heiser, 1995.
32 'Kinseyiana' file.
33 Anderson, op. cit., not dated. It could have been 1919. Thereafter, there is no record of it, and in the record no room for it.
34 Family archive, Joan.
35 Ch, p34.
36 K to Roeth, 1920, quoted Ch, p39.

37 Prohibition had begun to be enforced from January 1920. Anderson, op. cit.
38 Joan, int A.
39 Harvard biologist, quoted Ch, p38.
40 JB, pp154–5.
41 Clark, 1977, pp247–91.
42 Mac, taped int, Pom, 1970; Mac, int J, 10 December 1971.
43 Eigenmann to Bryan, 12 August 1920, quoted Clark, op. cit.

4 The Married Professor

1 Wells, int A.
2 *Male*, pp676, 677.
3 Lockridge, 1994, pp69ff. Mary G. Winther, int J, 11 March 1971, Mrs Edmondson, int J, November 1971; Joan, int A.
4 Jones, J, 1972. James Jones' recent (1997) biography had its origins in his unpublished PhD thesis, held in the Kinsey Institute. Usually, and especially where there is a conflict, I follow the biography – unless, of course, I disagree with it. But sometimes, for whatever reason, Jones does not include material he used in his thesis. Very occasionally, where I can check this (as here, in Clark, 1977), or sometimes where I can find no other source, I trust the youthful Jones and use the thesis.
5 Wells, int A cit.
6 Mac, int J.
7 Details in the last eight paragraphs from: Joan, int A; Mac, int Pom, tape, 1970; account by 'anon', 'Kinseyiana' file; Ch, pp44–5; Pom, p38.
8 K to Natalie Roeth, 10 April 1921.
9 Ch, p49, for details of the honeymoon.
10 Anon 'A', int Acit.
11 Ch, pp50–51.
12 Ibid., p69.
13 K to Roeth, 4 November 1921.
14 Tripp to A March 1999. Jones explains the difficulty by an adherent clitoris, but this would not prevent intercourse. It may well have been an additional problem however. JB, pp236, 816, note 15.
15 One can deduce the date roughly from the birth of their son Donald on 16 July 1922. This places the likely date of conception around 16 October. Since conception usually comes after intercourse has taken place a number of times, the first time was probably at the end of September, start of October.
16 JB, p174.

17 JB, p609.
18 *Female*, p327.
19 Miriam Hecht to A, 13 August 1996.
20 Geb, int A, November 1997.
21 Joan, int A.
22 Ch, p54.
23 That at least is a likely explanation given K's character and the run of events. Pomeroy (op. cit., Chap 4) gives as motive for the textbook Kinsey's course for high school biology teachers. But these courses did not start till 1929, years after the textbook was published.
24 Dr Frank Young, int A. And see Mrs Edmondson, int J; Dr Carl Hagen, int A, September 1995; Dr Herman T. Spieth to Geb, September 1961.
25 Bugbee, int J, 19 October 1971.
26 Prof. Frank Edmondson, int J, 8 November 1971. Quite apart from his irritation at stupidity, Kinsey was, like many who rise by their own efforts, an elitist. The eugenics movement (from the Greek *eugenes* – 'well born') was strong all over the West among intellectuals in the 1920s and 1930s, with results in Germany that we all know. 'Positive' eugenicists believed intelligent, educated and successful parents should be encouraged to breed and so increase the stock of 'good' genes in the pool; 'negative' eugenicists went further: those with 'defective' genes (alcoholics, the feeble-minded, etc.) should be discouraged, or even prevented, from breeding. (Sweden was still following the latter policy into the late 1970s.) It was never a major concern of Kinsey's, but by 1937, like many other intellectuals in America and Europe, he felt that something like this might offer 'the best hope of an improved race of mankind'. (Paul Binding, *House With Four Windows*, London, 1998, Part 3; Kinsey, *Methods . . .*, 1937, quoted JB, p195.)
27 Frank Young, int A cit.

28 Ch, p44; Rosenzweig, 1969.
29 Clark, 1977, pp247–91.
30 Account by Payne in 'Kinseyiana' file cit., see JB, pp182, 183, 806, note 27, for detailed account.
31 Ibid.
32 Mrs Frank Edmondson, int A cit.
33 K to Voris, 8 July 1936.
34 Spieth to Voris, 11 December 1937.
35 K to Pearson, 16 December 1950.
36 See for example Dr Carl Hagen, int A; Dr Heister, int A. There are many others.
37 Torrey, int J, 17 September 1971.
38 Ibid.
39 Edmondson, int J, 8 November 1971.
40 All unsourced details in this section and section 7 from Ch, Chap 4.
41 Joan Reid doubts he did. But the present owner, Dr Mary Gaither, assured me that Clara Kinsey had told her this. Kinsey could do carpentry. He made an exhibition stand for insects for Dr Copeland at Bowdoin (Ch, Chap 2). At Park Avenue the drawers run smoothly; the galoshes drawer is particularly attractive.
42 Anne, int A cit.
43 Joan, int A cit.
44 Yet where are these specimens now? I can find none.
45 Kroc, int A.
46 K to Voris, 26 March 1931.
47 Evelyn Spieth, int J, quoted JB, pp237, 238.
48 Rosenzweig, op. cit.; quoted Pom, pp45, 46.
49 Kinsey, 1926.
50 Ch, pp57–8.
51 Pom, p31.
52 Spieth, unpublished essay, quoted JB, pp190, 191.
53 Voris to K, 5 May 1933.
54 K to Voris, 30 December 1932.
55 Geb, int BBC.
56 Anne/Joan, ints A cit.
57 K to Voris, 14 December 1936.

58 Consuelo Lopez-Morillas, int A, October 1995.
59 Anne, int A cit.
60 Joan, int A.
61 Rosenzweig, op. cit.
62 Ibid.
63 Specimen, family archive, Joan.
64 K to Voris, 26 March 1935 and 10 June 1933.
65 K to Voris, 4 August 1930; 26 March 1935.
66 Helen D'Amico (née Wallin), int A, August 1995.
67 Dr Robert Reid, int A, September 1995.
68 K to Voris, 3 September 1934, Joan, int A.
69 JB, p249.
70 Ch sets this trip in 1926 but it is clear from Spieth's letter to Geb (1961), which she also used, that it was 1928. And see Pom, pp45, 46.
71 Bugbee, int J cit.
72 Dr Carl Hagen, int A cit; also Pom, p150.
73 Kinsey, 1930, p13.
74 Waterman Reports, 1925–9; also quoted Ch, p55–6.
75 The account that follows is drawn variously from Rosenzweig, op. cit.; June Keiser to Geb, 24 April 1962; Elizabeth Frazier, int A, July 1995; Ch, pp71–4, 178; Pom, pp34, 35, 45.
76 Dorothy Craig Collins, int J, 9 December 1971.
77 This is a deduction. I could not find any remnant of the gall code. Pomeroy says that from it K developed his unique sex code (Pom, p34). The *essence* of this, as we shall see, was its positional element. Since there is nothing unusual about a code which simply uses symbols to represent something else, I assume it was this *plus* the essential positional factor which K developed for his galls.
78 K to Voris, 3 September 1934.
79 Quoted Ch, p178.
80 K to Roeth, quoted Ch, p43.

5 Sex Life

1 Anne/Joan, ints A cit.
2 Mac, quoted Pom, pp48, 49.
3 Geb, int A, November 1997.
4 Far too many references, by innuendo or directly, to cite, but see for example: JB, pp77, 79, 123–4, 163, 171, 233, 262, 272, 343, 382, etc., etc.
5 Duberman, 1997.
6 Pom, p108.
7 Geb, int A cit.
8 Ibid.
9 Waugh, 1993, pp63–86.

10 K to RV, 29 July; RV to K, 31 July; K to RV, 20 September – all 1929; RV to K, 19 December 1931.
11 K to RV, 31 January 1937.
12 Geb, int A cit.
13 See for example K to RV, 14 November 1937; also JB, p268.
14 RV to K, 2 September 1931.
15 Breland to K, no date, but 1930s.
16 K to RV, 31 January 1937.
17 K to RV, 11 March 1938.
18 Breland to K, 10 March 1938.

19 RV to K, 10 May 1938.
20 E.g. Breland to K, 10 March 1938.
21 Breland to K, 11 July 1936.
22 See for an example, note, K to Breland, 3 January 1944.
23 Breland to K, 3 June, 11 April 1938.
24 K to Dickinson, 25 June 1941. For information in this section otherwise not referenced see Dickinson, 1931. Also the very useful Bullough, 1994.
25 See for example Breland to K, 29 December 1936.
26 K to RV, 30 December 1932.
27 You might think from the letters quoted that both families discussed such matters freely together, but I think this is just another instance of Kinsey using 'we' where most people would have used 'I'. Many other letters urge Ralph Voris to keep things from Geraldine which he wouldn't have done otherwise. (Geraldine was her name, incidentally, not Gwendoline as Kinsey seems to have thought at first, though it is likely he was jealous of her. Kinsey frequently mis-spelt the names of people who irritated him or whom he disliked.)
28 K to RV, 10 November 1934.
29 RV to K, 8 February 1935.
30 Van de Velde, 1930.
31 *Male*, p373.
32 Ibid., p374.
33 K to RV, 10 November 1934.
34 RV to K, no date, but November/December 1934. Jones interprets this straightforward exchange as Kinsey proffering, and Voris refusing, an invitation to group sex. (JB, p271.)
35 Breland to K, 11 April 1938.
36 Ibid., 24 January 1939.
37 Ibid., 14 May 1939.
38 Ibid., undated, but between May and September 1939.

39 Jim Kinsey, tel int A, December 1995.
40 Webster, 1995.
41 Dr L. Duncan Bulkey, *Syphilis in the Innocent*, quoted Brandt, op. cit.
42 Thomas Connelly, 1980, quoted Bullough, op. cit. The information in this section is drawn variously from Bullough; Brandt, op. cit., especially, and from other sources cited.
43 Quoted Brandt, op. cit.
44 David L. Gills, 1969, p588.
45 See JB, pp419–22; for a more detailed account, if something of a catalogue, see Corner, 1953.
46 *Fit to Fight*, quoted Brandt, op. cit.
47 Brandt, op. cit.
48 Quoted ibid.
49 Ibid.
50 Lockridge, op. cit., p84.
51 *Daily Student*, 15 December 1937.
52 William Armstrong, President of the IU Foundation for thirty years, int A cit.
53 Edmund White, 1983, quoted, John H. Gagnon in McWhirter, 1990.
54 Lockridge, op. cit., p72.
55 Bullough, op. cit.
56 Paul Robinson, 1989, p63.
57 *Male*, pp531–46.
58 Ch, p98.
59 JB, p274. In this passage, and many others, Jones assumes it was prurience that drove Kinsey here. *All* sex researchers are accused of prurience ('Craving for, or dallying with lascivious thoughts', according to *Chambers*). I will deal with this aspect of sex research later; but as regards Kinsey at this point it is an assumption, not a deduction from any evidence.
60 Bugbee, int J, 19 October 1971.
61 Pom, p41.
62 Mrs Shirley Backer, tel int A, December 1995. Her husband Herbert was a student of K's in the early '30s.

6 Gall Wasp Triumph

1 Ch, p68.
2 Lecture 'Individuals' by K to Phi Beta Kappa, 9.15 a.m., Monday 5 June 1939. Kinsey was at this time President of the IU Chapter.
3 K to Raymond Pearl, quoted Ch, pp70–1.
4 See Gould, 1985, Chap 16, for this and other insights. This is a marvellous book.
5 See K, 1922 (Studies[9]), 53:1–141, 163–71); and K, 1923.
6 See K, 1930.

7 Ibid., pp1–22 for this account and quotations.
8 All this, though begun in the above volume (see especially pp45ff) was completed in his second volume (K, 1936). I have included some of it here for the logic of the discussion.
9 Joan, int A cit.
10 K to RV, 15 September 1931, quoted JB, p208.
11 Pom, p40.

12 File No. 36693, Dept No. 2, in the Second Judicial District of the State of Nevada In and For Washoe County. Filed 21 September 1931. The details need not detain us, but the divorce was messy and contested. For a fuller account see JB, p243. Jones, incidentally, who was denied access to family archives, is wrong in saying this event ended Kinsey's relationship with his father. They met on a number of occasions, not totally unamicably.

13 Spieth to Geb cit. Other details in this section come from family letters: K to Mac, 28 October, 9 November, 14 December 1931.

14 K to RV, 26 March 1931.

15 RV to K, 4 April 1931.

16 K to Mac, 14 December 1931.

17 Joan, int A cit.

18 Joan, int J cit.

19 Joan, int A.

20 JB, p281.

21 *Male*, p76.

22 The points in these half-dozen paras from Anne/Joan, ints A.

23 Joan, int A.

24 Anne, int BBC.

25 Pom, p29.

26 K to RV, 3 September 1934.

27 Mac, taped int, Pom, 1970.

28 K to Mac, 14 November 1931.

29 Mac, int J, 10 December 1971.

30 K, int *Daily Student*, 4 December 1937. See also K, 1956.

31 Tripp, discussion A, October 1995.

32 Anne, int A cit.

33 Theodore Torrey, int J, 17 September 1971.

34 Ellson, int A, September 1995.

35 Edmondson, int A cit.

36 Dr Hagen, int A, November 1995.

37 Herman Wells, int A, 27 June 1995.

38 Elizabeth Frazier, int A cit.

39 Joan, int A cit.

40 Don Baxter, int A, November 1995.

41 Joan, int A.

42 K to RV, 8 July 1936.

43 I deduce this from Ch, p83. Here she says the Publishing Committee of the IU Science Series (publishers of the first volume) submitted the second, according to Kinsey, 'To a taxonomist and a geneticist for criticism. The taxonomist said the taxonomy was OK and important, but the genetics unprintably bad. The geneticist said the genetics was sound enough, but the taxonomy certainly not in accord with current work in taxonomy.' No doubt this annoyed Kinsey, who hated criticism, but it would hardly make sense just to imprison

the book unless he was being asked to make changes.

44 K to Mac, 28 October 1935.

45 K to Mac, 9 December 1935.

46 K to Mac, 18 December 1935; Coon, quoted Ch, p82.

47 Coon, ibid.

48 JB, p282. In fact, in his chapter on this trip (chapter 12) Jones seriously puts forward the suggestion that Kinsey had oral sex with his students and that he masturbated in front of them. It is not absolutely impossible, I suppose. But it is a serious allegation to make about a teacher and should not be made without overwhelmingly convincing evidence. Jones's only hard evidence is not just inadequate, it is silly, as I point out in my footnote to page 112. Kinsey, here and elsewhere, never made any bones about advocating nudity (often by example), encouraging masturbation, arguing fiercely against delayed marriage (by which he really meant sexual intercourse). It was all part of his crusade against the agonising and damaging inhibitions of his youth. It is Jones's failure, in my view, to give this side of Kinsey due weight which badly skews his portrait.

49 One can deduce this by an interesting route. Four years later Kinsey was reading *Sexual Life in Ancient Greece* by Hans Licht (see Kinsey to Voris, 17 January 1939). The edition he read (London, 1932) is extant and has been extensively annotated by Kinsey in the margins. On p336 there is an account of brothels in the Roman era describing how, in order 'to entice passers by' the girls sat before the hïspanira (brothels). Against this Kinsey has scribbled 'Still to be seen in Mexico'. Some time after he got back from this trip, in the letter to Voris already quoted about the burlesque in New York, he writes, 'I thought Tehuantepec was hot enough, and I do have some stories from it to tell you – but you will find New York [that is, the burlesque] more pointedly bothersome.' (Kinsey to Voris, 31 January 1937.)

50 K to Mac, undated but probably 20 December 1935.

51 Ditto, but probably about 10 January 1936.

52 Ibid.

53 Kinsey, 1936. The argument is taken from the first sixty pages. The rest of the book is taken up with his presentation of the evidence.

54 Gould, op. cit.; see also Spieth to RV, 11 December 1937.

55 Dolzhansky, a respected scientist, may have been impressed – all his critics were

impressed – but he also said that a 'species' in Kinsey was the same as 'races' to other authorities (*Genetics and the Origin of Species*, Dolzhansky, 1941, p377), Ernst Mayr (*Systematics and Origin of Species*, 1942) repeated this. Mayr was to become the next leader in the field, his work based not on subsamples like Kinsey's, but on whole populations. That is, he simply extended the principle Kinsey had pioneered. Kinsey's work continued to stand up. Dr Frank Young attended a seminar at the University of Florida in 1942 run by Professor Hubble on the Cynipidae books. The verdict was entirely favourable. (Young, int A, October

1995.) Note, incidentally, that the phrase *Origin of Species*, whose use might have seemed rather presumptuous of Kinsey, was perfectly usual in works of this sort then.

56 K to RV, 31 January 1937.
57 K to RV, 14 December 1937, and see 31 January 1937.
58 K to RV, 8 July 1936.
59 Bugbee, int J cit., Ramsey, int J, 15 March 1972.
60 K to RV, 11 March 1938.
61 Joan, int A.
62 Mac, int J cit.
63 Joan, int A.
64 *Daily Student*, 11 November 1937.

7 *The Marriage Course*

1 For this and the following, Robert Kroc, int A, November 1995.
2 'Biological Aspects of Some Social Problems', unpublished lecture by Kinsey, held at KI.
3 K to RV, 8 July 1936. Already implicit here is the position, thinly disguised, Kinsey later adopted in his *Reports*. By 'married' he obviously meant 'sexually active'. Since he at no point suggests that advanced education is itself an evil, the corollary has to be the advocacy of premarital sex.
4 Mrs Frank Edmondson, int J, November 1971.
5 Wendel W. Wright, 1939, Part 1, 102, IU Archives.
6 Herman B. Wells, int Dr Thomas D. Clark, January 1968.
7 Brandt, 1985.
8 See account in Bullough, 1994.
9 Brandt, op. cit.
10 *Daily Student*, 15 February 1938, IU Library.
11 Ch, pp99–101.
12 Ibid.
13 *Daily Student*, 8 March 1938, IU Library.
14 Pom, p58.
15 Cecilia Hardwick, int J, 22 January 1972.
16 See *Daily Student* of these dates; also Sydney Ditzon, 1969.
17 See Ch, pp99–100.
18 Hendrick, int J cit.
19 Dorothy Macrae, int A, September 1995.
20 Mrs Kate Mueller, int J, 1 April 1971; and see JB, pp339, 340.
21 Breland to K, 11 April 1938.
22 'Minutes of Board of Trustees', held IU archive, quoted JB, p326.
23 RV to K, 9 April 1938.
24 *Daily Student*, 24 September 1938.

25 Paraphrased from Morantz, 1983.
26 JB, p330.
27 Ref notes and lectures, Marriage Course, held KI. And see JB, pp327–85, 830, 831.
28 Mr and Mrs Weir, ints A, October 1995.
29 Alice Binkley, in *Sex and the Scientist*, TV film cit.
30 Marriage course comments.
31 Geb, ints A, August–November 1995.
32 Deutsch, 1949, p4.
33 K to Bugbee, 20 September 1938.
34 Glenn Ramsey, int J, 15 March 1972; 'Dr Donald Broadribb' to Lisa Wildey, BBC TV, 30 June 1995.
35 Kroc, int A cit.
36 K to Raymond Pearl, 7 July 1939.
37 Mrs Margaret Edmondson, int A, October 1995.
38 Marriage course comments.
39 Ramsey, int J cit.
40 'Questionnaire' to Marriage Course, autumn 1938.
41 Weirs, ints A cit.
42 'Herman S. Winton' to Lisa Wildey, BBC TV, 16 July 1995; female informant, telephone conversation, Wildey, July 1995.
43 See Mrs F. Edmondson, int J cit.
44 Pom, pp55, 56.
45 Marriage course comments.
46 Edmondson, int A, October 1995.
47 Quoted Ch, p103.
48 Ibid., p106.
49 K to Breland, 8 October and 13 December; Breland to K, 1 December 1938.
50 K to RV, 28 November and 13 December 1938.
51 K to RV, 17 January 1939.
52 Rice to K, 18 February 1939, quoted Jones, op. cit.; Pom, pp57, 58.

53 Dr Edith Schuman, int J, 1 April 1971.
54 Mrs Kate Mueller, int J cit.
55 *Daily Student*, 4 February 1939.
56 Alice Binkley, int A, September 1995.
57 JB, p348.
58 K to RV, 6 July 1939.
59 Anon A, int A; and see JB, pp369–72.
60 K to RV dated October 1939.
61 K to Frank Edmondson, 13 August 1939.
62 K to RV, 6 July 1939.
63 Elizabeth Frazier, int A cit.
64 K to RV, 19 September 1939.
65 Pom, int Bullough, op. cit.
66 K to Ramsey, 20 September 1940.
67 Taken from K to RV, 6 July 1939.
68 W. Ricker to Geb, October 1961.
69 Taken from K to RV, October 1939.
70 RV to K, 15 December 1939.
71 K to Ramsey, 16 November 1939; Ramsey
     to K, 23 January 1940.
72 Geb, int A, November 1997; see also JB,
     pp384, 385. Jones is particularly good on all
     this in his Chap 16.
73 K to 'Braine', 9 October 1940.
74 See K to 'Davie', 18 August; K to 'Ed', 4 July
     1939; K to 'Braine', 9 October 1940.
75 Geb, int BBC, 1995.
76 See K to 'Davie', 27 December 1945; 26
     April 1951.
77 Invitation card, 'Derek Hobbard' to K, May
     1948.
78 Joan, int A cit.
79 K to 'Braine', 9 October 1940; 'Dale' to Hall,
     BBC, 13/17 June 1995; Pom, pp76, 77.
80 From K's talk 'Individuals' to Phi Beta
     Kappa, 5 June 1939.

81 *Male*, p562.
82 G.M. Morris to A, 23 July 1996.
83 Some of this account is taken from Pom,
     pp86, 87.
84 Helen D'Amico (née Wallin), int A, August
     1995; Mac, int J, December 1971.
85 Joan, int A cit.
86 TV film *Sex and the Scientist* cit.
87 Payne, int J, 2 March 1971.
88 Martin, int A, October 1995.
89 Last 6 paragraphs from: Kroc, int A cit; Geb,
     int A cit; Geb et al., 1979, pp29–35 (?);
     'Nancy Long' to BBC, Wildey, 20 July
     1995; *Male*, pp38–104; for critics see
     Cochran et al., 1954.
90 Bill Armstrong, int A, November 1995.
91 Kate Mueller, int J cit.
92 Jones, 1972.
93 K to RV, March 1940.
94 Mrs Edmondson, int J cit.
95 Cards and telegrams of these dates, Jerry
     Voris to K. She did of course find a place, as
     people eventually do. There was
     correspondence for a while, particularly at
     first over Kinsey's 'dynamite' letters, which
     she rescued, as she wrote on 14 June 1940,
     with some difficulty: '. . . some people tried
     to make trouble . . . Their little game was
     spoiled.' The letters gradually cease until in
     August 1942 she married an airman in
     Miami. She is 'very happy'. (Geraldine Voris
     to Mrs Kinsey, August 1942.)
96 K to Breland, 17 May 1940.
97 JB, pp271–2.
98 Kroc, int A cit.
99 Robert S. Tangeman to Geb, 25 July 1962.

8 A Brief History of Sex Research

1 Geb, int A, August–November 1995.
2 Though Kinsey certainly became
    sufficiently familiar with his leading
    predecessors over time, which is why we
    must know something about them, I do not
    find Jones' assumption that he had read
    widely at this point convincing. Jones needs
    this to buttress his contention that Kinsey
    was pursued by his demons of
    homosexuality and 'masochism'. Desperate
    to understand them, according to Jones, he
    read everything he could. The only hard
    evidence of this period (1931 to 1939)
    comes from Robert Kroc who says as far as
    he knew Kinsey had only read Dickinson
    and Davis (Kroc, letter to A, 18 November
    1997), as well, of course, as the marriage
    course books listed above. *The list also
    comprised: Katharine B. Davis* Factors in the

    Sex Life of 2,200 Women, *New York 1929,
    also 'Periodicity of Sex Desire',* American
    Journal of Obstetrics and Gynecology, *Vol
    12, December 1926; G. S. Miller Jr, 'The Primate
    Basis of Human Sexual Behaviour',* Quarterly
    Review of Biology, *Vol. 6, December 1931;
    Paul Popeboe,* Problems of Human
    Reproduction, *William & Wilkins Co, 1926; O.
    Knoff,* The Art of being a Woman, *Little
    Brown & Co., 1932; W. S. Taylor, 'A Critique of
    Sublimation in Males',* Genetic Psychology
    Monographs, *Vol. 13, No. 1, January 1933;
    Robert Briffault,* The Mothers, *Macmillan &
    Co., 1927; Eric M. Matsner,* The Technique of
    Contraception, *Wm. Wood & Co., Baltimore,
    1936 (list held at Kinsey Institute).*
3 Malinowski, 1929; see also the discussion in
    A's 1977, pp356–64.
4 Licht, 1932. Page nos taken from this edition

(K's) held at KI.

5 Ibid., p261.
6 See for example, ibid., pp136, 137, 149, 183, 193, 242, 254, etc.
7 Ibid., p71.
8 Ibid., pp313, 314.
9 Ramsey, int J, March 1972.
10 For a translation, see Krafft-Ebing, 1922.
11 I am indebted throughout this section to Vern L. Bullough's excellent general study already cited.
12 Moll, A., 1891.
13 *Male*, pp618–20, 651.
14 Hirschfeld, 1910.
15 For Ellis I follow variously: Ellis, H. H., 1939; Ellis, H. H., 1928–1930, vol II; Calder-Marshall, A., 1959; Bullough, op. cit., and in particular, at the end, Paul Robinson's witty and penetrating book cited earlier.
16 Ellis, H. H., 1928–1930, op. cit.
17 *Male*, pp618, 619.
18 Pom, p69.
19 The small red mark against Learned Hand's name is in the list of the council of the American Law Institute contained in the bound Proceedings of their 32nd annual meeting. Louis B. Schwartz sent K a copy

(now in the KI) on 15 June 1955. Learned and Augustus Hand were not related to the Kenneth Hand with whom it is likely K had been in love when he was nineteen. (See Gunther, 1994.)
20 See for instance *Male*, p263; *Female*, pp170, 171. But K confined this aspect of his criticism of Freud largely to private converse (see Pom, pp68, 69). His written empirical criticism of Freud was far more extensive, as we shall see. At the same time, he found much in Freud with which he agreed and which he cited. Examples are too numerous to list, but can be found chiefly in the footnotes to *Female*.
21 Webster, 1995. How indebted I am to this fascinating and brilliant book will become evident.
22 John Burnham, quoted Bullough, op. cit.
23 Quoted Webster, op. cit.
24 Pom, p70.
25 Tape, Dr Earle Marsh to Geb, 25 November 1961.
26 Edgar Anderson to K, 16 July 1941.
27 For a fuller discussion and demonstration of this phenomenon see A, 1987.
28 Storr, 1997.

9 How to Get at the Truth

1 K to Ramsey, 20 September 1940.
2 Pom, p202.
3 Dr Carl Hagen, int A, September 1995.
4 *Female*, p287, note p289.
5 K to Mrs 'Cathage', 24 August and 6 September 1941.
6 Martin, int A cit.
7 Anne, int A. And see JB, p487.
8 Quoted Pom, p202.
9 Ch, p116.
10 Prof. Frank Edmondson, int A cit.
11 As I explain in the Preface, James Jones and I largely talked to the same people about Kinsey's private life. After Jones' book came out I talked to them again. This account is from them – in this particular case largely Gebhard, Tripp and Anon A, and JB, pp393–6. Martin refused to discuss it, either with me or Jones.
12 While Pomeroy, Gebhard and Kinsey all knew each other's sex histories, Martin in some respects seems to have been the odd one out. Gebhard made him a 2 on the H (homosexual) scale. Anon A made him 'a double o-oo' – i.e. extremely heterosexual. Since Kinsey and Martin had sex together for about four years, this seems odd.

Gebhard was closer to Martin than Anon A; on the other hand Anon A discussed these things with Kinsey. I noticed, too, that usually Anon A tended to make people more H than, to me, the evidence warranted. This is not vital, clearly, indeed it is almost academic, perhaps only interesting as an example of the arcane discussions that sometimes took place in the group about K. In this instance, I go with Gebhard.
13 Tripp, int A.
14 K to Ramsey, 20 September 1940.
15 K to 'William Timber', 29 September 1941.
16 K's lecture notes to lecture 10, autumn 1938.
17 K to 'Richard MacDonald', 4 December 1940.
18 Paul Robinson, 1989.
19 *Male*, p35.
20 Ibid., pp35–62.
21 See for example ibid., pp476, 511–13, 527–30; *Female*, pp194, 195.
22 *Female*, p8.
23 Much of this will emerge as we get into the *Reports*, but see for example *Male*, Chap 9, and pp4, 12, 42, 58; *Female*, pp642, 643.
24 Dr Stephanie Sanders, int A, November 1995.

25 Laumann et al., 1994.
26 Paul Robinson, 1972, pp99–102.
27 Robinson, int BBC.
28 Paul Robinson, op. cit., 1989.
29 *Male*, pp63–70.
30 It would now be possible to get most of it from Pom, 1960, and Geb, 1979, and from the lively account in the latter this is taken. What it would not be possible to obtain are the all-important positional meanings.
31 Frank Banta, int BBC.
32 Geb, int A cit.
33 See Freud, S., 1953–74, vol 12, pp115, 118, quoted Webster, op. cit.
34 *Male*, p42.
35 Pomeroy, 1960.
36 Pom, p129.
37 Geb, int A cit.
38 Pom, p129.
39 Dr Earle Marsh, tel int A, December 1995.
40 K, TV int, Arlene Francis's *Home Show*, broadcast 20 March 1955; also Dr Henry Remak's 'Home Movie' of a 1952 summer picnic in Martin's enormous garden.
41 Dr Vincent Nowlis, int A, October 1995.
42 *Male*, p44.
43 Dorothy Collins, int A, August 1995.
44 Helen D'Amico (née Wallin), int A cit.
45 Ch, p199.

46 Sam Steward to Geb, 19 October 1981.
47 Foucault, 1979, op. cit.
48 Quoted and adapted to K from Webster, op. cit., pp342–4.
49 Penis card, KI.
50 *Female*, p574; Taylor, 1996, p58.
51 Bair, 1995, p131.
52 Pom, pp317–18.
53 'Peter Dale' to BBC, Martina Hall, 13 and 17 June 1995.
54 *Female*, p618; *Male*, p510.
55 Pom, pp118, 119.
56 *Male*, pp485–6, 509. The connection between belief and method of masturbation, while logical, was told to Tripp by K and reported to A in his interview.
57 Ibid., p21 for examples.
58 Ibid., p10.
59 Ch, p119.
60 Records, IU Archives.
61 K to Harrison, 7 December 1940; Yerkes to Weed, 26 January 1946. Quoted JB, pp423, 424.
62 K to RV, 2 March 1940.
63 Glenway Wescott, int Jerry Rosco, December 1976.
64 Geb, int A cit.
65 Mrs Frank Edmondson, int J cit.

10 Money, Support, Attacks – The Shape of Things to Come: 1941–3

1 The hormonal paper see K, 1941; the paper on the variable winged Utah galls (*Biorhiza eburnea*) was part of a larger work, including *Xystoteras*, which he never finished.
2 Glass, S.J., et al., 1940. As I explained, Kinsey read these journals because of his dead son Don and because his sister had a thyroid problem. How his heart must have leapt when he read this article over his lunch!
3 K to Ramsey, 13 January 1941.
4 Dickinson to K, 18 June; K to D, 23 June 1941.
5 K to R, 19 February 1941.
6 Geb to A, 6 March 1996.
7 K to R, 21 February 1941.
8 K to R, 7 February 1941.
9 K to R, 21 March 1941.
10 K to R, 10 March 1941.
11 Pom, p98.
12 Last 5 paras: Gregg to Yerkes, 17 and 31 January 1931, quoted JB, and see JB, pp422, 423; Wells, int J, 3 December 1971.
13 K to Y, 14 May 1941.
14 K to Dr Walter B. Cannon, Dr George W. Corner, Dr Karl S. Lashley, Dr Adolf Meyer,

Dr Carl R. Moore, Dr Lewis H. Weed (Chairman NRC Medical Division). Letters, 1–5 July 1941.
15 These 2 paras from K's Report to Dean S.E. Start of IU and to NRC; also copies of his *Teaching Load*, 1941–1950 (all in IU Archives); K to Dr Robert Mihsen, 7 February 1941.
16 Jane Bolling to A, 27 September 1995. Her father, Professor Lawrence Wheeler, was a friend of the Kinseys, the first Executive Director of the IU Foundation and also taught journalism there. Although Mrs Bolling said she remembered quite clearly him telling her this about K, it has to be recognised that it has been ascribed to several other figures in the past. Great men attract good anecdotes. At the same time, there are examples of apocryphal exchanges taking place several times. See A, 1979, p142 (A. 1978, p129–30.
17 Dellenback, int A; Harry Benjamin to Geb, 1981.
18 Source for both Pom and Ch is Lester Dearborn to Geb, 17 April 1962.

19 Helen D'Amico (née Wallin), int A cit.
20 Tebbel, int A.
21 K to R, 11 January 1942.
22 Dr C to K, 13 June 1941.
23 R to K, 4 October 1941.
24 K to 'Timber', 6 November; to R, 6 November 1941; Pom, p128.
25 Wells, 1980, pp177–94.
26 See for example, *Sex and the Scientist*, TV, op. cit.
27 Martin, int J, April 1971.
28 Ramsey, int J, 15 March 1972.
29 Jones, 1972.
30 Ch, pp120, 128, 129.
31 R to K, 10 May 1940.
32 K to Y, 10 June 1942. The rest of these three paras has been condensed from letters about the case held in two large files. E.g. K to 'Wylie', 28 July 1941; to Y, 23 December 1941, 10 June 1942; to R, 11 January 1942; R to K, 13 January 1942. Also see Ramsey, int J cit.
33 K to R, 17 November 1942.
34 Pom, p100.
35 K to Yerkes, 24 March 1942.
36 Geb, int A cit.
37 Pom, p98.
38 *Male*, p374.
39 Ibid., pp339–63, 587.
40 Ibid., pp345, 521.
41 Gorer, 1971. An interesting survey as regards attitudes, but ineffective as regards behaviour, but insofar as it finds anything here it substantiates K. See table 43, p309, table 20, p274.
42 Johnson, Anne M., et al., 1994, pp80–3.
43 Mayhew, Henry, 1851/1862; *My Secret Life*, New York, 1966.

44 Joan, int A, 17 November 1995.
45 Last 3 paras Ramsey, int J cit.
46 Elizabeth Frazier, int A.
47 Mrs 'X' to K, 23 June; K to Mrs 'X', 30 June 1942.
48 K to Miss 'van ffeifer', 25 June 1942.
49 K to Dr 'Malcolm', 10 June; 10 November 1942.
50 K to B, 3 October 1942.
51 K to James V. Bennett at the Dept of Justice, quoted Pom, p210.
52 K to Mrs 'Glover', 24 October 1942.
53 Reverse of Yerkes to K, May/June (?) 1942, date obscured.
54 K to B, 11 December 1942.
55 These 5 paras from JB, pp432–6; Corner, int J, 5 August 1971; John Tebbel, int A cit.
56 Geb, int A.
57 Corner, 1953.
58 'Committee Opportunity and Responsibility in a Changing World', by Robert M. Yerkes. No date, but enclosed with draft of 20th Annual Report of the Committee for Research in Problems of Sex, 1 July 1940 to 30 June 1941. Sent to CRPS members 29 September 1941. Adolf Meyer Papers, series 11, Box 392, Folder 1241, The Alan Mason Chesney Medical Archives, The Johns Hopkins Medical Institution. Cited Gorchov, 1996.
59 Corner, int J.
60 Nowlis, int A.
61 Yerkes to Weed, 26 January 1946, quoted JB, p435.
62 JB, p437.
63 Pom, p100.
64 K to Mrs 'G', 9 December 1942.
65 *Male*, p10.

11 *Kinsey at his Exercise: 1943–4*

1 These next 5 paras from Hecht, correspondance A, 13 August, 1 October 1996; Hecht and Sarah Taubin, ints BBC, 1995.
2 K to Mac, 3 January 1943.
3 Thomas Clark, 1977, op. cit.
4 Pom, p100.
5 K to Yerkes, 20 January 1943; Harry Benjamin, int J, 23 August 1971.
6 Pom, pp157, 158.
7 Dr Earle Marsh, tel int A, December 1995; tape in KI.
8 'Glover' to K, 23 February; K to 'G', 10 March 1943.
9 Character sketch Pomeroy: ints, Martin/Mary J. Winther/Bugbee/

Dellenback with J; Helen D'Amico (née Wallin)/Pom/John Tebbel, with A.
10 Dr Paul Fuller to A, 20 August 1996.
11 Account from Geb, int J, int A; Pom, pp105–7 (but see his Chaps 7 & 8); Geb, 1979, op. cit.
12 Pom, p103.
13 Ibid., pp107, 108. James Jones takes this comment of Pomeroy's and inflates it until *power* becomes the major element in Kinsey's history-taking (now replacing the prurience he had earlier picked on); 'the power surge that results from psychic penetration'. (JB, p353). It was possibly an element – but in my view a small and diminishing one. All people involved in helping others –

counsellors, psychotherapists, doctors, etc. –
enjoy their authority to some extent. But
taking a sex history barely constitutes the
exercise of authority. Power, in any case, is
of little use unless it can be used – and no
one suggests Kinsey used his knowledge in
any but the stated way. In fact, the evidence
is that all the other things we have touched
on were far stronger with Kinsey:
compassion and anger at sexual suffering,
sympathy for homosexuals, the ability at last
to relate warmly on a human level – all
these, of course, in varying degrees
personally derived; and above all naked
scientific curiosity.

14 Tripp, int A cit.
15 Pom, p107.
16 Ibid., pp150, 152.
17 Geb, int J cit.
18 Martin, int J cit; K to Ramsey, 25 March, to
Yerkes, 5 April 1943; Bugbee, int J, 19
October 1971.
19 Geb int A; JB, pp481–4.
20 Tebbel and Geb, ints A. Anon A, typically,
made him a 3.
21 JB, p603; Geb, int A.
22 Tebbel, Nowlis, ints A.
23 JB, p503. Kinsey never set much store by
prostitute demonstrations – nor by the
various sex shows which were organised for
him. In both, the responses were mediated
through varying degrees of conscious acting
and to that extent were not genuine. (Paul
Gebhard, int A.)
24 Tripp, int A. Tripp also said that the
Everard Baths were built in 1888, which is
true, and that Oscar Wilde used them. I
suspect this last is gay apocrypha. Ellmann
does not mention it. Nor does Chauncey in
his, as always, full and interesting account;
his description of the Penn Baths is slightly
at variance with Tripp's. (Chauncey, 1994,
pp216–18.)
25 Y to K, 10 April 1943.
26 K to Y, 16 April 1943.
27 K to Y, 5 April 1943; K's *Teaching Load
Charts* and NRC/IU *Annual Reports*, 1942–4
held IU Archives.
28 K to Y, 5 April 1943.
29 Pom, pp126, 127.
30 K to Rev J. 'Jones', 14 May 1943.
31 K to Y, 5 April, 16 April 1943; Minutes, 23
April 1943 meeting NRC's CRPS. Y to K,
18 May 1943.
32 K, 1943.
33 K to N, 26 July 1943.
34 Typical K phrase in 1943–4 annual report.
35 Vincent Nowlis, 1995; Nowlis, int A,
October 1995.
36 Pom, p159.
37 K to Bugbee, quoted Jones, 1972; Yerkes to
K, 12 June 1943.
38 Beach, int J, 20 August 1971.
39 K to Beach, 17 September 1943.
40 Beach taped talk to KI, 1981.
41 Tripp, int A cit.
42 Beach, int cit, tape op. cit.
43 *Male*, pp293, 673–7; Robinson, 1989, op. cit.
44 K to Beach, 17 September 1943. Kinsey told
his circle what he was discovering as he was
discovering it. They responded in kind.
Beach wrote to him about sex with animals
in the past. 'The best one I have found so far
is the trial of one Benjamin Deschauffour on
25 May, 1726. This gentleman was taken in
the act of coition with a she-ass at Vauvres.
After due process of law he was sentenced to
death, but the animal was acquitted on the
grounds that she was the victim of violence
and had not participated of her own free
will. The Prior of the Convent, and the
principal inhabitants of the district signed a
certificate stating that they had known the
said she-ass for four years and that she had
... never given occasion for scandal to
anyone ...' (Beach to Kinsey, 25 January
1943. He cites E.P. Dutton, *The Criminal
Prosecution of Capital Punishment of Animals*,
New York, 1906.)
45 K to Wells, 21 October 1943, quoted J, op.
cit., from which these paras are taken.
46 K to B, 16 September, B to K, 9 October
1943.
47 K to N, 11 October, N to K, 22 October
1943.
48 E to K, 21 September 1943.
49 Pom, p122.
50 L to K, 26 October 1943.
51 Mrs 'G' to K, 13 October 1943.
52 K to Rev 'J', 26 November 1943.
53 K to Yerkes, 22 December 1943; *Male*, p21.
54 Beach, int J cit, among many others.
55 Deducible from D to K, 22 November 1943.
56 See D to K, 20 January 1944, 10 April 1945.
57 Nowlis, int A cit.
58 'Glover' to K, 15 January 1944, 6 June
1952; K to 'G', 18 January 1944.
59 See K to Beach, 23 February 1944; for
Beach's visit, his taped talk in KI.
60 *Male*, pp227, 234, 237.
61 Robinson, 1989, op. cit., p91.
62 Pom, pp219–21.
63 Mac, int J, December 1971.
64 *Male*, pp441–5, 498.
65 'Trend' to K, 18 July, K to 'Trend', 5 August
1948.

66 See William H. Masters, 1980. This contains interesting and frank discussions and quotes (p77 and 107) the *Report and Recommendations: Research Involving Children*, DHEW publication No (05) 77.0004, Washington, DC, US Govt Printing Office 1977 – National Commission for the Protection of Human Subjects of Biomedical and Behavioral Research.
67 Pom, pp217–21.
68 'Ruth Weinberg' to Hall/BBC, 15 June 1995 and subsequent tel int.
69 *Male*, pp416–36.
70 Tripp, int A cit.
71 Geb, int A cit.
72 See discussion of Mischel's work in *New Scientist Supplement*, 27 April 1996, pp8, 9.
73 *Male*, pp343–5.
74 K to LS, 27 November 1944.
75 K to Y, 9 May 1944.
76 Geb, int A cit.
77 Information from here to end of section variously from: ints J – Geb/Bugbee/ Martin/Ramsey/Dorothy Collins; ints A – Helen D'Amico (née Wallin)/Geb/Earle Marsh (telephone)/Dorothy Collins/John Tebbel. Scattered entries Pom. Nowlis, 1995, op. cit. Kinsey's appointment diaries.
78 My knowledge of Green's monumental diary comes from being shown specimen pages and tables and from lengthy questioning of Dr Paul Gebhard and Dr John Bancroft. They were reluctant to leave me alone with the complete work in case others should demand the same access.
79 *Male*, p161.
80 *Male*, pp157–92. For example much of pp166, 161 are from Green; so are tables 31–4, pp178, 179. And repeated observations throughout the chapter.
81 Though Lewis Terman did express anxiety

in a number of private letters and alluded to it in his review of the *Male* volume. JB, pp496, 592. Since I wrote this book, Judith Reisman has produced a further work to the one I refer to in the footnote on p223. The new book is full of errors, fake statements and is no more reputable than the first one. It does not require or merit discussion. Details in bibliography.
82 Martinson, Floyd M., 1972.
83 Taylor, Timothy, op. cit., p73. For ultra-sound he cites the Riverside Perinatal Clinic, Virginia; for eighteen months, Gene Abel of the Behavioral Institute of Atlanta.
84 See for example *Female*, p116–22.
85 Wescott, int Jerry Rosco cit.
86 Geb, int A cit.
87 See for example *Male*, pp237–8; *Female*, pp116–22, Robinson, op. cit., pp91–2.
88 Gregerson, Edgar, 1982, p198. This is a full, very useful compendium dedicated to K. Here his source was Evans-Pritchard, E.E., 1973.
89 Williamson, Margeret, 1995, pp122, 123.
90 Gregerson, op. cit., p202, or, racier, Lahr, John, 1986, pp155–225.
91 Webster, op. cit., p615.
92 Pom, p122.
93 Pom, p58.
94 Schuman, int J, 15 September 1971.
95 Wells, int J, 3 December 1971.
96 All NRC/Rockefeller details from JB, pp445–50.
97 K to Y, 22 October – but I get the actual date from Yerkes' reply, 22 October 1944. K's letter is missing from the KI's files.
98 N to Y, 21 October 1944.
99 Pom/Martin, ints A.
100 N, int A.
101 K to Y, 26 October 1944.

12 *Racing for the* Male *Report: 1944–7*

1 Pom, p159.
2 K to N, 4 January 1944.
3 N, int A.
4 Robert Latou Dickinson papers – Countway Library of Medicine, Harvard University. Box 1, Folder 36 – 'Other D Corres'. (Courtesy Lynn Gorchov.)
5 Pom, p157.
6 K to D, 10 January 1947.
7 Tebbel, int A cit.
8 Letters 20/10/44 from a tape Pomeroy made of extracts from K's letters to Mac.
9 *Male*, p10; NRC/IU Progress Reports,

1 April 1945, 1 April 1946, held IU Archive.
10 K to Dr Hugh Carmichael, 17 January 1945.
11 Mac to Pom, taped int, 1970.
12 IU Archive.
13 William Dellenback, 1994; K to Legman, 15 (?) March 1945.
14 K to Y, 4 February, 6 February 1945.
15 N to K, 9 December 1944.
16 See Pom, pp125–230.
17 Ibid., p223.
18 Nowlis, int A.
19 See for example, Saunders to Martin, 23 April 1948.

20 Beach, int J, 20 August 1971.

21 Mrs Frank Edmondson, int J, November 1971.

22 R, int A, October 1995.

23 GW, int Jerry Rosco, December 1976.

24 Cuttings, notes, appointment diaries, KI. Paul Gebhard says that Kinsey did not go to these burlesque shows but sent his team. I cannot absolutely prove Kinsey went but I think Gebhard felt he had to defend Kinsey here. Half the visits took place before Gebhard arrived on the scene and out of six recorded visits, Kinsey was in town at the same time as four of them. Why should he have forgone this valuable chance to do research?

25 Beach, int J cit.

26 Pom, p17.

27 K to D, 20 January 1944, D to K, undated but August 1945.

28 R to K, 1 April, 25 November 1945.

29 M, int J cit.

30 Pom, pp226–8; K to Y, 29 March 1945; but I am particularly indebted to Lynn Gorchov who allowed me to see a paper she delivered to the History Graduate Student Conference, University of Bielefeld/Johns Hopkins University, Bielefeld 24 May 1996: 'The Objective Scientist as Radical Reformer: Alfred C. Kinsey and the Politics of Homosexuality'. This was a preliminary fruit of her unpublished thesis.

31 Pom, pp216, 217.

32 K to Y, 4 September 1945.

33 K to Dr Elliott, 15 May 1945.

34 K to Ramsey, 12 July, 30 October 1945.

35 Dr C to K, 3 August, K to Dr C, 20 September 1945.

36 *A study of attitudes and knowledge related to venereal disease among two groups of soldiers in C-B-I,* Research department special service section HQ, USA – C-B-I. Held in KI.

37 K to MLK, 5 November 1945.

38 Sources last 5 paras: Nowlis/Geb/Collins, ints A cit; Nowlis, unpublished memoir cit; Pom, pp101–5.

39 *Male,* p13; sources for Huncke: Huncke ints, A and BBC, Pom, pp133, 134; *NY Times* obituary, 9 August 1996, p31; London *Times* obituary, 17 August 1996. Huncke was the model for Elmo Hassel in Kerouac's *On the Road* and for Junkey in his *The Town and the City.* More can be learnt about this interesting man from his autobiography *Guilty of Everything,* Hanuman Books, 1990.

40 Vidal, 1996, pp101, 102.

41 K to Dickinson, 25 January 1946; *Male,* p10; 'Teaching Load' Zoology Dept. summary, IU Archive.

42 'Viner' to K, 4 February; K to 'Viner', 20 February 1946.

43 Michael Eccleston to K, 14 March 1946.

44 Y to W, 26 January 1946, CRPS papers, quoted JB, pp451–4, from which this account largely comes. See also Gregg to K, 8 April 1946; Corner, int J, 5 August 1971, Y to K, 4 January 1946.

45 Details of salary records and purchases in IU Archive.

46 'Bocking' to D, 4 April 1946, plus encl.

47 D to K, 29 April 1946.

48 'AD' to K, 4 March 1946.

49 K to D, 4 May 1946.

50 'AD' to K, 4 March 1946.

51 See among several, *Female,* p11.

52 I have elided quotes from the following pages in *Male.* pp377, 381, 383, 557.

53 *Female,* p327.

54 Ibid., pp266, 328–30, 291.

55 Ibid., p13.

56 Ibid., pp104, 105, 115; Geb, int A.

57 Tripp, in *Sex and the Scientist,* TV programme cit.

58 *Female,* pp14, 285, 465; K to 'Mary S. Wagner', 20 December 1950.

59 Dr Robert Reid/Joan, ints A cit.

60 For this and following para: Geb, int J; Pom, pp231–7.

61 Joan to A, 19 March 1997.

62 K to Kluckhohn, 2 May; Kluckhohn to K, 20 May 1946.

63 Geb, int A; JB, p499.

64 Geb, int A.

65 JB, p603; Marsh, tel int A. In Jones' book, Earle Marsh appears as 'Mr Y'. Since then, Marsh has revealed himself to Clarence Tripp and allowed him to use his name in a long critique of the Jones biography (Tripp, 1999). Tripp was kind enough to let me see a pre-publication draft.

66 Pomeroy in discussion with Tripp, who relayed it to A. Pomeroy was referring to nine male partners – of whom I can locate six. I can also locate six female partners. These will emerge. Given Kinsey's secretiveness, there may have been additional ones but given Pomeroy's observation – and he knew Kinsey extremely well – probably not many.

67 I take all my details, much truncated, for this immensely complicated business from JB, pp455-61.

68 K to Beach, 6 August; to Nowlis, 26 September; and Nowlis to K, 30 September 1946.

69 JB, p510.

70 Ibid.
71 'Horace Cayton' to K, 8 October, 18 November 1946.
72 Pom, p235
73 Geb, int A, November 1997.
74 Geb, int A; Pom, p236.
75 Geb, int A. Jones cites an instance of staff refusal, but there are reasons to question motives here, to which I'll come in due course.
76 Remak, int A, July 1995.
77 Pom, p236.
78 Geb, int A.
79 Ch, p176.
80 Geb, int J, int A.
81 Geb/Joan, ints A.
82 *Male*, pp659, 600; *Female*, p19, *Male*, p315.
83 *Male*, pp239, 511, 515; *Female*, pp170, 171.

84 Webster, op. cit., p169; indeed see this excellent book for a full display of this whole theme.
85 *Male*, pp206–13.
86 See for example *Male*, pp160–80, and the refs above for child sexuality.
87 Pom, pp155–6.
88 Tripp discussed this at length with K (Tripp, int A).
89 K to Simpson, 11 November; Simpson to K, 1 December 1946.
90 I deduce this since Nowlis sent K a fairly long commentary on the first two-and-a-half chapters on 8 January 1947.
91 *Newsweek* 30 (1 December 1947), p52.
92 See Clark, Thomas D., 1977, pp247–91. Also Brinkman, Paul Delbert, 1971.

13 *Writing the* Male *Volume – Science and Self-expression: 1947*

1 K to Yerkes, 11 November 1946; Pom, p141.
2 Rosenzweig, op. cit.
3 Pom, p273.
4 Helen Dietz to Geb, October (?) 1961.
5 *Male*, p31.
6 Ibid., pp415, 416.
7 Ibid., p595.
8 Ibid., p521; K to Victor Weigel, 20 July 1951.
9 Robinson, 1989, op. cit., p91.
10 Compare the commentary in *Male*, p235 and chart on p236.
11 Ibid., pp235.
12 Ibid., p186.
13 Ibid., p125.
14 Ibid., p588.
15 Ibid., refs too numerous to cite but see for example, pp257, 307, 568, 569.
16 Ibid., refs too numerous but see for example pp377, 590.
17 Ibid., p580.
18 See for example, Morantz, 1977; Jeffrey Weeks, 1985; Irvine, 1990. In view of these long-held published views it is rather odd how in his recent biography Jones should write as if this was an extraordinary and revolutionary discovery.
19 *Male*, pp298, 650–1.
20 Geb to A, 21 February 1996. If, as Gagnon and Simon did, you concentrate on the college sample – where Kinsey was much sounder – and remove all adolescent activity, you are left with 3 per cent exclusively H behaviour and a further 3 per cent with extensive H activity. Figures still not greatly different from Kinsey's. See

Gagnon, 1973.
21 *Male*, pp610–66.
22 Robinson, 1989.
23 *Male*, pp326, 325.
24 The impression was gained from just four questions out of the possible 521: Special interests in sport; Athletic experience in high school and college organised teams; Fraternity and sorority membership in college; and something vaguely labelled 'Personality traits'. Of these, only half the sport question and the last would apply to the non-college educated sample. As regards this last, no details were given as to what these personality traits were, so presumably they were just further general impressions of the interviewers. There was also a question 'Psychological test ratings' – but this was restricted to a 'selected series of individuals'. Again no details are given as to who these selected people were, how they were chosen, who worked out the ratings, how they were obtained, what the results were or how they were used. Furthermore, the characteristics emphasized by Kinsey carry considerably less force when you realise that 31% of the early sexually active had a timid/taciturn rating, while 33% of the late adolescent, late active ones had the energetic/vivacious rating. Ibid., pp63, 64, 325–26.
25 Ibid., pp195, 197–203, 216.
26 Ibid., p393; Geb, int A; Pom, p223; Tripp, int A; K to Beach, 17 April 1946; 'Dale', int BBC, June 1995.
27 There is a strong, pro-culture anti-biology' current again in left-wing academia – especially in America – which would dismiss

Kinsey out of hand for his stance here. I
think this current is fundamentally wrong,
and it is likely, to mix metaphors, to have a
fight on its hands as the genome unfolds. For
an interesting discussion see Ehrenreich,
1997.

28 Pom, pp262, 263.

29 Raymond and Hitchcock to K, 5 February
1947. Publishing history is of limited
interest, but for a much fuller account see JB,
pp534–8.

30 Pom, p262.

31 Corner, int J, 5 August 1971; Corner to
Weed, 31 May; to K, 2 June 1947.

32 K to Corner, 9 June; Corner to K, 2 June
1947; Corner, int J (and see JB, pp457–64).

33 K to B, 22 May 1947.

34 K to N, 7 June; N to K, 14 June 1947.

35 N to K, 8 January, K to N, 11 January 1947.

36 K to Yerkes, 17 May 1947.

37 K to Saunders, 27 and 30 August 1947; *New
York Times*, 14 April 1970.

38 Brinkman, Paul D., 1971. Corner, int J.
Evidence for K desiring and engineering
publicity is everywhere. See for example K to
Saunders, 6 September; 25 November 1947.

39 *Male*, p678.

40 K to Treasurer, IU, 7 October 1947. IU
Archive.

41 Pom, pp263, 264.

42 Helen Dietz to Geb, October (?) 1961.

43 K to G, 1 October 1947.

44 Pom, p265.

45 Kubie to Corner, 6 April 1948, quoted JB,
p582.

46 Kubie to Dr Raymond Gosselin, 14 October;
K to Kubie, 18 October 1947.

47 See K to Dr Bentley Glass, 27 October or to
Dr Lloyd Warner, 29 October 1947. James
Jones, incidentally, condemns these moves
to get favourable reviews, energetic but
understandable, with high moral indignation
('to corrupt a system of peer review' etc.),
but it is by no means unknown in academe,
though perhaps more often left to publisher
or the writer's academic superior or
supporters. It is still more common in
general trade publishing and Kinsey's efforts
here are a further indication of how his work
attempted to straddle both worlds. Jones'
own book was plastered with extravagant
quotations of praise presumably solicited by
someone; nor do such pious strictures come
very well from an author who, in his search
for publicity, squeezed every last drop of
salacious material from his book and
concentrated it into a lengthy article in the
New Yorker (see JB, pp552–3 and dust jacket;
New Yorker, 25 August 1997).

48 K to Ramsey, 17 October 1947.

49 Clark, Thomas D., op. cit.

50 K to Lloyd Potter of Saunders, 3 November
1947.

51 Pom, p265.

52 Corner to K, 10 December; Gregg to
Saunders, 9 December; to K, 19 December
1947.

53 Brisco to Rice; Rice to K, 15 December
1947.

54 Quoted Pom, p247.

55 Helen Dietz to Geb, October (?) 1961.

56 D to K, 31 October; K to D, 10 November
1947.

57 K to Ramsey, 17 October 1947.

14 Publication: Criticism, Praise, Success!

1 Wells, Herman, op. cit., 1980, pp177–94.

2 Rather than continually reference these
separate figures I would simply direct the
interested scholar to the large Saunders files
for 1948 held at the KI. And see K to
Dickinson, 22 January 1948.

3 This figure is from Pom, op. cit., p360, and is
in fact for the *Female* volume, but this
duplicated in all other respects the *Male*
volume. Pomeroy gives no source, and in
fact global figures are oddly difficult to pin
down. Ch gives 250,000 total sale.
Brinkman, 270,000. There are a great many
individual figures in the Saunders files but
not these particular totals. JB seems to have
had equal difficulty.

4 Brinkman, 1971, op. cit.

5 *Indianapolis Star*, 30 November 1947,

quoting *Male*, p585 – one of K's no doubt
accurate guesses.

6 *Ashland Daily Press*, quoted Brinkman.

7 Pom, p283, 284.

8 See for example Pom, pp305, 306 on the
Survey published by Leo P. Crespi of
Princeton in *Public Opinion Quarterly*. Also
Saunders to K, 2 March 1948.

9 Beach, int J cit; Hecht, int BBC, 1995.

10 *Male*, pp397, 414–15, 556, 557.

11 Robinson, 1989, op. cit., pp85–7.

12 Geb, int A cit.

13 Robinson, 1972.

14 Trilling, 1954; Mead, 1948, pp60–9; JB,
pp334, 356, 504.

15 See for example Morantz Regina, 1977,
pp563–89.

16 Ehrhardt, Dr Anke, 1982.

17 Lowell Reed to Corner, 26 February 1948. Similarly, Robert S. Morison of the Rockefeller Foundation pointed out that anyone in the foundation business was in it for 'a better world', int J, 18 October 1971. And see JB, p556.

18 Kubie to Geb, 28 January 1970; Geb, int A.

19 Kubie to Corner, 6 April 1948; Kubie to Raymond Gosselin, 14 October 1947; K to Kubie, 18 October 1947.

20 K to Kubie, 8 March 1948.

21 Kubie to K, 14 January; 2 February 1948.

22 Kubie to Harriet Pilpel, 17 February 1959; K to Pilpel, 21 January 1956, on Kubie writing to Albert Deutsch.

23 JB, pp584, 585.

24 Tripp, int A.

25 K to H.D. Williams (Saunders), 27 May 1948.

26 Ibid., 13 September 1948.

27 Pom, pp297–8; Corner to Gregg, 10 January 1949.

28 K to C, 4 March 1948.

29 K to C, 26 November 1948; 7 January 1949.

30 K to D, 12 April 1949.

31 See for example K to Corner, 1 February; report of telephone conversation with Gregg; or Corner to K, 5 May 1948.

32 K to D, 10 February 1948; to Lloyd Potter of Saunders, 10 February and 2 March 1948.

33 K to Corner, 15 April 1950.

34 N to K, 17 November 1948, quoting Hans Sachs.

35 See M to Dr Clarence B. Farrar, 5 May; to K, 5 May; to Deutsch, 12 May; to K, 28 May 1948; K to M, 29 June 1948.

36 Much correspondence, but see for example K to Deutsch, 12 February and 23 June 1948; Ernst to K, 2 March; K to Ernst, 4 November 1948; K to Geddes, 24 March 1948.

37 E to K, 18 June 1948.

38 Lloyd Potter to K, 7 May 1948.

39 D to K, 31 July 1948.

40 See IU Archive and Pom, p288.

41 Haddon to Wells, 12 May; Wells to Haddon, 22 May 1949, IU Archive.

42 IU Archive.

43 K to Corner, 7 January 1949; memos, Wells to K, January 1949, IU Archive; Wells, int J.

44 Wells, int J; Wells, int Dr Thomas D. Clark, January 1968.

45 Pom, pp307–24; Collins/Edmondson/ Remak, ints A; Torrey/Payne, ints J.

46 Baxter, int A.

47 These three paras – Anne Call, int A/Int, *Daily Mail*, 23 March 1996, pp32–3; Clark, 1977; K to Saunders, 14 October 1948.

48 Gorer, 1971; N. Bajos, 1993; Anne M. Johnson et al., 1994; Edward O. Laumann et al. 1994.

49 Gorer, op. cit., pp30, 97, 224, 292–312.

50 *Female*, p79.

51 Laumann, op. cit., p35.

52 Ibid., pp30, 32, 34, 67, 167, footnote on p167.

53 Geb, int A.

54 Laumann, op. cit., p215.

55 Johnson, op. cit., pp185–96.

56 Ibid., pp195–6.

57 For example, there is evidence that there may have been a substantial drop in adolescent male H activity over the last fifty years. Certainly, this is so in Germany. The studies suggested, in explanation, first that young males, especially college males, have many more opportunities to engage sexually with females than they did fifty years ago (so supporting one of Kinsey's arguments). Second, that there is now a much greater awareness of the concept of 'homosexual' identity than there used to be, and that this (now again lessening) may have acted as a deterrent. See Schmidt, 1994.

58 Richard C. Lewontin, 1995.

59 E.g. Richard C. Lewontin and Stephen Jay Gould, 1979.

60 Johnson, op. cit., pp439–42.

61 *Male*, p128, *Female*, pp75–8.

62 *Male*, p153.

63 Laumann, op. cit., pp62–3, but see also pp55–70.

64 Ibid., p568.

65 E.g. Anke Erhardt, 1982.

66 Geb et al., 1979. See p9 for this discussion; see again note 20 to Chap 13.

15 Money – Branching Out – Kinsey's Sexual Experiments: 1948–9

1 K to Saunders, 17 January 1948.

2 Marsh, in conversation with Tripp.

3 JB, p604.

4 Tripp, int A.

5 JB, p607.

6 JB, pp82, 83; 779–80, notes 82, 83; note p79.

7 JB, p791, note 79.

8 JB, p604.

9 Weinberg, 1994, pp257–79.

10 Greven, 1992 (1991), pp174–86; JB, pp23, 779–80, note p83.

11 Geb, int A, November 1997.
12 Ibid.
13 Tripp, 1975/1987, pp115–16; Tripp, int A, November 1997.
14 Bill Gury, tel int A, October 1997.
15 JB, p604; Geb, int A.
16 Tebbel, Tripp, ints A; Pom, pp308–9.
17 Tripp to K, 10 February 1948.
18 Tripp, 1975/1987.
19 Tripp, int A.
20 K to Shadle, 26 January; Shadle to K, 29 January 1948; K to Beach, 8 October; Beach to K, 26 October 1943; Beach to K, 24 January 1948.
21 K to Saunders, 12 February; Saunders to K, 2 March; K to Saunders, 5 March 1948.
22 NRC IU Reports, IU Archive.
23 Saunders to Martin, 22 April 1948.
24 Almost none of Avinoff's letters is dated but this must be early 1948. And see Hellman, 1948.
25 In fact, this is the only Avinoff letter with a date – 14 December 1947.
26 Waugh, 1993.
27 Tripp, int A.
28 See for example, K to D, 12 February, D to K, 3 March 1948 – and many others.
29 Clark, 1977.
30 Anon A, int A.
31 Geb, int A.
32 Pom, p241; Dellenback, ints A and J; Tripp, int A.
33 D to K, 6 April 1948.
34 K to NR, 28 May, 23 August 1948.
35 Various undated letters A to K, May/June/July 1948; K to A, 29 June 1948.
36 Invitation on file, KI 'Hobhard'.
37 K to Avinoff, 26 September 1949.
38 K to EM, 10 August 1948.
39 Apart from itemised citations, I have drawn the disparate items in this section from: Pom, pp131, 132, 147–54, 161; Nowlis, int A; Tebbel, int A.
40 Geb, int A, November 1997.
41 Ibid.; Kroc, int A.
42 B to K, 9 July 1951; K to B, 16 June 1948.
43 Laurence E. Gichner to Geb, October (?) 1981; Dorothy Collins, int A.
44 K to 'DH', 6 May 1950.
45 K to D, 20 January 1944.
46 Geb, int A.
47 K to EM, 10 August 1948.
48 To reference all this would be excessive, but see for example: K to Mr B.B.D., 4 April 1949; Dickinson to K, August 1948; K to Dr Francis Childs, 22 September 1949; 'Female' to K, September (?) 1955; 'Mrs Mary Downside', 13 December 1952; 'Henry Zchloch', 17 October 1948; 'Klong' to K, 21 February, K to 'Klong', 25 April 1946.
49 This section from Dellenback/Geb/ Dorothy Collins/Wells/Edmondson/ Martin/Mac, ints J. Also K to Corner, 3 February 1950.
50 Reports to NRC and IU, in IU Archive.
51 Legman, 1966, p124.
52 Geb, int J.
53 Legman, op. cit., p94.
54 K to Mrs Mary Neil, Gotham Book Mart NY, 13 September 1949.
55 The only other letter dated A to K, 26 January 1949.
56 Paul Fuller to A, 26 September 1996.
57 Tripp, int A; Waugh, op. cit., 1993; Tripp to K, 3 November 1948.
58 Wescott, int Jerry Rosco, December 1976, Tripp to A March 1999.
59 Wescott, int Rosco cit.; Marsh, tel int A.
60 Martin, int A. Yet this seems a fantastic number, despite Martin's statement.
61 *Female*, Chap 15.
62 E.g. Taylor, 1996, p24.
63 *Female*, p634.
64 Telegram, 17 December 1948, KI.
65 K to D, 20 January 1948.
66 Dellenback, int A.
67 Pom, pp173, 174.
68 Collins, int A.
69 Tripp, int A.
70 Geb, int A.
71 K to Jebb, 15 June 1951, and see letters throughout the files to nudists, educationalists, liberal sex movements and so on. K to 'Anthony Beamish', 10 December 1955, for example.
72 Geb, int A.

16 Expansion – and Discovering the Female: 1949–50

1 Special Assistant to the President to K, 25 July 1948.
2 *San Francisco Chronicle*, 19 (?) February 1949; Pom, pp146, 147.
3 K to S, 4 April 1949.
4 K to J.A. Lutz (Saunders), 5 July 1949.
5 K to S, 27 January, 14 November; Martin to S, 13 December 1949.
6 Many letters. See for example K to S, 27 January 1949.
7 NRC/IU, 1 April 1949. Reports, KI and IU Archives.

8 Many letters. See for example K to C, 19 March, C to K, 24 March, 11 April, 27 May 1949. Pom, pp309, 310. Reports, op. cit.

9 These 3 paras: Torrey, int J, September 1971; Pom, op. cit., pp151, 152; Dellenback/Geb/Anger/Marsh (tel) ints, A, August-December 1995; Marsh tape, Geb, 25 November 1961.

10 Geb, int A.

11 Pom, pp401–2.

12 Gagnon, int BBC, 1995, for TV series *Reputations* – 'Kinsey' op. cit.

13 *Female*, pp375–91, 719; and see K to 'Dr Stephen F. Brandt', 3 May 1949.

14 Dr 'Alice Spears'; see Pom, pp179–80.

15 Tripp, int A cit; Geb, int A.

16 John Tebbel, int A cit.

17 Geb, int A.

18 Thomas Waugh, 1993.

19 Laidlaw to Geb, 2 May 1968.

20 Geb, int A.

21 Ibid. Also Geb to A, 14 July 1996.

22 Waugh, op. cit.

23 *Female*, Chaps 14 and (especially) 15; Masters/Johnson 1966.

24 Bullough, 1994, op. cit., quoting Joseph R. Beck, 1872.

25 *Female*, p633.

26 Bergler, E., 1936, quoted *Female*, p570.

27 Pom, pp304, 305.

28 Quoted *Female*, p583.

29 *Male*, p576, Trilling, op. cit., 1954.

30 These 3 paras, *Female*, pp157–63.

31 Ibid., pp567–93.

32 Ibid., pp573, 574, 591, 592.

33 Ibid., pp163, 164, 384, 385.

34 Ibid., p371.

35 K to Beach, 23 January 1950.

36 Helen Singer Kaplan, 1974.

37 *Female*, pp634, 635; Bullough, 1994, op. cit., citing Alice Lader et al., 1982; Bonnie Bullough et al., 1984.

38 Gertrude Stein, 1933.

39 Account in the last 8 paras mostly from the informative and amusing Introduction by Robert Phelps and Chronology by Jerry Rosco to Wescott, 1990, which they edited. Details also from James J. Martin, 1981; David Leddick, int A.

40 Wescott, int Rosco cit.

41 Wescott, op. cit., pp245, 246.

42 Ibid., p245.

43 Gore Vidal, 1965.

44 Vidal to A, 6 May 1996.

45 Vidal, 1997, p103.

46 K to GW, 6 December 1949; to MW, 17 December 1950.

47 Anger, int A, February 1997; Timmons, Stuart to A, 17 July 1997; D'Emilio, John, 1993.

48 K to Wheeler, 9 November 1949; Wheeler to K, 29 July 1953.

49 Geb ints, A/BBC.

50 K to Cochran, 12 January 1951.

51 Geb, int A.

52 Pom, pp202–5; Geb, int A.

53 Geb in William H. Masters, 1980, p18.

54 K to Potter, 6 September 1949.

55 Pom, p310.

56 K to August Vollmer, 26 September 1949. Important problems which, as far as I know, are simply not addressed today in either Britain or America. Kinsey's view on the first was that either some outlet should be provided (which partly solves the second) or that homosexuality should be allowed. 'We have never,' he told Dr Negley Teeter, 'worked in long-time institutions in which fewer than 60% of the men are engaged in such activity and in one such institution we had over 90% of the inmates admit such experience.' One would suppose tacit acceptance is what happens in UK and American prisons now. (Kinsey to Dr Negley Teeter, Department of Sociology, Temple University, Philadelphia, 1 August 1950.)

57 Quoted Pom, p206.

58 K to Douglas Rigg, 19 July 1950.

59 Collins, int A.

60 Wescott, int Rosco cit.

61 Wescott, op. cit., p266; Wescott, int Rosco cit.

62 K to B, 8 March 1950.

63 K to J.A. Franklin, IU Administration, 1 August 1949. IU Archive.

64 Collins, int A.

65 *Indiana Alumni Magazine*, April (?) 1950 (possibly March 1951); Wells, int A.

66 Clark, 1977; Eggert Meyer to Geb, 1961.

67 These 2 paras: Gregg to Corner, 7 March; K to Corner, 15 April; Corner to K, 24 April; Corner to Dr Lubin, 5 May – all 1950. (See also Corner to K, 23 January; Lubin to Corner, 14 June; Statistical Society to Corner, 15 June; K to Corner, 13 September – all 1950.) For a fuller account see JB, pp635–9.

68 Staff analysis by Geb and Dorothy Collins for A.

69 Edmondson, int A.

70 Collins, int J, 9 December 1971.

71 Collins, ints A and J. As far as I could ascertain, none of the fringe staff had any idea of the goings on among the central

figures. Except I did notice that when I asked a question in this direction in 1995, long before Jones' biography had miraculously loosened tongues, Dorothy Collins suddenly looked rather abstracted and after a pause said vaguely, 'I believe Paul had an affair with someone or other at some point.' I would be surprised if this extremely intelligent woman had not noticed more.

72 Geb, int A.

73 Roehr, int J., September 1971; the letter

information can be gleaned from the files because the letters she answers herself often have a more detached tone, but principally because the reference is simply ER (or ERG). When she is typing to Kinsey's dictation it is ER/ACK (or ERG/ACK).

74 Roehr, int J.

75 Geb, int A.

76 Tax returns, 1950–51. IU Archive.

77 Paper *Institute for Sex Research Inc.*, 1 June 1950.

17 Filming – 'Philosophy' – Women – Writing – Wescott: 1950–1

1 Pom, pp172–82.

2 Steward, Samuel, 1980, pp95–106; 1991, pp81–90 for next eight paras. Steward sets the sessions in 1949, but not till 1950 was the ISR Library on the ground floor, a fact he mentions in an amusing incident I haven't quoted.

3 Dellenback was a young, inexperienced, very 'green' young man at this time. 'But weren't you *shocked?*' his friend Tripp said, hearing his account of the S/M filming. Dellenback said he might have been but Kinsey treated it all as so normal, so run-of-the-mill, that 'I had nothing to hang my shock *on*.' (Tripp, int A.)

4 Wescott, int Rosco, Pom, pp172–82.

5 Earle Marsh, tel int A; John Tebbel, int A.

6 JB, p607.

7 Geb and Dellenback, ints A.

8 Wescott, int cit.

9 See Chap 19.

10 The facts in this and the next 3 paras come from JB, pp607, 608, and Anon A, int A. The discussion owes much to interviews with Dr Michael Perring of Harley Street, and Dr John Bancroft of the Kinsey Institute.

11 Tripp, 1987, Chap 6, esp. pp115, 116.

12 Interestingly, it does seem to apply to Earle Marsh. He, as we noted, had a very strict, sexually inhibiting religious upbringing. When he threw off his inhibitions he experimented boldly and joyfully for years with a whole range of sexual behaviours (the barriers can be almost anything that is disapproved of). When he read Tripp's book, Marsh told Dellenback (who told Anon A, who told me) that he had been fascinated to find how every word of Chapter 6 applied to him.

13 Geb and Dellenback, ints A.

14 Jones says vaguely that 'many' of the films 'involved sadomasochism' (JB, p611). He gives no authority or source for this and

Gebhard and Dellenback were completely clear in interview that there were only four. The figures for couple films are from Pomeroy (Pom, p177). Pomeroy greatly reduced the masturbation films which, as we noted, Martin, in interview, perhaps rather wildly set at 1,000. Kinsey's instinctive secretiveness here is interesting. While in general open with his team, something was always hidden from one or more of them. Thus, no one but Dellenback ever actually witnessed Kinsey's masturbating activity; nor did Dellenback ever see him or film him with a rope round the testicles alone, only round his entire genitalia. In fact, *no one* ever saw him with the rope round his testicles. The only sources for it are Anon A (JB, pp739, 885) and Earle Marsh. But Anon A's source was Pomeroy who said that he'd learnt it from Kinsey. Earle Marsh told Anon A that he too had been told it by Kinsey. Kinsey would not lie, but it is conceivable he would exaggerate or boast.

15 *Male*, pp60, 510; *Female*, pp88, 676–9, 681.

16 E. Roehr to Albert Deutsch, 13 June 1950.

17 K to D, 5 September 1950.

18 Dellenback, int A, among several informants.

19 Rigg to K, 12 September 1954 – this letter refers to K suggesting this 'years ago', so that it must have been about now. K wasn't again at San Q till April 1951.

20 See Bowman to K, 19 October; K to B, 14 November 1949; K to B, 20 March; B to K, 24 March: K to B, 30 March; B to K, 3 April; B to K, 2 October 1950.

21 Dellenback, int A.

22 *New York Close-Up* to Mac, 12 June; K to Mrs June Falkenburg McCrary, 21 June 1950.

23 K to Sh, 5 June; Sh to K, 8 August 1950.

24 'Field' to K, 8 August; K to 'F', August (?) 1950; 'F' to K, 20 September 1950; 'F' to K, 31 December; K to 'F', 31 December (?) 1951; K to 'F', 7 January 1952.

25 Pom, pp304–5; Bergler, 1954.
26 Too many letters in both directions to cite, but see for example telegram Dorothy Dickinson Barbour/Dickinson to K, 10 August 1950, 1 September 1950, 2 September to K; D to K, 17 September, 30 September; K telegram and letters over this period – all 1950. See D to K, scrap, 29 November 1948.
27 Corner to Lubin, 5 May 1950; K to Corner, 13 September 1950; Edmondson, int J; Cochran et al., 1954; K to Corner, 18 October, 9 November 1950; Cochran to Corner, 3 January 1951.
28 Cochran, 1954, pp693, 694; JB, pp641–4. My account differs somewhat from that in Jones, which is largely taken from an interview he had with Mosteller, then very old, in 1992. Most of this, as well as Mac's statement, applied to the *second* visit, as Paul Gebhard, Martin and Edmondson made clear to me. Why should the committee have expressed such belligerence, as Jones makes them do, when the purpose of their visit was to learn? It was on the second visit that they and Kinsey were advancing opposing views.
29 C to K, 2 January 1951.
30 Huncke, int A; Barney Miles, 1989, quoted Waugh, op. cit.
31 K's Engagement Diaries, K to Wheeler, 2 November; Wheeler to K, 22 December (telegram 26 December); K to Cadmus, 2 November – all 1950. Postcard Cadmus to K undated, but about now.
32 K to Tennessee Williams, 14 January; TW to K, 18 January; K to TW, 21 January; Tripp to K, 11 October; Wheeler to K, November (?) – all 1950.
33 K to Tennessee Williams, 21 November 1950; Cheryl Crawford to K, 19 July 1994; K to Crawford, July (?) 1954.
34 Pom, pp191.
35 Paragraph comment by Rosco, in GW int cit.
36 Pom, pp192–3; Collins, int A.
37 Wescott, op. cit., p307.
38 K to 'RJ', 10 October 1952 (possession 'RJ'); Dickinson to K, 5 January 1946, about 'van Hecht'; Report IU/NRC 1953, in IU Archive.
39 Discussion, Tripp with A; Frans de Waal, 1997.
40 Vern Bullough, op. cit.
41 Telegram Mrs A.P. Shirt to K, 29 November; telegrams K to Mrs Shirt, 29 November; property gift list K to D, 8 February 1946; Tripp, int A. In fact, Dickinson's daughter was not on Kinsey's side. She later disputed Kinsey's claims to her father's material, the legal right was not firm and Kinsey had to hand a lot of it over to the New York Academy of Medicine, who destroyed it.
42 Geb, int A.
43 Geb, int BBC; Clark, 1977, p277.
44 K to Corner, 13 December 1950; Clark, ibid.; and see Treasury Dept to Ernst, 13 February 1956.
45 Wells, int J; Pom, p388; Wells, int Clark, January 1968.
46 Joan/Dellenback/Geb, ints A.
47 Wescott, int Rosco.
48 K to Shadle, 15 January; Shadle to K, 31 January; K to Shadle, 5 February – all 1951.
49 K to Saunders, 10 July 1951.
50 Many refs but for example, *Female*, pp150, 200–7, 239–42, 293–5 and so on.
51 Ibid., pp160, 165, 384–5, 502 and so on. *Male*, p581.
52 *Male* throughout, but see pp154–8, 247–9, 304–6, 359, 424, etc.; *Female*, pp5, 180, 221, 271, 275.
53 *Female*, p688.
54 Ibid., pp661–3.
55 As Paul Gebhard pointed out in Geb, 1979; also, Geb to A, 6 March 1996.
56 *Independent on Sunday*, 10 November 1996.
57 Nancy Friday, 1975; or see Rachel Silver, 1995.
58 Many studies, but see for example, Johnson et al., 1994, pp70, 76–86, 115–19, 256–7, 616–27; I.E. Robinson, 1982, pp237–40; *American Review of Sex Research*, Vol V, 1994. And see Bancroft, 1989.
59 *Female*, pp490–501; Johnson, pp211–12.
60 *Male*, pp589–90; for K's discussion see *Female*, pp412–16.
61 Laumann et al., 1994, p210. And see Kate Fillion, 1997.
62 Baker, R, 1996; Taylor, T, 1996, p61.
63 *British Medical Journal*, Vol 313, p307.
64 Reports to NRC and IU (IU Archive).
65 Quoted, *Female* note, p739.
66 See report in *The New York Times*, 1 September 1996.
67 *Female*, p741 (and see additionally pp718–48).
68 'George E. Richards' to K, 25 January 1954; and see Bowman to K, 9 July, 19 July 1951.
69 Most of the information and quotations in this section come from the Rosco interview with Wescott in 1976. Some additional items are from Wescott's published journals, 1990, individually paged.
70 Wescott, op. cit., pp248–9, 316.
71 Ibid., note, p334; Wescott, int Rosco.
72 Ibid., pp292–3, 297–9; also int Rosco.
73 K int Rosco.

18 Bisexuality – and the Case Against Kinsey

1 Refs too numerous to list, but see for example JB, pp285, 411, 492, 500, 600, 602.
2 Informant A, int A.
3 The second was Informant A, int cit., himself the person Jones called Anonymous A.
4 Tebbel to author, 31 January 1996.
5 Wescott, 1990, pp245–6; Crump, 1994, p3 of article.
6 GW to K, 'Early January 1952'. That the letters have been censored by Wescott is suggested by the fact that the beginnings and endings are often missing. The dates are then added, as here, in Wescott's hand. This letter was originally longer than the thirteen pages devoted to explaining that his jack-knifing was not faked.
7 GW to K, 25 July 1951.
8 GW to K, 13 October 1951.
9 See for example GW to K, 1 August 1953.
10 Wescott, 1990, p313.
11 GW to K: 1 August 1949; 19 January 1950; 25 July 1951; 19 January, 24 February 1952.
12 Geb and Dellenback, ints A, November 1997.
13 Geb, int A; Tebbel, tel int A, November 1997.
14 Joan, tel int A, November 1997.
15 Geb, int A.
16 Will Chandlee, tel int A, November 1997.
17 Geb, int A. Given Kinsey's secrecy Miller may not have been the only one; alternatively, given K's diffidence in this respect, he may have been.
18 Chandlee, int cit.
19 Geb, int J. Tripp noticed this aspect too, but said Kinsey succeeded because a) he always knew the jargon of whatever discipline he engaged with and b) he was careful always to generalise and never particularise. 'Gebhard's blood had no need to curdle,' said Tripp.
20 *Male*, p666.
21 Ibid., pp655, 552.
22 Ibid., pp457–9, 631.
23 Waugh, Thomas, 1993.
24 Ibid., p70.
25 Geb/Dellenback, ints A.
26 Todd Smith, int A, July 1995.
27 Smith/Geb, ints A; A's own research.
28 Waugh, op. cit., p65.
29 Ibid., p86.
30 The references are too numerous to give all of them, but see, for example, JB, pp349, 376, 387, 516, 519, 522, 533, 541.
31 Tripp/Geb, ints A, November 1997. Kinsey

did not, as Jones suggests (JB, p677), secretly hope to do his H book after the *Male* one. The opposite was true. By 1953, he had decided, he told Tripp, that so important were the sex offender and the juvenile books, that homosexuals had to come fifth.
32 JB, p533.
33 Ibid., p349.
34 Wescott, int Rosco cit.
35 Anne M. Johnson et al., 1994, p211.
36 JB, pp270, 271. Kinsey has sent Voris two books about nudism. The relevant passage reads 'Are the Voris's [sic] shocked? Mrs Kinsey and I agree they have been a healthy part of our children's education. Read the Mason one first; it is a broader analysis of the movement.' That is all. K to RV, 10 November 1934.
37 JB, pp340–1.
38 Ibid., pp346, 347.
39 Ibid., p366.
40 Ibid., p417.
41 Ibid., p564.
42 Ibid., p566.
43 Ibid., p582.
44 Ibid., p568.
45 Ibid., pp684, 685.
46 *Chambers Twentieth Century Dictionary*.
47 JB, p490.
48 Nowlis, tel int A, November 1997.
49 JB, pp80–1, 255, 270–1, 273, 279–82, 284, 287–9, 481, 490–1, 501–3, 513, 605–14.
50 Ibid., pp604–5.
51 See respectively: *The Guardian*, 6 November; *TLS*, 5 December; *The Mail on Sunday*, 24 August – all in 1997.
52 *The Times*, 2 January 1998, p17.
53 See for example Julian Barnes: 'Detractors claim . . . that his desire to legitimate his hidden life resulted in his research being skewed in favour of homosexuals. This is probably correct . . .' – *The Sunday Times*, 9 November 1997. Blake Morrison: '. . . we can see how his own sexual agenda skewed some of his conclusions . . .' *Independent on Sunday*, 9 November 1997.
54 *The New Republic*, 24 November, *Gannett News Service*, 25 October, both 1997. Or, out of literally dozens, see Terry Teachout: 'The truth about Kinsey is that he was no impersonal gatherer of scientific data . . . But from the outset . . . sought out as many male homosexual interviewees as possible . . . [and] vastly overestimated the incidence of homosexual behaviour in America . . .' *The National Review*, 13 October 1997, pp69–70.

Or B.H. Ackelmire: 'Kinsey . . . was driven by personal demons that lured him to the extreme and the perverse . . . clouded his judgement and distorted his results.' *Indianapolis Star*, 22 November 1997.

55 I should perhaps note that, though I formulated my criticisms of Jones' book while I read it, I was reassured later to find quite a number of US reviewers agreed with some or all of my objections. See, for example, Kenneth Lewes, *Science*, vol. 278,

pp206–9, 19 December 1997; Martin Duberman, *The Nation*, 3 November 1997; Thomas Laquer, review posted 4 November 1997 in Slate, the Microsoft on-line journal, at http://www.slate.com/Book Review/97-11-04/Book Review asp. And Tripp, 1999.

56 Jones, 1981.

57 Nowlis, int A, October 1995; tel int, February 1998.

58 Lewes, *Science*, op. cit., pp206–9.

59 Duberman, *The Nation*, 3 November 1997.

19 *Writing and Publication of the* Female *Volume – Science as Sex and Literature*

1 Engagement diaries, KI; Dr Manfred Guttmacher to Geb, 26 October 1961; Collins, int A.

2 Ellis Memoir held at KI (and part used Pom, p436); K to Ruth D, 11 October 1951.

3 S to K, 21 November 1951.

4 Gebhard couldn't in interview remember the precise date, only 'during the writing of the *Female* volume', but he agreed it must have been about this time.

5 Geb to A, 6 March 1996.

6 Geb et al., 1979/Geb, int A; *Female*, pp30, 117–18. This course of events also disproves a recent suggestion that Kinsey dropped these statistics deliberately so that he would get fewer adult/child sex cases and so more easily challenge US sex laws. This is not how Kinsey operated. In any case, he would far rather have *kept* his prison sample. (See under Kenan, 1995.)

7 C to K, 27 August, 27 September, 8 October 1951; to Ford Foundation, 28 February 1952; Morison, int J.

8 C to K, 22 December 1951; K to Corner, 8 January 1952.

9 GW to K, 6 and 8 November (in KI); Wescott, op. cit., pp303–4.

10 Peter Parker, *The Observer Review*, 29 June 1997, p17; Wescott, op. cit., p307.

11 Wescott, op. cit., pp301, 302.

12 K to MW, 9 January, 7 December 1951.

13 See for example MW to K, 22 December 1950, 2 January and undated but January (?) 1952.

14 Anon A and John Tebbel, ints A cit.

15 K to Corner, 8 January; Cochran to Corner, 3 January 1952.

16 These three paras: Geb, Dellenback, Dorothy Collins, Corner, Mac, ints J cit; Geb, int A. For a much fuller account see JB, pp656–8, though included in this should be much of JB, pp641–4.

17 K to Wells, note 26, February 1952, IU

Archive.

18 K to Corner, 8 January 1952; Cochran et al., 1954; Corner to K, 5 February 1952.

19 Corner to Bernard Berelson, 26 February 1952 (and see Berelson to Corner, 6 March 1952). Also Morison, int J.

20 *Female*, footnote, p135.

21 Ibid., p352.

22 Ibid., p146. And see also, for example, pp230, 282, 283, 366, etc.

23 Ibid., many examples, see pp113–22, 166–221.

24 Ibid. Many refs. See, for example, pp137, 353, 355, 411, 412.

25 Ibid., pp410–11. But also see pp113–22, 166–221.

26 Ibid., pp17, 18. But still more specifically in lectures and conversation – Geb, int A.

27 Anne Johnson et al., 1994, p102.

28 For an informed discussion see Richard Webster, 1996, which as of writing (July 1997) awaits publication. Also Webster 1998, and K to Dr Agnes A. Sharp, 27 November 1952.

29 *Female*, pp116–22.

30 See the discussion in Bullough, op. cit., where he quotes or cites David Finkelhov, 1980, pp171–7; D.E.H. Russell, 1984; Geb et al., 1965; T.G.M. Sandfort, 1984, pp249–66.

31 K to R, 17 April 1952.

32 *Female*, pp39–42.

33 Geb to A, 6 March 1996.

34 *Female*, pp46, 511.

35 Ibid., p447.

36 John Gagnon in McWhirter, 1990, Chap 12. Gay gene: Richard Pillard and James Weinrich, 1986, pp808–12; Richard Pillard and Michael J. Bailey, 1991, pp1089–96; and see discussion Richard Pillard and Edward Stein, 1994, pp93–110. Chandler Burr, 1996; Dean Hamer, 1993, pp321–7. *New Scientist*, 4 November 1995, p5; 25 September 1996, pp32–5. Some of these

books and studies themselves have useful references. Intelligence: *New Scientist*, 14 June 1997, p16. Downs Syndrome: *New Scientist*, 7 June 1997, p49.

37 *Female*, pp89, 90.

38 Ibid., pp587; 673–4.

39 K to Univ of California, 3 August, 29 November 1951, 21 February 1952; Stanford University, 12 March 1952; K to Bowman, 20 February, 16 April 1952.

40 Deutsch to K, 28 April 1952; Reports, KI and IU Archive; Beach (tape) and Meyer to Geb, 1961; K to Jesse Bogue, 16 May 1952 (quoted Brinkman, op. cit.); K to Sharron, 9 September 1953.

41 K to Wheeler, 3 May, 27 May 1952; Meyer to Geb, February 1961 cit.

42 Collins, ints J/A; Geb, int A.

43 K to S, 12 July 1952.

44 Bullough, op. cit.; Geb and Nowlis, ints A.

45 Joan/Robert Reid, ints A.

46 K to GW, 7 July; GW to K, 14 July 1952.

47 Wescott, op. cit., p316.

48 See for example GW to K, 1 March 1953, 41 pages but an unknown number are missing.

49 Tripp, int A; *Male*, p593.

50 Octavio Paz, 1996.

51 Johnson et al., op. cit., p100.

52 Wescott, op. cit., pp250, 317.

53 K to Deutsch, 15 September 1952.

54 K to Saunders, 8 October 1952.

55 K to Auden, 10 October 1952.

56 N, int A.

57 Throughout this section I elide and take quotes sometimes several lines apart. Here, from *Female*, pp584–6.

58 Ibid., p590.

59 Ibid., p607.

60 Ibid., pp606–8.

61 Ibid., pp610–12.

62 Ibid., p613.

63 Ibid., pp607, 617, 618.

64 Ibid., pp606, 622.

65 Ibid., p622.

66 Ibid., p632.

67 Ibid., pp628, 631.

68 Ibid., pp637, 638.

69 Wescott, int Rosco.

70 See for example the letter to K from 'Mrs P. Gibson', 25 September 1953, a young woman who is so powerfully turned on by the book that she is having 'masses' of sex with her husband.

71 K to Saunders, 27 November 1952.

72 K to Wheeler, 26 November, 9 December 1952; to Wheeler, 11 September 1952.

73 Skutch to K, 4 December; K to Skutch, 15 December 1952.

74 Geb, in *Sex and the Scientist* film cit.

75 JB, pp608, 609.

76 E.W. Palmer to Saunders, 9 November 1951 (1952?).

77 Clark, 1977; Eggert Meyer to Geb, 1961.

78 See for example, K to Laidlaw, 26 March 1952.

79 See E.M.'s 'Comments', 22 February 1953. For a good account of K and Emily Mudd, see Judith Allen, 1997.

80 K to Saunders, 19 February; K to Corner, 19 February 1953; Corner to K, 11 February 1953; Tax return, April 1952/53 (IU Archive).

81 K to S, 11 May, S to K, 29 May; K to S, 4 August 1953.

82 Once again I follow Brinkman's unpublished dissertation for this section. Other sources are individually cited. Brinkman, 1971.

83 Grace Naismith, 'The Great Kinsey Hullabaloo', in *This Week Magazine*, 9 August 1953, quoted Brinkman.

84 K to Bob Rowan, 27 June 1953, quoted Brinkman.

85 Clark, 1977; Speaks, int A, July 1995.

86 Marsh, int BBC; Joan, int A.

87 Reid, int A.

88 Edgar Anderson in 'Kinseyiana File'; Kenneth Anger, int A, February 1996.

89 K to the accused's lawyer, Robert S. Smith, 14 August 1953.

90 *The Herald Telephone*, 19 August 1953, quoted Grant, op. cit. It is interesting that Bloomington still thought 'telephone' sufficiently modern to use like this then.

20 *The Paper Explosion*

Once again all unsourced material in this section and the next is taken from Paul Brinkman's careful and detailed unpublished doctoral dissertation on the subject (Brinkman, 1971). Other sources are individually cited.

1 Pom, p355.

2 Ibid., pp342, 361.

3 JB, p703.

4 Victor Cohen, int BBC.

5 Pom, pp364–5.

6 This and last 2 paras from letters in IU Archive.

7 Mead, 1928; Pom, p362. Margaret Mead was married three times and had numerous

affairs with men and women (including Ruth Benedict). See Jane Howard, 1984, pp51–59, 367.

8 Meninger's review in *Saturday Review of Literature*, 26 September 1953; The Associated New Wire Services, 10 May, *Time*, 17 May 1954.

9 Marsh, tel int A, December 1995.

10 Dellenback, int A.

11 Quotations, much of the information and some of the ideas in this section come from David Halberstam's excellent book on the period. Halberstam, 1994.

12 Halberstam, quoting Payne, in Goulden, 1976.

13 *Female*, pp310–11, 336, Table 78.

14 Johnson et al., 1994, pp79, 80.

15 Pom, p360.

16 The *Lancet*, 14 November 1953, pp1032–3.

17 Brinkman, op. cit.

18 As with the *Male* report, it doesn't seem possible to find completely accurate global figures. Ch says both books sold approximately the same. From tax returns in the IU Archives, royalties from the *Female* report totalled $318,171 by 1956/7, compared to $223,856 for the *Male* at 1952/3, but the former would include continuing royalties from the *Male* book since they are not differentiated. As before, we can't be far out if we follow Ch.

21 *Money – and Deterioration: 1953–5*

1 EM to K, 24 September; K to EM, 29 September 1953.

2 GW to K, 20 December 1953.

3 C to K, 2 December 1953; Pom, p373.

4 EM to K, 7 January; K to EM, 11 January 1954.

5 K to D, 25 November; D to K, 12 December – 1953; K to D, 6 March 1954.

6 Pom, pp373–81; Corner to K, 24 February 1954.

7 Pom, pp373–81; Halberstam, op. cit.; Robert S. Morison, int J, 18 October 1971; Wells, int J.

8 These 2 paras Morison/Warren/Corner, ints J; Pom, p373–81.

9 Corner, 1981.

10 K to Rusk, 3 March 1954.

11 Morison/Rusk/Corner/Warren, ints J. The above account is considerably truncated. For a much fuller one see JB, pp715–18, 725–7. Jones is excellent on this institutional history.

12 Rusk, int J; Pom, pp373–81; Cochran et al., 1954; JB, pp659–61, 722, 723, 730–7.

13 See, for example, K to Prof. Waters of IU, 10 June; Waters to K, 13 June 1952.

14 Morison, int J.

15 Geb's note 7 on Dr Morison's visit, November 1955.

16 Rusk, int J.

17 Geb and Dellenback to Corner, 17 April/Geb to Corner, 17 April 1954.

18 Tax returns, IU Archives.

19 Quoted Pom, p361.

20 K to Laidlaw, 3 March 1954.

21 Many examples. See K to Robert T. Wyatt, 27 December 1954, or Merck Institute New York, 15 November 1954. From K to Kretchmar, 21 May 1954, the usual fee

seems to have been $500. (Quoted JB, p886 note 30.)

22 IU Annual Report, April 1954, IU Archive.

23 Rosenzweig, 1969; Laidlaw to Geb, 2 May 1963.

24 K to Wheeler, 17 May; Wheeler to K, 24 May 1954.

25 Dingwall to Geb, 1 November 1981.

26 Dingwall to K, 17 July 1954.

27 Ch, p179.

28 Wescott, op. cit., p346, Wescott, int Rosco; Geb, int A.

29 Pom, p379.

30 K to Dr Wortis, 13 March 1947.

31 Geb, int A.

32 K to Dingwall, 11 October 1954.

33 Dellenback, int A.

34 Geb, Dellenback, ints A, July-December 1995; November 1997.

35 Wescott, op. cit., 7 September 1954, p351.

36 K to Ramsey, 24 September 1954.

37 Dellenback, int A (Pom, pp241–2).

38 Steward, 1980/81, p105.

39 JB, pp738–9, 885.

40 Geb, Dellenback, ints A cit.

41 Conclusion of discussion with Dr Michael Perring, int A cit.

42 Anon A, int A, November 1997.

43 JB, pp610, 864.

44 Geb/Dellenback, ints A, November 1997. Joan Reid, in an interview in 1995, but repeated by telephone in November 1997, said she remembered this incident, which was 'sometime after 1953'. Her father refused to let anyone but her husband Dr Robert Reid into the bathroom. She says it happened because her father dropped his razor on to his penis. Kinsey shaved with a safety razor. Either this was a separate

incident or it testifies to Joan's ignorance of
male shaving tackle and Robert Reid's
discretion.
45 Perring, int A cit.
46 Pom, p70.
47 K to D, 11 October 1954.
48 Wheeler to K, 25 November; K to Wescott,
26(?) November; K to Mr and Mrs Lloyd
Wescott, 30 November – all 1954.
49 K to Cadmus, 27 November 1954.
50 Wescott, op. cit., 30 November 1954, p355.
51 K to Laidlaw, 27 November 1954.
52 K to Dr R.M., 2 December 1954.
53 Many letters, see, for example, Dingwall to
K, 9 September 1954, 26 May 1955; Prof.
Lewis (Maudsley) to K, 16 March; K to
Lewis, 9 April, 4 May – all 1955.
54 K to Mikshe, 1 March; to GW, 1 March
1955.
55 See for example MW to K, 26 April; K to

MW, 4 May 1955; K to Wescott, 2 March
1955.
56 K to C, 9 February; C to K, 2 March; K to C,
8 March 1955.
57 K to Waterman, 2 March, 6 June 1955.
58 K to Dr Charles McLane, 30 December
1954; Mary S. Calderone to K, 10 January
1955 (I am indebted to Lynn Gorchov for
these references).
59 C to K, 16 May 1955.
60 C to K, 10 June (twice), K to Corner, 14
June (and see C to K, 20 June) – all 1955.
61 LS to K, 31 May; K to LS, 29 July – 1955; K
to LS, 9 April 1956.
62 Speaks, int A.
63 Benjamin, int J, 23 August 1971; Geb, int A.
64 Pom, p438; Geb, ints A and J.
65 Dingwall to K, undated, but 26 May; D to K,
undated but postmarked 14 August; K to D,
19 September – all 1955.

22 *Europe: October–November 1955*

1 The account which follows, and all
quotations not otherwise sourced, are taken
almost entirely from five sessions of two or
three hours each, made from brief notes he'd
taken as he went and delivered immediately
on his return, in which K described to his
staff what he'd seen. A stenographer sat in
and took it down as he talked.
2 Dingwall to K, 9 September 1954.
3 Mac, int J.
4 Dingwall to Geb, 1 November 1981.
5 Holmes, Richard, 1987, p460.
6 Anger, int A, 7 March 1997.
7 'R.J.', int A, July 1996; Anger, int A cit.

8 'R.J.', ibid.
9 Ibid.
10 Ibid.
11 K to Miss Roeth, 28 April 1921.
12 'R.J.', int A; Anger, int A.
13 'R.J.'/Tripp, ints A.
14 Anger, int A.
15 See under Chap 19.
16 Anger, int A.
17 See for example S to K, 15 March 1954; K
to S, 31 January 1955; K to S, 30 January
1956.
18 Wescott, op. cit., entry 6 December, p396.

23 *Death*

1 Dellenback, int A.
2 Dorothy Collins, int A.
3 Ibid.
4 Collins, int J.
5 See, for example, to 'Howard E. Erikson', 10
January 1955; Ch, p168.
6 Geb, int J.
7 Pom, pp433, 434.
8 Tripp, int A; Geb, int A; Collins, int J.
9 BBC transcript from Arlene Francis, TV
interview; video of int itself, at KI and
possession of A.
10 K to Gregg, 21 April; G to K, 28 April; K to
G, 10 May – all 1956.

11 NRC to K, 18 April 1956.
12 Wescott, int Rosco.
13 Tripp, int A; Pom, pp434, 435.
14 Wescott, int Rosco.
15 Pom, p435.
16 Ch, p199.
17 Corner to K, 1 May 1956.
18 K to Spieth, 11 April 1956; K to Jerry, 11
May 1956.
19 K to 'George Norton', 15 June 1956.
20 Unpublished paper 'The Right to do Sex
Research', probably dictated by Kinsey in
August 1956 (Ch prints this as an appendix).
21 K to Moskin, 15 May; the *Companion* to K,

22 May; K to *Companion*, 15 June – all 1956.
22 Earle Marsh, int BBC.
23 K to Spieth, 11 April; Spieth to K, 19 June – both 1956.
24 Wescott, int Rosco.
25 K to Carnegie Museum, 3 July 1956.
26 K to H. Most (Saunders), 18 July 1956.
27 Remak, int A; Remak to Ch, 28 August 1956.
28 Aswell to Wescott, 15 October 1956.
29 K to Pilpel, 2 July 1956; Pom, pp439, 440.
30 Wells, int A.

31 Pilpel to Geb, 21 October 1981; Pom, p438.
32 A, 1984.
33 K to Wise, 12 May 1956.
34 Clark, 1977, pp277–9 (?).
35 Wells, int J.
36 Mac, taped int, Pom; Anne, int A.
37 These last 3 paras largely from Joan, int A; plus Pom, p440; Geb, int A; Joan to A, 19 March 1997.
38 Torrey, int J; Wescott to Geb, 10 October 1956; Pom, pp440, 441.

24 Conclusions

1 NRC to Geb, 5 June 1957 and subsequent yearly letters.
2 Heffner, int BBC.
3 Pom, pp449, 540; Geb, int J.
4 Tripp/Collins/Joan, ints A.
5 Roehr, int J.
6 Geb, ints A/J.
7 'Jennifer Innes', from Nowlis, int A.
8 Pom, p454, and see Geb in bibliography.
9 Peek, tel int A, November 1995.
10 Blanchard, 1996.
11 NRC records – ser. 200, box 41, Folder 463, Rockefeller Foundation archives; United States v 31 photographs, 156 F. Supp, 350 (S.D. NY 1957). Cited Bullough, op. cit.
12 Beach, int J; Ch, pp187, 188.
13 Crump, 1994.
14 Smith, int A, July 1995.
15 Jennifer Pearson Yamashiro, Curator, int A, November 1997.
16 See for example Clyde Martin, 1975, 1981.
17 From Jerry Rosco's 'Chronology' in Wescott, op. cit.
18 This para and next, variously, Anne/Carol Zeller/Consuello Lopez-Morrilles, ints A; Mac, int J.
19 Hecht, int BBC.
20 Or so straw polls by A in the last two would suggest.
21 Guess estimate in Pom, probably a slight exaggeration (see Appendix B).
22 Interview in *The Observer*, 20 October 1996.
23 *Independent on Sunday*, 21 January 1996.

24 I am indebted for the suggestions in this sentence to Bullough, op. cit.
25 Bruce Voeller, Chap 3. McWhirter et al., 1990.
26 Quoted JB, p752.
27 Gorchov, op. cit.
28 *The Observer*, 30 March 1997.
29 American Law Institute, *Model Penal Code*, 1955.
30 Gregerson, op. cit., pp166–8; NGLTF Privacy Project Update, 14 January 1994.
31 Research is needed to find out when these statutes are used in this way, and when or if genuinely used against sexual behaviour. As far as I can discover there is none.
32 See under 'Dictionary' in bibliography. p584.
33 Michael White, 1997; Anthony Stevens, 1990.
34 Bullough, op. cit.
35 *Independent on Sunday*, 3 November 1996.
36 See McWhirter et al., 1990.
37 Califia, 1983.
38 Letitia Anne Pelau, Susan D. Cochrano, quoted in Chap 19, McWhirter, op. cit.
39 Koertge, Chap 22 (?); ibid.
40 Bullough, op. cit.
41 Kinsey, 1926.
42 *Female*, p642.
43 See for example, Isaiah Berlin, 1953, 1969.
44 Webster, op. cit., p445. I am not only indebted to this book in this section but also to Stephen Jay Gould, 1985/91.

Published Works by Alfred C. Kinsey

(Compiled with the assistance of material from the Kinsey Institute and Frank N. Young in *Indiana Academy of Science*, vol. 103, 1994, pp81–3; and private research.)

1919 'Fossil Cynipidae', *Psyche* 26: 44–9.
1919 'An African Figitidae', *Psyche* 26: 162–3.
1920 'New species and synonymy of American Cynipidae', *Bull. Amer. Mus. Nat. Hist.* 42: 293–317.
1920 'Life histories of American Cynipidae', *Bull. Amer. Nat. Hist.* 42: 319–57.
1920 'Phylogeny of cynipid genera and biological characteristics', *Bull. Amer. Mus. Nat. Hist.* 42: 279–95.
1922 'Studies of some new and described Cynipidae (Hymenoptera)', *Ind. Univ. Studies* (9) 53: 1–141, 163–71.
1922 'Varieties of a rose gall wasp (Cynipidae, Hymenoptera)', *Ind. Univ. Studies* 53: 142–71.
1922 With K.D. Ayers, 'Varieties of gall wasp distributions (Cynipidae, Hymenoptera)', *Ind. Univ. Stud.* 9 (53): 142–71.
1923 'The gall wasp genus Neuroterus (Hymenoptera)', *Ind. Univ. Studies* 53: 1–147.
1926 *An Introduction to Biology*, Lippincott/Philadelphia, 558pp.
1926 'Biologic sciences in our high schools', *Proc. Ind. Acad. Sci.* 35: 63–5.
1927 *Field and Laboratory Manual in Biology*, Lippincott/Philadelphia, 155pp.
1930 'The content of the biology course', *Sch. Sci. Math.* 30: 374–84.
1930 'The gall wasp genus Cynips. A study in the origin of species', *Ind. Univ. Studies* 16 (84–6), 577pp.
1933 *A New Introduction to Biology*, Lippincott/Chicago, 840pp.
1933 'Landscape picture with iris', *Bull. Amer. Iris Soc.*, July and October, pp1–11.
1934 *Workbook in Biology*, Lippincott/Chicago, 306pp.
1935 'The economic importance of the Cynipidae', *J. Econ. Entomol.* 28: 86–91.
1936 'The origin of higher categories in Cynips', *Ind. Univ. Pub. Sci. Ser.* 4, 334pp.
1937 'An evolutionary analysis of insular and continental species', *Science* 85: 56–7 (abstr).
1937 'An evolutionary analysis of insular and continental species', *Proc. Nat. Acad. Sci.* 23: 5–11.
1937 *Methods in Biology*, Lippincott/Chicago, 279pp.
1937 'New Mexican gall wasps (Hymenoptera, Cynipidae)', *Rev. Entomol.* 7: 39–79.
1937 'Supra-specific variation in nature and in classification. From the viewpoint of zoology', *Amer. Natur.* 71: 206–22.
1937 'Insects and arachnids from Canadian amber: order Hymenoptera; Cynipidae', *Univ. Toronto Stud.* 40: 21–7.
1937 'New Mexican gall wasps (Hymenoptera, Cynipidae)', II *Rev. Entomol.* 7: 428–71.
1938 *New Introduction to Biology (Revised)*, Lippincott/Chicago, 845pp.
1938 *Workbook in Biology*, Lippincott/Chicago, 164pp.
1938 'New Mexican gall wasps (Hymenoptera, Cynipidae)', IV *Proc. Ind. Acada. Sci.* 47: 261–80.
1938 'Cynipidae from Oceania', *Marcellia* 29: 1–8.
1938 'New Figitidae from the Marquesa Islands', *Bernice P. Bishop Mus. Bull.* 142: 193–7.
1941 'Criteria for a hormonal explanation of the homosexual', *J. Clin. Endocr.* 5: 424–8.
1942 'Seasonal factors in gall wasp distributions', *Biol. Symposia* 6: 167–87.
1942 'Isolating mechanisms in gall wasps', *Biol. Symposia* 6: 251–69.
1943 With M.L. Fernald, *Edible Wild Plants of Eastern North America*, A Gray Herbarium of Harvard University special publication, Idlewild Press/New York.
1948 With Wardell B. Pomeroy, Clyde E. Martin, *Sexual Behavior in the Human Male*, Saunders/Philadelphia, 804pp.

Published Works by Alfred C. Kinsey

1949 With Wardell B. Pomeroy, Clyde E. Martin, Paul H. Gebhard, 'Concepts of normality and abnormality in sexual behavior', *Psychosexual Development in Health and Disease*, Grune and Stratten/New York, pp11–32.

1953 With Pomeroy, Martin and Gebhard, *Sexual Behavior in the Human Female*, Saunders/Philadelphia, 842pp.

1956 'Music and Love', *High Fidelity Magazine*, July 1956, pp27–8.

1958 *Edible Wild Plants of Eastern North America*, revised by Reed C. Collins, Harper & Row/New York.

Bibliography

Key:
Long titles are shortened to the main title. KI = Kinsey Institute, IU = Indiana University.
Unpublished memoirs, studies, etc. are included if used.

A Study of attitudes and knowledge related to venereal disease among two groups of soldiers in C-B-I. Research department special service section HQ, USA – C-B-I. Unpublished. Held KI.
Allen, Judith A., *Strange Allies: Alfred Kinsey, Emily Mudd* . . . . Presentation at the KI, 14 November 1997.

Bair, Deirdre, *Anais Nin* . . ., London 1995.
Bajos, N., Spina, A., *Les Comportments sexuels en France*, Documentation Français/Paris 1993.
Baker, R., *Sperm Wars: Infidelity, Sexual Conflict and Other Bedroom Battles*, Fourth Estate/London 1996.
Bancroft, John, *Human Sexuality and its Problems*, Edinburgh 1989.
——, ed., *Annual Review of Sex Research*, Vol. 5, 1994.
Beach, Frank A., Clellan, Ford, *Patterns of Sexual Behavior*, Harper/New York 1951.
Beck, Joseph, 'How Do Spermatozoa Enter the Uterus?', *St. Louis Medical and Surgical Journal* 9, September 1872: 449.
Bell, A.P., Weinberg, M.S., *Homosexualities* . . ., Simon & Schuster/New York 1978.
Bell, A.P. et al., *Sexual Preferences* . . ., IU Press 1981.
——, *Sexual Preferences: Statistical Appendix*, IU Press 1981.
Bender, L., Blau, A., 'The Reaction of Children . . .', *American Journal of Orthopsychiatry* 22: 825–37, 1937.
Bergler, E., Hitschman, E., *Frigidity in Women* . . ., New York 1936.
Bergler, E., Kroger, William S., *Kinsey's Myth of Female Sexuality*, Grune & Stratton/New York 1954.
Berlin, Isaiah, *The Hedgehog and the Fox*, London 1953.
——, *Four Essays on Liberty*, London 1969.
Binding, Paul, *House with Four Windows*, Stockholm/London 1998, Part 3.
Blanchard, R., Bogaert, A.E., 'Handedness in homosexual and heterosexual men in the Kinsey Interview data', *Arch. Sex. Behav.*, vol 25 (4) 1996, pp373–8.
Blanchard, R., Bogaert A.E., 'Biodemographic comparisons . . .', *Arch. Sex. Behav.*, vol 25 (6) 1996, pp551–79.
Boswell, John, *Same-Sex Unions in Pre-modern Europe*, Villard Books/Random House, New York 1994.
Brandt, Allan M., *No Magic Bullet* . . ., OUP 1985.
Bredsdorff, Elias, *Hans Christian Andersen* . . ., London 1975.
Brewer, Joan S., ed., *The Kinsey Interview Kit*, 1981, unpublished. Held KI.
Brinkman, Paul D., *Dr Alfred Kinsey and the Press* . . ., unpublished PhD dissertation, IU August 1971. Held KI.
Buckley, J.M., 'Methodism, Methodism in the United States', in *Encyclopaedia Britannica*, 13th edition, 1926, pp293–7.
Bullough, Bonnie et al., 'Subjective Report . . .', *Nurse Practitioner*, 9 March 1984.
Bullough, Vern L., *Science in the Bedroom*, New York 1994.
Burr, Chandler, *A Separate Creation: How Biology Makes Us Gay*, Bantam 1996.

Calder-Marshall, A., *The Sage of Sex*, New York 1959.
Califia, P., 'Gay Men, Lesbians and Sex – Doing it together', *The Advocate*, pp24–7, August 1983.
Cecil, Hugh, *The Flower of Battle* . . ., London 1995.
Chauncey, George, *Gay New York* . . . *1890–1940*, Basic Books/HarperCollins, New York 1994.
Christenson, Cornelia V., *Kinsey: A Biography*, IU Press, Bloomington 1971.

Christiansen, H.R., Clegg, C.G., 'Changing Sex Norms...', *Journal of Marriage and the Family*, 32, 616–27 (1970).

Clark, Thomas D., *Indiana University: Midwestern Pioneer*, vol III 'Years of Fulfilment', IU Press 1977.

Cochran, William G., et al., *Statistical Problems of the Kinsey Report*, The American Statistical Association, Washington 1954.

Connelly, Mark Thomas, *The Response to Prostitution in the Progressive Era*, North Carolina Press 1980.

Corner, George W., Aberle, Sophie D., *Twenty-five Years of Sex Research...*, W.B. Saunders, Philadelphia/London 1953.

——, *The Seven Ages of a Medical Scientist...*, University of Pennsylvania Press, Philadelphia 1981.

Crump, James, 'Archiving Sexuality – The Photographic Collection of the Kinsey Institute', *Harm's Way*, Santa Fe: Twin Palms Publisher 1994.

Dellenback, William, *The Bloomington Herald-Times*, April 11, 1994.

D'Emilio, John, *Sexual Politics, Sexual Communities...*, University of Chicago Press 1983.

Deutsch, Albert, ed., *Sex Habits of American Men*, Prentice Hall/New York 1948.

Diamond, Milton, 'Bisexualities: A Biological Perspective', Paper to International Conference of Sociology, 1990.

Dickinson, Robert Latou, Beam, Lura, *A Thousand Marriages*, Williams & Wilkins, Baltimore 1931.

——, *The Single Woman*, Baltimore 1934.

Dictionary of Scientific Biography, ed. in Chief: Charles Coulston Gillespie, vol 4, p584, Scribners/New York 1970. Index dated 1980.

Ditzion, Sidney, *Marriage, Morals and Sex in America: A History of Ideas*, New York 1953.

Dolzhansky, Theodosius, *Genetics and the Origin of Species*, New York 1941.

Douglas, Anne, *Terrible Honesty: Mongrel Manhattan in the 1920s*, London 1996.

Duberman, Martin, 'Kinsey's Urethra', *The Nation*, 3 November 1997, pp40–43

Ehrenreich, Barbara, McIntosh, Janet, 'Biology Under Attack', *The Nation*, June 9, 1997, pp11–16

Ellis, Albert, *Sex Life of the American Woman and the Kinsey Report*, Greenberg, New York 1954.

——, *The American Sexual Tragedy*, Twayne/New York 1954.

——, *Sex Without Guilt*, New York 1958 – and many more.

Ellis, Havelock H., *Studies in the Psychology of Sex*, 6 vols, published 1897–1910. I follow the 7-volume edition published by F.A. Davis, Philadelphia between 1928 and 1930. It is completely typical of England that Ellis, an Englishman, should still not have been able to find a publisher here by this time.

——, *My Life*, London 1939.

Erhardt, Anke, *Address* to the 1982 re-dedication of the KI. Unpublished and held there.

Evans-Pritchard, E.E., 'Some Notes on Zande Sex Habits', *Am. Anthro.*, 75–1: 171–5, 1973.

Ewan, Joseph, Entry pp383–4, *Dictionary of Scientific Biography*, vol IV, ed. Charles C. Gillespie, New York 1970.

Fillion, Kate, *Lip Service: The Myth of Female Virtue...*, Pandora/London 1997.

Finkelhov, David, 'Sex Among Siblings...', *Archives of Sexual Behaviour* 9, 1980.

——, *Child Sex Abuse: New Theory and Research*, New York 1984.

Foucault, Michel, *The History of Sexuality – Vol 1. An Introduction*, trans. Robert Hurley, Random House, New York 1978/London 1979.

——, *The History of Sexuality – Vol 2, The Use of Pleasure*, London 1987.

Freud, S., 'Recommendations to Physicians Practising Psychoanalysis', in *Freud Standard Edition*, ed. James Strachey, Hogarth Press/London, 24 vols, 1953–74.

Friday, Nancy, *My Secret Garden...*, Virago/London 1975.

Gagnon, John, Simon, William, *Sexual Conduct: The Social Sources of Human Sexuality*, Aldine/Chicago 1973.

Gagnon, John, see McWhirter 1990.

Gallup, George, Rae, Saul, *The Pulse of Democracy...*, New York 1940.

Gathorne-Hardy, J., *The Public School Phenomenon*, Penguin/London 1979. (In US as *The Old School Tie*, Viking/New York 1978.)

——, *Love, Sex, Marriage and Divorce*, Cape/London, Summit Books/New York 1981.

——, *Doctors*, Weidenfeld & Nicolson/London 1984.

Gay, Ruth, *Unfinished People...*, Norton/New York 1997.

Gebhard, Paul H., et al., *Pregnancy, Birth and Abortion*, New York 1958.
——, *Sex Offenders*, New York 1965.
——, *Studies in Erotic Art*, Basic Books/New York 1970.
Gebhard, Paul H., Johnson, A.B., *The Kinsey Data – Marginal Tabulations of the 1938–1963 Interviews . . .*, W.B. Saunders 1979.
Geddes, D.P., ed., *An Analysis of the Kinsey Reports . . .*, London 1954.
Gills, David, ed., *International Encyclopedia of the Social Sciences*, New York 1969.
Glass, S.J., et al., *J. Clin. Endocr.*, 26, pp590–6, April 1940.
Gooren, Louis, et al., 'Biological Determinants of Sexual Orientation', *Annual Review of Sex Research*, 1990.
Gorchov, Lynn, 'The Objective Scientist as Radical Reformer: Alfred C. Kinsey and the Politics of Homosexuality', unpublished paper to History Graduate Student Conference, University of Bielefeld – Johns Hopkins University, Bielefeld, Germany 24 May 1996.
Gorer, Geoffrey, *Exploring English Character*, London 1955.
——, *Sex and Marriage in England Today*, London 1971.
Gould, Stephen Jay, *The Flamingo's Smile*, Norton/New York 1985, Penguin/London 1991.
——, *Adam's Navel*, Essays, Penguin 1995 (and see Lewontin, 1979).
Goulden, Joseph, *The Best Years – 1940–1950*, New York 1976.
Gregerson, Edgar, *Sexual Practices . . .*, Mitchell Beazley/London 1982.
Greven, Philip, *Spare the Child*, New York 1992, pp174–86.
Grosskurth, Phyllis, *John Addington Symonds*, Longmans/London 1964.
Gunther, Gerald, *Learned Hand – The Man and the Judge*, Knopf/New York 1994.

Halberstam, David, *The Fifties*, Ballantine Books/New York 1994.
Hallick, S.C., 'Emotional Effects . . .', in *Sexual Behavior and the Law*, ed. K. Slovenko, Illinois 1966.
Hamer, Dean H., et al., 'A Linkage between DNA Markers . . . and Male Sexual Orientation', *Science* 261, 16 July 1993.
Hamilton, G.V., *A Research in Marriage*, New York 1929.
Handbook for Boy Scouts, 1937.
Heiser, Charles B., 'Edgar Anderson, Botanist and Curator of Useful Plants', *Am Missour Bot Gdn* 82: 54–60, 1995.
Hellman, Geoffrey T., Profile 'Black Tie and Cyanide Jar', *New Yorker*, 21 August 1998, pp32–44.
Helweg, Hjalmar, *H.C. Andersen, En Psykiatrisk Studie*, H. Hagerup/Copenhagen 1927 (and 1954).
Hirschfeld, M., *Die Transvestiten . . .*, Berlin 1910.
——, *Die Homosexualität des Mannes und des Weibes*, Berlin 1920.
Hobbs, A, H., Lambert, R.D., 'An Evaluation of Sexual Behavior . . .', *American Journal of Psychiatry* 104 (12): 758–64, June 1948.
Holmes, Richard, *Shelley: The Pursuit*, Penguin/London 1987.
Howard, Jane, *Margeret Mead: A Life*, Simon & Schuster/New York 1984, pp51–9, 367.
Huncke, Herbert, *Guilty of Everything*, Hanuman Books/New York 1990.
Hunter, Nan D., et al., *The Rights of Lesbians and Gay Men*, American Civil Liberties Union Handbook, 3rd edition, 1992.

Irvine, Janice M., *Disorders of Desire . . .*, Temple University Press/Philadelphia 1990.

Johnson, Anne M. et al., *Sexual Attitudes and Lifestyles*, London 1994.
Jones, James H., *The Origins of the Institute for Sex Research . . .*, unpublished PhD dissertation, IU 1972.
Jones, James H., *Bad Blood . . .*, New York 1981.
——, 'Dr Yes', *New Yorker*, 25 August and 1 September 1997, pp99–113.
——, *Alfred C. Kinsey: A Public/Private Life*, Norton/New York 1997.
Kallmann, Franz J., 'Comparative twin study . . .', *Journal of Nervous and Mental Disease*, 115 (April 1952): 293–98.
Kaplan, H.S., *The New Sex Therapy . . .*, Brummer/Magel/New York 1974.
Kenan, Stephanie H., 'The Current Hysteria over Sex Offenders . . .', *Cheiron XXVII, International Society for the History of the Behavioral and Social Sciences*, Bowdoin College, Brunswick, Maine, June 22–25, 1995.
Kimmel, Michael, *Manhood in America*, Simon & Schuster/New York 1996.
Kinsey, Alfred C., see separate bibliography p497.
Koertge, Noretta, see under McWhirter, David P., pp387–97.

Krafft-Ebing, K., trans F. J. Rebman, *Psychopathia Sexualis*..., New York 1922.

Ladar, Alice et al., *The G-Spot and Other Recent Discoveries*..., New York 1982.
Lahr, John, ed., *The Orton Diaries*, London 1986.
Laumann, Edward O., et al., 'Monitoring the AIDS Epidemic in the US: A Network Approach', *Science*, 244: 1186–9, 9 June 1989.
——, *The Social Organization of Sexuality*, University of Chicago Press 1994.
Lederer, Wolfgang, *The Kiss of the Snow Queen*, University of California Press 1986.
Legman, Gershon, *Studies in Erotic Folklore & Bibliography*, New York 1966.
Lewontin, R., Gould, Stephen Jay, 'The Spandrels of San Marco and the Panglossian Paradigm...', *Proc. of the Royal Soc. of Lon.*, B205: 581–98, 1979.
Lewontin, R., 'Sex, Lies and Social Science', *New York Review of Books*, 42 (9), April 20, 1995, pp24–29.
Licht, Hans, *Sexual Life in Ancient Greece*, London 1932.
Lockridge, Larry, *Shade of the Raintree*..., Viking Penguin/London 1994.
Lynd, Robert S., Lynd, Helen Merrell, *Middletown*..., New York 1929, 1954, p251.

Macdonald, David, et al., ed., *The Encyclopaedia of Mammals*, Allen & Unwin/London 1984, pp26–55.
Malinowski, Bronislaw, *The Sexual Life of Savages*, New York 1929.
Marcus, Steven, *The Other Victorians*, Weidenfeld & Nicolson/London 1970.
Martin, Clyde E., 'Marital and Sexual Factors in Relation to Age...', in *Life History Research in Psychopathology*, vol 4, Wirt, R.D. et al., eds, Univ of Minnesota Press 1975, pp326–47.
——, 'Factors Affecting Sexual Functioning...', *Archives of Sexual Behavior*, vol 10, 5, 1981, pp399–420.
Martin, James J., ed., *The Dictionary of Literary Biography*, vol 9: American Novelists 1910–1945, Detroit 1981.
Martinson, Floyd Paul., *Infant and Child Sexuality*..., St Paul, Minn: Martinson 1972.
Masters, William H., Johnson, Virginia E., *Human Sexual Response*, Little Brown/New York 1966.
Masters, William H., et al., *Ethical Issues in Sex Therapy and Research*, Vol I, Boston 1977, Vol 2, Boston 1980.
Mayhew, Henry, *London Labour and the London Poor*, Vols 1–3, London 1851, Vol 4, London 1862.
Mayr, Ernst, *Systematics and the Origin of Species*, New York 1942.
McWhirter, David P., Sanders, Stephanie A., Reinisch, June M., eds., *Homosexuality/Heterosexuality: Concepts of Sexual Orientation*, OUP 1990.
Mead, Margeret, *Coming of Age in Samoa*, New York 1928.
——, *Sex and Temperament*..., New York 1935.
Mead, Margaret, 'An Anthropologist Looks at the Report', in Charles Walter Clarke, ed., *Problems in Sexual Behavior*, New York American Social Hygene Association/New York 1948.
Miles, Barney, *Ginsberg: A Biography*, New York 1989.
Moll, A., *Die Kontrare Sexualempfindung*..., Berlin 1891.
Morantz, Regina Markell, 'The Scientist as Sex Crusader...', *American Quarterly* 29 (1977), pp563–89. Also in *Procreation or Pleasure*..., ed. Thomas L. Altherr: Robert E. Krieger Pub. Co. 1983, pp145–66.
Murray, Jacqueline, ed., see Waugh, Thomas, 1993.
My Secret Life, anon, New York 1966.

Nowlis, Vincent, *Memories of Two Years with Alfred Kinsey 1944–1946*, unpublished memoir dated 4 September 1995.

Paz, Octavio, *The Double Flame: Essays on Love and Eroticism*, Harvill/London 1996.
Pillard, Richard C., Weinrich, James D., 'Evidence of Familial Nature of Male Homosexuality', *The Archives of General Psychiatry*, 43, 1986.
Pillard, Richard C., Bailey, Michael J., 'A Genetic Study of Male Sexual Orientation', *The Archives*..., 48, 1991.
Pillard, Richard C., Stein, Edward, 'Evidence for Queer Genes', interview in *GLQ – A Journal of Lesbian and Gay Studies*, vol 1, No 2, 1994.
Pomeroy, Wardell B., et al., *Taking a History*, The Free Press/New York 1960; London 1961.
——, *Dr Kinsey and the Institute for Sex Research*, Nelson/London 1972.
Porter, Roy, Hall, Lesley, *The Facts of Life: The Creation of Sexual Knowledge in Britain 1650–1950*, Yale

University Press/New Haven 1995.
Pulerbaugh, Geoff, ed., *Twins & Homosexuality: A Casebook*, New York 1990.

Raboch, Jan, 'Penis Size ...', *Sexology Magazine*, 16 June 1960.
Ramsey, Glenn V., 'The Sex Information of Younger Boys', *Amer. J. Orthopsychiat.*, 13: 347–52, April 1943.
——, *Factors in the Sex Life of 291 Boys*, published privately by Ramsey 1950.
Reisman, Judith A., Eichel, Edward W., *Kinsey, Sex and Fraud*, Lochinvar-Huntingdon, Louisiana 1990.
Reisman, Judith A., *Kinsey: Crimes and Consequences*, The Institute for Media Education, Arlington/Virginia, 1998.
Reiss, Ira L., 'Is This the Definitive Sexual Survey?', *Journal of Sex Research*, vol 32.1, 1995, pp77–91.
Reumert, Edith, *Hans Andersen The Man*, Detroit 1971.
Rice, Thurman B., *Sex, Marriage and the Family*, Lippincott/New York 1946.
Robinson, I.E., Jedlicka, D., 'Changes in Sexual Attitudes ... 1965 to 1980'; *Journal of Marriage and the Family*, 44, pp237–40, 1982.
Robinson, Paul, 'The Case for Dr Kinsey', *Atlantic Monthly* 229, May 1972, pp99–102.
——, *The Modernization of Sex ...*, Cornell University Press/New York 1989.
Rosenzweig, Louise, 'Notes on Alfred C. Kinsey's Pre-sexual Scientific Work and the Transition', *Journal of the History of the Behavioral Sciences*, Vol V, No 2, 173–81, April 1969.
Russell, D.E.H., Finkelhov, D., 'The Gender Gap among Perpetrators of Child Sexual Abuse', in *Sexual Explorations ...*, ed. Russell, Sage 1984.

Sanderson, Ivan T., *Living Mammals of the World*, Hamish Hamilton/London 1962, pp160–7.
Sandfort, T.G.M., 'Sex in Paedophiliac Relationships ...', *Journal of Sex Research*, 20, 1984.
Schama, Simon, *The Embarrassment of Riches*, Fontana/London 1991.
Silver, Rachel, *Where the Feet Dance*, Century/London 1995.
Shostak, Marjorie, *Nisa: The Life and Words of a !Kung Woman*, Harvard University Press 1981; Earthscan Publications/London 1996.
Skinner, Cornelia, Otis, 'Trial by Kinsey', *New Yorker*, 27 May 1950, pp29–31.
Stein, Edward, see Pillard, Richard.
Stein, Gertrude, *Autobiography of Alice B. Toklas*, New York 1933.
Stevens, Anthony, *On Jung*, Routledge/London 1990.
Steward, Samuel, M., *Chapters from an Autobiography*, Grey Fox Press/San Francisco 1980/81.
——, 'Dr Kinsey takes a peek at S/M: A reminiscence', in *Leatherfolk: Radical Sex, People, Politics and Practice*, ed. Mark Thompson, Boston: Alyson Publications 1991, pp81–90.
Stone, Abraham, Stone, Hannah, *A Marriage Manual*, Simon & Schuster/New York 1937.
Stone, Lawrence, *The Family, Sex and Marriage in England 1500–1800*, Weidenfeld & Nicolson/London 1977.
Storr, Anthony, *Feet of Clay: a Study of Gurus*, HarperCollins/London 1997.

Taylor, Timothy, *The Prehistory of Sex ...*, Fourth Estate/London 1996.
Terman, Lewis M., et al., *Psychological Factors in Marital Happiness*, New York and London 1938.
Time magazine, Gilbert Cane, '5,940 Women', August 24, 1953, pp51–58 and cover.
Timmons, Stuart, *The Trouble with Harry Hay*, Alyson Publications/Boston 1992.
Thompson, David M., ed., *Nonconformity in the Nineteenth Century*, London 1972.
Thompson, Mark, ed., *Radical Sex, Politics & Practice*, Alyson Publications Inc. 1991 (pp81–90).
Trilling, Lionel, 'Sex and Science: The Kinsey Report', *Partisan Review* 15 (April 1948), pp460–76. Endlessly reprinted, e.g. Geddes 1954.
Trilling, Lionel; Marcus, Steven, ed. and abridged, *The Life and Work of Sigmund Freud* by Ernest Jones, Penguin 1964.
Tripp, Clarence A., *The Homosexual Matrix*, McGraw Hill/Meridian/Penguin, New York 1975, 1987.
——, 'Doors Behind Doors and Wheels Within Wheels', *The Journal of Homosexuality*, 1999 (pre-publication draft).

Ullerstam, Eric, *Erotic Minorities*, Grove Press/New York 1966.

Van de Velde, Theodore, *Ideal Marriage – Its Physiology and Technique*, New York 1930.
Vidal, Gore, *The City and the Pillar*, London 1965.
——, *Palimpsest*, Abacus/London 1997.

Voeller, Bruce, 'Some Uses and Abuses of the Kinsey Scale', see McWhirter et al. 1990, pp32–38.

Waal, Frans de, 'Bonobo Sex and Society', *Sci. Am.*, 272 (3): 58–64, 1995.
——, *Bonobo: The Forgotten Ape*, University of California Press 1997.
Waugh, Thomas, 'Knowledge and Desire: Dr Kinsey as Arbiter of the Homoerotic Imaginary', in *Constructing Sexualities*, ed. Jacqueline Murray, pp63–87, University of Windsor, Ontario 1993.
Wallace, Irving, *The Chapman Report*, New York 1960.
Webster, Richard, *Why Freud Was Wrong...*, HarperCollins/London 1995.
——, *The Road to Pembroke*, 1996 (unpublished as of August 1997).
——, *The Great Children's Home Panic*, The Orwell Press/Oxford 1998.
Weeks, Jeffrey, *Sexuality and Its Discontents...*, Routledge & Kegan Paul, Boston/London 1985.
Weinberg, Thomas, 'Research in Sadomasochism...', *Annual Review of Sex Research*, vol V, 1994, pp257–79.
Weinrich, James D., *Why We Are What We Are...*, New York 1987.
Weiss, J., et al., 'A study of girl sex victims', *Psychiatric Quarterly*, 29: 1–15, 1955.
Wells, Herman B., *Being Lucky*, IU Press, 1980.
Wescott, Glenway, *Continual Lessons*, The Journals 1937–55, ed. Robert Phelps, Jerry Rosco/New York 1990.
Wheeler, William Morton, 'The Termitodoxa, or Biology and Society', in *Essays in Philosophical Biology*, ed. G.H. Parker, New York 1967.
Whitam, Frederick, L., 'A Cross Cultural Perspective...' in *Variant Sexuality: Research and Theory*, ed. G. D. Wilson, Croom Helm/London 1978.
White, E., *A Boy's Own Story*, New York 1983.
White, Michael, *Isaac Newton...*, Fourth Estate/London 1997.
Williamson, Margeret, *Sappho's Immortal Daughters*, Harvard Univ Press 1995.
Wilson, Edward O., *Naturalist*, Washington 1994.
Wilson, Paul R., *The Man They Called a Monster*, North Ride, Australia/Cassell 1981.
Wright, Wendell W., et al., *Report of the Self Survey Committee to the Board of Trustees of IU*, Part 1, 102, 21 March 1939.

Young, F.N., 'A Brief History of Biology at IU', *Proc. Indiana Acad. Sci* 92: pp297–312, 1983.
——, 'Zoology at IU: The Torrey Years', *Proc. Indiana Acad. Sci* 97: pp401–7, 1987.
——, 'Alfred Charles Kinsey as an Entomologist', *Proc. Indiana Acad. Sci* 103 (1–2) pp79–83 (1994) 1997.

Index

Compiled by Douglas Matthews

Note on ACK's Works: *Sexual Behavior of the Human Female* and *Sexual Behavior of the Human Male* appear as separate entries; ACK's other works are listed under his name. Where information was obtained from Kinsey Institute files, or where informants requested anonymity, their names are pseudonyms and have been placed in inverted commas.

gives history to ACK, 198; and Gregg's offer of Rockefeller aid, 263; and publication of ACK's *Male*, 266-7; and weakness in ACK's sampling, 273; Kubie attempts to stop funds from, 274; foresees end of NRC grants to ACK, 275; attends American Social Hygiene Association meeting, 297, 309; and ACK's statistical committee, 330, 374-5; and seizure of erotic material for Institute, 346; and Rockefeller Foundation's reluctance to fund ACK, 372, 406-8, 417; and ACK's estimate of *Female*, 389; finds funds for abortion research, 418, 432

Cornfield, Jerome, 384, 389

Cosmopolitan (magazine), 395

criminals *see* prisoners

Crowley, Aleister, 428

Crump, James, 356, 443

Cuba, 313-14

Cumming, Laura, 366

Customs (US): seize erotic material, 345-6; ACK's legal case against, 437, 442

Daily Express, 402

Daily Mirror, 402

Daily Student (Indiana University magazine), 98, 119, 123-4

'Dale, Peter', 140, 180, 262

Darwin, Charles: lament on science, 40, 415; influence, 159, 454; ACK compared to, 270; and natural selection, 279; and speciation, 453; *see also* evolution

Davis, Katharine B., 93, 151, 156

Dean, James, 400

Delisle, François, 155

Dellenback, Bill: ACK interferes with photographic equipment, 80; and ACK's lack of humour, 189; on Legman's deceptions, 232; photographing and filming for ACK, 296, 307, 333, 335; on ACK's abuse of Martin, 298; on ACK's tours, 304; on ACK's drinking, 313; Eleanor Roehr's infatuation with, 332; denies pressure on participants, 335; on ACK's pierced foreskin, 337; travels with ACK, 339; on Wescott, 346; films bull, 351n; films Wescott, 353; on ACK's discretion, 357; films homosexuality, 361; photographs meeting with statistical committee, 374; and ACK's reaction to criticisms of *Female*, 398; in Peru, 412-13; ACK admits self-circumcision to, 414; on soundproofing of ISR rooms, 430; at ACK's funeral, 438; later career, 444

Denmark, 254, 420-1

'Dent, Alice', 230, 242-3, 314, 316, 365n

Deutsch, Albert, 127, 338, 380, 434; (ed.) *Sex Habits of American Men*, 276

Dickinson, Robert Latou: ACK first writes to, 87; early sex research, 87-8, 151, 156-7; and incidence of VD among upper-level women, 123; writes to ACK, 186; ACK meets, 202-3, 213, 229, 242; and Green's material, 211, 220, 222, 267-8; visits ACK, 212, 268; and 'Alice Dent', 230; lectures at Philadelphia, 230-1; helps ACK with overseas material, 235; ACK seeks help from, 237; ACK reports 10,000 histories to, 239; on female orgasm, 245; introduces Marsh to ACK, 248; receives copy of *Male*, 269; ACK counsels silence on erotic material, 275; on reaction to publication of *Male*, 276; and ACK's attendance at American Social Hygiene Association meeting, 297; ACK writes to on abortion, 301; ACK

reports to, 308; on importance of clitoris, 321; illnesses, 340; death, 345; leaves erotic collection to ACK, 345; and Harry Benjamin, 418; *A Thousand Marriages*, 87-8

Dictionary of Scientific Biography, 449

Dietz, Helen, 256, 266, 381, 384, 389

Dingwall, D.E.J. (Eric): sends antique condom to ACK, 406, 411; visits ACK, 411-12; and ACK's illness, 412; and ACK's trip to Europe, 415, 417, 419, 421, 423, 425, 428

Dodds, Harold W., 96, 277

Dolores (prostitute), 167

Dolzhansky, Theodosius, 117

Doorbar, Ruth, 370-1

Dorn, Harry F., 384, 389

Doubleday (publishers), 435

'Downside, Mary', 302

drugs: erotic effect of, 257-8

Duberman, Martin, 83, 368

Dulles, John Foster, 407-8

'Edden, Jim', 298

Edmondson, Frank, 66, 109, 130-1, 167, 183, 186, 278, 330, 341

Edmondson, Margaret, 56, 64, 128, 141, 149, 183, 234, 278

Ehrhardt, Anke, 273

Eigenmann, Carl H.: engages ACK at Bloomington, 51; on picnic, 57; threatens ACK with dismissal, 64; death, 65; property speculation, 72

Einstein, Albert, 159

Eisenhower, Dwight D., 398, 400, 407

Eldredge, Niles, 103

Ellis, Albert, 370-1, 401

Ellis, Edith (*née* Lees), 155

Ellis, Henry Havelock: and the sermon, 31; ACK reads, 151; sex research, 154-7, 291; on homosexuality, 379n; *Studies in the Psychology of Sex*, 155

Ellson, Betsy, 109

Ernst, Morris, 158, 211, 346n, 384; *see also* Loth, David and Morris Ernst

Euripides, 152

Europe: ACK visits, 417, 419-29

evolution: ACK's commitment to theory of, 14, 46, 70-1, 103, 113-15, 117-18, 189, 208, 240, 351; *see also* Darwin, Charles

exhibitionism, 364

Exner, Dr M.J., 156

feminism: effect on sexual science, 451

Ferenczi, Sandor, 188

Fernald, Merrill Lyndon, 41-2, 46, 208, 449

Field, Alice, 238, 313-14

'Field, William', 339

Findlater, Rosemary, 462

Flood, Dr (of Massachusetts), 352

Foley, Mrs (Bloomington landlady), 58

Folsom, Joseph, 25, 202

Forbidden (film), 118-19

Ford Foundation, 372, 375, 389

Forster, E.M., 324, 348, 357

Fort Wayne, Archbishop of, 345-6

Fosdick, Harry Emerson, 406-7, 412

Foster, Jeannette, 330

Foucault, Michel: on the sermon, 31; and confession,

Index

Sex the Measure of All Things

Jonathan Gathorne-Hardy is the author of *The Rise and Fall of the British Nanny*, *The Public School Phenomenon*, and *The Interior Castle*, a biography of Gerald Brenen.